Legal Culture in the Age of Globalization

Legal Culture in the
Age of Globalization

Latin America and Latin Europe

EDITED BY LAWRENCE M. FRIEDMAN
AND ROGELIO PÉREZ-PERDOMO

Stanford University Press
Stanford, California
2003

Stanford University Press
Stanford, California
©2003 by the Board of Trustees of the Leland Stanford Junior University. All rights reserved.

Printed in the United States of America on acid-free, archival-quality paper

Library of Congress Cataloging-in-Publication Data

Legal culture in the age of globalization : Latin America and Latin Europe / edited by Lawrence M. Friedman and Rogelio Pérez-Perdomo.
 p. cm.
 Includes bibliographical references and index.
 ISBN 0-8047-4699-0 (cloth : alk. paper)
 1. Law—Latin America. 2. Law—Europe, Southern. 3. Democracy—Latin America. 4. Democracy—Europe, Southern. 5. Sociological jurisprudence. 6. Globalization. I. Friedman, Lawrence Meir II. Pérez Perdomo, Rogelio.
K561.L436 2003
340'.115—dc21

2003001559

Typeset by G&S Typesetters, Inc.

Original Printing 2003

Last figure below indicates year of this printing:
12 11 10 09 08 07 06 05 04 03

Contents

List of Tables   *vii*

List of Figures   *xii*

Contributors   *xv*

Acknowledgments   *xix*

1. Latin Legal Cultures in the Age of Globalization   *1*
   ROGELIO PÉREZ-PERDOMO AND LAWRENCE FRIEDMAN

2. Argentina: The Effects of Democratic Institutionalization   *20*
   MARÍA INÉS BERGOGLIO

3. Brazil: The Road of Conflict Bound for Total Justice   *64*
   ELIANE BOTELHO JUNQUEIRA

4. Law and Legal Culture in Chile, 1974–1999   *108*
   EDMUNDO FUENZALIDA FAIVOVICH

5. Justice and Society in Colombia: A Sociolegal Analysis of Colombian Courts   *134*
   CÉSAR A. RODRÍGUEZ, MAURICIO GARCÍA-VILLEGAS, AND RODRIGO UPRIMNY

6. The Rise of Lawyers in France   *184*
   ANNE BOIGEOL

7. The Italian Legal System, 1945–1999   *220*
   SABINO CASSESE

8. Italian Styles: Criminal Justice and the Rise of an Active Magistracy   *239*
   DAVID S. CLARK

9. "Faraway, So Close!" The Rule of Law and Legal Change in Mexico, 1970–2000   *285*
SERGIO LÓPEZ-AYLLÓN AND HÉCTOR FIX-FIERRO

10. Citizens Running to the Courts: The Legal System in Puerto Rico and the Modernization Process   *352*
BLANCA G. SILVESTRINI

11. The Organization, Functioning, and Evaluation of the Spanish Judicial System, 1975–2000: A Case Study in Legal Culture   *377*
JOSÉ JUAN TOHARIA

12. Venezuela, 1958–1999: The Legal System in an Impaired Democracy   *414*
ROGELIO PÉREZ-PERDOMO

13. Patterns of Foreign Legal Investment and State Transformation in Latin America   *479*
YVES DEZALAY AND BRYANT GARTH

14. SLADE: A Memoir   *499*
JOHN HENRY MERRYMAN

Index   *515*

Tables

1.1 Law Students   *8*

1.2 Changes in the Number of Lawyers in Selected Countries   *10*

1.3 Large Law Firms   *11*

1.4 Number of Judges   *13*

2.1 Litigation Rate, Córdoba, 1968–1995   *36*

2.2 Composition of Cases, 1983–1995   *37*

2.3 Mean Rates of Civil Suits   *40*

2.4 Mean Rates of Litigation, by Period   *41*

2.5 Mean Rates of Litigation Within Personal Relations   *42*

2.6 Mean Rates of Litigation of Family Suits   *43*

2.7 Correlations Between Litigation Rates and Judicial Costs, 1980–1995   *50*

2.8 Impact of Judicial Costs on Different Types of Suits   *52*

2.9 Mean Rates of Litigation, by Period   *53*

3.1 Situation of Judges in the State Courts, the Federal Courts, and the Labor Courts, 2000   *84*

3.2 Change over Time in the Number of Law Students   *86*

3.3 Fields of Study with Highest Enrollment in Brazil Overall and in Each Region, 1996   *86*

3.4 Fields of Study with Highest Number of Admission Slots in Brazil Overall and in Each Region, 1996   *87*

3.5 Number of Law Firms According to Size in Various Countries   *92*

3.6 Distribution of Urban Conflicts, by Type of Conflict, 1985–1988   *96*

3.7 People Eighteen and Older Involved in a Conflict, by Type of Action Taken, 1985–1988   *97*

4.1 Recourses of Protection   *124*

5.1 Types of Plaintiffs   *160*

5.2 Types of Defendants   *161*

5.3 Tutelas Granted and Denied by Colombian Courts   *162*

5.4 Types of Cases Pending (Average, 1992–1996)   *166*

5.5 Types of Services Rendered by Plaintiff Corporations (Average, 1992–1996)   *167*

5.6 Outcomes of Trials (Average, 1992–1996)   *168*

6.1 Changes in the Gender Profile of Law Students   *186*

6.2 Graduates in the Second and Third Levels of University   *187*

6.3 Traditional Legal Professions   *188*

6.4 Activity in Civil Courts (Rendered Decisions)   *190*

6.5 Number of Civil Cases   *191*

6.6 Activity in Administrative Courts   *193*

6.7 Activity in Penal Courts   *197*

6.8 Sanctioned Offenses   *198*

6.1A Increases in the French Population   *212*

6.2A Evolution of the Labor Force, by Sex   *213*

6.3A Progression of Unemployment   *213*

6.4A Households with Low Wages   *213*

6.5A Government Resources Allocated to Judicial System   *213*

6.6A Urban and Rural Populations   *214*

7.1 Civil Cases Filed in First Instance in All Italian Courts   *230*

7.2 Penal Cases Appealed in All Italian Courts   *230*

7.3 Cases Filed and Decided by the Council of State   *231*

7.4 Number of Referenda, by Year   *233*

7.5　Notarial Acts　*235*

8.1　Magistrates (Judges and Prosecutors) in Italy, by Region and Gender　*246*

8.2　Magistrate Positions in Italy, by Job　*247*

8.3　Reported Crimes in Italy, by Region　*250*

8.4　Persons Convicted in Italy, by Type of Crime　*252*

8.5　Convicted Persons in Italy, by Penalty and Type of Crime　*254*

8.6　Stage of Proceedings in Which Convictions Became Final in Italy, by Type of Crime, 1980　*255*

8.7　Incarcerated Persons in Italy, by Gender and Justification for Imprisonment　*256*

8.8　Penal Trials Requested with Italian Pretura Judges, by Region　*261*

8.9　Penal Trials Decided in Italian Tribunali and Courts of Assize, by Region　*265*

8.10　Penal Cases Appealed to Italian Tribunali and Courts of Appeal, by Region　*267*

9.1　Constitutional Amendments by Subject Matter, 1982– 2000　*295*

9.2　Comparison of New Laws Enacted, 1971–1976 and 1991– 1996　*297*

9.3　Crime in the Federal District, 1990 –1995　*302*

9.4　Number of Circuit and District Courts in Relation to Population, 1930 –2000　*307*

9.5　Federal Judicial Budget, 1970 –2000　*308*

9.6　Cases Before the Collegiate Circuit Courts, 1970 –2000　*309*

9.7　Civil and Criminal Appeals Before the Unitary Circuit Courts, 1970 –2000　*310*

9.8　*Amparos Indirectos* Before the District Courts, 1970 –2000　*310*

9.9　Federal Civil and Criminal Cases Before the District Courts, 1970 –2000　*311*

9.10　Filings Before the Courts of the Federal District, 1992–1999　*312*

9.11　Filings Before the Civil Courts and Civil Chambers of the High Court of the Federal District, 1992–1999　*313*

9.12   Filings Before the Criminal Courts and Criminal Chambers of the High Court of the Federal District, 1992–1999   *313*

9.13   Filings Before the First Instance Courts and Chambers of the High Court of the Federal District, 1995   *314*

9.14   Complaints Before the National Commission of Human Rights and Recommendations Issued, 1990–2000   *315*

9.15   Professionals in Mexico by Profession, 1990   *325*

9.16   Professionals in Mexico by Occupation Practice Setting, 1990   *326*

9.17   Biographical and Career Profiles of Circuit and District Judges, 1984   *328*

9.18   International Agreements by Subject Matter, 1972–1977 and 1990–1995   *333*

10.1   Criminal and Civil Cases Solved and Pending in Superior Courts, 1965–1966 to 1995–1996   *355*

10.2   New Cases Presented in Superior Courts, 1965–1998   *356*

10.3   Civil Cases in the Superior Court, Fiscal Years 1965–1966 to 1974–1975   *362*

11.1   "In your opinion, who is in a better position to give a fair decision: professional judges or lay jurors?"   *384*

11.2   "If you were the defendant in a criminal case, would you rather be tried by professional judges or by lay jurors?"   *385*

11.3   Contact with the Legal System, 1997   *389*

11.4   Practicing Lawyers in Spain, 1980–1998   *390*

11.5   Incoming Civil Cases in All First Instance Courts and Legal Transactions Supervised by Notaries, 1975–1998   *391*

11.6   Incoming Cases in the Spanish Courts, 1975–1998   *392*

11.7   Incoming Administrative and Labor Cases, 1975–1998   *394*

11.8   "Globally, how would you rate the way in which courts operate in Spain?"   *397*

11.9   Percentage of Interviewees That Rate as "Good" the Operation of Courts in Their Own Country   *397*

11.10 Political Chronology, 1975–2000   *399*

12.1   Political Chronology, 1958–1999   *416*

12.2   Principal Socioeconomic Indicators   *420*

12.3   Legislation Approved or Modified per Five-Year Period   *429*

12.4   Number of Courts, 1962–1997   *438*

12.5   Change in Distribution of Matters Heard in *Primera Instancia* and Superior Courts   *440*

12.6   Judicial and Police Activity   *441*

12.7   Criminal Trials Initiated and Concluded in *Primera Instancia*   *444*

12.8   Inmates in Venezuelan Prisons   *445*

12.9   Registered and Notarized Documents, Selected Years   *447*

12.10 Traffic and Cases Introduced Related to Traffic, 1992–1996   *448*

12.11 Cases Introduced in *Parroquia* Courts   *453*

12.12 Activity of Researchers of the Faculty of Legal and Political Sciences of the Central University of Venezuela   *461*

12.13 Lawyers in Venezuela   *464*

14.1   Analytical Framework   *503*

Figures

2.1 Debt-Collection Procedures *39*

2.2 Labor Litigation *41*

2.3 Litigation and Economic Growth *41*

2.4 Salaries and Judicial Costs *48*

4.1 Postgraduate Courses in Law at Chilean Universities: Total Enrollment and Degrees Obtained, 1980–1998 *120*

4.2 Total Annual Salary of Justices of the Supreme Court *122*

4.3 Salaries of Justices of the Courts of Appeals *123*

4.4 Comparison of Results Obtained with Recourses of Protection, 1980–1998 *126*

4.5 Regimes Analyzed by Year *128*

9.1 Constitutional Amendments by Presidential Period, 1920–2000 *295*

10.1 Case Distribution in the Superior Court, 1974–1975 *363*

10.2 Organization of the Judicial Branch, 1995 *368*

12.1 Workers' Real Wages, 1950–1997 *419*

12.2 Relative Size of Private Investment in Relation to GNP, 1950–1998 *420*

12.3 Homicides per 100,000 Inhabitants, 1980–1997 *442*

12.4 Number of *Asuntos Ingresados* in Noncriminal Matters in *Primera Instancia* Courts, 1985–1997 *447*

14.1 Social-Legal Interactions *507*

Contributors

María Inés Bergoglio is professor of sociology in the National University of Córdoba, Argentina. A summary of her research into legal culture and litigation appears in *Litigar en Córdoba* (Córdoba: Ed. Triunfar, 2001). She has been guest professor at Lund University and Strathclyde University.

Anne Boigeol is a researcher of the CNRS (Centre National de la Recherche Scientifique) attached to the Institut d'histoire du temps présent (IHTP), France. Her current research is concerned with the transformation of the judiciary and the feminization of the French legal professions.

Sabino Cassese is professor of administrative law, Law School, University of Rome La Sapienza; Doctor "honoris causa" of the Universities of Paris II; Aix-en-Provence, Athens; Castilla–La Mancha (Toledo); Macerata, Córdoba (Argentina). He has served in the Italian government as minister for public administration.

David S. Clark is the Maynard and Bertha Wilson Professor of Law, Willamette University. He earned his A.B., J.D., and J.S.M. degrees at Stanford University. He has been president of the American Society of Comparative Law and has taught in Europe, Latin America, and Asia and held the Alexander von Humboldt and Max Planck Society research fellowships. He has written or edited several books on comparative law, law and society, and procedural law and teaches in those areas.

Yves Dezalay is a director of research for the Centre National de la Recherche Scientifique (CNRS) located at the Centre de Sociologie Européenne, which is attached to the Collège de France and the Maison des Sciences de l'Homme in Paris. He and Bryant Garth have collaborated on several books, including *Dealing in Virtue: International Commercial Arbitration and the Construction of a Transnational Legal Order* (Chicago: University of Chicago Press, 1996), which won the Herbert Jacob book award of the Law and Society Association. He has degrees from Sciences-Po (Paris) and the École

Nationale de la Statistiques et de l'Administration Economique and the Doctorat d'État in lettres et sciences humaines from the École des Hautes Études en Sciences Sociales.

Héctor Fix-Fierro has a law degree from the National University of Mexico. He is a full-time researcher at the Institute for Legal Research of the same university.

Lawrence M. Friedman is the Marion Rice Kirkwood Professor of Law, Stanford University. He is the author or editor of more than twenty books and 150 articles and book chapters on legal history and law and society issues. He is a member of the American Academy of Arts and Sciences. He holds five honorary degrees from American and overseas universities.

Edmundo Fuenzalida Faivovich earned a degree in legal and social sciences from the University of Chile, an advanced degree in sociology from the Latin American Faculty of Social Sciences (FLACSO), and a Doctorate in Jurisprudence from the University of Rome. He has taught courses at the Universities of Zurich (Switzerland), Sussex (United Kingdom), Stanford (United States), and Catholic University of Chile. At present he is director of the Stanford University Overseas Studies Center in Latin America, in Santiago, Chile, and Titular Professor of Sociology of Law at the University of Chile.

Mauricio García-Villegas is professor of law at the National University of Colombia and Fellow of the Institute for Legal Studies at the University of Wisconsin–Madison. His publications include articles and books on the symbolic efficacy of law, judicial activism, and constitutional adjudication. His current work focuses on comparative sociology of law and legal culture.

Bryant G. Garth is director of the American Bar Foundation, located in Chicago. In addition to the books produced with Yves Dezalay, he has written a number of other books and served as coeditor with Mauro Cappelletti of the volumes on *Access to Justice* produced in the late 1970s. His degrees are from Yale, Stanford Law School, and the European University Institute in Florence. Prior to serving at the American Bar Foundation, he was dean of Indiana University School of Law (Bloomington).

Eliane Botelho Junqueira is a professor at the Catholic University of Rio de Janeiro, where she teaches courses on sociology of law and criminology. She is also the director of the Instituto Direito e Sociedade (IDES), Brazil.

Sergio López-Ayllón has a Ph.D. in law from the National University of Mexico. He serves as deputy director of the Federal Regulatory Improvement Commission of the Ministry of Economy and is a full-time researcher at the Institute for Legal Research of the National University of Mexico.

John Henry Merryman is the Sweitzer Professor of Law, Emeritus, and an affiliated professor in the Department of Art at Stanford University. His books include *The Civil Law Tradition,* 2d ed. (Stanford, Calif.: Stanford University Press, 1985), *Law in Radically Different Cultures* (with Barton, Gibbs, and Li; St. Paul, Minn.: West Publishing Co., 1983), and *The Loneliness of the Comparative Lawyer* (Boston: Kluwer Law International, 1999).

Rogelio Pérez-Perdomo is a dean of the law school at the Universidad Metropolitana in Caracas, Venezuela. He is a frequent visiting professor at Stanford Law School and has published extensively on different aspects of Latin American legal culture.

César A. Rodríguez is a professor of law at the University of the Andes (Colombia) and Ph.D. candidate in sociology at the University of Wisconsin–Madison. He is the editor of the journal *Beyond Law*. He has published articles and book chapters on sociology of law and legal theory, and his current research interests include the sociology of development, globalization, and labor.

Blanca G. Silvestrini is professor of history and director of the Institute of Puerto Rican and Latino Studies at the University of Connecticut. She has published extensively on Caribbean social history, women and work, and the study of social and legal changes in the transition to a "modern" society. She has a book in progress on conceptions of citizenship among Latinos in the United States.

José Juan Toharia is professor of sociology at the Universidad Autónoma de Madrid and has researched and published on the sociology of the judiciary as well as on public opinion on the system of justice. He hold a Ph.D. from Yale University and an LL.D. from the University of Madrid.

Rodrigo Uprimny is a professor of law at the National University of Colombia. He holds a Ph.D. in economics from the University of Paris I. His publications include articles on judicial reform, alternative dispute resolution, human rights, and constitutional adjudication in Colombia.

Acknowledgments

JOHN HENRY MERRYMAN has made and continues to make great contributions to the understanding of the civil law tradition. His work about the civil law tradition in the Italian style, as well as his other work about European, Latin American, and East Asian law, stands witness to his enormous contributions. In the 1970s, John Henry Merryman initiated one of his most ambitious projects in juridical investigation: SLADE, or Studies in Law and Development. It was an immense task. Very few people were trained in both law and the social sciences, and the available data were limited. The project was inspired by the idea that research on social change could help in understanding the function of the legal system comparatively—that is, in different societies. The project produced an impressive volume of information and works of great insight into the workings of law in the countries that participated in the study—but Merryman's goals have not been reached, at least not in the way that he wished.

This book was conceived as an act of homage to this great academic. We asked our colleagues in those countries that were Merryman's central focus of interest—countries of Latin tradition—to gather the necessary data from the last quarter century in their respective countries. We appealed to SLADE veterans who had continued research; and we were open to others who demonstrated a desire a participate. The chapters integrated into this volume, including the introductory essay by the editors, probably do not fully realize Merryman's dream of comparative and quantitative studies of law; but we feel that we are at least continuing his work, offering data and interpretations that others may be able to use. At the end of the day, science is a collective project that continues over time.

This book is therefore our way to render homage to John Henry Merryman. We are proud that our collective work concludes with his own essay on SLADE. It is the most fitting way to close this volume.

The chapters of this work were originally presented at a conference held at Stanford Law School in September 1999; the sole exception is the chapter about Colombia, whose origin, as explained in that chapter, was different. After the conference, these works were circulated and commented on, and most of the authors made considerable revisions. We thank these authors for their willingness to engage in dialogue and to accept academic criticism.

The works were originally presented in Spanish, English, French, and Portuguese. All were translated into English and Spanish. We thank those Stanford students who translated; they are mentioned in their respective chapters. The authors and editors have revised these translations.

Héctor Fix-Fierro deserves special mention. Besides being coauthor of a chapter, he was tremendous help in the editing and publishing of this book. Manuel Gómez was also of invaluable assistance in checking sources and helping to improve the text.

Above all we thank Stanford Law School, and especially the Stanford Law Library and its staff, for its institutional aid and facilitation, without which this book would not have been possible. We also want to express our gratitude to Mary Tye, our assistant, who did the entire job of preparing this manuscript for the publisher.

Legal Culture in the Age of Globalization

CHAPTER 1

Latin Legal Cultures in the Age of Globalization

ROGELIO PÉREZ-PERDOMO AND LAWRENCE FRIEDMAN

IT IS GENERALLY agreed that the Latin countries of Europe and America, as a group, are part of one of the world's great legal traditions. They are *civil law* countries, tied directly to this tradition (Merryman 1985). Some comparative scholars separate them from the Germanic countries as a Romanist subgroup (Zweigert and Kötz 1998). In this book, the term *Romanist* will refer to these legal cultures, because the word *Latin* is generally not applied to Latin Europe.

Latin countries in Europe have a common history. They were a central part of the Roman Empire. Their populations speak languages derived from the common language of the empire, Latin. They share many other aspects of collective history. For example, they are predominantly Catholic countries, which has marked many of their values and attitudes, as well as the content of their laws. Capitalist development took place relatively late, compared to that in northern European countries. Weber (1958) argued that Protestantism generated attitudes and beliefs that permitted early development of a capitalist economy in northern Europe.

The Latin American countries were colonies of France, Portugal, and Spain, and colonization brought the languages, religion, and values of the mother countries. A large part of the body of laws of these Latin countries is derived, ultimately, from Roman law. The diffusion of Roman law was first a result of the political and economic power of Rome, and later of the importance of the Catholic Church, which adopted and elaborated Roman law, in the form of canon law. From the twelfth century on, Roman law was studied in universities and became the formal knowledge base of jurists and lawyers. Until the eighteenth century, commentaries on great Roman texts constituted the European *jus commune*, the common core of European law. Only in the nineteenth century, with codification, did law take what is for us a familiar form: an aspect of the nation–state and an element of national character. These codes, though national, have similar structures, and they mutually influence each other, since legal literature circulates easily among Latin countries.

The common idea of law as a body of rules or norms emphasizes its strictly national character. One can talk, that is, about the *legal culture* of a particular country. This is a useful term, though different writers use it with different meanings. The term as used here means the cluster of attitudes, ideas, expectations, and values that people hold with regard to their legal system, legal institutions, and legal rules. Each person can have his or her own, unique cluster of such attitudes; but it is possible, no doubt, to generalize about classes of people—one can speak of the legal culture of women, old people, or the poor and the rich; of ethnic and racial minorities; and perhaps also of France, Spain, or Costa Rica as a whole. There is perhaps a legal culture of doctors and a legal culture of accountants. There is also, very definitely, a legal culture of lawyers, of judges, and of jurists in general. These occupations are, of course, of special importance in the study of the legal system and how it works. We can distinguish, perhaps, between the *internal legal culture* (the culture of lawyers and jurists) and the general or *external legal culture* (Friedman 1975).

What the legal culture consists of is an empirical question; and the literature in most countries is, unfortunately, very thin. Clearly, though, the legal culture is an extremely important variable. It is, in a way, the fuel that makes the law machine move and work. It determines the pattern of demands on the legal system. Without the legal culture, "law" is dead, inert, a skeleton—words on paper. Often, two societies will have the same formal rules (or very similar ones), and yet the living law may vary greatly because of differences in legal culture. This, of course, may not be the only difference between them. Institutions also vary. The living law is a product, not simply of legal culture but of legal culture in chemical reaction to the actual set of institutions. Not only does each country's legislation, like its political power, reach only to the borders, but legal institutions and policies gradually take on a national character as well. For example, Blankenburg (1994) has compared Holland with Nordhein-Westfalen, the neighboring German province. Even though Dutch law and German law are the laws of neighboring societies, fundamentally similar in development, and even though people and goods flow between the two regions, their courts and lawyers differ greatly. It is also interesting to analyze countries with a common legal tradition but with considerable disparity in economic and social development. The political and social challenges of *democratization* and *globalization* have affected all of them, but these economic and social processes have no doubt affected political and legal culture in different ways.

Democratization and Globalization

The Latin countries of Europe and America were estimated to have a population of 470 million at the beginning of the year 2000. The countries represented in this study have more than 90 percent of the population of this group. Nevertheless, the countries were chosen not on the basis of demography but simply because there were national academics able and willing to work on this project. We proposed to study the most recent period, as we were interested in the effect of democratization and globalization on these different countries. Each national investigator had complete liberty to choose the exact period—to adapt it to the particularities of his or her country. We who organized the study chose topics that we considered important; nonetheless, the individual authors had great freedom to use or alter the list of topics. Accordingly, country chapters do not have the same structure and content, though circulation of manuscripts and interaction among authors were sufficient to create a common base. We will describe this base so that readers of this book will have a common perspective.

At some points in the twentieth century, Fascist regimes governed Spain, France, and Italy. Spain began its process of democratization with the death of General Franco in 1975, the year that Toharia selected as the beginning point of his chapter. France, reestablishing its democracy after the Second World War, endured a political crisis that brought General de Gaulle to power in 1958, inaugurating a period of personalist democracy. Boigeol selected the end of de Gaulle's period in power as the beginning point of analysis. Italy has had a certain continuity in its contemporary political system, but the 1990s was a period of systemic crisis. The high point was the work of judges and prosecutors investigating the *mani pulite*, or cases of corruption. Spanish and French judges have taken similar actions. This has given judges an extraordinarily important political position, which has become an element of legal culture in these countries.

Argentina, Brazil, and Chile suffered from military dictatorship in the 1970s and 1980s. Their governments were notorious for their violations of human rights. Thousands of people in each country were executed extrajudicially; many of them "disappeared," leaving no corpse or information about the place of death. Thousands were tortured, raped, and imprisoned without trial. These countries are now in a period of democratic transition and of important transformations in their political and legal systems. The passivity or irrelevance of judges in the period of massive abuses of human rights has forced a recalibration of their role; the goal is to bind them to democracy and the rule of law and to induce them to take a more positive role in society.

Colombia, Mexico, and Venezuela have had more or less democratic governments in the second half of the twentieth century. In Mexico, one political party (*Partido Revolucionario Institucional*, or the PRI) controlled society and the state, including the electoral system. It tended to act in a way that perpetuated itself in power for seven decades. The hegemony of the PRI began to weaken in the 1980s, and Mexico recently elected its first president from a rival political party. Colombia has suffered from political conflict and violence; in 1958, a kind of treaty—really a coalition of the two principal political parties—led to a situation in which, for all practical purposes, the two parties alternate power. The political elite is remote from the public; guerrilla movements have sprung up and led in recent years to outright civil war. The guerrillas and drug traffickers pose a formidable challenge to the legal system. From 1958 on, Venezuela had a more conventional democracy that quickly ended a guerrilla movement that had been strong in the 1960s. Nevertheless, corruption and interventionist economic policies brought the country to a political and economic crisis that became especially severe in the 1990s. At the end of the century, a populist leader successfully changed the constitution and the rules of the political game—accumulating considerable political power in the process. It is still too soon to predict the results, but an era of political instability is likely.

Puerto Rico was included in this volume for another reason. Its language, popular culture, and intellectual life are clearly part of the Latin tradition, but it has been a colony of the United States since the Spanish-American War over a century ago. In the last fifty years, the colonial situation has matured, and the country enjoys considerable autonomy. Its legal system has closely followed that of the United States, and it is doubtful that it can be considered purely Latin American. Nevertheless, many of its problems, especially relating to globalization and democratization, have parallels with what is occurring in the rest of the Latin world.

The literature on democratic transitions in Latin American and southern Europe is abundant (see Santamaría 1982; O'Donnell, Schmitter, and Whitehead 1986a, 1986b). In the last twenty-five or thirty years, political processes in all of these countries have tended toward democracy, or in a similar direction, sometimes imperfectly; the final results, of course, are uncertain. The process has brought about a reconsideration of the role of judges; in some cases, judges have had an active role in beginning, ending, or molding political reforms. Judges are figures of some importance in the political and legal cultures of all of these countries. The creation of a constitutional court or the effective use of constitutional jurisdiction increases this importance. Reform is a theme in many countries. International banks and other global organizations have a growing interest in law and justice; and this, too, has been significant.

The period we analyzed was also one of intense and growing commercial and financial exchange among countries. Much investment has occurred within the group of countries—Spanish investment in Latin America, Brazilian investment in Argentina, Chilean or Mexican investment in Venezuela. Countries outside the group—the United States, Germany, and Japan—have also invested in the area. The world has become smaller since the 1970s. Isolation is no longer an option. Economic exchange is only one example of more general social and cultural diffusion across borders. Television, movies, and other means of mass communication, in general, have spread a global popular culture. Tourism has grown immensely. There is increasing immigrant pressure on rich countries. Millions of Mexicans have immigrated to the United States (legally or illegally), along with tens of thousands of emigrants and citizens from other countries of Central and South America. Mediterranean countries, for their part, have also been countries of immigration; they have become magnets for emigrants from less favored areas of the world.

To summarize, all countries in this study—and almost all countries in the world—share in the process of globalization. This is an economic process, but social and cultural aspects are equally important—perhaps more important, because the economic dimension of globalization depends at least in part on the global demand for the same kinds of consumer goods. In any event, these economic and cultural exchanges constitute what is usually referred to as *globalization*.

Its effects on the law are varied. For example, in each country, there is a group of lawyers who work on matters of international business and familiarize themselves with the law and legal culture of other countries. Exposure to foreign influences weakens the links of local culture (McLuhan 1964), evades tradition, accentuates individualism, and increases resort to law for the affirmation of individual rights (Friedman 1985, 1999). This indubitably generates a greater use of lawyers and legal instruments. The various chapters demonstrate the "legalization" of society (which is not the same as a rise in the number of lawsuits). Many other factors, such as cost and other barriers to access, affect the actual litigation rate.

Changes introduced by globalization and democratization are not so radical that they have unified legal regimes or judicial culture, in the general sense that these terms are used here. There are great differences still, even in the countries of the European Union, which share many aspects of development, political economy, and political and legal institutions. The differences are so great that it would not make sense to collect data for the countries of this study as a whole. Even within each nation-state, regional differences can be very significant, as is seen in the chapters on Brazil and Italy. Perhaps more research on these differences is needed, to study not only nations but also regions, as the SLADE project (Studies in Law and Development) originally intended. One of the greatest difficulties is that statistics are generally only national in scope.

This book presents experiences and data that the reader may appreciate and explore in greater detail. In this introductory chapter, we will briefly analyze the changes produced that affect the principal legal actors, without attempting to synthesize the subsequent chapters.

Students and Professors

The term *law student* has different meanings according to place and time. In the Latin tradition, law studies are undergraduate studies. That is, the young student who completes the secondary educational cycle (called *liceo* or *bachillerato* in various countries) enters the university directly into the study of law. In general, the students are eighteen years old. Law studies vary in length, according to the country and to the courses chosen. Five years is the typical duration of the program.

The study of law is supposed to provide general as well as professional training. In this regard, law studies are roughly equivalent both to undergraduate work in the United States, with a major in political science, for example, and to direct legal education. The comparison is not perfect, of course, because of differences in structure and duration and because in Latin countries, a legal education consists mostly of learning principles and rules of law.

Traditionally, the law curriculum is broken down into subdisciplines or subjects, each centered on a legal text. Constitutional law, civil law, penal (criminal) law, procedure, commercial law, and labor law are core studies in all countries of the group. Each course begins with a consideration of general principles, then enters into the details of legal principles and rules. The format is also basically uniform: the professor lectures, and the students listen and perhaps ask questions if some point is not clear. There may be courses with a different format—discussion courses, for example—but these are the exception rather than the rule.

The typical classroom is a rectangular room filled with students. The professor or an assistant teaches from the front of the room. In some countries, the professor teaches in an amphitheater filled with hundreds of students. Attendance is not strictly necessary; students can also learn through manuals that the professor (tenured chair) has written. These manuals are the written version of the professor's lectures.

During the period studied, not much in legal education has changed. In Europe, the university structure gives senior, and generally older, professors considerable power over younger ones. The careers of the latter depend to a great extent on the friendship and support of a senior professor (the system is termed a *mandarinat* by its French critics). This is a very important and conservative force. In France, the events of May 1968 and other forces of reform brought in more use of seminars, but the enormous numbers of students blocked any real reform.

The situation is different in Latin America, where the mandarinat does not have such concentrated power. This perhaps explains why more changes have occurred there. An important number of forces for changing the methodology of teaching and class discussion, and the preparation of readers and casebooks, came together in the 1970s. A number of professors and law schools reformed their methodology, first as a consequence of the so-called law and development movement, and later through the creation of private law schools. These new or reformed schools (for example, the Universidad Católica of Perú; the Universidad Diego Portales in Chile; the Universities of Belgrano, Palermo, and Torcuato di Tella in Argentina; CIDE, the Universidad Iberoamericana, and the Instituto Technológico Autónomo in Mexico [ITAM]) have also made important changes in the curriculum. They teach new skills (such as negotiation, oral presentation, and research) and new subjects (such as human rights and alternative dispute resolution). In Europe, the changes have been less sweeping and, in general, have taken place within public universities.

The number of law students has risen both absolutely and relative to national populations. But it has decreased relative to the total number of students in higher education. This suggests that, at least in part, the increase in law students is the result of greater access to higher education. There is also a perception that legal education offers good access to the labor market. The increased number of students has not led to corresponding increases in the number of those aspiring to the priesthood or studying arts and philosophy; these fields have greater difficulty in finding students than do law schools. Table 1.1 gives data about the numbers of law students in the countries studied.

Studies also show a "feminization" of the profession. In Mexico, for example, in only six years (1991–97), women rose from 41 percent to 46.7 percent of all law students. In France, the proportion rose from 50 percent in 1973 to 64.5 percent in 1998. Spain achieved 50 percent ratios in 1973 and has maintained that proportion ever since.

The number of law schools has also risen. In Latin America, as noted, private universities with law schools have come into existence. Many of these new law schools copy the curriculum and educational methods of the older ones and contribute to a certain "fossilization" of legal education; but in some private schools, important changes are taking place. These changes occur principally in those schools most oriented to training business lawyers. Some private schools have been very innovative and are also quite selec-

TABLE 1.1

Law Students

Country	Number of law students	Percentage of university students	Estimates of law students per 100,000
Argentina 1970	29,045	13.2	124
Argentina 1998	163,881	14.7	453
Brazil 1961	23,519	23.7	33
Brazil 1994 (a)	190,712	11.5	122
Chile 1950 (b)	2,284	25	19
Chile 1965 (a)	3,431	7.9	39
Chile 2000	24,478	5.4	163
Colombia 1950 (b)	1,985	20.5	18
Colombia 1965 (a)	5,274	11.9	29
Colombia 2001	66,976	6.9	155
Costa Rica 1950 (b)	205	13.3	24
Costa Rica 1965 (a)	328	4.5	22
Costa Rica 1994 (a)	4,262	5.4	125
France 1962	45,511	17.1	98
France 1978	131,460	15.6	248
France 1998	180,490	12.8	300
Italy 1950	27,035	11.7	60
Italy 1970	67,387	9.9	120
Italy 1996	324,889	18.3	560
Mexico 1965 (a)	16,808	12.6	42
Mexico 2000	188,422	11.9	193
Peru 1950 (b)	1,392	8.7	18
Peru 1965 (a)	4,624	5.8	40
Peru 2000	41,192	9.7	152
Spain 1950 (b)	16,853	30.9	61
Spain 1970 (b)	21,009	9.9	62
Spain 1988	180,516	11	458
Venezuela 1950	1,000	13.5	53
Venezuela 1965 (a)	6,766	12.6	78
Venezuela 2000	40,000	7.4	160

SOURCES: (a) UNESCO, *Statistical Yearbook* (Paris: Imprimerie Jean Lamour, 1973; Paris: Bernan Press, 1979); (b) Merryman, Clark, and Friedman (1979); Argentina: Sistema de Estadísticas Universitarias, Ministerio de Educación (data collected by Bergoglio); Brazil 1961: Falcão (1984); Chile 2000: Persico (2001); Colombia 2001: Fuentes Hernández, Educación legal y educación superior en Colombia: Tendencias recientes 1990–2002 (unpublished); France: Boigeol (in this book); Italy: Cassese (in this book); Mexico 2000: Fix-Fierro and López-Ayllón, La educación jurídica en México: Un panorama general (unpublished); Peru 2000: González Mantilla, La enseñanza del derecho en el Perú en la actualidad: Cambios, resistencias y continuidades (unpublished); Spain 1998: Toharia (in this book); Venezuela 1950: Pérez Perdomo (1981); Venezuela 2000: Pérez Perdomo (in this book).

tive; they have become as prestigious as the oldest, traditionally honored public universities. The most prestigious law schools offer postgraduate study, as the usual law degree is becoming insufficient for the best job opportunities. A postgraduate degree from a local university or from another country, such as the United States and England, is becoming a more useful credential. Parallel to the stratification of schools is a stratification of students and graduates. The more prestigious schools can be selective, taking students with the highest interest in and the most resources for a postgraduate degree.

In Europe, on the other hand, private universities have a more limited role, and postgraduate studies are usually restricted to preparation of business attorneys. The trend toward postgraduate work outside national boundaries is less general.

Lawyers

With the growth and stratification of students and law schools comes a similar growth in the stratification and number of lawyers. Table 1.2 gives data on the growth in the number of lawyers, both in absolute and relative numbers.

The first point is that the number of lawyers has increased enormously, in both absolute and relative numbers. The difference between countries is also substantial and does not appear to correspond to relative levels of development. In those countries in which legal studies lead directly to a professional title (as in Spain, Mexico, and Venezuela), the numbers tend to be very high. In those countries with additional requirements—examinations or additional training (France, Italy, and Brazil)—the resulting number of lawyers is comparatively lower. In other cases, such as Chile, the size of the profession had been regulated by limits on the number of persons who could attend law school; when university policies changed, the number began to rise substantially (De la Maza 2001). In other words, professional regulation, admission policies, or a combination of the two determines the number of lawyers in a country. It is also predictable that in those countries with a large number of law graduates but with relative restrictions on the number of lawyers, law graduates will find some type of occupation related to the legal system and will contribute in some way to the larger role of law in a society —that is, to the "legalization" of society.

Growth has also led to stratification in the profession. During most of the twentieth century, a law degree guaranteed access to elite occupations, and perhaps to a political position. This is no longer the case. Some lawyers have trouble even entering the professional labor market, other lawyers have high professional prestige (generally reflected also in high levels of income), and, of course, there are many gradations in between. This stratification is the product of both a rise in numbers and a democratization of access to law schools and to a professional degree. In a general way, it can be said that a person's social networks determine professional opportunities, even though the quality of legal education can be a very important factor: studying in the most prestigious schools and individual academic merit have an influence not limited solely to professional access.

TABLE I.2

Changes in the Number of Lawyers
in Selected Countries

Country	Number of lawyers	Lawyers per 100,000 people
Brazil 1950	15,666	30
Brazil 1960	30,066	42
Brazil 1970	37,710	41
Brazil 1980	85,710	72
Brazil 1991	148,671	101
Chile 1950 (a)	1,475	24
Chile 1960 (a)	2,602	34
Chile 1970 (a)	4,306	44
Chile 1982	6,546	58
Chile 1992	9,308	70
Chile 2000	11,400	75
Costa Rica 1950 (a)	467	54
Costa Rica 1960 (a)	682	55
Costa Rica 1970 (a)	968	57
Costa Rica 1990	4,400	157
Costa Rica 2000	10,800	309
France 1973	14,890	29
France 1998	42,092	70
Italy 1950	29,400	57
Italy 1960	36,916	73
Italy 1970	41,639	76
Italy 1996	98,258	171
Mexico 1960	8,426	24
Mexico 1990	141,539	174
Mexico 1998	200,000	208
Peru 1950 (a)	1,970	25
Peru 1960 (a)	2,960	31
Peru 1970 (a)	4,080	32
Spain 1980	27,983	75
Spain 1998	96,000	343
Venezuela 1950	2,087	41
Venezuela 1961	4,256	57
Venezuela 1971	8,102	76
Venezuela 1981	16,045	111
Venezuela 1990	31,350	159
Venezuela 2001	82,939	337

SOURCES: (a) Merryman, Clark, and Friedman (1979); Brazil 1950, 1960, 1970, 1980: Falcão (1984); Brazil 1991: Junqueira (in this book); Chile 1982, 1992, 2000: De la Maza (2001); Costa Rica 1990, 2000: information from Alfredo Chirinos, director of the Judicial School; France: Boigeol (in this book); Italy: Cassese (in this book); Mexico: Fix-Fierro and López-Ayllón (in this book); Spain: Toharia (in this book); Venezuela: Pérez-Perdomo (in this book).

TABLE 1.3
Large Law Firms

Country	100 or more	50–99
Argentina	2	7
Brazil	4	4
Chile	0	1
Spain	5	7
France	12	★
Italy	4	8
Mexico	1	4
Peru	0	1
Venezuela	0	2

SOURCES: For Latin America: 1999 *Latin lawyer: A who's who of Latin American law firms.* (London: Law Business Research, 1999); for Europe: J. Pritchard, ed., *Law firms in Europe and the Middle East,* 10th ed. (London: The European Legal 500, 2000).
★ The directory includes only 24 large firms, the largest having 68.

Traditionally, lawyers have worked in individual or family offices. In the second half of this century, U.S.-style law firms began to appear. The model spread more rapidly in Latin America, perhaps because in Europe the bar was tightly organized and controlled the progression more completely (see Abel 1988). The situation now appears to have changed, and large firms have emerged in Europe, some of which include both lawyers and accountants to give more integrated service to business clients. Truly large firms remain rare (see Table 1.3). Only seven firms in Latin America have more than 100 lawyers (210 is the largest); in Europe, there are twenty-one firms of this size. There are more firms in the 50–59 lawyer range—nineteen in Latin America. The total number of such firms in Europe is not known to us. (There are seven in Spain and eight in Italy, but the figure for France is uncertain.)

If Europe and Latin America have resented North American law firms (in particular, see the chapters on France and Venezuela), it is worth asking why European and Latin American firms tend to stay small or relatively small while those in the United States are in a stage of explosive growth (Galanter and Palay 1991). Various explanations are possible. One is the relatively closed environment until very recently: society was less "legalized," businesses were smaller, and the enormous accounting and legal requirements that characterize the gigantic multinational American corporations were relatively lacking. In addition, Latin businesses appear to trust their own legal departments—their in-house counsel. These legal departments process much of the daily legal work necessary for the business. When outside help is needed, businesses prefer "to buy in boutiques and not in department stores"

(Pérez-Perdomo 2001). Lawyers who are heads of legal departments have, in general, a status superior to that of their American equivalents.

Another explanation for the relatively small size of law firms is the narrow national nature of legal education. Lawyers are not well trained for work on problems of other legal systems. Finally, Latin American firms came late to the international legal services market, which was already occupied by the great international law firms (of the United States) and by equally great—if not greater—accounting firms with legal capabilities.

Judges and Lawsuits

In the Romanist tradition, judges had a modest role in society (Merryman 1985, 35). They were "the mouthpiece of the law" and, as a consequence, were not expected to be imaginative or to play a part in the drama of politics. Systems of justice commanded few resources; they were technologically primitive compared to the rest of the state apparatus. Judges and legal staff were relatively poorly paid. The *judicial power* was the Cinderella of the public system. This situation made it difficult to attract well-qualified people. In many Latin American countries, small-time corruption (*transaction bribes*, or illegal but customary payments to bureaucrats to speed up procedures) was a normal method of adding to this paltry salary. The elite did not need the justice system because the political system channeled public resources through personal networks. The political system was the general arbiter of conflicts. The process of privatization and the relative loss of power of the political system began to change this situation. Judges and justice are now gaining in importance.

The change can be seen, in the first place, in the prestige and compensation of judges. In all of the countries studied, the pay of judges has risen substantially, and the position of judge has greater social and professional prestige. The number of judges has also risen, even in relative terms, though the data are spotty, and the definition of *judge* can vary from country to country (see Table 1.4). In France, for example, we lack information on administrative judges of the 1970s. In Mexico, we have only been able to use figures for federal judges. We know that there were 3,677 state judges in 2000 (Concha and Caballero Juárez 2001), but we have no data from past years to compare. In Chile, available data show a significant decline in absolute terms and a 50 percent reduction in relative terms, but these results may have occurred because "assistant judges" were counted in 1970, and they do not appear to be included in the figures for 1995. In Venezuela, the number of judges appears to have decreased in relative terms, but this may be misleading. The figures do not include justices of the peace (some 200 in 1999), a jurisdiction created a few years ago. It might be controversial to include them, as they

TABLE 1.4

Number of Judges

Country	Number of judges	Number per 100,000 people
Argentina (Córdoba) 1971	167	8.0
Argentina (Córdoba) 1998	447	11.9
Argentina 1996	4,030	10.9
Brazil 1970	3,624	3.9
Brazil 1991	8,050	5.5
Chile 1970 (a)	604	6.2
Chile 1995	483	3.4
Colombia 1970 (a)	2,724	12.8
Colombia 1990	4,800	16.0
Colombia 1999	3,272	8.9
Costa Rica 1970 (a)	148	8.6
Costa Rica 1990	299	10.7
Costa Rica 2000	567	16.2
France 1973	4,538	8.9
France 1998	6,457	10.8
Italy 1970	5,992	11.0
Italy 1997	9,753	17.0
Mexico (federal) 1970	77	0.2
Mexico (federal) 1999	366	0.4
Mexico (states) 2000	3,677	3.7
Spain 1975	1,842	5.2
Spain 1985	2,328	6.3
Spain 1998	3,554	9.0
Venezuela 1971	783	7.3
Venezuela 1997	1,165	5.0
Venezuela 2000	1,772	7.5

SOURCES: (a) Merryman, Clark, Friedman (1979); Argentina: Bergoglio (in this book); Brazil: Junqueira (in this book); Chile 1995: Vargas, Peña, and Correa (2001); Colombia 1990: Giraldo Angel (1993; he includes instruction judges that became district attorneys); Colombia 1999: Fuentes-Hernández and Amaya-Osorio (2001); Costa Rica 2000: information from Alfredo Chirinos, director of the Judicial School; France: Boigeol (in this book); Italy: Cassese (in this book); Mexico (federal judiciary): Fix-Fierro and López-Ayllón (in this book); Mexico (states judiciary): Concha-Cantú and Caballero Juárez (2001); Spain: Toharia (in this book); Venezuela: Pérez-Perdomo (in this book).

NOTES: France: these numbers do not include administrative judges or business law justices; Mexico: the numbers refer only to federal judges; Venezuela: these numbers do not include the Supreme Court, military tribunals, or justices of the peace.

are seen fundamentally as mediators, are popularly elected, and are not necessarily law school graduates.

Numbers of judges are very crude indicators that do not say much about how the legal system functions. The work of judges can vary greatly from one country to another. However, judges usually do not lose function; the rise in the number of judges generally signifies a rise in work for the judicial system.

Another feature of judicial demography is the growing participation of women. For example, in Spain before 1977, less than 1 percent of the judges were women; in 1997, women made up more than half of the new judges. In France, women were 28.5 percent of the judges in 1982 and 48.5 percent in 1999. In Brazil between 1970 and 1991, the number of women judges rose from 5 percent to 20 percent. In the Mexican federal system, where at one time there were almost no women, they constituted 17 percent of the judges in 1999. The judiciary seems to have accepted women without any problems, though "feminization" is probably not a factor in the rise in judicial prestige.

We have little data on the socioeconomic origins of the judges. We know that in some countries, such as Spain, young people in the richest and most urban regions have become interested in judgeships. The growing social prestige of the judiciary is probably a factor.

Measuring litigiousness is an extraordinarily difficult task. Some categories of cases rise, at times rapidly; others fall or remain the same. The statistics are hard to interpret, and it is even harder to try to generalize from country to country (for detailed analysis, see the chapters on Argentina, Spain, and Puerto Rico in this volume). It is perhaps easier to measure legislative changes that "judicialize" certain types of conflicts and processes, or those that "dejudicialize" them. What is beyond doubt is the growing use of the judicial system to resolve political conflicts—to make claims and demands that were once impossible. The increase in suits against the state or against administrative agencies is especially noteworthy. It is now rare that a corruption scandal, for example, fails to generate some kind of judicial action. Sometimes, in fact, judicial action itself generates the scandal. In modern societies, the media expose these scandals to a broad public. Thus, judges become objects of intense public interest, which may perhaps pose a danger to the system of justice (Garapon and Sala 1996; Pérez-Perdomo 1998). One hears talk of the "penalization of the Republic" (Garapon and Sala 1996) or the "judicialization of politics and social relations" (Vianna et al. 1999). Constitutional and administrative justice has therefore grown substantially in importance, and this inflates the social and political importance of judges (García de Enterría 1997). Cases of judicial review, or those that are politically sensitive, are not *numerically* significant—most cases in court remain routine, even quasi-notarial, issues of debt collection, divorce, custody, or child support. But the numbers do not do justice to the globalization of judicial power (Tate and Vallinder 1995).

Most people still avoid courts at all costs. The reasons vary from country to country. In Latin America, the costs are too high for all but the rich, and there is no legal insurance. Legal aid is generally of poor quality. In Latin Europe, the obstacle is not so much economics as the strangeness of legal rituals and language (Carmena 1997; Garapon 1985). Increasing access to a painfully archaic and slow judicial system makes little sense. For this reason, all of the countries in this study, as is true elsewhere as well, are spending millions on judicial reform. The results are uncertain. The process is slow, and there is a shortage of serious social analyses and evaluations. More and more use is made of the system of justice, in crucial ways; but dissatisfaction with the system also runs high. Why is it that the political power of the judicial system is growing, even though there is so much dissatisfaction with the system in its day-to-day work?

There are, of course, obvious reasons for dissatisfaction. Justice in Italy is painfully slow. In countries with rapid and efficient justice systems (Finland is the best European example; Toharia 2001), there is a high level of confidence in judges. At the same time, in all the countries in this study, there has been a growing demand for justice as a *product*. After all, people do not bother to complain about institutions that have no meaning to them or from which they expect very little. People grumble when institutions that they deal with fall short of what they need and want from them.

In all the countries treated in this volume, people's expectations from their judicial systems have grown steadily over the years. This is, in part, a product of democratization. Democracy is more than a form of government. In our times, democracy is closely related to the rule of law. The demand for democracy is a demand for human rights, for a legal system that supports the type of life that the public demands. Of course, democracy means free elections, legislatures, and fundamental rights, but these rights are meaningless without institutions to protect and enforce them. Without such institutions, the "democracy" becomes unstable. This may be occurring in Venezuela.

In countries with a long democratic tradition, democracy is, in a way, taken for granted. People assume that the whole world wants it—that democracy is the natural, inevitable political system. It will develop everywhere, unless some form of artificial and despotic control crushes the free expression of ideas. But, of course, democracy is not "natural." No one (almost no one) in the Middle Ages even considered it an appropriate form of government; nor did most Latin countries, as late as the eighteenth century. The tendency to democracy, which has powerfully influenced all the countries we have studied, was produced by certain social forces that have become stronger and stronger over time.

One of these forces is globalization, especially in the cultural sense that we use this term. Television, roads, trains, planes, radios, movies: these aspects of modern life, and many others, have destroyed the peasant isolation and fatalism that kept many countries in a situation of turbulent quiet. The forces of modernization have destroyed the oligarchic equilibrium that existed in most of these countries (or in regions of these countries)—even though, in some cases, these same forces generated social and political processes that brought dictatorship to power. Modernity is a complex culture. It includes a set of beliefs, values, and attitudes—among them the belief in rights inherent in every person—that have spread all over the world and become a common currency for societies on every continent. Of course, there is no simple evolutionary line. Social processes are always complex and difficult to decipher.

The countries included in this study have modernized at different paces and at different historic moments. In 1975, only France and Italy could be considered completely modern and democratic. Argentina, Brazil, and Chile, the most industrialized countries of South America, had lost their democratic governments. In the year 2000, all of the countries in this study can be considered democratic. Only Venezuela, perhaps, appears to show signs of "caesarism." In most of the countries, there have been enormous political changes since 1975. Dictatorship in Spain died with Franco, and the domination of the PRI party in Mexico, after a period of decay, finally ended with the election of Vicente Fox. Colonial Puerto Rico gained in autonomy during this period and consolidated its democracy. Military dictatorships in South America gave way to freely elected governments. The Pinochet regime ended in Chile. That he was threatened with a criminal trial is perhaps a strong symbol of the end of an era.

As we have already indicated, contemporary democracies are basically tied to the rule of law (Dahl 1989). The "rule of law" means different things to different groups. For businesspeople, it means stable rules, honest judges, enforcement of contracts, and a reliable civil service. But authoritarian governments can, at times, produce *this* kind of "rule of law." For the ordinary person, rule of law means that there are limits to what the government and the bureaucracy can do; it means the right to live more or less as people wish, without midnight arrests or arbitrary treatment. Even constitutional rights are only words if there is no machinery to realize them. This explains why, in modern societies, courts play a more and more powerful role. Many countries now have constitutional courts or their functional equivalents. As a part of the same movement, many countries are reforming their systems of criminal justice. In almost all countries, proactive judges have appeared to fight the battles against corruption or tyranny. Di Pietro and Garzón are the most notable cases, but they are far from the only ones. Of course, most judges still work traditionally and anonymously, but there are signs that their roles are changing.

Each country in this study has its unique history and legal tradition. Nevertheless, all the countries have much in common, as we have noted. Formally, they share the Roman law inheritance. In Spanish-speaking countries, the common language facilitates a shared juridical literature and enables each to see what the others are doing. But this is true for the other countries as well. What is written and what happens in Italy or Spain are of interest to the French, and vice versa. Latin American attention to what happens in Europe is intense; and so, too, is the reverse. To this story of convergence is added the convergence of modernity itself, which brings countries closer together—including those of other legal traditions. North America and the rest of Europe are also more and more convergent. The convergence of legal systems is a hypothesis, but one that is becoming more plausible each day.

In all of these countries, law has grown in importance—however we care to analyze or measure it. International investors pressure the system and create a climate in which lawyers and law become established; society as a whole also puts pressure on the system to produce results. Businesses employ thousands of lawyers; but ordinary people also need the assistance of lawyers to buy houses, to get a divorce, and to do other mundane things. The growth of the middle class means more work for lawyers. Rights consciousness brings more claims against government and administrative agencies. There is a culture of claims developing (García de La Cruz 1999). For this reason, in one country after another the number of lawyers has increased. Of course, not all countries have embraced the rule of law, and all face problems of legality (see Méndez, O'Donnell, and Pinheiro 1999). The rule of law is best understood as an ideal. The chapters of this book provide data on which to reflect about the performance of the legal system. It is easy to be dissatisfied with the way the system works—the data reflect this dissatisfaction. But people also have high expectations. A vital, active, expanding legal order is part of life in Latin countries of Europe and America. The significance of law seems to be here to stay.

References

Abel, Richard L. 1988. Lawyers in the civil law world. Pp. 1–53 in *Lawyers in society: The civil law world*, edited by R. Abel and P. Lewis. Berkeley: University of California Press.

Blankenburg, Erhard. 1994. The infrasructure for avoiding civil litigation: Comparing cultures of legal behavior in the Netherlands and West Germany. *Law and Society Review* 28: 789–808.

Carmena, Manuela. 1997. *Crónica de un desastre: Notas para reinventar la justicia*. Madrid: Alianza Editorial.

Concha Cantú, Hugo, and A. Caballero Juárez. 2001. *Diagnóstico sobre la administración de justicia en las entidades federativas: Un estudio institucional sobre la justicia local en*

México. Mexico City: Instituto de Investigaciones Jurídicas de Universidad Nacional Autónomo de Mexico.

Dahl, Robert. 1989. *Democracy and its critics*. New Haven, Conn.: Yale University Press.

De la Maza, Iñigo. 2001. *Los abogados chilenos, entre el estado y el mercado*. Juris science master's thesis, Program for International Legal Studies, Stanford University.

Falcão, Joaquim. 1984. *Os advogados: Encino jurídico e mercado de traballo*. Recife, Brazil: Fundacão Joaquim Nabuco y Editora Massangana.

Friedman, Lawrence. 1975. *The legal system: A social science perspective*. New York: Russell Sage Foundation.

———. 1985. *Total justice*. New York: Russell Sage Foundation.

———. 1999. *The horizontal society*. New Haven, Conn.: Yale University Press.

Fuentes-Hernández, Alfredo, and C. Amaya-Osorio. 2001. Demanda y oferta judicial: Dificultades de ajuste. In *Nuevos enfoques para atender la demanda de justicia*, Conferencia Regional del Banco Mundial para América Latina y el Caribe, May, CIDE, México.

Galanter, Marc, and T. Palay. 1991. *Tournament of lawyers: The transformations of big law firms*. Chicago: University of Chicago Press.

Garapon, Antoine. 1985. *L'âne portant des reliques: Essai sur le rituel judiciaire*. Paris: Le Centurion.

Garapon, Antoine, and D. Sala. 1996. *La République pénalisée*. Paris: Hachette.

García de Enterría, Eduardo. 1997. *Democracia, jueces y control de la Administración*. 3d ed. Madrid: Civitas.

Garcia de La Cruz, Juan José. 1999. La cultura de la reclamación como indicador de desarrollo democrático: Tres perspectivas de análisis. *Politeia* 22:7–28.

Giraldo Angel, Jaime. 1993. Informe sobre Colombia. In *Situación y políticas judiciales en América Latina*, edited by J. Correa Sutil. Santiago: Escuela de Derecho Universidad Diego Portales.

McLuhan, Marshall. 1964. *Understanding media: The extension of man*. New York: McGraw-Hill.

Méndez, Juan, G. O'Donnell, and P. S. Pinheiro, eds. 1999. *The (un)rule of law and the underprivileged in Latin America*. Notre Dame, Ind.: University of Notre Dame Press.

Merryman, John Henry. 1985. *The civil law tradition*. 2d ed. Stanford, Calif.: Stanford University Press.

Merryman, John H., D. Clark, and L. M. Friedman. 1979. *Law and social change in Mediterranean Europe and Latin America: A handbook of legal and social indicators*. Stanford, Calif.: Stanford Law School.

O'Donnell, Guillermo, P. C. Schmitter, and L. Whitehead, eds. 1986a. *Transitions from authoritarian rule: Southern Europe*. Baltimore, Md.: Johns Hopkins University Press.

———. 1986b. *Transitions from authoritarian rule: Latin America*. Baltimore, Md.: Johns Hopkins University Press.

Pérez-Perdomo, Rogelio. 1981. *Los abogados en Venezuela 1780–1980*. Caracas: Monte Avila.

———. 1996. De la justicia y otros demonios. Pp. 117–73 in *Seguridad jurídica y com-*

petitividad, edited by M. E. Boza and R. Pérez-Perdomo. Caracas: Ediciones Instituto de Estudios Superiores de Administración.

————. 1998. Escándalos de corrupción y cultura jurídico política: Un análisis desde Venezuela. Pp. 31–47 in *Globalization and legal cultures*, edited by J. Feest. Oñati, Spain: International Institute for the Sociology of Law.

————. 2001. Oil lawyers and the globalization of the Venezuelan oil industry. Pp. 301–22 in *The legal culture of global business transactions*, edited by R. Appelbaum, W. Felstiner, and V. Gessner, Oxford, England: Hart.

Persico, Pablo. 2001. *Informe sobre la educación superior en Chile: Análisis de tendencias de la última década*. Santiago: Corporación de Promoción Universitaria.

Santamaría, Julián, ed. 1982. *Transición a la democracia en el Sur de Europa y América Latina*. Madrid: Centro de Investigaciones Sociales.

Tate, C. N., and T. Vallinder, eds. 1995. *The global expansion of judicial power*. New York: New York University Press

Toharia, José Juan. 2001. *Opinión pública y justicia: La imagen de la justicia en la sociedad española*. Madrid: Consejo General del Poder Judicial.

Vargas, Juan Enrique, C. Peña, and J. Correa. 2001. *El rol del estado y del mercado en la justicia*. Santiago: Universidad Diego Portales.

Vianna, Luiz W., M. A. R. de Carvalho, M. P. C. Melo, and M. B. Burgos. 1999. *A judicializacão de politica e das relacões sociais no Brasil*. Rio de Janeiro: Revan.

Weber, Max. 1958. *The Protestant ethic and the spirit of capitalism*. New York: Scribner.

Zweigert, Konrad, and Hein Kötz. 1998. *An introduction to comparative law*. 3d ed. Oxford, England: Clarendon Press.

CHAPTER 2

Argentina: The Effects
of Democratic Institutionalization

MARÍA INÉS BERGOGLIO

THE PRIMARY AIM of this chapter is to identify the main changes in law and legal culture in Argentina in the period 1970–98, a country that has gone through huge transformations, both economic and political, during this period. Examining legal transformations may help our understanding of the relationship between law and social structure.

The obstacles to this task are many because law and legal culture are complex phenomena. The task is particularly hard in Argentina, where socio-legal research is scarcely developed, and judicial statistics are a creation of the 1990s.[1] This chapter will concentrate on just one aspect of law and legal culture: litigation. The effects of changes in legislation, the courts, and legal culture become evident at this point where citizens confront the legal system.

The analysis is based on data from longitudinal research carried out in the Argentine province of Córdoba, 1970–98, by a team of the Centro de Investigaciones Jurídicas y Sociales de la Universidad Nacional de Córdoba.

Transformations in Argentina, 1970–1998

Before presenting these results, it is necessary to summarize the major changes in Argentina and in the legal context during the period. Social change was intense, politically and economically, and in terms of interna-

This research received a grant from the Consejo de Investigaciones Científicas de Córdoba (CONICOR). The project was directed by the author of this chapter at the Centro de Investigaciones Jurídicas y Sociales, Universidad Nacional de Córdoba. Julio Carballo and Mariana Sánchez were also part of the research team, as well as the student Lucas Vilanova.

tional relations. We limit our focus to transformations along two axes: the political-institutional context, deeply transformed by democratization, and social structure, where inequalities have widened. This description is just one among many possibilities, of course.

THE POLITICAL-INSTITUTIONAL CONTEXT

In 1970, the country was under military rule and seemed unable to find its way toward institutional normality. Today, democratic institutions are working regularly, and a fourth presidential term following the constitutional rules of succession has begun. As in other Latin American countries during this period, democratization has been a most profound change, as it is much more than institutional normalization: it entails changes within the power structure. The impact of these changes on the legal system and the legal culture is obvious.

However, building a genuine rule of law—a task still in progress—has not been easy.[2] We can distinguish four periods.

Political instability, 1970–1975. After the overthrow of Perón by the armed forces in 1955, none of the military or civilian presidents that followed ever completed his full term. Then, after an eighteen-year exile, Perón was elected to a third presidency in 1973. By that time, however, leftist urban guerrillas and paramilitary rightist groups were astir, and Perón was an old man. He died the following year, leaving his wife, Isabel, the vice president, to succeed him. Unable to unite the divided Peronist Party or to contain the mounting violence or control inflation, she, too, was ousted by the military in March 1976.

The junta dictatorship, 1976–1983. The military junta banned all political activity. The new regime surpassed all previous levels of military repression of the opposition and fought against guerrillas by all sorts of means, including torture. Illegal repression was used against nearly all political opposition, and human rights violations were, unfortunately, systematic and common. Several thousand people went "missing." After an unsuccessful war with Great Britain (1982) over possession of the Malvinas (Falkland) Islands, the military was compelled to call elections.

Restoration of democracy, 1983–1989. Civilian government returned in December 1983, with the election of Raul Alfonsin of the Radical Party as president. In an atmosphere of confidence in regard to the possibilities offered by the rule of law, Alfonsin's government prosecuted the officers responsible for violations of human rights. In 1985, former president Videla and other military leaders were sentenced to prison. Separately, former president Galtieri was also convicted in 1986 for negligence during the Malvinas (Falkland)

War. As a result of these trials, the prestige of the judiciary was enhanced, despite the military pressure that led to the grant of immunity to most officers in 1987.

In 1985, Alfonsin's austerity program succeeded temporarily in controlling chronic inflation. Later, inflation skyrocketed, leading to a hyperinflation crisis in 1989.

Consolidation of democracy, from 1989 onward. Presidential elections were held in May 1989 at a time of economic disintegration. Carlos Menem, the Peronist candidate, won the presidency. Democratic institutions seemed more solid as a second civilian president, from the opposition, came into office.

Menem, who pardoned the three former military leaders in 1989, launched a new economic austerity plan, which at first failed to halt inflation. Eventually, he restored the peso as the main currency unit. By 1993, Menem's anti-inflationary measures had succeeded, and the economy and stock market rebounded.

In 1994, the main political parties agreed to reform the 1853 constitution. This change of rules, together with economic success, allowed Menem to run for a second term, 1995–99. The stability of a ten-year-long political term in office is a vivid contrast to the sharp political oscillations of the 1970s.

CHANGES IN SOCIAL STRUCTURE

In 1970, after several decades of an industrialization strategy oriented toward import substitution, Argentina's social structure made Argentina one of the least unequal societies in Latin America. Economic growth following the Second World War and urban migrations fostered the expansion of the middle class, estimated at that time at 44.9 percent of the population.[3]

In spite of political instability, workers received a significant share of the national income.[4] Women's presence within the economy was also relevant: 27 percent of women aged 14 or older had a paid job (Wainerman 1995). Social inequalities could be classified as moderate, contrasting with acute social differences existing in Mexico, Brazil, or Venezuela (Treber 1996).

From 1976 on, the military government discontinued industrialization strategies aimed at the internal market and opened the economy, stressing anti-inflationary policies. When democracy was restored, the results of these policies were plain: decreased salaries, deteriorated living conditions, and severe economic recession. Difficulties with external financing, characteristic of the 1980s, aggravated the situation.

The first democratic administration set out to institutionalize the rules of the political game and devoted less effort to the economic situation. Although under Alfonsin there was a certain amount of recovery in salary scales, economic stagnation continued during the rest of the decade. In 1989, hyperinflation pushed poverty levels up. Poverty rates reached 41 percent in metropolitan Buenos Aires, and in some rural areas they were even higher (Minujin and Kessler 1995).

Checking inflation was a priority for the second civilian government. After 1991, the Convertibility Plan halted inflation and opened the economy. Structural reforms—privatization of public enterprises, refinancing of the external debt, and the consolidation of regional integration—led to economic growth. For the first time in many years, the gross national product (GNP) expanded in a sustained way.

But this new economic model was quite different from the recipes that were enforced during the 1970s. Employment became increasingly precarious, and unemployment rates grew. Reductions in public social expenditures led to deterioration of conditions in wide population groups, and economic growth did not translate into an improvement in wages: industrial wages in 1995 represented less than half of those registered in 1971.[5]

Poverty fell from the dramatic figures registered during the hyperinflation, but settled down at unprecedented levels. In metropolitan Buenos Aires in October 1998, 32.4 percent of the population was below the poverty line. The projection of these values for the whole country meant that 13 million Argentineans were living under these conditions.[6] In this context, women felt more and more the need to get a job, and female participation in the economy grew. Thirty-five percent of women aged 14 or older had a paid job in 1991.

As in other Latin American countries, economic structural adjustments in the 1990s produced higher levels of income inequality, surpassing levels registered forty years earlier (Altimir 1997).[7] There was downward mobility, within both the middle class and the working class. The pauperization of wide social groups was unparalleled in the recent history of the country. By the end of the 1990s, these trends had crystallized into a deeply segmented social structure; the distance between social classes had widened though the barriers between genders were being reduced.[8] Summarizing, we may say that fifteen years of democracy have not been enough to counterbalance the regressive trends toward social inequality initiated during the military governments. On the contrary, they have deepened in spite of the economic growth obtained over the last years.

SOME CONSEQUENCES

Crime rates reflect the importance of these processes in Argentina during this period. During the 1970s, political instability was associated with greater use of violence. Homicide figures—including those for political murders—

reached high levels, well above the historical averages for Argentina (10.8 per 100,000 in 1970–75). On the other hand, property crime (burglary-theft) rates were low due to general prosperity (182 per 100,000 for this period).

After 1976, the military government exerted state repressive force intensely. The atmosphere of fear and the harshness of legal punishment had a deterrent effect on potential delinquents. The frightening environment affected crime reporting as well. It is not surprising that crime rates were the lowest during this period.

When democracy was restored, there arose a new confidence in the institutions' ability to tackle social order problems within legal limits. Penal legislation was moderated. Within this optimistic environment, homicide rates continued to be low. But property crime (burglary-theft) rates experienced an upward trend, intensified during hyperinflation episodes. For instance, in 1989 the theft rate was 864 cases per 100,000 inhabitants, double the 1973 values.

Consolidation of democracy and a check on inflation came together. But social tensions, associated with unemployment, poverty, and rising inequalities pushed crime rates upward (Sánchez 1999). Fear of crime extended, as the general crime rate was double the levels registered during the military governments. The increase in the number of crimes was surely greater, because the proportion of unreported crime grew along with a dissatisfaction with democratic institutions. In 1996, an official victimization survey estimated the amount of unreported crime at 70 percent.[9] Hence, security became a central issue on the political agenda. The low efficiency of the penal system (Cerro and Meloni 1999) deepened citizens' discontent with the justice system. We have shown that crime statistics reflect the two major change processes registered within the country during this period: democratization and increasing social inequality. The following section summarizes the most important transformations within the legal field.

Normative Production

In Argentina, as in other civil law countries, written law is of vital importance. Laws are identified by a numeral; the numeric series began in 1862 after the national reunification, when the national Congress initiated its activities in Buenos Aires. Military government regulations are not laws, technically speaking, but they receive a number within the same series. We have then a good indicator of the intensity of normative activity.

Legislative production has been truly important during this period: 6,165 new national laws between 1971 and 1998. To summarize, from a substantive viewpoint, the change entailed by these norms is a task well beyond the limits of this chapter. To understand the scope of these changes, we must remember that the national constitution was restructured in 1994, following a trend that encompassed most provincial (state) constitutions. In 1999, the executive presented before Congress a draft of a new civil code to replace the one devised by Vélez Sársfield in 1869.

However, we may analyze the normative production from a quantitative viewpoint. The state's regulatory activity has intensified recently. The constitution was adopted a century and a half ago, but a quarter of all laws have been enacted since 1970. The trend toward higher normative production also has been observed in other countries (Galanter 1992). As Friedman (1990) points out, it is a central trait in modern legal culture. Analyzing normative production according to periods shows that it has been higher during the cycles of institutional instability: each change in the executive entailed a need for new regulations. In contrast, under democratic rule, the annual number of enacted laws has decreased 50 percent since the period 1971–76. For 1971–75, there were 2,338 laws enacted; but in 1984–89, only 623.

Legislative production in the province of Córdoba reveals similar trends. During the 1971–98 period, 3,530 new laws were enacted, about 40 percent of the total passed during the institutional life of the province. The intensification of regulatory activity can also be seen in administrative agencies of the national executive. Describing the normative production of two national agencies, the Banco Central de la República Argentina and the Dirección General Impositiva, since their creation in the 1930s up to the present, Lynch (1995) has been able to show the recent acceleration in regulatory activity. The hyperproduction of norms constitutes a sort of *legislative inflation*: if there are too many laws, people cannot know them, and the sheer number may be an obstacle to compliance.[10] Continuous changes in norms do not encourage observance of the law. It should also be noted that the norm of obedience to the law has been classically low in Argentina.

In an essay expressively entitled *Un país al margen de la ley*, Nino (1992) described the wide gap existing in Argentina between norms and practice. The fact that between 1930 and 1983 only one constitutional president was able to end his term is clear proof of this gap. Nino adds further proof, such as the high level of tax evasion and habitual violation of city traffic rules. Straying from the law has also become state behavior: state terrorism—systematic use of state force against political opposition, disregarding the legal limits— is a dramatic example. But this tendency not to use laws as guides to action is so deeply rooted in Argentine legal culture that it is also found under its democratic governments. Even though Congress has been functioning normally since December 1983, only after 1992, when inflation had been overcome, did the executive begin to send the national budget bill on time. The abuse of emergency decrees by the executive during the ten years of Menem's presidency is also a good indicator of this type of behavior.

This inclination to transgress legal rules, among both common citizens and government officials—so important in the genesis of political corruption—has perhaps abated, at least in some areas such as tax payment, but it is still a serious problem (Moreno Ocampo 1993; Grondona 1993; Isuani 1996). In short, normative production has been intense in these twenty-eight years. The brief duration of rules, which are easily replaced, and the complexity of the emerging normative structure do not encourage compliance. These traits, and the tendency toward normative transgression deeply rooted in Argentine legal culture, have flourished during the cycle of institutional instability. The return of democracy has weakened them, but they have not yet disappeared.

The Legal Profession and Legal Education

This section discusses the main traits of the legal profession and legal education in Argentina. It must be noted that scarcity of data is particularly serious in this field. As in other areas of the legal system, empirical research is almost nonexistent. Law studies have a long tradition in Argentina; they started at Córdoba University in 1791. Traditionally, most lawyers have come from the upper strata. Public university education began to offer a channel for upward mobility early in the twentieth century (Agulla 1968), and slowly lawyers began to come from diverse social origins. The legal profession has been a strong presence among the political elite (De Imaz 1964).

Since 1970, university education has expanded greatly. The total number of university students has increased by a factor of four. The traditional interest in legal studies has not declined, even if a number of new careers have opened up. At present, one out of seven university students follows this path. The expansion of university enrollment has been greater than population growth. There were 124 law students per 100,000 inhabitants in 1970; in 1996, this proportion reached 351, which is very high for this region. In 1970, there were 29,045 law students in public universities; in 1990, there were 117,348. The "massification" of universities has not been accompanied by a parallel increase in the education budget, and there have been difficulties in maintaining the quality of legal education.

In Argentina, it is sufficient to have a law degree and to be affiliated with a bar association to practice law as an attorney. Admission to a bar is a simple process and does not require any exam. The massification of legal studies entailed a democratization of the profession, as lawyers today are from quite heterogeneous social origins. Gender composition has also changed: the feminine presence in law faculties has been increasing steadily. In 1996, the proportion of women among law students had climbed to 56 percent. These

changes in the social origins of lawyers give a new meaning to their traditional presence in the political elite, still prominent. In 1990, there were
291 representatives in the national Congress; 125 of them had a law degree.
This meant that two-thirds of legislators with a university education came
from the law faculties (Gastron 1999).

There is no hard data available, but it may be assumed that the mean income of lawyers has decreased and that the styles of professional practice remain quite stable. Studying the attorneys in the province of Buenos Aires,
Fucito (1997) found that nearly 80 percent worked mainly in litigation. Preventive legal advice was the main task of less than 20 percent of the lawyers
interviewed. Fucito showed also that the law firms were still small; 46 percent
of the lawyers were solo practitioners. The rest carried on different forms of
associations with their colleagues. However, it was difficult to find a firm
with more than five lawyers. Probably the situation in the national capital,
Buenos Aires, is quite different. There, as in other big cities in the world,
new forms of professional practice are emerging. Still, Fucito's observations
—obtained in one of the richest and most highly urbanized provinces—are
a good indicator of the low development of law firms in the country.

The Administration of Justice

It is not easy to describe the evolution of the administration of justice in a
federal country. As in the United States, the justice system is dual in Argentina. It comprises federal courts, established and maintained by the federal
government, and also provincial courts. The federal system is more limited
than the provincial system in both size and competence. The fact that the
state finances just 30 percent of the total justice expenditure is a good indicator of the relative importance of both systems (Garavano 1998). Federal
courts have jurisdiction over cases in which the state is a party, as well as cases
involving foreign officials. Federal courts also hear "federal specialties," such
as drug trafficking or forgery. Provincial courts deal with the bulk of ordinary litigation. Even though we may distinguish the two levels clearly, we
should not forget that both are factors in the social construction of the public
image of the judiciary.

We know little about the evolution of federal justice. There are some
studies about the situation in the last years (Cavagna Martínez, Bielsa, and
Graña 1994) and historical studies on some specific issues (Kunz 1989), but
there is no global description of trends. This lack is not surprising, considering that the statistical bureau of the national Supreme Court was not created
until 1991. Availability of data at the provincial level is not much better because some provinces do not have such offices yet. Hence, the analysis will

focus on one province, Córdoba, for which this research team has built statistical series, employing the 1970–98 annual reports. Some references to the national level will also be made.

Is Córdoba representative of Argentina as a whole? From certain points of view, Córdoba, in the middle of the country, may be considered a synthesis of the nation. Like the whole country, it is divided into two different regions. On the one hand, the rich area of the pampas, which received European migration, contains the major urban concentrations. On the other hand, there is the northwest region, where scarcity of economic opportunities pushes people to the periphery of the big cities. It should also be noted that the province, where the oldest university of the country is located, has a higher average in levels of education and a greater concentration of lawyers than the rest of the country. These differences have an impact on the legal system: the availability of trained jurists has made the modernization of the administration of justice easier. For instance, in Córdoba, penal processes have followed an oral procedure since the 1920s; the federal justice system adopted oral procedure only after the restoration of democracy.

The differences are still visible today. Research evaluating the situation of the provincial administrations of justice (FORES 1998) placed Córdoba at the top of the quality ranking; its situation was described as normal for a democratic state. The other nine provinces—where the majority of the population lives—were classified in the same category, although their marks were lower. Acknowledging this situation, the administration recently prepared the National Plan for Judicial Reform, which proposed Córdoba as a model to be followed.[11] This position of Córdoba in the national context as a model for the administration of justice stimulated our interest in studying it. The following sections summarize the main changes in the administration of justice throughout the period 1970–98. The transformations have been numerous and can be seen in judicial organization, in the political role of the judiciary, and in efforts toward modernization.

JUDICIAL ORGANIZATION

In 1970, the judicial organization of the province included 185 magistrates of different levels of courts. The judges were relatively unspecialized and were divided into *fueros* (jurisdictions): civil, commercial, criminal, and justice of the peace. The latter dealt with minor civil cases. There was considerable centralization. All courts of appeal, as well as labor courts, were located in the capital of the province. The number of citizens per judge was not low (8.8 magistrates per 100,000 inhabitants),[12] but geographical concentration of courts was a real barrier to access to justice. Residents in some small cities had to travel more than 150 kilometers to find a court.

Twenty-eight years later, there has been a remarkable expansion in the administration of justice. The number of trial and superior courts has doubled. Courts today are far better distributed, and it is possible to file a case without having to travel long distances. The expansion of the magistracy has exceeded population growth, and the number of judges per 100,000 inhabitants has reached 14.23. Most of this expansion took place under democratic rule, showing the importance that civilian governments assign to the constitutional promise of justice for all. These transformations were made possible thanks to an increase in public expenditures for the judiciary, which are now at 7 percent of the total budget for Córdoba.[13]

The democratic administration's interest in facilitating access to justice could be observed also in the tax area. Although the tax contribution to the judiciary was increased, new tax exemptions were granted in lawsuits that may be important for ordinary citizens, such as alimony, adoption, or labor cases. Requirements to obtain free legal aid became a little more flexible. In 1998, a reform of the penal courts assigned the instruction and investigation of the cases to prosecutors, leaving to the judge the role of protecting rights and guarantees. More prosecutors were needed to fill these tasks, and their number increased by a factor of five.

As expected, the expansion of the judicial organization was accompanied by a specialization of functions. Justices of the peace, who dealt with minor civil cases, were eliminated in 1980, and new courts specializing in commercial matters were created. Family courts, whose tasks are assisted by social experts, were created in 1991. Administrative disputes were also assigned to a special court, reflecting the new importance given by the democratic state to judicial review of decisions of officials in the executive branch. In the new structure, penal courts have gained importance: they now include 47 percent of the magistrates. Considering the recent increase in crime rates, this importance is not surprising; it indicates the decision to fight crime—this time, within the limits of the law.

There has been a significant expansion of the judicial organization over the last few years, as well as some improvements in access to justice. A positive effect on civil litigation could therefore be expected.

THE IMPACT OF THE POLITICAL–INSTITUTIONAL CONTEXT

The political context has a significant influence on courts. During the period we are studying, political changes have been intense, and their effect on the administration of justice is clearly visible. The constitution assigns to judges the role of controlling the legality of the acts of the other organs of the state; judges are to be a barrier against irrational exercise of political power. For this reason, dictatorial governments have tried to control or, at least, neutralize the judiciary power.

Encroachments of the executive on the judiciary can be seen in the mechanisms involved in the nomination of judges. Until 1994, in the province, as well as on the federal level, the Senate appointed judges, following executive proposals.[14] Judges could not be removed except in cases of immorality. During the long succession of civilian-military governments, this constitutional rule was systematically violated, and the judiciary suffered the same instability as the state as a whole.

Each time the military dissolved Congress, they also removed some judges, appointing new ones in their places. The magnitude of these interventions grew over the years, at the same time that respect toward institutions gradually faded. Ves Losada (1991a) has documented this process of increasing delegitimization of the national Supreme Court.

Each time a civilian government took office, it removed the judges that had been nominated by the military and replaced them by means of constitutional regulations. The renewal was not complete at the lower levels, where it was not uncommon to find a military-appointed judge left in place by the Senate. But at the higher levels of the administration of justice, where the judicial role in legality is significant, this rarely happened. This vicious circle affected the independence of the judiciary and generated a paradoxical situation. For fifty years, each new government team had the opportunity of nominating judicial personnel with politically close ties, either defying the constitution or abiding by it. The consolidation of democracy required something different (Smulovitz 1995). When open intervention was no longer possible, civilian governments chose to create new positions in courts and assign their adherents to them. This strategy lay behind Menem's decision to increase the number of seats on the Supreme Court from five to nine. This way, he obtained a comfortable majority and prevented judicial revision of many controversial decisions.

The preceding discussion helps explain why the number of judges in Córdoba has grown more than needed. It also indicates that the desire to subordinate the judiciary, typical of military rule, did not disappear automatically when democracy was restored; though curbed by constitutional rules, it has also existed under democratic governments. Building a genuine rule of law is a long-term task. Traditionally, the judiciary has had little political importance in Argentina, due to its subordination to the executive. Court delays and social inequalities in access to justice also contributed to its delegitimization. However, as Smulovitz points out, democracy brought a demand for justice. The horror of human rights violations helped to emphasize the importance of legal rules to limit the abuses of power so that these aberrations would not be repeated. In 1983, democracy built its legitimacy through the demand for justice.

The trial against the military held responsible for human rights violations demonstrated the ability of the judiciary to satisfy—partially at least—this demand. The judges were able to produce formal legal data on a painful and divided past. After the *Juicio a las Juntas* (trial of the military junta), the judiciary was better placed within the political scenario.[15] Other significant cases —the trial against officers of the Malvinas (Falkland) War, for instance— reinforced the new political significance of the judiciary, seen also in other new democracies (Tate 1997a). These initial successes concealed the need for structural reforms, delaying the debate on the legal system's efficiency.

Judicializing the human rights issue had another effect: it broadened the cultural definition of potential legal disputes and stimulated further judicialization of conflicts. New types of conflicts were taken to court, such as cases involving military officers or labor leaders. This growth of social expectations of justice is also typical of modern legal culture. The *Juicio a las Juntas*, and its spectacular television broadcasts, also initiated a new and contradictory relationship between the judiciary and the mass media. Publicity was useful to judges, as it guaranteed some autonomy from the executive. It also helped to desacralize their authority, carrying their decisions into the light of public debate and exposing them to new critics. On the other hand, the discovery of the judiciary by the media, triggered by their interest in crime and drama, has helped generate expectations of quick solutions to conflicts within the population, in terms that were not consistent with the procedural norms of courts. In this way, discontent with the judicial system started to increase again.

During the consolidation of democracy, other factors also diminished the initial enthusiasm generated by the trials against the military. When decisions against the military were overturned and cases involving charges of political corruption went unresolved, skepticism toward the political role of the judiciary widened, as did the perception of its subordination to political power and its socially discriminatory character. A survey conducted by Graciela Romer in Buenos Aires in 1992 indicated that only 5 percent of the interviewees believed that the judiciary was independent. This proportion reached 18 percent in Córdoba in 1994. This research also showed that the magistrates' image was hurt by their weak role in the struggle against political corruption; the propensity to sue and the confidence in judges decreased (Bergoglio and Carballo 1996). But dissatisfaction with the judiciary also arose from other sources in regard to their function in the resolution of disputes. Delay no longer seemed acceptable in a society where the social value of time was growing[16] and where public expenditure on justice was high.[17] The debate concerning the efficiency of the administration of justice moved from academic circles into the political arena. It became evident that judges could no longer rely on their traditional prestige but had to appeal to instrumental legitimization. This dissatisfaction triggered the efforts toward modernization.

The admission of women into the judiciary is another important trend. Margarita Arguas, in the final years of the military regime, was the first woman to obtain a seat in the national Supreme Court. Today, there are only men in this high court. In Córdoba, women first became part of the Provincial Supreme Court in 1982; today, three out of the seven magistrates on this high court are women. As in other jurisdictions, breaching these gender barriers required special effort. Women appointed to these duties had outstanding credentials, far above those of their male colleagues. All of them were university professors (Mackinson de Sorokin 1987; Boigeol 1993).

INITIATIVES OF MODERNIZATION

During the consolidation of democracy, discontent about the administration of justice impelled efforts to renew judicial structures, adjusting working styles to technological changes and rationalizing procedures. As expected, the conservative judicial culture and scarcity of resources limited these efforts.[18] However, some advances were made. In the federal system, penal process was reformed and an oral procedure was designed. Computerization began, although the new technology was adopted in an unsystematic way. The 1994 constitution introduced the Consejo de la Magistratura, a tool to reduce the subordination to political power in the appointment of judges. Mediation was introduced as a compulsory step in many types of processes, an innovation that could reduce congestion in courts.

At the provincial level, this process followed different rhythms; it accelerated after the creation of the Junta Federal de Cortes Supremas Provinciales, a coordination organism that allows provinces to share innovation experiences and technical resources. In Córdoba, the push toward modernization can be seen in different initiatives. The incorporation of computer technology was slow, due to resistance to these techniques. An institution for the permanent training of judges was created, Escuela de la Magistratura. New procedures were adopted for the selection of judicial staff, more open and based on technical abilities. An experimental center for mediation was created within the court system, advancing the implementation of alternative dispute resolution mechanisms.

Among the innovations adopted during this period, the jury is particularly relevant. The constitutional clause (1853) prescribing the use of a jury in criminal cases had never been put into effect. Even so, this rule was not eliminated during various reforms of the constitution. This fact is a good indicator of the Argentine tolerance of the gap between legal rules and practices. In 1998, the Provincial Supreme Court decided to apply this institution experimentally. The decision typifies the inclination toward innovation and compliance with law, characteristic of this phase of the democratization process.

The initiatives we have cited illustrate the will to modernize the judiciary in recent years. The impact of these measures on the efficiency of the judicial system is not yet clear. However, citizens' discontent has not diminished. In a Gallup poll conducted in 1999 to evaluate Menem's ten years of government, the judiciary received a rating of 3.6 points (scale of 1 to 10, where 10 means excellent).[19] To understand thoroughly the roots of this discontent, we would need more knowledge about the basis of legitimization of judicial activity. However, we can suggest some explanations. Democratization enhanced the political role of the judiciary, and citizens' expectations regarding the judges' contribution to the solution of public problems grew. Success in confronting the weighty legacy of military governments brought demands for an active role in the struggle against political corruption and insecurity, but these demands remain unsatisfied.

Litigation

We analyze here the evolution of litigation in the province of Córdoba since 1971, focusing on possible changes following the restoration of democracy. Economic growth and judicial costs, two factors of significant influence on litigation, are also considered.[20] We have assumed that democratization could stimulate litigation levels through three mechanisms. First, it could be supposed that predisposition to turn disputes into judicial claims increases and that confidence in the independence of the judiciary could increase under the rule of law, as previous studies have found (Bergoglio and Carballo 1996). Changes in the cultural definition of potential legal disputes and the expansion of judicial organization brought by democratization could also increase the number and types of cases filed in the courts. For all these reasons, we expected higher litigation levels under democratic rule. However, in fact, the general litigation rate declined between 1979 and 1994.

The interpretation of this result is not obvious. Perhaps, after the crises of authoritarian governments, the climate of social integration achieved by the civilian administration reduced the frequency of social disputes. This effect would be stronger than the increase in the propensity to process interpersonal conflicts in state facilities, and so litigation rates would fall. This interpretation is consistent with a conception of litigation as a tool for dispute resolution. Nevertheless, to deepen our understanding of these results requires a refined measure of litigation, sensitive to the variety of social relations processed in the courts. To this end, we will describe the changes in the composition of litigation, as well as trends in particular rates of litigation. The research also produced a yearly series of private judicial costs for the 1980–95 period in Córdoba. These data will be useful to describe more precisely the economic barriers to access to justice within a context of increasing poverty and growing inequalities. The last section reviews the interpretation of the effects of democratization on litigation rates.

CONCEPTUAL NOTES

There is no single definition of *litigation*. According to Friedman (1989), "Litigation, in ordinary speech, refers to actions contested in court. The core meaning thus implies three distinct elements: first, a *claim*, that is, an active attempt to attain some valued end; second, a *dispute* or conflict, in other words, resistance to the claim; and third, the use of a specific institution, the *court* to resolve the conflict or dispute" (18 [emphasis added]). This definition stresses the contentious aspects of disputes. Under a perspective whose main interest is developing a tool to measure the global level of conflicts existing in a society, it emphasizes the function of law as a tool for social integration.

Toharia (1987, 1994), who has done research on litigation rates, excludes noncontentious matters from his analysis. He points out that dispute resolution is not the only function of courts, and consequently he does not consider as litigation cases where judicial intervention has an administrative character, such as certifying the change of a person's name. The fact that courts in contemporary societies perform multiple functions poses another problem: the definition of what a *civil court* is, an indispensable tool for comparative research. On this issue, we have followed Clark (1990) and have held courts to be the organisms identified as such in the Provincial Supreme Court reports.[21]

Similar problems arise with the concept of *case*. We have worked with an operational definition: cases refer to matters defined as such in official reports. In this way, matters of low contentious content (adoptions, successions, inheritances) are included in the research. However, other judicial interventions of strong administrative character (recordings in the Public Register of Commerce, for instance) are not included, as the report does not classify them as "cases." This procedure allows us to compare our results with Belgian, German, and Dutch data, since it is compatible with the definitions used by Van Loon and Langerwerf (1990), Blankenburg (1994), and Van Loon, Delrue, and Van Wambeke (1995). Unfortunately, comparison with the Spanish data reported by Toharia is not possible.

We use here the term *civil litigation* in a broad sense, to designate matters where citizens may choose to go or not to go to court seeking a decision. Therefore, we have included cases initiated in ordinary civil courts, in labor courts, and in commercial courts, which were created in 1980. The study also covers disputes brought to justices of the peace up until 1979. Only first instance cases have been taken into account. Family courts, created for metropolitan Córdoba in 1991, have also been included in the research. Their creation entailed significant changes in judicial procedure, as well as in the registration of data in official reports. Including them in the study required extensive redefinition of categories in order to maintain comparability of data. Juvenile courts have not been encompassed in the study because it is not easy to separate civil and criminal matters in their activities. The annual report of the Provincial Supreme Court was the source of the data.[22] As the classification employed for the cases changed several times during the period encompassed by the research, we faced serious difficulties in making data compatible. Because of the data available, we had to work with litigation series of different lengths. For example, the series of labor cases begins in 1970, whereas the divorce series begins in 1980.[23]

VOLUME OF CASES

First instance courts received 168,255 new cases in 1995—that is, 1 case per 17 inhabitants. But to understand this piece of information, we need some historical background. The data series concerning total volume of civil cases shows a wavelike movement of the caseload, and a long-term declining trend interrupted in 1993. In the years after 1993, there was an abrupt increase in the number of cases filed. We have not been able to consider more recent data due to profound changes in the classification of cases employed in these reports, but it seems there has been some stagnation since 1997.[24] Comparison of civil litigation over time, and between countries, has to take the size of the population into consideration. More people means more social and economic relations from which disputes may arise. All other factors being equal, the demand for judicial decisions must increase when population grows. During the twenty-eight years of the time series, the population increased 40 percent, while the absolute number of civil cases registered in 1995 is very similar to the 1968 figure. It is important to note that the percentage of the population aged twenty or under did not change between 1970 and 1990. An inspection of litigation rates shows a clearer declining trend registered up to 1993. The rate was considerably higher during the period of political instability: after peaking at 9,000 cases per 100,000 inhabitants around 1970, it dropped to 5,000 cases after 1973 under Perón's democratic administration (see Table 2.1).

After 1976, the line in the time series indicates a slightly upward tendency, reaching nearly 6,000 yearly cases just before the Malvinas (Falkland) War. Reinforced solidarity, typical of war times, initiated a downward trend, and a minimum of about 3,200 annual cases per 100,000 inhabitants was reached during the first years of Alfonsín's government (1984–85). It should be noted that this figure is approximately one-third of the litigation levels registered, for instance, in 1970.

With inflation getting more and more out of control, the litigation rate recovered slightly in the second half of the Alfonsín administration (1986–89).

TABLE 2.1

Litigation Rate, Córdoba, 1968–1995

Year	Population	Civil suits	Litigation rate per 100,000 inhabitants
1968	2,024,920	161,358	7,969
1969	2,049,310	158,269	7,723
1970	2,073,990	186,929	9,013
1971	2,098,860	169,263	8,065
1972	2,137,300	161,300	7,547
1973	2,175,350	13,279	6,085
1974	2,212,980	112,764	5,096
1975	2,250,160	112,742	5,010
1976	2,286,850	116,770	5,106
1977	2,323,020	122,520	5,274
1978	2,358,660	139,245	5,904
1979	2,393,730	129,256	5,400
1980	2,428,210	132,712	5,465
1981	2,462,090	147,951	6,009
1982	2,495,340	127,276	5,101
1983	2,527,940	97,566	3,860
1984	2,559,880	81,707	3,192
1985	2,591,150	81,134	3,131
1986	2,621,740	97,800	3,730
1987	2,651,640	112,196	4,231
1988	2,680,830	99,957	3,729
1989	2,709,320	96,187	3,550
1990	2,737,100	83,861	3,064
1991	2,764,180	85,440	3,091
1992	2,790,540	87,746	3,144
1993	2,816,180	125,349	4,451
1994	2,841,130	162,459	5,718
1995	2,865,360	168,255	5,872

A second trough in the line can be observed in 1990: only 3,000 civil cases per 100,000 inhabitants were filed per year at the beginning of the term of Menem, the second civilian president. Since 1993, the long-term trend has changed, and rates have risen sharply. They increased 80 percent in two years. The last report was of 5,800 cases filed annually per 100,000 inhabitants, similar to the figures registered fifteen years before during military rule. The historical perspective enables us to see that the 1993 increase is still moderate.

Can the Córdoba rates be considered representative of those for the whole of Argentina? As the province shows a higher average in levels of education, urbanization, and concentration of lawyers than the rest of the country, we may assume that national rates would probably be lower than provincial ones. Unfortunately, the federal organization of the nation makes such an analysis difficult. International comparison of contemporary litigation rates has shown that the incidence of lawsuits varies so widely that it seems impossible to regard any one figure as "normal" (Galanter 1983; Wollschläger 1990). As we noted earlier, this kind of comparison faces other important difficulties, such as the type of cases considered "civil" and the definition of what a court is. Even with these restrictions, it is possible to compare Argentine rates with those of other Western countries.

In Córdoba, 3,064 civil cases were filed per 100,000 inhabitants in 1990. The corresponding figure for West Germany (same year), including cases heard at labor courts and civil courts was 3,600; the figure for the Netherlands, 1,550 (Blankenburg 1994). Other countries, such as Japan, rank lower, with 940 civil cases per 100,000 inhabitants in the same year. These rates seem low compared to American rates, estimated by Wollschläger (1994) at 6,000 to 7,000 per 100,000 inhabitants. However, it should be noted that in 1970, the Córdoba rate also reached 7,000. We can sum up by saying that litigation levels in Córdoba are relatively high in international terms, although they are now still below their historical maximum, registered around 1970.

COMPOSITION OF CASES

Have variations in litigation levels been accompanied by changes in the type of litigation? Due to changes in the organization of official reports, this analysis is only possible for the 1983–95 period. As Table 2.2 shows, most cases now involve conflicts of a clear economic nature. *Ejecutivos* and *apremios* (quick debt-enforcement procedures) absorbed 63 percent of the workload of judges in 1995. If we consider these together with bankruptcy and evictions, we see that two-thirds of the first instance cases involve judicial intervention into social relations, within a market frame.

Ordinary suits are the most general type of case, where the requested judicial intervention may be oriented toward a variety of matters and where

TABLE 2.2

Composition of Cases, 1983–1995

Type of case	1983		1995	
	N	%	N	%
Debt enforcement	30,952	31.72	104,425	62.07
Ordinary suits	22,758	23.33	15,839	9.41
Evictions	3,637	3.73	3,242	1.93
Family cases	2,370	2.43	4,448	2.64
Successions	8,332	8.54	6,736	4.00
Amparos	—	.00	443	.26
Other voluntary	11,444	11.73	8,862	6.94
Bankruptcy	3,225	3.31	2,881	1.71
Labor cases	14,848	15.22	18,565	11.03
Total	97,566	100.00	168,255	100.00

procedural rules assign to judges long time periods in which to arrive at their decisions. They represent 10 percent of the workload. In contrast, cases of personal, private matters, such as family law or succession disputes, now make up only 6 percent of the caseload. Even though in most cases judges play the role of protector of rights, there are some cases where this role is more relevant. Within this category we place labor cases, just over 11 percent in 1995, as well as *amparos*, a procedure to deal with strictly constitutional matters, which register a very low frequency of below 1 percent.

Like debt-enforcement procedures (ejecutivos and apremios), evictions are quick procedures, where judicial intervention is limited by detailed normative prescriptions and where the chances of discussing the facts or the law are slim. These data indicate that we should pay more attention to the routine aspects of judicial work, which constitute two-thirds of the workload.

Table 2.2 also allows us to consider changes within the structure of litigation after democracy was restored. Clearly, the growth of litigation rates beyond 1993 is due to the rise of debt-enforcement procedures. There were nearly 31,000 of these cases per year by 1983, and by 1995 the number had tripled. As the workload did not generally expand, the significance of these cases in the workload grew. These changes, perceptible from 1993 on, reflect the impact of economic transformations brought about by the Convertibility Plan. The increasing importance of debt-enforcement procedures has also been observed in other countries. Souza Santos, Marques Leitao, and Pedroso (1996) found that in Portugal, this type of suit climbed from 39 percent of all cases in 1942 to 62 percent fifty years later.

Other cases have registered a slight upward trend accompanying the general rate movement. Family cases—where changes in legislation (divorce) and judicial organization had a stimulating effect—are an example. Their significance in the courts' workload has been stable. Labor cases have also increased, but at a slower rate. Consequently, today they absorb less effort than in 1983. Finally, it should be noted that ordinary processes, as well as succession and eviction proceedings, have reduced their absolute numbers since 1983.

Thus, we may observe that there have been qualitative changes within the structure of litigation since the restoration of democracy. The importance of quick debt-enforcement procedures has been stressed; their growth explains the reversal of the declining trend of the litigation rate in general since 1993. Family and labor cases have also experienced a mild upward trend, reflecting their affinity with the freedom ensured by democratic institutions.

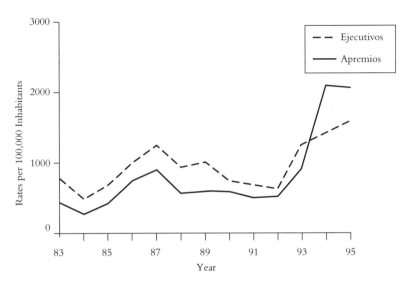

FIGURE 2.1 Debt-Collection Procedures

TRENDS IN ECONOMIC LITIGATION

Clearly, economic conflicts make up the majority of the disputes contested in courts, and their importance has grown recently. We have seen that the expansion of litigation after 1993 is principally due to increase in the number of these cases. Debt-enforcement suits embrace two different processes: ejecutivos, the most general type, and apremios, reserved for certain categories of debts, such as judicial costs or fiscal debts. Both processes are quickly executed when debts are documented; there is little scope for discussion of law or facts. A recent procedural reform has unified the two types of processes.

Our data on these suits start in 1983. Figure 2.1 shows clearly their recent expansion. Taken together, their number has tripled in thirteen years. Like the general litigation rate, they peaked in 1993, which can easily be connected to the first effects of economic transformations brought about by the Convertibility Plan.

In Argentina, bankruptcies are dealt with in provincial courts. The series for these processes starts in 1980, with the creation of specialized commercial courts. It shows important annual fluctuations. The annual number of bankruptcies indicates an important reduction (ten times) in the first years of democracy. In 1984, for instance, the rate was reduced by 90 percent, a good indicator of the impact of the optimistic climate induced by the restoration of institutions that raised business expectations (see Table 2.3). As with debt-

TABLE 2.3

Mean Rates of Civil Suits

Period	Debt = Enforcement procedures		Bankruptcies	General litigation rate
	Ejecutivos	Apremios		
1983	785.9373	438.4603	139.74	5,108.66
1984–89	887.9791	580.9669	34.35	3,593.90
1990–95	1,052.9649	1,110.6683	64.76	4,223.40
Total	956.2770	814.4824	67.59	4,208.65

NOTE: Rates per 100,000 inhabitants; 1983–95 figures are averages for the period.

collection procedures, these suits have increased since 1993. However, there are still not as many as the figures registered during the military government. Therefore, we may say that the profile of clearly economic litigation is very similar to the general litigation rate. There was an important peak in 1993, linked to Menem's liberal economic strategies. This abrupt increase explains the reversal of the declining trend in the general litigation rate.

LITIGATION IN THE LABOR FIELD

The series on labor suits is considerably longer; it encompasses the 1968–95 period. It shows annual variations and a clear upward trend, in contrast to the general litigation rate. Labor litigation was rather low in 1968; just 300 cases per 100,000 inhabitants. Until 1973, workers' propensity to sue grew rapidly along with union mobilization. During the period of the military government, the rate was stagnant, but it started to grow with the liberalization of the regime. Workers' claims increased continuously afterward, protected by the democratic climate of freedom.

As Figure 2.2 shows, since 1991, rising unemployment has reduced the number of labor suits.[25] Even so, the last figure (648 cases per 100,000 inhabitants) is double the initial values of the series. In 1995, labor suits were 11 percent of the total first instance caseload.

Mean rates by period (Table 2.4) allow us to observe the upward trend, leaving cyclical annual fluctuations aside. Connecting this continuous growth to the political context is not the only explanatory factor; we must also remember that filing a claim is free of court costs for workers. It is interesting to note the different evolution of the two longest series available. Whereas the general litigation rate falls and then turns around in 1993, the labor suit rate grows up to the 1990s and has fallen since then.

LITIGATION WITHIN PERSONAL RELATIONSHIPS

Succession proceedings.   We now consider processes where emotional, intimate relationships are involved: family cases and proceedings concerning

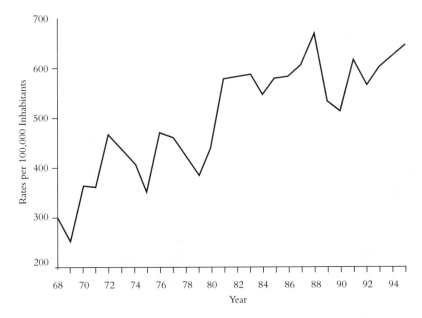

FIGURE 2.2 Labor Litigation

TABLE 2.4

Mean Rates of Litigation, by Period

Period	General litigation rate	Labor litigation rate
1968–72	8,063.22	348.11
1973–75	5,397.13	396.42
1976–83	5,264.79	490.12
1984–89	3,593.90	586.86
1990–95	4,223.40	593.89
Total	5,197.49	497.69

NOTE: Rates per 100,000 inhabitants; 1968–95 figures are averages for the period.

successions. Economic motivations are not absent from these processes, but they are not usually dominant. Due to these characteristics, these rates may evolve in a special way. We could expect, in principle, a high frequency of succession cases—death is, after all, a universal fact. But the procedure is compulsory only for estates of a certain size; hence, these processes are restricted to certain social groups. In 1995, succession proceedings were 4 percent of the caseload (Table 2.5).

Our series for these processes begins in 1983. Since the democratic res-

TABLE 2.5
Mean Rates of Litigation Within Personal Relations

Period	Succession proceedings	Family suits	General litigation rate
1983	329.5968	93.75	5,108.66
1984–89	284.1760	111.4067	3,593.90
1990–95	263.9109	156.7445	4,223.40
Total	278.3168	121.7025	4,208.65

NOTE: Rates per 100,000 inhabitants; 1983–95 figures are averages for the period.

toration, succession proceedings have decreased, even in absolute numbers. Starting with 329 cases per 100,000 inhabitants, the rate declined 40 percent up to 1990. With monetary stability, the rate grew slightly up to 1993. Nevertheless, the mean rate for the second democratic period (263 cases) is considerably below the initial values. The decrease in the number of these cases is undoubtedly significant because this process is compulsory for social groups with access to property. Hence, the decline is related to the contraction in the size of this group.

Family cases.   Family suits have quite a different profile (see Table 2.6). Most cases involve conflict between parties (divorces, alimony) or relate to situations that are relatively less common in contemporary society (adoptions, guardianship). It is not surprising that there are fewer of these suits than succession proceedings. There were 4,448 family cases in 1995, 2.64 percent of the caseload. In contrast to estate cases, family suits present an upward tendency. The series began with a rate of 93 cases per 100,000 inhabitants. The Divorce Act, which allowed remarriage following the separation of the couple, provoked a significant increase after 1987. The rate remained high afterward, with the exception of 1990. The low value reported for this year (73 cases) probably reflects incomplete data. Conceivably, redistribution of cases from ordinary judges to the new family courts caused an undercount. The mean rate in the 1990s (156 annual cases) is higher than the rate at the beginning of the 1980s.

Divorces make up two-thirds of all family cases. They increased immediately after Law 23.515 was passed in 1987, which allowed remarriage after divorce, as a number of couples whose relationship had been severed for many years became interested in a judicial declaration of their situation. In 1989—a difficult year, marked by the hyperinflation episode—the rate grew to 138 cases. Leaving aside the anomalous figure for 1990, the mean divorce rate in the 1990s is about 102 cases, 30 percent higher than the initial rate. Adoption cases show a similar rising trend following the organization of family courts.

TABLE 2.6

Rates Mean of Litigation of Family Suits

Period	Divorce	Guardianship*	Adoption*	Total family suits rate	General litigation rate
1980–83	79.4211	10.0082	10.6411	84.5834	5,108.66
1984–89	91.5253	11.8836	7.9978	111.4067	3,593.90
1990–95	102.5398	7.3978	11.8743	156.7445	4,223.40
Total	92.6297	9.6690	9.9903	121.7025	4,208.65

NOTE: Rates per 100,000 inhabitants; 1980–95 figures are averages for the period.
*Data available since 1983.

OTHER TYPES OF CIVIL PROCESSES

Ordinary processes are the most general types of civil suits. The judicial intervention required here may involve a great variety of matters; for instance, tort cases and issues concerning contract liability are usually filed as ordinary processes. In theory, any type of claim may be filed as an ordinary process if the law does not provide a special procedure. Procedural rules assign to judges a long period of time to arrive at their decisions in ordinary processes. More than 15,000 ordinary cases were filed in 1995, representing about 10 percent of the total caseload. The data show that they are declining, even in absolute numbers. The rate was near 900 annual cases in 1983 and fell to 440 cases in 1991. Since 1993, it has recovered somewhat, but the mean rate is now 516 cases. On the other hand, evictions have a quick, routinized procedure. The data show a pattern similar to that of ordinary suits, a continuous declining trend in the last year studied.

Economic Growth and Litigation

THE IMPACT OF ECONOMIC GROWTH ON LITIGATION

Having described the evolution and composition of litigation in Córdoba, we will now analyze the factors molding it, beginning with economic growth. Longitudinal studies of civil caseloads have shown that economic growth does not have a uniform effect on the use of civil courts. In fact, both a growing and a declining economy can cause a higher number of court cases. A growing economy signifies a rise in production and trade, more economic and commercial relationships, and, in consequence, more potential disputes. A declining economy also generates disputes—for example, debt collections, bankruptcies, and so on. Historical studies have revealed that as a country develops its industry, different patterns of civil litigation may emerge. In some nations, such as the Netherlands or Denmark, urbanization and industrialization have permanently added more work to civil courts, and litigation tends to increase together with the GNP. In others, such as Sweden and France, the line of the civil caseload in the time series runs downward, whereas population and GNP follow an upward course (Wollschläger 1994).

Since 1970, the economy has been stagnant in Argentina. Measuring the GNP in constant currency, there has been only a 6 percent increase in the two decades during the period 1970–90;[26] population growth in the same period was nearly 40 percent. Inflation during the period was chronic in the whole country, and there were two hyperinflation crises, in 1989 and 1991. The experience of hyperinflation led to deep economic transformations. Monetary stability was attained, and a liberal strategy was applied. Public enterprises were privatized, and external debt renegotiated. There was significant expansion of the GNP, but rising unemployment and income disparities accompanied it. Consequently, this period of rapid economic growth was also a period of increasing poverty (Altimir 1997; Treber 1996; Minujin and Kessler 1995).

As we have already reported (Bergoglio 1997b), economic growth and litigation in Córdoba do not follow the same direction. The coefficient of correlation between these two variables between 1968 and 1995 is negative. As in Sweden and Japan, prosperity reduces the need for judicial debt collection, and hence, litigiousness declines. However, it should be noted that this coefficient is lower than the one obtained with a shorter series. This suggests that the relationship between economic growth and litigation could be changing in recent years, following the economic transformation of the country.

ECONOMIC GROWTH AND LITIGATION: HISTORICAL VARIATIONS

We saw earlier that economic strategies developed in the country have changed during the twenty-eight-year period. To assess if these changes affected the economic growth–litigation relationship, we divided the whole series and calculated a correlation coefficient for each period.

Political instability was the main trait during the 1968–75 period. Even though the state's role in the economy was also changing continually, public social expenditures were high, stimulating redistribution of income. Mean salaries were relatively high, especially during the first years (Torrado 1992, 1995). While the GNP followed an upward trend, litigation rates declined. Economic growth and litigation are negatively associated; the correlation coefficient is highly significant ($R = -.803$, significant for $p < .016$).

Military governments opened the economy to international markets, abandoning previous industrialization strategies. They prioritized the struggle against inflation, but they merely controlled it temporarily. The first

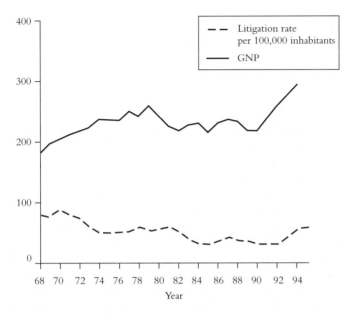

FIGURE 2.3 Litigation and Economic Growth
Source: Treber (1996).

civilian administration concentrated efforts on reestablishing political institutions and did not change much in the economy. By the end of Alfonsin's
term, a hyperinflation crisis was unleashed. During these two periods, the
economy was stagnant and so were litigation rates. Hence, the relationship
between litigation and economic growth changes direction: the coefficient
becomes positive, but without reaching significance. Structural economic
transformations initiated by Menem resulted in considerable rates of economic growth. However, this liberal program also had a clear concentrating
effect on income (Altimir 1997; Beccaria and López 1995). As of 1993, the
general litigation rate had grown with the expansion of the GNP. The coefficient between the two variables is positive and reaches statistical significance ($R = .888$, significant for $p < .04$), indicating the depth of economic
transformations introduced by the Peronist government (see Figure 2.3).

Changes in litigation, in response to transformation of the economic
model, indicate a strong link between the legal system and economic life.
This discussion also suggests that to explain the differential impact of economic growth on litigation in different countries, we should consider the influence of economic growth on income distribution.

THE IMPACT OF ECONOMIC GROWTH
ON DIFFERENT FORMS OF LITIGATION

In the last years of the series, economic growth brought about an increase in the general litigation rate, as well as changes in the nature of litigation. We explore here how growth affected different forms of litigation. We should remember that the analysis of different forms of litigation relies on series starting generally in 1983. The labor rate (1968–95) and the divorce rate (1980–95) are the only exceptions. On the other hand, the discussion of the general litigation rate is based on a longer series (1968–75). Debt-collection procedures (1983–95) are highly associated with economic growth. This type of process has strongly increased since 1993 and now constitutes two-thirds of the cases contested in court.

Litigation in the labor courts also grows when the economy expands, especially during recent years. The reforms of the second civilian administration have allowed economic growth, but its benefits have not reached the workers. This negative impact on salaries helps us to understand why the labor litigation rate grows along with the GNP. We must also include divorces among the group of cases that co-vary positively with economic growth. Their affinity with modernization contexts is probably the reason for this link. Taken as a whole, cases that increased along with the GNP (debt-collection procedures, labor cases, and divorces) in 1983 were 48 percent of the total caseload. They now represent 75 percent of the first instance processes. This marked effect of economic growth on some kinds of suits explains changes in the composition of litigation discussed earlier. In short, the impact of economic growth on litigation is strong, including changes both in the volume and in the composition of litigation.

The Influence of Private Judicial Costs

We have seen that during the period covered by the research, social inequalities deepened within the country. It is necessary to review the evolution of economic barriers to access to justice, because their deterrent effect on litigation may have become more pronounced recently. We will examine here the relationship between judicial costs and litigation rates. The economic barrier is considered to be the most important obstacle to access to justice (Cappelletti and Garth 1996). Previous empirical studies have shown the relevance of class differences in Argentina in this field (Bergoglio 1997a). Judicial costs are higher in Córdoba than in other provinces (Arjona 1996; Tappatá 1996); therefore, it should be easy to find this deterrent effect on litigation.

The analysis focuses on private judicial costs—those paid by the parties during a process. We do not take into account costs assumed by the state.

Total private judicial costs are difficult to estimate before the case is over. In this project, we considered only the expenses required to file a case; we assumed that these had the most influence on the decision to litigate. Argentina follows the English rule, where the loser pays all costs. An annual series of private judicial costs for Córdoba was constructed for the project. Due to gaps in data and methodological difficulties in expressing costs in current value where inflation is chronic, the series includes only the 1980–95 period. To illustrate the obstacles we are facing, it is worth remembering that the country changed its currency unit four times during that period.[27] The necessary data were obtained from the press and from law reports.

Costs required to file a case include the *tasa de justicia* (per-case filing fee) and compulsory contributions to the bar and to the lawyers' Social Security Agency.[28] The final amount may differ according to the type of case and its stakes. The indicator used takes into account the minimal costs for a first instance civil suit, on July 1 of each year.[29] Judicial costs were low during the period of the military governments. In 1985, the first democratic administration increased the fees to file a case. At the same time, new exemptions were granted for lawsuits that may be important for ordinary citizens, such as alimony, adoption, or guardianship. In 1989, during hyperinflation, the fees required to file a claim were fourteen times higher than in 1980. As was the case with other basic goods, justice passed far beyond the reach of many social groups. With monetary stabilization in 1991, the amounts fell. However, the final figures in the series are double the initial figure for 1980. This clear upward trend could have affected litigation rates.

LITIGATION COSTS AND SALARIES

This increase in judicial costs seems more significant when it is compared with the income trends of common citizens. Figure 2.4 compares the evolution of the mean industrial salary and our variable of judicial costs.[30]

Salary data offer a critical approach to the economic evolution of the country in the early 1980s; when costs remained low, salaries were relatively high. In contrast, since 1985, workers' wages have been falling steadily, but judicial costs have risen. The increasing gap between the two variables reveals that access to justice has diminished during the period covered by the research. The following section reviews the impact of these costs on the different litigation rates.

THE IMPACT OF JUDICIAL COSTS ON THE GENERAL LITIGATION RATE

We have documented the downward trend of the general litigation rate since 1970 and its recovery after 1993. It would seem reasonable to connect this evolution to the increase in judicial costs and presume that these have deterred litigation. The correlation analysis does not support this assumption.

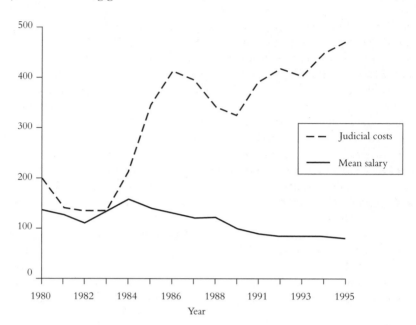

FIGURE 2.4 Salaries and Judicial Costs

The general litigation rate does not vary with judicial costs. Even if we omit the year 1989 to avoid the distorting effects of hyperinflation on the measure of costs, the correlation coefficient does not reach statistical significance. The strong expansion of the general litigation rate after 1993 — associated with the increase of debt-collection procedures — at a moment when judicial costs were also high, helps us explain these results. It is clear that high costs have little deterrent effect on some potential litigants. This discussion points out the complex nature of litigation, as it involves a particular form of public intervention into many different kinds of social relations. We must describe the effects of judicial costs variably, as they affect litigation rates in different types of cases.

JUDICIAL COSTS AND DIFFERENT LITIGATION RATES

It is necessary to specify the effects we expect in regard to different types of processes. Obviously, we do not expect a significant impact of costs on cost-free cases, such as labor cases, adoptions, alimonies, and guardianships. Although the exemption does not extend to mandatory payments to the bar association, it entails an important reduction of the costs.[31] We can safely assume that the effect of costs will not be visible in other kinds of processes where legal aid is easily obtained, such as divorces and other family cases.

Here, the deterrent effect of costs does exist, but it is exerted on a smaller group of users: the middle class. On the other hand, divorce cases are not good examples for observing restrictions to litigation. We know that changes in legislation and in judicial organization in this field have stimulated the propensity to sue. All the other kinds of cases provide conditions favorable for detecting the deterrent effects of high judicial costs, if these exist at all. The impact should be greater in processes with a low proportion of institutional actors, such as estate cases.

Table 2.7 reports correlations among litigation rates and judicial costs. The year 1989 has been omitted from the series to bypass the distortion introduced by hyperinflation. As expected, there is no covariation between costs and processes that are free, such as labor cases, adoptions, or guardianships, nor do costs affect cases of divorce. The second half of Table 2.7 presents the results of the correlation analysis in areas where exemptions are infrequent. We can see that there is an inverse relationship between judicial costs and rates for evictions, succession proceedings, and ordinary cases. The effect of high costs is especially great in cases with a high proportion of ordinary people as litigants, such as succession proceedings. We may assume that the situation affects middle-class families who are owners of some property and who have suffered important cuts in their income.

The deterrent effect of costs on ordinary suits is also noticeable ($R = -.765$, significant for $p < .004$). This category includes a variety of processes, including many tort cases arising out of traffic accidents. It is not surprising that these suits, which involve ordinary citizens, are affected by high costs.[32] The table also shows that debt-collection procedures are positively correlated with judicial costs. In many cases, the actors in these processes are corporations or individual businesspeople. For these, costs of suing are the price to pay to recover debts, and there is no deterrent effect. To understand the positive association between judicial costs and the rates for debt-collection procedures, we must assume that both are influenced by the general economic context. When prosperity rises, not only judicial but all costs are relatively low, making it easier to honor debts. Hence, the need for judicial intervention in these matters is reduced.

CONSEQUENCES

We can now summarize the impact of judicial costs on litigation from a more general perspective, taking into account the importance of the different kinds of cases in the caseload. Table 2.8 combines these data for the last year from which complete information is available, 1995. We can see that two-thirds of first instance cases are not affected by high costs. Where corporate actors predominate, such as in debt-collection procedures, obtaining the resources to file a case is not a problem. A second group of suits—labor

TABLE 2.7

Correlations Between Litigation Rates and Judicial Costs, 1980–1995

		Costs	Labor suits	Adoptions	Guardianships	Divorces	Total family suits
Costs	r	1.000	.444	.129	−.284	.433	.636★
	p	—	.097	.688	.371	.107	.011
	N	15	15	12	12	15	15
Labor suits	r	.444	1.000	.152	.410	.530★	.533★
	p	.097	—	.638	.186	.042	.041
	N	15	15	12	12	15	15
Adoptions	r	.129	.152	1.000	−.439	.549	.782★★
	p	.688	.638	—	.153	.065	.003
	N	12	12	12	12	12	12
Guardianships	r	−.284	.410	−.439	1.000	.150	−.165
	p	.371	.186	.153	—	.642	.609
	N	12	12	12	12	12	12
Divorces	r	.433	.530★	.549	.150	1.000	.893★★
	p	.107	.042	.065	.642	—	.000
	N	15	15	12	12	15	15
Total family suits	r	.636★	.533★	.782★★	−.165	.893★★	1.000
	p	.011	.041	.003	.609	.000	—
	N	15	15	12	12	15	15

and family—receive special treatment from the administration of justice. These are cases where constitutional rights are involved or where personal relations are affected. Tax exemptions, and legal-aid provisions facilitate the access to justice in these processes; they represent 14 percent of the caseload.

There remains a significant group of cases where costs have a restrictive effect: ordinary lawsuits, evictions, and estate and other civil suits. In 1983, when judicial costs were low, this group represented 47 percent of the total first instance caseload. This proportion fell to 22 percent in 1995. This helps us see that in spite of legal protection for some processes, economic barriers to access to justice in some fields have heightened during the last years. It is clear then that fiscal mechanisms developed by democratic administrations have not been able to stop the effects of increasing social inequalities.

Democratization and Litigation Rates

Mather (1990) pointed out the importance of political factors on the external environment of courts. Among these factors, democratization is undoubtedly significant, but the impact of this factor is difficult to assess in politically stable countries. It should be noted that most litigation studies have been conducted in developed countries, which are politically stable and have

TABLE 2.7

(*continued*)

		Costs	Ejecutivos	Apremios	Evictions	Bankruptcies	Succession proceedings	Ordinary suits	Other suits
Costs	r	1.000	.608*	.630*	−.584*	−.528	−.694*	−.765**	−.791**
	p	—	.036	.028	.046	.052	.012	.004	.002
	N	15	12	12	12	14	12	12	12
Ejecutivos	r	.608*	1.000	.895**	−.224	.499	−.333	−.283	−.150
	p	.036	—	.000	.484	.098	.290	.373	.642
	N	12	12	12	12	12	12	12	12
Apremios	r	.630*	.895**	1.000	−.160	.457	−.371	−.320	−.157
	p	.028	.000	—	.619	.135	.236	.311	.626
	N	12	12	12	12	12	12	12	12
Evictions	r	−.584*	−.224	−.160	1.000	−.012	.791**	.931**	.728**
	p	.046	.484	.619	—	.969	.002	.000	.007
	N	12	12	12	12	12	12	12	12
Bankruptcies	r	−.528	.499	.457	−.012	1.000	.088	−.005	.464
	p	.052	.098	.135	.969	—	.785	.988	.128
	N	14	12	12	12	14	12	12	12
Successions	r	−.694*	−.333	−.371	.791**	.088	1.000	.807**	.773**
	p	.012	.290	.236	.002	.785	—	.001	.003
	N	12	12	12	12	12	12	12	12
Ordinary suits	r	−.765**	−.283	−.320	.931**	−.005	.807**	1.000	.810**
	p	.004	.373	.311	.000	.988	.001	—	.001
	N	12	12	12	12	12	12	12	12
Other suits	r	−.791**	−.150	−.157	.728**	.464	.773**	.810**	1.000
	p	.002	.642	.626	.007	.128	.003	.001	—
	N	12	12	12	12	12	12	12	12

NOTE: The year 1989 has been excluded.
*The correlation is significant at 0.05 level (bilateral).
**The correlation is significant at 0.01 level (bilateral).

available statistical data on courts. Studies on developing countries are less frequent because in these nations it is difficult to collect the necessary statistical information.[33]

Democratization could be an influence on litigation, as it may have an impact on legal culture and on the availability of legal services. Few prior studies address this topic. Tate and Haynie (1993) reviewed how the Philippine Supreme Court performed the functions of conflict resolution, social control, and routine administration from 1961 to 1987. Authoritarian rule increased the social control activities (especially through criminal cases) of the Supreme Court; nevertheless, it had no impact on the conflict resolution function in ordinary civil cases.

We analyzed first the relationship between democratization and the general litigation rate. Data show that under the rule of law, the number of civil

TABLE 2.8

Impact of Judicial Costs on Different Types of Suits

Impact of costs	Types of cases	% of caseload, 1995
Positive or neutral	Ejecutivos	26.98
	Apremios	35.08
	Bankruptcies	1.71
	Total	63.77
Neutral due to legal protection	Labor cases	11.29
	Family cases	2.64
	Total	13.93
Negative	Ordinary suits	9.41
	Evictions	1.93
	Succession proceedings	4.00
	Other civil suits	6.94
	Total	22.28
Total cases		100.00

suits filed each year declined. During the 1968–72 military administration, the mean litigation rate was 8,063 cases per 100,000 inhabitants; this figure dropped to 5,400 when Perón came into office after the presidential elections in 1973. The average litigation rate remained at the same level in the next military turn and dropped again after the elections in 1983 (Table 2.9). It recovered during the Menem administration, but its present level is much below those registered during authoritarian governments.

We considered democratic rule a dichotomous variable, assigning the code 1 to the years in which government was elected and 0 to the years when the military was in power. Thus, we were able to calculate its correlation with litigation rates. This is rather rough, as it assumes a rigid contrast between civilian and military periods. As we have seen before, transition to democracy was not a sudden change but rather a gradual process.

If we keep these limitations in mind, it is interesting to observe the result: the coefficient is $-.642$ (significant for $p < .000$), indicating that democratization has a significant negative effect on litigation rates. The relationships between the two variables we are studying are complex. Democratization transforms political life and changes the actors and rules of the game of power; therefore, it has a multidimensional impact on litigation. To understand these effects, we must take into account that they may appear at different levels of the litigation pyramid. Litigation rates—the number of cases filed before the judges—are the end stage of a process of judicialization of a dispute (Felstiner, Abel, and Sarat 1980). The impact of democratization on the frequency of disputes and its propensity to judicialize conflicts may be quite different. The effect of democratization on different forms of litigation is an attractive subject. Unfortunately, owing to data limitations, we have only two series long enough for such an analysis: the general litigation rate and the labor litigation rate. The divorce rate and the bankruptcy rate—starting in 1980—include some years that fall within the military period. None of the other series are useful, as they start in 1983. Bearing in mind these limitations, as well as the complexity of relations between the two variables, we will specify some expected effects, indicating at the same time whether the available data support these assumptions.

EFFECTS ON SOCIAL RELATIONSHIPS

Democratization is a true process of change, and its effects go beyond the power structure to many areas of social life. Theoretical considerations suggest that crisis turmoil tends to increase the number of disputes and the frequency of litigation (Stookey 1990). From the viewpoint of consensus theory, long-term patterns of litigation may be taken as indicators of social harmony. During times of crisis, disputes of all types increase along with litigation. Conflict theorists generally agree that these relationships exist between crises, disputes, and litigation. Times of crisis are seen as periods of heightened group and class conflict, during which certain kinds of disputes increase—those that occur between an individual and an organization, such as labor cases or landlord-tenant disputes. Therefore, both theoretical approaches predict that total litigation rates will increase during times of crisis. However, the mechanism that provokes the increment is different under each theory. Consensus theorists predict a general increase in interpersonal disputes and in all types of cases; thus, they are interested in aggregated litigation rates. Conflict theorists claim that rates for cases where parties are very unequal—such as labor suits—will increase.

It is not difficult to presume that authoritarian rule, with its political violence, massive violations of human rights, and suppression of political parties and labor organizations, could be defined as a crisis period in Argentina.

TABLE 2.9
Mean Rates of General Litigation by Period

Period	Mean	Number of years	Standard deviation
1968–72	8,063.22	5	568.63
1973–75	5,397.13	3	597.59
1976–83	5,264.79	8	659.83
1984–89	3,593.90	6	405.11
1990–95	4,223.40	6	1,326.28
Total	5,197.49	28	1,688.86

NOTE: Rates per 100,000 inhabitants; 1968–95 figures are averages for the period.

Consequently, a greater frequency of disputes and higher litigation rates under military rule would be expected. From this theoretical standpoint, the negative correlation between the general litigation rate and democratization is comprehensible. The drop in absolute numbers of cases in 1984, considering the optimistic atmosphere of the country following the restoration of democracy, is consistent with this interpretation. This effect is also registered in different types of cases, such as divorces, labor suits, and debt-collection procedures. It is strong among bankruptcies, where it reaches statistical significance. Correlation between the bankruptcy rate and democratization has a coefficient of $-.823$, which is highly significant statistically.

The theoretical propositions considered so far are grounded in a concept of litigation as an instrument of conflict resolution. There are other perspectives. Grossman and Sarat (1975) suggest that litigation must also be considered as an alternative to orthodox political participation. If their position is correct, we should expect an increase in litigation when other participation channels are not available.

Analyzing litigation rates in a Missouri county between 1820 and 1970, McIntosh (1990) has shown that under a stable democratic regime, litigation rates increase when electoral participation decreases. These findings support the conceptualization of litigation as a specific form of interest mobilization, with clear political connotations. If this interpretation is correct, we should expect increased litigation levels during authoritarian periods, but for reasons different from those pointed out by Stookey.

We could also predict some variation in litigation rates during democratic periods, in line with levels of participation in public life. If this is correct, we could expect stronger reductions of litigation rates during the first democratic term, when political mobilization and electoral participation were high. Sarat's perspective is congruent with the general reduction of litigation levels that is seen at the beginning of each presidential term. It also offers an analytical frame in which to study the increasing judicialization of political conflicts in a context where electoral participation loses ground.

EFFECTS ON PROPENSITY TO SUE

On the other hand, democratization could affect not only the frequency of disputes within interpersonal relationships but also the propensity to process these conflicts in state facilities. First, we presume that democratization affects the way citizens view the courts: confidence in the independence of the judiciary and in the prestige of the judges—two variables that may have a bearing on the propensity to sue (Bergoglio and Carballo 1996)—are surely different in democratic and authoritarian periods. It might then be assumed that under the rule of law, litigiousness grows, because people are more willing to process their disputes through state facilities.

Second, we may consider that the legal culture itself—the general cluster of attitudes and beliefs related to the legal system—changes in a country where after fifty years of political instability, two constitutional presidents are able to serve out their terms.[34] Smulovitz (1995) points out that the cultural definition of potential legal disputes broadens and judicialization of conflicts is stimulated. If this proves to be correct, democratization should increase the propensity to sue.

Third, under democratic governments, the court system itself has changed, expanded, and become decentralized. Democratic administrations have created courts in smaller towns, improving geographic access to justice. Increased availability of justice may also favor a growth in the number of lawsuits.

The existence of these three mechanisms suggests that the propensity to sue is higher in democratic periods, and we could then expect increased litigation rates under the rule of law. We already know that the general litigation rate does not reflect these effects. But we did find them in some types of processes, especially where there is a high proportion of suits by individuals. The conceptual framework is useful for understanding the observed relationship between democratization and labor cases. These processes, generally brought by workers, tend to increase under democracy. The correlation coefficient reaches .520 (significant for $p < .005$). The relationship is particularly interesting because in labor cases, we are able to see the effects of democratization without the restrictive effect of costs. The length of the series (twenty-eight years) lends greater strength to these results.

Family cases are also a field where improved accessibility to judicial services should have visible effects. The divorce rate—the only series that includes data from the military period—shows a slight upward tendency under democracy. Even though the direction is as expected, this correlation does not reach statistical significance. Has improved accessibility to judicial services stimulated a propensity to sue in other fields? Unfortunately, the remaining available series are too short to answer this question. However, we may assume that the stimulating effects on litigation mentioned in this section cannot exist in many areas, as the general rate does not reflect them. It is clear, then, that democratization has promoted—through varied mechanisms—the judicialization of disputes, especially where the actors are individual persons, as in labor or family cases. Because these categories are a small share of the total caseload, the stimulating effects are not reflected in the general rate.[35]

SUMMARY

Detailed analysis of litigation rates has shown the dual effects of democratization. As we have observed from different perspectives, democratization improves social integration, offering a variety of institutional mechanisms to handle conflicts and protect individual rights. Consequently, under the rule of law, the number of interpersonal disputes decreases, and general litigation levels decline. At the same time, more alternatives for political participation are possible under a democratic regime. As Grossman and Sarat (1975) anticipated, this reduces the interest in litigation, which is a nonorthodox form of participation. However, democratic administrations have improved the accessibility of the administration of justice, especially in some fields of interest to common citizens. Consequently, the propensity to sue in such areas as labor or family courts is increased. Because these processes are such a small share of the caseload, the general rate does not reflect this effect. This is not surprising, as debt-collection procedures, in which there is a high proportion of corporate actors, are the bulk of court work.

At the End of the Road

Democratic institutionalization in Argentina has gone through deep transformations in law and legal culture. Political stability has brought normative stability; both have positive effects on the construction of the social order. The expansion of the judiciary and the increasing political role of the judges are also characteristic of this period. Transition to democracy is in itself an indicator of changes in legal culture; the way institutions function drives these changes. The trial against the military junta and the participation of judges in human rights issues have led to a broadening of cultural definitions of potentially judicial disputes. At the same time, expectations of justice have heightened, as is typical in modern legal cultures.

The country has gone through a long cycle of economic stagnation, followed by an acute hyperinflation crisis. In recent years, structural reforms have given way to economic growth once more. However, the negative impact of liberal policies on employment and salaries has deepened the tendency, which began during military rule, for wealth to be concentrated in the hands of relatively few people. Increasing inequality represents a serious challenge to the consolidation of democratic institutions. Growing poverty and unemployment breed higher crime rates, creating pressure for modernization of the administration of justice. The fear of crime places new pressure on judges, who must now watch their prestige, which rose in the early democratic years, decline.

Discontent with judges is aggravated by their inaction with regard to political corruption. Cases in which political figures are involved are dropped or delayed. The media comment on these cases, providing evidence that judicial subordination to political power has not disappeared under civilian rule. The analysis of litigation rates has been useful to illustrate the multiple effects of these processes of change. The pacification of the country under civilian administrations and the opening of new alternatives for political participation reduced conflicts within social relationships; and the general litigation rate reflects this effect. But changes in legislation and judicial organization, as well as the new atmosphere of freedom, stimulated the judicialization of claims in such areas as labor and family relations.

Later, economic structural changes pushed litigation rates up, also bringing about changes in the mix of types of cases. Debt-collection procedures, mostly initiated by corporate actors, have increased in importance and tend to absorb most of the working time of judges. At the same time, higher judicial costs and lower salaries discourage claims in areas where there are no cost exemptions. Economic barriers to access to justice heighten in such fields as succession proceedings or ordinary civil cases. The situation is hardly tolerable in a society where expectations of justice have increased since democratization.

The combination of a greater awareness of the possibilities offered by the judiciary in a democracy and the increasing economic difficulties with regard to access to justice for common citizens has eroded the legitimacy of the judiciary. The consolidation of democracy is not an easy task in a period of increasing social inequalities.

Notes

1. The Statistical Bureau of the national Supreme Court was not created until 1991.

2. O'Donnell (1997) uses the term *delegative democracies* to describe this situation in Argentina and other Latin American countries.

3. We follow here Torrado (1992, 1995), Treber (1996), and Altimir (1997).

4. In 1970, the real industrial average wage was double the figure for 1990 (Treber 1996).

5. Treber (1996) reports a value of 197.1 for 1971 and 81.4 for 1995 (base year = 1990).

6. These are preliminary results of a study based on the Encuesta Permanente de Hogares (INDEC) published by the *Clarín* newspaper, June 13, 1999.

7. The Gini coefficient, an indicator used to measure income inequality, changed from 0.40 in 1954 to 0.53 in 1995.

8. This pattern of inequalities—broadening distances between classes and reduction of gender barriers—is also found in empirical studies of access to justice (Bergoglio 1997a, 1999a).

9. *Hacia un plan nacional de política criminológica II*, Dirección Nacional de Política Criminológica, Buenos Aires (1997).

10. This situation is found today in many countries. Ferrari (2000) has argued that the excessive number of laws in many contemporary societies, as well as the increasing complexity of the normative system, does not help compliance.

11. The plan was published in the last year of Menem's administration.

12. Because the last legislative reform granted functions to prosecutors that were previously reserved to judges, we must consider the number of both types of public officials in observing the expansion of judicial organization. For this reason, the number of judges and prosecutors has been totaled to obtain the number of magistrates.

13. Public expenditure in the judiciary is between 3 and 6 percent in other provinces (Arjona 1996). Recently, the federal government has also increased the expenditure in the judiciary: courts absorbed 0.70 percent of the budget in 1978 and 1.40 percent in 1993 (Pásara 1995).

14. The new constitution created the Consejo de la Magistratura, which intervenes in the appointment of judges.

15. A bibliography on the role of the judiciary in this period may be seen in Acuña et al. (1995).

16. A survey conducted in Buenos Aires in 1995 showed that the average duration of debt-enforcement procedures amounted to 808 days; family processes were similar in length. In economic penal courts—where political corruption cases are filed—the mean duration of processes in first instance was more than five years (Gregorio 1995).

17. Total public expenditure on justice (including both federal and provincial) in Argentina was 0.65 percent of the GNP during 1991. This proportion grew to 0.9 percent in 2000. In absolute numbers, total public expenditure on justice for 2000 doubled the figures for 1991. Artana, Cristini, and Urbiztondo (1995) have shown that public expenses per case in Argentina are double the U.S. figures and triple Spain's. More international comparisons of public expenditures on justice can be found in Guisarri (1998).

18. See Mackinson de Sorokin (1987) for a description of conservatism in internal legal culture.

19. Results published in the newspaper *La Nación*, July 4, 1999. The same survey showed that the Menem administration, considered overall, obtained a rating of 6.6.

20. The research received a grant from the Consejo de Investigaciones Científicas de Córdoba (CONICOR).

21. Wollschläger (1998) follows a different route and chooses a "functional method" of international comparison. In so doing, he includes not only civil courts but courtlike institutions, such as the Chinese People Mediation Committees, in his analysis.

22. Each annual report details workload per court. This research team used this information to build the corresponding statistical series for the whole province.

23. The data in Córdoba are not usually available elsewhere in Argentina. In the Buenos Aires province, judicial statistical series start in 1979 (Ves Losada 1989, 1991b).

24. Since 1996, the prosecutor's office has been in charge of judicial statistics, and the registration procedures have changed. Their figures are not strictly comparable to those provided by the Provincial Supreme Court. However, we may observe that they reported 130,463 cases in 1996.

25. Unemployment rates in Córdoba went from 4.75 percent in 1991 to 15.55 percent in 1995.

26. Data from *Cuentas Nacionales: Oferta y demanda global 1980–1995*, Dirección Nacional de Cuentas Nacionales (1996), and *Producto Bruto Geográfico—un aporte a la determinación de la base imponible de los Impuestos sustitutivos del Impuesto sobre los Ingresos Brutos*, Ministerio del Interior (1997). Both series include recent technical corrections. When the analysis includes the 1970s, the historical series produced by Treber (1996) has been used. Correlation between both series is .99.

27. For details about the construction of the series, see Bergoglio (1999b).

28. The value of the *tasa de justicia* is fixed by the state for different types of cases. These resources help cover the judicial budget.

29. When inflation is constant, costs are different each week because of indexing of debts and taxes. The source used for our series was the legal newspaper *Comercio y Justicia*, which publishes daily information on legal costs. To make the comparison easier, we calculated the costs for one day each year (July 1) and constructed a table comparing the costs for all the years in the series.

30. We have employed the series of mean real industrial wages prepared by Treber (1996), using official data.

31. Costs required to file a case include a per-case filing fee and compulsory contributions to the bar (Colegio de Abogados) and to the lawyers' Social Security Agency. Tax exemptions refer only to the first item, the filing fee. Contributions to the bar and to the Social Security Agency must be paid in all cases; their final amount may vary according to the type of case and its stakes.

32. These negative effects were especially pointed out in interviews with lawyers.

33. An interesting exception is Clark's (1990) study that compares the tendencies of civil litigation in Europe and in three Latin American countries between 1945 and 1970.

34. For a detailed description of these changes, see García Delgado (1994).

35. Labor and divorce suits together represented 13 percent of the total caseload in 1995.

References

Acuña, Carlos H., Inés González Bombal, Elizabeth Jelin, Oscar Landi, Luis Alberto Quevedo, Catalina Smulovitz, and Adriana Vacchieri. 1995. *Juicio, castigos y memorias*. Buenos Aires: Nueva Visión.

Agulla, Juan Carlos. 1968. *Eclipse de una aristocracia*. Córdoba: Líbera.

Altimir, Oscar. 1997. Desigualdad, empleo y pobreza en América Latina: Efectos del ajuste y del cambio en el estilo de desarrollo. *Desarrollo Económico* 37, no. 145 (April–June):3–30.

Arjona, Flavio. 1996. La administración de justicia: Una comparación interprovincial. *Novedades Económicas* 18 (186):26–76.

Artana, D., Marcela Cristini, and Santiago Urbiztondo. 1995. *La reforma del poder judicial en la Argentina*. Buenos Aires: Asociación de Bancos Argentina.

Beccaria, Luis. 1992. Cambios en la estructura distributiva 1975–1990. Pp. 93–116 in *Cuesta abajo*, edited by Alberto Minujin. Buenos Aires: UNICEF-Losada.

Beccaria, Luis, and Nestor López. 1995. Reconversión productiva y empleo en Argentina. Pp. 191–216 in *Más allá de la estabilidad*, edited by Pablo Bustos. Buenos Aires: Fundación Friedrich Ebert.

Bergoglio, M. I. 1997a. Acceso a la justicia civil: Diferencias de clase. Pp. 93–107 in vol. 3 of *Anuario del centro de investigaciones jurídicas y sociales*. Córdoba: Universidad Nacional de Córdoba.

————. 1997b. Democratización y tasas de litigación en Argentina, 1969–1994. *Revista de Sociología del Derecho* 12:21–29.

————. 1999a. Desigualdades en el acceso a la justicia civil: Diferencias de género. Pp. 129–47 in *Anuario IV del centro de investigaciones jurídicas y sociales*. Córdoba: Universidad Nacional de Córdoba.

————. 1999b. *El impacto de los costos en la decisión de litigar*. Report to Secretaría de Ciencia y Técnica, Universidad Nacional de Córdoba. Mimeographed.

Bergoglio, M. I., and J. Carballo. 1996. Corrupción y opinión pública en Argentina. *Revista Politeia* 19:371–86.

Blankenburg, Erhard. 1994. The infrastructure for avoiding civil litigation: Comparing cultures of legal behavior in the Netherlands and West Germany. *Law and Society Review* 28 (4):789–807.

Boigeol, Anne. 1993. La magistrature française au féminin: Entre spécificité et banalisation. Paper presented at the 1993 annual meeting of RCSL, Oñati, Spain.

Cappelletti, Mauro, and Bryant Garth. 1996. *El acceso a la justicia: La tendencia en el movimiento mundial para hacer efectivos los derechos*. Mexico City: Fondo de Cultura Económica.

Cavagna Martínez, Mariano, Rafael Bielsa, and Eduardo Graña.1994. *El poder judicial de la nación*. Buenos Aires: La Ley.

Cerro A. M., and O. Meloni. 1999. *Análisis económico de las políticas de prevención y represión del delito en la Argentina*. Córdoba: Eudecor.

Clark, David. 1990. Civil litigation trends in Europe and Latin America since 1945: The advantage of intracountry comparisons. *Law and Society Review* 24 (2):549–69.

Comisión Nacional sobre Desaparición de Personas, Argentina. 1984. *Informe Nunca Más*. Prologue by Ernesto Sábato. Buenos Aires: Eudeba. Available at www.nun camas.org/investig/investig.htm. English edition: Argentina's National Commission on Disappeared People. 1986. *Report Nunca Más—never again*. London: Faber and Faber.

De Imaz, J. L. 1964. *Los que mandan*. Buenos Aires: Eudeba.

Felstiner W., R. Abel, and A. Sarat. 1980. The emergence and transformation of disputes: Naming, blaming, claiming. *Law and Society Review* 15:631.

Ferrari, Vincenzo. 2000. *Acción jurídica y sistema normativo*. Madrid: Dykinson.

FORES (Foro de Estudios sobre la Administración de Justicia). 1998. *La justicia de las provincias Argentinas.* Report for the Consejo Empresario Argentino, Buenos Aires.

Friedman, Lawrence. 1989. Litigation and society. *Annual Review of Sociology* 13: 17–29.

———. 1990. Opening the time capsule: A progress report on studies of courts over time. *Law and Society Review* 24 (2):229–40.

Fucito, Felipe.1997. *El perfil del abogado de la provincia de Buenos Aires.* La Plata: Colegio de Abogados de la Provincia de Buenos Aires.

Galanter, Marc. 1983. Reading the landscape of disputes: What we know and don't know (and think we know) about our allegedly contentious and litigious society. *UCLA Law Review* 31 (4): 4–71.

———. 1992. Law abounding: Legalisation around the North Atlantic. *The Modern Law Review* 55 (January):1–24.

Garavano, Germán. 1998. Eficiencia y justicia: Cuándo la justicia es eficiente? Paper presented at meeting, Justicia, Eficiencia y Derecho, Universidad Empresarial Siglo XXI, December, Córdoba.

García Delgado, Daniel R.1994. *Estado y sociedad: La nueva relación a partir del cambio estructural.* Buenos Aires: Flacso-Sociales.

Gastron, A. 1999. Los abogados y la clase política. Pp. 399–424 in *Ciencias sociales: Presencia y continuidades,* edited by J. C. Agulla. Buenos Aires: Academia Nacional de Ciencias de Buenos Aires.

Gregorio, Carlos. 1995. *Investigación sobre demora en el proceso judicial.* Buenos Aires: Centro de Estudios Judiciales de la República Argentina (CEJURA).

Grondona, Mariano. 1993. *La corrupción.* Buenos Aires: Planeta.

Grossman, J., and A. Sarat.1975. Litigation in the federal courts: A comparative perspective. *Law and Society Review* 9:321–46.

Guisarri, A. 1998. *Costos de la justicia y eficiencia en la asignación de recursos.* Proyecto Justicia y Desarrollo Económico. Buenos Aires: Colegio de Abogados de la Ciudad de Buenos Aires-FORES-Consejo Empresario Argentino.

INDEC (Instituto Nacional de Estadísticas y Censos). 1993. *Resultados definitivos del censo nacional de población y vivienda 1991.* Series B, no. 4, Buenos Aires.

Isuani, Ernesto. 1996. Anomia social y anemia estatal: Sobre integración social en Argentina. *Sociedad* 10 (November):103–28.

Kunz, Ana.1989. Los magistrados de la Corte Suprema de justicia de la nación (1930–1983). *Cuadernos de investigaciones no. 15,* Facultad de Derecho y Ciencias Sociales, Universidad Nacional de Buenos Aires, 1–36.

Lynch, Horacio. 1995. La ley y LA LEY. Foro de Estudios sobre la Administración de la Justicia (FORES). Unpublished manuscript.

Mackinson de Sorokin, Gladys. 1987. *Sociología del poder judicial.* Buenos Aires: Sociología del Derecho.

Mather, Lynn.1990. Dispute processing and a longitudinal approach to courts. *Law and Society Review* 24 (2):357–71.

McIntosh, Wayne. 1990. *The appeal of civil law.* Chicago: University of Illinois Press, Urbana-Chicago.

Minujin, A., and G. Kessler. 1995. *La nueva pobreza en Argentina.* Buenos Aires: Planeta.

Moreno Ocampo, Luis. 1993. *En defensa propia: Cómo salir de la corrupción.* Buenos Aires: Sudamericana.

Munger, Frank. 1988. Law, change and litigation: A critical examination of an empirical research tradition. *Law and Society Review* 22 (1):57–101.

———. 1990. Trial courts and social change: The evolution of a field of study. *Law and Society Review* 24 (2):217–27.

Nino, Carlos. 1992. *Un país al margen de la ley.* Buenos Aires: Emecé.

O'Donnell, G. 1997. *Contrapuntos.* Buenos Aires: Paidós.

Pásara, Luis.1995. La justicia en la Argentina. *Boletín Techint* no. 283 (July–September):57–72.

———. 1996. Reforma judicial: Urgencia y desafío. *Boletín Techint* no. 285 (January–March):33–57.

Sánchez, Mariana. 1999. *Delito y condiciones macroeconómicas.* Córdoba: Lerner.

Sanders, Joseph, and Lee Hamilton. 1992. Legal cultures and punishment repertoires in Japan, Russia and the United States. *Law and Society Review* 26:117.

Smulovitz, Catalina. 1995. El poder judicial en la nueva democracia Argentina: El trabajoso parto de un actor. *Ágora* 2:85–106.

Souza Santos, B., M. M. Leitao Marques, and J. Pedroso. 1996. The Portuguese courts: Distant citizens and close corporations. Paper presented at the Law and Society meeting, July, Glasgow.

Stookey, John A. 1990. Trials and tribulations: Crises, litigation, and legal change. *Law and Society Review* 24 (2):496–519.

Tappatá, Anahí de. 1996. Despejando la incertidumbre de los costos judiciales. *Novedades Económicas* 18 (186):22–26.

Tate, Neal. 1997a. La democracia y la ley: Nuevos avances teóricos y de investigación. *Revista Internacional de Ciencias Sociales,* no. 152 (June), published by UNESCO.

———. 1997b. El papel de los Tribunales de Justicia en la caída y la restauración de la democracia en Filipinas y su reflejo en el diario de sesiones del Tribunal Supremo. *Revista Internacional de Ciencias Sociales,* no. 152 (June), published by UNESCO.

Tate, Neal, and Stacia Haynie. 1993. Authoritarianism and the functions of courts: A time series analysis of the Philippine Supreme Court, 1961–1987. *Law and Society Review* 27 (4):707–39.

Tate, Neal, and Torbjorn Vallinder, eds. 1995. *The global expansion of judicial power.* New York: New York University Press.

Toharia, Juan José. 1987. *Pleitos tengas: Introducción a la cultura legal española.* Madrid: Centro de Investigaciones Sociológicas, Colec. Monografías 96.

———. 1994. *Conflicto y litigación en España.* Oñati, Spain: Instituto Internacional de Sociología del Derecho. Mimeographed.

Torrado, Susana. 1992. *Estructura social de la Argentina, 1945–1983.* Buenos Aires: De la Flor.

———. 1995. Notas sobre la estructura social de Argentina al comenzar los años 90. Pp. 67–102 in *Política social: La cuenta pendiente,* compiled by Gustavo Béliz. Buenos Aires: Sudamericana.

Treber, Salvador. 1996. La distribución por tramos o niveles de ingreso. Paper presented at the Conferencia Regional de la Asociación de Facultades, Escuelas e Institutos de Economía de América Latina, April, Buenos Aires.

Van Loon, Francis, Stephane Delrue, and Wim Van Wambeke. 1995. Sociological research on litigation: Perspectives and examples. *European Journal of Law and Economics* 2:379–85.

Van Loon, F., and E. Langerwerf. 1990. Socioeconomic development and the evolution of litigation rates of civil courts in Belgium, 1835–1980. *Law and Society Review* 24 (2):283–98.

Ves Losada, Alfredo. 1989. Indices de litigiosidad en la provincia de Buenos Aires (Primera parte). *La Ley*, T.C [vol. C], 1356–64.

———. 1991a. Crisis política y estabilidad judicial en la Argentina (1854–1990). *Revista de Sociología del Derecho* 6:17–22.

———. 1991b. Indice de litigiosidad en la provincia de Buenos Aires (Segunda parte). *La Ley*, T.A [vol. A], 1084–1110.

Wainerman, Catalina. 1995. Las mujeres y el trabajo en la Argentina. *Sociedad* 6: 149–58.

Wollschläger, Christian. 1990. Civil litigation and modernization: The work of the municipal courts of Bremen, Germany, in five centuries, 1549–1984. *Law and Society Review* 24 (2).

———. 1994. Acceptance and avoidance of litigation in Japan 1876–1991. Paper presented at the XIII Congreso Mundial de Sociología, Bielefeld, Germany.

———. 1998. Exploring global landscapes of litigation rates. Pp. 577–88 in *Soziologie des Rechts: Festschrift fur Erhard Blankenburg zum 60*, edited by J. Brand and D. Strempel. Geburtstag, Baden-Baden, Germany: Nomos.

CHAPTER 3

Brazil: The Road of Conflict Bound for Total Justice

ELIANE BOTELHO JUNQUEIRA

TO ANALYZE transformations in the law and legal culture of Brazil over a period of thirty years—from 1970 to 2000—is an ambitious project. Brazil experienced many political, economic, and social changes in these three decades—and as many legal changes. It is almost impossible to know how many laws, decrees, and administrative rules were written in these thirty years. It is even more difficult to analyze how the legal culture—the popular perception of and relationship with the world of law—has changed in this period. The task is not easy, but, perhaps for this reason, it is fascinating.

Four difficulties, however, should be confronted immediately. First, an analysis of the transformation of law and legal culture in the last thirty years must begin with a definition of "legal culture." About this topic, many pages have already been written, and in no way do I pretend to be original.[1] My point of departure is from Lawrence Friedman, who understands legal culture as "ideas, values, expectations and attitudes towards law and legal institutions, which some public or some part of the public holds" (1997, 34). But I recognize, as does Friedman, that it is a very slippery concept, with different meanings in different contexts (1999, 165). The *Dictionnaire Encyclopédique de Théorie et de Sociologie du Droit*, edited by André-Jean Arnaud, for example, lists four definitions of legal culture: (1) the techniques of explanation or interpretation used by operators of the legal system and the set of ideologies

This chapter was originally prepared for the seminar "Transformations in Law and Legal Culture in Latin America and the Mediterranean" held in September 1999 at Stanford Law School. I would like to thank the organizers of this event, Lawrence Friedman and Rogelio Pérez-Perdomo, for their invitation, as well as my research assistants, Alexandre Augusto Sivolella Barreiro, Luciana de Pontes Saraiva, Maria Neuenschwander Escosteguy Carneiro, and Monica Cristine de Rezende, for their help in collecting information.

into which these legal techniques translate; (2) the set of public opinions about the legal system; (3) the set of values, principles, and ideologies about law and the knowledge associated with the language of the operators of the legal system; and (4) the set of national and local differences in the thinking about and the practice of law (1993, 139).

More recently, Roger Cotterrell's (1997) criticism of Friedman's concept has spurred an intense debate.[2] Concerned specifically about the influence of professional practices on the construction and affirmation of the values and beliefs about the law, Cotterrell asserts that it is more appropriate to talk of "legal ideology" than legal culture.

This conceptual debate revives an old argument formulated by Friedrich von Savigny and Jeremy Bentham, among others: Is the law an independent or dependent variable? Are changes in the law a consequence of social changes, or, in contrast, are social changes produced by changes in the law? In the revival of this eighteenth-century question, we now ask: Is legal culture a result of legal change, or, in contrast, do changes in legal culture bring changes in the law? Does professional legal culture have a great potentiality to produce legal change? Or do legal changes correspond to changes in popular legal culture?

Cotterrell, without doubt, allies himself with the first position when, concerned with legal practices, he states that "the focus is more obviously on the power of the state legal system to produce structures of social understandings, attitudes and values among lay citizens than on the ways in which these kinds of diffuse understandings, attitudes and values shape the workings of the state legal system" (1997, 28). But this is not the meaning of the term as understood by Friedman, whose concept of legal culture has a center of gravity different from that attributed to the concept of legal ideology (1997, 38). Although Cotterrell's position is close to legal doctrine, Friedman situates himself closer to the perception of the law, whether it is by legal operators (internal legal culture) or by the general population (external legal culture).[3] More recently, Friedman has asserted that national identity is an aspect of culture and that culture is the progenitor of legal culture, which itself is the source of law, formal and informal. On the other hand, continues Friedman, the law produces a feedback in the culture even though the exact extent of this influence cannot be determined (1999, 164). Criticizing the position of Cotterrell, Friedman states:

[A]ny equation which takes the form social change X leads to legal result Y is simplistic and unsatisfying. A better form would be: social change X leads to a change in legal culture Y, which results in this or that kind of pressure on legal institutions, and what comes out is legal result Z. In other words, "legal culture" is a generic term for states of mind and ideas, held by some public; these states of mind are affected by

events, situations and the like in society as a whole, and they lead in turn to actions
that have an impact on the legal system itself. (1997, 35)

The term "consciousness of legality," coined by Bourdieu (1998) and developed principally in *Outline of a Theory of Practice* from an anthropological perspective, cannot be forgotten in this debate. Based on this concept, Patricia
Ewick and Susan Silbey (1998), for example, identified three attitudes in relation to the law—before law, with law, and against law—in the community
that they studied. Sally Engle Merry, analyzing the sense of law of a group of
workers, also makes use of this concept, defining it as "the way people con-
ceive of the 'natural' and normal way of doing things, their habitual patterns
of talk and action, and their commonsense understanding of the world. The
consciousness I am describing is not only the realm of deliberate, intentional
action but also that of habitual actions and practice" (1990, 5).

Merry explains the difference between concepts of consciousness and culture clearly: "Discourses are located in the world, rooted in institutional
structures. Consciousness, on the other hand, describes an individual's understanding of his or her world. It is produced by a person's interpretation of
the cultural messages provided by discourses, an active process in which the
person uses cultural categories to construct an awareness of self" (1990, 9).
However, if some scholars distinguish the objectivity of culture and the sub-
jectivity of consciousness, there are also compelling arguments against the
idea that these two can be separated. Perhaps trying to explain these differences, Blankenburg (1999) differentiates among law in books, law in heads,
law in action, and law in polls. Although the distinctions are important, I believe that it is not possible to dissociate the law in heads and the law in polls
(acknowledged by Blankenburg himself).[4]

My approach is to work with the concept of legal culture, including
within it the idea of legal consciousness. This is also the recent choice of
Friedman in *Horizontal Society*, where he admits that the concept of legal
culture is closely related to the concepts of legal consciousness and legal ideology (1999, 270). This decision solves my first conceptual problem at hand.
But another question persists. In which field of knowledge should we include the legal culture? Is it a subfield of cultural studies? Or is it a subfield
of civic culture? The latter is my approach. Legal culture is not seen as an
aspect of culture in general,[5] but rather as a following from the relationship
that is established with the state. I find my fundamental theoretical references
in the work of Robert Putnam (1996), with his analysis about the civic culture of different regions of Italy, and in the work of Wanderley Guilherme
dos Santos (1993), who analyzes the civic culture of the Brazilian population.

In addition to the conceptual difficulties, there are several operational
problems when we try to develop research about legal culture. How do you

study the legal culture of a country? Moreover, is it possible to speak of a Brazilian legal culture?

This is the second large problem to be confronted: it is difficult to think about a single national legal culture. Friedman, considering North American society, recognizes the diversity in legal culture: "There is not one culture, but many. There are legal conservatives, legal liberals, and all sorts of variants and subgroups. Within specific groups, legal culture consists of particular attitudes which, however, do tend to cohere, to hang together, to form clusters of related attitudes" (1987, 98). In other words, we must always ask "whose legal culture?" as there are different dialects circulating, although the culture of the elite is dominant (Friedman 1999, 165).

Although they exist, differences among legal cultures are not accentuated in the United States, where there is a large middle class and a relatively democratic and horizontal society. But in Brazil, the problem is quite serious. In addition to the obvious differences between external and internal legal culture, there is a deep fissure separating Brazil from Brasil.[6] There are poor cities and rich cities. Even within a single neighborhood, there are great social contrasts. The best example is the case of Rocinha, the largest *favela* (slum) in Latin America, located between two upper-middle-class neighborhoods in Rio de Janeiro (Gávea and São Conrado). Many of us, like the song of Chico Buarque and Roberto Menescal,[7] live in Brazil (the developed region of the country) and only see *Brasil* (the underdeveloped region of the country) on television, once in a while.

Third, the Brazil of the year 2000 is certainly not the same as the Brazil of 1970. The country has moved from an authoritarian regime to democracy, from the absence of political rights to the full protection of social rights, from the economic miracle to fiscal crisis, from a homogeneous society to a complex and atomized society, from an interventionist economy to a neoliberal economy. In thirty years, we have known various currencies: the *cruzeiro*, the new *cruzeiro*, the *cruzado*, the new *cruzado*, the *cruzeiro* (again), and the *real*. We have had various governments: the authoritarian regime; "a political opening (*abertura*): slow, gradual and secure" in a phrase coined by President Geisel; the New Republic; an impeachment. We have gone from predatory developmentalism to sustainable development; from the absence of environmental consciousness to greater environmental protection.[8] We have progressed from having to defend political rights to defending the rights of women, homosexuals, blacks, the indigenous, the disabled, the landless, and the homeless. We have entered into a regional economic arrangement as part of *Mercosur*. How do we compare the legal cultures of two moments so distinct in the history of Brazil?

Fourth, where do we analyze Brazilian legal culture? Almost twenty years ago Mario Brockman Machado defended the need for empirical research "mapping the principal beliefs, opinions, traditions, attitudes, values and norms that characterize our legal culture . . . [I]t would be interesting to have as careful description as possible of the manner in which the Brazilian relates himself, at the emotional and evaluative cognitive levels, to our legal system, its component parts and its functioning, that gives us an adequate vision of the image that he has of his own insertion—or lack of insertion—in this system" (1981, 22).[9] This chapter does not aim to develop this empirical research but to review what has already been done. And little has been done in this area. Official statistics exist, and various questions about the law are always included in official surveys.[10] However, the census statistics collected by the *Instituto Brasileiro Geográfico e Estatístico* (Brazilian Institute of Geography and Statistics [IBGE]), with a methodology that changes each decade, do not permit the construction of statistical profiles of the period,[11] and they tell little of legal culture. At best, there is information about the number of judges, lawyers, and lawsuits, which is insufficient to provide an X ray of the perception of law by society.

This chapter, therefore, is a patchwork quilt, bringing together data from various sources, combining the official statistics of IBGE with research conducted by other institutions. The investigation carried out by the Getúlio Vargas Foundation on Law, Justice, and Citizenship (hereafter referred to as CPDOC-FGV), for example, provides important lessons about the perception of law by Brazilians (although the study was restricted to Rio de Janeiro). Other research, such as studies conducted by Maria Guadalupe Piragibe da Fonseca (Guimarães 1999) and by Sérgio Adorno (1988), fill some—but not all—of the holes.[12]

This chapter consists of four parts. The first part analyzes social changes that occurred between 1970 and 2000. What were the characteristics of Brazilian society in 1970? What are they now? What is the rate of illiteracy? Did the living conditions, taking account of several indicators, improve or worsen in these thirty years? The second part analyzes regional disparities. To what extent is it possible to think about a national legal culture in the face of such diverse regional characteristics? The third part analyzes the changes in the law from 1970 to 2000, pointing to the impact of some legislative changes. This includes the laws that most directly affected the daily lives of people and those about which there were important national debates. The final part analyzes the internal legal culture, that of legal professionals including lawyers, judges, prosecutors, and public defenders, and the external legal culture, that of the general population.

From the Brazil of 1970 to the Brazil of 2000

What was Brazil like in 1970? What were its political characteristics? How did the Brazilian population live? How did the economy operate? And what has changed in thirty years? In sum, to what extent do these thirty years separate two different realities? In the 1970s, rapid economic development stood in contrast to the authoritarian regime and to the deficient living conditions of a large part of the population. Nowadays, Brazil is democratic, with a population that enjoys a better standard of living but that still confronts many economic problems, as well as difficulties in the areas of education, employment, health, and housing, among others.

FROM THE ECONOMIC MIRACLE TO THE CRISIS OF THE REAL

The data practically speak for themselves. In thirty years, the population of Brazil has almost doubled. From "ninety million in action," a refrain consecrated in the song of the World Cup in 1970, the population has become 163,833,384.[13]

As a population, we are ever more urban. Little by little, the rural areas have emptied out. As true in other countries of the Third World, almost everyone (78.4 percent of the population) wants to live in the cities, principally in large cities, which are thus transformed into megalopolises with all the problems that follow from a high population density. Pollution, traffic, and crime are challenges of our daily lives.

Through these thirty years, we have also conquered new geographic frontiers. Today, there are cities that did not exist in 1970, principally in the central-west region; the national agricultural frontier was opened in the 1970s by colonists from southern Brazil and by the cultivation of soybeans. And we continue to advance in the direction of the Amazon forest.

The best indicator of the changes in Brazil during these years is the Index of Human Development (IHD),[14] based on three characteristics: longevity (life expectancy from birth to death); the level of education (the rate of illiteracy combined with school attendance in the three levels of education); and income or gross domestic product (GDP) per capita. In 1970, Brazil (with an IHD of .507) was placed in the group of countries at the middle level of human development (countries with an IHD between .500 and .800). In 1996, the country received an IHD score of .830 and was placed among the countries with a high level of human development.[15]

The life expectancy of Brazilians increased in these thirty years. In 1970, we did not expect to live more than fifty-two years. Now the average life expectancy is sixty-seven years. We are more literate: we have moved from an adult literacy rate of 67 percent to 85.33 percent. We spend more time at

school, at all levels of education. In 1970, less than 50 percent of the Brazilian population of school age was enrolled in one of the three levels of education. Today there are 76.79 percent enrolled. Our GDP per capita almost
tripled (in constant monetary value). All of the indicators of the IHD—longevity, education, and income—had significant growth in the period, although their growth has been different: income has grown much more than
longevity or education.

We end the century with Mercosur, a regional agreement that seeks to
create a common market among the southern cone countries: Brazil, Argentina, Uruguay, and Paraguay (with Chile and Bolivia as associated countries). After the Treaty of Assunción that created Mercosur in 1991, a new
socioeconomic context emerged in South America. Considered before as
countries of medium importance in the international order, Brazil and Argentina have assumed a new posture as an economic bloc with more than
200 million inhabitants and a GDP of more than US$1 trillion in 1998.

The importance of Mercosur is not entirely economic; it also represents a
new vision of the legal order for Brazil. The country now sees its sovereignty
as limited, having to live with and work with other countries in the solution
of problems. The laws that emerge from Mercosur will have force in Brazil,
and this new source of rights and obligations will create conflict among the
member countries. This is a significant challenge for Brazilian legal culture
in the next decade.

FROM AUTHORITARIANISM TO DEMOCRACY

In the legal-political arena, the period between 1970 and 2000 was marked
by the end of the military regime, which in 1970 had reached its most repressive moment, ushered in by the Law of National Security and Institutional
Act 5 of 1968. After the military regime, there was a phase of liberalization
in which individual rights (for example, habeas corpus) were returned to
society, the politically persecuted were given amnesty, and political parties
began to restructure in preparation for the return to a constitutional democracy in 1988.[16] The following schema helps the reader understand this
historical process:

1964	military coup
1968	Institutional Act No. 5, with an increase in political repression
1970	economic miracle
1975	peak of political centralization
1979	reorganization of social movements
	political amnesty
	beginning of the political opening (abertura)
1984	unsuccessful movement for Direct Elections Now (*Diretas Já*)

1985   indirect civil election for president
          beginning of constitutional process
1985–88 worker strikes (more than five thousand)
1987   first meeting of the Constitutional Assembly
1988   approval of the federal constitution
1989   direct election of President Fernando Collor
1992   impeachment of President Collor
1994   beginning of the Real Plan (an economic plan)
          election of President Fernando Henrique Cardoso
1998   reelection of President Cardoso
1999   beginning of the new economic crisis, with a devaluation of
          the real

Without doubt, these changes were substantial. However, political scientists emphasize three main problems in the Brazilian democratic process. First, despite the high popular participation, the Constitutional Assembly was a locus of lobbying by diverse groups, among them the lawyers and the judiciary, which were able to impede important advances in the democratic process. For example, lawyers succeeded in obtaining a constitutionally protected monopoly on judicial representation, creating a barrier to direct popular access to the courts.[17] In addition, by writing into the constitution a large range of social rights without limiting itself to defining the rules of the game, the Constitutional Assembly succumbed to the belief, deeply rooted in Brazilian political and legal culture, that the legal norm can create social fact. It attempted to change the country through legal rather than political means (Helio Jaguaribe, quoted in Martins 1989, 244). Finally, the excessive constitutionalization of social rights, instead of being a positive indicator of the advance of democracy, reflects a lack of confidence in the democratic regime and a strategy to guarantee these "conquests" amid the instability of the political process.

In the sphere of civic society, in 1970 only the Bar Association, the Association of the Brazilian Press, and the Catholic Church were able to maintain a dialogue with the military regime. In the 1980s, the civic society was reinforced. The social movements, which reorganized at the end of the 1970s, opened up an alternative to traditional political parties for participation in public life and formation of new collective identities (Diniz and Boschi 1989, 43). Nongovernmental organizations and unions occupied an important place in political life and mobilized the population.

In 1984, the movement Direct Elections Now (Diretas Já), which was unfortunately unsuccessful, fought for direct presidential elections in the first great national mobilization in the process of democratization. Soon after, every Brazilian assumed the function of "Sarney's supervisor" (*fiscal do Sar-*

ney), referring to José Sarney, then president, overseeing the price freezes imposed by the economic plan of that time. In the second half of the 1980s, a high point of Brazilian civic spirit, popular mobilization was channeled into the constitutional process. The Pro-Popular Participation Plenary (*Plenário Pró-Participação Popular*) in the Constitutional Assembly, for example, collected nearly 12 million signatures. However, unable to break with the tradition of Brazilian politics and consolidate a civic culture, the Constitutional Assembly suffered discredit in public opinion: "The discredit that came to surround the so-called 'political class' . . . may have been associated with the more complex phenomenon of 'disenchantment' that has appeared in several transition processes. In the Brazilian case, however, this phenomenon was revealed in its most perverse form: the feeling of a progressive distancing between the citizen and his political representation, reintroducing the distance between political institutions and society that is presumed to be typical only of an authoritarian regime" (Martins 1989, 236–37).

The impeachment of President Fernando Collor in 1992, accompanied by a demonstration of thousands of students in the streets with faces painted green and yellow (the national colors), brought a revival of the civic spirit of the previous decade. The wave of privatizations undertaken by President Fernando Henrique Cardoso also led to attempts at popular mobilization in the second half of the 1990s, but the movement has been limited to the left and has lacked vigor. To a degree, it seems that the civic spirit has run out. A feeling of apathy and cynicism, little by little, has taken hold of Brazilian society and is present at all social levels.[18] It seems that the "communitarian language" of the constitution of 1988, known after its passage as the Citizen's Constitution, means little in 2000 (Cittadino 1998, 44).

Two contradictions characterize this process of democratization and popular participation. First, even while they seek to escape being swallowed by the state, social movements in Brazil seek more state regulation. In fact, the majority of their demands (84 percent) involve greater intervention by the state (Diniz and Boschi 1989, 44). Second, the return to legal normality itself translates into the ebbing of social movements.[19] A notable exception is the Landless Movement (*Movimento dos Sem-Terra*) (MST), undiscouraged in its fight for agrarian reform, which pressures the government through its occupation of private property and direct confrontation with the police and landowners, resulting in deaths and injuries on both sides.

After the moral reconstruction of the executive (brought by the impeachment of President Collor) and the moral reconstruction of the legislature (with the banning of several very corrupt politicians from the National Congress and the scapegoating of several other less corrupt congressmen), the morality wave arrived at the judiciary, which came into the public spotlight in the first half of 1999. Even as judicial reform was being discussed, including controversial proposals such as adopting stare decisis, instituting external control of the judiciary, and abolishing the labor court, a Parliamentary Commission of Investigation (*Comissão Parlamentar de Inquérito*) (CPI) was created with the objective of uncovering—and exposing—the judiciary's two principal blemishes, corruption and nepotism. But at the end of the century, no cause seems important enough to mobilize the Brazilian people, who watch from afar, very much afar. Discussion of the moral reconstruction and reform of the judiciary seems to be restricted to politicians, judges, and others within the legal system.

From Brasil *to* Brazil

Again, the data speak for themselves, leaving little to say. The situation of the southeast cannot be compared to the situation of the north and northeast. Although there has been an improvement in the living conditions of the population as a whole, strong regional disparities persist, particularly in the northeast, which has the highest rates of illiteracy (28.7 percent, as opposed to 8.7 percent for the southeast; the rate for Brazil as a whole is 14.7 percent); the lowest household incomes, as 40.6 percent of the population makes less than two minimum salaries a month, while the rate in the southeast is 14.1 percent; the poorest sanitary conditions and provision of electricity; the greatest birthrates; the lowest life expectancies (64.5 years, as opposed to 70.2 in the south); and the highest rates of infant mortality (60.4 per 1,000 births, while the rate in the south is 22.8).

The northeast has the highest rates of employment in the agricultural sector (40.6 percent) and consequently, the lowest rates of industrialization and the lowest rates of employed persons with more than eleven years of schooling (15.2 percent); for the southeast, the rate is 26.8 percent. The situation is even more serious considering that the northeast is the second most populous region of the country, containing 28.5 percent of the population—44,768,201 of Brazil's total population of 157,079,573.

The poorest regions, however, are not as poor as they were in 1970. There has certainly been improvement. Nevertheless, while the Index of Human Development demonstrates an improvement in all regions, the northeast and the north continue to have the poorest scores in the country. The poorest of 1970, although wealthier now, were still the poorest of 1996. And it is unlikely that this internal hierarchy will change.

Transformations in the Law

How do we assess the legislative output of the last thirty years? It is almost impossible. The objective in this chapter, as such, is not to give an exhaustive inventory of all the legal changes, but rather to point out the principal modifications that have taken place in the Brazilian legal order, especially changes that had an impact on the majority of the population. Brazil presently has about ten thousand federal laws, but not all are known by the general population, and very few affect our daily lives directly. Which laws, then, really changed our lives in these last thirty years?

FROM INDISSOLUBLE MARRIAGE
TO THE CIVIL UNION OF HOMOSEXUALS

In 1970, the Brazilian woman had already attained the full status of an adult, assured by the Statute of the Married Woman (*Estatuto da Mulher Casada*),[20] which modified the Civil Code of 1917, under which she had no full legal capacity. However, Brazilian couples still could not divorce. At best, they could legally separate, a process that left intact the marriage tie. Remarriages were not permitted. The opposition of the Catholic Church made divorce a taboo topic. The fight for the right to divorce was a hard one. Even when it was approved (1977), concessions to the Church (for example, limitations on the acceptable justifications for divorce and the prohibition of a second divorce) restricted divorce; legalizing divorce, nonetheless, represented a great step in the transformation of the Brazilian family.

The next steps were taken in the constitution of 1988. The concept of the family was altered to include any arrangement consisting of at least one parent and his or her offspring.[21] A stable domestic union was made equal to a civil marriage, although the latter remains the form considered most appropriate by the Brazilian state for the constitution of a family. The rights and obligations of partners who lived together were made equal to those of married couples. Children conceived through incest or adultery could be recognized. The man lost his authority in the home, no longer being the "head of the nuclear family." But the advances did not stop there. After 1992, a request for divorce no longer had to be justified. Couples had absolute liberty to break the marriage tie. Relationships outside of marriage were recognized, and rights of inheritance were protected.[22]

The century ended with a discussion of a very controversial bill regarding the civil union of homosexuals. If the bill is passed into law, homosexual couples will have the rights of inheritance, joint filing of tax returns, and ability to acquire Brazilian citizenship in case one of the partners is not a Brazilian citizen. This contract of civil partnership would not, however, have the status of marriage and would not permit the use of the last name of the partner, a change in the individuals' marriage status, or the joint adoption of children. These are, without doubt, limitations. But the advance is significant. In only thirty years, Brazil moved from not accepting divorce to making rules for the civil union of partners of the same sex.

FROM A POSITIVIST CRIMINAL APPROACH TO ALTERNATIVE SENTENCES

The influence of positivism in the Brazilian penal code in force in 1970 was unmistakable. Besides the prison sentence, there was a *medida de segurança*, a penal sentence applied to anyone considered dangerous (for example, anyone who had committed two crimes). The condemned was kept in prison until he or she was no longer considered dangerous. It was a kind of life sentence. The aim was to punish the guilty and defend society.

In 1984, the penal code was reformed: the medida de segurança was abolished, and the Brazilian penal system incorporated alternative sentences—suspension of certain rights; restrictions on weekend activities; community service requirements.[23] In 1998, the array of alternative sentences was broadened with the introduction of monetary installments and loss of property.[24] New punishments were created to relieve pressure on the overextended prison system and to make the state's response to crime more effective, particularly for less serious crimes. In the same period, the prisoners, for the first time in Brazil, had their rights formally respected[25] (although, in practice, these rights continue to be ignored, as a quick visit to a Brazilian prison would reveal). In theory (and unfortunately, only in theory), the new alternatives to the prison system were accompanied by a humanization of prison conditions. However, according to the prison census of 1995, only 2,098 people had been, up to that point, given alternative punishments (principally the obligation to perform community service), whereas 148,760 people were carrying out sentences in prison—while penal establishments had room for only 68,567 prisoners.[26]

FROM A FORMAL JUSTICE SYSTEM TO AN INFORMAL JUSTICE SYSTEM

The traditional forms of conflict resolution, centered in the judicial system, gave way during these thirty years to new, alternative dispute resolutions. Following an international trend, documented by Cappelletti and Garth (1988), Brazil entered the third wave of the movement for access to justice with an informalization of the judiciary. Small claims courts were created in the 1980s by the military regime,[27] which defended an informal judiciary more able to solve individual conflicts and avoid social upheaval.

Although the constitution expanded the possibilities of informal treatment for less serious crimes, only in 1995 did minor crimes come within the jurisdiction of the special criminal courts,[28] whose fundamental objectives are to repair the harm done under the rubric of conciliatory and compensatory justice, and to make use of alternative sentences. At the same time, the jurisdiction of the civil small claims courts was expanded. The lawyer ceased to be an indispensable figure in cases with low monetary value, despite the text of the federal constitution.[29]

Within this process of informalization and expansion of access to the judiciary, arbitration gained ground in the Brazilian legal order. In the 1980s, three bills were presented in the legislature on this subject, leading to the passage of an Arbitration Law in 1996,[30] an important step in the transformation of the concept of access to the judiciary.

FROM INDIVIDUAL RIGHTS TO COLLECTIVE RIGHTS

In the area of fundamental rights, there have been important changes over the last three decades. Habeas corpus, which was suspended in cases of political crimes, was reestablished in 1979. With the new federal constitution of 1988, other constitutional mechanisms for the protection of individuals were introduced, like the *habeas data*, assuring the right to know what personal information is contained in the public databases of government offices and permitting its correction when necessary. But this was not all. The public defender was recognized in the constitution as essential to the legal order as a defender of the poor, and a public defender system was to be established in every state (which, however, has still not occurred). The judiciary is now closer to the Brazilian people. Or at least it is easier for citizens to deal with.

But one of the most important changes in the area of fundamental rights is the enhanced protection of collective rights. With the reorganization of social movements at the end of the 1970s, the inability of the legal order to respond to collective conflicts was evident. Only individuals were able to bring lawsuits. In very few cases could groups seek redress in the courts for violations of their collective rights.

The first recognition of diffuse rights came in the Law of National Environmental Policy of 1981(Arantes 1999, 85).[31] In 1985, the public civil action was introduced for the protection of the environment, consumer rights, and artistic, touristic, and aesthetic values.[32] This transformation was made more substantive with the passage of the 1988 constitution. In the first place, the constitution established that no harm or threat to any right could be excluded from consideration by the judiciary.[33] Thus, it now encompasses collective as well as individual rights. Second, new mechanisms were created to defend the collective interests[34] and old mechanisms were expanded, such as the public civil action that came to include protection against governmental corruption as well as protection of the environment and the historical and cultural patrimony, ever more important.

FROM BARBARISM TO THE REGULATION OF PUBLIC SPACE

Brazil is famous worldwide for the flagrant disrespect of traffic laws—red lights run systematically, sidewalks used by cars, pedestrians at risk of their lives. Disobedience of the traffic code—and there is one!—has been the rule. The relationship of the Brazilian people with traffic laws has even become a running joke, an anecdote illustrative of the national culture. As stated in a book that tries to teach North Americans how to be a carioca,[35] "Have you ever dreamt you were behind the wheel of a Formula One race car, experiencing the thrill of overtaking another car by only a hair? Have you ever participated in a demolition derby? Great! You will feel right at home. Now is your chance to forget everything you ever heard about caution on the highways. Just keep in mind that driving in Rio is extremely fast, aggressive, and creative. Then put the pedal to the metal, and go for it!" (Goslin 1996, 44).

The first important change in the area of traffic rules was the mandatory use of seat belts in the mid-1990s, a rule that people quickly obeyed. The next step was the passage of a new national traffic code containing serious penalties for violating the law.[36] In addition to higher fines, a point system was adopted that leads to various penalties, including the loss of the driving license.

The new traffic code has deeply transformed the relationship between the citizen (the driver) and the law. From a no-man's-land of self-regulation and private appropriation of public space, we have arrived at rigid rules regulating traffic. Public space can no longer be freely appropriated, but rather is subject to the rules of the state. In no other area has the law had a greater impact. Thus, the traffic code, in some ways, symbolizes the passage from barbarism to civilization. Surprisingly, it is one of the few cases in which the law has really stuck.

FROM THE VIOLATION TO THE EXPANSION OF FUNDAMENTAL RIGHTS

In the 1970s, the violation of political and civil rights was pervasive. People were arbitrarily imprisoned. Torture was secretly used by the military regime. Political prisoners were frequently assassinated; it is estimated that three hundred people "disappeared" during the military regime. There was no right to vote. The free press was a memory of the past. There was no room for political opposition. There was no habeas corpus. Censorship crippled Brazilian art. Opponents of the government, principally the intellectuals, left the country.

In the year 2000, the political scene is completely different. Political rights were reestablished in gradual steps beginning in 1979 with amnesty for political prisoners. The constitution of 1988 expanded the right to vote to everyone aged sixteen and older. Social rights occupy a large chapter of the new constitution, carefully listed and detailed. Minority groups were recognized, and their rights were protected.[37] Child labor—the employment of those aged fourteen and younger—was prohibited.[38] Afro-Brazilians (48 percent of the population), women, and homosexuals were recognized as full citizens. Racial discrimination became a crime,[39] as did religious discrimination.[40] Indigenous groups (approximately three hundred thousand people)—along with their customs, languages, beliefs, and traditions—were constitutionally recognized, and their land holdings were legalized.[41]

The 1988 constitution, based on communitarian constitutionalism, also expanded the possibilities for popular participation. The people can propose bills, approve bills, and make policy decisions (through the people's lawmaking initiative, the popular *referendum*, and the plebiscite, respectively). Nowadays, we have many more legal mechanisms to participate in the public sphere and, by consequence, to feel ourselves as citizens (Cittadino, 1998).

FROM UNTAMED CAPITALISM TO CONSUMER PROTECTION

In the Brazil of the 1970s, there was no special legal mechanism for consumer protection. A liberal legal culture that presupposed the parties to a contract to be equals could not logically permit the protection of one of the parties. And by not protecting the weaker party in an unequal relationship, the law tacitly protected the stronger—industries, companies that provided services, commercial establishments. The civil procedure (*ação civil pública*), introduced into the Brazilian legal order in 1985 and used in the defense of consumer rights, was insufficient for the protection of consumer rights. In fact, consumer rights were still protected by a civil code dating back to 1917.

With the 1988 constitution, the state assumed the obligation to protect consumer rights.[42] In 1990, with the passage of the Code of Consumer Defense, the consumer received real protection.[43] Brazil thus entered the modern era of consumer relations, with a law that is well written, modern, and effective.

FROM RESTRICTED CITIZENSHIP TO FULL CITIZENSHIP

In Brazil, citizenship assumes a regulated form. At least, this is the phrase used by Wanderley Guilherme dos Santos (1979) to describe the special relationship between the individual and the state in Brazil. Citizenship is not related to political life, but rather to the system of occupational stratification. In order to be truly a citizen, it is necessary to have an occupation. But it is also necessary for the occupation to be recognized, defined, and regulated by the law.

In 1970, many workers, even rural workers with the passage of a rural labor law in 1963, had already "earned" citizenship. Almost all workers were thus citizens—except for domestic employees. Neither the rules of the social welfare system nor the labor legislation existing since 1943 was applicable to them. After all, how could the home—the personal space where the law is absent—be transformed into a space ruled by the state legal order? Roberto DaMatta's (1987) analysis of the characteristics of the home and the street may be the key to understanding the delay in the extension of workers' rights to domestic employees.

Only in 1972 did domestic employees begin to gain the status of citizens.[44] They gained the right to a minimum salary, annual vacation, a yearly bonus, a paid weekly rest day, maternity leave, and so forth. But not all workers' rights have been extended to domestic employees. In the area of social security, their rights are still limited. In sum, domestic employees are quasi citizens. They have still not achieved full citizenship. But fortunately, the century ended with the debate over a bill in the legislature that would regulate the profession of domestic employees.[45]

FROM THE LAW OF NATIONAL SECURITY TO HEINOUS CRIMES

The 1970s began with the ghost of political crimes. The Law of National Security was used by the military regime to fight opposition. A strong policy of national security was necessary, according to the official discourse of the period, to control subversion. The public demonstration of opinions considered contrary to the national interest as defined by the military was punished. Anything could acquire a political meaning and be interpreted as an attack on national security. Labor strikes, for example, fell under the purview of the Law of National Security (although existing antistrike legislation was already sufficiently repressive). The repression of terrorism created a reign of terror (Fragoso 1980).

With the beginning of political democratization in the 1980s, the panorama changed. There was no more talk of subversion. Those convicted of political crimes received amnesty. But common crimes, particularly crimes in the streets, grew in number. Or, at least, a sense of insecurity began to dominate Brazilian society, particularly in the large urban centers such as Rio de Janeiro and São Paulo. Fear was instilled in the Brazilian people by robbery, drug trafficking, property theft, homicide, and kidnapping, in this order. Demands for repressive measures, such as the death penalty, gained support. And torture continued to be used but was now applied for common crimes rather than political crimes. (Though the fact that torture is now a crime by law is indicative that Brazil is at least heading in the direction of the rule of law.)[46]

The state's response to urban violence came in 1990 with greater sentences for the most heinous crimes, such as rape, homicides by gangs of killers, armed robbery, violent sexual assault, adulteration of medicine, and kidnapping.[47] The frequency of kidnapping grew frighteningly in the mid-1980s, becoming one of the principal threats to the upper middle class. Organized crime took over the favelas of Rio de Janeiro. Drug trafficking spread throughout the country. In this context, repressive punitive measures gained popular support, principally the penalization of conduct that offended property rights.[48]

FROM OWNERSHIP OF OUR BODIES
TO THE PRESUMPTION OF ORGAN DONATION

From one day to the next, we were no longer the owners of our bodies. Or at least so thought the majority of Brazilians. A law had just been passed permitting the use of organs, tissues, and other body parts for transplants and treatments whenever there was no previous statement of the deceased forbidding the transplant.[49] By turning every person into a potential donor, the state seemed to have expanded its sphere of intervention. The human body became a "public good," making into "property" what before had been a family matter.

The reaction was inevitable. In many Brazilian states, the percentage that opted not to donate became very high. After the law was passed, people lined up to contest this state interference. The law generated a debate, one of the great national debates. For their part, the jurists questioned whether the law was constitutional or not. For some, the option adopted by the legislature offended constitutional provisions protecting personal rights such as the rights to self-determination, privacy, and human dignity. Others defended the law as constitutional, given that citizens had the opportunity to opt out. Meanwhile, people asked in amazement: Does the state have the right to decide what happens to my body?

The discussion of this law generated a broader debate about law in general. It affected the popular perception of the role of the state, particularly of the limits of state action in the name of the general good—in this case, satisfying the great need for organ donation in Brazil. And it demonstrated that, in certain cases, the law cannot change reality.

FROM ADULTERY TO SEXUAL HARASSMENT

Brazil began the 1970s with a penal code written in the 1940s—a penal code that punished adultery and abortion, a penal code that appealed to the idea of the "chaste woman" in contrast to the woman that could be easily seduced. Brazil ended the century with the same penal code. Adultery is still a crime, as are abortions. And only "honest women" continue to deserve legal protection against their male seducers.

Fortunately, however, there are signs of change. Since 1961, there have been several attempts to reform the penal code. Commissions have been formed and disbanded throughout the years. But many continue to work on this issue in the hope that one day a new penal code will be approved that revokes the most anachronistic provisions. Under the new code, euthanasia would be more tolerated. The possibilities for abortion, currently restricted to cases of rape and risk to the life of the mother, would be expanded to include pregnancies resulting from nonconsensual sex and nonconsensual use of reproductive technologies, and cases of mental and physical birth defects. The crime of infecting another with a serious illness would replace the crime of infecting another with a venereal disease. After all, we live in the world of AIDS more than in the world of syphilis (although syphilis is a greater problem than AIDS in Brazil). These are some of the planned reforms. All are important. The difficulty is that, because of the delay in its adoption, the new code is at risk of being born old—fashioned to fit the twentieth century rather than the twenty-first.

Transformations in the Administration of Justice

Viewing the legislative transformations in the period from 1970 to 2000, we cannot avoid an element of surprise. In the political arena, Brazil moved from an authoritarian regime to a democratic regime. The period began at the height of the military regime and ended with a democratic constitution. In the legal arena, there is greater intervention by the state in society. The law—and as such, the state—is more active in consumer protection, in the punishment of minor crimes, in increasing the punishment for heinous crimes, in divorce of married couples, in rules about extramarital relations, in the punishment of discrimination, in traffic rules, and even at our death with the organ transplant law.

Without doubt, there has been a process of legalization of personal conduct. Situations and relationships that until then had been outside the ambit of the state entered the world of law. But what has changed in the administration of justice in these past three decades? Has there been a litigation explosion? If so, are there enough judges, prosecutors, public defenders, and lawyers to respond to the legalization of conduct?

RATES OF LITIGATION

The outcome is not difficult to predict: as the population grows, becomes better educated, and obtains more rights, demands on the judicial system also grow. It is sufficient to take as an example the number of judicial cases between 1990 and 1998. At the appellate level, as well as in the lower-level courts, there was a significant increase in the number of new cases.[50] In 1990, there were 271,300 cases filed in state appellate courts, and in 1998 there were 421,578. In the lower courts, there were 3,617,064 filings in 1990 and 7,467,189 in 1998.

The increase in the number of cases from 1970 to 1999 in the Federal Supreme Court is also significant, particularly after 1980—there were 6,397 cases filed in 1970; 9,555 in 1980; 18,564 in 1990; 26,187 in 1999. The work of federal judges intensified at the end of the 1980s when the courts became a political arena for challenges to the federal government (and federal prosecutors assumed a "Robin Hood" posture, systematically positioning themselves against the federal government). Whereas there was an average of 1,216.7 cases per judge in 1989, ten years later the average was 3,916.4. In 1999, each judge decided, on average, 7.5 cases per day, whereas ten years earlier each judge had decided fewer than one case per day (not distinguishing here between working days and nonworking days).

It is also useful to analyze the lower federal courts, where the number of new cases grew at a rate even greater than that of the state courts and the Federal Supreme Court—from 58,460 filings in 1970 to 266,585 in 1990 and 800,107 in 1998; and from 62.8 per 100,000 people to 494.5 in 1998. Data clearly demonstrate that the growth of judicial actions in the federal courts occurred principally after the adoption of the federal constitution (1988).

Regional differences exist and are important. The numbers of new cases in the northeast and the north are lower than in other regions. There is one case for every 331.5 people in the northeast and one for every 365.6 people in the north, but there is one for every 199.6 in the southeast. The poorer regions, as would be expected, litigate less than the wealthy regions. The growth of cases in the labor courts expresses the intensification of labor conflicts (due to labor outsourcing and downsizing strategies pursued by many companies, with a resulting increase in unemployment).[51] Considering the period from 1970 to 1998, the number of cases filed in the labor courts grew, in relative terms, from 100 to 358, and in absolute terms, from just over 2 million filings in 1971–75 to over 7 million in 1996–98. Considering only the period from 1990 to 1998, the growth of the caseload of the Supreme Labor Court was even more striking—the number of filings in 1998 was over six times as great as in 1990. Actually, the increase in labor-related cases has occurred to a greater degree at the level of the regional labor courts than at the level of the lower labor courts. Even so, in all three levels of the labor courts there was an increase in cases per 100,000 in the period from 1991 to 1998—from 14 to 81 in the superior labor courts, from 100 to 238 in the regional labor courts, and from 852 to 1,204 in the lower labor courts.

Confirming that regional differences indeed imply differences in relations with the judiciary, it is symptomatic that in the southeast in 1996, there was one action in the lower labor courts for every 61.7 people, while in the northeast there was only one action for every 134.4 people. The same phenomenon is evident in the regional labor courts. The regional courts of the southeast received a new case for every 378.6 residents in 1996, but in the northeast they received a new case for every 749.9. A more informal economy and the strength of traditional work relations result in less awareness of workers' rights and of the mechanisms available to vindicate them, chronic problems of the poor regions where educational levels are lower.

The situation of the labor courts is no better than that of the federal courts in terms of the caseload per judge. In 1998, the 2,289 judges in the lower labor courts decided 1,925,250 cases.[52] In other words, each judge decided 841 cases. In the regional labor courts (appellate level), the 315 judges decided 413,502 cases, or 1,312.7 cases per judge per year. And in the superior labor courts, there were 111,814 cases in 1998, or 694.9 cases decided during the year by each of the 17 judges. In all these courts, the caseloads are clearly excessive.

LEGAL PROFESSIONALS

In this context of increasing demand, more lawyers, judges, prosecutors, and public defenders are necessary. And indeed, there is more of each category of legal professionals in both relative and absolute terms.[53] In the federal courts, the number of judgeships grew in this thirty-year period by a factor of eight. There were 110 judgeships in 1976; 112 in 1980; 279 in 1990; and 903 in 1998.

In general terms, the number of people per judge, for example, decreased from 25,700 in 1970 to 18,238 in 1991 as the number of judges rose from 3,624 to 8,050. The number of people per lawyer (including public defenders) decreased from 2,469 to 986 in the same time period, as the numbers of lawyers rose from 37,719 to 148,171. The number of people per public prosecutor also decreased, from 19,375 in 1970 to 14,685 in 1991. The number of people per judicial public servant decreased from 2,512 to 1,671. And the federal government expenditures on the judiciary increased by a factor of more than five between 1987 and 1997, as the number of employees rose from 37,083 to 87,849.

The data just presented permit an analysis of the changes in the number of legal professionals in relation to the national population. The greatest change is evidenced in the number of lawyers (up from 40.5 per 100,000 people in 1970, to 101.4) and judicial public servants (relative to which the increase in the numbers of judges and prosecutors is less significant). Comparative data may provide a better understanding of the significance of the number of lawyers. In the United States, there was one lawyer for every 303 people in 1995 (in 1947–48, there was one for every 790). In the state of Rio de Janeiro,

TABLE 3.1

Situation of Judges in the State Courts, the Federal Courts, and the Labor Courts, 2000

Type of court	Judgeships provided for by law	Judgeships filled	Vacancies	Male judges (%)	Female judges (%)	Vacancies (%)	Ratio of population to filled judgeships
State courts	9,543	7,007	2,536	71.15	28.84	26.57	23,089
Federal courts	903	610	293	72.62	27.37	32.45	265,230
Labor courts	4,507	4,089	418	69.23	30.76	9.27	39,567
Total	14,953	11,706	3,247	70.56	29.43	21.71	13,821

SOURCE: http://www.stf.gov.br (August 2000).

the number of lawyers has increased significantly. In 1996, there was one lawyer for every 234 people.[54]

As such, although it may not be advisable to compare state and national rates, it is notable that Rio de Janeiro has a population density of lawyers even greater than that of the United States.[55] But is the number of lawyers an adequate basis on which to compare Brazil and the United States in terms of the legal job market? What about the rate of litigation? How does the number of lawyers relate to litigiousness? It may be that one lawyer for every 303 people is not many for the United States. And perhaps it is very many for Rio de Janeiro. How can we know?

The number of judges, however, seems clearly insufficient in light of the number of unfilled judgeships. There was, on average, one state court judge for every 16,954 people; because 2,536 judgeships remained unfilled, the ratio should be somewhat better than it is. For the courts as a whole, see Table 3.1. The number of judges per 100,000 people remains low even today. In 1998, there were 7.1 judges per 100,000 people. Even so, the growth in the number of judges was greater than the growth of the general population. The situation has thus gotten better.

Transformations in the Legal Culture

The important questions in relating legislative changes to transformations in the legal culture focus on what has actually changed in people's behavior. How have Brazilians reacted to the larger presence of the state in the regulation of their daily lives? In these thirty years, did people get closer to the law? Are legal institutions, particularly the courts, perceived as more accessible? Or does a feeling of distance between the general society and the legal world persist? And what about legal professionals—how have they altered their behavior amid significant change in the Brazilian legal order? How have they been affected? How are future legal professionals being prepared?

TRANSFORMATIONS IN INTERNAL LEGAL CULTURE

We begin this topic by trying to answer the last questions posed. How have legal professionals changed in this accelerated process of social and legal transformation? To what new demands and necessities must they respond? How is this transforming their advocacy? What social classes are legal professionals being drawn from, and what are the consequences of changes in the social composition of the legal profession and the judiciary? How are law schools adapting to these changes?

From an elite profession to the proletarianization of the legal profession. It used to be that law students in Brazil all came from the elite. Indeed, the initial objectives of our law schools reinforced this characteristic. In 1827, we were in need of a political scenario that would build the nation-state—and actors that should, logically, come from the national elite. Law schools were thus destined to be filled with sons of the local elite—the sons of old sugar plantation owners in the northeast and the sons of the coffee growers in the southeast (Falcão 1984).

The situation today is no longer the same. Policies that expanded higher education implemented in the 1970s translated into an increase in the number of institutions of higher education, from 582 in 1970 to 893 in 1990 to 973 in 1998. The number stabilized in the 1980s but grew again in the 1990s, resulting in a 9 percent growth in the total number of enrolled students by 1998.[56] There were 6,252 college and university programs in 1996, and 274,384 people graduated in 1997.[57] In April 1998, there were 2,125,958 students enrolled in colleges and universities.[58] The number of law schools increased from 2 in 1827 to now more than 300 scattered throughout the country. The number of law students per 100,000 people grew from 113.46 in 1980 to 152.28 in 1996 (see Table 3.2).

The census of higher education published in June 1999 conveys the importance of these law schools at the national level. In 1996, law was the field of study with the greatest number of students (239,201), followed by business (225,456), engineering (146,376), and education (123,700). However, once again proving that we have a *Brasil* and a Brazil, law was not the most popular course of study in the northeast, but rather, education (largely preparing students to teach grade school). In the northeast, the law occupies a more modest fourth place (see Table 3.3). Nationwide, the greatest number of graduating students has also been in law (29,122 in 1995). After law has come business, education, and engineering. However, despite being first nationwide, when the regions are disaggregated, law comes in second in all five re-

TABLE 3.2

Change over Time in the Number of Law Students

	Number of law students		
Year	N	%	Students/100,000
1970	71,672	100	77.0
1980	137,373	192	115.4
1990	155,803	217	108.2
1996	239,201 ★	330	152.4

SOURCE: http://www.unescostat.unesco.org (August 2000).
★Sinopse Estatística do Ensino Superior/Ministério da Educacão (SEEC/MEC).

TABLE 3.3

Fields of Study with Highest Enrollment in Brazil Overall
and in Each Region, 1996

Brazil	North	Northeast	Southeast	South	Central-West
Law	Education	Education	Law	Business	Law
Business	Law	Business	Business	Law	Business
Engineering	Business	Liberal arts	Engineering	Accounting	Education
Education	Liberal arts	Law	Education	Engineering	Accounting

SOURCE: Sinopse Estatística do Ensino Superior/Ministério da Educacão (SEEC/MEC).

gions. It is second to education in the poorer regions of the north, northeast, and central-west, and it is second to business in the wealthier regions of the southeast and south.

But the study of law does not offer—or at least did not offer in 1996—the greatest number of admission slots (see Table 3.4). Business offered the most (71,453). Law was second overall in this regard (59,701), then education (50,671), and engineering (44,199). In the poorest regions, the number of admission slots for studying law is lower than the number for other fields of study such as education (in first place in the northeast, north, and central-west), business, and liberal arts. Even so, law still occupies a central place in the social imagination. It was the most sought after course of study in higher education in 1996 with 471,024 students taking the entrance exams for law. After law comes medicine, business, engineering, dentistry, and communications. In other words, the most desired fields of study are not necessarily those that admit the most students. The case of education is illustrative. Although education was the field that offered admission to the third highest number of students in 1996, it occupies a lowly seventh place in terms of national student preference. Law, in contrast, was the most desired field in all geo-

TABLE 3.4

*Fields of Study with Highest Number of Admission Slots
in Brazil Overall and in Each Region, 1996*

Brazil	North	Northeast	Southeast	South	Central-West
Business	Education	Education	Business	Business	Education
Law	Business	Liberal arts	Law	Law	Business
Education	Law	Business	Engineering	Education	Law
Engineering	Accounting	Law	Education	Accounting	Accounting

SOURCE: Sinopse Estatística do Ensino Superior/Ministério da Educacão (SEEC/MEC).

graphic regions, demonstrating that it is presently considered the best option in higher education. The strong interest in studying law in 1996 is shown clearly by the ratio of candidates to admitted students of 7.9 to 1, quite high considering the number of students offered admission.[59]

The result of this process is a change in the social profile of law students. Law students (at least, not the majority of them) are no longer from the elite. Recent data are revealing. In 1998, there were 41,159 law student graduates who came principally from the lower middle class. These are students who do not know English (45.3 percent); who do not read more than three books per year (51.1 percent); who study in night school (60.3 percent); and whose parents do not hold a degree (63.8 percent). As such, these students, on average, represent an improvement in social status or at least an improvement in educational status.

Three consequences of this process are fundamental. First, increasing the number of law students will tend to expand the supply of legal services. It increases the general knowledge of the law as more and more people have a relative who is a lawyer. It democratizes the law itself, the language of which becomes understood by a greater number of people. Without doubt, this has an important impact on popular legal culture, though the effect cannot be measured.

Second, this process translates into a growing proletarianization of legal careers. Little by little, the professional in the liberal tradition leaves the scene. The legal professional is increasingly an employee—of the state as a judge, a prosecutor, or a public defender; of a large business; or of a law firm. In this way, the ethos of the profession itself changes.

Third, it changes the social composition of the legal profession, making it younger and more feminine.[60] The average age of those who pass the public civil service exams has fallen recently, a function of the salaries of public legal careers that are too low to attract established lawyers. A greater number of women are now graduating from law schools throughout the country according to the data of the National Examination of Graduating Students (20,199 men and 20,959 women graduated in 1998). Although only a partial representation, the data from the state of Rio de Janeiro for 1996 are significant: women made up 28.1 percent of judges, 61.1 percent of public prosecutors, and 64.2 percent of public defenders. The national data reveal the same phenomenon of feminization in legal careers.[61] Men were 94.8 percent of the judges in 1970 and 80.2 percent in 1991. The *number* of women judges was 189 in 1970 and 1,596 in 1991. Men were 91 percent of the lawyers and public defenders in 1970 and 69.59 percent in 1991; the number of women rose from 3,408 to 45,266. A similar story can be told about public prosecutors. In 1991, women made up 45.9 percent of the public judicial servants.

Changes in how legal actors work and make decisions may result from this process of feminization, as discussed in the international literature (Abel 1989; Economides 1999). In the Brazilian case, however, it cannot be ascertained whether women are changing the legal professions or whether women are being changed by them.[62] Probably, it will be necessary to wait several years to be able to analyze this question.

From a technical approach to a humanistic approach in law schools.   The study of law, principally as a function of changes introduced in the early 1970s, was influenced by positivism and natural law theory. Rather than places to think about law, the law schools represented either places where codes were learned by heart or places where justice was idealized.

Criticism of the positivist and natural law paradigms gained ground in the 1980s, when a great part of what was written in the sociology of law involved the teaching of law. The 1990s thus began with a consensus on the need to reform the legal curriculum and replace positivism with a more humanistic and critical perspective. The 1994 joint report by the Committee of Legal Education Specialists and the Legal Education Committee of the Bar Association generated new curricular directives with the purpose of providing students with an education that was critical, humanistic, technical, practical, and policy oriented. The number of core classes was increased. In addition to taking classes in sociology and economics, required since Resolution No. 3 of 1972, the law student must study political science, general philosophy, the philosophy of law, general ethics, legal ethics, and sociology of law.[63] The abilities outlined by the Ministry of Education reveal the new professional that is being called for.[64] The future legal professional should have the following abilities:

1. Humanistic, technical-legal, and practical training, necessary for an adequate interdisciplinary understanding of legal phenomena and social transformation
2. Professional-ethical judgment, associated with social responsibility, with

an understanding of the causes and the results of legal norms and the continual striving toward human freedom and the improvement of society
3. The ability to perceive, critically transmit, and creatively use the law, tied to logical reasoning and awareness of the ever-present need to stay current in the field
4. The capacity to solve problems and look for solutions that harmonize with social needs
5. The capacity to develop extralegal means of preventing and solving individual and collective conflicts
6. An up-to-date view of the world and, in particular, awareness of the problems of one's time and place

The results of this process cannot yet be quantified. However, these changes not only affect the curriculum but also translate into more oversight in legal education and evaluation of graduating students through a national examination. We began the 1970s trying to increase the number of law programs. We end the 1990s afraid of the uncontrolled proliferation of law schools and worried about the quality of law programs and future legal professionals. The on-site inspections of all law schools attest to the low quality of the programs, which have large classes, little infrastructure, and professors without credentials.

Only 7.77 percent of the law schools were considered to have a very good teaching faculty, and only 8.29 percent had professors classified as having very good academic credentials.[65] In addition, the role of the professors in academic life was considered insufficient in 30 percent of the programs. This problem arises because in Brazil, in contrast to the United States, law professors are primarily legal professionals—judges, public prosecutors, public defenders, or lawyers—and only secondarily professors (in terms of dedication as well as remuneration). Teaching is more like a hobby, with the main benefit being the prestige it offers.[66]

The Brazilian Bar Association, which has a monopoly on representation, selection, and discipline of lawyers,[67] is also worried about the technical and ethical preparation of lawyers. In 1994, for example, a new ethics code was approved. Also, beginning in 1994, law students had to take a bar exam to enter the profession. An important qualitative filter is thus introduced—another form of trying to control the excessive number of law students graduating from law schools. And the numbers are surprising. Only 42.83 percent of graduated law students in the state of Rio de Janeiro passed the bar exam given in December 1998. Soon Brazil will be a country with many graduated law students but fewer lawyers.

From legalism to the alternative use of law. Democratization also brought changes to the judicial branch—in the manner in which decisions are made and whom decisions benefit. At the beginning of the 1970s, the judges tried first and foremost to be legalists—strict interpreters of the law. And it could not have been otherwise, given the political moment. The law functioned as a protective shield. To be daring carried risks. After the mid-1980s, some judges began to confront the legal order, to oppose themselves to government policy in their decisions. The actions of the judiciary amid the privatizations undertaken by the Cardoso government are representative of this new position. Injunctions requested by a variety of civic society organizations against privatization were liberally granted in the lower courts toward the end of the twentieth century, although they were later reversed in the Federal Supreme Court. In 1990, the Supreme Court had to decide only 5 injunction cases, but in 1998 it decided 1,298.[68]

This movement of "alternative judges" (that is, critical and activist) had an influence in changing the posture of the judges—or at least of some judges—and not only of judges as the movement expanded to include public attorneys. Despite being concentrated in the country's southern states, it is an important movement both locally, where the decisions increasingly tend to favor less privileged social groups, and nationally, as it introduces a debate about the function of the judiciary (Guanabara 1996; Junqueira 1992). In more conservative states, such as Rio de Janeiro, the judges see their function principally as the resolution of individual conflicts and the application of the law (Junqueira, Vieira, and Fonseca 1995); but the alternative judges make decisions that consider the implications of the lawsuit for the collective good. Prioritizing social implications, their interpretations can even be contrary to the law as long as they accord with the fundamental principles of the legal order. Little by little, the legalistic posture is questioned—or at least "strict legalism" is questioned—although it is recognized that even bad law is better than no law (Carvalho 1993).

From lawyers for political prisoners to lawyers for causes.   In 1979, political prisoners were amnestied. Political repression slowed. Democratization, a process that still continues, was begun. The consequences were felt even in the work of lawyers. Politically involved lawyers who defended those persecuted by the military regime became unnecessary now that there were no more political prisoners to be defended. At the same time, social movements began to be organized. Lawyers who had represented political prisoners transformed themselves into cause lawyers. The provision of alternative legal services surged, sometimes tied to the Church but always tied clearly to political parties on the left, particularly the Workers Party (*Partido dos Trabalhadores*).[69] The involvement of these lawyers went beyond legal representation, assuming the more basic functions of awareness building and group organization.

In the beginning, these legal services were principally in opposition to the state. Nongovernmental organizations were in truth more like antigovernmental organizations (Moura 1992). The state was the great target of complaints, and no partnership was considered possible. External financing guaranteed even greater autonomy from the state.

In the 1990s, this situation was turned around. Now the state is run by allies of alternative legal services—by the people who in the past were in the opposition and in exile. Although demands continue to be directed at the state, the antagonistic relationship has eased. The present difficulty of obtaining external financing, now directed toward either ex-Soviet countries or African countries, accentuates the possibilities for partnership. Legal services have begun to be financed by the state itself. Antigovernmental organizations have been transformed into quasi-governmental organizations. The debate grows about the "third sector" and its role in the state at the end of the century.

Although there are some tensions, the link between alternative legal services and the movement of alternative judges is obvious. For cause lawyers, it is important above all to rescue the insurgent legal forms, the forms that are unofficial, of the people, found in the street—to use some of the many terms that were used in the 1990s to refer to another way of thinking about legal relationships outside the ambit of the state. For the alternative judges, of primary importance is the alternative use of law, in the mold of the movements of the 1960s in Italy and France. In other terms, while cause lawyers may defend authoritarian legal forms when they benefit the people, for alternative judges, the general principles of law must constitute the outer limits (Carvalho 1993).

From the local to the global. At the beginning of the 1970s, a traditional form of lawyering based on the solo practitioner, the general practice attorney, was still dominant. Today, the general practice lawyer still exists, but other forms of lawyering have gained ground. Lawyering may now take the form of a large firm, with dozens of lawyers, interns, staff, a library, and a human resources department. Lawyering may be more specialized and more globalized, breaking down national borders. Lawyering may take place not only locally but also with interconnections with London, Lisbon, or New York. These new forms of lawyering (taught by the American law firms) require professionals with other technical competencies, distinct from those possessed by general practice lawyers who take care of family matters, leases, inventories, and, when willing to take a risk, perhaps a criminal case.[70] The new lawyer must act more to prevent than to resolve conflicts, more in mediation and arbitration than in litigation—the traditional way of resolving conflicts.

Certainly Brazil at the end of the twentieth century[71] cannot be com-

TABLE 3.5

Number of Law Firms According to Size in Various Countries

	Number of lawyers		
Country	More than 50	26 to 50	11 to 25
Brazil	6	18	67
United States	901	—	—
France	14	20	69
Argentina	9	9	34
Canada	58	56	91
Germany	9	31	130
Japan	7	10	25
England/Wales	44	51	47
Mexico	3	10	34

SOURCE: Martindale-Hubbell (www.martindale.com). For the United States, this source does not provide data for firms with fewer than 50 lawyers.

pared to the United States, where there are 901 law firms with more than fifty lawyers.[72] In Brazil, there are only 6 firms with more than fifty lawyers, all of them in São Paulo; of the 18 firms with twenty-six to fifty lawyers, 4 are in Rio de Janeiro and 12 in São Paulo. The number of large law firms in countries such as France, Argentina, and Mexico (see Table 3.5) is also still small. In the end, large law firms represent a phenomenon prototypically North American, as Richard Abel has recognized: "[S]uch firms have become the most conspicuous feature in the American legal landscape. Furthermore, they are virtually unique to the United States, although firms are growing in England, Canada, and Australia, some Latin American countries, and most recently in Europe" (1989, 182).

Maybe the origin of this new advocacy can be found in the law and development movement of the 1970s, which was translated in Brazil into an attempt to modernize law and introduce the case method. Since the end of the 1960s, there has been a recognized need for modern lawyering that could work out conflicts of a modernizing country and that was in tune with the policies of development and legal reform.

Even though the law and development movement has eroded in Brazil as in the United States because of internal criticisms developed by the participants in the movement itself, a whole generation in Brazil was undoubtedly influenced by the ideas of modern law and modern lawyering. The economic growth of the following years and the growing complexity of business relations contributed to an expansion of these new law firms that now, with the economic liberalization policies implemented by Presidents Collor, Franco, and Cardoso, keep on growing. As Brazilian businesses increasingly have a vision of the market that goes beyond Brazil's borders, these law firms are prospering.

TRANSFORMATIONS IN THE EXTERNAL LEGAL CULTURE?

We can now return to the questions that began this discussion. Brazil has more laws, and more democratic laws. There are more lawyers, judges, and prosecutors. The judicial apparatus has grown, but what has changed in the behavior of people? How are the Brazilian people reacting to the greater presence of the state in the regulation of their daily lives? Have the people and the law grown closer in the last thirty years? Are legal institutions, especially the judiciary, perceived as more accessible?

Toharia (1999) suggests that analysis of popular legal culture should be centered around (1) familiarity with the law, (2) experiences of the law, (3) confidence in legal institutions, (4) attitudes about the law and the administration of justice, and (5) attitudes about conflict. All these topics are analyzed in the following discussion, though not in a systematic form, given that the data were collected from a wide variety of sources.

The point of departure is from Putnam (1996) and Santos (1993). The legal culture is part of civic culture or of "the system of beliefs shared by the population regarding public authority, the society in which we live, and the rights and obligations that each person believes he has" (Santos 1993, 105). Institutions—whether political or legal—are part of the history of a people. They express a political trajectory. As pointed out by Arturo Israel, a specialist in Third World development, it is easier to build a road than to maintain the road. We can take this further and say that it is easier to build a road than to convince people accustomed to using trails and dirt paths to use this road (cited in Putnam 1996, 25). Taking it even further, it is helpful to recall Alexis de Tocqueville's observation that there is a connection between the customs of a society and its political (and legal) practices.

To consider how the popular legal culture changed (or did not) in the process of institutional modernization begun in 1980, it is necessary to consider the concept of citizenship as related to participation in the public arena (Putnam 1996, 101). The interest in public affairs is fundamental. It is an attitude that stands in contrast to "amoral familialism," under which people try "to maximize the immediate advantage of the nuclear family assuming that others will act similarly" (Edward Banfield, quoted in Putnam 1996, 102). In a civic society, there is a public spirit; in less civic societies, there are just individual interests. In a civic society, relationships are horizontal and cooperative; in less civic societies, relationships are vertical and hierarchical. Civic societies have citizens; less civic societies have patrons and clients.[73] In a civic society, citizens are involved in politics through having and expressing political beliefs; in less civic societies, the hierarchical relations of clientelism guide voters. In a civic society, we believe in the rules and everybody must follow them; in a less civic society, it is assumed that the rules will not be respected by others, thus justifying our own disrespect for them. In civic societies, solidarity and self-discipline prevail; in less civic societies, the "forces of order" and hierarchy govern. Public interest and civic duty give way to corruption and cynicism about democratic principles. Political participation is weak, and its place is taken by religious activities (Putnam 1996, 125, 128).

And what is happening in Brazil? Does it continue to be, as in the last century, a country without citizens? (Louis Couty, quoted in Carvalho 1987, 10). In the nineteenth century, the number of stable families was small, and the prevalence of informal employment caused a significant contingent of the population to live between legality and illegality (Carvalho 1987, 17). In truth, legality manifested itself as repression. There was not a well-defined line between the citizen and those on the margins (38). There was no political community, or in other words, a community of citizens that felt they belonged to a collectivity. The world of law was not to be taken seriously (159). Formal law was the subject of jokes and irony. Order could only be imposed by force. In an exclusionary republic such as Brazil, the people "related to the government through an indifference to the official mechanisms of participation; through pragmatism in their search for jobs and favors; through, overall, violent reactions when the law touched that which was considered out of the reach of the law. In all of these cases, there was a view of power between cynicism and irony, an absence of any sense of loyalty—the flip side of the coin when rights do not exist" (163).

The military regime contributed nothing to the development of Brazilian legal culture. On the contrary, authoritarianism reinforced the idea that the government would look after everyone. Laws decreed by the executive— dressed up as provisionary measures—were perceived as a way of bypassing the legislature (Caldeira 1984, 219). The two principal problems of this Prussian road of institutionalization are obvious. In the first place, legality and the rule of law are divorced from each other. Second, rights are not won but granted—from the time of Getúlio Vargas, who "gave" us labor legislation. In Brazil, in order to have rights, it is necessary to be right, to obey the law. An outsider has no rights (232).

A little over fifteen years ago, José Murilo de Carvalho pointed out that there was not much difference between the Brazil of the present and the Brazil of the nineteenth century: "[E]ven today, . . . the citizen is not able to transform his capacity for community participation into a capacity for civic participation. The popular attitude toward the law still oscillates between indifference, physiological pragmatism, and a violent reaction. The collision of order with disorder, law with law-breaking . . . continue[s] in full force under a tacit accord between the authorities and the dealers of illegal lottery tickets of the *jogo do bicho*" (1987, 164).[74] Not by chance, the research of CPDOC-FGV shows that Brazilians trust only religious leaders (Carvalho

1999a, 39). As in the nineteenth century, we end the twentieth century with a low degree of political participation. Only 2 percent of those interviewed were affiliated with a political party; even participation in civic society organizations such as neighborhood groups and parent associations is small.

In our hierarchical society, there are three types of citizens: the "doctor" (rich, well bred, educated, white); the "believer" (an honest worker, unaware of his or her rights); and the "loafer" (a worker in the informal sector, guilty until proven innocent) (Carvalho 1999b). For each type, there is a different legal code: for doctors, the civil code; for believers, the labor code; for loafers, the penal code. Rights are thus not for everyone. Worse still, they are not even known by everyone. According to the research of CPDOC-FGV, 56.7 percent of the respondents were not able to identify even one of their rights. And, of course, the ability to identify rights was inversely proportional to the respondent's level of education. Among those that had only four years of schooling, 64.2 percent were not able to identify their rights, whereas only 30.3 percent of those who had spent at least some time in college demonstrated this inability. But the duties inherent in the exercise of citizenship in a democracy were also unknown: 55.7 percent of those surveyed were not able to list even one citizen duty. This lack of awareness also increased as the respondent's level of education declined.[75]

Being unaware of their rights, people easily become victims of arbitrary treatment. They believe that lack of a worker card or identity card, or mere suspicion from the police, justifies imprisonment. In other words, they legitimate arbitrary police practices. This even occurs among high school graduates, though, logically, it is a greater problem among the less educated.

The distance from laws and rights is aggravated by two factors. First, the informal economy has grown in this period. According to research by IBGE in 1999, the informal sector employs 25 percent of workers in Brazilian cities and produces 8 percent of the gross national product (GNP). The number of "loafers" thus grows—those who have no labor rights and illegally inhabit the public urban space.[76]

Second, urban violence has grown during this period. As legal scholars were looking for "the law of the street," the psychoanalyst Jurandir Freire Costa revived the topic of the centrality of the law and of institutions for the existence of civilized lifestyles: "[W]hat is observed in arrogant delinquency is the absolute disdain for the other. Wearing a tie or having bare feet, the arrogant delinquent lives in an illusory world, considering himself above the law and challenging in a grotesque manner all those that do not want to make themselves an appendage of his omnipotence" (1989, 134–35). Costa problematizes "urban violence" as a crisis of ethics. His interpretive horizon is "the narcissistic culture . . . where the expression of omnipotence and powerlessness is carried to such a point that it becomes conflictual and ex-

TABLE 3.6

Distribution of Urban Conflicts
by Type of Conflict, 1985–1988

Type of conflict	%
Labor	18.3
Marital separation	18.9
Criminal	17.1
Inheritance	9.2
Neighbor	8.6
Debt collection	9.4
Abandonment of property	9.4
Alimony	6.8
Land ownership	2.4

SOURCE: *Plano Nacional de Amostra Domiciliar*, Instituto Brasileiro Geográfico e Estatístico (1988); Santos (1993).

tremely difficult to engage in social solidarity" (127). In a narcissistic culture of violence, this new ethic would be related to social decadence and to the growing discredit of the people in the institutions and laws.

The genealogy of the "violent" urban citizen as a subject of a particular-ist ethic is a question explored by Maria Célia Paoli (1982) in her study of the production of the so-called inverted citizen. The "inverted citizen" is the perverse outcome of the intersection between the lack of recognition of "popular culture" by the autocratic sphere, which defines the public space in Brazilian society, and the juridical-legal mechanisms that repress these so-cial actors in public life. Paoli seeks to link the question of urban violence with the problem of citizenship, turning around the legal focus on the uni-versalization of rights and asserting that certain social actors are deprived not only of rights but also of a publicly recognized identity. This fundamental absence of political and cultural citizenship represents a condition in which these individuals do not understand themselves, and as such, do not envision themselves as right-holders, organizing their actions through the "recogni-tion of other universal and collective authorities, such as the natural, the di-vine, a moral guarantee . . . , an eternal, day-to-day, violent, and intimate world, ruled by cultural codes of private conduct" (50).

Understanding citizenship as the possibility of incorporating collective experiences and the self-images of specific groups into the public space and not as an abstract body of rights and obligations, Paoli defines the criminal justice system as the only public space in Brazil.[77]

The consequences are obvious. First, there is a very fragile belief in the law as a mechanism to regulate and resolve conflicts in all social classes, even the more educated. The perception of law held by law students in the state of Rio de Janeiro is symptomatic and frightening, especially considering that they are the future legal professionals.[78] For them, conflicts in Brazil are resolved principally through the *jeito* (47.2 percent)[79] and the law of the strongest (46.8 percent). Only 6.0 percent of the students believe in the law and its institutions for the resolution of conflict. Second, there is a sense of distrust of legal professionals and the judiciary. Research by the magazine *Veja* revealed that the lawyer is the professional least trusted by the Brazilian public. In line with this, only 49.9 percent of Rio de Janeiro law students trust the judiciary.

In the same manner, the judicial system is little used, a fact that does not mean that Brazilian society has little conflict. There are a lot of conflicts, mainly family and crime related, particularly for the large population that belongs to the lower middle and lower classes (see Table 3.6).

It is not amazing then that 67 percent of people who acknowledged having had some type of legal conflict in 1988 did not take it to the judiciary (IBGE 1990, xxxi) and that 43 percent of these people resolved the conflict on their own (see Table 3.7).

Regional characteristics, although important, do not explain the behavior of people. With regard to victims of theft and robbery, there is similarity among all regions of Brazil. For Brazil as a whole, 68 percent of the victims of theft or robbery did not go to the police, nor did 61 percent of the

TABLE 3.7

People Eighteen and Older Involved in a Conflict,
by Type of Action Taken, 1985–1988

Response	Brazil (%)	North (%)	Northeast (%)	Southeast (%)	South (%)	Central-West (%)
Participants that did not go to police	67.0	60.0	65.0	64.0	68.0	67.0
Participants that resolved the conflict on their own	43.0	41.0	34.2	42.0	50.0	55.0
Participants that feared reprisals	1.5	1.2	1.8	1.8	0.8	0.5
Participants that did not believe in the courts, did not want to involve the court, or saw indifference as less costly	28.7	35.5	36.0	28.4	21.8	22.8
Participants that sought assistance from other persons or entities	6.0	7.0	6.3	6.0	6.2	5.0

SOURCE: *Plano Nacional de Amostra Domiciliar*, Instituto Brasileiro Geográfico e Estatístico (1988).

victims of physical aggression. In all regions and for all types of victimization, there is the same estrangement from the law and legal institutions, as seen in Table 3.7. For the Brazilian people, distrustful of the state, the most natural path is to reject conflict (Santos 1993) or, when this is impossible, resolve it without the intervention of the state. The literature of the period 1970 to 2000 demonstrates a decline in availability of community standards for the resolution of conflict. Neighborhood associations as a locus of conflict resolution in the favelas, celebrated in the Pasárgada of Boaventura de Sousa Santos, were replaced by drug traffickers (Junqueira and Rodrigues 1992). After the mid-1980s, the favela was transformed into a territory where residents were continuously subject to two forces: drug trafficking and the police, who continue to disrespect citizen rights daily. Thus, 30.5 percent of the victims of theft (from research by CPDOC-FGV) did not report it to the police because of fear or distrust (the rate of crimes reported increased with the level of education of the respondent: 24 percent of respondents who had attended high school reported the crime, whereas only 11 percent of those with a grade school education did so).

Violence generates violence, especially among those with less education: 63.4 percent of the sample of CPDOC-FGV felt that the rights of criminals should not be respected, given that they did not respect the rights of others. The arbitrariness of the police themselves is accepted: 40.4 percent justify violent methods to obtain confessions from criminal suspects, again with greater approval among those with less education. Even lynching is acceptable to 11.2 percent of those surveyed, with an acceptance rate of 18.4 percent among respondents with less schooling, and of 1.3 percent of high school graduates. Many (40.6 percent) consider lynching a wrong, but understandable, practice.

Only 13 percent of the CPDOC-FGV sample had resorted to the labor courts, 8.2 percent to the state courts, and 1.9 percent to the small claims courts. Overall, the justice system itself is discriminatory. Clients of the penal system are the poor and blacks: 68.8 percent of the convicted are black (Adorno 1996, 284).[80] And the people know this. Of those surveyed, 90.7 percent say the law is applied more strictly to some than to others. It is more strictly applied to men (38.5 percent), to blacks (66.4 percent), to the poor (95.7 percent), and to employees (43.9 percent). The justice system not only is discriminatory but is deadly slow: 46.3 percent think the labor courts are slow, and 54.1 percent see the state courts as slow. This perception increases with the respondent's level of education.[81]

The attempts to bring the judiciary closer to the people through, for example, small claims courts and courts for minor crimes have not always worked (D'Araujo 1996). The number of cases brought to the court established in Rocinha, the largest favela in the city of Rio de Janeiro, is much less than the number of cases brought to courts not located in favelas: "[T]he rich bring more cases and . . . the poor are more often defendants in cases even in courts that are, by definition, meant to democratize the judicial system. This leads us to two important teachings of the sociology of law: the first is that justice is rarely equitably distributed; the second is that there are different legal cultures characterizing the poor and the rich, the more educated and the less educated, which explain the different use of the courts by these groups" (314 [emphasis added]).

Conclusion

Lawrence Friedman (1987) identifies two important characteristics of the North American legal culture—the general expectation of justice and the general expectation of recompense. The United States is a society with a high degree of claims consciousness and rights consciousness that, little by little (at least according to Friedman), is advancing toward "total justice"—or, in terminology he used more recently, toward a "horizontal society" (43).

Are we in Brazil also heading toward total justice? Will we one day live in a civic society? Will we be a horizontal society? Paraphrasing Caldeira (1984) in her work on the idea of the "politics of others," can we think about the legal order in terms of the "law of the others"? It is difficult to respond. In contrast to the United States, where there is a "pervasive expectation of fairness," throughout Brazil there is a pervasive expectation of unfairness. It is clear that the Brazilian legal order has improved over the last thirty years. But this legal order still does not regulate the social relations of the majority of Brazilians. It is not easy to overcome the history of Brazilian legal culture, marked by the confluence of bureaucratic-patrimonial practices brought from Portugal and liberal-individualistic ideas (Adorno 1988; Wolkmer 1998). The counterpoint to the persistence of the Iberian vestiges on Brazilian public culture can perhaps be found in the recent expansion of Protestantism in the popular classes, forcing the retreat of the secularized public cultures of Catholicism and Afro-Brazilian religions.

Several problems are still present in Brazilian society. First, the absence of political capability is making constitutional advances "illusory" (Souza and Lamounier 1990, 103). Second, the modern, liberal, individualistic, and universalistic logic coexists with the private or particularistic logic (DaMatta 1987).[82] In the words of Santos, "we continuously pass from polyarchical to non-polyarchical institutions, as if we were co-inhabiting the same institutional universe" (1993, 104). Third, the legal culture in Brazil seems not to depend on legal transformation—or at least not in the short term. Finally, the popular legal culture does not approach the internal legal culture, or vice versa. There is no communication between the two.[83] The research coordinated by Fonseca proves this argument (Guimarães 1999). For the people, private property represents a source of security; for the legal professionals, a source of liberty. For the people, the state should be a supreme power; for the legal professionals, a limited power. For the people, obligations should be fulfilled for ethical reasons; for legal professionals, for technical-legal reasons. For the people, law and justice are difficult to acquire; for legal professionals, they are in the reach of all (209).

In any case, there is no doubt that changes in the civic culture, and consequently in the legal culture, are not immediately forthcoming. Changes may require a number of generations (Putnam 1996). It would not be plausible, thus, to expect that a more democratic legal order would have already produced effects among the Brazilian people. We need to be patient and wait. However, it is worrisome to realize that sometimes we seem to be moving away from total justice, from a horizontal society. In these thirty years, in spite of political and legal democratization, only the degree of individual uncertainty, the sense of impotence and unpredictability, has seemed to grow (certainly the high inflation rates of the 1980s contributed to this feeling). The consequence is obvious: "the erosion of social norms, the tendency towards isolation, and the return to a state of nature" (Santos 1993, 108). It is not without reason that the Durkheimian notion of anomie has been resuscitated in analyses of Brazilian society at the end of the century. In other words, as happened in the nineteenth century with the laws that gradually abolished slavery, our laws continue to be made "for the English to see" (*para inglês ver*).[84]

Notes

1. See, for example, the definition of Antonio Carlos Wolkmer: "representations stamped by (il)legality in the production of ideas, the practical behavior, and the institutions of legal decision, transmitted and internalized within a determined social formation" (1998, 5).

2. On the conceptual and methodological difficulties in research on legal culture, see Nelken (1995).

3. Maria Guadalupe Piragibe da Fonseca utilizes the terms "popular legal culture" and "legal culture of legal operators" (in Junqueira, Vieira, and Fonseca 1995).

4. "My own position in the end will therefore be to reserve the term 'legal culture' to none of these layers alone, but rather to the most illuminating relations between the various layers" (Blankenburg, 1999, 12).

5. I am not adopting here the perspective of Steve Redhead (1995), who analyzes the origins of law and public culture through cultural studies (in the representations of law in art, music, etc.).

6. The author plays with the English and the Portuguese orthography to show that the country is divided into two areas, one more developed than the other. *Ed.*

7. *Bye Bye, Brasil.*

8. The year 1974 is considered the beginning of the environmental movement in Brazil. In these thirty years, Brazil has progressed from environmentalism to environmental politics, with the environmentalization of the modern middle class (Viola 1987).

9. Machado makes an important criticism of the law and development movement: The change of a legal culture does not happen merely through a change in the form of transmission, because in a society "where democracy has not been more than rhetoric," it is unlikely that it will have a democratic legal culture (1981, 23).

10. The *Plano Nacional de Amostra Domiciliar* (National Plan for Sampling of Domiciles) (PNAD) of 1988 included important questions for analyzing the relationship of the people to the justice system. It asked, for example, what recourse was taken in cases where rights were violated. Unfortunately, this question was not included in later PNADs.

11. Brazil carried out its census of 1990 in 1991, which in some ways makes comparison with other countries difficult.

12. Roberto Kant de Lima (1989) has also worked with the concept of legal culture, specifically analyzing police practices and the existence of an inquisitorial legal culture, despite Brazil's adoption of accusatorial criminal procedures.

13. Information obtained on July 19, 1999, on the Web site of IBGE: http://www .ibge.gov.br.

14. The Index of Human Development measures development using social indicators rather than economic indicators.

15. The indices are calculated according to the old methodology of the United Nations Development Program (UNDP). Because of a change in the IHD methodology, in 1997 Brazil was lowered to the group of countries with a middle level of human development.

16. On the difference between liberalization and democratization, see Przeworski (1982).

17. Federal constitution (hereafter, FC), art. 133.

18. A recent article by Jurandir Freire Costa (1997) shows that the Brazilian elite presently live in a state of depression, infected by the dream of *sex, lies, and videotapes.*

19. "[T]o the extent that the redefinition of citizenship and political rights are transferred to the constitutional level, movements lose their centrality as a provider of a sense of civic identity and as a defender of these rights" (Diniz and Boschi 1989, 45).

20. Law No. (hereafter, LN) 4121/62.

21. FC, art. 226, para. 3: "For purposes of protection by the State, the stable union between a man and a woman is recognized as a family entity, and the law should facilitate the conversion of such entity into marriage"; para. 4: "The community formed by either parent and their descendants is also considered as a family unit."

22. LN 8791/94 and LN 9278/96.

23. LN 7209/84.

24. LN 9714/98.

25. LN 7210/84.

26. Data available at http://www.mj.gov.br/depen/censo.

27. LN 7244/84.

28. LN 9099/95.

29. FC, art. 133.

30. LN 9307/96.

31. LN 6938/81.

32. LN 7347/85.

33. FC, art. 5, sec. XXXV.

34. FC, art. 5, sec. LXX.

35. Carioca is a person born in the city of Rio de Janeiro.

36. LN 9503/97.

37. Law of the Child and Adolescent (LN 8069/90). As this chapter was being completed, the government announced the prohibition of paid labor to persons younger than sixteen.

38. However, in practice, it continued to exist. In 1991, there were 1.9 million children between the ages of ten and thirteen working.

39. LN 7716/89, also known as Lei Caó, and LN 8081/90.

40. LN 9459/97.

41. FC, art. 231 and art. 232.

42. FC, art. 5, sec. XXXII, and art. 170, sec. V.

43. LN 8078/90.

44. LN 5859/72.

45. Bill proposed by Senator Benedita da Silva.

46. LN 9455/97.

47. LN 9455/97.

48. In September 1999, the Ministry of Justice announced a proposal to expand alternative punishments and revoke the law of heinous crimes as part of a more liberal crime policy based on a minimalist conception of criminal law.

49. LN 9434/97.

50. Unfortunately, the available data do not permit an analysis of the increase in cases within specific areas of law.

51. Regarding the crisis of the paradigm of the labor law, see Alvim and Fragale Filho (1999).

52. Data available at http://www.tst.gov.br.

53. Entrance to judicial careers occurs through a public civil service exam. But judges on the Federal Supreme Court are chosen by the president and approved by the Federal Senate (FC, art. 101).

54. Rio de Janeiro has a population of 13,406,308, according to the data of the IBGE for 1996 (http://www.ibge.gov.br/defaulttesto.htm). A total of 57,256 lawyers are registered with the Rio de Janeiro section of the Brazilian Bar Association.

55. For the entire country, the ratio of people to lawyers would be much higher, as the states of Rio de Janeiro and São Paulo have the greatest concentration of lawyers.

56. According to the Ministry of Education, the maintenance of a 7 percent rate

of growth in enrollment (the rate of growth from 1994 to 1998) will result in approximately 3 million students in undergraduate programs by the year 2004 and will require the addition of 875,000 admission spots in Brazil's institutions of higher education (http://www.inep.gov.br).

57. The new programs created 32,674 new admission spots in 1998. The Ministry of Education received 5,257 requests to create new programs but authorized the opening of only 647 (http://www.inep.gov.br).

58. However, only 62.4 percent of the students finished their studies (http://www.inep.gov.br).

59. Medicine had an even greater candidate/admitted student ratio (29 to 1).

60. The number of blacks is less significant, but certainly within the next few years there should be a greater number of blacks in law school and in legal careers. In any case, it is important to remember that according to the Plano Nacional de Amostra Domiciliar (IBGE) of 1996, only 6 percent of the population was classified as black (*pretos*); 38.2 percent as part black (*pardos*); 55.2 percent as white (*brancos*); 0.4 percent as Asian (*amarelos*); and 0.2 percent as indigenous (*índios*). The greatest concentration of blacks is in the southeast (7.4 percent), followed by the northeast (6.1 percent), central-west (4.0 percent), urban north (3.7 percent), and the south (3.1 percent).

61. More recent data are contained in Table 3.1.

62. Research conducted among judges of the state of Rio de Janeiro found that, according to the interview subjects, the gender of the judges makes no difference except in cases of requests for food assistance by women, which the female judges tended to be more unwilling to grant (Junqueira 1998).

63. Other important changes include the requirement to write a final paper and take practice-oriented legal classes, and a growing philosophy of individualization in the course of study achieved through allowing students to choose complementary activities and areas of specialization.

64. In accordance with Decree No. 163 of 1998.

65. If we disaggregate the data according to the type of institution, 25.71 percent of the federal law schools obtained a ranking of very good with regard to the credentials of the faculty, as opposed to 4.72 percent of the programs at private law schools.

66. This situation is a little different in the public schools where, at least formally, the professors are more dedicated to teaching (but in practice, the situation is not very different than in the private institutions). If we disaggregate the data according to type of institution, 88.58 percent of the federal law school faculties were ranked as very good with respect to their work performance, but only 14.96 percent of private law school faculties achieved this evaluation.

67. Statute of the Bar Association, art. 44, sec. II.

68. Data available at http://ww.stf.gov.br.

69. This phenomenon is not specific to Brazil (see Rojas 1986).

70. The new lawyers should understand business negotiations, capital markets, international contracts, debt conversion in risk capital, financial institutions, foreign investment in Brazil, Brazilian investment in foreign markets, loans and financ-

ing, liquidity of financial institutions, privatization, mining, aerospace law, computer technology, intellectual property, telecommunications, art, culture, leisure (fiscal exemptions in cases of donations and cultural and artistic events), ecology, real estate transactions, immigrant labor, importation and exportation, maritime law, fiscal consulting, fiscal contention, labor consulting, contention in the higher courts, consumer relations, antitrust, the European Economic Community, Mercosur, applications for public jobs, and legal auditing.

71. Unfortunately, comparative data for earlier years are not available.

72. According to a survey conducted in July 1999.

73. Putnam states, "In a civic region, when two citizens see each other in the street, *both* have probably read the daily newspaper; in a less civic region, when two people see each other, *neither* [has] probably read the newspaper" (1996, 111 [Putnam's emphasis]).

74. *Jogo do bicho* is an illegal lottery in which each number corresponds to an animal.

75. Among respondents with up to four years of education, 62.8 percent could not identify rights; this falls to 38.2 percent among those who have at least some high school education.

76. From 1980 to 1991, the population in favelas in the state of Rio de Janeiro grew 53.14 percent according to IBGE.

77. "The lack of a constituted civil space that could effectively mediate the relations between state and society seems to have had the political effect of making daily conflicts resolvable in only one of two ways: privatization or repression" (Paoli 1982, 55).

78. Research conducted in 1996 by the Department of Research and Documentation of the Brazilian Bar Association of Rio de Janeiro and by the Instituto Direito e Sociedade.

79. On the importance of the *jeito* in Brazilian legal culture, certainly one of the most important works is by Keith Rosenn (1998), who characterizes our legal culture as paternalistic, legalistic, and formalistic. According to the author, the idea of *jeito*, which in the finest Brazilian tradition is untranslatable, would correspond roughly to a "knack," "twist," "way," or "fix."

80. Adorno does not discard the possibility that this difference is a result of the differential access to lawyers, with blacks more subject to representation by the public defender.

81. The Institute Vox Populi conducted an opinion poll under a contract with the Liberal Party, a member of which is one of the principal politicians pressuring for judicial reform, Senator Antonio Carlos Magalhães. The poll shows that 58 percent of those surveyed consider the judiciary incompetent, 89 percent consider it slow, 40 percent think it is biased, 67 percent think it is for the rich, and 59 percent think that justice is not attainable by the poor (*Estado de São Paulo*, 7 April 1999, p. 21).

82. "When I am getting a driver license or trying to get a telephone line, I am personalistic and I use the *jeito* with the bureaucratic officials. I do the same when I am talking to a policeman as I opt for the 'do you know who you are talking to?' approach. But when the situation involves buying, selling, electing, or being elected, I am a universalist and I demand that laws and institutions be trustworthy. It is as if

modern universalism is demanded in the public sphere, but personalism and particularism continue to function in the personal or private sphere" (DaMatta 1987, 20).

83. This point is fundamental in relation to the perspective of alternative law that seeks precisely to rescue the vision of the law and norms of the marginalized sectors of society.

84. Responding to English economic pressure, Brazil passed many laws to abolish slavery gradually. But, in practice, the laws were not respected.

References

Abel, Richard. 1989. *American lawyers*. New York: Oxford University Press.

Adorno, Sérgio. 1988. *Os aprendizes do poder*. Rio de Janeiro: Paz e Terra.

————. 1996. "Racismo, criminalidade violenta e justica penal: Reus brancos e negros em perspectiva comparativa." *Estudos Historicos* 9 (18): 283.

Alvim, Joaquim Leonel de Rezende, and Roberto Fragale Filho. 1999. Justiça do trabalho: Um paradigma em crise? *Trabalho & Doutrina* 21 (June):113–26.

Arantes, Rogério. 1999. Direito e política: O Ministério Público e a defesa dos direitos coletivos. *Revista Brasileira de Ciências Sociais* 14 (39):83–102.

Arnaud, André-Jean, ed. 1993. *Dictionnaire encyclopédique de théorie et de sociologie de droit*. Paris: Librarie Générale de Droit et de Jurisprudence.

Blankenburg, Ehrard. 1999. Legal culture on every conceptual level. In *Globalization and legal cultures*, edited by Johannes Feest. Oñati, Spain: Oñati International Institute for the Sociology of Law.

Bourdieu, Pierre. 1998. *Outline of a theory of practice*. Cambridge: Cambridge University Press.

Caldeira, Teresa Pires del Rio. 1984. *A política dos outros*. São Paulo: Brasiliense.

Cappelletti, Mauro, and Bryant Garth. 1988. *Acesso à justiça*. Porto Alegre: Sergio Fabris.

Carvalho, Amilton. 1993. *Direito alternativo na jurisprudência*. São Paulo: Acadêmica.

Carvalho, José Murilo de. 1987. *Os bestializados*. São Paulo: Companhia das Letras.

————. 1999a. O motivo edênico no imaginário social brasileiro. Pp. 19–43 in *Cidadania, justiça e violência*, edited by Dulce Pandolfi, José Murilo de Carvalho, Leandro Piquet Carneiro, and Mario Grynszpan. Rio de Janeiro: Fundação Getúlio Vargas.

————. 1999b. Brasileiro: Cidadão? In *Pontos e bordados*, edited by José Murilo de Carvalho. Belo Horizonte: Universidade Federal de Minas Gerais.

Cittadino, Gisele. 1998. *Pluralismo, direito e justiça distributiva*. Rio de Janeiro: Lumen Juris.

Costa, Jurandir Freire. 1989. Narcisismo em tempos sombrios. In *Tempo de desejo*, edited by Heloisa Rodrigues Fernandes. São Paulo: Brasiliense.

————. 1997. A ética democrática e seus inimigos: O lado privado da violência pública. In *Ética*, edited by Frei Betto, Jurandir Freire Costa, and Eugenio Barba. Rio de Janeiro: Garamond.

Cotterrell, Roger. 1997. The concept of legal culture. Pp. 13–31 in *Comparing legal cultures*, edited by D. Nelken. Aldershot, England: Dartmouth.

DaMatta, Roberto. 1987. *A casa e a rua*. Rio de Janeiro: Guanabara.

D'Araujo, Maria Celina. 1996. Juizados especiais de pequenas causas: Notas sobre a experiência no Rio de Janeiro. *Estudos Históricos* 9 (18):301–22.

Diniz, Eli, and Renato Boschi. 1989. A consolidação democrática no Brasil: Atores políticos, processos sociais e intermediação de interesses. Pp. 17–75 in *Moderniza- ção e consolidação democrática no Brasil: Dilemas da Nova República*, edited by Eli Diniz, Renato Boschi, and Renato Lessa. Rio de Janeiro: Vértice/IUPERJ.

Economides, Kim. 1999. Lendo as ondas do "Movimento de Acesso à Justiça": Epistemologia versus metodologia? Pp. 61–76 in *Cidadania, justiça e violência*, edited by Dulce Pandolfi, José Murilo de Carvalho, Leandro Piquet Carneiro, and Mario Grynszpan. Rio de Janeiro: Fundação Getúlio Vargas.

Ewick, Patricia, and Susan Silbey. 1998. *The common place of law*. Chicago: University of Chicago Press.

Falcão, Joaquim. 1984. *Os advogados: Ensino jurídico e mercado de trabalho*. Recife, Brazil: Fundação Joaquim Nabuco/Massangana.

Fragoso, Heleno. 1980. Sobre a lei de segurança nacional. *Revista de Direito Penal* 30 (July–December):5–10.

Friedman, Lawrence. 1987. *Total justice*. Boston: Beacon Press.

———. 1997. The concept of legal culture: A reply. Pp. 33–39 in *Comparing legal cultures*, edited by D. Nelken. Aldershot, England: Dartmouth.

———. 1999. *Horizontal society*. New Haven, Conn.: Yale University Press.

Goslin, Priscilla Ann. 1996. *How to be a carioca*. Rio de Janeiro: TwoCan.

Guanabara, Ricardo. 1996. Visões alternativas do direito no Brasil. *Estudos Históricos* 9 (18):403–16.

Guimarães, Ana Cristina Rodrigues. 1999. Coincidências aparentes, diferenças na essência: Um relato das tendências da cultura jurídica. *Plúrima* 2 (5):201–10.

Junqueira, Eliane. 1992. O alternativo regado a vinho e a cachaça. Pp. 94–114 in *Lições de direito alternativo 2*, edited by Edmundo Lima de Arruda Jr. São Paulo: Acadêmica.

———. 1998. A mulher juíza e a juíza mulher. Pp. 185–216 in *Horizontes plurais*, edited by Cristina Bruschini and Heloisa Buarque Holanda. São Paulo: Editora 34.

Junqueira, Eliane, and José Augusto de Souza Rodrigues. 1992. Pasárgada revisitada. *Sociologia: Problemas e Práticas* 12 (October):9–18.

Junqueira, Eliane, José Ribas Vieira, and Maria Guadalupe Piragibe Fonseca. 1995. *Juízes: Retrato em preto e branco*. Rio de Janeiro: Letra Capital.

Lima, Roberto Kant de. 1989. Cultura jurídica e práticas policiais: A tradição inquisitorial. *Revista Brasileira de Ciências Sociais* 10 (4):65–84.

Machado, Mario Brockman.1981. Comentários. In *Direito, cidadania e participação*, edited by Bolívar Lamounier, Francisco Weffort, and Maria Victoria Benevides. São Paulo: Queiroz.

Martins, Luciano. 1989. Ação política e governabilidade na transição brasileira. Pp. 223–62 in *Dilemas da consolidação da democracia*, edited by José Álvaro Moisés and J. A. Guilhon Albuquerque. Rio de Janeiro: Paz e Terra.

Merry, Sally Engle. 1990. *Getting justice and getting even*. Chicago: University of Chicago Press.

Moura, Alexandrina Sobreira de. 1992. *Organizações não governamentais e o uso do solo da Região Metropolitana de Recife*. Recife, Brazil. Mimeographed.

Nelken, David. 1995. Disclosing/invoking legal culture: An introduction. *Social & Legal Studies* 4:435.

Paoli, Maria Célia, Maria Victoria Benevides, Paulo Sérgio Pinheiro, and Robert DaMatta. 1982. *A violência brasileira*. São Paulo: Brasiliense.

Przeworski, Adam. 1989. Como e onde se bloqueiam as transições para a democracia? Pp. 19–48 in *Dilemas da consolidação da democracia*, edited by José Álvaro Moisés and J. A. Guilhon Albuquerque. Rio de Janeiro: Paz e Terra.

Putnam, Robert. 1996. *Comunidade e democracia: A experiência da Itália moderna*. Rio de Janeiro: Getúlio Vargas.

Redhead, Steve. 1995. *Unpopular cultures: The birth of law and popular culture*. Manchester, England: Manchester University Press.

Rojas, Fernando. 1986. *A comparison of change-oriented legal services in Latin America with legal services in North America and Europe*. Madison, Wis.: Institute for Legal Studies.

Rosenn, Keith. 1998. *O jeito na cultura jurídica brasileira*. Rio de Janeiro: Renovar.

Santos, Wanderley Guilherme dos. 1979. *Cidadania e justiça*. Rio de Janeiro: Campus.

———. 1993. *Razões da desordem*. Rio de Janeiro: Rocco.

Souza, Amaury, and Bolívar Lamounier. 1990. A feitura da nova Constituição: Um reexame da cultura política brasileira. In *De Geisel a Collor: O balanço da transição*, edited by Bolívar Lamounier. São Paulo: Instituto de Estudos Econômicos, Sociais e Políticos de São Paulo.

Toharia, José Juan. 1999. La cultura legal: Cómo se mide. In *Globalization and legal cultures*, edited by Johannes Feest. Oñati, Spain: Oñati International Institute for the Sociology of Law.

Viola, Eduardo J. 1998. O movimento ecológico no Brasil (1974–1986): Do ambientalismo à ecopolítica. *Revista Brasileira de Ciências Sociais* 3 (1):5–26.

Wolkmer, Antonio Carlos. 1998. *História do direito no Brasil*. Rio de Janeiro: Forense.

CHAPTER 4

Law and Legal Culture in Chile, 1974–1999

EDMUNDO FUENZALIDA FAIVOVICH

BETWEEN 1974 and 1999 Chilean society weathered a transcendental change, which deeply affected it economically and socially, as well as politically. This fact is well known.[1]

In the economic sphere, the country shifted from a system of production characterized by the active participation of the state and protection from international competitiveness through high tariffs and prohibitions on imports, to an economy open to world markets, in which the presence of the state was constantly reduced, except in the case of large copper mines. In the social sphere, labor and social legislation was dismantled, and rights and recognition achieved by workers and unions were canceled. Politically, a representative democracy, in general respectful of the law and of individual rights, was replaced by a military dictatorship that committed grave violations of human rights.

These changes were imposed initially by the military government, presided over by General Augusto Pinochet after the military coup d'état of September 11, 1973. Democratically elected governments since 1989 have essentially maintained the policies of opening the economy to world markets and privatizing public businesses, while at the same time have put a stop to the violations of human rights; they have adopted social policies designed to combat poverty and diminish the inequality of income distribution.

Between 1974 and 1999 two periods can be distinguished: The first corresponds to the military dictatorship as such, which extended from the consolidation of the authoritarian regime during the year following the coup

Special thanks to José Cayuela, Fabia Fuenzalida, and Sandra Fuenzalida for their great help in the final version of this chapter.

d'état against the government of Salvador Allende, until the plebiscite of 1988 and the restoration of a democratic system through the election of President Patricio Aylwin at the end of 1989. The second period begins when Aylwin takes control in March of 1990 and ends with the third electoral victory of the Union of Parties for Democracy (CPD) and their presidential candidate, the Socialist Ricardo Lagos, who came to power in March 2000.

This chapter attempts to answer two issues relating to each of these historic phases: What role did the legal system play in the process of economic, social, and political change occurring between 1974 and 1989? Was the legal system an obstacle to the transformations imposed by the authoritarian government, or did it passively adapt, or even collaborate?

Once democracy was reestablished in 1990, how did the system react to the attempts of democratic governments to humanize the economic and social regime inherited from the dictatorship? What was its role during the design and implementation of new democratizing policies: collaborator, passive executor, or obstacle?

The Notions of a Legal System and of a Legal Culture

The questions formulated in the previous discussion arose not only from definitions of legal systems and the good they bring to society, but also from the exceptional situation in which Chilean legal culture found itself after the military coup d'état and the political reforms of the military government, headed by General Pinochet. The Chilean legal system was very solid. It appeared even more ingrained and stable than those in the Mediterranean countries discussed in this volume—Spain, France, and Italy—which passed through eras of totalitarian dictators and foreign occupation in the twentieth century.

In this chapter, a "legal system" refers not only to constitutions, rules, and laws created by competent authorities, or conventions and contracts generated by individuals, but also the courts, from the lowest level to the highest, the lawyers, and other auxiliary functionaries of the law, such as notaries, archivists, librarians, law professors, and police and prison services.[2] Understood as a sociocultural system, the legal system includes not just the legal texts but also the more or less qualified and specialized personnel, and elements as varied as financial support, buildings, and equipment. Regarding its dynamics, the system receives demands from society, processes them, and generates results. It includes, for example, the formation and enforcement of contracts and other transactions, judicial decision making, the elaboration of manuals and legal treatises for the correct application of law, the use of human resources, and also detentions, imprisonment, and other legal acts.

In spite of the strong relationship between legal systems and political regimes, the two should not be confused: the political sphere determines norms of conduct to which citizens must adjust, whereas the legal system gives certainty and security to established rights and obligations drawn from those norms, utilizing for this purpose the power of the state.

One important aspect of all legal systems is the culture of its operators and that of its subjects; that is to say, the amalgam of ideas and beliefs that each has regarding the system and its obligations to it and to society. How have both cultures changed in Chile during the last twenty-five years? In the same direction, or in opposite directions? Or, put another way, do they tend to draw together or draw apart? How much and in what way (in which directions) has Chilean legal culture been modified under the impact of the radical transformation of the normative framework for human life that occurred between 1974 and 1999? From a sociolegal research perspective, this is perhaps the most general question that one could ask with respect to Chile in this period. Nevertheless, one could ask an even broader question as well: How and in what way has the change in the legal culture contributed to the change in the Chilean normative framework?

I do not agree with the assumption that the change in the normative framework is independent from, and causes changes in, legal culture. Such an assumption is natural to sociology, a discipline that, in general, asserts that cultural changes are consequences of changes at the level of the normative framework. I think that this assumption should be treated as a hypothesis susceptible to scrutiny through investigation. Does this assumption hold in the case of Chile, or is cultural and legal change one of the elements that generates fluctuations in the normative framework?

The Chilean experience is a particularly interesting way to verify this hypothesis. In the second half of the twentieth century, this country has seen great changes in the normative framework. Between 1950 and 1974 the change was slow and consensual, effected through democratic methods of citizen participation in collective decisions, but the period 1974–89 saw an abrupt change imposed by one sector of the citizenry. Therefore, what role did the legal culture have in the process of changing the normative framework between 1950 and 1974? Did it come before, or did it develop at the same time, or was the change simply a consequence? Did it play the same role, whatever that role may be, in the later period of 1974–89? Put in another way, did the *type of change* in the normative framework in society (whether slow or abrupt) influence in some way the *type of change* experienced by legal culture? If it is slow and consensual, could the legal culture easily adapt, or even advance and guide such change? On the other hand, if it is abrupt, was the legal culture left behind, becoming an inert obstacle to change, incapable of reacting to the direction of change in the normative mold until it was overtaken and became a new legal culture?

Further, admitting that legal culture has two axes, one directed internally toward the system's operators and another directed externally toward the subjects of the norms, is there a difference between internal and external legal culture regarding its relationship with the *type of change* in the normative framework?

Last, legal culture is only a segment of the cultural life of a society, which includes the cognitive aspect (philosophy, natural and social sciences, and technologies) and the expressive aspect (literature and the arts). Changing the normative mold of human life also changes the culture of that society in its totality, though not every segment in a simultaneous way. In certain cases, the transformations occur in the cognitive segment, while other segments remain stable for long periods of time. In other cases, the expressive part of culture changes first, and other segments remain momentarily unaltered.

It is logical to think that the change in other segments of a culture should have some effect in changing legal culture, but what effect would that be? Only an investigation of individual cases can generate hypotheses in this respect.

This chapter investigates only what occurs in legal culture when an abrupt and nonconsensual change is produced in the normative framework of a society. This is precisely what happened in Chile between 1974 and 1999, given that Chilean legal culture was formed through a century and a half by slow and consensual change in the normative framework, which became tradition. Suddenly this culture saw itself confronting an abrupt change in the normative framework, propelled by an authoritarian government ignoring the traditional urge to search for social consensus.

The Historical "Legalistic" Tradition and Its Demise

To understand the Chilean legal tradition in all of its dimensions, one should remember that the country had thought of itself, beginning with its political independence from Spain in the early nineteenth century, as one of the few Latin American countries not ruled by a *caudillo* (charismatic leader) but instead by a president elected by the citizenry, with powers strictly regulated by a constitution and a body of laws, rules, and decrees. It is true that there was a distance between social and political reality and this normative vision of its political elites, but in Chile, unlike other countries of the region, the president, with a limited term, governed according to law, demanded that his citizens comply, and finally transferred his power to a newly elected president.

In the last quarter of the nineteenth century, this conception of the nature of political authority, which belonged to the oligarchic elite who organized the republic, was transformed into a historical truth by a distinguished generation of historians, who recognized it and drafted essays and texts about it. Then, a no less distinguished generation of university professors and secondary schoolteachers closed the circle, using those texts to teach this truth from the podium (Jocelyn-Holt 1997).

At the beginning of the twentieth century, Chile could present itself before the international community as a democratic state "in form"; that is to say, with an effective legal system of long standing. Chile was recognized as such by the most distinguished foreign intellectuals of the time.

This process of consolidation and legitimation of political power would not have been possible without the efforts of a large body of jurists, from the executive, the Congress, the judiciary, and the universities, who generated the codes, laws, doctrine, and jurisprudence that constituted the normative dimension of the legal system. Men of the caliber of the Venezuelan Andrés Bello, author of the civil code, and of the Argentine José Gabriel Ocampo, author of the commercial code, were only the most visible of this community of legislators, judges, lawyers, and professors. Curiously, these two men of law were political exiles who found in Chile the conditions to generate legal masterworks that their own governments and societies would not let them realize. The Chilean community produced great men, such as Luis Claro Solar, with his monumental work, *The Chilean Civil Code Explained and Compared*. In the same vein, the works of Valentín Letelier, and especially his *Genesis of the Law* and *Genesis of the State*, remain as testimony to the level of maturity reached by legal science in Chile in the first quarter of the twentieth century.

This process of state construction, in which the Chilean elite joined forces with jurists and academics and used legal instruments to exercise power, gave Chile its exceptional political stability. The system resisted two wars with neighboring countries (against the Confederation of Perú and Bolivia in 1836, and against Perú and Bolivia in 1879) and a civil war (between the executive and Congress in 1891) without seriously affecting its democratic succession. This solid institutional "order" was abruptly interrupted by the fall of the main export of the country, sodium nitrate, in the 1920s, and then by a worldwide recession in the 1930s. Chile suffered a great deal as a consequence of this crisis. Social tensions deepened to the point that the legal and political fabric gave way, and the century of democracy was interrupted by a succession of short-term military dictators.

Nevertheless, the institutional process began again in the same decade, the 1930s, through reforms introduced by nontraditional authors and actors: the traditional elite was slowly displaced and replaced by a middle class. From this middle class came a succession of political leaders, chosen by a successively broader electorate and controlled by the new constitution of 1925 and profuse legislation.

Chile began again to think of itself as a democratic state "in form." By replacing leaders according to constitutional and legal principles, the country recovered international recognition and prestige. Important political reforms, such as women's suffrage (1949) and the introduction of the state-printed voting form to guarantee voting secrecy (1958), were adopted without delay or violence. Great social and economic transformations, such as the industrialization of the country and agrarian reform, were introduced by adapting the legal system and the constitution itself without problems or serious uprisings. In this period, from 1933 to 1973, the constitution served as a framework for economic and political progress, thereby renovating and reinforcing the "legalistic" tradition.

These notable advances in the economic, political, and social spheres, achieved without altering legal stability, came to pass in an era in which many countries, some with a long democratic tradition, suffered from deep institutional crises and abandoned democracy to experiment with other forms of political organization. In Chile, the process of profound change, to be achieved within the "legal order," produced an unexpected effect in the new generation of the leading elite. This generation, called in this discussion the "1941s" for the date in which Eduardo Frei Montalva reached his thirtieth birthday,[3] began to think that Chile could continue indefinitely to introduce those transformations in its economic and social structure required by a new consciousness of social justice, in full accordance with and respect for democratic institutions and legality. The idea that the law is an efficient instrument to achieve changes in social structure was conceived and concretized by jurists of that generation, who theorized beyond contemporary ideological and partisan borders.

A variety of projects of reform were prepared, as much by the believers in the "Revolution in Liberty," propagated by the Christian Democrats and their followers, as by the militants and sympathizers of the Marxist left, the Socialists and Communists. The victory of the Christian Democrats under Montalva in the presidential election of 1964 signified the practical application of and confidence in the law, especially relating to agrarian reform. The Socialist government of Allende, elected in 1970, took the same notion to its extreme, forwarding a global transition in social organization from capitalism to socialism through the utilization of existing legal instruments. In this case, the occupation of farms and industries by workers was understood as a way of accelerating the necessarily slow process of transferring the means of production from the private sector to the public sector through legal channels.

Beginning in the 1970s, most people shared an unlimited confidence in legal instruments as efficient means to produce large and immediate changes in the economic and social structure. In fact, it became a defining characteristic of Chilean legal culture, internally (the culture of judges, lawyers, law professors, and other auxiliary functionaries in the administration of justice) and externally (that of the general population). It is true that some political groups denounced this thinking as illusory, but their influence was very weak.

The history of "Chilean legalism" that we have outlined can serve to explain this naive conception of the law. What never fails to surprise is its general acceptance. The rapid deterioration of the economy after the first year of Allende's administration and the worsening of social conflicts at the beginning of the second year, as a consequence of government actions and the reaction of the opposition, should have made a dent in such an optimistic vision of the role of law in social change. Nevertheless, the vision remained unchanged, as much in the government's public discourse as in the opposition's. For this reason, when the commanders in chief of the armed forces conducted the coup d'état on September 11, 1973, they produced a crisis, not only of democratic institutions but also of the legal culture constructed around them and of the attitudes and behavior of many jurists who had contributed to its development.

The history of a new era (1974–89) from the point of view of transformations of legality and legal culture of the country, following the criteria used until now, is the history of the new behavior of Chilean jurists and the way in which they viewed and taught the law. Now they had in front of them a reality, unknown in Chile, of a military government de facto that defined itself as foundational and that, exercising its power without counterweights, proceeded to reorganize the economy and the society according to neoliberal prescriptions without respecting human rights.

FROM 1974 TO 1980: VIOLENCE AS A SYSTEM

The military dictatorship lasted sixteen years without interruption (with a fraction of a year between September 11, 1973, day of the coup, and the end of that year, and another fraction of a year between December 31, 1989, and March 11, 1990, the date on which a democratically elected president took control). In this extensive period it is necessary to distinguish two subperiods: between 1974 and 1980, and between 1981 and 1989. Both are separated by the introduction of the constitution of 1980.

Regarding the period immediately after the ousting of President Allende until January 1, 1981, the day in which the new constitution entered into force, the role of the legal system can be described in very general terms as follows.

In the first months of the military government, many Allende sympathizers were detained and jailed, without a warrant and without promptly putting them before a judge as the law required. Because the jails were filled, concentration camps, like the tragically famous National Stadium of Santiago, were created. Relatives and friends of the detainees filed habeas corpus petitions before the appeals courts, which were refused, leaving the detainees in the hands of the captors. The quantity of petitions was so large that the president of the Supreme Court, in his official inaugural speech of the judicial year of 1974, stated that dealing with these petitions would take too much time away from other judicial business.

The military leadership, initially pronouncing edicts (*bandos*), began to govern by decree-laws, that is to say, norms that are laws but that have not been approved by the procedure contemplated in the Political Constitution of 1925. The military government defined the constitution's place as "partially in force." In fact, the government did not respect many of its provisions.

The decree-laws of this period adopted a model of economic development that was drastically different from the one that had guided the state's public policies from the government of Pedro Aguirre Cerda (1939–42) to that of Salvador Allende (1970–73). Tariffs and customs duties on the importation of manufactured goods, which had been raised to protect national industry, were reduced. New rules facilitated foreign investment (Decree-Law 600). On the other hand, workers' rights were limited to facilitate layoffs of workers.

Other important decree-laws ended the privileged legal status of professions, transforming the professional colleges (such as those for lawyers and doctors), which had disciplinary jurisdiction over their members, into simple voluntary associations with moral supervision over the conduct of their members.

The official operators of the legal systems confined themselves to enforcement of this new legislation, even though individual members of the Order of Lawyers provided free services to the Vicariate of Solidarity, created by the Catholic Church to receive denunciations for violations of human rights and to try to protect the victims. In addition, given that the military government had appointed a commission of jurists to draft a new constitution, another group of lawyers formed the Committee of 24 to monitor the process closely and formulate alternative propositions. These actions were not completely safe, as is demonstrated by the case of the lawyer, professor, and former dean of the law faculty at the University of Chile, Eugenio Velasco Letelier, who was detained while leaving the Palace of Justice and expelled from the country.

The constant violation of human rights by the security services (DINA and then CNI) was ignored in the yearly inaugural speeches of the judicial year by the president of the Supreme Court (Cuneo 1980).

In terms of legal education during this period, the law faculty of the University of Chile made drastic changes and returned to the curriculum and the teaching methods of the 1930s. All of the efforts of the 1960s and early

1970s to modernize teaching methods and incorporate social sciences into the preparation of future lawyers and judges were erased (Fuenzalida 1997).

In brief, the superior courts, as components of the legal system, did not perform their role and allowed the military government to pursue a policy of elimination of the opposition. As a large number of citizens disappeared or were exiled, the majority of judges and judicial functionaries did not raise their voices in protest. They could not have done much more, given the concentration of power in the hands of the military, but this gesture would have been important for the internal and the external legal culture. A change occurred in both external and internal legal culture: a change from a historical attitude of respect toward the superior courts to a vision increasingly more critical of their behavior. As stated previously, within the body of lawyers we did find a group of professionals who supported habeas corpus petitions, provided free services to the Vicariate of Solidarity of the Catholic Church, formed the Committee of 24, and, in general, protested against abuses of military power. In terms of legal education, the new policies of reactionary reform drove out various professors of the law faculty of the University of Chile, who found themselves forced to work only as practicing attorneys.

FROM 1981 TO 1989: A NORM FOR THE DICTATORSHIP

The enactment of the new constitution of 1980 could have made a difference, in terms of the certainty and security of the citizenry and their rights. The new document was approved in a plebiscite in which the result could not have been other than approval. The alternative was the continuation of an arbitrary regime, without limitations. Nevertheless, the constitution was of little importance because the text contained transitional articles that permitted the military government to continue to exercise its power arbitrarily until the election of new authorities. For example, according to Transitional Article 24, during the eight-year presidential term that Pinochet would serve, starting with the enactment of the constitution, he could keep people under house arrest for five days or in other places that were not jails; could restrict the right of free association and freedom of information; could prohibit from entering or expel those who propagated certain doctrines and those who acted in ways contrary to Chilean interests or who constituted a threat to internal peace; and could order persons to remain in an urban area of the country for up to three months. To exercise these powers, President Pinochet merely had to declare a danger of disruption to internal peace; there would be no recourse against his decrees, unless he himself reconsidered.

The new constitution maintained the separation of powers that had been a mainstay since the beginning of the republic. Nevertheless, it increased executive power and decreased congressional power. It stated that the president of the republic would be elected every four years and could be reelected only once.[4] The number of senators and congressmen was modified, and a category of institutional senators was created; that is to say, not elected by the people but instead appointed: two by the president of the republic, three by the Supreme Court, and four by the National Security Council. In addition, former presidents of the republic would become senators for life at the end of their presidential period. The judiciary remained a power independent of the other two, headed by the Supreme Court. A Constitutional Tribunal was formed, with authority to declare laws unconstitutional. The new constitution also introduced a National Security Council, comprising the president of the republic, the president of the Senate, the president of the Supreme Court, the general comptroller of the republic, and the commanders in chief of the four branches of the armed forces. That is to say, it imposed a framework in which civil power, democratically formed, had the same weight as military power. Military power was, in fact, outside democratic political control, given that the chiefs of staff of the armed forces were designated by the president of the republic, although from lists of five names prepared by each branch and for a period of four years. The president of the republic could not dismiss these chiefs during their term, except with the approval of the National Security Council. This body had, among its powers, the power to present to the president of the republic, the National Congress, or the Constitutional Tribunal its opinion on a situation, an act, or material that, in its judgment, gravely threatened the fundamentals of the institutions or compromised national security.

Nevertheless, more important than these constitutional norms, temporary or not, was the maintenance or change in the patterns of behavior of the courts relative to the consideration and resolution of habeas corpus petitions, or of the new *recurso de protección*. The latter permitted appeals to the courts in cases of violations, not only of personal liberty, but also of any other right guaranteed by the constitution in Article 19.

The military regime termed 1981 the year of "modernization." Decree-laws were enacted that changed the rules of the game in areas of great importance to social life. They created a private health system, parallel to the public one and based on health insurance contracts with private businesses called Institutes of Health and Social Prevention (ISAPRES). In addition, they introduced contracts of insurance against other risks, such as aging, with institutions called Administrators of Pension Funds (AFP), which ended up controlling the obligatory donations of workers. The labor code was modified, limiting workers' rights to collectively contract and organize strikes and making it easier to fire workers. Private universities could be established, and the public university financing system was modified.

The financial crisis of 1982 led to massive protests in the next three years and to a resurgence of political opposition to the military regime. The failed assassination attempt on President Pinochet in 1986 convinced an important sector of the opposition that the only way to return to democracy was through the procedure proposed by the government. In the October 1988 plebiscite, with due guarantees and under international observation, the opposition triumphed. Over 50 percent voted no, which meant not allowing General Pinochet to continue as president after the end of his term. In December 1989, in the first presidential election since 1970, Patricio Aylwin, the candidate of the unified opposition, ran against Hernán Büchi, Pinochet's former finance minister and the candidate of the political right and the military regime.

The 1990–1999 Period

After the victory of the "no" vote and the triumph of the candidate for the Unified Parties for Democracy over the candidate who stood for the continuation of the Pinochet regime without Pinochet, a new era began for law and legal culture in Chile. This period lasted from March 1990, when President Aylwin assumed power, until the last year of the term of his successor, Eduardo Frei Ruiz-Tagle (1994–99). In general terms, this period is characterized by attempts of the democratically elected authorities to purge and reform the inherited legal system, in the face of a political opposition that leaned on the authoritarian provisions of the 1980 constitution, the Supreme Court, and one faction of lawyers and academics (Fuenzalida 1996).

Various reforms had been introduced into the constitution, particularly regarding temporary measures that limited the exercise of public liberties. Nevertheless, a group of rules that assured the continuing participation of the military and its sympathizers in government affairs was maintained. One of the most important was the maintenance of the National Security Council, with the participation of the highest authorities of the state and of the chiefs of staff of the four branches of national defense. Another was the existence of nine institutional senators, two appointed by the president of the republic, four by the National Security Council, and three by the Supreme Court. To these were added senators for life: the former presidents of the republic, but only those who had served six years. As a result of this article, former president Pinochet became a senator for life, but former president Aylwin, who governed only the four years originally contemplated by the constitution, did not.[5]

The democratic period also began with a Supreme Court, inherited from the military regime, some of whose members were questioned on their professional conduct by many sectors of the country. Two of them were accused by the newly installed House of Deputies of gravely shirking their duties and were sued by the Senate. One of them was impeached. Besides these extreme cases, the Supreme Court constituted the biggest obstacle in the legislative reform of the judiciary, which the government of President Aylwin tried to carry out (J. Correa 1999).

With the idea that part of the problem that impeded the reform proposals of the democratic government was the internal legal culture of judges, a group of academics and lawyers organized conferences to understand and debate the ideas and beliefs of the judges, with the participation of some magistrates and even some superior court judges (Squella 1992, 1994). This group of scholars had maintained a high level of critical analysis of law in society, even under the dictatorship, which led many people to think that once a democratic regime was reestablished, a period of great creativity and a variety of sociolegal studies would follow. This, however, did not occur (Fuenzalida 1999).

What happened instead was an explosive growth in the number of law schools and in the number of law students, as a consequence of the proliferation of private universities that the military regime promoted before handing over its power. The number of universities that led to a career in law did not change during the military regime: five, all state run. In 1990, however, they increased to nineteen, adding fourteen private universities to the original five. In 1998, there were thirty-six: thirteen state universities and twenty-three private ones.

Applications for law careers also grew explosively. In 1973, there were something over four thousand law students; in 1990, about nine thousand. But in 1998, Chile had a grand total of nearly twenty-five thousand law students, the majority registered at private universities.

Obviously, internal legal culture is related to legal education, but the growth in the number of law schools, their wide distribution across the country, and the growth in the number of law students do not necessarily contribute to a change in internal legal culture. The effectiveness of the expansion depends on the renovation of the curriculum and professorial quality. According to a recent study (Zavala 1999), new law schools have reproduced the established curriculum and have contracted successful lawyers to teach their courses, which means that it is unlikely that a new internal legal culture would come from these schools. There are exceptions to the general rule: the law schools of Diego Portales University in Santiago and the Atacama University in Copiapó. Postgraduate legal education could be a more efficient mechanism than undergraduate education to modify internal legal culture. This type of legal education has expanded considerably (see Figure 4.1), though the initial impetus waned during the years of transition from a military to a civilian government and only began a resurgence in 1992. On the other hand, postgraduate legal education has emphasized legal spe-

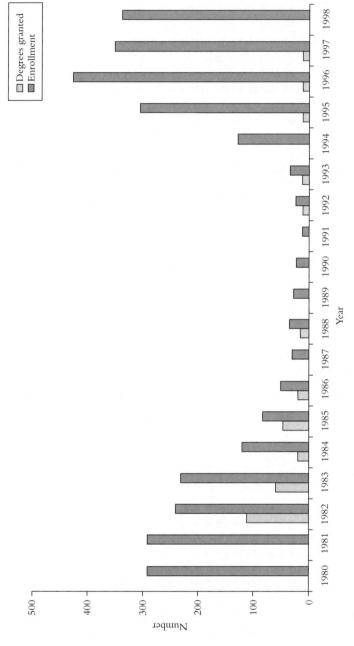

FIGURE 4.1 Postgraduate Courses in Law at Chilean Universities: Total Enrollment and Degrees Obtained, 1990–1998
Source: Herrera (1999), based on statistics from the Rector's Council.

cialization over reconstructing the approach to law and legal institutions (Herrera 1999).

Under the military regime, the infrastructure of the legal system was ignored, though studies to improve the administration of justice were carried out, and some civil courts were given computer equipment that allowed the public direct access to the status of their suits.

After 1990, democratic governments made a systematic effort at improving the infrastructure of the legal system, raising the percentage of the national budget earmarked for the judiciary, with the aim of duplicating that percentage in five more years. Expenses for modernization and technology grew (in 1999 pesos) to more than double the first budget designed by the democratic government of President Aylwin between 1991 and 1992. Then it doubled again between 1997 and 1998, during the presidency of Eduardo Frei Ruiz-Tagle. Something similar happened with infrastructure. Between 1990 and 1999, the fiscal contribution to the judiciary rose 199 percent (Correa 1999).

With these new resources, buildings have been constructed for the courts, both in the metropolitan region and in other regions, equipped with appropriate technology. Special attention has been given to modernizing prison infrastructure, constructing new jails, and repairing old ones. In general, new democratic governments gradually raised fiscal appropriations to the judiciary. Starting with Aylwin's presidency, the percentage of the budget destined for the judiciary rose from 0.57 percent in 1991 to 0.94 percent in 1999. In 1999 money, the appropriations rose from 2,701,350 pesos in 1978 to 7,066,912 pesos in 1999 (see Figure 4.2). Democratic governments understood that it was necessary to raise the traditionally low salaries of judicial functionaries in Chile. The salaries of ministers of the Supreme Court and of the courts of appeals rose sharply between 1980 and 1999, in 1999 currency (see Figure 4.3).

One of President Aylwin's initiatives that bore fruit was the creation of the Judicial Academy, devoted to the education of future judges and to the betterment of present ones. The idea of creating a judicial school was not new. Under the military regime in 1983, the Ministry of Justice had planned a judicial school. A set of regulations was drafted but not put into force. Professor Antonio Bascuñán of the University of Chile and Professor Hernán Correa de la Cerda, the main force behind the idea, both drafted projects of long-distance training in the early 1990s. The University of Chile offered a master's degree in judicial law in the 1980s. Two private organizations, the Centro de Estudios Publicos and the Corporación de Promoción Universitaria, and one of the new private universities, Diego Portales, sponsored preparatory studies for the creation of a judicial academy.

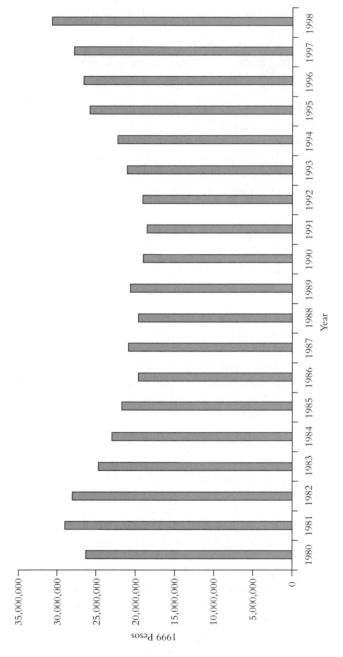

FIGURE 4.2 Total Annual Salary of Justices of the Supreme Court

Source: Department of Human Resources, Administrative Corporation of the Judiciary.

Note: Values calculated on the basis of a UF mean value in December of the previous year; UF (*unidad de fomento* or "unit of promotion or fomentation") is the unit of calculation used to correct public and private debts for inflation, in pesos, and is published daily by the Central Bank; as of August 9, 1999, UF = $14,911.00.

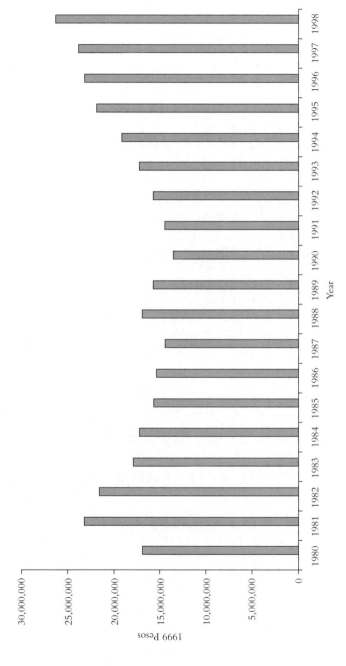

FIGURE 4.3 Salaries of Justices of the Courts of Appeals

Source: Department of Human Resources, Administrative Corporation of the Judiciary.

TABLE 4.1

Recourses of Protection

				Recourses of protection						Population	
Year	Submitted	% Rise	Finished petitions	No information	Accepted	Denied	Abandoned	Other	Total Partial	Population	% Rise
1980	155		132	6	28	90	2	6	126	1,1146,726	
1981	315	103	330	11	41	238	23	17	319	1,1318,558	1.5
1982	495	219	365	7	36	272	44	6	358	1,1492,991	3.1
1983	530	241	492	12	87	299	22	72	480	1,1671,524	4.7
1984	787	407	710	83	87	473	34	33	627	1,1855,655	6.4
1985	920	493	855	116	123	542	56	18	739	1,2046,884	8.1
1986	1,102	610	1,161	175	200	695	83	8	986	1,2246,720	9.8
1987	1,127	627	1,052	142	189	641	68	12	910	1,2454,160	11.7
1988	1,234	696	1,395	272	181	771	140	31	1,123	1,2666,946	13.6
1989	1,654	967	1,395	272	181	771	140	31	1,123	1,2882,818	15.6
Total	8,319		7,887	1,096	1,153	4,792	612	234	6,791		
%					17	71	9	3	100		

SOURCE: Ramírez (1999).

Nevertheless, it took until November 18, 1994, to pass Law 19.346, which formally established the Judicial Academy, given the task of training future judges and perfecting present ones. The prerequisites to enter were having Chilean citizenship, having earned a law degree, not being included in the exceptions list (that is, not having a criminal record), and having performed well academically during the five years of study and the final exam. Also, prospective students were tested with analyses of concrete cases and with a psychological evaluation.

By 1999, the Judicial Academy had around 160 alumni, 66 of whom were already in the court system, either as judges, secretaries, or court reporters. The academy has developed a methodology in its teaching, including internships in the courts. During this time, the student is guided by a mentor judge who allows him or her to participate in proceedings and in decisions. These mentor judges have previously received the training necessary to be a tutor. Further, the school hosts workshops and seminars where technical topics are discussed and holds court simulations of normal proceedings, such as witness interrogation.

To correct the situation inherited from the military regime, the governments of the Democratic Alliance have sent various law proposals to Congress that would give new rights to citizens or would protect nonrenewable resources subject to intensive exploitation. Nevertheless, the public tends not to get excited concerning the judiciary, despite the important reforms and innovations approved by Congress, because an external legal culture has been formed in which the legal system and its functionaries are held in low esteem (Correa and Barros 1993).

As mentioned earlier, the 1980 constitution created a "recourse of protection" that should have been used broadly by citizens whose rights were affected. This, in fact, has occurred, according to a study that includes all of the appeals courts of the country during the 1980–89 period (that is, still under a military regime) and shows that the number of these petitions rose year after year, at a rate much faster than the growth of the population (Ramírez 1999). Nevertheless, as if to prove the overwhelming negative public opinion about the conduct of the judiciary, 71 percent of those petitions were denied (see Table 4.1).

The situation did not change with the transition to a civilian government in 1990. In a study of this legal instrument that covers the first five years of civilian government (1990–95), the number of recourses of protection presented to the Appeals Court of Santiago rose considerably, from 224 in 1990 to 546 in 1991, and to 632 in 1992; but then it fell to 511 in 1993, and to 312 in 1994 (González 1999). It is natural to relate the falling number with the answers given by the appeals court to these petitions. More than 80 percent were denied or declared inadmissible (see Figure 4.4).

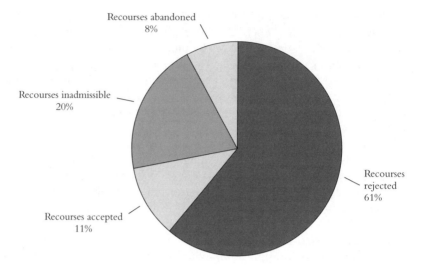

Recourses abandoned
8%

Recourses inadmissible
20%

Recourses
rejected
61%

Recourses accepted
11%

FIGURE 4.4 Comparison of Results Obtained with Recourses of Protection, 1980–1998
Source: Gonzalez (1993).

Another similar case is Law 19.325 (August 27, 1994) against intrafamilial violence, whose detailed ruling is stated by Supreme Decree 1415 (February 5, 1996). This law represents a great advance over common penal legislation, as much substantively as procedurally, in terms of precisely defining the concept of intrafamilial violence, facilitating its denunciation to authorities, giving jurisdiction to the civil judge (and not to the criminal judge), and establishing special sanctions. With respect to what intrafamilial violence comprises, the law states in its first article: "Intrafamilial violence is understood as every bad treatment which affects the physical or mental health of that person who, being of age, has a relationship with the offender, in the quality of older relative, spouse, or live-in, or, being under age or incapacitated, has the relationship of descendant, adoptee, pupil, blood relative to four generations, or is under the care and dependency of whoever lives under the same roof."

The act of intrafamilial violence can be denounced not only by the victim or his or her relatives but also by anyone who has direct knowledge of the facts, without need of a lawyer. The denunciation can be oral or written and can be presented to the civil judge with jurisdiction over the area where the victim lives, to the *carabineros* (preventive uniformed police), or to the investigative police. The judge who receives the denunciation is to draft a summons or subpoena within the next eight days. The law allows the judge to also adopt immediate precautionary measures, such as enjoining the offender from entering the home or authorizing the victim to abandon the home. Once the hearing is initiated, it should continue until it is concluded, even extending to the next day. The judge can try to induce the parties to reconcile, but if this is not achieved, he or she must hear the merits of the case. Given proof, the judge must call the parties to hear the sentence or can order measures to better resolve the problem within three days. The sentence has to be dictated at the end of the hearing or at a maximum of ten days later. Concerning sanctions, the judge can punish the offender with prison, in whichever grade—minimum, medium, or maximum—with a fine, or with obligatory attendance at a therapy or family orientation program for up to six months.

The enforcement of this intrafamilial violence law has not satisfied the high expectations under which it was written. One indicator of this is the variation in the number of denunciations presented. According to the carabineros, denunciations by women rose from 34,094 in 1996 to 38,671 in 1997, but fell to only 24,408 in 1998. In the case of men and children, one can see the same slow rise followed by a fall. In the case of the elderly, denunciations fell to 220 in 1996, to 181 in 1997, and to only 82 in 1998. This "retreat" of victims from the courts appears to be related to the refusal of judges to dictate precautionary measures when they find out about an episode of intrafamilial violence during the hearing, allowing the offender to continue to persecute his or her victim. According to journalists, other factors could be that the judge's decision is announced very late and that the judicial preference is to reconcile the victim and the offender. To confront this situation, the government has created an interministerial committee that has taken various steps: the creation of a Task Force on the Family by the carabineros and an office for the reception and distribution of the denunciations among the twenty-three civil judges of Santiago; preferential treatment of victims of intrafamilial violence in hospitals; training actuaries, judges, and police officers; and preparing instructional material for students in primary schools about nonviolent means of conflict resolution.

Something similar occurred—that is, the public's expectations were not met—with regard to Law 19.335 (September 23, 1994), which created a new property regime for married couples in addition to the traditional one, called "participation in earnings." The public's demand for the new regime has been minimal.

Historically, the system of the "regime of conjugal society" (RSC) has been preferred, although there is a rising tendency toward the "separation of property" system (RSB). When the law allowed for a "participation in earnings" (RPG) system, it was thought that it would be accepted broadly, but this was not so, as one can see in Figure 4.5 (Saavedra 1999).

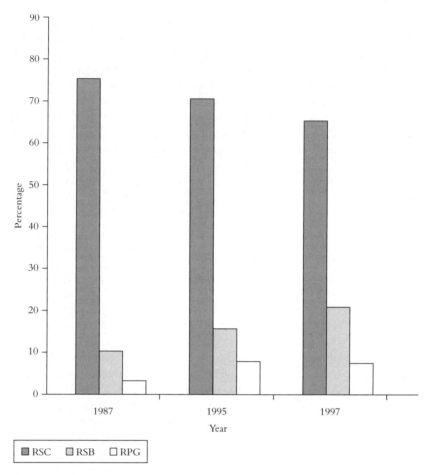

FIGURE 4.5 Regimes Analyzed by Year
Source: Saavedra (1999).
Note: RSC: regime of conjugal society; RSB: regime of separation of property; RPG: regime of participation in earnings.

Similar results occurred regarding other laws enacted by the democratic governments, such as Law 19.300 (March 9, 1994), which concerns general principles for environmental protection, specified by Supreme Decrees 86, 93, and 94 (all from October 26, 1995), and further defined by the regulations on Environmental Impact, dictated by Supreme Decree 30 (April 3, 1997). Other cases are those of the law against violence in football stadiums;

the law on siblings, which concedes equality of rights to all offspring, born in or out of wedlock; and that on freedom of religion.

One of the most notable initiatives of President Frei has been the reform of the penal process. According to the reform, the inquisitorial, written procedure will be replaced by an oral, accusatory procedure. To make this possible, a new agency was created, the Public Ministry, which, through the national attorney general and the regional attorneys, will direct police investigations of crimes and will bring those presumably responsible for them before the courts. The Public Defender's Office was also created to give indigents accused of crimes adequate defense of their rights. The Judge of Guarantee was established to oversee the criminal process and to ensure that the rights of the accused are respected.

Conclusions and Answers to the Questions

The legal system was no obstacle to the policies of the military government, which were directed at eliminating its adversaries and imposing a new normative mold for human life on the country. In particular, the courts of appeal, directed by the Supreme Court, denied the numerous habeas corpus petitions submitted to help those who were detained by the armed forces or the police and who were not brought before a judge. Acting in this way, the courts did not follow through with their constitutional and legal obligations, and graver still, caused the citizenry to lose confidence in the idea that there existed an institution of the state to which they could turn to protest abuses committed by government functionaries. That is to say, they helped destroy the legacy of the history of a country respectful of the law and of human rights.

It must be emphasized that this harsh judgment refers to the legal system as a system, and not to each of those involved in it, many of whom did what they could to protect the rights and the lives of the citizenry. Not all judges were insensitive to the tragedy that the country endured during the dictatorship, and when democracy was restored, many dedicated themselves to giving justice. There were judges who did not deserve their high positions (from which they benefited), but to generalize about the entire judiciary from these few is a step that should not be taken, considering the facts. For example, under the democratic regime, Adolfo Bañados, minister of the Supreme Court, indicted retired general Manuel Contreras for his role as leader of DINA, the military government's secret police, and his dedication and drive led to a seven-year prison sentence for the accused.

The Order of Lawyers lost its public character, and many of its members continued to work in their profession, showing little interest in the global situation of the country, with its lack of certainty and legal security during the military dictatorship. There were, nevertheless, a relatively large group of lawyers that, ignoring their own professional progress, dedicated themselves to working with the Vicariate of Solidarity, receiving petitions about arbitrary detentions and disappearances. Others did so on their own time, running serious risks. Special recognition goes to the lawyers that formed the Committee of 24, with the goal of monitoring the work of the Commission of Jurists designated by the military government to draft a new constitution and formulate alternatives to its proposals.

Law professors continued teaching as they had done before the institutional crisis, emphasizing the acquisition of legal dexterity and ability more than the acquisition of liberal and democratic values. It is again necessary to point out the exceptions: law professors who pushed themselves to perpetuate the sense of law as a guarantee of liberty, and some law schools in private universities, such as Diego Portales University.

The collective effort to return to the rule of law under the new constitution of 1980, which included "authoritarian enclaves" that could not be eliminated because the government lacked a necessary majority in Congress, had an undesired effect in the external legal culture: a mix of fear of returning to an era of violent confrontations and a growing disillusionment with the capacity of democratic governments to bring to justice those responsible for violations of human rights during the military regime. Public opinion viewed the judges, with some notable exceptions, as not having put the necessary energy in the search of "detainees–disappeared persons" and their persecutors. In particular, the former military officers seemed to be outside the reach of ordinary justice.

This environment changed radically after Pinochet, the former president of the republic and senator for life, was detained in London on October 16, 1998, at the petition of the Spanish judge Baltasar Garzón, who wanted to submit him to trial in Spain for his responsibility in the violation of human rights during his government. The legal battle that began then and that, as of 2002, created fear for the institutional stability of the country because of the nationalistic reaction of many Chileans who saw in these actions of both Spanish and British judges a violation of Chilean national sovereignty. After some tense months, the internal political situation calmed down, but now with an extremely important difference with respect to the previous situation: the new conviction of the external legal culture that no one is above the law. If the Chilean legal system could not, for internal political reasons, prosecute Pinochet, the world's legal system would do it.[6] This new conviction had immediate consequences: starting prosecutions against those alleged to be responsible for violations of human rights, and the filing of numerous criminal suits against the former dictator. It also permitted the rapid election of the first national attorney, the head of the new Public Ministry responsible for the prosecution of crimes.

In this way, at the end of this traumatic period in the life of the law and legal culture in Chile, the legal system can be said to be moving, pushed by the external legal culture, slowly but surely toward its reconstruction as an integral part of a new democracy.

Notes

1. The literature is vast. The most recent works are more balanced than earlier works. See Moulian (1997), Jocelyn-Holt (1998), and Menendez and Joignant (1999). For a well-qualified witness of national developments, see De la Parra (1998).

2. I recognize the great influence of Lawrence Friedman (1975) in my theoretical analysis. Nevertheless, I alone am responsible for the definitions and their use.

3. I have broadly developed the idea that, in Chile, there are five generations in the second half of the twentieth century and that there exists a great difference in the "political culture" between the first two and the last three (see Fuenzalida 2001).

4. This norm would be later modified, and the presidential period would be fixed at six years, without reelection.

5. At the beginning of the presidential administration of Lagos, the political forces of the government and the opposition negotiated a constitutional reform that attempted to achieve two goals: give Aylwin the status of senator for life and allow for resignation from that status, something not contemplated in the constitution adopted during Pinochet's administration. They wanted to facilitate the exit of the former dictator from Parliament. They therefore debated a new question: Did the status of "ex-president" and "retired senator" confer two sets of powers, one for each position? To solve the impasse, President Lagos initiated a new project that clarified that point and left Pinochet subject to a resolution to remove such power, just as any former president or parliamentarian would be.

6. In March 2000, a week before the installation of President Lagos, General Pinochet was freed by Jack Straw, the British interior minister. Straw interrupted Pinochet's extradition process, initiated by Judge Garzón, declaring that for health reasons, Pinochet would be incapable of facing prosecution in Spain. Once in Chile, Pinochet found himself facing a large number of criminal suits (ninety-four at the time this chapter was completed) handled by the minister of the Appeals Court of Santiago, Juan Guzmán Tapia.

References

Correa, Jorge. 1999. Cenicienta se queda en la fiesta: El poder judicial chileno en la década de los 90. Pp. 281–315 in *El modelo chileno: Democracia y desarrollo en los noventa*, edited by Paul Drake and Iván Jaksic. Santiago: LOM.

Correa, Jorge, and Luis Barros, eds. 1993. *Justicia y marginalidad: Percepción de los pobres.* Santiago: Corporación de Promoción Universitaria.

Correa, Luis. 1999. *El aporte fiscal al poder judicial en los gobiernos democráticos: Años 1978 a 1999.* Santiago: Escuela de Graduados, Facultad de Derecho de la Universidad de Chile.

Cuneo, Andrés. 1980. La Corte Suprema de Chile, sus percepciones acerca del Derecho, su rol en el sistema legal y la relación de éste con el sistema político. Pp. 71–83 in *La administración de justicia en América Latina*, edited by Consejo Latinoamericano de Derecho y Desarrollo. San José de Costa Rica: Universidad de Costa Rica.

De la Parra, Marco Antonio. 1998. *La mala memoria: Historia personal de Chile contemporáneo.* Santiago: Planeta.

Friedman, Lawrence. 1975. *The legal system: A social science perspective.* New York: Russell Sage Foundation.

Fuenzalida, Edmundo. 1996. El sistema jurídico chileno ante la globalización. *Anuario de Filosofía Jurídica y Social* 14:331–40.

———. 1997. La investigación básica en derecho y sociedad: Un enfoque de sociología de la ciencia sobre el caso de Chile. *Anuario de Filosofía Jurídica y Social* 15: 225–40.

———. 1999. Dictatorship, democracy and legal scholarship. Paper presented to the World Congress of Sociology of Law, Warsaw and Cracow, July.

———. 2001. *Generaciones políticas en Chile: Bases para entender la generación del Bicentenario.* Santiago: Cuadernos del Segundo Centenario, 16, Centro de Estudios para el Desarrollo (CED).

Gonzalez, Moisés. 1999. *El recurso de protección y el sistema jurídico chileno.* Santiago: Escuela de Graduados, Facultad de Derecho de la Universidad de Chile.

Herrera, Matías. 1999. *Evolución de los estudios de postgrado en derecho en las universidades chilenas en los últimos veinte años.* Santiago: Escuela de Graduados, Facultad de Derecho de la Universidad de Chile.

Jocelyn-Holt, Alfredo. 1997. *El peso de la noche: Nuestra frágil fortaleza histórica.* Santiago: Planeta/Ariel.

———. 1998. *El Chile perplejo: Del avanzar sin transar al transar sin parar.* Santiago: Planeta/Ariel.

Menendez-Carrión, Amparo, and Alfredo Joignant, eds. 1999. *La caja de Pandora: El retorno de la transición chilena.* Santiago: Planeta/Ariel.

Moulian, Tomás. 1997. *Chile actual: Anatomía de un mito.* Santiago: LOM–Universidad de Artes y Ciencias (ARCIS).

Ramírez, Cristián. 1999. *Recurso de protección: Análisis comparativo del número de recursos interpuestos frente al aumento de la población chilena, 1980–1989.* Santiago: Escuela de Graduados, Facultad de Derecho de la Universidad de Chile.

Saavedra, Ricardo. 1999. *Innovaciones al régimen de bienes del matrimonio: Consideraciones sobre su efectivo impacto: Estudio sobre la realidad de Valparaíso en los años 1987, 1995 y 1997.* Santiago: Escuela de Graduados, Facultad de Derecho de la Universidad de Chile.

Squella, Agustín, ed. 1992. *La cultura jurídica chilena.* Santiago: Corporación de Promoción Universitaria.

———. 1994. *Evolución de la cultura jurídica chilena.* Santiago: Corporación de Promoción Universitaria.

Zavala, José Luis. 1999. *Evolución de la oferta de enseñanza del derecho en los últimos 25 años.* Santiago: Escuela de Graduados, Facultad de Derecho de la Universidad de Chile.

CHAPTER 5

Justice and Society in Colombia:
A Sociolegal Analysis of Colombian Courts

CÉSAR A. RODRÍGUEZ, MAURICIO GARCÍA-VILLEGAS,
AND RODRIGO UPRIMNY

IN THE LAST decades, the Colombian judicial system has not only experienced profound transformations but has also forcefully entered the political scene. Thus, many institutional reforms, some of them linked to the 1991 constitution, have profoundly modified the judicial system. Likewise, the judiciary has acquired an unusual salience because the debate about judicial reform has turned into one of the principal topics in the political agenda and because judicial decisions have in many cases had a considerable impact on Colombian politics and society. This protagonism was illustrated by the events of the political crisis during President Ernesto Samper's administration (1994–98). President Samper's actions were investigated by a judicial body, the attorney general's office (*Fiscalía*), and numerous judicial actors, through their declarations and decisions, occupied a central place in the different events of the protracted crisis.[1]

The activism of the judiciary is a recent phenomenon in Colombia. In

The research project on which this chapter is based was conducted by the authors within the context of a broader project about justice in Colombia directed by Boaventura de Sousa Santos and Mauricio García-Villegas. The results of this broader project can be found in Santos and García-Villegas (2001b). The articles on which the present text is based and that form part of the broader project are Uprimny (2001), Rodríguez (2001a), García-Villegas and Rodríguez (2001), Santos (2001a), Santos and García-Villegas (2001a), and Rubio (2001). The theoretical framework and research methodology of this study are the fruit of a nearly five-year joint work project with Boaventura de Sousa Santos, whose study about justice in Portugal (Santos et al. 1996) and influence as the director of the Colombian project were decisive in the orientation and the realization of our investigation. This work would not have been possible without Santos's generous support and dedication, over many years, to build a community of sociologists of law in Colombia.

the past, judges were not at the center of political debates, nor were they a particularly attractive study area for academics. This was so partly because judicial practices were seen as a variable dependent on other social processes, such as the evolution of the economy or political struggles. The current centrality of justice is not exclusive to Colombia. Judicial protagonism has taken hold in countries around the world (Santos 2001a, 2001b).[2] Nevertheless, in Colombia the judicial theme has acquired an unusual academic and political importance. This is demonstrated by the fact that justice has been one of the axes of all the political and constitutional reforms of the last twenty years and that the scholarly studies in this area have grown notably (Rodríguez and Uprimny 2003; Nemogá 1995).

Such growing scholarly attention to justice in Colombia is partly the result of the intensification of violence and the salience of political corruption, which are often attributed to the inefficiency and weakness of the judicial system. This weakness is a symptom of a broader phenomenon—that is, the structural precariousness of the Colombian state (González 1989; Pécaut 1997), which, to some authors, verges on the possibility of the collapse of state institutions (Hoskin 1988). This situation explains the enormous number of crimes that go unpunished, which has led people and organizations both on the right and the left to clamor for judicial reform, particularly concerning criminal courts. Whereas some propose such a reform as a part of a probusiness agenda seeking to create the political stability and economic conditions conducive to private investment (Montenegro and Posada 1994), others do so to ensure the punishment of the crimes of the powerful and of serious violations of human rights (Comisión Andina de Juristas 1992).

In this chapter, we set out to offer an account of some of the most important transformations of the judicial system from the mid-1980s and of their impact on the political process and on democracy in Colombia. We prefer to speak of "transformations" rather than of "reforms" to show that the actual changes have not always corresponded to the plans of the reformers. For example, originally the *Fiscalía General de la Nación* and the introduction of the adversarial system in Colombia were proposed by the authoritarian sectors, which were interested in increasing the executive's interference in criminal investigations.[3] Nevertheless, the modifications to the original project introduced by the Constitutional Assembly of 1991 placed the Fiscalía in the judicial branch. A hybrid was created, which has enormous risks but also great virtues. This body has assumed positions and conducted investigations that compromise governmental responsibility and that would not have been possible if the initial proposal, whereby its head, the *fiscal general*, would have been appointed and removed freely by the president, had triumphed. Ironically, one of the figures that most fervently defended the Fiscalía's independence in the Constitutional Assembly was Horacio Serpa, who later became the key defender of President Samper during the above-mentioned political crisis. Without the Fiscalía's autonomy, there probably would not have been a case brought against the president, nor a political crisis.

In the following discussion, we examine such transformations by highlighting the paradoxical character of the recent evolution of justice in Colombia. On the one hand, as noted previously, some sectors of the judicial system have gained great political salience and visibility. On the other hand, some parts of the judiciary have become or remained highly routinized and socially irrelevant. To flesh out this contrast, we will divide the remainder of this chapter into four parts. First, we will describe the generalities of the transformation of the judicial system and the social context in which it operates. Second, based on primary empirical research, we will focus on the visible, activist sector of the judiciary, specifically on the role of constitutional justice in the protection of fundamental rights. Third, we will look at the evidence on the operation of civil and criminal courts to illustrate the relative invisibility and routinization of some sectors of the judiciary. Finally, we will offer some conclusions.

Society, Politics, and Courts in Colombia

A cogent sociolegal account of justice in Colombia must begin by specifying the social context in which courts operate—and which they also help to shape. Thus, in this section we will begin by sketching the central long-term trends of Colombian politics and society. Thereafter, we will focus on the recent social and political changes and examine the transformations of the judicial system.

LONG-TERM TRENDS IN COLOMBIAN SOCIETY AND POLITICS

Colombia is a complex and paradoxical country that for a long time escaped the theoretical generalizations about peripheral capitalism and Latin America. From a political point of view, although military intervention has been a constant in Latin America's history, Colombia has experienced very few years of military dictatorship in its nearly 180 years of independent life. According to the English historian Malcom Deas, "[T]his Republic has been the scene of more elections, under more systems than any other Latin American or European country which could pretend to contend for the title" (1973, 29). Similarly, although institutional instability has been a common feature of Latin America's history, Colombia has been characterized by the surprising stability of its political system. As Rouquié (1984) has pointed out, Colombia's bipartisan system enjoyed throughout the twentieth century a constitutional continuity that rarely occurs on this continent.

This political continuity was accompanied by considerable economic stability, at least when measured against the parameters of Latin American capitalism. In Colombia, the economic cycles have been less extreme than those in other countries of the region. Both economic expansions and recessions have been relatively mild. Indeed, while most Latin Americans have lived through dramatic economic downturns throughout the last quarter of the twentieth century, Colombians came to experience such a situation only in the late 1990s, when the country plunged into its worst economic crisis since the 1930s.

Nevertheless, political and economic stability has not led to a greater democratization. On the contrary, stability has promoted an exclusionary development in which the "dominance of the oligarchy has been more solidly established than in other parts" (Touraine 1976, 85). Neither has this stability led to peace in social relations. Violence and armed conflicts have been recurrent. As a result, the current Colombian homicide rate as measured per 100,000 inhabitants—more than 80—is much greater than the same rate for such countries as the United States, Mexico, Brazil, and Sri Lanka, which are generally considered to be violent countries. In fact, Colombia's homicide rate is ten times greater than that of the United States, three times that of Brazil, and four times that of Mexico (Montenegro and Posada 1994; Uprimny 1993).

Colombia has also lived through numerous internal armed conflicts in both the nineteenth and twentieth centuries. Particularly, in the 1950s, Colombia endured the period known as *La Violencia* (The Violence), which pitted the armed groups of the liberal and conservative parties against each other and which deeply affected all Colombian society, especially in the countryside. During the most critical years of that period—between 1948 and 1950—more than 1 percent of the population, or around 110,000 people, were assassinated (Oquist 1978, 321). Also, over the course of the last three decades, a guerrilla war has been developing in the country with increasing intensity.

Nevertheless, this does not mean that violence and armed conflict have been a constant of Colombia's history. There have been periods of peace—for example, between 1910 and 1945. It would be more accurate to say that there have been cycles of violence. At the end of the 1950s, the homicide rate in Colombia was very high, at 45 per 100,000 inhabitants. During the following years, the homicide rate decreased drastically. In the mid-1960s, the rate was 25 per 100,000. It then kept decreasing, though at a slower pace, to its lowest level during the mid-1970s. From that period on, the homicide rate started to increase anew, at the beginning slowly, but then much more rapidly, especially during the second half of the 1980s. As a result, in 1990 the homicide rate was considerably higher than at the end of the 1950s.

The combination of a lack of militarism and political and economic stability with the persistence of inequality, poverty, armed conflicts, and violence is noteworthy. In addition to these paradoxical traits is the existence of a precarious and low-profile state, which is also singular. In fact, although in many semiperipheral and peripheral countries there has been a tendency toward what some authors have labeled an "overdevelopment" of the state's structures (Evers 1977), in Colombia the state's intervention into Colombian society has been negligible. Due to the absence of political modernization and to an incomplete construction of the national identity, the Colombian state has not been able to differentiate its interests from those of the dominant economic and political sectors. The state has not successfully mediated and institutionalized social conflicts because it has been unable to appear as the representative of the general interests of all of society's groups. As Fernán González puts it, "[T]he state concluded by coinciding with the hegemony of one of the two parties, or with the cohabitation of both in power, which impeded the creation of a modern bureaucracy" (1989, 9). In addition, the generalization of the practices of clientelism, which privatized the management of public resources through patron-client relations between politicians and their constituencies, has broken the "differentiation between the public and the private, which is expressed by a marked privatization and fragmentation of power" (12). According to Touraine, due to the long hegemony of the Colombian oligarchy, "the state does not appear differentiated from the social and political forces" (1988, 445). The precariousness of the state on the political front has been accompanied by a traditionally low level of intervention in the economy relative to the intervention characteristic of other Latin American states (Kalmanovitz 1988).[4]

Finally, popular movements in Colombia have been very weak, a weakness caused by certain evolutions in particular. Some historians point to the parochialism of Colombian politics. The absence of strong European immigration during the republican era in Colombia, in contrast to countries such as Venezuela, Chile, or Argentina, precluded Colombia from assimilating the socialist and revolutionary ideology. Other studies have emphasized the capacity of bipartisanism to coopt the popular and opposition movements, as well as the particularities of the coffee economy that have created a historical structural weakness of the Colombian working-class and peasant movements (Berquist 1988).

Now it is possible to establish some connections between these traits in order to attempt to explain the logic of the "Colombian paradox." The precariousness of the constitution of a modern bourgeois state does not imply instability. This is due to the existence of very effective decentralized mechanisms of dominance founded on the clientelist and patrimonial control of the population. Bipartisanism's role in the framing of the subaltern classes was central, although it impeded the formation of a modern state capable of mediating social conflicts.

The stability of state institutions also gained from the lack of strong divisions within the ruling class. In Colombia, due to the peculiarities of the coffee economy that permitted the convergence of interests between industrialists, bankers, exporters, and large landowners, there did not exist the acute conflicts between agricultural exporters and industrialists that occurred in countries such as Argentina and Brazil. This is explained by the fact that in the Antioquia and Caldas regions, the commercial monopoly of coffee exporters was based in large part on their control of an industrial activity—the *trilla* (the grinding and processing of coffee beans)—which led to a great homogeneity of interests between agricultural exporters and antioqueño industrialists, who oftentimes were part of the same families (Arango 1981, 214; Kalmanovitz 1988, 240).

At the same time, this bourgeoisie was peculiar—in contrast to other dominant classes in Latin America—because it apparently did not need the state to organize itself and, thus, attempted to take the defense of its interests away from sectarian party conflicts. This meant that partisan politics was not the mechanism through which the dominant classes expressed and advanced their interests. To further their interests, they relied on semiprivate organizations—business associations (*gremios*)—especially after the failed state-led modernization of the 1930s.

In sum, three elements converge to explain the coexistence of institutional stability and the precarious constitution of the national state in Colombia: (1) effective, albeit relatively decentralized, mechanisms of control of the population, represented paradigmatically by the institutionalization of bipartisanism between the late 1950s and the early 1970s under the so-called National Front (*Frente Nacional*); (2) great cohesion among the sectors of the ruling class, notwithstanding their partisan divisions; and (3) functioning mechanisms of articulation of interests among factions of the ruling class wherein the state as an autonomous power plays a minimal role. The joint effect of these elements has given rise to a precarious state subject to cooptation and control by the ruling class, and, at the same time, to relative political stability, given the hegemonic consensus within the ruling class and the control of the subaltern classes. In addition, these elements help explain the absence of sudden turns in Colombian politics, as social conflicts do not play themselves out in the political arena. Stability, however, is achieved at a high cost—that of the dramatic separation between the political and the social. Politics does not function as a field of mediation for social conflicts, which are thus solved by other, often violent, means.

RECENT DEVELOPMENTS: THE GOVERNABILITY CRISIS

Since the end of the 1970s, such paradoxical stability has been affected by multiple factors. First, the erosion of the Catholic Church's ideological and political leverage and of the population's political loyalty to the traditional parties, as well as urbanization and an increment in education levels, undermined the effectiveness of the traditional mechanisms of dominance by eroding the ideological context that sustained the legitimacy of the partisan division, which conferred a natural appearance to social inequalities.

Second, in the 1970s, the military gained greater autonomy in controlling public order and considerably increased its influence on the state apparatuses, thus accentuating the fragmentation of the political regime. Indeed, according to some analysts, one of the reasons for Colombian political stability, especially during the period known as the National Front that started in 1958, was the "partitioning of the state among the dominant agents" (Gallón 1989). This partition sought to avoid conflicts within the different factions in power, assuring the most powerful social contenders the control of a predetermined state parcel—that is, public administration to the liberal and conservative parties, the economy to the business associations, and public order to the military. Unsurprisingly, this distribution has tended to translate itself into growing institutional fragmentation.

Third, the guerrilla movements, which had ebbed in the early 1970s, considerably increased their bellicose and territorial presence in the 1980s and 1990s. This increase was accompanied by the development of the *guerra sucia* (dirty war), associated with the emergence of paramilitary groups that, drawing on the complicity of sectors of the military and the support of large landowners and drug traffickers, spread across vast spans of the Colombian territory. While ostensibly pretending to combat the guerrillas by undermining their social support, the paramilitary groups' actions affect large sectors of civil society and give rise to gross violations of human rights. Given these circumstances, the Colombian state, which never truly achieved control of its territory nor effectively monopolized the exercise of coercion, is now being confronted by powerful, armed actors, with which it has very complex relationships of confrontation, dialogue, and even cooperation. Therefore, the population finds itself under the cross fire of the diverse armed actors in conflict—that is, institutional armed forces, paramilitary groups, drug traffickers, insurgent guerrilla forces, and other forms of private violence.

Fourth, all these transformations took place during a time when drug trafficking caused profound changes in Colombian society. Drug money gave rise to the reconfiguration of the economy, society, and politics, while providing the means for the expansion of both guerrilla and paramilitary groups (Uprimny 1994).

Finally, the international context changed and modified the insertion of Colombia into the global dynamic. On the one hand, the processes of economic restructuring associated with globalization have led to the modification of the Colombian economic growth model in the direction of neoliberalism. These changes started taking shape during the Barco government (1986–90) and were consolidated during the Gaviria administration (1990–94). On the other hand, U.S. pressure on Colombia increased in many areas as the war on drugs obtained greater international importance during the Reagan and the first Bush administrations. In addition, with the end of the cold war, the alleged threat posed by drug trafficking and organized crime started to play the ideological role that the communist threat had played earlier. This led the United States to reconsider its role in global politics and to reevaluate its ties to its traditional allies, among them Colombia.

The combined effect of these factors has provoked a growing institutional and economic instability. Consequently, Colombia faces a deep governability crisis and since the 1980s has entered into a turbulent and uncertain phase. Diverse strategies have been developed to deal with these problems. In some periods, the politics of authoritarian control of the public order have been favored, through ample concessions of power to the military and strong restrictions on human rights. At other times, processes of political openness and negotiation with the insurgent groups have been attempted. Within this context, the 1990 election of a Constitutional Assembly with the purpose of writing a new constitution that would reestablish and legitimize the political order in Colombia was of particular importance. The assembly had a pluralist composition, as indicated by the participation of members of the traditional parties as well as demobilized guerrillas and representatives of social and religious groups traditionally excluded from Colombian politics, such as indigenous groups and religious minorities. As will be discussed later, the assembly also introduced important political and institutional innovations.

Nevertheless, the war continued because only a few guerrilla groups turned over their guns and assimilated into civil life. Moreover, during the Samper administration (1994–98), Colombia faced a grave political crisis, which was unleashed by accusations that the Cali cartel had contributed to the president's campaign and that of other politicians (Leal 1996). The effects of endemic violence and institutional fragmentation have been compounded during the current Pastrana administration (1998–2002) by the unleashing of a deep economic recession and the continuation of the civil war, despite the government's efforts at promoting negotiation with the major guerrilla groups. It is within this complex social and political setting that the historical characteristics and recent transformations of the Colombian judicial apparatus must be understood.

THE HISTORICAL FEATURES OF THE COLOMBIAN JUDICIARY

During the mid-1970s, the first attempts at reforming the Colombian justice system were undertaken without success. Thus, the processes of transformation truly began to materialize in the second half of the 1980s, during the Barco (1986–90) administration, and they took shape for the most part during the Gaviria administration (1990–94), due not only to the 1991 constitution but also to the numerous procedural innovations introduced through decrees issued by the executive based on state of emergency powers. Before turning to the content of such transformations, in what follows we offer a brief account of the historical features of the judiciary in Colombia, some of which were the target of the reforms attempted since the mid-1980s.

Organic autonomy and administrative dependence. The historical context in which such reforms were implemented was characterized by a widespread perception that the judiciary was in a state of crisis. Such crisis entailed, among other things, persistent court backlogs, delays, and impunity, as the analysis of criminal and civil courts offered later in this chapter will show. The inefficiency of the judicial system was particularly evident when courts had to face complex problems—for example, when criminal courts had to tackle such issues as organized crime, violations of human rights, white-collar crime, and political corruption. Contributing to this crisis was the contradictory structure of the judiciary whereby absolute organic independence was accompanied by a nearly complete administrative and financial dependence on the executive. Judicial independence had been assured since the plebiscite of 1957, which established a system whereby the justices of the highest courts appointed appellate judges, who, in turn, appointed trial judges. The political sphere, therefore, exerted no direct influence over the composition of the judicial power. For good or for bad, this peculiar system helped distance the judges from the dynamics of politics.

However, it is worth noting that the judicial system's structural autonomy was not the result of a campaign by members of the judiciary, nor was it a triumph of citizen movements in defense of the rule of law. It was not even the result of the project of a political party. Due to one of those paradoxes of Colombian history, the independence of the judicial branch is a result of the military junta of 1957. In fact, before the plebiscite that gave birth to the National Front, the justices of the Supreme Court and the State Council used to be elected for five and four years, respectively, by the legislative chambers from lists presented by the president.[5] The court elected appellate judges, who, in turn, appointed trial judges. At that time, the political body exercised great influence over the composition of the courts. The agreements between the political parties for the plebiscite did not provide for anything related to the judicial power, but the military junta proposed that an article be added to the text stating that the Supreme Court justices would have life tenure and that they should be named by the incumbent justices. According to the military, this modification was necessary to make the court independent of the executive and legislative powers and, particularly, from "a political class who because of its parties' interests had led the country into barbaric violence" (Charria Angulo 1988, 40). According to some, in this way the heads of the military junta sought to avoid the possibility that once the civil government had been reinstated, the Supreme Court, selected by Congress and, thus, influenced by the parties, would take them to trial for their support of the Rojas dictatorship. In fact, according to the constitution approved through the 1957 plebiscite, it was the Supreme Court's obligation to judge the commanding generals. The Supreme Court's self-selection mechanism considerably reduced these risks because the military junta would appoint the first justices. In this way, the military achieved the judicial power's complete organic autonomy, which neither the judges nor any political power had sought, and whose importance was initially overlooked.

Thus, it is not surprising that the judicial branch, whose structural independence was for the most part the result of a fortuitous combination of historical factors, remained budgetarily and administratively subordinate to an agency belonging to the executive branch—the *Fondo Rotatorio de Justicia*. In practice, the everyday management and the pay scales were strongly conditioned by governmental decisions, such that not until the Gaviria administration was the judicial system well budgeted.[6] It is important to remember that the absolute independence of the judicial branch can have both positive aspects and negative effects in a democratic society. In fact, the self-selection mechanism of the judicial system, in effect from the 1957 plebiscite until the 1991 constitution, gave rise to a judicial elite with aristocratic tendencies, independent from the democratic political process and controlling the appointment of all of the country's judges. In this way, the Colombian political powers did not directly influence the composition of the judicial branch, which was positive insofar as it allowed the judiciary to preserve its independence and to escape political clientelism. However, according to its most ardent critics, the self-selection mechanism created a damaging clientelism within the judicial branch itself. Such a mechanism froze the renovation of judicial interpretation, as the selection process prevented those who critically distanced themselves from the positions of the high courts from becoming part of the judicial branch.

The persistence of the state of emergency and its impact on the judiciary. The permanent use of state of emergency powers by the executive to tackle political crises—particularly those associated with violent disruptions of the public order—led to numerous reforms of different aspects of the judicial system, according to the changing views of the government on the best strategies to counter increasing violence and social fragmentation. Throughout the second half of the twentieth century, Colombian governments resorted invariably to the declaration of the state of emergency and the use of emergency legislation to reform the judiciary, particularly the criminal justice system. While most Latin American countries went through protracted dictatorships, Colombia's constitutional democratic order proved highly stable. It was, however, a peculiar constitutional regime, because the permanent recourse to state of emergency legislation meant that, in practice, many of the abstract principles incorporated in the constitution were not applied. Instead, a legality of exceptions that limited public liberties applied. From 1949, the time of La Violencia, until 1991, when the new constitution was issued, Colombia was almost permanently under a state of emergency, which allowed the president to concentrate legislative powers and suspend some constitutional rights. Indeed, for thirty-two of those forty-two years, the country lived under a state of emergency. Therefore, for the government, the judiciary, and the citizenry at large, a regime of transitory laws and exceptions became the rule.

The declaration of the state of emergency allowed for the introduction of legislation ostensibly aimed at the control of public order, particularly through the establishment of restrictive measures on the rights of free assembly, movement, and expression and limitations on organized labor's rights. It allowed, above all, for the detention and trial of political opponents, union leaders, and those who headed diverse forms of social protest before military courts of doubtful impartiality. This recourse to military justice lasted for more than twenty years, from May 1965, when this custom was established, until March 1987, when the Supreme Court declared it unconstitutional. The law gave military courts jurisdiction over 30 percent of the crimes established in the criminal code (Gallón 1979).

The common recourse to state of emergency powers and the constant legislative changes it entailed had serious consequences not only with regard to the protection of constitutional rights but also with regard to legal certainty. This translated into greater ineffectiveness in the judicial system. The preference for punitive measures downplayed other more consensual and negotiated options for resolving social conflicts. This explains the tendency to criminalize many forms of social protest with excessive punitive measures, as occurred in the application of the antiterrorist statute, which was presented as an instrument designed to confront organized crime, strikes, and student protests. It also allowed for the rise of ad hoc justice, which greatly undermined the functioning of the judicial system as a regular, stable, and efficient arena for dispute resolution. Similarly, the circumstantial nature of official state responses considerably increased the difficulty of formulating a consistent and long-term criminal policy based on democratic debate and social support.

The combined effect of the use of emergency legislation and the worsening of the civil war, entailing the growing presence of armed groups across the national territory, has given rise to a marked legal pluralism that directly affects the judicial system. At the state level, a judicial dichotomy has operated. While ordinary courts busy themselves with conflicts that do not affect the status quo, military courts and otherwise exceptional courts decide cases concerning public order and the repression of popular discontent. Moreover, in many rural areas different armed groups, which tend to develop informal structures of private justice and maintain very complex relationships with the official bodies, exert direct control. Thus, in many cases the rural paramilitary groups have acted in conjunction with the public forces. Even more surprising, in many instances guerrilla justice and the official state justice have developed, in certain rural zones, complex forms of interaction and even informal cooperation.[7]

Special features of justice in Colombia.   Finally, in order to understand the recent transformations of justice in Colombia—to which we turn in the next section of this chapter—it is important to take into account two special features of the country's judiciary in the early 1980s.

First, beginning in the mid-1970s, there were clear signs of political independence in the judiciary, which seemed to be an effect of the judiciary's structural autonomy, as well as of growing activism vis-à-vis the legislative and executive powers. Indeed, a sizable group of judges and judicial officials joined the *Asonal Judicial,* a union independent of the traditional parties. In addition, high courts became gradually more activist in controlling the actions of the political branches of government. In particular, the Supreme Court began to exert tighter constitutional control. Until that time, constitutional jurisprudence had been excessively complacent about presidential powers and had permitted long-term use of emergency powers. In the late 1970s, however, the court began to hand down decisions that had a strong impact on Colombian society and politics. The court became the target of strong criticisms levied by the political elite when it voided two constitutional reform projects and cut back the president's emergency powers, notably by declaring unconstitutional the application of military justice to civilians.

Second, the judiciary came under intense violent attack. There were 290 judges and judicial officials assassinated between 1979 and 1991. Undertaken by drug traffickers and paramilitary groups—and to a lesser but growing extent by the guerrillas—such attacks greatly affected the functioning of the judicial system and its capacity to bring to completion certain important investigations (Comisión Andina de Juristas 1992). This added to the corrupting effect of the enormous amounts of capital mobilized by drug trafficking and further destabilized the judiciary.

RECENT TRANSFORMATIONS OF THE JUDICIAL SYSTEM

In little over five years, between 1987 and 1992, the judicial apparatus was the object of reforms that affected a broad range of institutions, including criminal justice—for example, the introduction of the Fiscalía, plea bargaining, and anonymous, "faceless" judges (*jueces sin rostro*); alternative mechanisms of conflict resolution; the administrative structures—for example, the introduction of an autonomous system for the administration of the judiciary, changes in territorial distribution of courts, and a considerable increase in the judicial budget; the transformation of the system of constitutional review, represented by the creation of the Constitutional Court; and the creation of legal actions for the protection of human rights before the courts, such as the *tutela* action,[8] class actions, and the *acción de cumplimiento*.[9] All of this took place within an extensive process of constitutional reform that strengthened the symbolic power and the legitimacy of such changes.

Among these profound transformations, the most important changes and debates have dealt with criminal justice because violence, violations of human rights, and delinquency have been at the center of public debates in recent Colombian history. In this area, the most significant development has been the creation of the Fiscalía (Attorney General's Office) because it signaled not only an essential change in the structure of criminal investigation but also a change in the relations between criminal law and the political process.

The introduction of the Fiscalía and the so-called adversarial system.   Initially, as mentioned before, the Fiscalía was conceived of as an instrument to increase the effectiveness of criminal investigations and the executive's control over them. Before the creation of the Fiscalía, specialized judges were responsible for carrying out criminal investigations. According to the critics, this system had several problems. On the one hand, it had led to lack of investigative specialization because such judges had to confront the most diverse crimes on their own. This lack of specialization meant that the same judge could issue indictments for traffic accidents, petty thefts, homicides, and financial crimes and led to criminal justice's growing ineffectiveness in responding to the most complex crimes, which were often linked to organized crime. On the other hand, it was thought that such judges did not have the capacity to resist the pressures and threats of the collective actors involved in criminal activities, such as guerrillas, paramilitary groups, or drug traffickers.

Moreover, the relations between these judges and the investigative police agencies were on many occasions problematic because each acted under its own logic. Judges specializing in criminal prosecution were keen on respecting judicial procedures but had great difficulty in achieving investigative successes because they did not have the requisite training or any technical resources of their own. In addition, the judges' requests for the judicial police to perform certain tasks were not well received. Police agencies, which belonged to the executive branch, preferred to obey instructions from the government, the high police ranks, and the military rather than the "judicial orders" of an isolated judge, whom they saw as someone who, because of judicial formalities, slowed down successful investigations. Thus, according to the critics, the management of public order, which was the responsibility of the president, and judicial investigations, which were advanced by the judges, were totally separated from each other. The separation forced the government to turn to military criminal justice to confront the great problems—for example, guerrilla violence and drug trafficking.

Finally, given the extant system, there did not seem to be any official or government agency that could be accountable for the alarming level of impunity in the country. The government could point its finger at the inefficiency of the investigative judges, as they were responsible for the judicial processes. The judges, in turn, responded by saying that they lacked resources and the collaboration of other powers and that their responsibility was limited to advancing, to the best of their ability, the indictments of their respective chambers.

As a result of all these factors, proposals were often made to create a high-profile agency as part of the executive branch, which, drawing on the model of the U.S. Attorney General's Office, would centralize criminal investigation. According to the defenders of this model, the above-mentioned deficiencies would be corrected because there would be no isolated judges, but instead prosecutors who would be responsible to the fiscal general. In this way, there would be a political figure responsible for investigative effectiveness, and the officials would be able to specialize and coordinate the various investigations and, in turn, obtain better results against crime. In addition, the importance of the Fiscalía and its common interests with the executive branch would permit better collaboration between the police and prosecutors and, thus, better coordination between the management of public order and judicial investigation.

This explains the tenor of some of the projects that were debated in the Constitutional Assembly of 1991, like that of President Gaviria, who proposed that the attorney general (fiscal general) should be freely named and removed by the government and that the Fiscalía should lack judicial powers because of its role as an investigative body of the executive. In response to this proposal, individuals and organizations concerned with the protection of human rights and the rule of law proposed placing the Fiscalía in the judicial branch to give it autonomy so that it would not be dependent on governmental instructions. There was the reasonable fear that in a country marked by a long tradition of presidential authoritarianism and immunity for crimes committed by the powerful, justice would be used as a mechanism for persecuting the opposition. This second proposal triumphed, but with substantial changes, because it was thought that if the Fiscalía belonged to the judicial branch, it should be given judicial faculties. The result was a hybrid, unique system that differs markedly from the classic adversarial systems (Uprimny 1995).

In countries with a classic adversarial system, such as Italy and the United States, prosecutors lack the power to detain persons and to tap communications because, except in emergencies, they are supposed to solicit authorization from a judge, who is responsible for controlling the legality of the investigative activity. This separation of responsibilities is not capricious. It seeks to place the limitation of citizens' rights in a person or institution different from one whose responsibility it is to investigate and criminally accuse suspects. The reason for this is as simple as it is profound. It is necessary to separate the official charged with executing the punitive powers of the state (the prosecutor) from the official who must protect the rights of the individual vis-à-vis the prosecutor (the judge). This separation is necessary to establish external controls on the prosecutors in order to avoid the arbitrariness that could arise from prosecutors being tempted to utilize their judicial faculties to pressure those accused to obtain confessions from them. Thus, it is unlikely that the same person can be both a good prosecutor and a good judge. The good prosecutor needs to construct a culpability hypothesis to guide his or her investigations, but the good judge should be impartial. It is hard to believe that the same official, a few days after considering somebody a suspect and interrogating him or her, can impartially determine whether the suspect should be detained or liberated.

The Fiscalía involves great risk because it concentrates an enormous amount of power within one body as a result of combining judicial and investigative functions. Colombian prosecutors can independently issue warrants, eavesdrop on communications, detain people, and carry out raids, among other things. Nonetheless, the Fiscalía's relative judicial autonomy reduces the risk that its actions respond to orders from the executive, thus avoiding the type of criminal system typical of dictatorships in Latin America and elsewhere, in which criminal policy is an instrument of persecution in the hands of the government. The Fiscalía is not a simple reproduction of military criminal justice or of the politicized judiciaries of other countries because the prosecutors are not obligated to respond to the executive's instructions. This does not mean that the government never exerts an important influence over the investigative agency. After all, the president has great influence over the selection of the fiscal general, who is elected by the Supreme Court from a three-person presidential list. Nevertheless, once chosen, the fiscal general is autonomous for four years, during which time the government cannot remove the person from office. This has notable effects not only over criminal investigations but also over the related political process because the Fiscalía can prioritize some investigations and, thus, design its own criminal policy, which can be very different from that of the government.

The Colombian Fiscalía, in sum, escapes the traditional classifications of comparative law and is a dangerous but promising entity. Investigators have judicial functions, which could be dangerous for procedural guarantees. At the same time, however, the Fiscalía is an entity that is autonomous from the government, which is potentially important for the construction of the rule of law in Colombia.

"Faceless" justice, the policy of surrender, and the normalization of the exceptional. A second important axis of the modifications to the criminal system was the normalization of the so-called courts of public order. This jurisdiction began to develop in 1987 when the Supreme Court declared unconstitutional the application of military criminal justice to civilians. The government attempted to fill the void created by the court's ruling through laws issued by the president based on state of emergency powers that introduced public order courts. Thus, these exceptional courts have gradually become responsible for investigating and punishing political crimes, terrorism, and drug trafficking, which were considered the principal problems faced by the government. In addition, the processes handled by these courts are characterized by a strong restriction of procedural guarantees, similar to that in military courts. For example, people can be detained indefinitely, as the only two factors that can lead to one's release are fulfilling one's sentence or being over seventy years old.

Nevertheless, public order courts have distinctive traits. Thus, they cannot simply be considered the functional equivalent of the application of military criminal justice to civilians as in preceding years. On the one hand, public order courts reside in the judicial branch and, thus, are not docile instruments of the executive or the military chiefs. In fact, on some occasions public order courts have denounced the complicity of some military authorities with the expanding paramilitary groups. This situation explains why the government passed numerous state of emergency laws aimed at administratively controlling such courts. For instance, the government created an agency residing in the executive branch that would be in charge of the administrative aspects of public order courts and of the distribution of cases among such courts. On the other hand, this new branch of the judiciary contains far-reaching procedural innovations. Through state of emergency legislation, the government authorized the creation of so-called secret judges and witnesses—judges and witnesses whose identity is kept secret—in order to protect these people from threats and attacks. In addition, this legislation eliminated juries in criminal trials in general and public hearings in trials before public order courts.

During President Gaviria's administration, such courts were promoted in conjunction with legislation aimed at inducing high-profile criminals to surrender. Indeed, at the beginning of his term, Gaviria offered drug traffickers the opportunity to turn themselves in to the state in exchange for receiving reduced sentences for confessed crimes and a no-extradition guarantee. Thus, the mechanism of plea bargaining, which had not hitherto been part of the Colombian criminal justice system, was introduced.

All these reforms have been the product of state of emergency legislation, which was converted wholesale into permanent legislation thanks to the transitory powers given to the government by the Constitutional Assembly in 1991. The Colombian Constitutional Court later decided that most of these mechanisms were constitutional, although it did introduce important limitations.[10]

Changes to punishment: Structural tendencies and circumstantial changes. The previous transformations are mostly of a procedural nature. The criminal system has also undergone important modifications in substantive areas. In the last few years there has been a clear tendency to criminalize more activities and to make the punishment of existing crimes more severe. For example, Law 40 of 1993 establishes sanctions of up to sixty years in prison for kidnapping and aggravated homicide. In Colombia, the maximum sentence had traditionally been thirty years. However, almost simultaneously, there was an important decriminalization process. Sentences for certain crimes were reduced, and many actions were decriminalized and converted, through Law 23 of 1991, into misdemeanors that can now be resolved before administrative authorities. Finally, as mentioned before, many forms of plea bargaining were recognized, generally for the most serious crimes. Plea bargaining was later extended to all crimes through the procedural reforms of Law 81 of 1993.

How can this complex and contradictory process of criminalization, decriminalization, and negotiable justice be explained? A possible interpretation is the following. The threefold movement reflects the fashioning of a differentiated criminal policy. A core of tough criminal policy is built to deal with the many organized actors that the state has defined as its main enemies. Nevertheless, the very weakness of the judicial system in confronting these actors leads the state to incorporate negotiation mechanisms. These mechanisms allow the state to elicit the cooperation of criminal organizations' insiders who have struck a deal with the state to dismantle such organizations and also give the state a certain flexibility in the execution of criminal policy itself in order for it to be able to adapt to volatile social and political circumstances. It is, thus, a hard but negotiable nucleus, which is accompanied by an informal periphery, in which the citizens themselves resolve, in a consensual fashion, the problems that the state considers minor conflicts. In this way, the criminal system is relieved of routine cases that increase docket congestion. In addition, justice is socially legitimated, and mechanisms of informal control are generalized. Getting tough on crime and implementing the negotiation policy are not necessarily contradictory to the processes of informalization. The protagonism and visibility of public order courts thus goes hand in hand with the routinization of other criminal courts, as we will explain in more detail later.

In addition to these structural tendencies, circumstantial and somewhat improvised reforms were implemented that responded to the recurring tendency in Colombia of criminalizing rather than seriously tackling social problems and their roots. Thus, in August 1995, the Samper government declared a state of emergency, arguing that it was necessary to confront the increase in common criminality. In response, the punishment for street crimes was increased. Because the Constitutional Court ruled unconstitutional such a declaration of a state of emergency, the government turned to Congress to pass these measures without much debate. The result of such legislation was that the number of prisoners increased considerably (by almost 30 percent), causing a further increase in the congestion of the prison system and the backlogs of criminal courts. Not surprisingly, protests and mutinies in the prisons soon intensified, which, in turn, justified a new declaration of a state of emergency.

A significant silence in criminal policy: The military courts. As important as the changes just described are what can be called the silences in criminal reform —that is, those institutions linked to criminal justice that have not been substantively altered. Undoubtedly, one of the most evident silences has to do with the preservation of judicial privileges for the military. After all, the discussion about human rights in the late 1980s had concentrated on the impunity of the military courts, which were criticized for not sanctioning members of the state armed forces who appeared to be linked to serious crimes. Nevertheless, the Constitutional Assembly kept such judicial privileges for the military and even extended them to the police.

This indicates that there is a tacit agreement between the members of the Colombian elite, including those represented in the Constitutional Assembly, to respect such privileges as if they were a central element of the current political regime. Such consensus became evident a few years later in response to the Constitutional Court's controversial decision that active military personnel could not form part of military courts because as long as they were subject to the hierarchy inherent in the military, they could not have the impartiality required of judges.[11] This decision produced a profound restructuring of military justice; until that moment, the judges had been the commanders of the different armed bodies. Nevertheless, Congress and the government decided to close ranks behind the armed forces, and in a few months one of the quickest constitutional reforms in Colombia's history took place. This reform explicitly declared that the military courts would be composed of members of the state armed forces, including both active and retired members.

However, it should be noted that since 1997, there have been important changes concerning military courts. For instance, in Decision C-358/97, the Constitutional Court stated that the gravest violations of human rights— murders, torture, or disappearance—should be under the jurisdiction of ordinary courts, not military courts, because the gravity of these crimes could not allow them to be considered acts done in the line of service. Congress did not attempt to modify this decision through a new constitutional reform, although the court's ruling considerably restricted the judicial privileges of members of the state armed forces. Therefore, the Fiscalía has been able to investigate various military members for violations of human rights. The Colombian elites' consensus in favor of military privileges could be weakening, because of repeated criticisms from certain sectors of civil society concerning the errors and abuses of the military courts, and because of the growing international pressure against the grave human rights violations attributable to the armed forces.[12]

Political process, justice, and the fight against corruption.   Other reforms concern the role of the judiciary in checking the behavior of public officials and other political actors. Because of the anticlientelist spirit of the 1991 Constitutional Assembly, due to its pluralist composition, the assembly intended to introduce substantial reforms on the manner in which the business of politics is carried out. The members of the assembly favored the correction of political vices through the judiciary. In other words, they considered that such a task should not be carried out by improving the system of political representation—through political parties and electoral system reforms—but by introducing an uncompromising system of judicial control over political activities, especially those of members of Congress. To apply this regime, judges were given new powers. The new constitution eliminated various privileges given to members of Congress that used to exempt them from judicial control and created a system whereby the Supreme Court can investigate and judge them at any time. However, a judicial mechanism was created whereby any person can ask the State Council to deprive members of Congress of their position whenever it is proven that they have engaged in practices of political corruption—for example, influence trading, violating the rule against holding another job while serving in Congress, or even by missing more than six sessions in which votes are taken on law proposals.

This demonstrates that the recent transformations in the sanctioning power of the judicial branch, and especially those stemming from the new constitution, did not intend solely to increase the effectiveness of the criminal apparatus and strengthen the mechanisms of social control. Reforms have also been implemented that increased the Colombian judicial system's capacity to combat the traditional immunities of the powerful sectors, thus helping to guarantee the respect for constitutional rules and human rights, as we will explain in more detail later. Through these reforms, the constitution attributes to the judicial branch an important responsibility in the construction of a more transparent political process.

ALTERNATIVE MECHANISMS OF CONFLICT RESOLUTION

The 1991 constitution created or reinforced mechanisms for the resolution of conflicts outside courts, such as mediation, arbitration, informal adjudication (through the so-called judges of the peace), and adjudication by administrative authorities in certain types of conflicts. The 1991 constitution also gives jurisdictional functions to the customary authorities of indigenous groups. In spite of their evident differences, all these mechanisms stem from a certain distrust of the state's formal justice system—that is, from the belief that such a system does not constitute an effective, transparent, and adequate instrument to deal with everyday disputes. All of them aim at offering alternatives for ordinary citizens to resolve their conflicts in a quicker, consensual manner.

Some of these alternative mechanisms of dispute resolution have resulted in important legal and institutional changes. For instance, the range of conflicts subject to conciliation has considerably increased, particularly in the realm of family law. Likewise, it was established that conciliation could be used in certain types of suits against the state. Procedural innovations were also established to reduce the courts' backlogs. It was decided that negotiable disputes brought before courts, which include most conflicts outside the jurisdiction of labor, criminal, or administrative courts, could end through conciliation between the parties at any time before the issuance of the court decision.

To put these reforms into effect, the law authorized the creation of centers of conciliation and arbitration by nonstate organizations, such as associations of lawyers, chambers of commerce, law firms, and universities. The legislation on alternative mechanisms of dispute resolution also allowed for conciliators in equity—that is, lay citizens designated by the parties—to definitively solve any conflict concerning a negotiable issue, on the basis of norms of equity or fairness. The institution of the judges of the peace, which has only recently begun to be implemented, was also approved during the constitutional transition.

Finally, in major cities, pilot programs were implemented that sought to offer alternatives for the poor so that they would have effective access to justice. Such programs were embodied in the so-called houses of justice, community centers in which every major institution of the judicial system was represented and in which alternative mechanisms of dispute resolution were allowed (Pearson 1997). These houses of justice seek not only to decentralize the administration of justice, in order to make it more accessible to citizens, but also to combine elements of "formal" justice with the development of alternative mechanisms of conflict resolution and practices of community justice.

These reforms have had positive results and have democratic potential, as they restore to the community and to the citizens the capacity to resolve their own disputes in a voluntary manner, while relieving the judicial apparatus of excess disputes. However, they also have antidemocratic risks. On occasion, the central criterion for the promotion of informal justice has been simply to relieve courts of the tasks they should—but have been unable to—perform efficiently. It is, thus, a strategy that operates more to the benefit of judges and judicial employees than of those who use the system. Instead of strengthening the judicial system so that it can adequately process the conflicts between citizens, the strategy tends to exclude poor people's conflicts from courts. A second-rate informal justice is thus created for the poor, as courts tend to be reserved for the members of the middle and upper classes and for firms that can afford the costs associated with litigation or sophisticated forms of informal justice (for example, commercial arbitration), as the empirical analysis of civil litigation that follows will make clear.

Administrative changes in the judicial system.   The judicial branch has undergone important administrative and bureaucratic transformations, which have centered on four aspects. First, there has been a noteworthy increase of public allotments to security and justice. Between 1990 and 1993, for example, "the public resources allotted to the justice sector have been increased by 105 percent in real terms, while those of the defense sector have grown 60 percent" (Presidencia de la República 1993). As stated in *El Tiempo* on

July 30, 1993, the joint security and justice costs equaled 2.4 percent of GNP in 1990, and they had climbed to 3.5 percent in 1993. *El Tiempo* reported on October 21, 1996, that in 1991, the expenses in this sector of the justice system equaled 0.6 percent of GNP; in 1992, these expenditures represented 1.1 percent; and later they reached 1.2 percent—an increase of 100 percent in real terms in only a few years. Thus, the public allotments for this sector in the national budget went from 2.9 percent in 1990 to 5.4 percent in 1995. Of these expenses, almost 50 percent corresponded to the growth in the Fiscalía, which increased from ten thousand officials in 1992 to twenty thousand in 1996 (Comisión de Racionalización del Gasto y las Finanzas Públicas 1996).

Second, the administration of the justice sector has been separated from the executive and become autonomous, through the creation of the *Consejo Superior de la Judicatura* (Administrative Council for the Judiciary). The Consejo, which was established by the 1991 constitution as part of the judicial branch, handles the budget and the organization of the judiciary.

Third, the constitution made more flexible some procedures involving territorial divisions and personnel administration. In the former regime, the spatial distribution of the courts and tribunals had to correlate with the general division of the national territory into regions, provinces, and towns. This requirement generated many practical difficulties, given that such a division does not always make sense from the point of view of the distribution of the resources of the judicial branch. Likewise, the creation and elimination of courts were subject to rigid legal procedures. Thus, it was difficult to rationalize the distribution of work among the different courts. In contrast, the new constitution authorized the Consejo to redivide the national territory specifically for judicial purposes, to relocate courts, and to create, eliminate, and combine positions within the judiciary.

Fourth, the system of selecting judges and judicial officials has changed in some ways. Although the structural autonomy of the sector continues to be considerable, in practice, there has been increased interference between the judicial branch and the political sectors in terms of appointments. For example, the high courts have to participate in the selection of other officials. The State Council elects the members of the National Electoral Council from candidate lists presented by political parties. At the same time, the political apparatus has acquired a certain influence in the appointment of some high court judges. For example, the justices of both the Constitutional Court and of a section of the Consejo are elected by the chambers of Congress.

However, along with this incipient politicization of the judicial branch, there have been attempts to strengthen its autonomy and professionalism through the implementation of the judicial career. The majority of the new judicial officials have been appointed through competitive examinations. Although there have been problems in the development of these competitions, they guarantee a greater impartiality in selection than the preceding system, which was based on the discretion of the nominator.

In sum, Colombian justice has undergone profound changes over the last two decades that have created both new opportunities and new risks for the implementation of the progressive principles established in the 1991 constitution. Meanwhile, the social context in which the judicial system operates has become increasingly marked by violence and social polarization. As we have set out to argue throughout this section, it is against this sociolegal background that the operation of courts in Colombia must be understood. For it helps explain the central contrast that, in our opinion, characterizes the functioning of the judicial system in the country—that is, that between the protagonism and visibility of some courts and the routinization of other courts. Drawing on empirical research, in the following two sections we elaborate such a contrast by looking into the operation of high-profile courts—namely, the Constitutional Court—and routinized courts—namely, civil and ordinary criminal courts.

The Protagonism of Constitutional Justice

THE ROLE OF CONSTITUTIONAL JUSTICE IN COLOMBIA

Within the recent transformations of the Colombian judicial system that have a closer relationship to the protective—as opposed to the repressive—function of law, the creation of the Constitutional Court and the introduction of the tutela action and of other judicial mechanisms for effectively implementing constitutional rights stand out.[13] In fact, constitutional justice has come to be the most visible means of justice for the common citizen and, through activist decisions in both judicial review and tutelas, has come to be a protagonist in the institutional life of the country.

The introduction of the Constitutional Court in Colombia was not uncontroversial. Critics of the institution—whose nine members are elected by the Senate for eight-year terms from lists submitted by the president, the Supreme Court, and the State Council—feared that the intervention of the Senate in the appointment of the justices would erode judicial independence ensured under the previous system by the fact that judicial review was carried out by the Supreme Court, which was structurally independent from the political powers. However, such politicization of the appointments of justices was expressly defended by various members of the Constitutional Assembly, who believed that it would avoid control being exercised by an elitist, aloof ensemble of jurists disconnected from the social and political dynamics of the country.

Along with the intervention of the Senate in the appointment of the court's justices, the 1991 constitution included key provisions that gave the court (and, in the case of the tutela action, all courts) ample powers to protect constitutional rights. For instance, the constitution includes not only civil and political rights but also social and group rights and establishes judicial mechanisms for their protection. In contrast, the previous constitution contained a very inadequate listing of rights. More important, the effective force of those constitutional rights under the previous regime was precarious because most lawyers and judges did not consider the constitution to be a legal norm directly applicable in concrete cases, but rather a collection of procedures through which the "real" laws (those passed by Congress) were created. In contrast, the constitution of 1991 introduced mechanisms for the prompt and direct application of constitutional rights by courts (more on this later). As Justice Carlos Gaviria (1996) has pointed out, the central characteristic of the new constitution is that rather than being a mere proclamation of rights, it contains effective mechanisms so that it can be applied in judicial decisions.

Although its role and decisions have been the matter of much controversy over the last ten years in Colombia, the Constitutional Court has demonstrated a noteworthy independence and a desire to interpret and apply the constitution in a progressive manner. Through judicial review—that is, in cases in which citizens ask the court to declare unconstitutional an act of Congress or a decree of the executive that has the same effect as a law of Congress—the court has taken very controversial positions in favor of the individual's rights, such as the decriminalization of drug consumption (Decision C-221/94) and euthanasia (Decision C-239/97). Likewise, it has protected minorities traditionally discriminated against, such as AIDS patients and homosexuals. The Constitutional Court has also tended to favor religious, ideological, and ethnic pluralism. Thus, it has actively enforced the guarantee of equality among the religions—for example, through the annulment of the privileges of the Catholic Church. It has given indigenous groups a large realm of discretion for the resolution of conflicts according to their own customs. The court has also protected—albeit in a rather reluctant and tentative manner—basic social rights. Finally, the court has severely curtailed the use of state of emergency powers by the executive through several decisions rendering unconstitutional either the very declaration of a state of emergency or the legislation produced based on state of emergency powers (Decisions C-300/94 and C-466/95).

Furthermore, the new constitution established judicial mechanisms aimed at conferring greater effectiveness to constitutional rights in everyday life. Among them, the tutela stands out. This action has brought about not only a substantial transformation of judicial activity but has, above all, brought the constitution closer to the citizens by endowing them with a supple instrument for the protection of their rights. It is not surprising, thus, that in the first ten years of the new constitution, over 450,000 tutela actions have been brought before the courts, encompassing the most diverse social relations, as the following empirical analysis will bear witness. For instance, the tutela has reshaped the relationship between state agencies and citizens, for, among other things, it has quickened the payment of pensions and social services and has forced the governmental entities to respond in a comprehensive way to users' claims. Moreover, the tutela action has made constitutional rights enforceable in relationships between individuals, between individuals and private firms, and among private firms. Thus, children who are victims of abuse, abandonment, or the religious dogmatism of their parents have been protected by the court through decisions in tutela cases (for example, Decisions T-128/94 and T-205/94). The tutela has also been amply used to protect the rights of students vis-à-vis the actions of school and university authorities (Decisions T-420/92, T-114/95, and T-015/94). The court has protected the rights of vulnerable sectors of the population, such as the elderly (T-036/95) and AIDS patients (ST-082/94). Likewise, the court has repeatedly enforced the rights of indigenous groups regarding the preservation of their culture and the protection of their territories (ST-380/93). Tutela decisions have also protected workers' rights. For instance, the court has protected workers' freedom of association by sanctioning corporate anti-union practices, such as discriminating against unionized workers through salary increases limited to nonunionized workers or through exclusion of union workers from the possibility of working overtime to increase their income (ST-23/94; ST-079/95; ST-143/95; ST-326/94, SU-342/95; SU-510/95). All this bears witness to the substantial impact of this legal action on the dynamics of the judicial apparatus. Indeed, it can be said without exaggeration that the popularity of the tutela and its instrumental and symbolic effects have led to the "constitutionalization" of law and of important aspects of Colombians' life.

A CLOSER LOOK AT THE FUNCTIONING OF THE TUTELA ACTION

In order to empirically ground our arguments on the role of constitutional justice in the protection of rights, in this section we present a brief quantitative analysis of the tutela based on a representative sample of cases extracted from the information available in the Constitutional Court about all the tutela cases decided in the country since the court was created in 1991. The random sample we studied (García-Villegas and Rodríguez 2001) consists of 631 cases (which yields a margin of error of 5 percent).[14] Based on this information, we discuss in this section (1) the conflicts that give rise to the tutela (the events giving rise to the conflict, as well as the kinds of parties involved) and (2) the response that judges have given to such conflicts. The study covers the period January 1991 through December 1996.

Before turning to the data, however, it is important to consider the key features of the tutela. The tutela can be utilized by any person without the need of a lawyer or any written documentation. It is meant to protect what the constitution calls "fundamental" rights (generally, civil and political rights), rather than social rights. Nevertheless, the court's jurisprudence has established that when a social right is directly connected with a fundamental right, this legal action can be employed, thus making all rights potentially subject to tutela. Tutela actions can be brought before any judge in the country, as all judges have legal authority over this kind of action. All the judicial decisions involving tutela reach the Constitutional Court, which reviews those that it considers most important (approximately 1 percent of all cases). The tutela procedure is simple and quick. The judge must decide in eight days and take the necessary measures to protect the fundamental right. Tutela actions can be filed against both public and private authorities, individuals, or organizations. Finally, tutela actions proceed only when there are no other judicial mechanisms available to effectively protect the allegedly violated right.

Events that give rise to tutela actions. More than 21 percent of the events that give rise to the tutela action originate in government agencies' failure to respond to claims formulated by the citizens, particularly those that provide health services and retirement income (11.57 percent). More than a fifth of the tutelas seek the fulfillment of the public administration's duty to respond appropriately to the claims raised before it by individuals. This demonstrates the tutela's importance as an instrument for protecting citizens' rights against the state bureaucracy. Many tutelas concern labor disputes—for example, disputes concerning the payment of salaries and services (6.18 percent) or the firing of workers (3.33 percent). Given the availability of several regular mechanisms for solving such disputes before labor courts, this type of action is unlikely to proceed.

Education is the third theme in importance, as is shown by the percentage of tutelas concerning unjustified denials of admission or of opportunities to continue one's studies in an education center (3.01 percent). In this case, contrary to what happens with the labor claims, the tutela seems to be the appropriate mechanism for solving the conflict, as long as the student, or his or her parents, cannot resort to any other judicial action to ask for the student's quick reintegration or admission to the school or university. The plaintiffs who allege irregularities in the application of sanctions or disciplinary procedures by schools or universities are in the same situation; this event, likewise, represents a significant percentage of the tutelas filed (2.54 percent).

In terms of the rights involved, the highest percentage of tutelas corresponds to the violation or threat to the right to have a prompt answer to one's petitions from the government (23.93 percent). The right to work and to social security is involved in 16.32 percent of the tutelas. Also, there is a high percentage of tutelas filed for violation of due process (12.84 percent) in judicial, disciplinary, and administrative procedures. An important area of violation or threat to due process can be found in the procedures through which sanctions are imposed by educational institutions, events that, as explained, are a common source of tutelas.

Plaintiffs.   The analysis of the selected case files gives an idea of the type of person who turns to the tutela action. Table 5.1 identifies the top ten types of plaintiffs. The most frequent users of the tutela action are workers (21.71 percent). They use this mechanism chiefly to ask courts to protect their rights regarding job stability and the timely payment of social security and health benefits. Public-sector workers most often turn to the tutela, as shown by the fact that the most common defendants are state agencies and municipalities (see Table 5.2). Next are those plaintiffs who represent minors (5.07 percent), who rely on this recourse mainly to protect the rights of education and due process guaranteed to minors. These rights are violated or threatened mostly in the disciplinary procedures advanced in schools.

The third significant plaintiff group consists of prisoners (4.75 percent), who bring tutela actions seeking their liberty or the improvement of their conditions of detention. Likewise, they use this action to protect their right to due process (particularly that prosecutors and judges follow the laws about criminal process) and their right to obtain timely responses to actions and claims that they bring before the jail authorities, judges, and prosecutors.

TABLE 5.1

Types of Plaintiffs

Type of plaintiff	%
Worker	21.71
Representative of a minor	5.07
Prisoner	4.75
Elderly person	4.44
Civic associations	4.44
Minor	2.06
Group of workers	1.9
Commercial corporation	0.16
Group of students	0.95
Neighborhood association	0.63

SOURCE: García-Villegas and Rodríguez (2001).

TABLE 5.2
Types of Defendants

Type of defendant	%
Municipality	11.25
Individual	8.24
Cajanal	7.45
Instituto de Seguros Sociales	6.02
Private business	4.75
Private school	4.28
Civil judge	4.12
Public utilities firm	3.8
State or municipal social security agency	3.01
Police officer	2.22
Public school	2.06
Criminal judge	1.74
City secretary	1.74
Municipal mayor's office	1.58
Private university	1.58
Jail establishment or authority	1.43
Governor	1.43
State secretary of education	1.43
Data management business	1.27
Hospital	1.27

SOURCE: García-Villegas and Rodríguez (2001).

Elderly people (4.44 percent) turn to the tutela to seek the protection of their rights to social security and rights of petition, which would be threatened or violated by social security entities that do not attend to their claims for granting, readjusting, or substituting their pensions or other types of social services.

Defendants.   Through the tutela action, one can solicit the protection of a fundamental right against individuals or organizations, public or private. Table 5.2 lists the twenty most common types of defendants.

The predominance of the public sector among those sued is noteworthy. In fact, nearly 80 percent of the suits are brought against state entities of all types (territorial entities, firms in the service sector, administrative and judicial authorities, and so forth). Nevertheless, the percentage of tutelas against private organizations and individuals is also significant. This shows the importance of the application of fundamental rights in the private sphere, which before 1991 lacked effective constitutional regulation.[15]

In the public sector, municipalities are the most frequent defendants (11.25 percent). Next in order, social security entities, which includes the most often sued entity in the country, the *Caja Nacional de Previsión Social* (*Cajanal*), the National Social Security Institute (7.45 percent). The great

TABLE 5.3

Tutelas Granted and Denied by Colombian Courts

	Granted		Denied		Total	
	Number	%	Number	%	Number	%
Trial courts	180	28.53	451	71.47	631	100
Courts of appeals	41	76.57	134	23.43	175	100

SOURCE: García-Villegas and Rodríguez (2001).

majority of these suits solicit information through the right of petition. The *Instituto de Seguros Sociales* (ISS), Institute of Social Securities, is also a frequent defendant (6.02 percent) in trials that have origins similar to those of the Cajanal (failure to respond to claims or failure to pay for social services). Additionally, in the case of the ISS, frequently suits are brought for failings in the provision of health services. When the percentages corresponding to agencies providing social security services are considered as a whole, such agencies represent 17.48 percent of the total, which makes the social security sector the one that is sued most frequently.

Finally, it is important to note the use of tutela against decisions issued by judicial authorities of various ranks and specialties (close to 10 percent, composed of judges and prosecutors).

The tutela decisions.   Judges grant only 28.5 percent of the requests they receive. Nevertheless, this percentage varies according to the type of right whose protection is being sought. When dealing with civil and political rights, judges grant 31 percent. In contrast, when the request concerns social, economic, or cultural rights, judges grant only 19 percent.

All tutela decisions can be appealed before a higher court before reaching the Constitutional Court for its review. The court reviews approximately 1 percent of tutelas. Table 5.3 presents the number and percentage of tutelas granted and denied by trial courts and courts of appeals. The percentage of tutelas granted and denied varies according to whether they are resolved by trial courts or courts of appeals. In trial courts, the percentage of tutelas granted (28.53 percent) is higher than in courts of appeals (26.25 percent). The slight difference between these percentages shows a strong tendency of courts of appeals to uphold the decisions of trial courts. The principal reason for denying a tutela is the existence of another means of judicial defense (25.07 percent in trial courts; 32.1 percent in courts of appeals),[16] followed by the lack of violation or threat of the right invoked (13.5 percent in trial courts; 12.35 percent in courts of appeals).

Routine Justice: Civil and Criminal Courts

As we argued in the first part of this chapter, a contrast characterizes the Colombian judicial system. On the one hand, there exist highly visible lawsuits (for example, those of tutela) and courts (for example, the Constitutional Court) that have taken on a protagonist-like role by specializing in these lawsuits. On the other hand, there is a large sector of the judiciary that remains generally invisible to the public and that is dedicated chiefly to the resolution of a massive number of routine lawsuits. In the previous section, we discussed constitutional justice to illustrate the functioning of the most visible part of the judicial system. In this section, we explain, based on a detailed empirical study, the way in which a key sector of the less visible part of the judicial system—that is, civil and ordinary criminal courts—operates.

CIVIL COURTS

In order to inquire about the parties, conflicts, and results of civil trials, we used two sources of quantitative data for this research project (Rodríguez 2001a). First, a long series of data covering the period from 1938 to 1995 was compiled from an analysis of the information collected annually by the National Department of Statistics (DANE 1996). This long series offers a diachronic and general vision of the most significant variables of the demand for and supply of civil justice.[17] Second, we obtained a short series of data through primary empirical research entailing the study of a representative sample of cases handled in the courts of the three principal cities (Bogotá, Cali, and Medellín) between 1992 and 1996. We selected a random sample containing 276 trials, which gives rise to a 5 percent margin of error. The sample was collected in twelve courts in Bogotá, nine in Medellín, and seven in Cali. This sample is proportional to the number of courts in each city. This short series offers a synchronic and detailed perspective of a large number of variables in the operation of civil justice. In both series, the data correspond to the cases handled in trial courts.

Types of civil trials in Colombia. In order to understand the data presented below, one must bear in mind that the great majority of civil conflicts in Colombia are dealt with through two types of processes: the declaratory and the executory.[18] The object of the former is the judicial recognition of the existence of a right. In a declaratory trial (*juicio declarativo*), the parties debate the facts and provide evidence aimed at clarifying an uncertain legal situation (such as the possible breach of a contract), which is resolved by the judge handling the case. In contrast, in an executory trial (*juicio ejecutivo*), a person seeks to enforce the fulfillment of a clear and express obligation embodied in a document (such as a check) that the plaintiff must provide for the case file. It is through these trials that, for example, the collection of debts guaranteed with checks and promissory notes is processed. Besides the declaratory and executory trials, the Colombian system handles a small volume (less than 5 percent) of liquidation trials and of voluntary jurisdiction.[19]

The general evolution of civil litigation: Demand, supply, and backlogs in civil courts. The most general data about civil justice refer to the evolution of the demand for and the supply of civil justice. The demand concerns the number of cases that enter civil courts over a specified period. The supply is composed of the number of cases that the civil courts are able to resolve in the same period. In an ideal situation, the demand and the supply would be equal, so that there would be no accumulation of cases during the period analyzed. When this does not occur and the demand is greater than the supply, the cases are continued into the next period, causing court backlogs.

Our research shows a chronic situation of backlogs in civil justice. This situation is observed by analyzing the data of the long series concerning the pending trials at the beginning of each year—that is, those that have accumulated over the course of the previous years.[20] Besides a huge jump in the numbers between 1955 and 1957—as a result of changes in the counting method used to obtain the official statistics—we observe a sustained growth of the number of cases pending in Colombia until the beginning of the 1990s. Indeed, 200 to 300 cases per 100,000 inhabitants accumulated annually between 1956 and 1990. In absolute terms, these numbers signify a growth in the annual inventories of close to 30,000 cases in the 1960s; 50,000 in the 1970s; and 80,000 in the 1980s. The number of pending cases grew from 329,412 in 1956 to 402,331 in 1960; to 663,338 in 1970; to 1,175,536 in 1980; and to 1,885,361 in 1989. Nevertheless, since 1990, a considerable reduction in the number of pending cases has occurred. The number decreased to 1,562,886 in 1990 and to 1,376,204 in 1991. Since 1992, the backlog has increased, although it has stabilized below the level registered until 1989. In fact, since 1992, the number of cases pending per 100,000 inhabitants has stabilized to around 4,700; in 1989, this number reached almost 6,000.

The decrease in the number of cases pending during this period is due to two factors: (1) the transfer of a considerable number of cases concerning inheritance, alimony, and other matters to the specialized family jurisdiction since its inception in 1989; and (2) diverse mechanisms introduced near the end of the 1980s and the beginning of the 1990s to relieve congestion in the judicial system, such as the obligation to hold conciliation hearings in civil cases, the authorization granted to notary publics to perform marriages, and the promotion of alternative dispute mechanisms such as arbitration and mediation. These measures seem to have stimulated the decrease in the inventories of executory cases, which were reduced from 1,349,694 in 1989 to

1,040,026 in 1991. This reduction was temporary, as is shown by the fact that the number of executory cases pending in 1994 increased, but was still only 1,127,751.

Nevertheless, the two above-mentioned measures—the creation of a specialized family jurisdiction and the promotion of extrajudicial solutions to disputes—had only a partial impact on the reduction of the inventories of civil cases. In fact, after the decreases in 1990 and 1991, the number has stabilized to a level of case backlogs that is still too high: in 1994, the number of pending cases was 1,586,956. This number, however, can be misleading because close to 60 percent of the pending cases have been abandoned by the parties and, as a consequence—given that the resolution of civil cases depends on whether or not the parties carry them forward—they do not involve any ongoing proceedings.

The most frequent types of conflicts and cases: The predominance of debt collection. Our study carefully dissected the general data concerning civil litigation in order to determine what types of conflicts and cases predominate. As we explained earlier, civil conflicts vary greatly—from breach of contracts to traffic accidents and marriage disputes—but some are more important than others in terms of frequency.

The most interesting results of the research concern the clear predominance of debt collection. This is reflected by the fact that Colombian civil justice is fundamentally dedicated to resolving executory cases—that is, cases geared toward the payment of debts guaranteed by such documents as checks and promissory notes. The executory cases are the majority of all pending cases during the period for which complete data on the composition of the pending cases exist (1973–94), by a wide margin.

In Colombia, during the whole period, the executory trials (juicios ejecutivos) represented between 60 percent and 70 percent of the pending cases. This predominance continues today, as shown by the results of the short series of data for the cases being processed in the civil courts of the three principal cities, condensed in Table 5.4.

In fact, 70 percent of the trials studied from 1992 to 1996 are executory, whereas the declaratory trials account for 17 percent. The declaratory-executory trials are relatively scarce, accounting for 3 percent.[21] This composition of civil litigation allows the formulation of a central conclusion with relation to civil justice in Colombia. The great majority of the disputes do not follow the classic model of litigation, in which both parties dispute the facts and present evidence in an attempt to obtain a favorable decision from the court. In place of this type of litigation in which the judge's role is to adjudicate, the typical process in Colombian civil justice is one that seeks a coercive mechanism to enforce undisputed obligations (Rodríguez 2001a). As

TABLE 5.4

Types of Cases Pending (Average, 1992–1996)

Type of case	Number	%
Executory	192	70
Declaratory	46	17
Declaratory-executory	8	3
Tutela	5	2
Liquidation	3	1
Voluntary jurisdiction	3	1
Other	11	4
No data	8	2
Total	276	100

SOURCE: Rodríguez (2001a).

will be seen later, the result of the executory processes is highly predictable, given the existence of a document (for example, a check) that clearly embodies the obligation of the defendant vis-à-vis the plaintiff.

The most common declaratory trials concern torts (30 percent), generally related to traffic accidents. Other significant cases pertain to the removal of tenants (22 percent) and adverse possession (11 percent).

The users of civil courts. We investigated in detail the characteristics of the plaintiffs and defendants in the cases included in the short series of the study. The central objective of this analysis was to identify the main characteristics of what Galanter (1974) calls "repeat players"—that is, those litigants who participate in civil trials (generally as plaintiffs) in a routine manner and, therefore, have considerable advantages over "one shotters." These advantages exist, in part, because repeat players have greater experience in dealing with courts, better legal advice, and less aversion to the risk entailed in participating in a judicial process than one shotters do.

In order to create a profile of frequent litigants, we focused our analysis on the parties that participate in the most common procedures—the executory trials. As shown in the preceding section, this type of trial is used mainly for debt collection. Therefore, the investigation concentrated on determining who relies on civil justice to collect debts and against whom they litigate. For this purpose, it was determined that the most relevant characteristic of the plaintiffs and the defendants was whether they were individuals or organizations, since studies in other countries show that repeat players tend to be organizations—more specifically, corporations—whose participation in civil procedures is a routine element of their economic activities (Jacob 1996; Santos et al. 1996). In Colombia, individuals are 41 percent of the plaintiffs, and organizations are 59 percent.

Nevertheless, this participation varies if the executory and the declaratory procedures are examined separately. In the executory cases, individuals and organizations are each 50 percent of the plaintiffs; in declaratory procedures, individuals are 91 percent of the plaintiffs, and organizations, 9 percent.

These data show that while individuals predominate in declaratory trials, organizations have a significant rate of participation in executory trials, in which they represent 50 percent of the plaintiffs. This percentage is composed mainly of companies that are repeat players and have distinctive characteristics concerning their legal status and economic activity. The results of the study show that the majority of them are midsize, limited-liability corporations (40 percent) or large stakeholder corporations (39 percent). The preponderant economic activity among the plaintiff corporations is services (61 percent), followed by commerce (17 percent), manufacturing (4 percent), and construction (4 percent).

The predominance of service-sector companies as plaintiffs in general and as debt collectors in particular in executory trials can be better understood by examining the distribution of these companies in accordance with the type of services they render (Table 5.5).

This table reveals a central characteristic of the executive trials: finance-sector corporations are the quintessential repeat players in Colombian civil litigation and mobilize the judicial system for the collection of debts that originated in credit operations (mortgage credit, credit cards, and so forth). Such corporations have experience in litigation and initiate numerous trials in which they claim relatively small amounts of money. These companies are mainly banks (46 percent), savings and loan corporations (18 percent), and commercial finance companies (17 percent) that, in the normal development

TABLE 5.5

Types of Services Rendered by Plaintiff Corporations
(Average, 1992–1996)

Type of service	Number	%
Financial		
Bank	31	46
Savings and loan corporation	12	18
Commercial finance company	11	17
Other	3	4
Corporation	1	1
Debt-collection company	1	1
Professional services	1	1
Health and social security	2	3
Real estate	2	3
Other	4	6
Total	68	100

SOURCE: Rodríguez (2001a).

TABLE 5.6

Outcomes of Trials (Average, 1992–1996)

Outcome	Number	%
Court ruling	170	78
Settlement	10	5
Payment	10	5
Abandonment	3	1
Other	26	11
Total	219	100

SOURCE: Rodríguez (2001a).

of their credit activities, use the courts as means of portfolio recovery (Rodríguez 2001a).

In Colombia, the great majority of these debt-collection trials, as well as of civil trials in general, are brought against individuals. The study found that in 84 percent of the civil cases, the defendant is an individual, whereas the defendant is an organization in only 16 percent of the cases.

The outcomes of civil trials.   Finally, our investigation inquired into the outcomes of civil trials in Colombia, and Table 5.6 presents the results.

Most trials reach the final phase—the court's ruling (78 percent)—and a very low percentage of trials end in a settlement between the parties (5 percent). This shows that in Colombian civil courts, cases initiated tend to go through all the stages because effective intermediate filters to prevent the continuation of the litigation do not exist. If analyzed from a comparative perspective, this phenomenon can be seen as the main cause of court backlogs in Colombian civil justice. Indeed, in countries such as the United States, the high number of suits brought before the civil courts does not give rise to the backlogs registered in Colombia largely because a generalized negotiation practice exists during the trial, in which the judge and the parties' lawyers play a central role. In fact, less than 10 percent of the civil trials initiated in that country reach the sentencing phase, as there exists an intense negotiation phase between the parties within a short time after the suit is filed. This intimate union between litigation and negotiation has given rise to what is called "litigotiation," to characterize the operation of American civil justice (Jacob 1996, 56).

Moreover, our study found that the results of the trials are highly foreseeable. In fact, a detailed analysis of the trial results demonstrated that in Colombia, 87 percent of the civil trials favor the plaintiff. This tendency is even more marked in the most frequent types of cases, those concerning debt collections. Indeed, 94 percent of such cases end with a favorable result for the plaintiff. Therefore, in Colombia the task of the judge is frequently limited to the validation of a result that is virtually determined beforehand, either because the defendant does not respond to the claim or because, when the defendant does respond, a financial document (for example, a check or a promissory note) clearly proves the existence of the debt and, thus, prevents controversy between the parties.

ORDINARY CRIMINAL JUSTICE

The thesis of the routinization of a considerable part of Colombian justice can be extended to other areas of the Colombian judicial system. In other words, the dedication of justice to routine and repetitive conflicts is not a phenomenon exclusive to civil courts but is also present in other vital areas of the judicial system. This is shown, for example, in the results of the investigation of ordinary criminal justice (Rubio 2001).

It is important to remember that the administration of criminal justice in Colombia has been traditionally divided between ordinary criminal courts and courts that are part of a special, exceptional criminal jurisdiction based on state of emergency legislation. The latter jurisdiction has taken different names throughout recent Colombian history, some more expressive than others, among which are "justice of public order," "faceless justice," and "regional justice." The line that divides the ordinary from the extraordinary is highly unstable and arbitrary. Exceptional criminal justice—about which systematic information does not exist because of the secrecy that characterizes its trials and that makes access to court documents very difficult—has taken care of the crimes considered especially grave, although the criteria of "graveness" has fluctuated considerably or has given rise to overly broad definitions of crimes. In practice, exceptional criminal justice has tended toward two harmful extremes. First, it has extended, based on overly broad criminal classifications, to harmless behavior.[22] Second, it has been unable to punish highly destabilizing conduct, such as massive homicides with terrorist aims and kidnappings. These vices are common to the ordinary criminal justice system, which is analyzed in this section. In spite of having under its jurisdiction the resolution of some of the most destabilizing crimes in the country —such as homicides committed by common criminals or by people involved in personal disputes, which account for the majority of the homicides committed in Colombia, as well as aggravated thefts—it has concentrated on less serious crimes that are more easily resolved (Deas and Gaitán 1995; Pécaut 1997).

General aspects of the Colombian criminal system.   Criminal trials in Colombia begin with an investigative phase, advanced by the Fiscalía, an agency created by the constitution of 1991 whose origin and features were explained earlier. On some occasions, this phase is preceded by a preliminary investigation when there are doubts about the viability of the case. During the investigation, prosecutors gather evidence with the purpose of determining if there is a basis for prosecuting the suspect before a criminal judge. In this same phase, prosecutors working for the Fiscalía may order that the suspect be arrested and held in custody. If the prosecutor responsible for the case determines that sufficient evidence against the suspect exists, formal charges are formulated, and the case goes to the trial phase, at which time the criminal judge hands down a sentence. If the evidence is insufficient, the public prosecutor orders the filing of the investigation, and the case is deemed finished.

The "pyramid" of criminal litigation. A sociolegal understanding of criminal justice entails analyzing how many crimes out of all committed actually enter the criminal judicial system. This type of analysis has become a common feature of sociolegal studies of judicial systems throughout the world. This is shown, for instance, in studies of the "pyramid of litigation" (Santos et al. 1996) or the "legal iceberg" (Galanter 1974) in various legal systems. The idea behind the pyramid of litigation is a simple one. The base of the pyramid is made up of the estimated total number of crimes committed in a country, which can be resolved through various means, such as the state's failure to hear of the crime, the victim's inaction or self-help, settlement, litigation, and adjudication. Criminal conflicts solved through inaction, self-help, or settlement constitute the intermediate layers of the pyramid. When conflicts cannot be solved through these means, they reach the stage of litigation and, absent a successful negotiation between the state and the defendant, adjudication. Thus, litigation and adjudication constitute the peak of the pyramid. The shape of the figure is a pyramid because the number of crimes is much larger than the number of cases that reach the litigation and adjudication stages.

According to the results of our study, during 1995 in Colombia, a little more than half a million families (close to 15 percent of the total) were victims of some crime. The rate of global criminality was slightly higher than 4,800 criminal incidents per 100,000 inhabitants. This means that for a population of 38 million inhabitants, the total number of infractions amounts to 1,824,000 (Rubio 2001). These cases constitute the base of the pyramid.

It has been estimated that in Colombia, only 31.5 percent of these criminal incidents are investigated. This percentage is very low in the international context.[23] The Fiscalía brings charges against defendants only in one-third of the crimes reported to it, and the criminal courts' rulings—that is, the peak of the pyramid—represent around 1.75 percent of the total crimes committed. In 1994–95, this percentage meant 31,920 rulings (Rubio 2001). This reveals that only a tiny portion of crimes are cleared through court rulings.

The reasons that people do not denounce a punishable act in Colombia are linked not only with lack of confidence in the results and the performance of judges and the Fiscalía, but also with the fear of retaliation. This second reason is very significant. It indicates that a negative association between violence and reports exists. In the most violent zones, people report less.

The crimes investigated and sanctioned by the criminal justice system. The following overview of the chronology and types of crimes litigated is based on the statistics that became available in the mid-twentieth century. In the 1940s, the percentage of cases initiated was distributed 40/40 between crimes relating to property (for example, thefts) and those relating to people's lives and physical integrity (for example, homicides and kidnappings). However, 60 percent of the accusations were made concerning crimes against people and 30 percent, concerning crimes against property (Rubio 2001).

From the mid-1950s, property crimes and those crimes labeled "others" began to gain ground in the courts, to the disadvantage of crimes against people. In the mid-1970s, serious problems of congestion appeared in the Colombian judicial system.[24] To help solve these problems, important procedural reforms of the system were devised, which restricted the number of trials through several mechanisms, including the exclusion of cases in which there was no known suspect.[25] In this way, (1) the increasing tendency to litigate crimes against persons was halted, (2) the rate of litigation of property crimes decreased, and (3) the rate of litigation of new types of crimes increased significantly.

The current situation confirms this tendency. According to the most recent home surveys, 90 percent of the criminal incidents in Colombia are related to property rights.[26] The percentage of crimes against property in claims made before the national police is, nevertheless, only 50 percent. This percentage diminishes to nearly 30 percent for cases that actually enter the judicial system. Crimes against life and personal integrity, in contrast, make up about 40 percent of reports filed with the national police. About 20 percent of these cases reach both the indictment stage and the trial phase. Also, the so-called other crimes constitute less than 20 percent of the total reports filed with the national police. Nevertheless, they represent close to 44 percent of the investigations and 42 percent of the convictions.

Rubio (2001) also studied the consequences of procedural reforms introduced in 1971 and 1987. According to his study, in 1994 the criminal investigations that were initiated in response to crimes against property had been reduced to approximately 10 percent of those begun in the mid-1980s, crimes against life to about 25 percent, and those against individual freedom to about 20 percent. The new priorities concentrate on crimes against the family, whose number of investigations increased by a factor of four between 1989 and 1994 and which currently constitute nearly 12 percent of the investigations, and drug trafficking crimes, which constituted an almost nonexistent category in 1985 but increased to a current rate of nearly 12 percent of the investigations.

The second consequence of this structural change is related to the relative negligence of the system regarding homicide. In the last twenty years, there has been a large increase in crimes against people, specifically, homicide. The criminal justice system does not investigate two out of every three homicides committed in the country. Judging by the data related to court rulings, nearly 95 percent of the violent deaths in Colombia are not resolved through judicial means. In fact, "the probability that a homicide leads to an accusatory resolution, that in the 1960s surpassed 35 percent, is currently slightly superior to 6 percent. Whereas in 1975 for every 100 homicides the criminal system captured more than 60 suspects, by 1994 that percentage had been reduced to 20 percent. The probability that a murderer is condemned, which was 11 percent in the 1960s, barely exceeds 4 percent today.[27] It is difficult not to think that such precarious indicators of performance have not played some role in the evolution of violence in the country in last the two decades" (Rubio 2001).

The third consequence is seen in the relation between crimes, accusations, and sentences. According to Fernando Gaitán, the probability that someone in Colombia in 1990 would have been accused of a crime he or she committed was 3.2 percent, and the probability that the person would have been condemned was 2.6 percent (Deas and Gaitán 1995, 328). Since the mid-1970s, however, the number of accusations has fallen drastically and the number of convictions has begun to increase, as well as the percentage of court rulings entailing a conviction. Thus, "from a relatively severe atmosphere in terms of investigation—an important percentage of investigations led to trials—but with some degree of uncertainty at the trial stage—between 70 percent to 75 percent of the trials ended in convictions—the criminal system shifted to a much more relaxed environment in terms of investigations ending in formal charges and thus trials, but much more severe, and predetermined, in the trial phase itself" (Rubio 2001).

The overall result of these three phenomena is what we have called the routinization of justice, which in the realm of ordinary criminal courts means the primary dedication of the judicial apparatus to cases of easy solution. These are the cases in which the identity of the accused and the circumstances of the crime are clear from the beginning and, therefore, generally lead to the Fiscalía bringing formal charges and to condemnatory sentences by the criminal judges. At the same time, the criminal system dedicates insufficient time and resources to the investigation and conviction of difficult cases, precisely those that generate greater instability in Colombian society.

These include common homicides—that is, those committed by common criminals or people involved in personal disputes, which, as explained previously, constitute the great majority of the homicides committed in Colombia. This tendency is compounded by the recent imposition of quantitative criteria of efficiency in the criminal justice system, which creates incentives for prosecutors to focus on easy cases that improve their record of "successful" investigations—that is, those that end in formal charges against the defendant.

Finally, court backlogs have been a chronic problem during the last three decades. The following mechanisms have been used to try to relieve the system: (1) procedural exclusion of cases in which the suspect is not known, (2) the introduction of criteria of efficiency in the performance of prosecutors, and (3) the improvement in the levels of qualification and remuneration of the judges and prosecutors. The manipulation of the justice system and its transformation in terms of efficiency have played an important role in the operation of the criminal justice system. This is especially serious if one considers that this manipulation affects prosecution of criminal incidents that cause a great deal of fear in society, such as homicide and aggravated robbery, which are frequently excluded from the system because of the difficulties that their investigation entails.[28] Efficiency thus results from a substitution of the criterion of ease for that of importance.

Conclusions

Throughout this chapter, we have set out to substantiate our claim about the contrast between visible and activist justice, on the one hand, and invisible and routine justice, on the other, as an essential feature of the operation of courts in Colombia. In this section, we end our study by formulating some conclusions about the central challenges for Colombian justice in the new century that can be extracted from the preceding analysis.

First, a noticeable characteristic of the judicial system in Colombia is the dissociation between the demand for and the effective supply of justice. The pyramid of litigation has a very small judicial peak. In other semiperipheral countries, strong social networks give rise to community systems of justice that lessen the risks of this dissociation.[29] In Colombia, the strains of urbanization, the sudden secularization, the crisis of institutional legitimacy, the weakness of social movements and of collective strategies, and the persistence of a culture of violence, among other factors, have dramatically deteriorated the internalization of values that in some way gave stability to the social expectations before the 1980s (Pécaut 1997; Santos and García-Villegas 2001a). Under these circumstances, and above all in the great urban areas, the lack of access to justice translates not only into a feeling of frustration, but also into violence (García-Villegas 2000a). In addition, in Colombia the culture of the judicial defense of rights is very precarious. In sum, whereas in other countries the effects of the dissociation between the supply of and the demand for justice are lessened by the effectiveness of the social mechanisms of conflict resolution, in Colombia such dissociation is aggravated by the deterioration of these mechanisms.

Second, the Colombian judicial system operates in a selective way. For example, the fact that civil courts busy themselves mainly with suits initiated by corporate repeat players against individuals without experience in litigation belies the principles of equality and fairness that constitute the core of judicial discourse. Such selectivity reveals a judicial system given over to commercial and financial interests. In addition, it entails a low-profile judicial apparatus that devotes itself mainly to procedures of administrative and even notary nature. This tendency debases the judicial system and undermines the important social role it must play.[30]

When viewed against the background of judicial selectivity, the issue of court efficiency becomes much more complex than advocates of judicial reform usually present it. The obsession with quantitative efficiency tends to overlook such central issues as who uses the judicial system, how accessible courts are for most citizens, and which sectors of the population benefit most from judicial decisions. For instance, Rodríguez (2001b) commented on an official study showing that in Colombia the likelihood of conviction for a criminal defendant represented by a state-appointed lawyer is 80 percent higher than for a defendant represented by a private lawyer. He pointed that no matter how much money is spent on providing criminal courts and prosecutors with computers, the system as a whole will continue to be highly unfair if the issues of legal aid and access to justice are not tackled.

The combination of inefficiency and selectivity is especially worrisome in the realm of criminal prosecution. In Colombia, the concentration in the justice system of certain types of crimes is not due solely to changes in the number of cases brought to court and to the introduction of new crimes, but to the filters introduced by the system in relation to the crimes without a known suspect—that is, in relation to that part of the case that is most difficult to process and to crimes that cause the greatest social alarm. Thus, the increased seriousness of the ineffectiveness of criminal justice in Colombia is based on (1) the deterioration of the social mechanisms of conflict resolution, (2) the increase in homicides during the last two decades and the consequent social alarm that it entails, and (3) the incapacity of the criminal system to deal with the most serious crimes.

Third, in general terms, semiperipheral countries such as Colombia are characterized by great social and institutional heterogeneity. In the judicial area, this has at least two consequences. There is a gap between the functional scheme of a classic liberal type that prevails in judicial discourse and legal procedures and the social conditions that do not correspond—nor have they ever corresponded—to the liberal societies from which such a scheme was copied. Also, because Colombia, as do all semiperipheral countries, combines political, cultural, and economic features corresponding to different stages of development—thus the coexistence and (skewed) cooperation, for instance, between formal postfordist and informal prefordist firms, and between elite sectors of the population fully inserted in the global economy and global culture and sectors that will never have a chance to have access to phone lines or running water—courts are asked to simultaneously deal with all sorts of conflicts. Uprimny and García-Villegas (1999) have made this point in the following way:

> The developed European constitutional regimes can be seen as buildings with several floors, that were successively built in different centuries, by absolutism—that set the ground for peace—, by liberalism—that controlled the state's arbitrariness—, by movements in favor of the universal vote—that extended citizen and democratic participation—, and by the fights against poverty and economic inequality—that launched the welfare state. In the Colombian case, the problem is that it seems we have to build the building all at once. Thus, we live situations of acute armed conflict and of precariousness of the state monopoly on violence, which means that Colombia faces typical state creation problems. However, our country must deal with these challenges in a very different context than that in which the European experiences of state construction of the 16th and following centuries developed. The human rights culture, at the national and international level, as well as the demands of the social and democratic movements, luckily prevent that the construction of a national state in Colombia be done without recognizing the principles of the rule of law, blocking democratic participation or forgetting social justice. Colombia must reach an internal public order in an ideological, legal and social framework that, currently, makes the absolutist formulas unsustainable, illegitimate, and even counterproductive in purely pacifying terms.

Fourth, the study of the relationship between the criminal justice system and the political regime is essential to understanding the operation of justice in Colombia. For thirty-six out of the last fifty years, the country has been under state of emergency. This situation of "normalized" abnormality has had enormous consequences on the national legal culture, on the institutional configuration, and, of course, on the structure and operation of the criminal jurisdiction. State of emergency legislation has created a large part of the criminal categories dealt with by the system and of the procedures that must be followed to sanction them. In this way, a type of exceptional criminal justice system parallel to the ordinary system has been created, with the limits of each insufficiently clear.

This study discusses why social conflicts that await a judicial solution have grown in proportion to judicial rulings in the last three decades. This is not true for all areas in which justice operates. Some crimes with implications for institutional stability of the country have caused the weakening of a special type of justice aimed at the reestablishment of the public order. This area of the criminal justice system leaves much to be desired and deepens the gap between judicial conflicts and results. On the other hand, the growth of the exceptional criminal justice has had repercussions by decreasing the number of ordinary judicial conflicts, criminal as well as civil. This results in a double dissociation between justice and conflict. In general terms, although exceptional criminal courts have not been highly effective, they have been gaining ground vis-à-vis ordinary criminal courts thanks to the expansion of their jurisdiction through emergency legislation. All this has brought with it a type of "trivialization" or "routinization" of the exceptional.

Fifth, in sum, the current institutional circumstances in Colombia raise important challenges and dangers for justice. On the one hand, courts have acquired an unexpected protagonism in the definition of the principal problems in the criminal justice system. The deterioration and corruption of the political class have made possible the intervention of judges in multifarious matters, ranging from the enforcement of social rights to the sanctioning of political corruption. On the other hand, the increasing inability of justice to respond to the demands arising from social conflicts makes evident a profound crisis of its traditional instrumental function. Judicial activism and court performance are intrinsically connected. Unless Colombian courts manage to raise their performance to an acceptable level of efficiency and to become actually accessible and useful to most citizens rather than to only a small minority, their highly visible—and oftentimes indispensable and welcome—incursions into the realm of politics will prove insufficient for the effective protection of rights in Colombia.

Notes

1. President Samper faced judicial action for receiving political contributions from drug traffickers during his presidential campaign. This process was named "Proceso 8000" by the press. See Uprimny (1996).

2. "Judicial protagonism" is related to "judicial activism." Like judicial activism, it requires a high level of involvement by judges in actions and decisions that help shape the country. However, unlike judicial activism, judicial protagonism requires that judges' actions and decisions be highly visible and accompanied by media attention. [*Trans.*]

3. The *Fiscalía General de la Nación* is closest in structure and function to the United

States attorney general. However, as will become evident later on, there are some important differences. [*Trans.*]

4. For instance, government expenses equaled 7.8 percent of the gross national product (GNP) in 1960, 10.6 percent in 1970, and 11 percent in 1975. For those same years in Brazil, they were 18.6 percent, 24.3 percent, and 23 percent; in Chile, 18.6 percent, 24.3 percent, and 23 percent. For all of Latin America, the figures were 15.1 percent in 1960 and 18.4 percent in 1970 (Wright 1981, 43). See also Kalmanovitz (1988) and González (1987).

5. The State Council (*Consejo de Estado*) is the equivalent of the French *Conseil d'État*—that is, the highest court in matters involving administrative law.

6. Until the 1990s, the funds allotted for the justice department equaled only between 2 percent and 3 percent of the national budget, the military's share of the same was between 15 percent and 18 percent, and the payments on the foreign public debt of the central government represented approximately 20 percent. According to numbers from the General Accounting Office, in 1987 justice counted on 1.9 percent of the national budget, defense expenses totaled 18.3 percent, and the payments on the foreign debt accounted for 17.6 percent.

7. These cooperative relationships are multifarious. A judge that works in a zone where there is an important presence of the *Fuerzas Armadas Revolucionarias de Colombia* (FARC), narrated the following two episodes, which are very illustrative. On one occasion, when he worked in a remote rural municipality, some guerrilla members brought to him a person they had tied up and said: "This man committed a homicide. We bring him to you, your honor, so that you can sentence him because we cannot keep him and he does not deserve to be shot. The deceased's body is at such and such a place and so-and-so witnessed the killing." According to the judge, based on those facts, the killer was condemned, and he is currently in jail. In this case, the official justice system took advantage of the investigative labor of the guerrillas to sanction a crime. But other times it is the opposite: it is the guerilla who administers justice based on the evidence collected by the official authorities. This same judge said that on another occasion, he had to investigate a lawyer who, in association with a corrupt judicial official, had stolen money from a widow. The investigation culminated with the sanctioning of the lawyer and of the corrupt official, but the judge explained to the widow that he, as a criminal judge, could not do anything to recoup the money. Then the woman told the judge that it did not matter; she only needed copies of the investigation's files to fix the problem. A little later the judge found out that with such copies, the woman went to the guerrilla commander of the area, who forced the lawyer to return the money to the woman.

8. For an explanation of the tutela action, see the section on constitutional justice.

9. The *acción de cumplimiento* is a legal mechanism whereby any person can ask courts to order a governmental agency to fulfill (*cumplir*) its duties whenever the latter's negligence or tardiness creates a serious damage to such a person.

10. See, among others, Decisions C-053/93, C-093/93, and C-150/93. In particular, the court decided that the period of detention could not be indefinite, because this violated the right to trial without unmerited delays, and added that secret judges and witnesses were constitutional insofar as the specific regulation of these institu-

tions permitted an effective right to defend. Thus, the court, according to these criteria, decided that it was unconstitutional to sentence someone based solely on secret witnesses because this "makes vulnerable the principles of judicial certainty and the publication of the sentence, the guarantees of the defendant and the right to due process" (Decision C-275/93). In this same line of thought, in Decision C-394/94 the court established that the extension of the right of secrecy beyond the information that would identify the witness was unconstitutional because it violated the right to defense, as it did not permit the defendant to contradict the testimony.

11. See Decision C-141/95.

12. International pressure has assumed various forms. Since the mid-1980s, many reports from prestigious human rights nongovernmental organizations (NGOs), such as Amnesty International, have denounced grave human rights violations attributable to the Colombian state. Since the end of the 1980s and throughout the 1990s, the Interamerican Commission of Human Rights has issued twenty resolutions condemning the Colombian government for disappearances, massacres, and murders. Likewise, in a decision handed down in December 1995 in the case of Caballero Delgado and Santana, the Interamerican Court condemned Colombia for the disappearance of two teachers. The United Nations established a permanent office of its High Commissioner of Human Rights, and the Commission of Human Rights has expressed on various occasions its preoccupation with the Colombian humanitarian crisis. Equally important is the fact that the reports of the U.S. State Department concerning the human rights situation in Colombia have been increasingly more severe in their condemnation of the Colombian government.

13. The *tutela* action is a legal mechanism whereby a person can ask any court to immediately protect his or her constitutional rights whenever they have been violated or are seriously threatened and there are no other similarly effective judicial mechanisms at the plaintiff's disposal. Thus, this action—which has equivalents in other legal regimes, such as the *amparo* action in Mexican law—amounts to a control of constitutionality in concrete cases, as opposed to the abstract control of constitutionality of laws exerted only by the Constitutional Court (more on this distinction later). The tutela action has been enormously popular since its introduction in the 1991 constitution.

14. We present a brief summary of the main results of this investigation. The complete explanation of the results and the statistical methodology can be found in García-Villegas and Rodríguez (2001), as well as in a previous, extended version of the study (CIJUS 1995). The updating of the statistical data has been done with the collaboration of Henrik López.

15. A paradigmatic case of this constitutional absence was the lack of a mechanism of protection for students against the arbitrary actions of the boards of educational institutions. This situation explains the explosion of the number of proceedings related to these conflicts through the tutela.

16. As explained previously, according to the constitution, the tutela can be used only when no other recourse for judicial defense exists, except when it is used to avoid an injury that cannot be remedied. The Court's jurisprudence has added that, for the tutela to be unavailable, the judicial defense must exist and must be effective for the protection of the right violated or threatened.

17. To understand precisely the study's results and the reach of civil justice in Colombia, one must know that until 1989, civil courts decided all types of matters related to what in the continental judicial tradition is known as "civil law" or "common law," including conflicts related to family law. In that year, nevertheless, the jurisdiction specializing in family matters was created, so civil justice does not currently deal with this matter. For this reason, the data covering civil justice before 1989 include family matters, while after that year, separate statistics for civil and family courts exist. To simplify, in this section we talk about "civil justice." However, one must understand that the long series of data covering civil justice includes family conflicts, and the short series includes only civil conflicts as understood narrowly.

18. The declaratory trial (*juicio declarativo*) is similar to a normal civil trial in the United States, in which it is likely that each party will present evidence supporting his or her position and dispute the evidence presented by the other party. Executory trials (*juicios ejecutivos*) in Colombia are most similar to summary proceedings in the United States, except that they are even more limited. In Colombian executory trials, all the plaintiff is seeking is the enforcement of a clear and undisputable legal right. [*Trans.*]

19. In Colombia, liquidation proceedings include, besides the liquidation of bankrupt corporations, the execution of wills, the dissolution of marriages for causes other than death, and the nullification and dissolution of corporations. In the voluntary jurisdiction trials, temporal declarations, concerning matters that have not been tried, are made about diverse matters, such as the presumed death of a missing person or a holding that a person is mentally incompetent with regard to civil affairs.

20. The calculation of the data per number of inhabitants is based on the demographic data published by DANE in the period studied. The estimated current population of Colombia is 38 million.

21. The declaratory-executory trials are initially declaratory trials that seek the recognition of a right (such as the right to be indemnified because the defendant breached a contract), but then become executory when the plaintiff within the same trial seeks to enforce the decision coercively (for example, through the seizure and auction of the defendant's property).

22. The criminal classification of "terrorism," for example, is so broad in Colombian legislation that several crimes based on it have been prosecuted that do not represent any social danger (Nemogá 1997).

23. The percentage is usually double this in most countries (Almeida 1992). But the most important difference between Colombia and other countries is related to crimes against human life and bodily harm or kidnapping. Although the volume of intentional homicides per 100,000 inhabitants in Colombia for 1996 was 59, for Portugal, it was 3. In addition, according to the Colombian Commission of Jurists (Comisión Colombiana de Juristas 1999, 27), half of the kidnappings in the world occur in Colombia.

24. As of 1940, investigations began to grow at an almost constant annual rate of 7 percent. The capacity to dispose of indictments, on the other hand, grew at an average rate of only 1.3 percent annually. According to numbers obtained by Rubio (2001), between 1940 and 1964, the criminal proceedings that the system decided to investigate increased fivefold, from 30,000 to 150,000 per year. For the same period,

the annual number of cases that the system could actually handle increased by less than 50 percent, from 10,000 in 1940 to nearly 15,000 in 1964. For 1964, the number of cases that entered the criminal system annually was ten times greater than the number that could be investigated. By the beginning of the 1960s, the situation was such that the accumulated cases that had not been classified equaled ten years of entries. With the capacity of the system at that time, it would have taken nearly a century to deal with the backlog, if no new cases had been accepted.

25. Decree No. 1450 of 1984 voided the power of the police to carry out criminal investigations without the authorization of a judge. Decree No. 50 of 1987 restricted the opening of criminal cases to those criminal incidents that had known suspects.

26. The National Survey of Homes No. 72 of 1991 and No. 90 of 1995 included samples of 17,203 and 21,130 homes, respectively.

27. With such doubtful effectiveness, any attempt to control homicide based on an increase of the sanctions contemplated in the legislation seems weak. For every ten years added to the legal punishment of this conduct, there is an increase in the expected sentence of just five months.

28. The number of these crimes has skyrocketed in Colombia over the last twenty years (see Deas and Gaitán 1995; Pécault 1997).

29. For example, according to Santos et al. (1996), the strong networks of mutual recognition and collaboration based on kinship and neighborhood relations that characterize Portuguese society favor the mechanisms of communitarian and peaceful conflict resolution.

30. As Santos and his colleagues rightly comment in presenting similar results in their investigation on Portuguese justice: "[T]he fact that our judges are dominated by low-intensity disputes reinforces their vulnerability, their routinization, their bureaucratization and, lastly, their social irrelevance" (1996, 688).

References

Almeida, María Rosa Crucho de. 1992. *Inquérito de vitimaçao.* Lisbon: Gabinete de Estudios e Planeamento.

Arango, Mariano. 1981. *Café e industria: 1850–1930.* Bogotá: Carlos Valencia Editores.

Berquist, Charles. 1988. *Los trabajadores en la historia latinoamericana: Estudios comparativos de Chile, Argentina, Venezuela y Colombia.* Bogotá: Siglo XXI.

Charria Angulo, Alfonso. 1988. *Plebiscito, referendum o dictadura?* Bogotá: Impresores Iberoamericana.

CIJUS (Centro de Investigaciones Jurídicas y Sociales). 1995. *Incidencia social de la acción de tutela.* Bogotá: Universidad de Los Andes.

Comisión Andina de Juristas. 1992. *Justicia para la justicia.* Bogotá: Comisión Colombiana de Juristas.

Comisión Colombiana de Juristas. 1999. *Tercer informe.* Bogotá: Comisión Colombiana de Juristas.

Comisión de Racionalización del Gasto y las Finanzas Públicas. 1996. *El sistema judicial y el gasto público.* Bogotá: Imprenta Nacional.

DANE (Departamento Administrativo Nacional de Estadísticas). 1996. *La justicia Colombiana en cifras*. Bogotá: Imprenta Nacional.

Deas, Malcom. 1995. Canjes violentos: Reflexiones sobre la violencia política en Colombia. Pp. 3–5 in *Dos ensayos especulativos sobre la violencia en Colombia*, edited by Malcom Deas and Fernando Gaitán. Bogotá: Fonade.

Deas, Malcom, and Fernando Gaitán, eds. 1995. *Dos ensayos especulativos sobre la violencia en Colombia*. Bogotá: Fonade.

Evers, Tillman. 1977. *El estado en la periferia capitalista*. México: Siglo XXI.

Galanter, Marc. 1974. Why the "haves" come out ahead: Speculations on the limits of legal change. *Law and Society Review* 9:95–160.

Gallón, Gustavo. 1979. *Quince años de estado de sitio en Colombia: 1958–1978*. Bogotá: Editorial América Latina.

———. 1984 Leyes y excepciones en el derecho a la vida. *Controversia* 119:25–36.

———. 1989. *La arbitrariedad mesurada*. Unpublished manuscript.

García-Villegas, Mauricio. 2000a. Contexts of law and justice in Colombia: With some glances at Latin America. Paper presented at the Law and Society annual meeting, Miami.

García-Villegas, Mauricio, and César Rodríguez. 2001. Justicia constitucional: La acción de tutela. Pp. 423–54 in *El caleidoscopio de las justicias en Colombia*, edited by Boaventura Santos and Mauricio García Villegas. Bogotá: Uniandes-Siglo del Hombre-Colciencias- Centro de Estudos Sociais (CES).

Gaviria Díaz, Carlos. 1996. *La tutela, instrumento de paz*. Unpublished manuscript.

González, Fernán. 1989. *Un país en construcción*. Bogotá: Centro de Investigación y Educación Popular (CINEP).

González, Jorge Iván. 1987. Empleo público y estado en Colombia. In *Controversia*. Bogotá: CINEP.

Hoskin, Gary. 1988. Modernización social, populismo frustrado y esclerosis política: Reflexiones sobre la democracia Colombiana. *Pensamiento Iberoamericano* 14:16–29.

Jacob, Herbert. 1996. *Courts, law and politics in comparative perspective*. New Haven, Conn.: Yale University Press.

Kalmanovitz, Salomón. 1988. *Economía y nación: Una breve historia de Colombia*. 3d ed. Bogotá: Siglo XXI, CINEP, Universidad Nacional de Colombia.

Leal Buitrago, Francisco, comp. 1996. *Tras las huellas de la crisis política*. Bogotá: Tercer Mundo, Fundación Friedrich Ebert en Colombia (FESCOL), Instituto de Estudios Políticos y Relaciones Internationales (IEPRI), Universidad Nacional de Colombia.

Montenegro, Armando, and Carlos Esteban Posada. 1994. *Criminalidad en Colombia*. Bogotá: Planeación Nacional.

Nemogá, Gabriel Ricardo. 1995. Crisis judicial: Enfoques diferentes y elementos constantes. *Pensamiento Jurídico* 4:24–47.

———. 1997. *La justicia sin rostro*. Bogotá: Universidad Nacional.

Oquist, Paul. 1978. *Violencia, conflicto y política en Colombia*. Bogotá: Biblioteca Banco Popular.

Pearson de González, Annette. 1997. *Informe de evaluación sobre las experiencias de las*

Casa de Justicia de Ciudad Bolívar en Bogotá y de Aguablanca en Cali, presentado al Banco Interamericano para el Desarrollo. Santafé de Bogotá. Mimeographed.

Pécaut, Daniel. 1988. *Crónica de dos décadas de política Colombiana*. Bogotá: Siglo XXI.

———. 1997. Presente, pasado y futuro de la violencia. *Revista Análisis Político* 30: 41–54.

Presidencia de la República.1993. *Seguridad para la gente: Segunda Fase Estrategia Nacional contra la violencia*. Bogotá: Imprenta Nacional.

Rodríguez, César. 2001a. La justicia civil. Pp. 547–614 in *El caleidoscopio de las justicias en Colombia*, edited by Boaventura Santos and Mauricio García-Villegas. Bogotá: Uniandes-Siglo del Hombre-Colciencias-CES.

———. 2001b. Globalization, judicial reform and the rule of law in Latin America: The return of law and development. *Beyond Law* 18:13–42. Bogotá: Instituto Latinoamericano de Servicios Legales Alternativos.

Rodríguez, César A., and Rodrigo Uprimny. 2003. Justicia para todos o seguridad para el mercado? El neoliberalismo y la reforma judicial en Colombia y en América Latina. Pp. 34–89 in *La Falacia Neoliberal*, edited by Darío Restrepo. Bogotá: Universidad Nacional de Colombia.

Rouquié, Alain.1984. *El estado militar en América Latina*. Bogotá: Siglo XXI.

Rubio, Mauricio. 2001. Justicia penal: Juicio sin sumario. Pp. 485–547 in *El caleidoscopio de las justicias en Colombia*, edited by Boaventura Santos and Mauricio García-Villegas. Bogotá: Uniandes-Siglo del Hombre-Colciencias-CES.

Santos, Boaventura. 2001a. Los paisajes de las justicias en las sociedades contemporáneas. Pp. 85–150 in *El caleidoscopio de las justicias en Colombia*, edited by Boaventura Santos and Mauricio García-Villegas. Bogotá: Uniandes-Siglo del Hombre-Colciencias-CES.

———. 2001b. Derecho y democracia: La reforma global de la justicia. Pp. 151–208 in *El caleidoscopio de las justicias en Colombia*, edited by Boaventura Santos and Mauricio García-Villegas. Bogotá: Uniandes-Siglo del Hombre-Colciencias-CES.

Santos, Boaventura, and Mauricio García-Villegas. 2001a. Colombia: El revés del contrato social de la modernidad. Pp.11–84 in *El caleidoscopio de las justicias en Colombia*, edited by Boaventura Santos and Mauricio García-Villegas. Bogotá: Uniandes-Siglo del Hombre-Colciencias-CES.

———, eds. 2001b. *El caleidoscopio de las justicias en Colombia*. Bogotá: Uniandes-Siglo del Hombre-Colciencias-CES.

Santos, Boaventura, Maria Leitão, Joao Pedroso, and Pedro Lopes. 1996. *Os tribunais nas sociedades contemporâneas: O caso Português*. Oporto, Portugal: Afrontamento.

Touraine, Alain. 1976. *Les sociétés dépendantes*. Paris: Duculot.

———. 1988. *La parole et le sang: Politique et société en Amérique Latine*. Paris: Odile Jacob.

Uprimny, Rodrigo. 1993. *Las violencias en Colombia: Hechos, interpretaciones y búsquedas de alternativas*. Bogotá: PNR. Mimeographed.

———. 1994. Narcotráfico, régimen político, violencia y derechos humanos. Pp. 104–29 in *Drogas, poder y region en Colombia*, edited by Ricardo Vargas. Bogotá: CINEP.

————. 1995. Fiscal General o General Fiscal? Nuevo procedimiento criminal y derechos humanos en Colombia. *Revista del Colegio de Abogados Criminalistas del Valle* 29 and 30:67–89.

————. 1996. Jueces, narcos y políticos: La judicialización de la crisis política. Pp. 120–46 in *Tras las huellas de la crisis política*, edited by Francisco Leal Buitrago. Bogotá: Tercer Mundo Editores, FESCOL, IEPRI.

————. 1997. Administración de justicia, sistema político y democracia: Algunas reflexiones sobre el caso Colombiano. FESCOL. Pp. 78–117 in *Justicia y sistema político*. Bogotá: FESCOL.

————. 2001. Las paradojas de la justicia en Colombia. In *El caleidoscopio de las justicias en Colombia*, edited by Boaventura Santos and Mauricio García-Villegas. Bogotá: Uniandes-Siglo del Hombre-Colciencias-CES.

Uprimny, Rodrigo, and Mauricio García-Villegas. 1999. El nudo Gordiano de la justicia y la guerra en Colombia. In *Armar la paz es desarmar la guerra*, edited by Alvara Camacho and Francisco Leal Buitrago. Bogotá: FESCOL.

Wright, Philip. 1981. El papel del Estado y las políticas de acumulación de capital en Colombia. *Cuadernos de Economía* 3 and 4:14–36.

CHAPTER 6

The Rise of Lawyers in France

ANNE BOIGEOL

LAWYERS ARE AT the heart of the production and diffusion of legal culture. Since the 1970s, they have seen their role, their practice, their social position, and their influence in society change appreciably. Judges now extend beyond their role as servants of the law, and the emergence of a business bar has shaken up the legal profession. A changing conception of the judicial system among legal practitioners is at the heart of these transformations. For certain judges, judicial authority "is no longer merely a secondary element, but is a central marker of genuine authority" (Salas 1998, 12).

These changes are bound by complex links to more general societal transformations that are not brought about solely by changes in the social structure and are not specific to French society: changes in the economic situation, with the development of an economic crisis and then with changes imposed by the liberalization and globalization of economic markets; changes in the demand for justice, with the evolution of family models or with the emergence of victims as a new collective actor; as well as transformations generated by the unification of Europe and the internationalization of the legal field.

The early 1970s mark the beginning of this period of societal transformation (see Appendix 1). No precise date marks this beginning; it is defined rather by a series of intertwined events and tendencies. The early 1970s saw the end of a period of continuous economic expansion, in particular, with the first oil crisis in 1973. This period is also marked by the entry into the professional labor market—and, specifically, admission to the bench and to the bar—of baby boomers. Also after 1970, recourse to the legal system for

Thanks to Cécile Bargue for her help with documentation and her comments.

the resolution of divorce matters intensified, considerably amplifying a development that began in 1964. For the legal profession, the end of the 1960s was a period in which a small number of lawyers realized that the fragmentation of the legal profession into several vocations would not enable them to resist the increased competition from lawyers that would accompany the unification of Europe. They recommended a process of integration that was first articulated in the professional reforms of 1971. The beginning of the 1970s also follows a period marked by the movement to unionize judges, initiated in 1968 (see Appendix 1). All of these changes, in addition to others, are evidence of a turning point in the evolution of the law and of legal culture.

In this chapter, the approach to the evolution of legal culture will be from the perspective of the professional actors, and more precisely, *magistrats* and *avocats*.[1] This approach requires that the evolution of the role of law and courts in certain disputes be taken into account. Therefore, the approach will be from a particular angle, primarily empirical, which will illuminate the transformations that have taken place in the legal field since the 1970s. This approach also takes into account some of the diverse ways of analyzing legal culture—either by describing the attitudes of the public and the professionals with regard to the law (Friedman 1985, 1997), or by using an analysis of civil disputes (Blankenburg 1990), ideological analysis (Cotterrell 1997), or other approaches.

The chapter initially deals with the evolution of French legal culture through an analysis of the education of lawyers at universities and then addresses the question of whether the increase in the number of lawyers during the early 1970s led to more lawsuits. This is followed by an inquiry into the manifold consequences of changes in the criminal justice system. The final discussion deals more specifically with the evolution of the two most significant legal vocations: avocats (practicing attorneys who belong to bar associations) and magistrats.

The Increase in the Number of Lawyers

Lawyers are at the heart of the production and diffusion of legal culture. Their numbers have increased appreciably since the 1960s—that is, since the entry of the generation born after the Second World War into universities and subsequently into the professional market. The number of students studying law in 1973 was two and a half times that in 1962 (as shown in Table 6.1). Since that time, the increase has been much less appreciable. Between 1973 and 1993, the number of law students grew by 74 percent, but the proportion of law students among all students declined.[2]

This growth is explained mainly by the increase in graduates from high school,[3] combined with the relative democratization of access to higher edu-

TABLE 6.1

Changes in the Gender Profile of Law Students

Year	Number of students	% Law students	% Female among new students	% Female among all students
1962	45,511	17.1	—	—
1973	112,954	16.2	50.4	52.3
1978	131,460	15.6	53.2	51.9
1983	134,432	14.4	57.8	54.9
1988	142,504	13.7	57.9	55.4
1993	196,236	13.9	61.8	59.7
1997	186,870	12.9	—	—
1998	180,490	12.8	64.6	57.3

SOURCE: Ministère de l'education nationale, Direction de la programmation et du développement, "Repères et références statistiques sur les enseignements, la formation et la recherche" (publications for each year listed in table).

cation. Under the socialist government of François Mitterand, whose goal was to bring 80 percent of the generation to the baccalaureate level (end of high school), the number of graduates increased by 70 percent, from 282,000 in 1987 to 492,000 in 1995 (*Données sociales* 1999, 81). With the onset of the economic crisis, providing young people with greater access to universities also became a means of managing youth unemployment. The universities —with some rare exceptions—are public organizations that do not practice selective admission. The university course comprises three levels: access to the first level is conditional on obtaining a baccalaureate, and entry to the other levels, on the successful completion of examinations; access to the third level is not automatic. It is necessary to submit an application to be registered in the third level and to be allowed to work for the DEA (Diploma of Advanced Studies) or the DESS (Diploma of Specialized Higher Studies). The DEA is, in theory, a year of introduction to research, but in practice, it comes close to the DESS, which is essentially professional training. With the growth in the number of students, the third level has become very selective.

The number of graduates in law is significantly lower than the number of students registered at the university due to the high rates of failure and the high dropout rate during the first year (46 percent). Nevertheless, the number of graduates in law consistently increased during the last quarter of the twentieth century. Although a decline in the number of registered students began in 1996, this decline is not very noticeable today at the graduate level (see Table 6.2).

The number of graduate students has more than doubled in twenty years for those at the bachelor's level (baccalaureate plus three years) and the master's level (baccalaureate plus four years). Many students, however, stop at the

TABLE 6.2

Graduates in the Second and Third Levels of University

Year	Second level		Third level		
	License* (3 years)	Master's degree (1 year)	DEA (1 year)	DESS (1 year)	Doctorate (3 years)
1977	8,191	6,983	1,890	900	409
1983	8,912	6,712	2,162	1,393	478
1988	9,528	8,622	2,359	2,330	956
1993	14,578	12,483	1,753	3,949	416
1997	17,262	15,582	4,454	4,472	588

SOURCE: Ministère de l'education nationale, Direction de la programmation et du développement, "Repères et références statistiques sur les enseignements, la formation et la recherche" (publications for each year listed in table).
*License is equivalent to a bachelor's degree; the course takes one year after two years at
the first level.

master's level. More than two-thirds of the master's degrees conferred were in the area of private law; only 11 percent, in public law (the rest were without specialization). However, beyond the increase in diplomas conferred, university legal culture appears to have changed in other ways.

UNIVERSITY TRAINING DIRECTED MORE
TOWARD THE NEEDS OF THE MARKET

The most significant change is the success of and increase in the professionalization of higher education. Under market pressure, universities are no longer exclusively places of "legal science" and of academic knowledge but are becoming, perhaps more and more, professional schools and places of vocational training, where both professors and experts play an educational role, actively intervening in professional training. The success met by the DESS evinces this new tendency. This training, which is often very selective, makes it possible for students to have a diploma known and recognized in professional contexts and that allows for changes in training to meet market demands.[4] At the end of their studies, the students have a professional anchoring, which is often a key to entering the professional world. DESS is particularly sought after by students and thus extremely selective.[5]

A similar change can be observed concerning another sphere of activity among professors of law: legal consultation. As experts in their fields, they can be requested to provide opinions on points of law and legal doctrines. However, consultations in the field of business law appear to be much more practice oriented; these consultants are asked not only to give a report on doctrinal matters related to a particular question but also to analyze the application of the law in various scenarios (Bancaud and Boigeol 1995).

TABLE 6.3

Traditional Legal Professions

Profession	1973	1998
Law professors	—	1,261
Lecturers	—	1,644
Judges and prosecutors	4,538	6,457
Administrative magistrate	—	858
Clerks	4,028	7,810
Avocats	8,307	34,078
Notaries	6,338	7,624
Bailiffs	2,544	3,241
Avoués	245	390

SOURCE: Annuaire Statistique de la justice 1999 (Paris: La documentation française); Ministère de l'education nationale 1999, Note d'information 92-25.

CHANGES IN THE SOCIOLOGICAL PROFILE OF LAW STUDENTS

The increase in the number of students was accompanied by a change in
their sociological profile, notably its feminization. Certain university disciplines have been more feminized than others. Law is one of the disciplines
that is rather strongly feminized in the first two levels of higher education;
as in the other disciplines, feminization is weaker at the doctorate level. In
1998, women accounted for 56 percent of all students and 61 percent of law
students (78 percent of the students in literature, 21 percent in sciences and
technology, and 64.6 percent of the new entrants in law school [Table 6.1]).
Although there has been a certain democratization in education, students
in law generally come from relatively affluent social backgrounds, as do their
counterparts in medical school.

These law students will then occupy various positions in society. Some of
them will join one of the traditional legal occupations by becoming practicing attorneys, professors, bailiffs, clerks, and so forth (see Table 6.3). The majority of these occupations recruit only a small number of new entrants annually due to their small size. A significant number of those trained in law
will be practicing attorneys.

One consequence of the mass production of new lawyers is increased
competition to enter certain legal fields for which entry is controlled by entrance exams or other restrictions. The educational qualifications required
for these positions have become significantly higher. Candidates who successfully complete the entrance examination at the *École nationale de la magistrature* (National School of Magistracy [ENM]) have more advanced university diplomas than required by the school and, more often, have double

specializations, including, for example, a diploma in law and a diploma delivered by an institute of political studies.

The rise in academic competition and the complexity and increasing technicality of the problems that arise also lead lawyers working in business law firms or in the legal offices of banks and companies to have dual training: a diploma in law plus a more technical diploma (banking, finance, trade). The culture of legal professionals has thus become less strictly "legal" and more diversified.

In addition to traditional legal occupations, new work opportunities have been available to students during the last few decades due to the increased legalization of social relations. These include working as a lawyer in a corporation, an insurance company, or a bank. In order to expand, companies are now forced to have access to extensive and effective legal services. For example, a large construction and public works company had 20 lawyers in 1986; ten years later it had 120 lawyers. The number of lawyers is correlated with the volume of business. In this same company in 1986, there was a lawyer for each billion francs of sales. In 1996, there were two lawyers for each billion francs in sales.[6]

It is extremely difficult to know the exact number of lawyers in French society apart from those in traditional legal professions. Law is a type of general training suitable for various occupations. Some trained lawyers do not practice law, and many provide administrative legal services. The difficulty in counting the trained lawyers is indicative of their position in French society. Although one can estimate only the number of lawyers in the traditional legal professions, it is clear that it has increased appreciably. The presence of more lawyers logically leads to the legalization of social relations and to an increase in legal services. The level of litigiousness and the practice of law are somewhat dependent on how many experts are available, but the relationship between the two is not simple.

Recourse to Justice by Citizens

In the mid-1970s, a survey of the French population revealed the extent to which the public perception of the civil justice system was more favorable than that of the criminal justice system, an institution that many French citizens saw as repressive and punitive (Baraquin 1975). The survey also revealed the schism between the system of civil justice and the culture of the citizens. For citizens, it was better to avoid recourse to the system, because of its cost, its slowness, its association with social stigma, and general ignorance of the institution. At the time, only 10 percent of citizens were estimated to have a good knowledge of the legal system and its operation, and only 13 percent possessed a good knowledge of their personal rights. Overall knowledge of the system of civil justice increased somewhat because of greater use and a relative improvement in public access to law and justice. A few years ago the public image of the judicial system did not appear particularly positive, as illustrated by an opinion poll in 1997 (Jean 1999). More than 65 percent of the population did not trust it and had a bad impression of it, more than 75 percent criticized it for functioning poorly and found it to be slow and expensive, and more than 80 percent judged it "antiquated" and "subject to political influence." Their claims related mainly to the perceived lack of access to the justice system and to the necessity to accelerate the processing of cases in courts. Those who had come into contact with the justice system judged its operation even more severely. In spite of these trends, the number of citizens having recourse to civil justice has actually increased.

THE INCREASE IN CIVIL CASES

The increase in the recourse to justice occurs both at the level of adjudicated cases and at the level of *procédures de référés* (summary procedures), which are special procedures allowing the court, in the event of an emergency, to take interim measures (repair damage, preserve evidence, and so forth) while awaiting judgment. Very often the procedure stops there, as the parties are satisfied with the decision. All the courts are concerned by an increase of their activity (as shown in Table 6.4). (See Appendix 3 for information on the French judicial system.)

The growth in the number of people filing claims in the civil justice system since the 1970s is undeniable. Reports confirm this trend by demonstrating the increase in disputes and the workload of the magistrats. Many such reports estimate that courts cannot continue to function in this manner (Coulon 1996). During this period, the French population increased (information available in Appendix 2); but a comparison of the number of cases

TABLE 6.4
Activity in Civil Courts (Rendered Decisions)

	1973	1978	1983	1988	1994	1998
Ordinary Courts						
Court of Cassation	6,518	8,777	13,648	19,255	18,456	20,463
Courts of appeal	54,704	75,554	114,439	163,973	186,426	207,125
Courts de grande instance	181,913	247,353	349,652	460,022	601,991	631,728
Courts d'instance	219,984	264,842	384,338	480,624	499,237	453,060
Special Courts						
Commerce Tribunal	170,077	209,861	264,051	190,275	297,746	236,094
Conseils de prud'hommes	73,163	81,201	137,251	148,970	165,815	165,235

SOURCE: Annuaire statistique de la justice 1973–1999 (Paris: La documentation française).

TABLE 6.5

Number of Civil Cases

Year	Court of cassation		Courts of appeal		Courts of grande instance		Court d'instance	
	Filed	Decided	Filed	Decided	Filed	Decided	Filed	Decided
1973	14	12	119	105	364	350	433	423
1978	21	16	172	142	509	465	508	497
1983	28	25	247	210	690	643	755	707
1988	31	29	275	283	807	815	1,189	1,074
1993	34	31	350	306	968	910	962	950
1997	34	34	359	340	1,082	816	787	754

SOURCE: Annuaire statistique de la justice 1973–1999 (Paris: La documentation française).
NOTE: Number of cases per 100,000 inhabitants.

—new or adjudicated—with increases in the population shows that population growth cannot adequately account for the relative increase in disputes, as shown in Table 6.5.

Cases are assigned to one of the two general first instance civil courts, depending on their importance. The number of cases per 100,000 inhabitants brought before ordinary civil courts and courts of appeal increased threefold between 1973 and 1997 (except for the courts of instance because of the transfer of some of their responsibilities to the courts of *grande instance*). In fact, the courts of appeal saw the highest increase in its activity, resulting in an increase in the average processing time for cases (16 months in 1989; 17.4 months in 1998). However, since 1977 the amount of civil litigation as a whole has decreased. The number of judges and prosecutors has increased but not in proportion to the increase in disputes: 4,538 in 1973 and 6,327 in 1998, a 40 percent growth that explains, at least in theory, the longer time period required to process cases.

Have the French become more litigious, a phenomenon that would demonstrate a change in attitude toward law and the justice system? An analysis of the principal disputes enables us to give a qualified answer. Recourse to the civil justice system occurs when it is inevitable, as in the case of divorce or when one is summoned to court for breaching a contract.

FAMILY AND CONTRACT DISPUTES

The greatest increase in disputes during the period studied was in family law, specifically, proceedings related to divorce disputes and their aftereffects.[7] This type of dispute, which in 1973 accounted for 36 percent of the activity of the courts, today accounts for 60 percent of the cases processed at the court of grande instance level. Changes in the traditional family model have resulted in a rise in the divorce rate and thus in the number of people resorting to court intervention, because divorce, even by mutual consent, must be validated by a judge. (The plan to deregulate divorce by consent, suggested by a former minister of justice, ran up against a lobby of avocats who did not want to lose what is a significant source of income for many practicing attorneys.) Not only has the number of divorces grown, but divorce provisions concerning children are more often contested and modified: there are often modifications to custodial arrangements and to the amount of alimony awarded, the latter being particularly numerous during periods of economic crisis and high unemployment.

The rise in divorce was also accompanied by changes in the role of judges and the judicial system—the creation of specialized courts (that is, a family court that was in place for only a few years, which was replaced by a judicial post to deal with matrimonial cases, an office that has since been revamped to include the adjudication of other familial disputes). Judges in charge of family affairs gradually moved away from their traditional role, receiving training that enabled them to better understand the divorce process: they now endeavor to convince spouses to reach a mutual agreement rather than impose a decision.

The other significant field of civil dispute is contract law. Whereas family law disputes are heard in courts of grande instance, contract disputes are dealt with primarily in the courts of instance, which have become, to some extent, courts of contract. In the majority of these cases, the financial stakes are low. Most of the time (75 percent of the cases) the applicants are creditor organizations (coming before the court for nonpayment of rent, for example) and not private individuals. The courts of grande instance also hear disputes relating to contract law in which the economic and financial stakes are sometimes considerable, representing a significant shift in the work of judges. Due to the internationalization of the economy and the legalization of economic relations, judges are increasingly asked to intervene as arbiters of economic relations. The legal institution is thus becoming "not only one of the arenas, but also one of the privileged instruments for the resolution of disputes which take place in the economic sphere" (Dezalay 1995, 121).

The economic crisis of the early 1990s was marked by an increase in disputes, many of which concerned excessive debt, layoffs, breached contracts, and the liquidation of companies. Between 1990 and 1996, cases relating to breach of employment contracts brought before the labor relations board, the *conseil des prud'hommes* (a tribunal composed of nonprofessional judges), increased by 12 percent. In addition, the number of receivership or bankruptcy cases grew by 63 percent during the same period (Lumbroso and Timbart 1999). These types of disputes are treated by a specialized court—the commercial court—composed of nonprofessional judges. The lack of legal rigor in some of these jurisdictions has inspired critics to call for the intro-

TABLE 6.6

Activity in Administrative Courts

	Conseil d'état		Administrative courts of appeal		Administrative courts	
Year	Filed	Decided	Filed	Decided	Filed	Decided
1973	8	8			43	41
1978	9	8			57	48
1983	16	13			85	78
1988	16	13			195	122
1993	19	18	13	12	164	164
1998	17	17	28	19	221	184

SOURCE: Annuaire statistique de la justice 1973–1999 (Paris: La documentation française).
NOTE: Cases per 100,000 inhabitants; the administrative courts were created in 1989.

duction of a professional judge into the decision-making process, a suggestion that would further expand the role of professional judges in the system. But opposition from members of the commercial court to this reform has been strong.

DISSATISFACTION OF CITIZENS REGARDING THE FUNCTIONING OF THE STATE

Disputes processed through administrative hearings increased nearly six-fold beginning in the 1970s, which attests to the dissatisfaction of the citizens vis-à-vis the operation of the state (see Table 6.6). In spite of a 50 percent growth in the number of administrative judges, from 0.8 per 100,000 inhabitants in 1973 to 1.5 in 1998, the duration of administrative proceedings increased appreciably, thus demonstrating the difficulties faced by these courts in responding to demands for governmental accountability. The processing time for a case before the administrative court is two years, whereas in the judicial courts of first instance, it is nine months.

THE VARIABLE SUCCESS OF ALTERNATIVES TO JUSTICE

Alternatives to the judicial system have existed for a long time in the economic sphere. Companies prefer nonpublic, quick arrangements and are slow to resort to legal institutions. The development of a system of arbitration for private transactions met these needs (Dezalay and Garth 1995). Another alternative has existed in France since 1978: the institution of the *conciliateur.* Its mission is to facilitate, apart from any legal procedure, the amicable settlement of legal disagreements.[8] The role of the conciliateur is limited; he or she cannot definitively resolve the dispute but must simply endeavor to reduce the tensions and the aggressiveness of the parties. The conciliateur is supposed to function more in a social than a legal way. However, when the role of conciliateur was created, these individuals found their position rather difficult. They were regarded as intruders who lacked legitimacy and encroached on the territory of legal professionals such as judges and avocats. The conciliateurs reacted by asking for more institutionalization of their position, with special training, particularly in law, establishing themselves as a specific and legal vocation. In 1999, the number of conciliateurs was increased to support the amicable resolution of small claims (according to the data of the Department of Justice, there were 1,605 conciliateurs at the beginning of 1999). But their role is still modest.

Other more modern forms of "evading the civil judge" appeared (Guinchard 1998), such as mediation, with relative success. The first formalization of mediation in French law dates back to 1955 and occurred in the area of labor law, where mediators help resolve collective labor disputes. In 1973, mediation developed in administrative matters, with the creation of a mediator of the republic charged to settle disagreements between citizens and the administration.

The history of mediation in France shows a relative increase since the 1980s. The development of mediation in North America, in particular the emergence of criminal mediation in the United States and of family mediation in Quebec, created great interest in France in professional and institutional circles to such a degree that American experiments are being imported and tested.[9]

The greatest efforts to institutionalize mediation's role in the legal system have been carried out in the field of family law, especially in the last ten years.[10] At the same time, there has been an increase in the number of mediation facilities and in associations practicing mediation. The process of professionalization of mediators began with the publication of works, often written by mediators, to promote mediation as an institution. Yet, after a period of enthusiasm, when people spoke of an "irresistible rise" in family mediation, the success of this practice is still so limited that there is talk of "invincible stagnation" (Cardia Vonèche and Bastard 1995). The importance of mediation in the speeches and in the literature seems out of proportion to its effective place in dispute resolution (Lazerges 1997).

Mediation has been officially recognized as a legal procedure since its incorporation into the code of criminal procedure in 1993 and the code of civil procedure in 1995. More recently, the minister of justice has called for developing alternative modes of litigation (Jean 1999). In commercial matters, the development of mediation as a legal practice is under way; lists of mediators and the rules of mediation have been prepared, but the practice itself appears less developed (Bessard 1997). Until now, except for arbitration, the implementation of alternatives to the legal resolution of conflicts has been limited. Alternatives have met with professional and institutional re-sistance and also certain judicial reservations.

In order to limit the tendency of avocats to press lawsuits rather than to encourage the amicable resolution of disputes, a recent law (1998) allows re-imbursement for avocats who opt to settle civil disputes rather than submit the cases to the courts.

In other fields, initiatives have come from judicial authorities who want to promote nonadversarial modes of resolution to ease the caseload of the courts. One such initiative targets cases of excessive debt through a 1992 law that aims at an amicable settlement of these cases; the law creates a mecha-nism that ensures that the courts are used as a means of last recourse. The law mandates the creation of commissions organized on the departmental level that are charged with working out plans to restructure the debt with the par-ties. As a result of the surge in excessive debt cases, whose importance had been largely underestimated at the time of the law's enactment, the com-missions' workload was heavy, and the parties often ended up turning to the judicial system for the resolution of their cases (Sadaume de Oliveira 1997). A new law was passed in 1995 to limit the possibility of recourse to judicial intervention in these cases.

ACCESS TO LAW AND JUSTICE

Increasing the public's access to law and the judicial system is a concern that appears throughout this period. The cost of obtaining justice, the lack of legal knowledge among citizens, their general fear with respect to unfamiliar legal institutions, and the dominant "penal" image of the legal system have dissuaded citizens from commencing legal proceedings. "It is better to have a bad arrangement than a good lawsuit," says a French proverb. Today, ac-cording to surveys, the majority of French still consider it better to avoid re-course to the judicial system.[11]

Initially, access to the judicial system was the primary focus of the public's attention (law of 1972) and then, more generally, access to the law (law of 1991).[12] Questions regarding the costs of accessing the legal system are often articulated in surveys and in speeches on judicial matters. These questions became more important as the economy declined with the first oil shock of 1973, which affected the income of a significant part of the population. Be-tween 1983 and 1997, unemployment continued to rise; the proportion of those earning minimum wage grew from 11.4 percent to 15.1 percent, which is related somewhat to the increase in part-time work (see Appendix 2). This resulted in an appreciable growth in the cases handled by legal aid. In 1998, the number of civil and administrative applicants increased 4.6 times com-pared to the number of applicants in 1975 and 1.8 times compared to 1985.

Less than 25 percent of the cases brought before the courts of grande instance receive legal aid, while 30 percent of divorce cases receive aid (Millet 1999). The cost of legal aid is supported by the state: in 1991, the cost amounted to 367 million francs; in 1998, it was 1,240 million francs—that is, more than three times the amount in 1991. Legal aid was extended to criminal defense in 1982.

Concerns related to access to legal advice were not addressed in the initial reform of legal aid in 1972. Since 1991, access has been dependent on local initiatives, more precisely, those of the president of the court and its local partners (such as bar associations and local community organizations), who have the means of creating departmental councils of legal assistance. These initiatives, which are still few in number, coincide with the significant responsibility undertaken in recent years by municipalities and associations to facilitate access to the legal system for the most underprivileged populations. Certain community organizations did not wait for state subsidies to address their citizens' lack of legal knowledge and have been providing a permanent service of free legal aid for some time. Many of these organizations have acquired very good legal skills in certain areas of law and provide excellent service. Unions and consumer associations have also developed legal aid offices. In addition, bar associations arrange for free legal consultation to be provided in town halls or local courts.

Social workers are often the privileged interlocutors between the legal system and members of the population who are marginalized in relation to the legal system. They are charged with informing these groups on the law. Although social workers are not lawyers, they contribute a great deal to the dissemination of information on law and individual legal rights.

The increase in publications dealing with how to assert one's rights and in the popularity of legal discussions on television or radio shows intended for consumers, owners, tenants, and accident victims are a sign of the growing public interest in law and its implementation, even though it is difficult to evaluate the precise impact of this phenomenon. This diffusion of law is probably not without consequence in the recourse to courts. However, as a significant share of the increase in court files can be attributed to creditor organizations for debt recovery, the number of citizens who take advantage of their legal rights is still limited.

Perspectives on the Criminal Justice System

There has been much talk about the "historical turning point" when the judiciary liberated itself from political influence (Salas 1998). The result of this historical change was the impingement of criminal justice on aspects of the political and, to a lesser extent, the corporate spheres. But political and eco-

TABLE 6.7

Activity in Penal Courts

Year	Complaints received by the *Parquet*		Sentences	
	Number (in thousands)	Per 100,000 inhabitants	Number (in thousands)	Per 100,000 inhabitants
1987	5,353	9,627	586,719	1,055
1988	5,073	9,099	355,626★	637★
1993	5,395	9,382	553,289	962
1997	4,941	8,431	537,353	916

SOURCE: Annuaire statistique de la justice 1987–1998 (Paris: La documentation française).
★Effect of the amnesty decided at the time of the election of the president of the republic.

nomic elites were not the only ones to be subjected to the increased intrusion of the criminal justice system in their lives. The crackdown on both minor and major infractions has never been so forceful. Sanctions handed down are harsher than ever (Burricand and Timbart 1996). The prisons are overflowing. At the same time, the legal system more and more ignores complaints from citizens and attempts to deal with petty criminality in other ways.

The data that legal institutions provide give an account of police behavior and the response of courts that differs from the account of "delinquency" experienced by private individuals. Changes in the law and in the political leanings of public authorities can affect the general evolution of social behavior and can lead to an increasing number of convictions, even though the number of crimes committed does not increase in the same proportion. The studies undertaken on criminal justice show that judges pay little attention to citizen complaints of criminal activity, primarily because the police have not clarified these complaints (Robert 1999). The proportion of police reports that arrive at the *parquet* in which the offender is unknown grew from 42 percent in 1990 to 63.4 percent in 1998.[13] The cases that are not processed continue to increase, particularly complaints filed by the victims of misdemeanors; moreover, many victims do not file complaints because of their slim chances of succeeding in a legal action against the offender (Crenner 1999).

The trends reflected in police statistics and cases transmitted to the parquet give an imperfect image of the reality of delinquency. Even though all the infractions are not handled by a legal institution, the rise in legal actions has gradually led to a freezing of the criminal justice system, resulting in frequent case delays, and a judgment handed down several years after the crime is not uncommon. The criminal justice system thus loses much of its effectiveness.

Between 1987 and 1997, the number of offenses sanctioned by the criminal justice system decreased (as shown in Table 6.7). But this reduction is

TABLE 6.8

Sanctioned Offenses

	Number of Infractions		
Nature of infractions	1984	1993	1996
Crimes	2,729	3,247	3,383
Homicides	640	615	612
Assaults and armed robbery	308	357	336
Rapes[a]	700	1,329	1,550
Misdemeanors	532,325	591,651	589,118
Burglary; concealment	202,558	168,992	147,113
Traffic infractions[b]	85,877	132,979	131,087
Driving Under the Influence	48,220	101,536	97,910
Illegal labor[c]	241	5,027	8,128
Narcotics related	20,966	51,235	71,647

SOURCE: Timbart (1999).
[a] Rape totals include figures for statutory rape (rape of a minor fifteen years old or younger: 129 in 1984; 764 in 1993; 864 in 1996).
[b] Traffic infraction totals include driving under the influence.
[c] Work by illegal aliens or work that is part of the underground economy. *Ed.*

apparent only because it comes primarily from the decriminalization of certain activities that are now handled by administrative authorities (for example, bounced checks, which have been managed by the banking authorities since 1991). Here, one encounters the problems of comparison analyzed by Blankenburg (1990). With no meaningful change in the legislation, the variation in crime rates and sanctioned offenses reveals not a reduction but an increase during the same period (Timbart 1999).

Cases of theft and receipt of stolen property are the most frequent types of cases, but their proportion of the total has decreased; the crimes actually punished have increased, in particular, rapes (26 percent of all of the crimes sanctioned in 1984, and 46 percent in 1996). Guilty verdicts for statutory rape (sexual intercourse with a minor fifteen years or less in age) have increased sufficiently to explain the total increase in crimes that are punished. This growth does not reflect only a rise in this type of criminality but, at least to some extent, a change in the behavior of the victims who are now less hesitant to file complaints. In 1996, convictions for statutory rape were six times greater than in 1984 (as shown in Table 6.8) and now constitute more than half of the crimes reported.

Criminal justice appears increasingly centered on public policies relating to sensitive problems that, at some point in time, lead to a crackdown. Thus, the fight against drug trafficking has been particularly intense. Between 1984 and 1993, the number of drug cases grew by 244 percent. The fights against illegal immigration and underground work were also the subjects of political attention.[14] Illegal labor cases are more numerous than before, which does not correspond to an increase in this type of work but to the political will to crack down on these situations through increased control. This is also true of the crackdown on intoxicated motorists, a problem that became particularly severe because of the high number of fatal accidents.

To limit the number of cases filed for which no action is taken and the feeling of impunity that this inaction generates, as well as to modernize the methods of cracking down on certain activities and to better facilitate the protection of the victims, alternatives to criminal litigation were put into place for the parquet. Mediation-conciliation mechanisms have emerged gradually in this context along with summons by the prosecutor or the prosecutor's delegate for a solemn reminder of respect for the law. The use of alternatives to court proceedings has increased regularly: more than 8.8 percent between 1995 and 1996, more than 12.4 percent between 1996 and 1997, and 60 percent between 1997 and 1998. In 1998, 13.7 percent of the colorable claims in this area were handled through an alternative procedure.

These initiatives led to the creation of the "houses of justice and law," the first of which was created at the beginning of the 1990s. These "houses" assist the judicial system by providing access to justice, preventing delinquency, assisting crime victims, and overseeing alternative modes of dealing with conflicts (Wyvekens 1996). They are still few in number, but increases are planned. In certain jurisdictions, they are used a great deal. In Lyon, two out of three criminal cases in the parquet go to the correctional justice system and one to alternative measures (Dalle 1999).

In addition to this justice "de masse," during the last decade one could observe a rise in so-called *affaires*, or criminal actions aimed at political personnel, high-ranking civil servants, or the heads of corporations for corruption or failing to perform their public duties. This phenomenon has had a profound impact on the public perception of criminal justice primarily because these affaires are heavily reported on by the press. Thus, public and administrative life—the life of the republic itself—has been subjected to "criminalization" (Garapon and Salas 1996). This complex process has been analyzed as resulting from outside forces and, of course, from changes in the magistracy (Bancaud and Robert 2001).

The malfunctioning of administrative and political responsibility and policy leads to a process of criminalization. Criminal penalties become substitutes for otherwise ineffective regulations of political and corporate conduct. Also, weakened legitimacy of political and administrative elites as a result of the erosion of the welfare state and their implication in these scandals heightens the investigative curiosity of judges and causes a certain level of indignation among the citizens.

In addition, in recent years some groups of victims—victims of contaminated blood, of asbestos poisoning, of oil slicks (following tanker shipwrecks)

—have mobilized, and many now use the legal system to demand justice and reparations.

The demands made on judges and on the judicial system take many forms. Society simultaneously demands that the judicial system be a place of memory (Papon lawsuit), that it establish the historical truth, that it take sides in questions of bioethics, and that it evaluate public health policies or the contents of the planning of social policies.[15] The legal system is increasingly implicated and engaged in diversified and expanded areas of society.

Judges and prosecutors are confronted with a complex set of demands. They must manage large caseloads, consisting principally of crimes committed by those left behind by society, and more sophisticated disputes, such as those involving political and economic elites in cases of corruption, financial crimes, or "corporate crimes." These are extremely complex and often require a broad understanding of specialized fields not traditionally within the competency of magistrats. A small number of magistrats, examining judges, and prosecutors have acquired knowledge in these fields and have therefore become specialists, all the more dreaded by litigants because the media play up their actions. But the evolution of the magistracy itself constitutes an explanation of this criminalization.

Judges and Prosecutors

Because of the changes mentioned, the magistracy is becoming, according to some, an "autonomous political actor." If the sociopolitical context partly explains this evolution, which is characterized by the breakdown of judicial subordination to the political sphere, these changes cannot be understood without examining changes in the magistracy itself. The situation is no longer a matter of socialist trade union judges who, in the 1970s, engaged in symbolic actions aimed at denouncing the class aspect of justice, but of judges who present themselves as professionals and who, through their practice, endeavor to redefine their social and professional identity (Roussel 1998).

THE PROFESSIONALIZATION OF THE MAGISTRACY
AND CORPORATIST TEMPTATION

In a trend that has been evident for a number of decades, the magistracy has continued to bureaucratize. It has come closer to the model of other public offices, in particular in aligning its methods of selection with those of the highest level of the French administration. To understand the French situation, it should be noted that the administrative and political elites and many economic elites belong to what appears to be a specificity of French bureaucracy: *les grands corps de l'État.* They are educated at the *École nationale d'administration*, the National School of Administration (ENA) created in

1945, and are among the highest ranked at the final examination. The ENA and the grands corps de l'État, such as members of the *Conseil d'État* (Supreme Court of administrative justice), have always constituted a model for the judicial magistracy, which often compares its position to theirs. The National School of Magistracy (ENM) was created in 1958 on the model of the ENA. Since 1958, magistrats have been recruited by competitive exam, and their training has been provided within this school;[16] the ENM has not, however, been able to compete with the ENA for qualified applicants. Until now, no student who has been admitted to both the ENA and the ENM has ever chosen the ENM. The prestige of the magistracy slowly declined until the mid-1990s, as demonstrated by the progressive decrease in the use of magistrats in official ceremonies.

Today, four out of five magistrats have been recruited and trained within the ENM.[17] They receive training that lasts thirty-one months, with both theoretical and hands-on training. In addition to this initial training, the ENM offers continuing education courses that magistrats may pursue throughout their careers.

The training of young judges and prosecutors within a specialized school, where they are gathered for rather long periods, has an effect on the conception of the profession. One of the consequences of the creation of a national school of magistracy was the formation of a professional esprit de corps, with its solidarity and its shared values. Solidarity between magistrats develops to the detriment of vertical solidarity with legal professionals at higher levels of the professional hierarchy. The magistrats are identified as belonging to the group they were trained with at the ENM, which becomes, to some extent, a reference group, such that magistrats appear to have less need of their superiors to guide their conduct.

The level of competition to enter the magistracy is an interesting indicator of the institution's capacity to attract individuals and therefore of its prestige. Although the institution was rather selective in the early 1970s, this selectivity had decreased by the end of the decade, and the magistracy had significant problems recruiting magistrats during the 1980s. Since the 1990s, the number of candidates for the magistracy has grown, and the competition has become very fierce (one candidate in seventeen is successful). Is this the result of a significant rate of unemployment or the result of a renewed attraction to the magistracy?

The feminization of the magistracy constitutes the most outstanding feature in the evolution of the sociological profile of this institution. In 1999, women made up 48.5 percent of the magistrats (in 1982, they accounted for 28.5 percent), and the process of feminization is progressing; of the candidates who currently take the entrance examination, 70 percent are women. This feminization reflects an increase in the number of women in the legal labor market, but it also shows the lack of interest among young male law-yers, who prefer to direct their professional ambitions elsewhere, mainly to the business bar (Boigeol 1993). The feminization of the magistracy has changed the model of the bench somewhat. The male gender, with some of its attributes, such as physical force and voice power, is no longer associated with judgeship. Now the profession includes both males and females, and this modifies the image of authority, making it more strictly professional (Boigeol 1997).

In addition to feminizing the magistracy, the mode of recruitment previ-ously discussed allows for a relative democratization of the legal profession. The magistracy now recruits from the middle class, with women coming from slightly higher-status social backgrounds than men (Bodiguel 1991).

The manner in which judges and prosecutors are selected and trained has given rise to much criticism; people have denounced the inexperience of the young magistrats and recommended a system more in accord with the British/American model, in which magistrats are selected from among con-firmed professionals, lawyers in particular (Soulez-Larivière 1990). The criti-cisms were particularly strong during the 1980s when the magistracy was ex-periencing recruitment problems.

The esprit de corps that evolved among magistrats resulted in a mistrust, even a distrust, of lawyers who attempted a lateral move into the judiciary. Besides recruitment by open competition following the completion of legal studies and legal training at the ENM, professional experience in the general legal profession is another route to the magistracy. This mode of recruitment has been encouraged in recent years, with the aim of diversifying the profes-sional background of the magistracy and avoiding "cultural monolithism." The magistrats who came to the magistracy through the traditional route of the ENM never approved of the integration of former practicing attorneys into their ranks. They believed that these new members of the institution lacked the professional culture forged at the school and were suspected to have entered the magistracy because they had failed elsewhere (a claim that is not always false). In the same manner, the small number of magistrats who temporarily leave the magistracy to pursue other activities are not always well received on their return (Boigeol 2000).

In their careers, magistrats have become less dependent on political per-sonnel for advancement, at least as far as judges are concerned. Since 1993, the *Conseil supérieur de la magistrature*, the Higher Council of the Magistracy (CSM), which is responsible for assigning magistrats to their posts, has been made up primarily of judges and prosecutors elected by their peers.[18] It was given greater power to recommend nominations for president of courts of grande instance. The CSM opinion now has binding effects on the minister of justice when dealing with judges, and the council provides a consultative

opinion when dealing with public prosecutors. During the socialist government of Lionel Jospin (1996–2002), the ministers of justice committed
themselves to nominating only those who received a favorable opinion from
the CSM for positions at the public ministry.

The creation of specific professional organizations also attests to the transformation of the magistracy, which gave up part of its individualism that used
to make the institution particularly sensitive to the pressures of hierarchy.
The first magistrats' organization was created in 1946. But the birth of the
Magistrats' Trade Union in 1968 reflected an institutional awareness of the
importance of collective political action. At the beginning of its existence,
this trade union approached topics that went beyond simple corporatist defense: justice and money, justice and immigration. It introduced new forms
of demand and protestation into the magistracy, hitherto not very inclined
"to be in politics or to make politics." The labor union movement also made
its mark: the oldest organization, located at the center of the political chess-
board, took its trade union form in 1973. With the arrival of leftist political
power in 1981, a third organization, marked as politically "rightist," formed
itself within the magistracy.

THE MAGISTRACY AND THE PRIVATE MARKET FOR LEGAL SERVICES

The criminalization of political and business life had unforeseen consequences. A certain number of companies and administrative agencies were
affected when their leaders were implicated in criminal conduct; the crackdown had been anticipated neither by law firms nor by internal legal departments. Many large companies, directly or via headhunters, thus "hired"
particularly qualified magistrats, examining judges, or members of the financial parquet and offered them higher salaries in order to obtain their advice
on actions to be taken in relation to certain disputes. Even certain business
law firms, which did not use the courts, sometimes sought the assistance of
these magistrats. Those who left the magistracy "sold" their knowledge of
the legal system and its clerks. Not all solicited magistrats responded positively to private-sector requests; the spirit of public service and a certain distancing from money matters remain significant components of the professional model of the magistracy (Boigeol 2000).

THE "JUDICIAL JUDGE": A NEW ACTOR IN THE POLITICAL FIELD

When entering the magistracy, judges and prosecutors seek to exert functions of authority and to occupy a privileged position in society.[19] The magistracy does exert functions of authority, with a specific duty toward society
and progress: magistrats manage a large number of disputes ranging from divorce cases to the condemnation of minor offenders and repeat offenders.
They have become a kind of ordinary civil servant, "workers of the law"

(Bancaud 1991) who are more suited to clearing files than to processing them. There is a strong temptation among magistrats to become disenchanted with, or to endeavor to redefine the meaning of, their occupation. Less constrained by social networks, which imply a certain unquestioning submission to legal and political authority, more confident in their own competence, "they [magistrats] hold an intransigent belief in the official values of justice and show an acute sensitivity to the symbolic dysfunctions of justice and to contradictions between practice and the official line" (Bancaud and Robert 2001, 180).

To a certain extent, the advent of a leftist government in 1981 accelerated changes in the judicial system, and disappointment with leftist leadership among those who expected radical leftist reform "facilitated the shift in policy disputes to political disputes" (Bancaud and Robert 2001, 182). The socialist government of François Mitterand, apart from carrying out certain symbolic reforms, such as the abolition of the death penalty and the abolition of special courts (the state security court and military tribunals), failed to meet the aspirations of the magistrats by privileging high-ranking civil servants within the hierarchy of state administration. Last, and perhaps most significant, a 1990 amnesty law favoring politicians deeply irritated judges and contributed to their radicalization, shocking the ethos of a new generation of magistrats concerned with equality before the law.[20] Politico-financial matters would give these magistrats the opportunity to display their presence and their authority.

But it is not solely in relation to politics that the role of judges changed. In the economic sphere, too, they are more frequently asked to intervene, and in a different manner.

THE "LEGAL JUDGE": A NEW ACTOR IN THE ECONOMIC FIELD

Traditionally, magistrats, like lawyers, maintained a distant relationship with and even displayed mistrust toward the business world, which was convinced of magistrats' relative incompetence in this field and considered them to be more at the periphery of the economic world than in the center. Because of internationalization of the economy and "legalization" of economic relations, judges are now often solicited by economic actors. Justice tends to become "not only one of the arenas, but also one of the privileged instruments [used in] the battles that take place in the field of economic relations" (Dezalay 1995, 121). A few years ago, the position of judges in this new system was said to depend on the system's capacity to operate what the president of the Supreme Court of Appeal called a "cultural revolution." In the economic field, judges are in territory unfamiliar to them, where they are obliged to set aside prudence and are required to go beyond their role of guardians of the letter of the law and stability. According to Bancaud and Boigeol (1995),

In the area of economic law, more remains to be done than has been done. Very often the law does not exist, or it is too general or too old to be applicable. Moreover, the business community needs predictable, explicit, fast and flexible answers to legal questions, and not answers that are rigid, constantly put off, or made incomprehensible and unpredictable by imprecision and indecision. Fundamentally, a new conception of the law, the way it is created and its authority, is in the making—a new, less ritualized, less general, less abstract law, that takes into account the realities of the business world. (110–11)

Paradoxically, law firms play a significant part in redefining the role of judges. As crafters of the internationalization and legal codification of the market, they tend to see judges as referees between corporations and the state, between the corporations themselves (through the "legalization" of arbitration), between the members of the European Community (EC) and their national institutions, and between national law and EC law, to whose creation these law firms have contributed (Dezalay 1995).

THE INDEPENDENCE OF THE MAGISTRACY: TOWARD A SEPARATION OF THE JUDGES AND PROSECUTORS

Judges and prosecutors belong to the same body of magistrats, receive common training, and can pass from the bench to the parquet and vice versa without a problem. Until now, the magistrats of the parquet were responsible to the minister of justice. Recent reform proposals envisage an increase in the independence of prosecutors, whose nomination would be subject to the approval of the CSM. Without severing the links between the minister of justice and the parquet, the proposals aim to limit the power of the minister of justice over prosecutors. The reforms have not been voted on.

However, within the magistracy a minority of judges and prosecutors predict that change in the practice of the parquet makes the dogma of unity problematic (Dalle 1999). The position maintained at the Conference of First Presidents of Courts of Appeal in 1998 attests to this evolution: they unanimously decided in favor of a separation in status between judges and prosecutors. The evolution of judges and prosecutors was analyzed as symmetrical: "As the prosecutors left the courts and immersed themselves in society, in order to carry out public policy, judges, on the other hand, focused on courts and became more preoccupied with impartiality" (Dalle 1999, 56). More and more often, prosecutors were brought in to intervene at the local level. With the decentralization that began in the 1980s, prosecutors have come closer to the new local centers of power to implement policy in the fight against crime, particularly in the suburbs. One prosecutor notes that "[w]e are on the ground more, ensuring a legal presence at the point where decisions are made, to respond to requests and . . . to find concrete solutions to the problems which arise as well as to regain the confidence of the citizenry" (Donzelot and Wyvekens 1998, 31). Is there then an increased cultural divide between judges and prosecutors that requires a differentiation of their status? Although it is extremely controversial within the magistracy, this perhaps suggests, in the long run, the principle of the duality of judicial power. Does this signal an end of the French model of the magistracy (Dalle 1999)?

The Difficulties in the Emergence of a French Business Bar

Lawyering during this period underwent a significant transformation in its professional culture with the fast development of a business bar, along with the growth of business law and the internationalization of economic relations. The bar thus shifted from a model centered on the primacy of private individual clients, traditional civil law, criminal defense, and the role of the attorney as a defender to a model where business law dominates, the clients are corporations, consultation is more prevalent than defense before the courts, and lawyers are concentrated in structures that become enterprises.

The practice of law is the traditional legal field that displayed the strongest growth rate during the last three decades, increasing from 8,307 in 1973, to 17,683 in 1988, to 34,097 in 1997, and absorbing a great number of young graduates in law. (It should also be noted that during this period, in 1991, the legal profession also integrated *conseils juridiques*, or legal consultants—that is, between 5,000 and 6,000 people.) Today, young avocats are attracted to the practice of corporate law and the high remuneration associated with it.

Until the 1960s, the practice of law was a profession whose size was relatively stable, made up primarily of somewhat older men. The situation has changed completely. Not only has the profession become younger, but it has also been feminized. In 1983, women made up 33 percent of lawyers, and 24 percent of them were younger than thirty (Boigeol 1988). In 1998, more than half of avocats were less than forty years of age; women accounted for 45 percent of all the bar and 65 percent of the avocats under thirty years of age. But there are also a number of older women who are avocats; the bar has been open to women for over one hundred years (since 1900).

The territorial distribution of avocats is very unequal. On average, in France there are 58 avocats for every 100,000 inhabitants, but in Paris there are 612. In 1998, this amounted to more than 13,000 avocats—half of all trained lawyers—which testifies to the ability of the Parisian bar to attract lawyers (Munoz Perez and Moreau 1998). The concentration of avocats in the capital has increased. The bar associations of Paris and Nanterre (a business district in Paris) contain 41.7 percent of all French avocats (38.2 percent and 3.5 percent, respectively). The second-largest contingent of practicing attorneys in France is in Lyon and comprises 1,360 avocats—4 percent of all French avocats. The situation of the Parisian bar accords with France's centralist image, a reality impossible to circumvent, in spite of the progress of decentralization. It is in Paris that the registered offices of large companies, the principal economic institutions, the stock exchange, and many international organizations are concentrated. It is thus in Paris that the largest business consultancies and the large legal institutions have been established.

The evolution of the bar is very closely related to the development of the business legal market that began in the 1970s. The internationalization of the economy and its deregulation reinforced the importance of legal formalization of business relations and the increased recourse to contracts, whose clauses are the subject of intense negotiation. With the increase in takeover bids in the 1980s, contractors discovered or rediscovered the tactical use of law both to defend against and to attack their competitors. Economic warfare thus took place on the legal level, requiring lawyers of a new type and resulting in the emergence of a business bar in France.

Today, the bar is strongly differentiated and hierarchically arranged according to fields of law and clients. At the top of this hierarchy are large firms specializing in business law (taxation, commercial law, and so forth), composed primarily of men, with high incomes; at the base are young people, very often women, working as sole practitioners with general law practices, but with a propensity toward family or criminal law, and earning relatively low salaries (the disparity between the two is so great that some speak of the impoverishment of a fraction of the bar). Between the two, there is an intermediate bar, with a diverse clientele and varied legal specializations (Karpik 1995, 1999).

The conversion of the general bar to business law did not take place easily; for a long time, work that touched on commerce or trade was regarded as undignified work, and it was not certain that the process would succeed (Boigeol and Dezalay 1997; Karpik 1999). In fact, the emergence of a French business bar met with two major obstacles. The first came in the form of internal resistance, from those clinging to a small-scale model of lawyering; the division of function between several legal professions delayed and obstructed the construction of a strong profession able to face international competition. The second was a consequence of the first: because national professionals found it hard to organize as a strong entity able to control legal services for French business, the establishment of foreign firms and legal departments of multinational corporations was facilitated.

A brief word about the way in which the neglect of legal services for businesses sheds light on the French situation. From the beginning of the century, only a very small fraction of the bar was interested in the legal problems of large companies. Other occupations then met those needs—notaries in particular, but especially an unofficial group that offered many services to businesspeople and traders, the *agents d'affaires*, some of whom became legal consultants. Legal consultants developed and offered companies a variety of services in tax, accounting, civil law, labor law, and so forth (Boigeol and Dezalay 1997).

In the mid-1960s, some members of the Parisian bar became aware of the danger inherent in the division of the profession in France in light of the competition from European lawyers, and accordingly proposed a single, merged, and large profession, on the model of the American legal profession, in a way that would encompass all legal professions and would have a monopoly on legal work. The proposal succeeded partially; *agréés* (who represented cases before the commercial court) and *avoués* (who were a type of solicitor) of first instance were integrated into the bar. The majority of the bar associations were hostile to the project, and legal consultants did not react favorably to the proposal, believing that the ethical rules of the bar—which, for example, prohibited going to see clients at their places of work—were incompatible with the services provided to companies.

As French avocats began to explore the market for corporate legal services, they also discovered foreign competition. Law firms and multinational firms of auditors with multidisciplinary practice, the "big eight," arrived in France, not working within the bar (which was not open to them) but as legal consultants or in-house counsel, gradually occupying an increasingly significant role. The expansion of American and British firms, and especially the ambitions displayed by the multinational firms of auditors, placed into question the viability of the national monopoly on legal services built by generations of clerks (Dezalay 1992).

To face this competition—which proved to be more threatening than was initially anticipated—French avocats realized the urgent need to again regroup their dispersed forces. In the 1980s, the modern faction of the Paris bar mobilized again, and after two years of conflicts, confrontations, alliances, and reversals of alliances, the new legal profession, which joined avocats and legal consultants, was created in 1990. With the reform, the lawyers employed by legal subsidiaries of six giant accounting firms (at that time) were now fully recognized avocats of the bar. Their competition would take place from then on within the bar. Also, as soon as lawyers from the EC could establish themselves in France, American and British law firms would be able to practice without major restrictions. Moreover, the reform ratified the modes of organization that were completely foreign to French avocats, such as salaried work or the practice of legal work in commercial firms, which upset the traditional practices of lawyers.

The creation of a French business bar requires institutions that, by their size, can compete with foreign offices. Since the reform, the process of concentration of law firms has proceeded, but with less drastic results. Although reliable information on large French law firms is not yet available, they still appear to be very few in number:[21] "the French firms seem seized by an irremediable tendency to split up, which does not cease to deprive them of the benefit of growth, whereas the foreigners are engaged in maneuvers to control the French market" (Karpik 1999, 81). Now that lawyers working in the legal subsidiary companies of the major accounting firms and in the Parisian offices of the British and American law firms are fully recognized by the bar, the future of the French business bar appears, at the very least, dubious. The situation is all the more difficult for the French bar, as its mode of organization and its mode of "government," which continue to be a source of dispute within the profession, are increasingly seen as unsuited to the problems and the real stakes at issue (Karpik 1999).

Conclusion

This chapter has approached French legal culture through its professional actors. This approach is incomplete, but it appears to afford a key to enhance understanding of the evolution of French legal culture, whose transformation can be seen in the increase in the number of lawyers since the end of the 1960s. This rise in the number of lawyers was accompanied by a significant transformation in the training provided at universities—training that is not purely academic but more professional—and by a diversification of the positions offered to lawyers. Even though the traditional legal professions, and particularly the bar, absorb a rather significant number of lawyers each year, companies and organizations such as banks and insurance companies continue to constitute new outlets for young lawyers. As a result lawyers are becoming more and more present in French society.

The relationship between the number of avocats and the importance of their use of the courts is complex. Nevertheless, one can say that there is a link between the two.[22] The strong increase in civil disputes observed during the last thirty years can be seen as related to the improvement in access to the legal system and the institution of legal aid in 1972, and to the increasing number of avocats, but external factors also play a major role: transformations in the family, the development of a consumer society, the economic crisis and its impact on the level of employment, the levels of income, and thus the capacity of citizens to adhere to contractual engagements. The change is also in the profile of the user of the justice system. Economic actors frequently seize on legal processes and use them in a tactical way within the framework of economic disputes.

The change in the legal culture can be seen in the transformation of the role of the judge. In civil matters the judge's role goes beyond simple implementation of the law; apart from dealing with ordinary cases of divorce and debt recovery, the judge is now asked, in the economic field for instance, to serve as referee between corporations and between private corporations and the state. In criminal justice, changes are quite visible and are most spectacular because of media coverage.

The criminalization of political and administrative life, seen through the prosecution of some of its members, is significant evidence of the rise of judicial power in the state and of the creation of what certain magistrats call the "third power [*tiers pouvoir*]" (Salas 1998). Together with this new role, the criminal justice system and its judges must address ordinary and massive criminality, although a growing number of cases are not resolved by the police.

The explanation of the increasing prosecution of political, administrative, and economic elites must be sought, in particular, in the malfunctioning of administrative mechanisms of regulation, but the evolution of the magistracy is part of this development. This discussion has attempted to demonstrate, first, how professionalization and the corporatist development of the magistracy led it to a rather dominated position with regard to the highest level of French administration and, second, how these influences allowed the magistracy, in a particular sociopolitical context, to reposition itself.

The change in the French legal culture can also be seen through the transformation of the bar, through its relation with the business law market. The evolution of the bar during these thirty years is marked by the difficulty faced by French legal professionals in creating a business bar, because of their late arrival in the business law market, divisions in the legal profession, and the presence of new, powerful competitors: the Parisian offices of British and American law firms, as well as the legal departments of the major accounting firms in France. The growth and ambitions of these latter entities made the development of a French business bar a difficult task. The particular structure of their professional organization has not enabled them to react quickly, collectively, and effectively to this situation.

French legal culture evolved under the influence of societal transformations and also as a result of the influence, whether sought or imposed, of other legal systems and of other societies. The intrusion of international law firms or the legal departments of multinational consultancies on the French legal market has allowed these institutions to take the lead and has thereby shaken the French legal system. They are seen as the vehicle for penetration in France of British and American law, particularly in the drafting of contracts.

Simultaneously, with the displacement of national culture as a "center of gravity" by the European Union, the French model of justice is being influenced by a new model built on a European—and international—mold characterized by a mix of legal traditions. Thus, for example, the criminal legal process, largely inquisitory in its investigative phase, could be replaced with a mixed model, with the accusatory model constituting one phase of the investigation (Guinchard 1999).[23] Such an evolution, among others, appears to be a process of globalization of legal culture.

Appendix 1
Chronology of Major Events

1958 Fifth Republic established. Vast judicial reforms, including (1) reform of the Higher Council of the Magistracy, (2) creation of the National Center of Judicial Studies (CNEJ), reorganized in 1970 as *Ecole nationale de la magistrature* (National School of the Magistracy), and (3) reform of the judicial system.

1965 Clerks become public functionaries.

1968 Creation of the *Syndicat de la magistrature*, Magistrats' Trade Union (politically leftist).

1971 First reforms of legal professions. Failure of the grand professional project, but (1) partial fusion: the *avoués* of first instance (a type of solicitor) and the *agréés* (counsel in the commercial courts) become avocats, with the latter now providing their clients both an oral defense before the courts and preparation of papers for filing; and (2) the title of *conseil juridique* (legal consultant) is protected.

1972 Reform instituting a system of legal aid for civil actions. The benefits of legal aid are subject to certain financial conditions, fixed by law. The appointed avocats receive an allowance paid by the state.

1975 Reform instituting divorce by mutual consent.

1981 François Mitterand becomes president of the republic.

1981 Abolition of the death penalty.

1981 Creation of the *Association Professionnelle des magistrats* (politically rightist).

1982 Removal of the *Cour de sûreté de l'État* (State Security Court).

1982 Legal aid extended to criminal actions.

1985 Passage of the law on the protection of victims (simplified indemnification scheme).

1988 Reelection of Mitterand to the presidency. Passage of the amnesty law.

1990 Passage of a law mandating amnesty for offenses related to the financing of political parties and election campaigns.

1991 Reform of legal aid distinguishes (1) jurisdictional aid and (2) aid in access to the legal system, which is left to local authorities.

1991 Reform of the judicial professions, including (1) fusion of avocats with legal consultants, (2) introduction of salary for avocats, and (3) ability of avocats to organize in law firms.

1993 Unification of the European common market. European legal market liberalized.

1995 Jacques Chirac elected president of the republic.

1996 Lionel Jospin becomes prime minister.

1998 Passage of law relating to access to the legal system and the friendly resolution of legal disputes.

1998 New reform of the Higher Council of the Magistracy, voted on separately by the two Assemblies (Chambers of Deputies and Senate), to (1) reinforce the weight of the CSM in the nomination of judges and prosecutors, in particular the latter, and (2) broaden the composition of the CSM to include representatives of civil society. Judges and prosecutors become a minority within CSM (to avoid corporatism). This law, which includes a constitutional change, had to be approved by the two Assemblies in a joint meeting, the Congress, with a two-thirds majority. The meeting was held on January 24, 2000.

2000 The president of the republic postponed the meeting of the Congress after a change of position by the parliamentary opposition. A judge of freedom and imprisonment was established, which controls, among other things, detention pending trial.

Appendix 2
Transformations of French Society

TABLE 6.1A
Increases in the French Population

Year	Number in Millions
1970	50,772
1980	53,880
1985	55,284
1990	56,735
1995	58,139
1999	60,400

SOURCE: Institut national de la statistique et des études économiques (INSEE), *Données sociales* (1999, 36).

TABLE 6.2A

Evolution of the Labor Force, by Sex (%)

	1970	1980	1990	1995	1998
Men	74.3	69.4	64.0	62.3	62.0
Women	38.2	42.8	45.5	47.2	47.6
Total★	55.6	55.6	54.4	54.5	54.5

SOURCE: INSEE, *Données sociales* (1999).
★Total refers to the number of people working or registered as unemployed (15–64 years old) in relation to the total number of people of the same age, for each sex.

TABLE 6.3A

Progression of Unemployment (%)

	1970	1975	1980	1985	1990	1995	1998
Men	1.5	2.9	4.3	8.4	6.7	9.8	10.2
Women	4.3	6.1	9.5	12.7	11.7	13.8	13.8
Total	2.5	4.1	6.4	10.2	8.9	11.6	11.8

SOURCE: INSEE, *Données sociales* (1999).

TABLE 6.4A

Households with Low Wages (%)

Year	Percentage
1983	9.2
1985	10.2
1987	11.2
1989	11.5
1991	11.0
1993	12.2
1995	14.0
1997	13.2

SOURCE: Concialdi and Ponthieux (1999, 168).
NOTE: "Low wages" refers to an amount less than two-thirds of the household median wage.

TABLE 6.5A

Government Resources Allocated to Judicial System

Year	Percentage
1965	0.65
1973	0.76
1981	1.05
1999	1.56

SOURCE: Millet (1999).

TABLE 6.6A
Urban and Rural Populations

Year	Urban (%)	Rural (%)
1970	67	23
1982	73	27
1990	74	26

SOURCES: UN *Demographic Yearbook* (New York: UN, 1989, 1997).

Appendix 3
Brief Presentation of the French Judicial System

The judicial system in France is regulated by the principle of separation of administrative and judicial powers.

JUDICIAL JURISDICTIONS

Courts of first instance.   France has 181 courts *de grande instance*. This court is empowered to hear civil matters involving amounts greater than 7,600 euros and adjudicates matters relating to business, familial relations, and real estate. In the criminal field, this tribunal is called a court of corrections and adjudicates crimes punishable by a maximum of ten years of imprisonment and/or a fine.

There are several types of special courts, including 473 courts *d'instance*, jurisdictions with a single professional judge who is responsible for simple litigation generally involving sums of less than 7,600 euros. When this court rules on criminal matters, the court is referred to as a police court. It is qualified to rule on infractions punishable with a fine amounting to a maximum of 1,500 euros. The 139 juvenile courts adjudicate offenses committed by minors. A juvenile court is made up of a presiding juvenile judge and two nonprofessional assessors. The proceedings of this court are not open to the public. The 191 commercial courts are made up solely of merchants elected by their peers; these courts hear disputes between merchants and litigation relating to commercial activities. The 271 *conseils de prud'hommes* (labor courts, or industrial courts) are composed of an equal number of employees and employer representatives, elected respectively by their peers. Their mission consists of resolving litigation emanating from employment contract disputes. The procedure includes an obligatory phase of conciliation.

Courts of appeal.   The 35 courts of appeal are composed only of professional judges and prosecutors; these courts are competent to hear on appeal all of the cases on which the courts of first instance rule. A court of appeal can rule on both questions of law and fact in relation to the cases that are submitted to it. It can either affirm the decision or overrule it. In the latter instance, the court evaluates the case de novo. Decisions of this court can be reversed through an appeal to the Court of Cassation.

Cours d'assises. These courts deal with crimes—that is, criminal acts punishable by criminal detention (loss of liberty of greater than ten years). A cour d'assises is made up of three professional judges and nine jurors selected at random from the population, using election lists. They deliberate together on the guilt of the accused and on the punishment to be imposed. Until 2000, because of its popular character —the jury represents the French people—the cour d'assises made final decisions: it ruled in the first and last instance, and its decisions were not subject to the review of any court other than the Court of Cassation. The possibility of an appeal before a new cour d'assises with twelve jurors was voted on in 2000, on the grounds of the enormous differences observed between the behavior of the courts.

Court of cassation. In principle, a final decision from any jurisdiction, criminal or not, can be reviewed by the Court of Cassation. This court does not reexamine the facts but only reviews questions of law to verify that the law has been correctly applied. The general parquet of the Court of Cassation plays a decisive role in proposing new doctrines, in settling jurisprudential interpretation of different chambers of the court on the same question of law, and for maintaining continuity within the court's own line of doctrine.

ADMINISTRATIVE JURISDICTIONS

The 33 administrative courts adjudicate disputes between citizens and administrative agencies. There are 5 courts of administrative appeal. The *Conseil d'État* has supreme jurisdiction over administrative actions. It is a court of appeal for cases decided by administrative courts and administrative courts of appeals. The government consults this court on legislation and solicits advisory opinions on other matters. The court of conflict has jurisdiction when there is a jurisdictional conflict between the administrative courts and judicial courts.

Notes

1. French *magistrats* are professional judges and include judges and prosecutors. When the name magistracy is used, it is in its special French meaning. *Avocats* has not been translated because of its specificity.

2. The groups of disciplines that accommodate the most students are the social sciences (38,046 new graduates in 1997–98), followed by law and political science (30,312), then hard sciences, literature, and languages (Ministry of National Education 1998, *Note d'information* 98–09). Law loses ground to other fields such as economics and social administration.

3. These graduates are baccalaureate holders who qualify for entry to university through a national examination.

4. This arrangement makes it possible for universities to receive money from corporations.

5. For example, at the University of Paris 2, which is the largest law school in France and also the most prestigious, DESS are offered in the areas of the law of business and taxation, human resource management and labor relations, and notarial law.

6. Data from conference given in April 1996 at the University of Paris 2 by the director of the legal department of Bouygues.

7. The divorce rate began to rise in 1964, however, following passage of a law that allowed divorce by mutual consent. In 1975, the number of divorces significantly increased.

8. Thus, human rights law, criminal law, and administrative law are excluded. See Jobert and Rozenblatt (1981).

9. Some authors advance the hypothesis that common law countries are more receptive to mediation experiments than civil law countries. The common law system, in which law is made by judges according to social norms and customs, is generally more receptive to social experiments. Conversely, the civil law system is more rigid (see, in particular, Faget 1997). Of course, there are some exceptions, as illustrated by the system in Japan.

10. This trend was reflected in a conference devoted to a ten-year assessment of mediation. The conference, held in December 1999, was organized by various associations of mediators.

11. The surveys were carried out in 1991 and 1997, and an account of them was given in articles in Le Monde (February 1, 2000) by Phillipe Chriqui, "Les justiciables sont les plus critiques à l'égard de l'institution judiciaire" (The litigants surveyed were most critical with regard to the legal system) and Jérome-Jaffre, "La justice et la politique sont accablées du même opprobre" (Justice and politics are heaped with the same opprobrium). The litigants surveyed were most critical with regard to the legal system.

12. The law of 1972 provides litigants who have few financial resources with the services of an avocat. Legal aid financed by the state is provided based on the economic status of the recipient of such services. The avocats and other professionals involved receive an allowance from the state (see Appendix 3).

13. Roughly, parquet is the office of the public prosecutor; but the prosecutor in France is considered part of the judicial system. Ed.

14. At this time, political leaders were preoccupied with attempts to dissuade the French citizenry from turning to the extreme right in their political views.

15. Maurice Papon was the last French high civil servant of the Vichy regime to be judged, in 1998, for his collaboration with the Nazis in deporting Jews. Papon was found guilty of complicity of "crimes against humanity." During his trial, many historians were called as "witnesses," both by the plaintiffs and by Papon. A question regarding the articulation of historical truth and judicial truth was raised.

16. Between 1908 and 1958, magistrats have been recruited through a professional examination.

17. There are several ways of gaining acceptance to the ENM. A preliminary competition is open to candidates holding a master's degree, provided they are under the age of twenty-seven. A second competition, created in 1972, is open to civil servants, government officials, and local authorities with four years of public service who are under the age of forty. Since 1992, a third competition has been open to professionals who have worked for at least eight years in a professional activity or who have been elected to an office in a territorial assembly.

18. Since the reform of 1993, the CSM has consisted of sixteen members. In addi-

tion to the president of the republic and the minister of justice, these include twelve magistrats elected by their peers and four external functionaries who do not belong to the legal profession. Previously, the members of the CSM were named by the president of the republic.

19. The term "judicial judge" excludes administrative judges and nonprofessional commercial judges. *Ed.*

20. This law gave amnesty for all infractions related to the financing of political parties and election campaigns committed before June 15, 1989. It supplements another law of amnesty passed after Mitterand's reelection to the presidency in 1988.

21. See Barsck (1977), although the data are not exhaustive. Some offices refused to provide this information.

22. Japan is an example of a country in which recourse to the courts is not high and the number of lawyers is therefore comparatively low.

23. The first attempt at this reform appeared in 1993 with a law that increased the rights of people who are investigated by the examining judge, and so, of avocats. In June 2000, a law established a *juge des libertés et de la détention* (judge of individual freedom and of imprisonment), who deals with the question of detention and release.

References

Bancaud, A. 1991. Les désarrois des magistrats. *Regards sur l'actualité* 171 : 51–69. Paris: La documentation française.

———. 1993. *La haute magistrature judiciaire: Entre politique et sacerdoce.* Paris: Librairie générale de droit et de jurisprudence (LGDJ).

Bancaud, A., and A. Boigeol. 1995. A new judge for a new system of economic justice. Pp. 104–13 in *Professional competition and professional power*, edited by Y. Dezalay and D. Sugarman. London: Routledge.

Bancaud, A., and Ph. Robert. 2001. La place de la justice française: Un avenir incertain. In *Les mutations de la justice: Comparaisons européennes*, edited by Ph. Robert and A. Cottino. Paris: L'Harmattan.

Baraquin, Y. 1975. *Les Français et la justice civile Paris.* Paris: La documentation française.

Barsck, Caura. 1997. *Radiographie des cabinets d'affaires français en France.* Paris: Les juristes associés.

Bessard, C. L. 1997. La médiation commerciale. In *Actes du colloque du 10 octobre 1996*, edited by Christian-Nils Robert, with the collaboration of Nathalie Bornoz and Noelle Languin. Geneva, Faculté de droit, Travaux du CETEL 49 (September): 69–84.

Blankenburg, E. 1990. Culture juridiques comparées. *Droit et Société* 16.

Bodiguel, J. C. 1991. *La magistratur: Un corps sans âme?* Paris: Presses Universitaires de France.

Boigeol, A. 1988. The French bar: The difficulties of unifying a divided profession. Pp. 258–94 in *Lawyers in society, Vol. II: The civil law world*, edited by Richard L. Abel and Philip S. C. Lewis. Berkeley and Los Angeles: University of California Press.

————. 1993. La magistrature française au féminin: Entre spécificité et banalisation. *Droit et Société* 25:489–523.

————. 1997. Les magistrates de l'ordre judiciaire: Des femmes d'autorité. *Les Cahiers du MAGE* 1:23–36.

————. 2000. Les magistrates "hors les mur." *Droit et Société* 44–45:225–48.

Boigeol, A., and Y. Dezalay. 1997. De l'agent d'affaires au barreau: Les conseils juridiques et la construction d'un espace professionnel. *Genèses* 27:49–68.

Burricand, C., and O. Timbart. 1996. Infractions sanctionnées, peines prononcées: Dix ans d'évolution. *Infostat Justice* 47.

Cardia Vonèche, L., and B. Bastard. 1995. Unaufhaltsamer Aufstieg oder unüberwindbare Stagnation? Die Frage nach den Schicksal der Familienmediation. Pp. 205–14 in *Mediation: Die andere Scheidung: Ein Interdsiziplinärer Überblick*, edited by Joseph Duss-von Werdt, Gisela Mähler, and Hans-Georg Mähler. Stuttgart: Klett-Cota.

Commaille, J. 1999. Une sociologie politique de la justice en oeuvre. *Droit et Société* 42–43:467–510.

Concialdi, P., and S. Ponthieux. 1999. Les bas salaires en France depuis le début des années quatre-vingt et quelques éléments de comparaison avec les États-Unis. In *Données sociales*. Paris: Institut national de la statistique et des études économiques (INSEE).

Cotterrell, R. 1997. The concept of legal culture. In *Comparing legal cultures*, edited by D. Nelken: Aldershot, England, and Brookfield, Vt.: Dartmouth.

Coulon, J. M. 1996. *Réflexions et propositions sur la procédure civile*. Paris: La documentation française.

Crenner, E. 1999. Insécurité et préoccupations sécuritaires. Pp. 366–72 in *Données sociales*. Paris: INSEE.

Dalle, H. 1999. Juges et procureurs. *Justices* 1:55–65.

Dezalay, Y. 1992. *Marchands de droit*. Paris: Fayard.

————. 1995. Des justices du marché au marché international de la justice. *Justices* 1:121–33.

Dezalay, Y., and B. Garth. 1995. Merchants of law as moral entrepreneurs: Constructing international justice from the competition for transnational business disputes. *Law and Society Review* 29 (1):27–64.

Données sociales. 1999. Paris: INSEE.

Donzelot, J., and A. Wyvekens. 1998. La politique judiciaire de la ville: De la "prévention" au "traitement," les groupes locaux de traitement de la délinquance. Report for the Ministry of Justice, mission de recherche "droit et justice."

Faget, J. 1997. *La médiation, essai de politique pénale*. Paris: Erès.

Friedman, Lawrence M. 1985. *Total justice*. Boston: Beacon Press.

————. 1997. The concept of legal culture: A reply. In *Comparing legal cultures*, edited by D. Nelken. Aldershot, England, and Brookfield, Vt.: Dartmouth.

Garapon, A., and D. Salas. 1996. *La République pénalisée*. Paris: Hachette.

Guinchard, S. 1998. L'évitement du juge civil. Pp. 221–28 in *Les transformations de la régulation juridique*, edited by J. Clam and G. Martin. Paris: LGDJ.

————. 1999. La procédure: Une liberté fondamentale? *Justices* 1:91–130.

Jean, J. P. 1999. Les réformes de la justice. *Regards sur l'actualité* (February):17–36. Paris: La documentation française.

Jobert, A., and P. Rozenblatt. 1981. *Le rôle des conciliateurs et ses relations avec la justice (The role of conciliators and their relationships to justice)*. Paris: Centre de recherche pour l'étude et l'observation des conditions de vie.

Karpik, L. 1995. *Les avocats*. Paris: Gallimard.

———. 1999. Les avocats: Le renouveau et la crise. *Justices* 1:67–82.

Lazerges, C. 1997. Médiation pénale et politique criminelle. In *Actes du colloque du 10 octobre 1996*, edited by Christian-Nils Robert, with the collaboration of Nathalie Bornoz and Noelle Languin. Geneva, Faculté de droit, Travaux du CETEL 49.

Lumbroso, S., and O. Timbart. 1999. Pourquoi se tourne-t-on vers la justice? Pp. 378–85 in *Données sociales, 1999*. Paris: INSEE.

Merryman, J. 1985. *The civil law tradition: An introduction to the legal systems of Western Europe and Latin America*. Stanford, Calif.: Stanford University Press.

Millet, D. 1999. La justice et ses moyens. *Justices* 1:133–56.

Muñoz Perez, B., and C. Moreau. 1998. *Statistique sur la profession d'avocat*. Paris: Ministère de la justice, Direction des affaires civiles, Cellule Etudes.

Robert, Ph. 1999. *Le citoyen, le crime et l'État*. Geneva and Paris: Droz.

Roussel, V. 1998. Les magistrats dans les scandales politiques. *Revue Française de Sciences Politiques* 48 (2):245–73.

Sadaume De Oliveira, D. 1997. *L'Institution judiciaire, la profession de magistrat et la loi Neiertz*. Thèse, France: Université Paris X.

Salas, D. 1998. *Le tiers pouvoir*. Paris: Hachette.

Soulez-Larivière, D. 1990. *Justice pour la justice*. Paris: Seuil.

Timbart, O. 1999. La délinquance mesurée par l'institution judiciaire. Pp. 373–77 in *Données sociales, 1999*. INSEE.

Verin, J. 1994. *Pour une nouvelle politique pénale*. Paris: LGDJ.

Wyvekens, A. 1996. Justice de proximité et proximité de la justice: Les maisons de la justice et du droit. *Droit et Société* 33:363–88.

CHAPTER 7

The Italian Legal System, 1945–1999

SABINO CASSESE

IN THE YEARS immediately after the Second World War, judicial decisions were seldom the subject of public opinion in Italy. In the 1970s and 1980s, however, the judiciary was often on the front page of daily newspapers; judges and prosecutors were frequently interviewed, and judicial cases were matters of public discussion.[1] In the 1990s, major changes in the Italian political system were brought about by the combined action of prosecutors and judges: as a consequence of the *mani pulite* (clean hands) initiatives, two leading Italian political parties, the Christian Democrats and the Socialists, have disappeared, and new electoral laws have been enacted for municipal councils and mayors, regional councils and presidents, and the national Parliament.

The purpose of this chapter is twofold: to identify, assess, and analyze the main changes in the Italian legal system; and to explain the reasons for them. The important reforms over the last twenty-five years contain many ambiguities and contradictions, as continuity and change overlap. The analysis of these changes will highlight four features: (1) the stability of the judiciary and the progress of litigation, (2) the stagnation of the state and the growth of peripheral powers, (3) the stability in the number of law teachers and the increasing number of lawyers, and (4) the inertia of legal stereotypes and the cultural revolution. This chapter first sketches a brief history of the Italian legal system and then analyzes the ambiguities of the state in the second half of the twentieth century and presents its current structure.

Presented at the seminar "Las transformaciones del derecho y la cultura jurídica en Europa Mediterránea y América Latina en los ultimos venticinco años," Stanford Program in International Legal Studies, Stanford Law School, September 9–10, 1999. I would like to thank Gerolamo Giungato for his help in producing the statistical data used in this chapter and Lawrence Friedman, Bernardo Mattarella, and Giulio Napolitano for their comments.

The History of the Italian Legal System

The Italian legal system has a short history compared to the French, English, and Spanish systems; the political unification of the peninsula took place only in 1861. The legal system established then had the following characteristics:

1. The 1848 constitution of the Kingdom of Sardinia (Sardinia and Piedmont) was extended to the new Kingdom of Italy.
2. A civil code, a commercial code, and about ten major administrative statutes were approved in 1865.
3. Among the three branches (legislative, executive, judiciary), the leading role was given to the executive, headed by the Crown, while the legislative played a residual role, and the judiciary was only partly independent.
4. In 1889, the Council of State was given a judicial role in solving disputes between citizens and public authorities, thus establishing a dualistic system of courts.
5. The administrative system was highly centralized, through the prefects, who were field officers with the power to keep local governments under control.

The main institutions of the legal system were influenced by the French legal tradition (for example, civil code, Council of State and judicial dualism, prefects). There have been three turning points in the legal system: the end of the nineteenth century, when electoral participation was enlarged; the 1920s, when the so-called Fascist period began; the end of the Second World War, with the republic and a new constitution. During the Fascist period there were no elections, and authoritarian institutions were established.

By the middle of the twentieth century, industry had become more important than agriculture, and in 1947 the republican constitution was adopted, to go into effect in 1948; it is still in force today. The new constitution has given Parliament a central role, in reaction to the previous Fascist regime, in which the executive played a pivotal role. Under the new constitution, the judiciary was granted an independent status.[2] The executive, on the other hand, was given a limited role.

In the years that followed, in spite of the Italian "economic miracle," the legal system encountered many difficulties:

1. The constitution of 1948 was implemented very slowly: the Council for the Economy, for instance, was established in 1953; the Constitutional Court, in 1956; the Council of the Judiciary, in 1958; the regions, in 1970.
2. The executive was very unstable; the average life of governments was one year.

3. Parliament produced a great deal of legislation, which, in turn, gave rise to overregulation and led to a certain rigidity in the economy.

There has been, therefore, a widespread feeling that changes are needed in the constitution. For this purpose, over the last fifteen years, three ad hoc parliamentary commissions have been established. They have produced various proposals, but those proposals have not been followed up.

A second important step was the signing of the Treaty of Rome in 1957, establishing the European Community. In the first part of its life, the Community was chiefly of economic importance. Since the 1980s, its importance in the field of law has increased for two main reasons. First, the European Court of Justice has established its supremacy over national courts, while integrating them into a network of courts. Today, the Community (or Union) is a system of functionally integrated judiciaries. According to Article 177 (now 234) of the 1957 treaty establishing the European Community, any court or tribunal of a member state may request the European Court of Justice to give a preliminary ruling if it considers that a decision on a question of interpretation of the treaty, of validity and interpretation of acts of the institutions of the Community, and of interpretation of the statutes of bodies established by the Council of the Community is necessary to enable it to give judgment. Second, a series of European Union directives enacted in the 1980s and in the 1990s has obliged national governments—including the Italian government—to privatize most of the industrial sector under public control and liberalize public utility sectors, which were previously the domain of state monopolies.

A third important development was the approval in 1990 of an administrative procedure act, establishing principles such as the right of parties to a hearing and access to administrative documents.

The fourth important change came in 1992, with the mani pulite investigation by the prosecution office of Milan, which brought about some major changes in the political arena. The leaders of the two major political parties in power since the Second World War—the Christian Democrat and Socialist Parties—were charged with violating the law on the financing of political parties and with corruption; subsequently, the two parties went through a crisis, and the center-right of the political arena has now become occupied by a new political movement, *Forza Italia*, headed by industrialist Silvio Berlusconi.

Three Paradoxes of the Italian State
in the Second Half of the Twentieth Century

From the middle of the twentieth century up to the present day, the Italian state has been characterized by three fundamental flaws or contradictions. The first is a fear of "Caesarism" or "Bonapartism"; the second can be summed up as "the elusiveness of the state"; and the third concerns the welfare state and its funding.

THE FEAR OF CAESARISM OR BONAPARTISM

The second half of the twentieth century has been dominated by the fear of Caesarism or Bonapartism, which has been fed in at least two ways. Above all, it has been conditioned by the French cultural experience; France has always exercised a considerable degree of influence over Italian political affairs. This fear has also been fed by direct experience. During the Fascist period, the executive was dominated by a single figure, who claimed a direct, personal link to the people.

Reaction to this has produced numerous effects since the end of the Second World War. First, it led to the choice of an electoral system based on proportional rather than majority representation, to avoid the possibility that the electorate's choice would concentrate in a single person. Second, a multiparty constitutional system developed in which the parties designated candidates to Parliament, and the elected candidates and their parties were able to choose the government without any direct electoral mandate. Third, it produced what the French called in the nineteenth century "government by assembly," by affirming the centrality of Parliament, where power is largely concentrated. In Italy, the fear of Caesarism and Bonapartism—fear of an overweening executive—contributed to turning the political parties into institutions in their own right.

All of this helped produce serious government instability; from 1948 to 1993, there was a total of fifty administrations, each lasting an average of twelve months, more or less comparable to the average duration of the administrations that governed Italy between 1861 and the Fascist era, and slightly longer than the average length of the administrations of the French Third Republic, from 1871 until the Second World War. Despite the instability of the government, the same party remained in power. This places Italy in the category of an "uncommon" democracy, characterized by chronic government instability despite an absence of parties that alternate in holding power.

THE ELUSIVENESS OF THE STATE

From the fall of Fascism until the 1990s, Italy's civil service has proved to be a shapeless animal with a soft, white underbelly. On the one hand, it displayed a fondness for wielding its powers of veto and prevention; on the other, it displayed a consistent inability to achieve its aims (a good example of this is that Italy, unlike other countries such as France, has in the postwar era managed to construct only one major infrastructure of national dimension—the motorway network). At the same time there has been massive corruption as the parties vied with each other in carving up public-sector industries into competing spheres of influence. The state-run industrial sector has long been an object of prey for the parties of government, so much so that it is often referred to as *sottogoverno*, or a subbranch of government. The juridical concept of "the state" may have been real; but the state as a body, as a coherent entity, hardly existed.

The traditional Italian civil service has, to be sure, given work to people from the south of Italy (an area of the country that has only 35 percent of the population but that supplies the civil service with 55 percent of its workforce), mitigating the otherwise serious problems of the labor market in the south; but it has always been slow, Byzantine, and anything but innovative. (According to reliable estimates, systematic bureaucratic delays annually cost Italian society and the economy about 1 percent of Italy's gross national product.)

Southern Italians who have scaled the heights of the civil service and the so-called Boyars of the State (the name given to those appointees, who, faithful to their respective parties, are supposed to run the state-owned enterprises) are not chosen according to merit and are not motivated by criteria of efficiency or of productivity, but only by the desire to guarantee themselves a place in the sun and faithfully execute the orders of their respective political lords and masters.

THE WELFARE STATE AND ITS FUNDING

Between the 1970s and the 1980s, Italy built up its benefits network and its health and education systems, in much the same way as other European countries did. Most Italians (and above all, the trade unions) vigorously defend the welfare state as it stands. However, three problems are emerging. The first is that the welfare system remains incomplete; education, health, and pensions are well covered, but there is no comprehensive benefit system for the unemployed. The second is its poor cost-effectiveness ratio. The treasury is obliged to spend more while providing less than other comparable countries do, especially in education and health, and above all, in the south of Italy. The welfare state may mitigate the effects of certain aspects of social inequality, but in doing so, it creates others—by protecting the old at the expense of the young, by offering high-quality services in the north but poor services in the south, and by an unfair division of the tax burden to pay for what is an already too expensive system.

The Structure of the Law Machine

At the center of the legal system is Parliament, which is divided into two chambers with equal powers, whose members are elected through the same procedures. The two chambers have too many members (a total of 945) and wide powers to legislate and control. Although the first power (to legislate) is much used (producing many statutes, often in exaggerated detail), the second (to control) is not.

Regarding legislation, a few trends can be highlighted. The first is the growing amount of regional legislation since 1970, when regional authorities were established. The constitution conferred legislative power on the regions in order to relieve the national Parliament of the burden of having to handle so much detail. But in fact, there is more legislation than ever.

In the 1990s, especially after the political crisis, the government made frequent use of so-called law-decrees (acts approved by the Council of Ministers in cases of urgency and subsequently submitted to Parliament for ratification), until the Constitutional Court put a stop to this practice (Decision 60 of 1996, which treats law-decrees as exceptional and states that they are not to be approved again by the government if Parliament has not had time to ratify them). From then on, delegated legislation (statutes approved by Parliament, authorizing the government to adopt laws as a delegated power) have been common. Parliament can control the government because it has the power to investigate; it can invite public officials to give their opinions before permanent or ad hoc commissions, and it receives hundreds of reports. The first and second powers are used from time to time. The reports submitted to Parliament are, on the contrary, rarely discussed and are often not even read, in spite of the fact that their submission is mandatory under statutes approved by the Parliament.

The executive is the weakest part of the system. Governments are unstable and short-lived, and the public administration is large (including approximately 4 million civil servants, teachers, and military personnel) and badly organized, with eighteen central departments, about one thousand public bodies, twenty regions, one hundred provinces, and eight thousand municipalities.

Stability is the main problem of the executive. The attempts made in the

1990s to strengthen governments and make them last five years (for the duration of the legislature—Parliament is elected for five years according to Article 60 of the constitution) have been, up to now, unsuccessful.

In 1991–93, two referenda were held on the subject of electoral reform. Following these referenda during the course of 1993, the Eleventh Legislature approved two new electoral laws regulating the election of members to the Senate and the Chamber of Deputies; then, at last, amid great expectations, new general elections were held in 1994. These were the first elections in the history of the Italian republic to be held under the first-past-the-post system.

In the following two years (between 1994 and 1996), there were two governments, one lasting for eight months and the other, for fifteen months. Then, due to the impossibility of forming a stable majority, Parliament was dissolved once more, with elections held on April 21, 1996, which led to the formation of the Prodi government, also based on an unstable majority. In 1998, the Prodi government was replaced by the D'Alema government, which was followed by a second D'Alema government (1999) and then by the Amato government (2000). In short, the problem of unstable parliamentary majorities has not been solved, nor indeed the problems of the duration of the legislature (the last two have lasted no more than two years) or of unstable governments (there were six from 1994 to 2000).

Italy does not have a legal tradition like that of England, where the courts play a central role in the legal system. At the apex of the system is the Constitutional Court. Below are civil and penal courts. There are also regional administrative tribunals and the Council of State. But only the civil and penal courts constitute the "judiciary" according to the constitution. Under Article 104, the civil and penal courts (*magistratura*) are autonomous and independent from state power. Article 107 provides that magistrates are irremovable. They can only be moved to a different court or dismissed by the Council of the Judiciary (*Consiglio superiore della magistratura*) and only after a hearing.

Civil courts are on four levels: justice of the peace, court of the first instance, appeals court, and court of cassation. Penal courts are also on four levels: justice of the peace, court of first instance, court of assize, and court of cassation.

There are approximately seventy-eight hundred members of the judiciary. But this number includes not only judges but also prosecutors, as these are considered part of the judiciary, with the same selection procedures, careers, and salaries. The Ministry of Justice provides staff and means to the judiciary; but it has no control over the judiciary and cannot interfere with it. Selection, career, job assignment, and so forth are responsibilities of the Council of the Judiciary, which consists of thirty members, twenty of whom are elected by the judges and ten by Parliament, with the president of the republic as president and only two other ex officio members: the president and general prosecutor of the court of cassation.

The Council of the Judiciary, in spite of its limited number of functions, has become the body that governs (*organo di autogoverno*) civil and penal judges. This body debates the problems of justice, approves motions on the policies of the judiciary, and acts as the parliament of the judges.

Two statutes passed by Parliament between 1966 and 1973 have made changes in the career possibilities of magistrates (and prosecutors). After being selected by competitive examination, the members of the judiciary can rise up to the Court of Cassation, the highest court, only by seniority. This rule, introduced in order to avoid interference in the careers of the judges, has many drawbacks; the chief one is the lack of selectivity after entry into the judiciary. After entry through a competitive examination, a judge goes through a twelve-month period of training (*tirocinio*) and then follows an established and automatic itinerary. Promotions are entirely independent from the functions assigned and from performance. There is also no hierarchy among magistrates. They only differ in their functions (Article 107 of the constitution).

There are four other characteristics relevant to the members of the judiciary. First, they are highly unionized and have established a strong tradition of colleagueship. Second, they receive good salaries compared to those of the public sector. Prosecutors have gained a very high degree of visibility; the best law graduates enter the judiciary. Third, members of the judiciary see their role as political actors: they are not only *bouche de la loi* but also *bouche de la constitution*. They see themselves as having a mission and a high degree of responsibility toward the people. They believe that their job is not merely the interpretation of written law but also the interpretation of social values (Morisi 1999).

Finally, prosecutors and judges are, as already noted, on an equal footing. They belong to the same body; are selected under the same procedure; follow a similar career, moving from one role to another; and have the same status, salary, and degree of independence. In other countries, such as France and Germany, prosecutors have the status of a judge but are hierarchically dependent on the executive or the chief prosecutor; in Italy, prosecutors are accountable to no one. The chief prosecutor (*procuratore capo*) is only a senior prosecutor who has a very limited power of coordination over the other members of the prosecuting office (*procura*). The chief prosecutor cannot even assign cases; cases are assigned automatically to the prosecutors who are on duty (Guarneri 1993).

Although the current performance of the civil and penal courts is good (La Torre 2000), there are many cases pending. For penal cases, in the period

July 1998–June 1999, there were 5,914 cases pending; 8,986 cases were filed; and 8,571 were decided. The number of pending cases is lower than the number of cases decided in one year; for civil cases, it is more than double the cases decided in one year (3,575 pending; 1,536 filed; 1,480 decided). The average duration of a case before penal courts is ten months, and before civil courts, two and a half years.

The role of the Constitutional Court and the administrative courts is no less important. Every important decision at the constitutional and administrative levels (from the admission of referenda to the decisions of independent regulatory authorities) is brought to these courts. The Constitutional Court has fifteen judges. Five are appointed by the president of the republic, and ten are elected: five by the Parliament, three by the Court of Cassation, one by the Council of State, and one by the Court of Accounts.

The Constitutional Court can declare a law void on the grounds that it is unconstitutional. But only a court can open a case before the Constitutional Court. The Constitutional Court has played an important role in many fields, ranging from family law to civil rights, and from referenda to property rights (Rodotà 1986).

The administrative courts (the twenty administrative tribunals and the Council of State) play an even greater role. A large number of important administrative decisions are submitted to these courts, ranging from issues of insurance to telecommunications, and from banking control to police. The administrative courts have the power to force the executive branch to comply with the rules of law.

The role of some independent administrative agencies falls halfway between those of the courts and the executive authority. These agencies include the antitrust authority; regulatory authorities for electricity, gas, and communications; the institute responsible for controlling insurance companies; the council controlling the stock exchange and private companies; the privacy authority; the authority responsible for ensuring transparency in public works; and the commission that regulates strikes in public services. The members of these agencies are generally appointed by the chairmen of the two assemblies of Parliament or are elected by Parliament. The agencies are accountable neither to the government nor to Parliament. They have rule-making power or the power to adjudicate, or both, and a high degree of independence.

There are now three branches of the legal profession. First, there are the lawyers themselves. They used to be divided into two sections, *procuratori* and *avvocati*. (Having passed the exam to enter the profession, a lawyer used to be a *procuratore* for ten years and could only appear before the lower courts; after that period of time, or after having passed another selection procedure to shorten that period, the lawyer could become an *avvocato*.) A 1998 statute abolished this distinction, and now there are only avvocati. They are organized as a legally recognized, but self-regulated profession. Second, notaries are legally recognized. As lawyers do, they elect their representatives in provincial and central bodies, which are public corporations; set rates; and decide on disciplinary matters. The third profession, that of law professors, is not a legally recognized profession but is highly regarded because doctrine (professor's opinions) plays a very important role in judicial decisions.

Legal education is a branch of undergraduate studies and plays an important role in general education (as politics, philosophy, and economics courses in British universities do). A legal education is, therefore, required in the civil service, where the majority of personnel have a law degree. There is thus a common legal culture that unites the legislative, the civil service, and the judiciary. This legal culture is paradoxically positivistic, though it accepts judge-made law. Textbooks affirm that the only sources of law are European regulations, the national constitution, statutes approved by the Parliament, law-decrees, and delegated laws. But, de facto, everyone knows that judges make law. For example, the major turning point in the history of administrative justice of the last twenty years was Decision 500 taken in July 1999 by the Court of Cassation, which provided a different and more open interpretation of Article 2043 of the civil code.

This law machine, with all its ambiguities and contradictions, is considered inefficient by the people but has not, apparently, led to a refusal by the public to take part in political life. According to a statistical survey by Istituto Nazionale di Statistica (Istat 1998a, 145), of more than 1 million persons who preferred not to bring an action before the courts, over 40 percent made this choice because of the complexity of the procedures or because of long delays in obtaining a decision. In spite of the widespread corruption that emerged from the mani pulite investigations, political participation from 1993 to 1997 did not diminish (turnout for national ballots has remained around 80 percent).

The Judiciary, Litigation, and Quasi-Judicial Bodies

In the postwar period, the machinery of justice has been relatively stable, judging by the number of judges and the number of cases filed and decided in the Court of Cassation, although there has been a sizable increase in both numbers since the 1970s. In 1945, there were 10 judges per 100,000 inhabitants, 11 in 1970, and 17 in 1997. The number of cases filed and decided in the Court of Cassation, the highest judicial body, is a good indicator of changes occurring inside the machinery of justice, but behind the scenes. In 1945, there were 19 cases filed and 15 decided per 100,000 inhabitants; the figures for 1970 were 57 filed and 50 decided; for 1997, there were 111 filed

TABLE 7.1

Civil Cases Filed in First Instance
in All Italian Courts

Year	Filed	Decided
1945	381	107
1970	824	324
1980	1,335	595
1997	1,978	884

SOURCE: Istituto Nazionale di Statistica, *Annuario Statistico*
Italiano, Rome.
NOTE: Cases per 100,000 inhabitants.

TABLE 7.2

Penal Cases Appealed
in All Italian Courts

Year	Filed	Decided
1945	72	75
1970	121	147
1985	210	144
1990	30	21
1997	134	114

NOTE: Cases per 100,000 inhabitants.

and 107 decided. Thus, from 1945 to 1970, cases filed and decided both grew by a factor of three, whereas from 1970 to 1997, the figures doubled.

If we move toward the lower courts, the picture changes in respect to the following five indicators: total number of civil cases, number of civil cases appealed in superior courts, total number of penal cases, number of administrative cases, and number of cases in the court of justices of the peace. For civil cases, see Table 7.1.

Growth in the number of civil cases was continuous in the two periods; decided cases increased by a factor of eight, and cases filed, by a factor of five. For appealed cases, there was also growth—17 per 100,000 population in 1945 and 129 in 1997. For these cases, too, in 1945, there was stability or little increase, whereas in 1997, cases filed and decided grew by a factor of seven or eight.

For penal cases, see Table 7.2. These data are of particular importance, as there was, in the late 1980s, an attempt by Parliament to reduce the number of cases brought before the courts, through a *depenalizzazione*—a certain number of violations of law no longer fell within the jurisdiction of penal judges; these violations were subject only to administrative sanctions. In

TABLE 7.3
*Cases Filed and Decided
by the Council of State*

Year	Filed	Decided
1945	2	0.50
1970	19	9★
1980	5	7
1998	20	19

SOURCE: Istituto Nazionale di Statistica, *Annuario Statistico Italiano,* Rome.
NOTE: Cases per 100,000 inhabitants.
★For 1966.

spite of this sharp reduction in 1990, the number of cases filed and decided, which increased by factors of three and two, respectively, from 1945 to 1985, increased by factors of four and five, respectively, in the seven-year period 1990–97. The case of administrative justice is similar. For cases filed and decided by the Council of State per 100,000 inhabitants, see Table 7.3. For regional administrative tribunals, 68 cases were filed per 100,000 inhabitants in 1970 (35 decided); the figures for 1998 were 156 and 91, respectively.

As in the case of penal justice, an attempt was made to relieve the burden of the demand for justice on the Council of State by establishing twenty regional courts in 1971. But these courts have become rapidly overloaded (with an increase by factors of two to three from 1970 to 1998 alone), and cases filed and decided by the Council of State have more than tripled.

A final and highly enlightening example of the growing demand for justice and the pressure it puts on the judicial machine is that of the justices of the peace, honorary judges introduced in 1995 to decide minor penal and civil cases: in 1997, the number of cases filed was 309,000, with a 40 percent increase over the previous year.

In the period 1945–97, litigation increased because of the increase in the demand for justice. The judiciary has not been able to cope with the volume, and new initiatives have proved unable to contain the increasing pressure on the courts.[3] Consequently, Italy is subject to an increasing number of sentences and fines by the Council of Europe Court at Strasbourg because of court delays.

The result of this bottleneck is a flight from justice. This takes various forms, especially a search for alternatives to courts, as in the following examples:

1. Since 1993, the provincial chambers of commerce have established sixty-seven chambers of arbitration (*camere arbitrali*), which decided 90 cases in

1995 and 164 in 1996, and ten conciliation bodies (*sportelli di conciliazione*) (Istat 1997, 313; 1998c, 143).
2. The majority of the twenty regions and many municipalities have established ombudsmen.
3. More than twenty quasi-judicial (and regulatory) authorities have been established at the national level: among them, *Commissione nazionale per le società e la borsa* (Consob) (1975) for securities and exchange; *Istituto di vigilanza sulle assicurazioni private e d'interesse collettivo* (Isvap) (1982) for private insurance; *Garante per la radiodiffusione e l'editoria* (1981 and 1990) for broadcasting; *Autorità garante per la concorrenza e per il mercato* (1990) for competition; *Commissione di garanzia per l'attuazione della legge sullo sciopero nei servizi pubblici essenziali* (1990) for solution of conflicts arising from strikes in the public services; *Autorità per l'energia elettrica e per il gas* (1995) for electricity and gas; *Autorità per le garanzie nelle comunicazioni* (1997) for broadcasting and telecommunications. The antitrust authority has decided thirty-five hundred cases in seven years.
4. Delegated Law 2908 (February 3, 1993), regulating the civil service, has established alternative dispute settlement procedures, such as conciliation (Articles 69 and 69 bis).

Thus, over the last twenty-five years in Italy, there have been two contrasting trends: (1) greater powers for judges (Zannotti 1994) and (2) a flight from justice, toward new quasi-judicial bodies.

The State, the People, the Union, and the Regions

There is another sharp contradiction: while the core of the state is stable or in retreat, more power is exercised directly by the people, by the European Union, and by the new *meso* level, the regions. For the state, there are three factors involved: the number of laws enacted by Parliament, the number of public employees in the nonindustrial sector, and the size of the industrial public sector. Since 1970, the national Parliament has passed fewer laws in relation to the size of the population than in earlier years. The number of public administration staff has increased—in 1945, there were 2,140 per 100,000 inhabitants; 3,200 in 1970; and 4,082 in 1992.

Data on the personnel in the industrial public sector are not available, but it appears that the number of personnel has decreased by two-thirds since the late 1980s because of the government's privatization policy. In the nonindustrial sector, the legislative branch has remained stable in the last half of the twentieth century, whereas the size of the staff of the executive branch has almost doubled since 1970. Although the number of personnel in the industrial sector has sharply decreased, an important and growing role has been

TABLE 7.4

Number of Referenda, by Year

Year	Number	Year	Number
1974	1	1990	2
1978	2	1991	1
1981	5	1993	8
1985	1	1995	12
1987	5	1997	7
1989	1	2000	7

SOURCE: Chimenti (1999).

acquired by the once "peripheral" forces—the people, the Union, and the regions.

Article 75 of the 1948 constitution introduced the idea of referenda to repeal laws. No referendum was held until 1974. The subsequent growth in referenda is shown in Table 7.4.

There might have been more than these 52 referenda, but the Constitutional Court turned certain ones down. Four of these referenda concerned the judiciary: one on the responsibility of judges (1987), one on judges' careers (1997), one on the extrajudicial duties of judges (1997), and one on the responsibility of judges (2000).

The impact of the European Union (established in 1957), latent until the 1980s, has grown quickly since then: public utilities, government contracts, state subsidies, competition, access to the professions, agriculture, and so forth are now governed by European Union directives, which regulate even electric plugs, lawn-mower noise, and marine pollution levels.

A third change occurred in the 1970s. In 1970, fifteen regional councils were elected; in 1972, 1977, and 1998, many areas of responsibility were devolved to the regions. These local bodies have the power to enact laws. They have 2 percent of all public personnel and manage 16 percent of total public expenditure. Many local bodies were given more autonomy, with the power to choose their charters (*statuto*) and levy taxes (with some limitations): municipalities in 1990, chambers of commerce in 1993, and universities in 1989 and 1993. Thus, new actors are taking the stage, and the law machine becomes more complex.

Law Teachers, Law Students, and Lawyers

Although the number of law teachers has doubled, law students and lawyers have increased more significantly. In 1950, there were 60 law students and 57 lawyers per 100,000 inhabitants. For 1970, there were 120 and 76, respectively, and in 1996, 560 and 171. The number of law students increased by a factor of two from 1950 to 1970 and by a factor of five from 1970 to 1996; lawyers increased a little in the first period and more in the second. In absolute terms, the number of lawyers in Italy is three times the number of lawyers in France (99,000 versus 34,000).

The Inertia of Legal Stereotypes and the Cultural Revolution

In legal textbooks, legal positivism, formalism and dogmatism, and rejection of judge-made law are still the rule.[4] If we look at decided cases, the work of scholars, and the way in which those involved in the legal profession actually behave, the picture becomes quite different.

Traditional legal positivism is challenged by (1) competition from different sources of law, European and regional, alongside the law produced by the national Parliament; (2) the active role played by the European Court of Justice and the Italian Constitutional Court in developing constitutional principles; (3) transplants of legal principles from one legal system to another; and (4) the creative role played by the civil, penal, and administrative courts (well known are *sentenze-comandamenti* [decisions establishing how the parties shall behave] and the judges' so-called *potere monitorio* [power of prescription]).

Doctrine has been ready to draw attention to and study the courts as lawmakers. For example, two books published in 1998 were devoted to the principle of proportionality, which is a judge-made principle of law. Attention to foreign legal cultures was once directed primarily toward French and German doctrine; it has now turned toward English and American doctrine. Moreover, judicial decisions are more systematically and critically studied.

External and Internal Reasons for the Law Explosion

To explain the great changes that have occurred in the second half of the twentieth century, but mainly during the last twenty-five years, we have to consider both external and internal factors. There have been active external economic, social, and political pressures on the system. Economic changes are reflected in Table 7.5, which suggests how rapidly Italy has changed from an agricultural and static economy into a dynamic and industrial one.

Social changes are harder to assess. There has been a kind of turning point since 1968; more egalitarian social relationships have developed, and the traditional deference to authorities (from fathers to public authorities) has lessened. The student protest movement was an important catalyst. In 1990, Parliament passed the Administrative Procedure Act, giving new rights to citizens vis-à-vis public authorities and providers of public utilities, and providing new incentives for litigation to protect such rights. This opened a door to additional lawsuits, reflecting the social changes in society. In 1993, the

TABLE 7.5

Notarial Acts

Year	Wills	Real estate mortgages	Land sales	Automobile sales	Incorporation of business associations
1945	177	28	760	1,820★	43
1970	58	297	1,840	5,990	42
1997	43	419	1,736	11,036	262

SOURCE: Istituto Nazionale di Statistica, *Annuario Statistico Italiano*, Rome.
NOTE: Acts per 100,000 inhabitants.
★For 1955.

new electoral law abandoned the purely proportional system and introduced a first-past-the-post system. But high expectations, mainly for constitutional reform, have not been satisfied.

Pressure from "inside" (legal) forces, such as the European Union, has also been important. The European Union has developed first and foremost as a legal community, where close links are established between national courts and the two supranational courts (the first instance Tribunal and the Court of Justice).

In Italy, more regulations and more regulators (for instance, competition law and antitrust authority) produce more litigation. This is a paradox. The antitrust authority was established in 1990 to avoid burdening the judiciary with the additional task of enforcing the new antitrust law. But all the important decisions of this quasi-judicial body (and other similar authorities) can be and are attacked before the administrative courts. Therefore, non-judicial adjudication produces more judicial adjudication.

An additional incentive to litigation is produced by the opening of public utilities to competition. Indeed, the liberalization of public utilities (telecommunications, electricity, gas, railways, and so forth), which started in the 1990s with European Union directives, has produced the need for more regulation, establishing rules for incumbents in favor of the newcomers and of the users. These rules have, in turn, produced more litigation (and competition through litigation).

A final set of factors is structural in nature. First, Italian courts do not have at their disposal the means to keep the increased demand for justice under control (such as the "leave to apply" of British courts, granted only if an arguable case is shown in proceedings against public authorities). Second, Italian judges managed to acquire new rules for themselves in the period 1963–79; according to these rules, their careers are automatic, without any limitation in terms of the posts available, and there is no hierarchy among judges. Third, thanks to their powerful associations and the Superior Council of the Judiciary, judges are able to act as a highly politicized, institutionalized pressure group (all parties are keen to have judges among their candidates, and the number of judges in Parliament is proportionally high) (Righettini 1995).

Conclusion

Italy provides a good example of a legal system in which the judiciary has acquired a leading role at the expense of the executive and of the lawmaking branches and in which all important decisions are sooner or later challenged in courts. But this situation contains numerous ambiguities. In the first place, the success of the judiciary is due more to the prosecutors than to the courts. However, because both roles are played by people with the same career and status as a magistrate, people do not easily see the difference.

Second, the performance of courts as such is not good. They are understaffed, and magistrates are not well distributed among courts, due in part to a constitutional guarantee under which they cannot be removed or transferred against their will.

Third, the judiciary as a whole is gaining power and political prestige. A growing number of magistrates are entering the political arena (for example, Antonio Di Pietro, one of the prosecutors of many of the mani pulite cases in Milan). But the more the judiciary becomes an important political actor, the less independent it becomes from politics. Judicial decisions are more and more often subject to public debate and become the object of partisan politics. Yet Italy also provides an example of a legal system undergoing great change, though unable to introduce the widely debated reforms established in the constitution. Three different ad hoc parliamentary commissions have provided numerous well-elaborated proposals in the last fifteen years, but without success.

Constitutional reform has been on the agenda since the 1980s. The Bozzi Commission looked into it between 1983 and 1985. The De Mita-Jotti Commission had another go between 1992 and 1994. The D'Alema Commission followed between 1996 and 1998.

Problems yet to be addressed include consolidating the prerogatives of the government with regard to Parliament while giving the prime minister a position of clear preeminence over the other ministers, the direct election of the president of the republic, and the strengthening of the president's powers according to a "semipresidential" definition.

The tendency is to import elements of other countries' constitutional systems, such as those of France, the United Kingdom, or Germany, but without due regard for the overall context. Some are in favor of the French system, where the president is chosen by the people through direct elections and has a voice in foreign affairs and defense. Others are in favor of the British prime minister system, where members of Parliament and the prime minister are chosen at the same time, in a first-past-the-post system. Others are in favor of the German *Kanzler* system, where a government cannot be dismissed if the Parliament does not have a new majority and a new government ready to replace the previous one. But there is a general concern that government instability can further weaken the efficacy and effectiveness of public institutions and that there is a need to relieve government of some of its burdens (for example, public enterprises). There is also agreement on the need to modify (1) the first part of the constitution, regarding the rights and duties of citizens, and (2) the second part, regarding the organization of the state.

The structure of the European Union poses two dilemmas: commitments laid down by the Treaty of Maastricht on state public finances conflict with measures to safeguard the welfare state; and the principles of liberalization and the opening up of the public sector to free market competition conflict with the state's obligations in terms of its social policies.

The political debate often overlooks that democracy does not merely mean government by the people; it also stands for mitigation of the "dictatorship of the majority." The parliamentary majority should consider itself bound by rules that protect not only the parliamentary minority but other interest groups as well. It means ensuring that everyone has access to the political forum; otherwise, instead of democracy, there is simply an alternation of majorities.

Italy also needs to pay attention both to the rules of democracy and to the problem of training future generations of leaders. In the Italian Parliament, there was a turnover of about 80 percent of members between the Eleventh and the Twelfth Legislatures (1994). There was a further turnover of about 40 percent between the Twelfth and the Thirteenth Legislatures (1996). But precious little attention was paid to the competence and experience of the newly elected members; what seemed to matter much more was their popularity rating, on television or in the printed media.

Governmental stability is not beneficial in itself. It is a necessary but not sufficient condition of efficiency in public institutions. A stable government, unfortunately, does not automatically imply a well-governed state.

Notes

1. Prosecutors in Italy have the same status and degree of independence as judges.

2. On the independence of the judiciary in Italy, see the contributions by Di Federico (1995) and Guarnieri (1995); in general, see also Jacob et al. (1996).

3. Only in the last few years has Parliament enacted laws that could solve some of the major problems, devolving more cases to first-degree courts (*pretori*), establishing special courts (*sezioni/stralcio*) in 1997 with one thousand honorary judges recruited from among retired judges and lawyers to deal with the caseload pending, and reducing the number of collegiate judicial bodies at first instance level (*giudice unico di primo grado*) in 1998.

4. For an account of traditional Italian doctrine, see Merryman (1965).

References

Cassese, S. 1998. *Lo Stato introvabile*. Rome: Donzelli.

Chimenti, A. 1999. *Storia dei referendum*. Bari, Italy: Laterza.

Di Federico, G. 1995. Italy: A peculiar case. In *The global expansion of judicial power*, edited by C. N. Tate and T. Vallinder, pp. 233–42. New York: New York University Press.

Guarnieri, C. 1993. *Magistratura e politica in Italia: Pesi senza contrappesi*. Bologna: Il Mulino.

———. 1995. Judicial independence and policy-making in Italy. In *The global expansion of judicial power*, edited by C. N. Tate and T. Vallinder, pp. 243–60. New York: New York University Press.

Istat. 1997. *La situazione del paese nel 1997*. Rome: Istat.

———. 1998a. *La vita quotidiana nel 1996*. Rome: Istat.

———. 1998b. *Rapporto sull'Italia—edizione 1998*. Bologna: Il Mulino.

———. 1998c. *La situazione del paese nel 1998*. Bologna: Il Mulino.

Jacob, H., E. Blankenburg, H. M. Kritzer, D. M. Provine, and J. Sanders. 1996. *Courts, law and politics in comparative perspective*. New Haven, Conn.: Yale University Press.

La Torre, A. 2000. *Relazione sull'amministrazione della giustizia nell'anno 1999*. Rome: Stamperia reale.

Melis, G. 1996. *Storia dell'amministrazione italiana*. Bologna, Italy: Il Mulino.

Merryman, J. H. 1965. The Italian style I: Doctrine. *Stanford Law Review* 18:39–65.

Morisi, M. 1999. *Anatomia della magistratura italiana*. Bologna: Il Mulino.

Righettini, S. 1995. La politicizzazione di un potere neutrale: Magistratura e crisi italiana. *Rivista Italiana di Scienza Politica* 2:227–65.

Rodotà, C. 1986. *La Corte Costituzionale*. Rome: Editori Riuniti.

———. 1999. *Storia della Corte Costituzionale*. Bari, Italy: Laterza.

Scoppola, P. 1991. *La Repubblica dei partiti: Profilo storico della democrazia in Italia*. Bologna, Italy: Il Mulino.

Zannotti, F. 1994. L'organizzazione giudiziaria italiana e l'espansione dei poteri della magistratura. *Amministrare* 3:363–412.

CHAPTER 8

Italian Styles: Criminal Justice
and the Rise of an Active Magistracy

DAVID S. CLARK

The norms, institutions, and processes of Italian law become
truly Italian only when seen through Italian eyes. A common
lawyer who approaches the Italian law should attempt to acquire
the Italian legal outlook.

[T]he future would seem to hold an expanded role and greater
prestige for Italian judges. In part this will come about through
deflation of the bloated conception of the legislature that has
loomed over continental legal thought since 1804. In part it
will flow from reconsideration of the nature and the rigidity of
the separation of powers.

—JOHN HENRY MERRYMAN

John Henry Merryman's Contribution
to Comparative Legal Studies

In a series of three articles in 1965 and 1966 on the style of Italian law, John
Henry Merryman redirected the course of American comparative law studies (1965, 1966a 1966b).[1] First, he made it attractive to investigate legal systems other than those of France and Germany, which had dominated Ameri-

I am grateful to Luisa Antoniolli and Luca Castellani for providing advice and materials useful in preparing this chapter. I thank the USIA Fulbright Senior Scholar Program and the
Commissione per gli Scambi Culturali fra l'Italia e gli Stati Uniti for financially supporting my
stay with the spring 1999 Fulbright Chair in Comparative Law at the Università degli Studi di
Trento Facoltà di Giurisprudenza. I also thank Dean Roberto Toniatti at the Trento Law Faculty for his encouragement and support in carrying out this research and the Willamette University College of Law for a summer research grant.

can comparative law up to that time (1965, 39–42). Second, he emphasized a particular legal system's style.[2] John Merryman's many ideas from the Italian law series were further developed in 1969, especially the legal tradition idea (1969, 2; 1985, 2),[3] to apply generally to Western Europe and Latin America in the best-selling *The Civil Law Tradition* (1969, 1985, see 1973).

In an effort to break mainstream comparative law away from its frozen preoccupation with legal norms as the principal object of study, Merryman obtained funding for and directed the Stanford Studies in Law and Development (SLADE). This multinational, multidisciplinary investigation was based on certain premises: (1) social change drives legal change; (2) most of what is interesting about law is found in the legal institutions' structures and processes, the resources they consume, the roles of professionals who work with these institutions, and these professionals' and the general population's legal culture; (3) change over time in these matters might be measured; and (4) comparative change across regions and nations is the most interesting of all (Merryman, Clark, and Friedman 1979, 21–35).

The SLADE scholars—from Italy (Sabino Cassese, Stefano Rodotà), Spain (José Juan Toharia), Chile (Edmundo Fuenzalida), Colombia (Fernando Rojas), Costa Rica (the late Carlos José Gutiérrez, Ricardo Harbottle), Peru (Lorenzo Zolezzi), and the United States (John Merryman, Lawrence Friedman, David Clark)—devised a research plan, collected and analyzed data, and wrote articles and monographs (Merryman, Clark, and Friedman 1979, v–vi). The concept of legal culture entered the lexicon of comparative law, law and society studies, and general legal scholarship (for example, Friedman 1969, 1975, 193–267; Friedman and Macaulay 1977, 979–81, 1028–31; Merryman and Clark 1978, 28–29, 355–91, 1277 [index entry for "legal culture"]; Nelken 1997). John Merryman proposed (1974, 1977, 1998) that comparative law refocus its lens on law and social change. His comparative law casebook with SLADE data from Europe and Latin America was used in many American law school classrooms (Merryman and Clark 1978, xlv–xlvii [table of tables, listing fifty-four tables]). Its successor edition added East Asia and continued with a clear empirical and legal culture orientation toward the study of comparative law (Merryman, Clark, and Haley 1994, vii–viii, 582–85, 656–704, 1255–56 [table of tables, listing forty-two tables]).

Comparative Regional Judicial Studies

In this chapter I attempt to use these insights, incorporated in earlier SLADE studies, by analyzing several legal and social indicators for two historically relevant regions in Italy: the area south of Rome known as Mezzogiorno (land of the midday sun) and the remainder of the country (north and center).[4]

Sabino Cassese considers many of these same indicators in their social and cultural context for Italy as a whole (see Chapter 7 in this volume). Our concern is to describe and perhaps explain legal change in the post–World War II period, noting certain demographic, economic, and political developments over this half century that significantly influenced the work and structure of the Italian criminal justice system.

The expanded power of independent magistrates (judges and prosecutors), whom many accused of carrying out their own political agenda, illustrates one emerging Italian style. This development might not seem surprising to an American lawyer describing post-1950s federal and some state judiciaries in the United States. But to a civil law jurist, describing a judiciary largely modeled on the nineteenth-century French idea of strictly insulating courts from the political branches of government, this violates the separation of powers doctrine. In the 1990s economic and political pressures built up on the Italian system of justice that only some accommodation between the judiciary and the legislature could solve. John Merryman predicted in 1966 that there would be an expanded role for the judiciary, but its eventual course surprised everyone.

I try to shed some light on the patterns and pressures restructuring the Italian judicial system by focusing on its response to crime in the context of Italy's two principal regions. In 1990, using updated SLADE data, I wrote about civil litigation trends in Europe and Latin America since 1945 and argued for the advantage of making intracountry comparisons (Clark 1990). I found that Durkheim's socioeconomic development thesis that modernization leads to increased civil litigation did not explain trends from 1945 to 1984 in the six SLADE nations examined. However, it did hold for regional synchronic comparisons within single nations grouped according to their socioeconomic development. There was one exception: Mezzogiorno Italy (Clark 1990, 557–58 n. 7).[5] Intrigued by this deviation, I now compare developments since 1950 in the Italian south with those in north and center Italy as they relate to the magistracy's growth and its response to crime.

Regional Population Shifts and Economic Growth

The Italian population grew moderately after World War II until the mid-1970s, when it slowed to a pace that in the 1990s was the lowest in Europe (Eurostat 1998, 2–3).[6] The population of Italy was 47,516,000 in 1951, rising to 56,557,000 in 1981; in 1997, it was 57,563,000. Just over a third lived in Mezzogiorno, the Italian south (Istat, *Annuario* 1998, 39, 642; 1973b, 8, 10; 1963, 12–14; 1953, 33). Overall, Italy's population increased 21 percent between 1951 (the first postwar census) and 1997, with a slightly larger 23 percent in the north and center region (hereafter NC) compared to 19 percent in Mezzogiorno (hereafter MG). Most of this expansion, 14 percent, occurred from 1951 to 1971 (the original SLADE period) versus only 2 percent from 1981 to 1997. In fact, NC grew barely at all during these latter two decades, and what population increase there was occurred in MG. Although there was some fluctuation in Italy's population distribution living in MG, beginning at 37 percent in 1951 and falling to 35 percent in 1971, MG has since that time almost recouped its original 1951 population share. If social dislocation causes crime, it might have been the great migration from south to north in the 1960s that triggered resort to criminal activity in Italy.

In 1997, 6.5 percent of Italy's economically active population worked in agriculture, about average for the European Union (EU) member states (Eurostat 1998, 16–17).[7] This figure represented a dramatic transformation in Italian social life since World War II. In 1951, 57 percent of MG's workers and 35 percent of NC's were employed in agriculture, which by the SLADE period's end in 1970 had already declined to 31 percent in MG and 13 percent in NC (Merryman, Clark, and Friedman 1979, 522, 528).

The Durkheimian theory, positing elevated civil litigation related to this type of socioeconomic change, would predict much higher civil litigation rates in the more urbanized NC than in MG, with gradual merging of rates by the 1990s (Clark 1990, 556–57). In fact, this did not happen. In 1950, MG's civil filing rate per capita in first instance courts was 17 percent *greater* than the NC rate, which moved toward parity (only 7 percent larger) in 1970. However, in 1997, MG's civil litigation rate, at 3,740 cases per 100,000 population compared to NC's 1,870 cases, was 100 percent higher (Istat, *Annuario* 1998, 147; Merryman, Clark, and Friedman 1979, 162, 507). What caused this huge difference in litigiousness between Mezzogiorno and north and central Italy? Would the difference suggest a similar gap with much higher criminality and penal caseloads in MG than in NC?

Another dimension to the Italian postwar story was its economic miracle, equal almost to Germany's. From one of the poorest European countries in 1945, Italy steadily expanded its goods and services production so that an economic spurt between 1985 and 1990 overtook (*il sorpasso*) the United Kingdom's gross domestic product (GDP) to rank Italy the fifth-largest economic power in the world—after the USA, Japan, Germany, and France (Cassese 1993, 316; Sassoon 1997, 75).[8] In the mid-1990s Italy's per capita GDP continued to exceed the United Kingdom's, in both current exchange prices and by even more when adjusted for purchasing power (Eurostat 1999, 6–7; 1998, 14–15).[9]

Italian per capita GDP in 1997 was 33.9 million lire, having increased from 4.9 million lire in 1951 (in constant 1997 prices) (Istat, *Annuario* 1998, 296). Few other European Union member states have the large geographical discrepancy in economic production that exists between MG and NC. In 1995, per capita income in MG was only 55 percent of that in NC. The closest parallel might be Germany, which is proceeding to integrate former communist lands into a larger reunified economy (Eurostat 1999, 4–7).[10] Italy experienced strong sustained economic growth from 1951 until the early 1980s, followed by the jump (sorpasso) between 1985 and 1990 that overtook the United Kingdom. The 1990s, however, was a decade of slow growth. The government embraced pragmatic neoliberalism involving austerity, deregulation, and privatization (Sassoon 1997, 85–88). What impact should this difference in strong economic development up to 1989 versus the recent relative stagnation have on the overall judiciary's penal caseloads?

Italy's MG started our period with a per capita GDP only 52 percent as large as that of NC, but then fell to 45 percent in 1960. Large central government intervention and below-average tax revenues in MG helped to raise the relative economic production to 61 percent of that of NC in 1975, but that was the high point, which has slowly declined to 55 percent today.[11] This entrenched dualism is not likely to lessen in the coming years, because MG generates only about 10 percent of Italy's exports and sustains about triple the NC's unemployment rate. Moreover, the legislature abolished the resource redistributing *Cassa per il Mezzogiorno* in 1992 (Sassoon 1997, 82–83). What importance might this gap between the two regions have for NC and MG criminal activity and the use of the penal process to control it?

Italian Political Culture and the Rule of Law

Italy embraces a Mediterranean legal culture that distinguishes it from its northern European neighbors. As long as the Alps isolated Italy or larger external forces such as the cold war convinced allies to ignore differences in the Italian political and legal systems, it continued as a "democratic paradox" (LaPalombara 1987, 3–24) or a "difficult democracy" (Spotts and Wieser 1986).

Nevertheless, Italy was a founding member of the 1957 European Economic Community, which established a legal framework that could draw Italy closer to its northern fellow members. However, it was the 1991 Maastricht Treaty on European Union and provisions for economic unity and a single currency that significantly increased external pressure for Italian political and economic change by reducing the room for divergence between word and deed. In addition, the Soviet Union's collapse eroded anticommunist support for the traditional political leaders in the Christian Democrat and Socialist Parties. In 1993, partly due to massive corruption scandals, the five postwar ruling parties (*pentapartito*) and their final coalition disappeared. A center-right alliance led by media mogul Silvio Berlusconi and his *Forza Italia* won the March 1994 election (Ginsborg 1996, 19–23; Gundle and Parker 1996, 1–11).

The 1992–94 political crisis clearly revealed that the Italian "blocked democracy" was systematically corrupted because illicit governance was routine. The political class (*partitocrazia*) had turned governmental institutions to its own use by "privatizing" the public sphere. Political appointments required a party card. A self-perpetuating cycle of extensive networks of clientelistic exchange (*scambi occulti*) throughout the legal system created a hidden power structure behind what Sabino Cassese (1998) called the *stato introvabile* (unfindable state).[12] The civil service was no better. Cassese, minister for public administration during the crisis preceding the March 1994 election, calculated that the average Italian lost three weeks each year trying to deal with the bureaucracy. The government's speed or efficacy in acting depended primarily on the pressure, ranging from the use of contacts to bribery, that a citizen could exert on public officials (Bull and Rhodes 1997, 3–6; Ginsborg 1996, 23–24; Olgiati 1985, 91–96).

Was it likely between 1950 and the 1992 crisis that ordinary citizens' frustration with politicians and the public administration affected the magistracy, penal court caseloads, and the criminal justice system in general? What do the 1990s political developments mean for the rule of law (*Rechtsstaat*) ideal?

One answer to this latter question is that most important pressures for change related to the rule of law came from abroad through Italian connections with the European supranational framework and other agents of economic globalization. Lawrence Friedman (1998) made a similar general argument that the rule of law is tied to modernization; it is not peculiarly Western nor universal. First, the European Union (and the Council of Europe) introduced a new style of politics and law into Italy based on northern Protestant, technocratic rules that were inconsistent with more clientelistic, Mediterranean, personalized norms.[13] Although the latter tended to subvert the former for much of the period under study, inadequate implementation of EU directives and widespread fraudulent abuse of EU aid created an obvious dissonance noticeable to the highly pro-EU Italian population. The Maastricht Treaty signing in 1992 exerted the final pressure on Italian politicians, who then had to begin meaningful political and economic reforms. Second, market globalization and intensified competition exposed deficiencies in the national legal system and economic capital markets. Foreign investors signaled their lack of confidence in traditional Italian collusive practices and informally regulated investments (Bull and Rhodes 1997, 7–8; see Dezalay and Garth 1997).

An alternative interpretation is that an indigenous Italian official morality supported the rule of law when the vices just detailed became excessive. This morality was found in the 1948 Constitution and in strong popular support for Europeanization. Although substantial tension existed between the everyday practice of favors, connections, and corruption and the loftier offi-

cial rule of law morality, it was the latter that brought down the venal political class.[14] The increased popularity of referenda was another sign that Italians were taking legal rules more seriously (Ginsborg 1996, 24–26).

An Active Magistracy's Emergence: Judges and Prosecutors

Italy has attained a strong independent judiciary. This independence extends
also to prosecutors, who share the same education and recruitment. Together
judges and prosecutors, who make up the career magistracy, enjoy autonomy
or external independence from the political branches of government as well
as a certain internal independence from other magistrates (Cost. arts. 101[2],
104[1]; see Appendix for a list of statutes). Prior to the 1948 Constitution,
the minister of grace and justice determined a judge's assignments and other
career possibilities, which under Fascism led to many abuses. The constitution's solution authorized the Superior Magistracy Council (*Consiglio superiore della magistratura*, or CSM), which the Parliament finally created in 1958
(Cost. arts. 104–107; Legge no. 195). It is an elected body of twenty judges
and prosecutors (selected by the entire magistracy), ten law professors and
lawyers (selected by the Parliament), the Court of Cassation's first president and procurator general, and the republic's president serving as presiding chair.[15] The CSM makes most important decisions related to the judicial branch's personnel and internal operation (Cappelletti, Merryman, and
Perillo 1967, 102–9; Certoma 1985, 61–71).[16]

Table 8.1 illustrates the Italian magistracy's growth since 1950. From a
small corps of 4,281 in 1950, the number of career judges and prosecutors
increased to 8,275 in 1996 (plus 3,300 *giudici di pace* judges, noncareer magistrates added in 1995 to help with the civil caseload crisis). In relative terms,
the increase was from 9 to 20 magistrates (including justices of the peace) per
100,000 population. By comparison, there were 22,100 career judges and
5,400 prosecutors in Germany in 1995 or 33 per 100,000 population (Clark
1999, 90, 101).

Successful candidates taking the judicial apprentice (*uditore giudiziario*) examination tend to have top grades as law graduates from Italian universities.
To reduce the vacant position number, some law faculties in the 1980s coop-
erated with the CSM to offer supplemental courses to prepare graduates for
the rigorous exam. Magistrates after the apprenticeship enjoy life tenure as
civil servants in the upper governmental salary range until age seventy, with
substantial pension rights. In 1963 women became eligible to take the test.
The female magistrate percentage gradually increased to 18 percent in 1991
and 27 percent in 1997. Traditionally, this legal career appealed to young jurists from the south, who have fewer alternatives with corporations or law
firms. In 1963, for instance, 77 percent of magistrates were born in MG (Al-

TABLE 8.1

Magistrates (Judges and Prosecutors) in Italy, by Region and Gender

Year	Italy			North and central (NC)			Mezzogiorno (MG)		
	Number	Per 100,000	% Female	Number	Per 100,000	% Female	Number	Per 100,000	% Female
1950	4,281	9		2,342	9		1,939	10	
1955	5,517	10		2,827	10		2,330	11	
1960	5,213	10		2,833	10		2,380	11	
1965	5,509	10		3,072	10		2,437	11	
1971[a]	6,701	12	3	4,197	12	4	2,504	13	1
1981[b]	6,965	12	9	4,308	12	10	2,657	13	8
1991[c]	7,516	13	18	4,386	12	19	3,130	15	17
1996[d]	11,575	20	27	6,683	18		4,892	23	

SOURCES: Istat (1994, table 4.5; 1984b, table 8; 1977, 3, 13, 96–153, 485); Merryman, Clark, and Friedman (1979, 448–51, 506); Pellegrini (1997, 220–24); Violante (1997, 156–58); see Cassese (1994, 211).

NOTE: Data in absolute numbers and per 100,000 population; these magistrates worked in the ordinary court system; their total excluded authorized but vacant positions; the north and central region included Court of Cassation judges, who decided petitions from throughout Italy.

[a] These figures subtracted from the census data approximately 505 magistrates in the Constitutional Court, Council of State, Court of Accounts, and certain judicial staff (of whom 140 were in MG); the jump in the magistrate number between 1965 and 1971 was overstated in NC (and accordingly understated in MG) by 223 because Marche and Umbria were included in NC in 1971 but were part of the SLADE semiagrarian (MG) region in 1965.

[b] These numbers excluded from the census figures approximately 555 magistrates (of whom 165 were in MG) in the Constitutional Court, Council of State, and Court of Accounts and certain judicial staff.

[c] The percentage of female magistrates was for the supervisory corps.

[d] Pellegrini (1997, 225); included 3,300 *giudici di pace*, who were judges but not career magistrates; they first decided cases in 1995 (Nebbia 1998, 171); they were allocated to the two regions according to the percentage of career magistrates; the female percentage was from the justice ministry (1993) and is reported at http://www.ojp.usdoj.gov/bjs/pub/ascii/wfbcjita.txt.

lum 1973, 157, 199–200; Certoma 1985, 71–72, 74).[17] In addition, for the entire postwar period a disproportionately greater number of magistrates relative to population worked in MG compared to NC (see Table 8.1).[18] Table 8.2 illustrates the division between prosecutors and judges and their assigned duties in 1993.

Judicial activism tendencies can be traced to the 1960s, when a substantial number of postwar-educated judges had replaced the earlier generation appointed under Fascism. The 1958 CSM enabling statute caused resentment among younger magistrates, because it continued to permit the practice of allocating larger salaries to higher-level judges on a basis other than seniority. It also left some power over status (promotions and transfers) and discipline outside the plenary CSM dispersed in the Ministry of Justice, a CSM special section controlled by higher level judges, and the Council of State. The *Associazione Nazionale Magistrati*, controlled by younger judges, criticized the CSM statute, which led higher court judges to form their own *Unione dei Magistrati Italiani*.

The fault line was drawn by generation and by political ideology, especially as it related to differing ideas of judicial independence. Center-left

TABLE 8.2
Magistrate Positions in Italy, by Job

Magistrate position	Number
Court of cassation judges	305
Court of appeal judges	962
Tribunale judges	2,790
Pretura judges	1,847
Specialized tribunale judges (minors, guardianship)	286
Apprentice judges	150
Subtotal, judges	6,340
Prosecutors at all courts	2,148
Ministry of Grace and Justice	128
Anti-Mafia National Office	21
Superior Magistracy Council	2
Total	8,639

SOURCE: Pellegrini (1997, 220).

magistrates opposed continued hierarchical career structures and preferred equal pay for both higher and lower court judges based solely on seniority. They also resented outside political influence tied to continued justice ministry involvement and court review of certain CSM decisions. Between 1963 and 1975, Parliament gave in on many of these demands and eliminated competitive examinations for promotion (relying instead on seniority), reduced salary differentials, and gave more power to the CSM. By the mid-1970s the Italian magistracy had acquired significant political force. This was further supported by the significant number of magistrates, such as Luciano Violante, former president of the Chamber of Deputies, who became politicians (Allum 1973, 201–4; Guarnieri 1997, 158–60; Nelken 1996b, 197; Spotts and Wieser 1986, 160; see Legge no. 195, arts. 10–13, 17).

The rise of organized political factions (*correnti*) within the magistracy helps to explain the nature of Italian judicial and prosecutorial activism. Younger magistrates realized in the 1960s that the dominant Christian Democrats (DC) supported magistracy leadership through coordinated activity of the justice minister and higher-ranking magistrates. As a result, they turned to the Socialist Party (PSI) during the years in which it shared power in the center-left governing majority for assistance in dismantling the traditional career structure. Strong relationships developed between correnti, political parties, and the media. After many breaks and reconfigurations, the magistracy today is thoroughly factionalized among four groups: left to right, the *Magistratura Democratica, Movimento per la Giustizia, Unità per la Costituzione,* and *Magistratura Indipendente.*

After 1968 the Communist Party (PCI) overcame its traditional mistrust of a "bourgeois," repressive judiciary and supported PSI magistracy reforms. By the 1970s "democratic" judges, particularly in labor cases (including workplace safety), were sympathetic to the workers' movement. Some activist prosecutors gained fame by bringing criminal initiatives (*protagonismo*) against environmental pollution, tax evasion, and bank fraud. With electoral success in 1975, the PCI assisted the PSI in enacting the coup de grace to judicial hierarchy: proportional representation with competing candidate lists for electing the twenty magistrates to the CSM (Legge no. 695, art. 5, amending Legge no. 195, arts. 25–27; Di Federico 1995, 238–39; Guarnieri 1997, 160–64; Spotts and Wieser 1986, 158–61).[19]

Since 1976 all elected CSM magistrates have belonged to a corrente. From that time until 1994, the CSM gained members from the far left Magistratura Democratica and lost those from the far right Magistratura Indipendente, with the centrist Unità per la Costituzione holding a plurality. This magistracy politicization and shift to the left clearly affected the nature of career decisions. Since transfers and promotions were now based solely on seniority, the CSM chose among equal-rank candidates on a faction- or party-affiliation basis in a reciprocal exchange process. The CSM, thanks to the justice minister's decline, was now the key institutional link between political parties and the magistracy.

This structure helps to explain the rise of prosecutorial and judicial activism. Leftist judges argued in the 1970s for a less positivistic approach to statutory and codal interpretation that could rely on constitutional principles such as equality. Sometimes they easily granted leave in civil or criminal cases to refer an issue to the Constitutional Court, an innovative entity that frequently found provisions in Fascist-era codes and statutes unconstitutional, much to the more conservative Court of Cassation's chagrin (see Merryman and Vigoriti 1967). Gustavo Zagrebelsky, a Torino law professor who sits on the Constitutional Court, carries on this tradition. Judges on occasion backed up these ideas with vocal participation in mass meetings and demonstrations.

There was also a steady expansion of prosecutorial-judicial intervention in politically sensitive matters, such as terrorism and, later, organized crime. Parliament in the late 1970s, supported by the Communist Party, granted expanded powers to prosecutors and investigative judges to fight terrorism on both the left and right. Some first instance prosecutor-judges, known as *pretori d'assalto*, used these tools to bring controversial pollution, labor relation, and consumer protection cases. People began to see the magistracy rather than the executive as the instrument for fighting society's ills and for public order. But at the same time, the magistracy's substantial ability to act arbitrarily, to allege matters that could not be proved, and to detain for long periods individuals who were later found innocent at trial led to accusations of political partisanship (Di Federico 1995, 239; Guarnieri 1997, 160–64; Spotts and Wieser 1986, 158–61).

In summary, the 1970s saw substantial growth in the magistracy's investigative powers, especially over the police. In the 1980s these instruments began to be used against mafia organizations, not only in MG but increasingly in the north. This time government parties were less supportive, unlike the PCI, which continued to praise judicial activism. Some prosecutors and judges discovered examples of "hidden power" fueled by administrative and political party corruption. The PSI, led by Bettino Craxi, struck back by instituting constitutional reform via referendum to rein in the magistrates' autonomy and arbitrariness, for instance, by increasing judicial civil liability for malfeasance. In 1990 President Francesco Cossiga, a Christian Democrat, even launched an attack on the CSM. It was in this setting that magistrates began the *Tangentopoli* (Bribesville) or *mani pulite* (clean hands) investigations and prosecutions against politicians, administrators, and business leaders in 1992, which led to the 1992–94 political crisis. Eventually, four hundred magistrates took part in these prosecutions. Emboldened by favorable public opinion for magistrates, President Oscar Scalfaro in 1993 and the Carlo Ciampi government from April 1993 to March 1994 cautiously supported the magistrates' efforts (Allum 1973, 201–4; Ginsborg 1996, 26–28; Guarnieri 1997, 164–66; Nelken 1996a, 200, 204 n. 13; Pizzorusso 1985, 116–17).

But public sentiment toward the magistracy has been ambivalent. After all, voters in 1987 overwhelmingly supported the referendum to make magistrates civilly liable for harm that they might cause. In addition, judges were too slow in processing penal cases in the mid-1970s and late 1980s and civil cases from the late 1980s, resulting in severe caseload crises (Pellegrini 1997, 242–43). The magistracy's poorer reputation in the late 1980s provided the Socialist government with an opportunity to replace the Fascist-era, inquisitorial Penal Procedure Code with one adopting an accusatorial ideology. The magistracy had previously thwarted reform efforts for a new code because they did not want to lose any of their hard-won, largely unsupervised investigative powers (Guarnieri 1997, 164–65).[20]

Italy's magistracy was, and was believed to be, a body primarily focused on penal rather than civil matters. Penal judges, of course, have more political visibility than civil judges (Ferrarese 1997, 464–71; 1988, 168–69; Nelken 1996a, 197). This was particularly true at the Court of Cassation, whose penal caseload since 1950 always exceeded 70 percent. Below Cassation, 57 percent of the remaining judges processed penal cases, leaving only 43 percent for civil cases (Varano 1997, 660). Of course, most prosecutors worked on penal matters. The magistracy's focus on criminal proceedings in large part explains its increased importance in the Italian legal system and in society overall.

TABLE 8.3

Reported Crimes in Italy, by Region

	Italy			North and central			Mezzogiorno		
Year	Number	Per 100,000	% No Suspect	Number	Per 100,000	% No Suspect	Number	Per 100,000	% No Suspect
1950	710	1,501							
1955	709	1,453							
1960	820	1,628							
1965	889	1,705							
1970	1,015	1,886	55	706	2,264	59	309	1,640	46
1976	2,145	3,842	80	1,437	4,007	81	708	3,643	79
1980	1,920	3,400	76						
1981	1,952	3,453	72	1,251	3,427	74	701	3,496	70
1985	2,000	3,497	69	1,317	3,621	70	693	3,423	67
1990	1,998	3,461	84	1,457	4,017	85	541	2,640	82
1991	2,817	4,875	83						
1993	2,680	4,700	81	1,981	5,447	82	698	3,376	78
1995	2,938	5,129	83	2,003	5,489	82	935	4,493	83
1996	2,974	5,176	83	2,100	5,745	83	874	4,187	82
1997	2,856	4,962	81	2,020	5,516	82	836	3,992	78

SOURCES: Istat (1998b, 34, 439); Annuario (1994, 199; 1991, 221; 1986, 222; 1982, 107; 1978, 109; 1971, 111).
NOTE: Data in absolute numbers (in thousands) and per 100,000 population; reported crimes (notizie dei reati) were those for which judicial authorities initiated a penal action; due to difficulties in implementing the 1989 Penal Procedure Code, some 1990 crime reporting was delayed until 1991; thus, 1990 figures were lower than would otherwise have been the case, and 199 data were higher (Istat, Annuario, 1994, 199).

Criminal Activity

Although a few magistrates may undertake matters of great public interest and importance, the ordinary magistracy is primarily concerned on a day-to-day basis with routine criminal cases and civil disputes. The public's opinion about prosecutors' and judges' competence, fairness, and honesty will thus primarily be based on these activities. Before we consider specific penal court caseload statistics, we will look at the ebb and flow of criminal activity in Italy since World War II. We also look at the judiciary's response measured by penal convictions and their relationship to prison policy. To a large extent, prosecutors and judges merely react to crime, but the incidence and severity of monetary punishment or incarceration may themselves influence future criminal activity.

Table 8.3 traces the reported crime (delitti) history in Italy, by region, between 1950 and 1997 in the aggregate and by holding population constant. Reported crimes only provide a surrogate for the actual criminality level, because many people do not report certain types of crimes. Since we consider the same data class over time, underreporting errors should have less effect on comparative analysis.[21]

From 1950 until 1970, Italian criminality gradually increased, about 26 percent overall in relative terms per 100,000 population. However, in 1970 the crime rate in NC was 38 percent higher than in MG. At the same time, average income in NC was 74 percent higher, so reported crime tended to flourish in an area with greater economic resources. Because many farmers left the land throughout Italy, the resulting social transformation was not confined to only one region. But MG in the 1960s actually lost population while NC grew by 13 percent. Attracted by greater economic opportunity north of Rome, many leaving agriculture or leaving the south in general nevertheless could not obtain work. Some of these individuals turned to crime. The reported crime differential between NC and MG continued for the entire postwar period (as did higher income in NC), although the crime gap became smaller in the 1970s and 1980s but increased again during the 1990s crime wave.

The first great postwar crime surge occurred between 1971 and 1976, when the rate per capita more than doubled. Police efficiency declined dramatically as the percentage of crimes with no suspect increased from 55 percent in 1970 to 80 percent in 1976. The efficiency rate improved somewhat during the 1980s as the percentage of crimes without suspects dropped to between 69 and 76 percent, but deteriorated again in the 1990s when the police could identify suspects in fewer than one-fifth of the crimes reported. Overall, the criminality level was relatively flat between 1976 and 1990, when the second postwar crime wave began. This pushed the total number of crimes from about 2 million to close to 3 million annually (or nearly 5,000 per 100,000 population) during the 1990s.

The first crime wave in the 1970s was largely due to an increase in theft, which coincided with the smallest postwar five-year income per capita increase up to that time. But theft also became Italy's defining crime for the remainder of the twentieth century, usually ranking above 60 percent and sometimes 70 percent of all reported crimes. During the second crime wave in the 1990s (which paralleled another economic slowdown), the theft rate per capita again increased significantly. Other crime types show a similar pattern, portraying the 1950s and 1960s as a low and even declining criminality period. For instance, the homicide rate in 1950 was a high 5.1 per 100,000 population, declined to half that in 1970, jumped to 3.5 during the first crime wave, and then remained flat until the second crime wave in 1990, when it again exceeded 5 homicides per 100,000 inhabitants. Another example is the robbery, extortion, and kidnapping category. It followed the homicide pattern, except that the early 1970s jump did not level off but continued to grow with the rise of 1970s terrorism until the rate reached a high plateau in the 1990s, when it was over twelve times greater than in 1950 (Istat 1998b, 30–31, 439).

TABLE 8.4

Persons Convicted in Italy, by Type of Crime

Year	Total Number (thousands)	Total Per 100,000	Homicide and attempted homicide Number	Homicide and attempted homicide Per 100,000	Robbery, extortion, and kidnapping Number	Robbery, extortion, and kidnapping Per 100,000	Theft Number (thousands)	Theft Per 100,000	Theft % Total convicted
1950	140	296	540	1.1	1,549	3	51	108	37
1955	91	187	791	1.6	1,037	2	22	45	24
1961	120	237	636	1.3	1,096	2	21	40	17
1965	102	196	524	1.0	1,195	2	19	36	19
1970	65	121	304	0.6	885	2	10	18	15
1976	81	146	364	0.7	1,501	3	12	22	15
1980	134	238	494	0.9	3,382	6	22	39	17
1985	112	196	692	1.2	3,446	6	16	28	14
1990	118	205	473	0.8	4,818	8	21	36	18
1991	158	274	496	0.9	6,510	11	32	56	20
1993	193	339	766	1.3	7,235	13	33	59	17
1995	204	357	722	1.3	7,432	13	30	52	15
1996	245	427	593	1.0	8,466	15	36	62	15
1997	293	509	736	1.3	9,222	16	43	75	15

SOURCE: Istat (1998b, 37, 440).
NOTE: Data in absolute numbers and per 100,000 population; homicide figures excluded negligent homicide and murder endangering public security (*strage*) (Istat, 1998b, 37).

Penal Convictions

Although there was a gradual increase in criminality from 1950 to 1970, the persons convicted declined 59 percent from a 1950 high of 296 to 121 per 100,000 inhabitants in 1970 (see Table 8.4).[22] Thus, the 1950 conviction-crime ratio was 20 percent, but it deteriorated to 6 percent in 1970, reflecting the postwar low point in conviction rates at 121.

Judges responded to the first postwar crime surge by increasing convictions per capita to 146 in 1976, but the conviction-crime ratio further declined. There was only a 4 percent probability that a person would be convicted for committing a reported crime. The situation improved somewhat for the remainder of the 1970s and 1980s, but there were still only 205 convictions per 100,000 inhabitants in 1990, resulting in a 6 percent conviction-crime ratio. Finally, judges responded vigorously to the 1990s crime wave by raising the conviction level 148 percent to 509 per 100,000 inhabitants in 1997, resulting in a 10 percent conviction-crime ratio.

The magistracy's success in obtaining convictions varies among crimes. For homicide, the conviction-crime ratio reached a 41 percent high in 1955, falling to 23 percent in 1970 at the beginning of the first crime wave, which ended in 1976 at 18 percent. The ratio then reached a 13 percent postwar low in 1991 at the second crime wave's beginning but improved to 24 percent in 1997, close to the 23 percent level for homicide in 1950.[23]

Theft tells another story. The 1950 conviction-crime ratio was its all-time 18 percent high point. It declined significantly in the 1950s and 1960s until the 1970 leap in thefts signaled the response of criminals who believed the legal system no longer credibly punished thefts. A series of political forces merged with economic and social factors favoring criminal activity in 1970. First, Parliament authorized amnesties as an inexpensive solution to growing criminal case backlogs in the late 1960s and as a political statement from the left that theft represented a substitute for ineffective government-sponsored wealth distribution via social programs for the poor (see Mantovani 1988, 799–800). Sympathetic leftist prosecutors and judges also abandoned most efforts to punish theft, and the conviction-crime ratio fell to 2 percent (see Pavarini 1994, 50–53; Spotts and Wieser 1986, 159–60). During the first crime wave, ending in 1976, this ratio dropped to its postwar low below 1 percent, which even by 1990 had returned to only 2 percent. However, prosecutors renewed efforts during the 1990s crime surge to obtain theft convictions, which nevertheless reached only a 3 percent ratio. Even though thefts increased 440 percent from 1950 to 1997, there were actually fewer convictions at the end of the period than at the beginning.

Recall that the crime rate tended to be higher in NC than in MG (see Table 8.3), which continued during the 1990s crime wave. What is surprising was that MG's conviction rate per 100,000 population was higher than that in NC, and increasingly so during the 1990s. Thus, MG magistrates dealt more effectively with crime than their more liberal colleagues to the north, which in turn likely fed higher NC crime rates. For instance, the overall 1993 NC conviction rate was 339 persons per 100,000 inhabitants compared to 357 persons in MG. By 1997, this gap increased to 442 for NC versus 626 for MG. Moreover, if one considers the 1997 convicted person's birthplace, the differential expanded to 294 to those from NC versus 752 for those from MG. The fact that southerners were two and a half times more likely than northerners to be convicted for crime clearly fed northern popular opinion that crime was part of southern culture (Istat 1998b, 38).[24] As theft represented most crime since 1970 and the NC crime rate always exceeded that in MG, crime became an important southern export to NC that yielded significant (although unreported) income for MG.

Recidivist convictions occurred more often at a crime wave's end than at its beginning. The judiciary overall probably responded to public concern about rising crime by incapacitating those whom they could and deterring others likely to continue the crime spree. Thus, in 1970 and 1990, at the two Italian postwar crime-cycle beginnings, the recidivist conviction percentage (for all crime categories) was lower than in the subsequent reported year near each crime wave's peak. Moreover, Table 8.4 lists higher conviction rates in 1980 and 1997, which suggest that the magistracy reacted to each crime wave by increasing convictions in general, as well as against persons who had previously committed a crime. There was not a significant relative increase in the percentage of women convicted of crime during the fourfold growth in convictions since 1970. The major exception to this general condition was for thefts, a category in which women in the late 1990s exceeded their ratio with men for overall crime.

Italian criminal sentencing in general has been lenient (Pavarini 1994, 50–53; see Table 8.5). Since the first crime cycle's beginning in 1970, judges levied only a fine in 40 to 51 percent of their sentences. Where a prison term was required, the average sentence did not exceed six months. In 1997, for example, judges fixed sentences as follows: 30 percent at less than three months, 28 percent for a term of three to six months (the modal category), and only 7 percent at over two years (Istat, *Annuario* 1998, 159). The only major shift in sentencing policy since 1970 discernible in Table 8.5 was the use of fines in lieu of imprisonment for thefts in the 1990s.

If an accused were subject to preventive detention, Table 8.6 illustrates why, due to lenient sentencing, the average defendant's advantage would be to admit guilt and obtain an early conviction. In 1980 the average processing time for convictions finalized in first instance proceedings took nineteen months, while we saw in Table 8.5 that the typical sentence was merely a fine. Even if the sentence required incarceration, it averaged between only three and six months.

Most 1980 final convictions (70 percent) occurred and ended in first instance proceedings, which lasted an average of nineteen months.[25] For those

TABLE 8.5

Convicted Persons in Italy, by Penalty and Type of Crime

Year	Total % Fine only	Total Average prison sentence (months)	Homicide and attempted homicide % Fine only	Homicide and attempted homicide Average prison sentence (months)	Robbery, extortion, and kidnapping % Fine only	Robbery, extortion, and kidnapping Average prison sentence (months)	Theft % Fine only	Theft Average prison sentence (months)
1970	40	<6	0	36–120	0	12–36	0	<6
1980	51	3–6	0	>120	0	12–24	<1	3–6
1990	44	3–6	0	>120	0	12–24	4	3–6
1997	46	3–6	0	>120	1	12–24	31	3–6

SOURCES: Istat, *Annuario* (1998, 159; 1991, 226; 1982, 111; 1972, 150).
NOTE: Fines are typically nominal; in 1997, of those penalized by fine only, 59 percent owed less than 1 million lire; 4 percent owed more than 5 million lire (Istat, *Annuario* 1998, 159).

TABLE 8.6

TABLE 8.6

*Stage of Proceedings in Which Convictions Became Final in Italy,
by Type of Crime, 1980*

Type of crime	Instruction and first instance %	Instruction and first instance Time*	Appeal %	Appeal Time	Cassation %	Cassation Time	All cases Time
Total convictions	70	19	23	44	7	65	28
Homicide	8	35	49	48	43	66	55
Robbery, extortion, and kidnapping	14	29	58	31	28	47	35
Theft	53	24	38	39	9	59	33

SOURCE: Istat (1983, 372–75).
*Average processing time (in months).

23 percent who appealed, the process was delayed an additional twenty-five months, whereas those 7 percent who then sought cassation review of legal issues waited another twenty-one months, for a total of 5.4 years between filing the criminal report and final conviction. The average delay for all convictions, however, was twenty-eight months. This period became longer for more serious crimes because they were more likely to be appealed and taken to cassation.

If an accused were free during penal proceedings, his or her lawyer's strategy might be just the reverse of pleading guilty—that is, delaying ultimate sentencing. When the crime's limitations period was not too long, the approach of the accused would be to stretch out the proceedings, including appeal, so that the period ran before a conviction became final (see CP arts. 158, 160).[26] In addition, Italy's frequent use of parliamentary amnesty (*amnistia*) terminated many cases for all but the most serious crimes.[27] The period 1968 to 1971 illustrates this situation. The number of accused acquitted, based on an amnesty, during these four years (with those accused of theft in parentheses) was 20,517 (3,646); 9,688 (1,815); 248,733 (21,043); and 111,576 (15,847) (Istat, *Annuario* 1974, 157).[28] What better incentive was there to delay proceedings than to wait for amnesty?

The 1989 criminal procedure reform to increase efficiency and equity also made it necessary to amend the constitution's article 79 on amnesty and pardon (*indulto*) (Legge costituzionale no. 1, art. 1). This was an attempt to restrain parliamentary coalitions, by requiring a two-thirds vote, from using amnesty as a principal method for resolving criminal matters. In the early 1990s defendants still often refused to use the new code's summary procedures, even with the incentive of reduced penalties, because they continued to hope for amnesty to extinguish the crime (Panagia 1992, 431–37; see CP arts. 151, 174; new CPP art. 672).

TABLE 8.7

Incarcerated Persons in Italy, by Gender and Justification for Imprisonment

	Total incarcerated at year end			Convicted (%)	Preventive detention (%)	Security measures (%)	New prisoners during year
Year	Number	Per 100,000	% Female				
1950	47,648	101	6	32	68	—	129,243
1955	32,351	66	6	35	65	—	88,702
1959	33,794	68	6	31	59	10	63,746
1965	36,158	70	5	26	66	8	56,657
1970	21,391	40	5	27	63	10	48,760
1975	30,726	56	4	22	73	5	91,369
1980	31,765	56	5	20	73	7	92,576
1985	41,536	73	5	21	74	5	95,329
1990	26,150	46	5	21	74	5	57,736
1991	35,485	62	5	18	78	4	80,234
1993	50,212	88	5	19	78	3	99,072
1995	47,759	83	4	22	75	3	93,051
1996	48,564	85	4	19	78	3	89,517
1997	50,527	88	4	18	79	3	88,024

SOURCE: Istat (1998b, 521–24; 1973b, 390).
NOTE: Data in absolute numbers and per 100,000 population; Istat did not report figures for persons incarcerated for security measures in 1950 and 1955; thus, the total incarcerated and new prisoner figures were underestimated for those years, and the conviction and preventive detention percentages are too high; preventive custody (*custodia cautelare*) may occur at any time before sentence becomes final, including the period during appeal.

Besides crimes (delitti), Italian courts also process misdemeanors (*contravvenzioni*), which include traffic offenses (often driving while intoxicated), penal code offenses against public order, and special laws on taxes, food safety, industrial waste disposal, and other similar matters. In 1997 there were 111,510 misdemeanor convictions, most of which were punished by a (usually small) fine (Istat, *Annuario* 1998, 160).

Prison Policy

One might think that imprisonment would be the natural consequence for conviction of a serious crime, that regular patterns would emerge between the number of persons convicted and those imprisoned, that the 1989 Penal Procedure Code would make a difference in the reasons why people were incarcerated, and that most incarceration would be justified on the grounds that an accused had been duly convicted of a crime. The Italian style tends to belie these suppositions, but not completely (see Table 8.7).

There was a rough correlation between the number of persons convicted and the average number incarcerated. Just as convictions fell in the period up to 1970 (although crime increased), the number imprisoned declined 60 percent between 1950 and 1970 to a postwar low of 21,391 prisoners, or 40 per

100,000 population. However, in response to the 1970s crime wave, convictions rose and imprisonment expanded 40 percent between 1970 and 1975 to 56 per 100,000 population (or 30,726 prisoners). This number remained level until 1981, when it increased again until it reached 42,795 in 1984, falling to a 1990 low of 26,150. The conviction level (see Table 8.4), alternatively, increased dramatically in the late 1970s only until 1980, when it began to decline until 1987. Both variables again coincided in the 1990s in response to the second major crime surge. In this last period, the relative number imprisoned on an average day grew 93 percent, from 46 in 1990 to 88 in 1997 (or 50,527 prisoners), which still was fewer than the 101 per 100,000 inhabitants in 1950.

The average Italian jail residence remained under one year throughout the postwar period. In part, this was due to the policy of Parliament of alleviating prison overcrowding by granting amnesties, but also to the magistracy's liberal policy on early release. In 1976, for example, judges released 55 percent of the total prison population provisionally, granted another 25 percent amnesty, and required only 20 percent to serve out their terms (Spotts and Wieser 1986, 166–67). One can calculate a rough average stay indicator from Table 8.7 by dividing the prisoner number at year's end by the new prisoner number entering jail during the year. This ratio began at 37 percent in 1950, rose to 53 percent (slightly over half a year) in 1959, and declined to 34 percent at the first crime wave's end in 1975. The ratio then rose to 44 percent in 1985, again exceeded half a year in 1992, and reached its 57 percent high in 1997. Thus, in the 1990s the judiciary attempted to fight the rise in criminality with both average jail terms beyond six months and higher conviction rates.

These figures do not refer to average judicial *sentences*, but to prison stays. It is important to emphasize that the judge at a preliminary hearing may order a person to jail for either preventive detention (*custodia cautelare*) if there is substantial evidence of guilt (new CPP arts. 273[1], 275[3], 285)[29] or as a security measure (*misure di sicurezza*) if the person is "socially dangerous" (CP arts. 202, 206; see new CPP arts. 312–13).[30] From 1959 to 1997 the average proportion of Italian prisoners incarcerated because they had been convicted of a crime gradually declined from 31 to 18 percent. Preventive detention has been and continues to be, by far, the dominant reason for imprisonment in Italy (see Spotts and Wieser 1986, 165–66).

The 1989 Penal Procedure Code attempted to improve defendants' rights with regard to the decision about preventive detention, which was further reformed in 1995 to stem abusive judicial use (new CPP arts. 272–315, as amended by Legge no. 332). These rules permitted preventive detention only if the prosecutor showed substantial evidence that an accused had committed a crime with at least a two-year maximum term and that the accused was likely to flee, tamper with a witness or other evidence, or commit a serious crime. In addition, the code set maximum detention periods for each stage of the proceedings and permitted compensation up to 100 million lire for grossly negligent judicial decisions (new CPP arts. 274–75, 303–6, 314–15).[31]

Nevertheless, judges in 1997 used preventive detention to place 87 percent of new prisoners in custody, although only 13 percent were to be punished for actual conviction of a crime (Istat 1998b, 453).[32] The 1997 preventive detention rate was similar regardless of the major crime category of the accused. This situation was different from that in 1980, when a person accused of the most serious crime was more likely to be incarcerated pending the proceeding's outcome. Thus, the 90 percent overall preventive detention rate was exceeded for homicide at 97 percent and for robbery and theft at 94 percent. In 1970, before the first crime wave, the new prisoner preventive detention rate was 82 percent (Istat 1998b, 451–53; 1983, 528–30; 1973b, 292).

The magistracy and Parliament made other significant changes in incarceration policy. In 1970, 13 percent of all new prisoners had been accused or convicted only of a misdemeanor, which actually increased to 17 percent in 1980. However, after Parliament depenalized many misdemeanors, subjecting them to administrative sanctions (Legge no. 689, arts. 1, 33, 102), and later implemented the 1989 Penal Procedure Code, the new percentage of prisoners convicted only of a misdemeanor declined by 1997 to less than 1 percent.

Prison has also been used less for those accused or convicted of theft. Between 1980 and 1997, although the new prisoner number remained similar (see Table 8.7) and convictions almost doubled (see Table 8.4), the new percentage of prisoners accused or convicted of theft declined from 35 to 21 percent (Istat 1998b, 451–53; 1983, 528–30; 1973b, 292).[33]

Another major development in 1990s Italian prison policy has been the shift toward putting foreigners in prison. More *new* prisoners are foreigners than ever before, rising from 21 percent in 1993 to 31 percent in 1997, when foreign prisoners made up 21 percent of the *total* inmate population (Istat, *Annuario* 1998, 162–63).[34] In addition, between 1990 and 1992, the drug abuser proportion in prison expanded from 20 percent to over 60 percent (Pavarini 1994, 57). Prisoners in 1997 were also less likely to be released before they had completed their term. Judges released only 6 percent early (on conditions) and none for amnesty or pardon. By contrast, judges in 1970 granted amnesty to 19 percent of those imprisoned and released conditionally another 3 percent (Istat 1998b, 445; 1973b, 286–87).[35]

The Penal Court System

The Italian judicial structure in the immediate postwar period looked much like its predecessor at the nineteenth century's end. Largely modeled on the French judiciary, its form was a hierarchical pyramid with the Court of Cassation on top to maintain national uniformity in the law's interpretation. Beneath were courts of appeal (with collegiate panels) to guarantee lower court factual and legal decision correctness, and multiple first instance courts differing in the importance of their jurisdiction. These courts included *uffici di conciliazione* (now *giudici di pace*) for minor civil cases and two court levels (*pretura* and *tribunale*) for both civil and penal matters.[36] As in the French system, there were also courts of assize (with their own appellate courts) to adjudicate the most serious criminal cases, with a mixed panel of professional and lay judges, subject finally to review in cassation. In addition, appeal from minor jurisdiction courts went either to superior first instance courts or directly to cassation because of several factors.

Over the second half of the twentieth century, the Italian judicial structure was substantially remade. First, the Italian crime rate increased 231 percent from 1950 to 1997 (see Table 8.3). Even with sympathetic judicial and legislative attitudes toward some types of crime, processing many more cases inevitably led to more penal trials and appeals. In addition, civil case filings per capita grew 217 percent over the same period (Istat, *Annuario* 1998, 147; Merryman, Clark, and Friedman 1979, 162).[37] These caseload pressures convinced jurists and legislators that the overall system should be simplified, primarily by unifying the first instance level around its core task of initial adjudication. This entailed eliminating uffici di conciliazione and improving pretura distribution, removing penal appellate jurisdiction from tribunali and transferring it to courts of appeal, and ending three-judge collegiate tribunale panels so that only unitary first instance courts remained (Decreto legislativo no. 51; Legge no. 30; see Luiso 1999, 676–78).

Second, republican democratic ideology—reacting against the Italian Fascist experience from 1922 to 1944—argued for both structural and procedural changes in the judiciary. One structural change was to add a Constitutional Court with judges sympathetic to republican values. Another was to create the Superior Magistracy Council to support an independent third governmental branch. A third change was to surrender at an early stage some national sovereignty to the European system of supranational courts, for which Italian litigants had standing to request the review of Italian judicial decision.

This same liberal individual-rights focus supported change in Italian procedure, particularly penal procedure. It was no accident that the only new postwar code was one for penal procedure in 1989. The Italian Constitutional Court, scholarly legal doctrine, and the European Court of Human Rights brought substantial pressure for change through their critical decisions and writings about Italian rules and practices. Unlike reform attempts for a new civil procedure code, which lawyers tended to resist (Chiarloni 1999, 263, 276–81), Parliament with lawyer support succeeded against a weakened magistracy at the end of the 1980s in authorizing a new Penal Procedure Code (Legge no. 81).

The 1989 Penal Procedure Code rejected the French inquisitorial model and adopted a more accusatorial criminal process. Aimed at better protection of individual rights, the code reduced prosecutorial power, required trial judges to hear evidence independently where possible, and increased defense counsels' ability to confront adverse witnesses. One might expect this approach to utilize more judicial resources, a serious problem in light of growing caseloads. The code's drafters foresaw this issue and improved certain alternatives to the traditional process and adopted summary trial and plea bargaining procedures with sentence reductions to divert cases away from trials (see Grande 2000).

To understand Italian penal cases better, it is important to emphasize the magistracy's involvement in the criminal justice process from judicial police supervision to the time of an individual's release from prison. Before 1989 the "judicial police," a concept including most police forces (new CPP art. 57), were required to make a timely report of a crime (*notizia di reato*) (see Table 8.3) to a pretura judge (acting also as a prosecutor) or a tribunale prosecutor (1930 CPP arts. 2, 231–34). Since introduction of the 1989 code, police make this filing with a prosecutor (*pubblico ministero* or *procuratore*) tied to one of these two first instance courts (new CPP arts. 330, 347). The Constitutional Court and dominant scholarly doctrine have interpreted the obligatory prosecution mandate (Cost. art. 112.) to require prosecutors to review reported crime files even though no suspect is named.

Preture

Table 8.8 lists the number of "trials" requested with pretura judges (*pretori*). An entry in this category meant that a *pretore*, acting as both the prosecutor and examining judge through the secret instruction stage (*istruzione*), decided to issue a citation for trial (1930 CPP arts. 220, 230–31, 406–9).[38] At this public trial, the pretore acted as judge, and another magistrate (or delegate) assumed the prosecutorial role. The abuse or perceived abuse of rights of the accused in this mostly secret inquisitorial process was an important reason for the 1989 code's reform (see Certoma 1985, 243, 245).

Since 1990, on receiving the crime report, the prosecutor opens a prelim-

TABLE 8.8
Penal Trials Requested with Italian Pretura Judges, by Region

Year	Italy		North and central		Mezzogiorno	
	Per 100,000	Number	Per 100,000	Number	Per 100,000	Number
1950	249	536	112	418	137	697
1955	254	517	118	413	137	660
1960	273	539	135	454	139	660
1965	312	590	170	538	142	666
1970	217	405	116	333	101	538
1976	351	635	210	585	141	725
1980	328	583	186	511	142	715
1983	293	518				
			1989 Penal Procedure Code in effect			
1990	116	205	61	169	55	267
1991	195	343				
1993	354	620	199	547	155	747
1995	425	742				
1996	434	756				
1997	449	781	238	650	212	1,010

SOURCES: Istat, *Annuario* (1998, 155–56; 1994, 197–98; 1986, 219; 1978, 107); Istat (1993, 239; 1983, 286; 1973b, 171); Merryman, Clark, and Friedman (1979, 276, 507).
NOTE: Data in absolute numbers (in thousands) and per 100,000 population.

inary inquiry. This work and any recommendation made are reviewed by a preliminary inquiry judge (*giudice per le indagini preliminari*), commonly known as GIP. The GIP controls evidence taking and guarantees cross-examination within time limits set by the code, which should not normally exceed six months but may extend to eighteen months or even two years for certain crimes. During the investigative stage a prosecutor may ask the GIP for dismissal (*richiesta di archiviazione*), use of a special procedure, or trial (new CPP arts. 326–28, 335, 358, 392, 401, 405–11, 415–17, 549–55; see Grevi 1994, 147–61).

Before the 1989 code, misdemeanors and those crimes carrying a three-year maximum incarceration, or with solely monetary punishments, were filed with preture (1930 CPP art. 31).[39] The 1989 code increased pretura jurisdiction to cover crimes levying a maximum four-year term plus other important crimes such as aggravated theft, fraud, and negligent homicide (new CPP art. 7). From 1950 to 1997 the relative number of penal trials requested before pretori per 100,000 population grew 46 percent (see Table 8.8). Over the same period, the relative number of career magistrates expanded a much larger 122 percent (see Table 8.1), so more magistrates were available to deal with this caseload unless other matters demanded their attention. These other matters included a decline in tribunale filings but an increase in courts of appeal filings and cassation petitions.

From 1950 until 1965 pretori requested a relatively constant number of trials. By the late 1960s younger magistrates, pushing for social democratic values, had replaced many of those, particularly at the preture level, who had served during the Fascist dictatorship. Collectively, these younger magistrates implemented a de facto depenalization policy for "unjust" crimes, even as the crime rate increased, by assigning 31 percent fewer cases per capita to trial by 1970 compared to 1965. This impulse was significantly stronger in NC (38 percent reduction) than in MG (19 percent decrease).

Could this action have been a partial cause of Italy's first postwar crime wave from 1971 to 1976, when the per capita crime rate more than doubled? Whether or not this was true, pretori responded by requesting 57 percent more trials between 1970 and 1976, rising to 635 per 100,000 inhabitants, a level that declined in the 1980s and was not seen again until the second postwar crime wave in the 1990s. Once the 1989 Penal Procedure Code was fully implemented in 1993, the trial rate increased 26 percent by 1997 to 781 per 100,000 inhabitants, the highest postwar level. Even though the crime rate was consistently lower in MG than in NC, the MG trial rate was always greater, from 67 percent higher in 1950 to 55 percent higher in 1997. The south, at least in this respect, took a more conservative, punitive approach to law and order.

Data on pretori deciding penal trials broadly reflect, but with less volatility, the same patterns described for trials requested. This is also true for the greater relative use of pretura courts in MG than in NC. The overall work rate was steady, usually in the 500s per 100,000 population, except for the 28 percent expansion during the first crime wave, the decline during the 1989 code changeover, and the 26 percent increase in trials decided between 1993 and 1997 (Istat, *Annuario* 1998, 155–56; 1994, 197; 1991, 217; 1986, 219; 1978, 107; Istat 1998b, 41–41; 1993, 239–40; 1973b, 171–72; Merryman, Clark, and Friedman 1979, 270, 277–78, 507).

Average processing time for pretura criminal cases proceeding to trial (including the instruction or investigation phase) exceeded one year only in 1976, at the end of the first crime wave, until the 1989 code procedures collided with the second crime wave in the 1990s. Between 1993 and 1997 average delay rose from thirteen to twenty-one months, with MG judges seemingly less willing to utilize the new methods. The irony of this is that one of the new code's principal aims was to increase the Italian judiciary's efficiency with plea bargaining and other procedures alternative to full trial.[40]

One of the 1989 code's innovations was the summary trial (*giudizio abbreviato*), which grants a defendant the right to request quick resolution of his or her case based on the GIP's investigative file plus testimony from the defendant. The prosecutor and judge should grant this request if the case can be resolved from the file. In exchange for saving the state judicial resources, a judge must reduce the defendant's sentence by one-third if found guilty (new CPP arts. 438–42; see Pizzi and Marafioti 1992, 23–28, 31–33). This procedure actually has been less important in preture, falling from 4,355 to 2,569 cases between 1993 and 1997.[41]

The situation was different in tribunali (see Table 8.9), where GIP summary trials increased from 6,708 to 7,009 cases, which is about one-eighth the number of traditional trials tribunale judges decided. Persons guilty of more serious crimes processed in tribunali might well prefer the one-third sentence reduction, which is suggested by the guilty proportions of 84 percent in 1993 and 86 percent in 1997 (Istat 1998b, 43; *Annuario* 1994, 197).

Another innovation was explicit plea bargaining (*applicazione della pena su richiesta*). The prosecutor and accused may agree to reduce the normal sentence up to one-third if the negotiated term does not exceed two years. The prosecutor may also offer a conditional suspension of this two-year or shorter sentence (CP art. 163; new CPP art. 444[3]).[42] Either the GIP or trial judge, depending on the proceeding stage, must agree to the arrangement (which does not bargain away charged crimes). In fact, an accused may directly ask the judge for such a bargain even if the prosecutor refuses to concur (new CPP arts. 444–48; see Pizzi and Marafioti 1992, 21–23).

Plea bargaining has become an important part of Italian criminal procedure in less than a decade, although more efficiency could be achieved if this option were further encouraged among prosecutors at GIP preliminary inquiries. In 1993 and 1997 pretura GIPs agreed to only 15,790 and 13,550 plea bargains, respectively. But at trial (usually the first hearing), preture resolved 44 percent of 165,844 convictions in 1993 and 42 percent of 201,635 convictions in 1997 by plea bargain.[43]

Tribunale GIPs more easily accepted the plea bargain alternative to terminate a substantial number of minor cases: 13,800 in 1993 and 16,693 in 1997. Moreover, tribunale judges resolved 37 percent of 32,003 convictions in 1993 and 41 percent of 39,857 convictions in 1997 by plea bargain (Istat 1998b, 43; *Annuario* 1994, 197).[44]

A final alternative to trial is the penal decree proceeding (*procedimento per decreto penale*), which was used before 1989 but now is more attractive to defendants. Although the penal decree proceeding is primarily intended for pretura to resolve crimes for which a fine is adequate punishment, prosecutors may offer to terminate such a case with a 50 percent discounted fine. If the accused and GIP agree, the latter executes a conviction decree (new CPP arts. 459–60; 1930 CPP arts. 506–7; see Pizzi and Marafioti 1992, 20–21). Between 1993 and 1997, however, the penal decree number dropped from 170,229 to 128,051 (Istat 1998b, 43; *Annuario* 1994, 197).

TABLE 8.9

Penal Trials Decided in Italian Tribunali and Courts of Assize, by Region

Year	Italy Tribunali number	Italy Per 100,000	Italy Assize time[a]	Italy Number	North and central Tribunali number	North and central Per 100,000	North and central Assize time	North and central Number	Mezzogiorno Tribunali number	Mezzogiorno Per 100,000	Mezzogiorno Assize time	Mezzogiorno Number
1950	107	230	11		52	193	10		55	280	11	
1955	65	131	10		30	104	11		35	169	9	
1960	63	124	14		29	99	15		34	160	14	
1965	43	81	15		24	76	17		19	88	13	
1970	107	199	12	1.3	62	178	11	0.6	45	238	14	0.7
1976	117	211	24	1.1								
1980	148	264	18	0.9	90	248	19	0.4	58	292	17	0.5
1983	146	258	20	0.9								
1988	135	238	33	1.0								
1989 Penal Procedure Code in effect												
1990[b]	166	293	12	0.8	88	242	10	0.3	78	382	14	0.5
1991	44	78	16	0.4								
1993	50	87	19	0.4								
1995	48	85	24	0.4								
1996	64	111	23	0.5								
1997	59	103	25	0.6	33	91	21	0.2	26	125	30	0.4

SOURCES: Istat, *Annuario* (1998, 155–56; 1994, 197; 1991, 217; 1986, 219; 1978, 107); Istat (1998b, 41–42; 1993, 239–40; 1983, 286–87; 1973b, 171–72); Merryman, Clark, and Friedman (1979, 274–75, 507).

NOTE: Data in absolute numbers (in thousands) and per 100,000 population; I calculated average processing time by adding the periods for the prosecutor's preliminary investigation (*istruzione* prior to 1990), its judicial supervision, plus the tribunale trial; for before 1993, I used the SLADE method of calculating average delay (adding three months for instruction to the tribunale trial time from 1950 to 1965; see Clark and Merryman 1976); for 1993 on I relied on Istat figures (Istat, *Annuario* 1998, 144).

[a] Average first instance processing time (in months).

[b] I included 132,133 tribunale trials and 528 court of assize trials decided under the 1930 Penal Procedure Code (Istat, *Annuario* 1991, 217); the regional figures include these trials, which were allocated according to the division for 1989 code trials; the average processing time was for both 1930 code and 1989 code cases.

Tribunali and Courts of Assize

Tribunale penal procedure has been more elaborate than that in preture. For instance, before 1989 all instructions in preture were summary. In tribunali, an instruction, depending on the circumstances, might have been summary (conducted by a prosecutor) or formal (conducted by an examining judge, *giudice istruttore*). Tribunale public trials took place before three judges, none of whom was the examining judge. Too often the trial was merely a formal reception of the instruction file's written summaries of testimony and other evidence (1930 CPP arts. 295–96, 389, 423, 437; see Certoma 1985, 231–45). After 1989 pretura and tribunale processes came closer together, as both courts used GIPs to control prosecutors' work (see new CPP arts. 549–67).

Although the relative number of pretura trials requested between 1950 and 1997 rose by 46 percent (see Table 8.8), tribunale trial requests declined 37 percent from 198 per 100,000 inhabitants in 1950 to 124 in 1997, a low rate that had occurred before only during the late 1950s and early 1960s. These opposing overall trends between the two types of courts can be attributed to the jurisdictional shift of certain crimes from tribunali to preture in 1984 and 1989.

Beyond the jurisdictional shift, there were similar caseload patterns between the two courts. Thus, during the first crime surge (1970–76), the relative number of trials requested grew 24 percent. But unlike preture requests, which then experienced a downturn, tribunale requests reached a postwar high in 1983, which led to the 1984 jurisdictional reform. Similarly, during the second crime wave the relative number of requested trials rose 38 percent. The MG regional preference for trials compared to that of NC is similar for tribunali and for preture. For courts of assize, which adjudicate the most serious crimes, the relative MG incidence of trials over NC was often double and even triple in 1997 (Istat, *Annuario* 1998, 155–56; 1994, 197–98; 1991, 217; 1986, 219; 1978, 107; Istat 1993, 239; 1983, 286; 1973b, 171; Merryman, Clark, and Friedman 1979, 173, 507).[45]

The situation for tribunale trials decided was broadly similar to that for trials requested, except that the overall decline for trials decided from 1950 to 1997 was even greater (see Table 8.9).

In general the pre-1990 pattern was U-shaped, with the low in 1965 at only 81 decided trials per 100,000 population, and the two arms of the U at 230 in 1950 and at 293 in 1990. There were two periods of substantially increased productivity from 1965 to 1970 and from 1988 to 1990, which significantly reduced average delay, in both cases bringing average processing time down to one year. Otherwise, delay usually exceeded one year (except during the 1950s), reaching crisis points in 1976 (twenty-four months) at the

TABLE 8.10

Penal Cases Appealed to Italian Tribunali and Courts of Appeal, by Region

	Italy				North and central				Mezzogiorno			
	Tribunali		Courts of appeal		Tribunali		Courts of appeal		Tribunali		Courts of appeal	
Year	Number	Per 100,000	Number	Per 100,000	Number	Per 100,000	Number	Per 100,000	Number	Per 100,000	Number	Per 100,000
1950	25	54	23	49	11	41	11	42	14	71	12	60
1955	36	73	23	46	17	61	11	36	19	90	12	59
1960	43	85	25	50	21	69	12	42	22	107	13	61
1965	45	85	26	49	24	77	14	44	21	96	12	57
1970	44	82	23	43	28	79	15	42	16	87	8	44
1976	2	112	35	64	36	101	21	59	26	133	14	74
1980	59	105	43	77	32	87	26	72	28	139	17	86
1983	46	82	42	74								
1988	6	11	108	191								
					1989 Penal Procedure Code in effect							
1990*			59	104			37	102			22	107
1991			37	65								
1993			59	104			32	88			27	131
1995			59	103								
1996			73	127								
1997			77	134			38	104			39	185

SOURCES: Istat, *Annuario* (1998, 155–56; 1994, 197–98; 1991, 217; 1986, 219; 1978, 107); Istat (1993, 239; 1983, 286; 1973b, 171); Merryman, Clark, and Friedman (1979, 79, 82, 507). NOTE: Data in absolute numbers (in thousands) and per 100,000 population; about 80 to almost 100 percent of the decisions in courts of assize were appealed to an assize court of appeal; thus, the absolute and relative number of appeals, and their regional division, closely track in the statistics.
*I included 41,446 court of appeal filings under the 1930 Penal Procedure Code (Istat, *Annuario* 1991, 217); the regional figures include these appeals, which were allocated according to the 1980 ratio.

first crime wave's end, in 1988 (thirty-three months) before the caseload shift to preture under the new code, and finally in 1997 (twenty-five months) during the second crime wave. As with pretori, tribunale judges faced with increased trial requests seemed unable to meet the new code's efficiency goals in the 1990s. And as with MG preture, MG tribunali worked slower than their counterparts in NC under the 1989 code's procedures.

Appellate Courts

Until 1984 prosecutors or defendants appealed preture decisions to a three-judge tribunale panel (1930 CPP art. 512; Legge no. 400; Ord.Giud. arts. 43, 48), except for certain nonappealable matters filed at cassation.[46] All tribunale cases, and both pretura and tribunale cases that commenced after 1984, were appealed to a court of appeal three-judge panel, again except for nonappealable matters appropriate for cassation. Overall, between 1950 and 1997, the number of appeals per 100,000 inhabitants increased 30 percent from 103 (adding the figures for tribunali and courts of appeal) to 134 (courts of appeal) (see Table 8.10).

Appeal against both pretura and tribunale penal decisions became more common in the 1950s. Thus, while the relative number of penal trials decided was flat from 1950 to 1960, the number of appeals filed increased 57 percent. Similarly, while the number of tribunali trials decided dropped 65 percent between 1950 and 1965 (see Table 8.9), the number of appeals remained level. Another way to illustrate this phenomenon is to compare the incidence of appeal to first instance decisions between 1950 and 1965. This rose for pretura trials from 10 percent to 16 percent and for tribunale trials from 21 percent to 60 percent. During the first crime wave between 1970 and 1976, the relative number of appeals to tribunali grew 37 percent and to courts of appeal, 49 percent, with the respective appeal incidence at 18 percent and 30 percent (growth from 1970).

The second postwar surge in crime increased filings to courts of appeal by 29 percent between 1993 and 1997. The appeal incidence from preture and tribunali combined rose slightly from 28 percent to 29 percent, which is much closer to the rate in 1976 for tribunali appeals than that for preture appeals. MG litigants again demonstrated a greater penchant than those in NC to use the criminal justice system. MG's appeals per 100,000 population exceeded the levels for NC in both tribunali and courts of appeal throughout the postwar period. During the second crime wave, moreover, MG's relative number of appeals increased 41 percent to 185, whereas NC's number rose only 18 percent to 104 between 1993 and 1997.

The pattern for tribunale penal appeals decided generally followed that for filings (see Table 8.10 and cited sources). MG was more active per capita than NC. The national level of decided appeals consistently increased from 1950 until 1982, but average delay never exceeded one year except at the first crime wave's end in 1976 (at thirteen months). These appellate duties, however, took resources away from first instance cases, whose processing time suffered (see Table 8.9 and cited sources). Parliament thus terminated tribunale appellate jurisdiction in 1984.

The courts of appeal work pace was stable from 1950 until 1976. But their inability to decide more appeals during the first crime wave when filings increased 49 percent between 1970 and 1976 led to the courts' first postwar average delay beyond one year (at twenty-one months) (see Table 8.10 and cited sources). Efforts to attack the caseload between 1976 and 1980 improved the decision rate 54 percent from 50 to 77 appeals per 100,000 inhabitants, which reduced average processing time to fourteen months. Nevertheless, these efforts waned in the early 1980s. Coupled with the 1984 reform and the shift of all penal appellate jurisdiction to courts of appeal, even the higher decision rate of 114 appeals per 100,000 population still yielded a postwar average delay record of thirty-two months. Only substantially improved productivity to clear out the backlog in 1990 brought average processing time down to twenty months.

During the second crime wave between 1993 and 1997, the courts of appeal managed to increase their work rate 73 percent to 114 decisions per 100,000 population. This permitted average delay to stay between nineteen and twenty-four months, which is still almost twice the twelve-month delay in 1970. MG throughout the postwar period was more active per capita than NC (except for 1990), and MG's processing time became shorter after 1965.

The Italian Court of Cassation has been primarily a criminal law court. After World War II, between 70 and 88 percent of its petitions concerned penal rather than civil matters. This ratio stood at 75 percent in 1997.

The Court sits in five-judge panels. Cassation cases filed and decided grew rapidly from 1950 to 1955. Per 100,000 inhabitants, filings rose 46 percent, but decisions increased 133 percent, so that average delay dropped from its postwar twenty-month high in 1950 to seven months in 1955. After that time, filings per capita remained stable through 1991. For instance, during the first crime wave between 1970 and 1976, cassation petitions filed rose only 11 percent.

The same was not true with the second crime wave's collision with the need to authoritatively interpret the 1989 Penal Procedure Code. Between 1991 and 1997, filings expanded 60 percent to 83 per 100,000 population. Nevertheless, the Court was able to keep up with its caseload: during the 1990s, average delay remained under six months. In fact, from 1955 (except for 1965), the Court's average processing time was one year or less (Istat, *Annuario* 1998, 147, 155; 1994, 187, 197; 1991, 201, 217; 1986, 203, 219; 1981,

86, 96; 1978, 95, 107; 1971, 100, 109; Merryman, Clark, and Friedman 1979, 62–64).

In 1997, the Court's 46,665 penal decisions were divided between 31,660 ordinary proceedings, which reviewed appellate court judgments and certain nonappealable lower court decisions about the guilt or innocence of an accused individual, and 15,005 special proceedings. Of the ordinary proceedings, the accused or civil party initiated 87 percent; the prosecutor, 12 percent; and the civil party and prosecutor together, 1 percent. The Court declared 57 percent of these ordinary petitions inadmissible, rejected another 21 percent on the merits, and reversed the lower court in only 22 percent of the cases.[47]

The Court of Cassation's preoccupation with ordinary proceedings declined after 1970, when they represented 91 percent of the total penal workload. This fell to 87 percent in 1980 and 1990, then dropped further to 68 percent in 1997, reflecting the 1989 code's greater concern with provisional detention abuse, which could only be reviewed with special proceedings. Statistics also confirm the extent to which the judicial pyramid's rationale of winnowing cases to the top was progressively implemented between 1970 and 1997. In 1990, 40 percent of the Court's ordinary petitions came from courts of appeal and appellate courts of assize, but by 1997 this ratio had grown to 67 percent (Istat 1998b, 48; *Annuario* 1991, 219; 1981, 96; 1971, 109).[48] Finally, as with the judicial hierarchy's lower levels, MG prosecutors and other parties used the Court of Cassation much more per capita than did those in NC, with 77 compared to 42 ordinary petitions decided per 100,000 inhabitants (Istat 1998b, 47–48; *Annuario* 1991, 219; 1981, 96; 1971, 109).

In 1997, 50 percent of the Court's special proceedings dealt with provisional personal or property detention and security measures, 26 percent with postconviction sentence and prison condition review, and 4 percent with jurisdiction (competence) and venue issues. The Court granted relief in 23 percent of the detention and postconviction review cases (Istat 1998b, 48). Before 1990, jurisdiction and venue issues were a significant portion of special proceedings: 23 percent in 1970, 33 percent in 1980, but falling to 7 percent in 1990 before reaching 4 percent in 1997. MG again was more active than NC, with 36 compared to 20 special proceedings decided per 100,000 inhabitants. The difference for provisional detention cases was almost triple: 20.7 from MG compared to 7.5 from NC (Istat 1998b, 47–48; *Annuario* 1991, 219; 1981, 96; 1971, 109).

The Italian Styles

Comparatists frequently distinguish between civil law and common law countries by referring to the latter's more prestigious judiciary. In the United

Kingdom and United States, for example, this prestige stems from several factors characteristic of developed common law nations.[49] The judiciary is an elite corps. Its membership is small compared to the number of private lawyers, from whose ranks judges generally are appointed late in their careers. Appellate judges explicitly create law and actively confront important social and sometimes political issues, for which they are famous (or notorious) among jurists and occasionally the general public. They express their own individual views about legal issues in their written opinions. Judicial independence from executive power is unquestioned.

Foreign jurists often think of Italy as another typical, even derivative, civil law nation. John Merryman certainly fought against such a facile and erroneous characterization. His 1966 statement prefacing this chapter predicted greater prestige for Italian judges. At that time, Italian judges shared several characteristics usual in developed civil law judiciaries. Collectively, its size was large relative to the number of lawyers in private practice. Judges entered a civil service career shortly after law school and before they had any significant law practice experience. Judges were not supposed to make law (a task for Parliament), and they did not explicitly confront important social issues (although the new Constitutional Court judges might do so). Judges were essentially anonymous, as their individual views were hidden in unsigned panel opinions. And some questioned the independence of judges whose career steps were subject to justice ministry or higher magistracy control.

The first Italian style identified in this chapter was the magistracy's changed position within the legal system. Since the mid-1960s judges and prosecutors have achieved further independence vis-à-vis the justice ministry and even against senior magistrates. Promotion, transfer, and salary since the 1970s have been almost completely dependent on seniority, with minimal attention to productivity. Italian judges (and also prosecutors), as a result, are as independent of governmental pressures as common law judges.

Some of these frontline prosecutors and investigative judges, supported by sympathetic colleagues at trial and on appeal, aggressively tackled serious social and political issues. Although proworker decisions involved civil cases, most activism occurred in penal cases fighting pollution, terrorism, the mafia, and in the 1990s, business and political corruption. Unlike the situation in the United States, where activist federal judges in the 1950s and 1960s explicitly shaped civil rights and criminal procedure norms under the constitutional umbrella, Italian magistrates, guided by obvious political party ideology and internal party-related magistrate factions, used legal tools provided by Fascist-era codes and a few helpful parliamentary statutes increasing investigative powers.

The average Italian had little trust in the magistracy and criminal justice system for much of the postwar era. On the one hand, from the early 1970s, an individual was not adequately protected from crime and, on the other hand, could suffer grave abuse of authority from prosecutors and investigative judges (Spotts and Wieser 1986, 169).

The successful Italian struggle against terrorism in the 1970s and early 1980s might well have altered the popular consensus about crime and punishment, providing magistrates with greater support. But trust only went so far, as the 1987 referendum to ratify judicial civil liability illustrated. In addition, against most magistrates' wishes, the 1989 Penal Procedure Code promised that its accusatorial procedure would be fairer toward those accused than the 1930 code's inquisitorial dominance by a pretura prosecutor-judge or tribunale investigating judge. The 1992–94 political crisis, with prosecutors and investigative judges pursuing politicians, business leaders, and mafiosi, made some magistrates household names, which gained further support for the penal process. The magistracy, not the executive, was the government branch that could successively confront social ills (Pavarini 1994, 59).

The second Italian style concerns the special position of prosecutors within the "judicial" branch and their opportunity for inefficiency and abuse of authority. Prosecutors are bound by the constitutional principle of compulsory prosecution, reflecting the post-Fascist desire to hedge in prosecutorial discretion in the interest of equal law enforcement. This is clearly inefficient. The prosecutor must open a file and request the judge's decision every time some (although insufficient) evidence suggests a crime has occurred, even in a case in which an accused is named who the prosecutor believes is innocent. To cope, prosecutors open the file but often do nothing more until the limitations period lapses. They then ask the judge to close the case.

To make matters worse, rather than confront the discretion issue realistically within the magistracy, the Italian style to achieve independence dismantled hierarchical control from the Ministry of Justice and even from the chief of an individual prosecutorial office. Now the 1989 Penal Procedure Code, in promoting an accusatorial model, gave prosecutors increased investigative powers. Parliament added to these after the mafia killed two prosecutors in 1992, and Constitutional Court rulings further consolidated investigative power away from judges and toward adversarial prosecutors.

Despite the new code's purported aim to increase fairness for defendants, the current structure may in fact disadvantage those accused of high-visibility crimes. For instance, prosecutors have discretion when to notify the accused that an investigation has begun, up to immediately preceding the first court appearance. Normally this does not matter, but in politically sensitive cases the media often hear about the "secret" investigation and notification, taking the latter in the former inquisitorial spirit as the equivalent of guilt. After prosecutors opened so many corruption crime files against politicians and businesspersons beginning in 1992, the 1994 Berlusconi center-right government proposed CSM reform to depoliticize it and legislation to make preventive detention more difficult to utilize. Magistrates opposed further safeguards on preventive detention, but Parliament enacted the reforms (Legge no. 332; Di Federico 1995, 237–39; Guarnieri 1997, 167–69; Nelken 1996b, 190, 194, 203 nn. 16, 18).[50]

The third Italian style favors leniency toward crime and punishment. This resulted from at least two peculiar social and cultural circumstances. First, there was a strong perception—not only among leftists—that crime was a political and not a legal question. Marxists, although admitting that criminals were working-class enemies, rhetorically supported integrating these socially deprived individuals into society rather than isolating them by penal repression. Others, particularly among lower classes, felt that the criminal justice system was simply a violent, state-sanctioned mechanism to preserve an unequal society. From this standpoint, a criminal could be compared to the resistance fighter, struggling against those in power.

Second, southerners constituted the great majority of prisoners, further exacerbating economic, political, and cultural tensions between the two sections of Italy. The underlying theme was that NC, the "legal Italy," should not adopt too harsh a stance toward MG, the "criminal Italy" (Pavarini 1994, 51–52).

If we compare incarceration rates from other countries, the leniency of the Italian criminal justice system is put into perspective. From lowest to highest, these rates per 100,000 inhabitants at the end of 1991 were Holland, 36; Sweden, 61; Italy, 62; England and Wales, 98; Canada, 109; South Africa, 332; and the United States, 455 (Morris 1995, 237). The Italian rate jumped to 88 in 1993, a level it maintained through 1997 (see Table 8.7). This could signal a renewed interest (not seen since 1950) in confronting crime with imprisonment. After 1991 judges attacked the serious rise in crime by keeping defendants in prison for longer stays, resulting in a total prisoner population that reached postwar highs near a full capacity of fifty thousand. It could also be that magistrates, and Italians in general, now view the social order question differently, with prison reserved not for suppressed southerners but for undeserving foreigners and drug addicts.

The fourth Italian style concerns judicial inefficiency. In general, the judiciary did a poor job beginning in the mid-1970s to meet the challenge of larger caseloads. This was partly due to magistracy understaffing, but also to dysfunctional judgeship allocations and lax work habits fostered by the dismantlement of promotion incentives (Guarnieri 1997, 170, 175 n. 29; Nelken 1996a, 202–3; Pellegrini 1997, 217–40; Verde 1999, 86–87). Parliament's willingness to intervene with periodic amnesties certainly did not encourage judicial productivity.

Several factors served to reduce the effectiveness of the ordinary judiciary. First, there were in 1993 actually 9 percent fewer magistrates in service than positions authorized (see Table 8.2), and this gap ranged as high as 15 percent in some years. Also, the vacancy rate for judicial staff usually has been quite high. Second, judges constituted only 73 percent of the Italian magistracy, while the ratio of judges to total German magistrates was 80 percent in 1995 (Clark 1999, 101).[51] Third, many Italian judges were actively involved in outside social, political, and economic activities, including serving on government commissions, teaching law courses, or even resolving private arbitrations. Magistrates also took leaves of absence to serve in Parliament (Di Federico 1995, 239; Guarnieri 1997, 165, 174 nn.18−19; Nelken 1996a, 198; Pellegrini 1997, 220−21, 224−25; Verde 1999, 91). Fourth, the CSM was unable for structural and cultural reasons to rationally manage judgeship allocation to those districts or regions where the need was greatest. Fifth, judges did not adequately control the many lawyers barely earning a living, who purposely delayed civil cases to force settlements or obtain more money from their clients (Chiarloni 1999, 276−78; Vellani 1999, 715).

The cultural and social division between Mezzogiorno and north and central Italy brings us to the final Italian style. MG certainly was the more legalistic of the two regions, a situation that did not change over the past half century. Thus, more magistrates per 100,000 inhabitants worked in MG than in NC (see Table 8.1). MG plaintiffs brought many more civil cases per capita, almost double the NC rate in 1997 (Istat, *Annuario* 1998, 147). But in the 1990s the average NC pretura judge decided 34 percent more civil cases than the average MG pretore, who accumulated proportionately a much larger backlog of files (Pellegrini 1997, 217−40).[52] Consequently, MG residents were more litigious than their northern neighbors, but their judges were less productive (referring to the fourth style).

MG's criminal trial rate at all court levels—preture, tribunali, and courts of assize—was always higher than NC's rate per capita (see Table 8.8). This carried through for appeals and eventually petitions in cassation (see Table 8.10). In this respect, the south took a more conservative, punitive approach to law and order. For criminal cases, MG magistrates worked as efficiently as those in NC until the 1989 Penal Procedure Code's implementation. In the 1990s, MG judges seemed less willing to use the code's new summary procedures, and their average processing time (except for appeals) increased significantly over NC judges' productivity and average delay.

In spite of MG's greater civil litigiousness and use of penal trials, its crime rate per 100,000 population was always *lower* than NC's, a gap that even increased during the 1990s crime wave (see Table 8.3). However, MG's conviction rate was higher than that in NC and increasingly so during the 1990s. Thus, MG magistrates dealt more effectively with crime than their more liberal colleagues to the north, which in turn likely fed higher NC crime rates. By 1997 the gap in conviction rates increased to 442 for NC versus 626 for MG. Moreover, if one considers the 1997 convicted person's birthplace, the differential expanded to only 294 for those from NC versus 752 for those from MG. The fact that southerners were two and a half times more likely than northerners to be convicted for crime clearly fed northern popular opinion that crime was part of southern culture. As theft represented most crime since 1970 and the NC crime rate always exceeded that in MG, crime became an important southern export to NC that yielded significant revenue for MG. Ironically, NC was the land of crime, and MG was the land of the law.

The Italian republic in its first fifty years saw massive change. There emerged an independent, active magistracy that today plays a significant role in addressing major social issues. But each of the two functions within the magistracy—prosecution and adjudication—exhibited substantial inefficiencies that in the past two decades caused major crises in the administration of justice. In addition, prosecutors who abused investigative powers and judges who abused preventive detention prompted a reaction in favor of limits to protect individual rights. For most of the postwar era, Italian politicians and judges favored leniency toward crime and punishment. This attitude may be changing because crime boomed in the 1990s, more perpetrators were foreigners and drug addicts, and there was the common perception that organized crime had systematically spread from the south to the north. Organized crime has globalized and is involved with illegal immigrants, arms traffic, drugs, and cigarettes. What did not change materially was the cultural and social division between north and central Italy and Mezzogiorno. NC had wealth and was the engine for growth, but MG (residence for Cosa Nostra, 'Ndrangheta, Camorra, and Sacra Corona Unita) was the land of the law.

The Italian legal system demonstrated the ability to face some of its legal styles' negative aspects. Delay in civil litigation by the late 1980s was so long that there was a substantial flight from justice (*fuga dalla giustizia*) and general public disappointment in the civil justice system (Chiarloni 1999, 270–71; Ferrarese 1988, 168–69). This prompted Parliament to enact major structural changes. One solution was to increase the supply of justice by hiring thirty-three hundred (of an eventual forty-seven hundred) noncareer justices of the peace and the first four hundred (of an anticipated one thousand) honorary judges (*giudici onorari*) (Decreto legislativo no. 51; Legge no. 374; see Nebbia 1998, 171; Varano 1997, 657–60; Vellani 1999, 708–9; Verde 1999, 86, 89–90; Table 8.1).[53] In 1990 Parliament tried to improve efficiency by transforming civil tribunali for most matters from three-judge courts to single-judge courts (Legge no. 353, art. 88, amending Ord.Giud. art. 48). Continued long court delays convinced Parliament in 1997 to authorize the justice ministry (which acted in 1998) to merge civil preture into tribunali. These courts will be staffed by unitary judges using tribunale procedures (Luiso 1999, 676–77).

The 1989 Penal Procedure Code's attempt to augment productivity by diverting cases to summary procedures largely failed in the face of the 1990s crime wave. As a result, the justice ministry, at the same time in 1998 that it merged civil preture into tribunali, also abolished penal preture, its special procedure, and accompanying prosecutor offices. It transferred pretura jurisdiction to tribunali and their prosecutor offices. In addition, penal tribunali in 1999 became primarily single-judge courts.[54] To further improve case processing efficiency, the 1998 statute assigned certain pretura administrative duties to the public administration (Decreto legislativo no. 51, amending Ord.Giud., CPC, CPP). Finally, Parliament authorized the justice ministry, whose norms took effect in 2000, to depenalize many misdemeanors and make them merely administrative offenses (Decreto legislativo no. 507).

Further magistracy and court system reform could yield productivity gains. First, judges should have a career structure tied to performance and reward, so that salary increases and promotion would be granted by a collegiate body representing nonpolitical divisions within the magistracy. Independence is sustainable only with accountability. Second, careful analysis of regional differences in the demand for justice should control the allocation of magistrate posts. The CSM should do what it can to equalize the quality of justice between the north and central and Mezzogiorno. Third, granting the Court of Cassation discretion to review both civil and penal petitions would reduce the need for judges at that level, and these posts could be shifted to levels at which delay has been the longest (Chiarloni 1999, 284–88).

For Italy to successfully implement the procedural reforms enacted since 1989 will require a fundamental change in legal style and culture. But just as north and center Italy serves as a model to Mezzogiorno, so too does the European Union and the Council of Europe provide discipline to the Italian legal system. Perhaps jurists place too much emphasis on the ideology of rule of law. After all, Italian economic success was accomplished not by governmental programs but by strong entrepreneurial spirit together with the diligent efforts of workers and managers. Entrenched individualism meant that Italy functioned best when government and its laws were largely ignored or not involved. Political fatalism built the popular capability to absorb governmental crises and scandals. Italians knew they were on their own and sensed they could protect themselves best by making the legal system minimally effective or bypassing it entirely (Kostoris 1996, 291; Spotts and Wieser 1986, 290–92). Only the twenty-first century will reveal whether the Italian style can succeed in balancing law and politics so that court system efficiency fulfills its promise of justice to a skeptical citizenry (see Pulitanò 1997).

Appendix

STATUTES

Codice di Procedura Civile [CPC], regio decreto no. 1443, 28 Oct. 1940.

Codice di Procedura Penale [1930 CPP], regio decreto no. 1399, 19 Oct. 1930.

Codice di Procedura Penale [new CPP], decreto no. 447 del Presidente della Repubblica, 22 Sept. 1988, in effect 24 Oct. 1989.

Codice Penale [CP], regio decreto no. 1398, 19 Oct. 1930.

Costituzione della Repubblica Italiana [Cost.], promulgated 27 Dec. 1947, in effect 1 Jan. 1948.

Decreto legislativo no. 51, 19 Feb. 1998, Norme in materia di istituzione del giudici unico di primo grado, in effect 2 June 1999, in *Gazzetta Ufficiale della Repubblica italiana* [G.U.] no. 66, 20 Mar. 1998.

Decreto legislativo no. 507, 30 Dec. 1999, Depenalizzazione dei reati minori e riforma del sistema sanzionatorio . . . , in *G.U.* no. 306, 31 Dec. 1999.

Legge no. 30, 1 Feb. 1989, Costituzione delle preture circondariali e nuove norme relative alle sezioni distaccate, in *G.U.* no. 30, 6 Feb. 1989.

Legge no. 81, 16 Feb. 1987, Delega legislativa al Governo della Repubblica per l'emanazione del nuovo codice di procedura penale, in *G.U.* no. 62, 16 Mar. 1987.

Legge no. 195, 24 Mar. 1958, Norme sulla costituzione e sul funzionamento del Consiglio superiore della Magistratura, in *G.U.* no. 75, 27 Mar. 1958.

Legge no. 332, 8 Aug. 1995, Modifiche al codice di procedura penale in tema di semplificazione dei procedimenti, di misure cautelari e di dirritto di difesa, in *G.U.* no. 184, 8 Aug. 1995.

Legge no. 353, 26 Nov. 1990, Provvedimenti urgenti per il processo civile, in *G.U.* no. 281, 1 Dec. 1990.

Legge no. 374, 21 Nov. 1991, Istituzione del giudice di pace, in *G.U.* no. 278, 27 Nov. 1991.

Legge no. 400, 31 July 1984, Nuove norme sulla competenza penale e sull'appello contro le sentenze del pretore, in *G.U.* no. 210, 1 Aug. 1984.

Legge no. 689, 24 Nov. 1981, Modifiche al sistema penale, in *G.U.* no. 329, 30 Nov. 1981.

Legge no. 695, 22 Dec. 1975, Riforma della composizione e del sistema elettorale per il Consiglio superiore della magistratura, in *G.U.* no 343, 31 Dec. 1975.

Legge costituzionale no. 1, 6 Mar. 1992, Revisione dell'art. 79 della Costituzione in materia di concessione di amnistia e indulto, in *G.U.* no. 57, 9 Mar. 1992.

Ordinamento Giudiziario [Ord.Giud.], regio decreto no. 12, 30 Jan. 1941.

Notes

1. These essays in modified form are also in Cappelletti, Merryman, and Perillo (1967, 164–277). They have recently been republished in Merryman (1999).

2. "The most productive approach to Italian law is by way of prevailing Italian attitudes toward law and legal process" (Merryman 1965, 39).

3. "A legal tradition . . . is a set of deeply rooted, historically conditioned attitudes about the nature of law, about the role of law in the society and the polity, about the proper organization and operation of a legal system, and about the way law is or should be made, applied, studied, perfected, and taught. The legal tradition relates the legal system to the culture of which it is a partial expression. It puts the legal system into cultural perspective."

4. Mezzogiorno is defined according to Istat's (Italy's bureau of statistics) standard, which includes the islands of Sardinia and Sicily and all the regions from Abruzzi south with the exception of Lazio (Rome) (Istat, *Annuario* 1998, 39). SLADE's Italian semiagrarian region included Mezzogiorno plus the two northern regions (Umbria and Marche) adjacent to Lazio and Abruzzi. These two regions had a population of 2.2 million in 1951 and 2.3 million in 1997 (Istat, *Annuario* 1998, 39). I used the SLADE regionalization for legal indicators from 1950 to 1965 when the following 1979 source was cited (Merryman, Clark, and Friedman 1979, 33–35, 507). The disjunction with Istat's regionalization is minimal as most legal indicator data will be provided on a per capita basis.

5. Called the semiagrarian region, Mezzogiorno had the lowest socioeconomic level in Italy but the second- or third-highest civil litigation rate throughout the period 1945 to 1984 (Clark 1990, 559).

6. Italian and Spanish population growth for 1990–97 was tied at 1 percent (Eurostat 1998, 2–3).

7. This compared to 8.3 percent agricultural workers in Spain (Eurostat 1998, 16–17).

8. The average life expectancy for men as well as women in Italy exceeds that in the United States by two years (Eurostat 1998, 2–3). In 1996, however, U.K. GDP at current prices surpassed Italian GDP, due primarily to the strength of the U.K. pound over the Italian lira (*Sunday Times*, 19 March 2000, pt. 3, p. 9).

9. Current exchange prices used the three-year average 1994–96 (Eurostat 1999, 6–7). By 1996 purchasing power, Italy exceeded Sweden and almost met France and the Netherlands (Eurostat 1998, 14–15).

10. France and the United Kingdom, for instance, have much more homogeneous economies (Eurostat 1999, 4–7). Of course, all countries have substantial disparity between income earned in the principal cities and that earned in smaller towns.

11. In the early 1990s, the average MG consumption level was two-thirds that of NC (Sassoon 1997, 82). It is likely that more of the MG economy is not captured in official statistics because it is informal or illegal.

12. The informal *Manuale Cencelli*, named after a Christian Democrat operative, provided guidelines on how to allocate positions among parties, and within parties, among factions (*correnti*).

13. All political (and legal) systems rely on some ascriptive norms and clientelistic relations; it is always a matter of degree.

14. Paul Ginsborg (1996, 24–25) related the story of Mario Chiesa's curtain. Chiesa, the first Socialist caught taking kickbacks, was the director of a retirement home in Milan. His arrest in February 1992 marked the beginning of the corrup-

tion scandals known as *Tangentopoli*. Illustrating the symbolic importance of the official morality, Chiesa told the investigating magistrate Di Pietro that when contractors came to make illegal payments, he would draw the curtain so that no one could see what happened.

15. From 1959 to 1975, the CSM had twenty-four elected members (Guarnieri 1997, 159, 173 n. 3).

16. The executive branch minister of grace and justice still has certain power over judicial organization, including a veto over management position allocation, entrance exams for probationary magistrates, and judicial clerk and other auxiliary personnel administration (Legge no. 195, arts. 14–16; see Certoma 1985, 66–67).

17. Sabino Cassese (1977, 69–118) traced the overall public administration southernization from the 1930s for elite positions and from the 1960s for ordinary posts.

18. In actuality, there were even more magistrates per capita in MG because NC included 305 judges and 46 prosecutors (*procure generali*) at the national *Suprema corte di cassazione* in Rome in 1993 (Pellegrini 1997, 220).

19. The ten Parliament-selected CSM members were also chosen along party lines (Guarnieri 1997, 173 n. 8).

20. Magistrates also fought against the 1995 preventive detention reform (Nelken 1996b, 194, 203 nn. 16, 18).

21. It may be that fewer petty thefts are reported in the south because the insurance for that type of coverage is too expensive.

22. There was a period of increased convictions from 1960 to 1962, reflected in the 1961 rate of 237 per 100,000 population, as shown in Table 8.4 (see Istat 1998b, 440).

23. The pattern for the robbery, extortion, and kidnapping category was similar. The conviction-crime ratio began in 1950 at its 43 percent high point, gradually declining to 28 percent in 1970. At the first crime wave's end in 1976, the ratio had fallen further to 11 percent and continued to fluctuate around that level, with an 8 percent low in 1990. But as with the homicide ratio, convictions for robbery, extortion, and kidnapping improved to 16 percent in 1997.

24. The 1980 conviction rate gap was 215 convictions per 100,000 inhabitants in NC compared to 281 in MG. This difference was much larger for homicide cases, which was 4 percent in NC and 117 percent in MG (Istat 1983, 377).

25. Under the 1989 Penal Procedure Code conviction finalization in first instance increased from 79 percent in 1993 to 85 percent in 1997 (Istat 1998b, 36).

26. For crimes with a maximum punishment of less than five years, the prescription period is five years. It begins to run from the date of the crime but may begin anew when the investigation is completed and the "trial" begins (*decreto di citazione a giudizio*). But even when interrupted, the overall limitations period may not be increased by more than 50 percent, or seven and one half years in this example (CP arts. 157, 158, 160).

27. Cost. art. 79 regulates amnesty. It requires a parliamentary act, followed by the president's decree. Presidents have left political details to the legislature and simply copied the laws as decrees. There were several specific amnesties immediately after World War II, followed by more general *decreti del Presidente della Repubblica* numbers

922 (1953), 460 (1959), 5 (1963), 332 (1966), 1084 (1968), 283 (1970), 413 (1978), 744 (1981), 865 (1986), and 75 (1990). Certain amnesties dealt only with tax crimes: numbers 834 (1973), 525 (1982), and 43 (1983) (Panagia 1992, 431–37).

28. In 1970, for instance, judges convicted 65,295 persons of a crime (see Table 8.4). At the same time, they acquitted or released (*prosciolti*) 408,522 persons, 61 percent of whom were granted amnesty. For theft, 60 percent were granted amnesty (Istat, *Annuario* 1972, 150).

29. Time served in preventive detention will be deducted from a judicial sentence if the individual is convicted of a crime (CP art. 137; see new CPP art. 657).

30. Delinquent minors, drunks, drug addicts, the insane, and others as provided by the law may be detained in a special prison ward or reformatory, a psychiatric hospital or sanatorium, an agricultural colony, or a workhouse (CP arts. 206, 215). In 1970 there were 2,230 persons held for security measures on December 31: ward or reformatory (1 percent); hospital or sanatorium (79 percent); agricultural colony (9 percent); and workhouse (11 percent) (Istat 1973b, 287).

31. The code also set overall caps on detention (including the period after sentencing while an appeal was pending): detention of two years for crimes with up to a six-year maximum penalty; detention of four years for crimes up to twenty years in prison; and detention of six years for other crimes (new CPP art. 303[4]).

32. Less than 1 percent was incarcerated as a security measure (Istat 1998b, 453).

33. Between 1980 and 1997, the new prisoner percentage accused or convicted of homicide remained the same at 2 percent but increased for robbery, extortion, and kidnapping, from 8 to 11 percent (Istat 1998b, 451; 1983, 528–29).

34. This phenomenon occurred mainly in NC, where 30 percent of the 1997 resident prison population was foreign compared to only 9 percent in the south. Fifty-six percent of new female prisoners in 1997 were foreigners, who represented 25 percent of the total women incarcerated at the end of 1997 (Istat, *Annuario* 1998, 163).

35. In 1980, judges granted conditional early release to 13 percent of those leaving prison and freed less than 1 percent for amnesty (Istat 1983, 525). But these numbers fluctuated widely. For instance, Parliament in 1978 and 1981 authorized amnesty to seven thousand and fourteen thousand prisoners, respectively (Spotts and Wieser 1986, 166–67).

36. The Italian structure, unlike the French, does not maintain separate commercial courts.

37. Excluding conciliazione and justice of the peace courts, there were 623 first instance civil filings per 100,000 population in 1950 compared to 1,978 in 1997 (Istat, *Annuario* 1998, 147; Merryman, Clark, and Friedman 1979, 162).

38. Reported instructions always exceeded reported crimes (see Table 8.3) because instruction transfers to another court were counted again. Most cases filed with prosecutors were dismissed (*decreto di archiviazione*) for reasons such as lack of evidence or lapse of the prescription period.

39. In 1984 a few additional crimes were added, such as aggravated theft, which increased by about thirty-seven thousand the trials filed with preture (Legge no. 400; Istat, *Annuario* 1986, 219).

40. MG prosecutors, GIPs, and pretori all took longer to process cases than did NC magistrates (Istat 1998b, 41–42).

41. GIPs reduced the percentage found guilty in summary trials from 66 to 61 percent between 1993 and 1997 (Istat 1998b, 43; *Annuario* 1994, 197).

42. If the defendant does not commit another crime within five years, the original criminal sentence is extinguished; if the defendant does commit another crime, the judge may revoke the suspension (CP arts. 167–68; new CPP art. 445[2]).

43. The overall ratio of convictions to acquittals (*proscioglimento*, including *assolu-zione*) was 2.0 in 1993 and 1.5 in 1997 (Istat 1998b, 43; *Annuario* 1994, 197).

44. The overall ratio of convictions to acquittals was 2.4 in 1993 and 2.6 in 1997 (Istat 1998b, 43; *Annuario* 1994, 197).

45. An assize court sits with eight judges (the president from the court of appeal, another career judge from a tribunale, and six lay judges) who together decide both factual and legal issues. Its jurisdiction includes crimes against the state, homicide, and slavery (1930 CPP art. 29). In 1989 jurisdiction for crimes against the state was limited to those with at least a ten-year sentence but was also expanded to cover most other crimes with at least a twenty-four-year sentence (new CPP art. 5).

46. Preture crimes committed before November 29, 1984, were appealed under the pre-reform path to tribunali, which accounts for the 1988 tribunale statistics in Table 8.10.

47. Of 6,957 reversals, 41 percent were returned to the lower court for implementation or further proceedings (Istat 1998b, 48).

48. Because courts of assize try the most serious crimes, about one-third to one-half of the appellate courts of assize decisions were further pursued before the Court of Cassation (see Table 8.9 and Table 8.10 note).

49. Generalizations about the United States refer to the federal judiciary and a few state appellate court systems.

50. Besides maximum detention periods for each proceeding stage, the new law called for audio- or videotaping custodial testimony to prevent police and prosecutorial misconduct (Legge no. 332 arts. 2, 15, amending new CPP arts. 141-bis, 303–4).

51. In addition, about 2 percent of the nonprosecutor Italian magistrates have, in fact, nonjudicial duties (see Table 8.2).

52. This regional differential was smaller for tribunale judges, where the gap favored NC judges, who decided, on average, 6 percent more cases than their MG counterparts (Pellegrini 1997, 230–33).

53. Career judges may treat honorary judges, who tend to be less successful lawyers, as second-class colleagues with unattractive assignments, which could adversely affect productivity (Chiarloni 1999, 283; Luiso 1999, 678).

54. Three-judge panels remain for certain cases and decisions. For example, preventive detention decisions require a three-judge panel. Preture will continue to function as such until they have completed their 1999 case backlogs (Decreto legislativo no. 51, arts. 14, 42, 179–81).

References

Allum, P. A. 1973. *Italy—Republic without government?* New York: W. W. Norton.

Bull, Martin, and Martin Rhodes. 1997. Between crisis and transition: Italian politics in the 1990s. Pp. 1–13 in *Crisis and transition in Italian politics*, edited by Martin Bull and Martin Rhodes. London: Frank Cass; *West European Politics* 20:1–13.

Cappelletti, Mauro, John Henry Merryman, and Joseph Perillo. 1967. *The Italian legal system: An introduction.* Stanford, Calif.: Stanford University Press.

Cassese, Sabino. 1977. *Questione amministrativa e questione meridionale: Dimensioni e reclutamento della burocrazia dall'unità ad oggi.* Milan: Dott. Antonino Giuffrè.

———. 1993. Hypotheses on the Italian administrative system. *West European Politics* 16:316–28.

———. 1998. *Lo Stato introvabile: Modernità e arretratezza delle istituzioni italiane.* Rome: Donzelli Editore.

———, ed. 1994. *Guida alla facoltà di giurisprudenza.* 2d ed. Bologna: Società editrice il Mulino.

Certoma, G. Leroy. 1985. *The Italian legal system.* London: Butterworths.

Chiarloni, Sergio. 1999. Civil justice and its paradoxes: An Italian perspective. Pp. 263–90 in *Civil justice in crisis: Comparative perspectives of civil procedure*, edited by Adrian A. S. Zuckerman. Oxford: Oxford University Press.

Clark, David S. 1990. Civil litigation trends in Europe and Latin America since 1945: The advantage of intracountry comparisons. *Law & Society Review* 24:549–69.

———. 1999. Comparing the work and organization of lawyers worldwide: The persistence of legal traditions. Pp. 9–155 in *Lawyers' practice and ideals: A comparative view*, edited by John J. Barceló & Roger C. Cramton. The Hague: Kluwer Law International.

Clark, David S., and John Henry Merryman. 1976. Measuring the duration of judicial and administrative proceedings. *Michigan Law Review* 75:89–99; *Sociologia del Diritto* 1976:363–76.

Dezalay, Yves, and Bryant Garth. 1997. Law, lawyers and social capital: "Rule of law" versus relational capitalism. *Social & Legal Studies* 6:109–41.

Di Federico, Giuseppe. 1995. Italy: A peculiar case. Pp. 233–42 in *The global expansion of judicial power*, edited by C. Neal Tate and Torbjörn Vallinder. New York: New York University Press.

Eurostat. 1998. *Des chiffres pour se connaître: Condensé de l'annuaire Eurostat.* Luxembourg: Office des publications officielles des Communautés européennes.

———. 1999. *Statistiques en bref: Statistiques générales (Theme 1-1/1999).* Luxembourg: Office des publications officielles des Communautés européennes.

Ferrarese, Maria Rosaria. 1988. Civil justice and the judicial role in Italy. *Justice System Journal* 13:168–85.

———. 1997. Può la Magistratura essere considerata istituzione della libertà? Pp. 459–75 in *Diritto, cultura e libertà: Atti del convegno in memoria di Renato Treves*, edited by Vincenzo Ferrari, Morris L. Ghezzi, and Nella Gridelli Velicogna. Milan: Giuffrè Editore.

Friedman, Lawrence M. 1969. Legal culture and social development. *Law & Society Review* 4:29–44.

———. 1975. *The legal system: A social science perspective.* New York: Russell Sage Foundation.

———. 1998. Some thoughts on the rule of law, legal culture, and modernity in comparative perspective. Pp. 1075–90 in *Toward comparative law in the 21st century,* edited by The Institute of Comparative Law in Japan. Tokyo: Chuo University Press.

Friedman, Lawrence M., and Stewart Macaulay. 1977. *Law and the behavioral sciences.* 2d ed. Indianapolis, Ind.: Bobbs-Merrill.

Ginsborg, Paul. 1996. Explaining Italy's crisis. Pp. 19–39 in *The new Italian republic: From the fall of the Berlin Wall to Berlusconi,* edited by Stephen Gundle and Simon Parker. London: Routledge.

Grande, Elisabetta. 2000. Italian criminal justice: Borrowing and resistance. *American Journal of Comparative Law* 48:227–59.

Grevi, Vittorio. 1994. The new Italian code for criminal procedure: A concise overview. Pp. 145–77 in *Italian Studies in Law 2,* edited by Alessandro Pizzorusso. Dordrecht: Martinus Nijhoff.

Guarnieri, Carlo. 1997. The judiciary in the Italian political crisis. Pp. 157–75 in *Crisis and transition in Italian politics,* edited by Martin Bull and Martin Rhodes. London: Frank Cass; *West European Politics* 20:157–75.

Gundle, Stephen, and Simon Parker. 1996. Introduction: The new Italian republic. Pp. 1–15 in *The new Italian republic: From the fall of the Berlin Wall to Berlusconi,* edited by Stephen Gundle and Simon Parker. London: Routledge.

Istat (Istituto Nazionale di Statistica or Istituto Centrale di Statistica [before 1990]). 1971, 1972, 1978, 1982, 1986, 1991, 1994, 1998. *Annuario statistico italiano [Annuario].* Rome: Istat.

———. 1973a. 3 *Annuario di contabilità nazionale: Tomo 2, edizione 1973.* Rome: Istat.

———. 1973b. 20 *Annuario di statistiche giudiziarie: Edizione 1970–71.* Rome: Istat.

———. 1977. *11th Censimento generale della popolazione (24 ottobre 1971): Vol. 6 (Professioni e attività economiche), book 2 (Professioni).* Rome: Istat.

———. 1983. 28 *Annuario di statistiche giudiziarie: Edizione 1980–81, book 2 (Materia penale; Materia penitenziaria).* Rome: Istat.

———. 1984a. 12 *Annuario di contabilità nazionale: Tomo 2, edizione 1983.* Rome: Istat.

———. 1984b. *12th Censimento generale della popolazione (25 ottobre 1981): Vol. 2 (Dati sulle caratteristiche strutturali della popolazioni e delle abitazioni), book 2 (Fascicoli regionali).* Rome: Istat.

———. 1993. *Statistiche giudiziarie: Anno 1990.* Rome: Istat.

———. 1994. *Popolazione e abitazioni: Fascicolo regionale (13th Censimento generale della popolazione e delle abitazioni, 20 ottobre 1991).* Rome: Istat.

———. 1998a. *Contabilità nazionale: Tomo 3, Conti economici regionali, anni 1980–95.* Rome: Istat.

———. 1998b. *Statistiche giudiziarie penali: Anno 1997.* Rome: Istat.

Kostoris, Fiorella Padoa Schioppa. 1996. Excesses and limits of the public sector in the Italian economy: The ongoing reform. Pp. 273–93 in *The new Italian republic:*

From the fall of the Berlin Wall to Berlusconi, edited by Stephen Gundle and Simon Parker. London: Routledge.

LaPalombara, Joseph. 1987. *Democracy Italian style*. New Haven, Conn.: Yale University Press.

Luiso, Francesco P. 1999. L'ordinamento giudiziario in rivoluzione. *Giurisprudenza Italiana* 151:676–78.

Mantovani, Ferrando. 1988. *Diritto penale: Parte generale*. 2d ed. Padova: CEDAM.

Merryman, John Henry. 1965. The Italian style I: Doctrine. *Stanford Law Review* 18: 39–65.

———. 1966a. The Italian style II: Law. *Stanford Law Review* 18:396–437.

———. 1966b. The Italian style III: Interpretation. *Stanford Law Review* 18:583–611.

———. 1969. *The civil law tradition: An introduction to the legal systems of Western Europe and Latin America*. Stanford, Calif.: Stanford University Press.

———. 1973. *La tradizione di civil law*. Milan: Dott. A. Giuffrè Editore.

———. 1974. Comparative law and scientific explanation. Pp. 81–104 in *Law in the United States of America in social and technological revolution*, edited by John N. Hazard and Wenceslas J. Wagner. Brussels: Establissements Emile Bruyland.

———. 1977. Comparative law and social change: On the origins, style, decline and revival of the law and development movement. *American Journal of Comparative Law* 25:457–91.

———. 1985. *The civil law tradition: An introduction to the legal systems of Western Europe and Latin America*. 2d ed. Stanford, Calif.: Stanford University Press.

———. 1998. Comparative law scholarship. *Hastings International and Comparative Law Review* 21:771–84.

———. 1999. *The loneliness of the comparative lawyer and other essays in foreign and comparative law*. Boston: Kluwer Law International.

Merryman, John Henry, and David S. Clark. 1978. *Comparative law: Western European and Latin American legal systems*. Indianapolis, Ind.: Bobbs-Merrill.

Merryman, John Henry, David S. Clark, and Lawrence M. Friedman. 1979. *Law and social change in Mediterranean Europe and Latin America: A handbook of legal and social indicators for comparative study*. Stanford, Calif.: Stanford Law School.

Merryman, John Henry, David S. Clark, and John O. Haley. 1994. *The civil law tradition: Europe, Latin America, and East Asia*. Charlottesville, VA: Michie.

Merryman, John Henry, and Vincenzo Vigoriti. 1967. When courts collide: Constitution and cassation in Italy. *American Journal of Comparative Law* 15:665–86.

Morris, Norval. 1995. The contemporary prison: 1965–present. Pp. 227–59 in *The Oxford history of the prison: The practice of punishment in Western society*, edited by Norval Morris and David J. Rothman. New York: Oxford University Press.

Nebbia, Paolisa. 1998. *Judex ex machina*: The justice of the peace in the tragedy of the Italian civil process. *Civil Justice Quarterly* 17:164–74.

Nelken, David. 1996a. A legal revolution?: The judges and *Tangentopoli*. Pp. 191–205 in *The new Italian republic: From the fall of the Berlin Wall to Berlusconi*, edited by Stephen Gundle and Simon Parker. London: Routledge.

———. 1996b. Stopping the judges. Pp. 187–204 in *Italian politics: The stalled tran-*

sition, edited by Mario Caciagli and David I. Kertzer. Boulder, Colo.: Westview Press. Reprint with the same pagination as 11 *Italian Politics: A Review* (1996).

————, ed. 1997. *Comparing legal cultures*. Aldershot, England: Ashgate.

Olgiati, Vittorio. 1985. Legal systems and the problem of legitimacy: The Italian case. Pp. 87–97 in *Legal systems & social systems*, edited by Adam Podgorecki, Christopher J. Whelan, and Dinesh Khosla. London: Croom Helm.

Panagia, Salvatore. 1992. Codice penale: Art. 151 (Amnistia). Pp. 431–37 in *Commentario breve al codice penale*, edited by Alberto Crespi, Giuseppe Zuccalà, and Federico Stella. Padua: CEDAM.

Pavarini, Massimo. 1994. The new penology and politics in crisis. *British Journal of Criminology* 34:49–61.

Pellegrini, Stefania. 1997. *La litigiosità in Italia: Un'analisi sociologico-giuridica*. Milan: Dott. A. Giuffrè Editore.

Pizzi, William T., and Luca Marafioti. 1992. The new Italian code of criminal procedure: The difficulties of building an adversarial trial system on a civil law foundation. *Yale Journal of International Law* 17:1–40.

Pizzorusso, Alessandro. 1985. The Italian constitution: Implementation and reform. *Jahrbuch des öffentlichen Rechts der Gegenwart* 34:105–21.

Pulitanò, Domenico. 1997. La giustizia penale alla prova del fuoco. *Rivista Italiana di Diritto e Procedura Penale* 40:3–41.

Sassoon, Donald. 1997. *Contemporary Italy: Economy, society and politics since 1945*. 2d ed. London: Longman.

Spotts, Frederic, and Theodor Wieser. 1986. *Italy: A difficult democracy*. Cambridge: Cambridge University Press.

Varano, Vincenzo. 1997. Civil procedure reform in Italy. *American Journal of Comparative Law* 45:657–74.

Vellani, Carlo. 1999. Riflessione sugli ultimi anni di interventi nel processo civile. *Rivista Trimestrale di Diritto e Procedura Civile* 53:703–23.

Verde, Giovanni. 1999. La giustizia italiana agli albori del 2000. *Il Foro Italiano* 122 (pt. 5): 85–91.

Violante, Luciano, ed. 1997. *Mafia e società italiana: Rapporto '97*. Rome: Laterza.

CHAPTER 9

"Faraway, So Close!"
The Rule of Law and Legal Change in Mexico, 1970–2000

SERGIO LÓPEZ-AYLLÓN AND HÉCTOR FIX-FIERRO

THE MAIN ARGUMENT in this chapter is that demographic, social, economic, and political factors affecting Mexican society during the last thirty years are causing the increased intervention of legal rules and institutions in social life. Ultimately, these factors appear to require a new role for the legal system as a whole. Such a role means that legal rules and institutions should begin to serve more and more as an effective means of regulation and conflict resolution rather than as a primarily symbolic resource or a mere point of reference for bargaining (López-Ayllón 1995).

Indeed, there have been major transformations in the legal system during this thirty-year period, and particularly in the last seventeen years. It is during this latter period that an almost completely new legal infrastructure (rules, institutions, and procedures) has been set in place (López-Ayllón 1997). These changes correspond with a new social awareness of the significance of the law for the achievement of modernity: both the government and important sectors of society have come to consider that the law is becoming more and more an indispensable instrument for the consolidation of a democratic political system and a market-oriented economy. This idea is reflected, for example, in the current (official and nonofficial) discourse on the crucial role of the "rule of law" (*estado de derecho*) for the country's development (1995–2000, chap. 2; see also Centro de Investigación para el Desarrollo [CIDAC] 1994, chap. 1).

The factors just mentioned include long-term trends and developments, such as population growth, higher levels of urbanization, education, life expectancy, political participation, media exposure, and the like. All of them reflect social change processes pointing toward a more developed and modern society. However, we can identify also other growth processes in relation, for example, to poverty and the unequal distribution of wealth, environmental degradation, migration, social exclusion and violence, drug trafficking and organized crime, corruption, unemployment, regional imbalances, and so forth. Other accidental but no less significant factors include natural disasters, recurrent economic crises, political assassinations, and guerrilla movements. If we add to this picture a visible erosion of political authority in the context of a very diverse and heterogeneous society, we may then understand why Mexico also presents a growing image of disorder and instability.

In view of this, we are led to a much more skeptical assessment of the emerging rule of law in Mexico and its chances for success.[1] As will be shown in the following sections of this chapter, the positive transformations in the Mexican legal system during the past thirty years are somehow counteracted by negative factors that obstruct and resist change and, ultimately, prevent the rule of law from taking hold in society and becoming embedded in social life. On the one hand, we have new laws and legal institutions, a higher number of law schools and law graduates, a stronger judiciary, and increasing rights awareness among the population. On the other, we find an often technically poor legislation, low-quality legal training, a weak legal profession, a formalistic judicial mentality, and a pervasive distrust of legal institutions and procedures.

It is our impression, therefore, that the bottlenecks presently facing the rule of law in Mexico lie less in the shortcomings of the legal infrastructure and more in the lack of the basic social support it requires to operate. There is not enough social support for the rule of law in the external legal culture, mainly because of the prevalence of group interests and social networks over individual rights, values, and merits. Also, there is an incipient and insufficient internalization of the meaning and consequences of the rule of law in social practice. At the same time, we find that the social agents in charge of the operation of the legal infrastructure (lawyers, judges, and other state officials) are, for the most part, a product of the existing system. Consequently, they do not find enough incentives to facilitate change and to operate in a more demanding environment. And where there is such an incentive, the professional groups concerned either lack the "critical mass" necessary to sustain the process of change or they do not have a clear perspective of the direction and meaning of such change.

It is fairly evident to us that legal change is, on the whole, dependent on broader processes of social change (Merryman, Clark, and Friedman 1979). This seems to be clearly the case for the Mexican legal system between 1970 and 2000. However, we do not observe a legal system changing, adapting, and responding gradually to social change and social expectations, but rather an avalanche of social transformations that engulfs a legal system not quite able to absorb and process such levels of change.

Indeed, given the level of social expectations, the legal requirements of the government and, most important, the limited demand for, and access to, legal services, it could be said that until the 1970s, Mexico had a legal system that, on the whole, worked reasonably well. In its own way, and considering the constraints flowing from an authoritarian regime and the obvious differences between legal areas, there was a reasonable degree of respect for ordinary legality and legal forms, cultivated by a small elite of "enlightened" lawyers, many of whom occupied the highest posts in government at one time or another; a reasonably independent (federal) judiciary, with an informal but effective judicial career; a fairly good legal education, under the leadership of the School of Law of the National University (UNAM) and other public law schools with regional prestige; and a respectable body of legal doctrine. All of this was supported by a secular legal tradition that found its most prominent virtue in the mixing and adapting of various influences from different legal traditions.

After 1970, however, both state and society seemed to "explode," and later on, after 1982, when the inevitable growth crisis ensued, the state acknowledged that a more-of-the-same strategy was no longer viable and that new domestic and international realities required that the existing "national project" be redefined. The legal system also responded to these changes by growing and transforming itself, but apparently not at the required scale. Thus, a maladjustment between law and society was produced, with potentially dire consequences for both.

In sum, we observe that the last thirty years have produced a legal system with visible summits and abysses, with sectors that are more advanced than others, with differential levels in law enforcement, and with Mexican society showing a strong ambiguity regarding the value of law as a legitimate and effective means of regulation and conflict resolution. So, we arrive at a much more circumspect assessment of the state of the rule of law in Mexico and its future development. Many features of a modern, Western-type legal system seem to be closer than ever to becoming reality. At the same time, we observe developments that make us believe that such achievement is still far away. For this reason, we have borrowed the title of Wim Wenders's celebrated film as a title for this chapter.

This chapter is divided into three sections. The first section will address the main methodological and theoretical issues raised by our research. After a very brief description of the Mexican legal system prior to 1970, the second section describes change and continuity processes, both in quantitative and qualitative terms, in the Mexican legal system during the last thirty years.

Finally, the concluding section provides a very short discussion of the meaning of the rule of law in the present context of Mexican society.

Methodological and Theoretical Aspects

THE MEXICAN LEGAL SYSTEM

Before analyzing legal change in the period between 1970 and 2000, it is important to present a few broad features of the Mexican legal system as it has historically developed.

The first important consideration is that Mexican law is a product of the mixing and acculturation of elements originating in different legal traditions at different periods. Thus, after the Spanish conquest, Castilian law was transplanted to the new territories. This system was supplemented by special laws issued for the governance of the Spanish colonies in America (*leyes de Indias*). The indigenous peoples, which were then the majority of the population, were allowed to keep their usages and legal customs, insofar as they did not conflict with the fundamental political and religious principles of the Spanish state (González 1998).

After independence in 1821, Mexico underwent a period of civil wars and political instability. During this period, several constitutional models were tried, with elements taken from American and European public law. It was not until the second half of the century that, under the 1857 constitution, the first national codes (civil, criminal, commercial) were drafted and enacted, superseding the colonial laws and institutions. These new national laws were again modeled on the European codes, basically blending elements from the Spanish, French, and Italian legal systems (González 1999).

It is worth noting that such national laws were mainly elaborated by a small elite of jurists and that they had scarce connection with a primarily agrarian society that still carried strong indigenous features. Nevertheless, a formal legal system was established and operated by the legal elite, serving the interests and needs of the small but powerful sectors of landlords and urban middle classes.

From a broader perspective, law accomplished a very important function for the Mexican nation. Having rejected the monarchical and religious foundations of political legitimacy and having chosen a liberal and republican model instead, the only way to construct and legitimize an otherwise artificial structure resided in the law and its symbolic authority. This meant, however, that nobody could really expect that the law would or should be strictly enforced (López-Ayllón 1997, 250–59).[2]

The Mexican Revolution of 1910 provided a new social and political foundation to the Mexican state. From the legal perspective, the constitution of 1917 incorporated the liberal legal tradition of the previous century. However, by also introducing other "alien" elements, taken mainly from the colonial tradition (for example, the communal property of land of the Indian population), the constitution generated an internal ambiguity. Specifically, such ambiguity resided in the somewhat awkward coexistence of an orthodox, Western-type model of constitutionalism with other reformist constitutional elements designed to provide the constitution with minimum conditions of effectiveness (Díaz y Díaz 1999, 177–78). Thus, although the distance between the constitution and social reality was attenuated, stabilized, and internalized in the legal system itself, for the most part the reformist provisions of the constitution served to modulate, even to the point of utter disregard, the interpretation and application of its more orthodox sectors.

PERIOD

Our research comprises the period between 1970 and 2000. We have chosen 1970 as our starting year for several reasons. Most observers agree that by the end of the 1960s, the political and economic system that had been consolidated in the 1930s and 1940s started to show its first symptoms of exhaustion. Different social movements, for example, indicated that the new urban middle classes no longer found a place within the political structures of the system. The import-substitution model implemented in the 1940s, which had been very successful until the 1960s in terms of economic growth (the so-called *desarrollo estabilizador*), began to appear insufficient for sustaining development, especially as a means to diminish poverty and foster higher levels of employment (Medina Peña 1995, 169–76).

The thirty-year period can be clearly divided into two parts. The first part includes the years from 1970 to 1982. During these twelve years, two federal administrations tried to respond to and cope with these first symptoms of exhaustion through the growth of state intervention and public debt, as well as through the partial modernization of some sectors, while allowing for a very limited degree of political and economic openness. This strategy was carried out to such extremes that when the final collapse came in 1982, in the form of a severe financial crisis, no other way out seemed possible than a radical change of direction.[3]

The second part of the period extends from 1983 to December 2000. At first timidly, and then with increasing vigor, especially after 1992, a new economic policy was implemented. This new policy was based on open markets and a significant reduction in state intervention. At the same time, a process of political liberalization was started, and its most visible manifestation lay in increasingly contested elections.

Particularly during the latter period, very significant changes in the legal system took place. For example, between 1982 and 1996, almost 80 percent of the federal laws either were newly enacted or were extensively amended. Also, a new and more complex institutional framework was created (new specialized courts, ombudsmen for human rights, and autonomous regulatory agencies, among others). Following economic liberalization, a traditionally closed legal system began to have increasing contact with international law, especially through the ratification of trade, environmental, and human rights treaties and agreements (López-Ayllón 1997, 172–223).

The federal elections of July 2, 2000, put an end to more than seventy years of one-party rule, but they also meant the symbolic demise of a legal order based on the undisputed authority of a single person. Although this chapter documents the gradual but deep process of change affecting the Mexican legal system, especially after 1982, the year 2000 can undoubtedly be considered as a turning point whose consequences may not fully appear for a long time.

DATA AND INFORMATION SOURCES

Sociolegal research encounters significant handicaps in Mexico. There is an almost complete absence of empirical studies on the legal system, and therefore, we found very limited direct support in the literature for this overview. Indirect sources, contained mainly in political and sociological studies, are more readily available, but the law has not been an explicit object of study for the social sciences, although this has been changing in recent years.

In general, data regarding legal indicators are fragmentary and scattered, and their comparability and reliability are often unknown. This problem is especially significant for the period between 1970 and 1988. After 1988, it is relatively easier to find reliable sources that allow for the construction of data series, particularly at the federal level. With few exceptions, it is extremely difficult to find any source at all for the states.

We relied mainly on official federal sources and records. Particularly, we used data produced by the *Instituto Nacional de Estadística, Geografía e Informática* (INEGI), the statistical annexes of the annual *Informes de Gobierno* and the periodical reports of the *Banco de México*. We also made extensive use of the data compendium "México Social 1996–1998," published by Banamex-Accival. With respect to the federal judiciary, we relied on the *Informes anuales de labores de la Suprema Corte de Justicia de la Nación*. The data on the number of law students and law schools were taken from the *Anuario Estadístico de la ANUIES (Asociación Nacional de Universidades e Instituciones de Educación Superior)*. In other instances, we obtained data directly from sources such as the *Diario Oficial de la Federación*, the *Diccionario biográfico del Gobierno Mexicano*, or the official compilations of court decisions and interpretations.

A valuable source of indirect but significant data was found in opinion polls and surveys, which have become commonplace in the 1990s for a variety of topics (elections, values, standard of living, victimization, and so forth). It should be noted that very few of these surveys deal explicitly with legally relevant issues. However, many of them provided interesting insights for our research. Although a comparison between different time periods is not possible yet, as most of these studies are quite recent, we have nevertheless used them, considering that they lend some empirical support to our hypotheses and observations.

Finally, we also conducted a series of eighteen individual interviews with a selected group of lawyers. We chose our subjects to include a wide spectrum of legal activities (judges, public officials, private practitioners, legal scholars), as well as representatives of different generations and legal-training backgrounds. Each interview was conducted on the basis of the same open questionnaire and lasted, on average, one and a half hours. The interviews had several purposes. First, we tried to obtain general elements of orientation for our research. Second, because quantitative data are not self-explanatory, the interviews helped us in the interpretation of the data. And third, the perceptions and opinions expressed in the interviews have provided us with additional elements for analyzing the meaning of processes both of change and of continuity in the legal system. In the end, we try to give a more complete overview, taking into account both macroprocesses and microphenomena, through a combination of quantitative and qualitative research.

THEORETICAL ISSUES

This paper shares SLADE's (Stanford Studies in Law and Development) main approach, in the sense that we attempt also to link social and legal change through quantitative data and indicators. We also share the assumption that this influence runs both ways (Merryman, Clark, and Friedman 1979, 26–27). However, we cannot completely agree with the expectation that "the stronger effect is that of social change on legal systems" (27), although this seems to be clearly the case with the Mexican legal system between 1970 and 2000, as the overall process of social, economic, and political change was followed or accompanied by considerable changes in the legal infrastructure. We believe that, depending on the point of observation adopted, it is less a question of "before" and "after," and perhaps more an issue of "demand" and "response." This is especially true in the political and economic spheres, where some changes are not even possible without previous changes in the existing laws.

The amendment of a law for the purpose of implementing a new policy may be relatively easy, but this modification may have broader and unpredictable consequences for the rest of the legal system (for example, in the development of new judicial doctrine or in the behavior of attorneys). Such internal response of the legal system may turn out to be inadequate or insufficient in view of specific social demands or expectations. In fact, any response by the legal system will always be considered inadequate or insufficient from an external point of view because it follows its own internal logic and processes (in this sense, the legal system is autonomous). In times of social turmoil, the distance between social expectations and legal responses may become so extreme that the legal system runs the risk of losing a substantial part of its social legitimacy.

This seems to be the situation in Mexico today.[4] Social demands and expectations are so high and put such a tremendous pressure on the legal institutions that it is no wonder that legal responses are perceived as unfair or insufficient. The important point here is not whether the legal system does satisfy, or not, those demands or expectations, but the fact that they are addressed to the legal system at all. In order to determine the conditions and limitations of an adequate response of the legal system, however defined, we have to raise the issue of the influence of law on society, or more precisely, of the social effects of legal change.

Here, we assume that legal change generates particular social expectations or affects specific behaviors (including those of legal professionals), and the relevant question is how and to what extent legal change will produce social change, which, in turn, will have a further impact on the legal system. From the point of view of the legal system, the relationship can be framed in terms of supply and acceptance. This means that legal change opens up new possibilities for legally relevant behavior, which social agents may use or not, depending on multiple social and legal (cultural) factors. It is very important to stress that, whatever the response of the legal system and whatever its evaluation by social actors, such response will always produce both social *and* legal consequences.

The main theoretical questions that we would have to address with respect to Mexico are the following: Once legal change has occurred, what are the further consequences for the social and the legal systems? Does legal change have equal or differential impacts on different social groups, and why? To what extent can the promises of the rule of law be fulfilled, and what are the consequences of nonfulfillment? What are the thresholds and conditions under which such legal change will take permanent hold in social practice?

These questions are of particular interest in the Mexican situation. Social and legal changes have occurred, but they have not quite translated into stable and solid institutional arrangements. There is much talk of a "democratic transition," but a transition process is not a one-way street. As much as we may desire its final outcome, the result is still uncertain. And this uncertainty is related, to some degree, to the fate of the rule of law in Mexico.

The Dimensions of Mexican Legal Life, 1970–2000

BRIEF DESCRIPTION OF THE MEXICAN LEGAL SYSTEM PRIOR TO 1970

Before proceeding to a detailed description of the changes in the Mexican legal system after 1970, it is useful to present a schematic characterization of its main features prior to that year.

Revolutionary legitimacy. The political and the legal systems derived their legitimacy from the Mexican Revolution of 1910 and the national project contained in the constitution of 1917. The invocation of the revolution and its political and social project served as a justification for legal change and as a material criterion for judicial and academic interpretation (see Cossío Díaz 2001, chap. 2).

The presidency. The president of the republic enjoyed undisputed political supremacy and therefore dominated, directly or indirectly, all processes of creation, interpretation, and enforcement of the law. Through his political control of the Congress, the president was the key factor in almost all constitutional and legislative changes, as well as in international treaty making. The political dominance of the presidency is reflected also in a relatively simple governmental structure.[5]

Law enforcement. Law enforcement was highly selective and discretionary, to the extent that it could be used as an instrument of political and social control (particularly in administrative, criminal, and labor law).

Judiciary. The federal judiciary enjoyed an effective degree of independence and respect as a guarantor of constitutional rights. However, its resources and powers were limited, especially in sensitive political matters (see Schwarz 1977). There existed an informal, endogamic judicial career. The judiciary was relatively isolated from external developments, and it voluntarily cultivated a very low public profile. The local judiciaries were subject to a much higher degree of political control and generally had very precarious resources.

Amparo *suit.* Despite its broad scope as a legal remedy for the protection of constitutional rights, the amparo had generally limited effects and access.

Legal profession. The legal profession was relatively small, segmented, and weak. Private practice did not require bar affiliation or exam, and generally speaking, it depended more on social relationships than technical skills. A considerable number of middle- and high-level public officials, including the president, had a law degree.

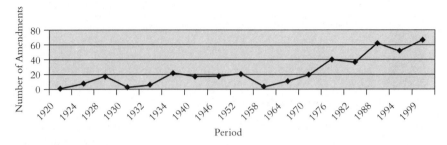

FIGURE 9.1 Constitutional Amendments by Presidential Period, 1920–2000
Source: Own calculation using the Diario Oficial de la Federación (1920–2000).

Legal education. The most prestigious and influential law school was the School of Law of the UNAM, which also served as a center of political recruitment.

Legal culture. It can be assumed that a majority of the population regarded legal institutions and the legal profession with distrust, partly as a consequence of its exclusion from the formal legal system.[6] Such exclusion, as well as the corporatist and clientelistic nature of the political regime fostered both informal legal practices (for example, in land tenure) and periodic attempts to legalize them.[7]

Legal nationalism. The legal system was relatively closed to outside influences. A sort of "legal nationalism" was shared and transmitted by a majority of lawyers. Only a small group had any interest in external legal developments (comparative law).

QUANTITATIVE OVERVIEW OF LEGISLATION

The quantitative analysis of legislative activity, as well as of law enforcement, presents several methodological problems that are not examined in this chapter. Nevertheless, we will try to present a broad quantitative review of the changes in the period 1970–2000. Then we will explore some of the qualitative dimensions of these matters.

In the Mexican legal system, laws and regulations (*leyes y reglamentos*) have always been the main source of the law. Based on a long tradition, change in the laws, including the constitution, has been considered one of the principal means to induce or sustain social and political change. Therefore, it would not be surprising that major changes occurred in Mexican legislation during the last thirty years. We will examine those changes on two levels: the federal constitution and federal legislation.

The federal constitution. The Mexican federal constitution is the foundation of the legal and political systems. Besides its legal function, the constitution of 1917 has a major political and symbolic value. Although it is formally a "rigid" constitution, in reality it has been easy to modify, and every president has used his legal and political powers to introduce amendments to the constitution as a means to ensure or to legitimize his policies.

Between 1917 and December 2000, the Mexican constitution has undergone 397 amendments.[8] Figure 9.1 shows the number of changes introduced by each president since 1917. It is clear that the number of changes has grown significantly since 1970. Out of the 397 amendments, 253 were passed between 1970 and December 2000. In other words, 65 percent of the total number of modifications occurred in the last thirty years, and 46 percent of them alone belong to the 1982–2000 period.

Table 9.1 shows the distribution of constitutional amendments by subject matter between 1982 and 2000.

A significant number of amendments between 1982 and 2000 are related to the electoral system and to the reinforcement of the organization and powers of the Congress and the federal judiciary. Other important changes concern individual and social rights and their protection, the economic system, including state control of "strategic" areas, and the accountability of public servants. Although the number of amendments to the economic articles of the constitution is relatively small, they have a very significant impact. Indeed, during the same period, some of the supposedly "untouchable" principles of the revolution incorporated into the constitution (education, state-church relationships, and agrarian reform) were also modified. It could be even asserted that a new, more complex and modern institutional design was introduced and superimposed over the institutional model constructed in the decades following the revolution. At least in some respects, both institutional designs coexist within the same constitution (see Díaz y Díaz 1999).

TABLE 9.1

Constitutional Amendments by Subject Matter, 1982–2000

Subject matter	Number	Percentage
Individual and social rights	57	22.1
States, municipalities, Federal District	14	5.4
Economy	18	7.0
Executive power	14	5.4
Legislative power	65	25.2
Judicial power	42	16.3
Nationality and citizenship	6	2.3
Electoral system	19	7.4
Accountability of public servants	17	6.6
Other	6	2.3

SOURCE: Own calculation using the *Diario Oficial de la Federación* (1982–2000).

Federal legislation.   Out of 211 federal laws in force as of December 2000, 158 had been newly enacted, 29 had been amended, and 24 had not been modified between 1971 and 2000.[9] In other words, 75 percent of the existing federal legislation was "born" during the time we are analyzing. If we add the 29 laws amended during the same period, the result is that 89 percent of the existing federal legislation was either enacted or amended during the last thirty years. Only 54 predated 1970, and 29 of these were amended after 1970.

According to a more detailed analysis, a comparison between two "activist" six-year periods can be made. The first one runs from 1971 to 1976, when a significant number of laws were enacted or modified, introducing new matters into the Mexican legal system, as, for example, environmental, urban, and economic law. During this time, legislation tended to reinforce the intervention of the state in social and economic life. Also, there was a clear intent to renovate the laws enacted before 1970 (for example, laws related to education and the military). The second runs from 1991 to 1996 (the last four years of the administration of President Salinas and the first two of President Zedillo). During this time, we observe a complete shift in the orientation of the laws and an almost complete renewal of the legislative framework, mainly in the economic, financial, agricultural, trade, services, and human rights sectors.[10] A very significant percentage (over 50 percent) of the existing legislation was enacted or modified during this second period. Table 9.2 shows a comparison of the number and subject matter of new laws enacted and the percentage of laws still in force for both six-year periods.

THE QUALITATIVE APPROACH

Between 1970 and 2000, important qualitative changes took place in the role of the constitution, the legislative process, and the technical quality and general substantive orientation of legislation.

Toward a normative constitution.   It is commonplace to hear in Mexico that the 1917 constitution has not been a "normative" constitution—that is, a constitution that actually regulates the political process and is otherwise enforced and respected as the supreme law and the foundation of the legal system. On the contrary, a very widespread perception finds a considerable gap between the constitutional text and the political and legal process. This gap is ultimately explained by the authoritarian nature of a regime that has been able to instrumentalize and change the constitution at will, instead of subordinating itself to it.[11]

Obviously, the gap has existed and still exists, just as in other countries. This does not justify, however, denying the constitution any normative value altogether. The 1917 constitution has been a normative constitution to the

TABLE 9.2

Comparison of New Laws Enacted, *1971–1976 and 1991–1996*

Subject matter	1971–76	Percentage	1991–96	Percentage
Total laws enacted	56	100.0	64	100.0
Total laws still in force	21	37.5	63	98.4
Agriculture	2	3.6	1	1.6
Business	1	1.8	3	4.7
Communications/transportation	0	0.0	7	10.9
Criminal law	3	5.4	3	4.7
Economy	6	10.7	13	20.3
Education and research	8	14.2	1	1.6
Electoral	1	1.8	1	1.6
Financial services	3	5.4	1	1.6
Taxation	9	16.0	5	7.8
Health	2	3.6	2	3.1
Human rights	1	1.8	5	7.8
Judiciary	0	0.0	4	6.2
Labor and social security	3	5.4	2	3.1
Military	2	3.6	1	1.6
Natural resources and environment	6	10.7	6	9.4
Other	4	7.7	4	6.2
Private law	1	1.8	0	0.0
Public administration	4	7.1	5	7.8

SOURCE: Own calculation using the *Diario Oficial de la Federación* (1971–76; 1991–96).

extent that it reflected a basic political arrangement and fundamental social values that effectively channeled Mexican institutional life for a long time. Within this basic arrangement, there was plenty of room for political expediency, which required the frequent amendment of the constitution. However, any attempt to change or go beyond the defining points of reference of this arrangement (for example, the interdiction of presidential reelection or the guarantee of individual rights and private property) either failed or was reversed not long thereafter.[12]

It is not surprising that constitutional scholars, for the most part, tended to have a political view of the constitution, in the sense that they approached constitutional issues in terms of their political significance rather than as a problem for legal-technical interpretation (Cossío Díaz 2001, chap. 2).

However, political and social change seems to require now that the constitution should begin to operate as a normative constitution in a narrow, technical sense. This is indeed occurring, and we provide two clear examples of this process:

We refer first to the *electoral system*. The constitutional and statutory rules regarding federal elections have become normative in a strict sense. First, they have been the product of a process of political democratization in which political actors increasingly accept and recognize the legitimacy of electoral outcomes. This attitude has been fostered by the growing participation of political parties in the process of designing electoral laws and institutions. In 1996, culminating a twenty-year process of electoral changes, a very important constitutional amendment regarding the federal electoral process was agreed to by the three major national political parties. This amendment included, for the first time, the judicial review of the constitutionality of electoral laws and of other determinations by electoral authorities. It can be said that until that moment, the electoral rules of the constitution were not normative, in the sense that there was no legally effective means to enforce them (De la Peza 1999, 335).

Second, the Supreme Court has an increasingly active role in *constitutional interpretation*. The 1994 judicial reform introduced new constitutional remedies (constitutional controversies and actions of unconstitutionality) (see Fix-Fierro 1998a), through which the court can begin to play a more prominent role in constitutional life and in the enforcement of constitutional provisions.[13]

The trend toward a more normative constitution has, at the same time, exposed the technical deficiencies of the constitution itself and the lack of reflection on, and experience with, the technical and political problems of constitutional interpretation.

The legislative process.   Since at least the 1940s and until 1997, the federal legislative process was clearly controlled by the president of the republic. The ruling party, the *Partido Revolucionario Institucional* (PRI), had control of both chambers of the Congress, and, in turn, the party and the Congress were politically subordinated to the president. Legislative bills, including proposals for constitutional amendments, were prepared by administrative agencies, as well as by the office of the presidency. According to some of our informants, even the bill's evaluation (*dictamen legislativo*) by the Congress was also frequently prepared by administration officials. In other words, presidential bills faced no major political obstacles, and the president was able to ensure that the Congress passed such laws as he considered appropriate for the implementation of his policies. His overwhelming political control allowed him to effectively prevent, without using his broad veto powers, the passage not only of bills introduced by the fledgling opposition parties but also of those bills introduced by the president or his party that for some reason had ceased to be politically convenient. One of our informants found a telling parallel between this legislative process and European absolutism: "The president (the king), surrounded by a group of his experts (ministers), created a rational order, with a claim to universality, for a chaotic world (the country)."

In reality, the legislative process was not as straightforward as it appears —that is, that presidential will was necessary and sufficient to produce legislation. Rather, there were significant modalities, according to the political circumstances and the administration's particular profile. In most cases, during the elaboration of legislative bills, a broad, mostly closed consultation process was implemented among interest groups and government officials before the bills were introduced to Congress.[14] This informal consultation and discussion process facilitated compromise where necessary and the achievement of reasonable and practicable solutions. In other cases, the Congress, or more precisely, the members of Congress, representing specific interests, did play a role in the negotiation of modifications. However, the president remained the ultimate arbitrator, and his decision was final.

This type of legislative process allowed for stricter control of the technical aspects of legislation. In any case, legal form and legal-technical considerations played an important role if only because most decision makers, including the president himself, had had legal training. Also, the legal universe to be regulated and the number of participating actors were relatively small.

The "way of doing things" just described slowly started to change by the end of the 1970s as a consequence of successive electoral reforms that opened up broader spaces for the political participation of opposition groups in the Congress.[15] The gradual decline in the presence of the hegemonic party (the PRI) in the Congress, a process that accelerated during the 1990s, has translated into a different legislative dynamic.[16] Several studies carefully describe and explain these changes, especially in recent years.[17] We may summarize them by saying that although most bills introduced to Congress are still drafted by the executive, their enactment into law is less and less guaranteed by this fact alone. The chambers of Congress, through political negotiations conducted between the political parties and between the latter and the executive, increasingly introduce changes to the president's proposals.[18] The number of bills coming from the political parties or their members in Congress is also on the rise.

However, particularly in socially sensitive matters or in those with international implications, the participation of interest groups and nongovernmental organizations (NGOs) in the legislative process has also increased significantly. We find recent examples of this development in the discussion and enactment of amendments to the environmental and cinematographic laws.[19] The principle of transparency—that is, public consultation and prepublication of proposed regulations—is also being increasingly recognized and has been timidly established in some laws and regulations. However, it is important to point out that the increasing openness in the legislative process is far from a general trend in the legal system. In reality, it concerns only some legal areas, those where a clear link exists between particular social groups and the law. In other areas, the level of participation is significantly lower. We are told that the technical level of legislation diminishes to the extent that a particular law incorporates political compromises. One of our informants puts it this way: "The legislative process has become a task of achieving consensus rather than a technical one." Another factor that contributes to a relatively low technical level of legislation is the almost complete absence of legal-technical support for the activities of Congress, which would help in the "legal translation" of the political work of the members of Congress.

It is not difficult to understand why this has been so. The growing size and complexity of Mexican society, as well as the political and economic reform process of recent years, generated a need to legislate intensively on new and more technical issues, relatively unknown to the Mexican legal profession.[20] Because the number and technical skills of lawyers were limited (see following discussion), and considering that during the last twelve years the final decision makers have no longer been the lawyers, it is not surprising that there is a perception that the technical level of the new laws and regulations has diminished.[21] In the 1970s, there was already a perception of a growing proliferation and dispersion of laws and regulations that were contrary to the systematic ideal of codification and legislative order (Vázquez Pando 1978, 116–17).

The existence of inconsistent legal provisions or strong ambiguities in the laws opens up a space for interpretation and contributes to a potentially stronger role for both judicial and administrative authorities. The risk, however, is that the victory achieved by political compromise in the legislative arena can suffer a defeat at the hands of law-enforcing officials, simply because of the practical difficulties encountered by its implementation.

Orientation.   The second significant change in Mexican legislation has been a major transformation in its general orientation. This is a complex process due to several factors, mainly determined by the change in the model of economic development and the composition of the political elite between 1982 and 2000. We could generally characterize the new orientation as the full acceptance of an open-market economy; the reduction of the size (privatization) and functions (deregulation) of the state; a new institutional design aimed at achieving more effective checks and balances vis-à-vis the executive power (judicial and political reforms), and between the federal, the state, and the municipal governments; and finally, the enhancement of civil and political rights.

All of these factors had a direct impact on the legal system. As mentioned before, between 1982 and 1999, a major transformation of Mexican law occurred. The scope of this transformation was such that we can even say that a "new legal order" was put in place (see Sáenz Arroyo 1988; Valdez Abascal and Romero Apis 1994). This new legal order was less the result of an explicit design and more the consequence of the new economic and political orientations of public policy. The absence of an overall plan for legal reform does not mean that it had no clear objectives in terms of the modernization process (Valdez Abascal 1994, 46–47).

Changes in legislation were structured along three main lines. The first sought to achieve a more rational and predictable legal infrastructure for a market economy. The second required a new definition of the functions and the structure of the state. The third attempted to open or enlarge spaces for the public action of groups and individuals (López-Ayllón 1997, 203–19). The overall result would be a modern and rational legal infrastructure for the needs of a market economy articulated with the world system, a smaller but more effective state, and the enhanced guarantee of the civil and political rights of its citizens.

LAW ENFORCEMENT

Law enforcement is much more difficult to assess than the creation of laws and regulations. In general, there is a very widespread perception, in the media and among the population, that laws and regulations are not enforced. However, although there are practically no systematic empirical studies on law enforcement, not even in recent times, a more careful analysis would soon show significant differences in the levels of law enforcement between legal areas. We observe, for example, that whereas the tax and social security legislation is normally enforced, criminal and labor law is, for the most part and for different reasons, perceived as ineffective. In this section, we will provide a few elements that can be useful for the general description and analysis of law enforcement in Mexico. For this purpose, we have chosen three different legal areas.

Criminal prosecution. In recent years, a significant aspect of Mexican society is the perception of growing crime rates. Although there are no empirical studies that allow for a detailed diagnosis of the causes and trends in criminality, some of the most frequently alleged reasons for growing crime rates are linked to recurrent economic crises, political instability, and the lack of a strong and efficient law-enforcement apparatus. Simultaneously, there is strong distrust of the police and other agents responsible for criminal prosecution. Victimization surveys are still scarce and partial. However, they show clearly that, on average, only about a third of crimes committed are ever reported to the public authorities. Some recent studies have tried to find, on the basis of official statistics on reported crimes, where the source of the ineffectiveness of the criminal justice system lies.

TABLE 9.3

Crime in the Federal District, 1990–1995

Year	Population of Federal District (in thousands)	Reported crimes	Cases resulting in criminal charges	Impunity (%)	Index (per 100,000 inhabitants)
1990	8,235.7	133,352	8,392	93.71	1,619.2
1991	8,284.7	136,927	6,474	95.27	1,652.8
1992	8,334.0	143,999	4,467	96.90	1,727.8
1993	8,383.6	137,568	4,904	96.44	1,640.9
1994	8,433.5	161,496	4,170	97.42	1,914.9
1995	8,483.6	218,599	5,479	96.25	2,576.7

SOURCE: Ruiz Harrell (1996, 19).

According to one of these studies (Ruiz Harrell 1996), in 1995, there were 218,599 criminal offenses (*delitos*) reported to the Office of the Attorney General of the Federal District (*Procuraduría General de Justicia del Distrito Federal*). During the same year, a total of 5,479 individuals were charged before a criminal court. This means that in about 97.5 percent of all reported crimes, the authorities were not able to identify the persons responsible for committing those crimes, to gather sufficient evidence against them, and to arrest or present them before a judge. This situation has worsened since 1990 (see Table 9.3), although criminal prosecution has never been very effective: between 1930 and 1990, the "impunity index" was never less than 90 percent (Ruiz Harrell 1996, 18–20).

Ruiz Harrell finds that this situation is partly explained by the lack of resources invested in the criminal justice system. Whereas crime rates per 100,000 inhabitants remained almost stable between 1950 (1,193) and 1980 (1,190) (Ruiz Harrell 1996, 24–29), the number of cases processed by each public prosecutor increased from around 60 in 1950 to about 220 in 1995. By contrast, the number of police officers in charge of public security has grown in relation to the number of reported crimes. Mexico City has the highest number of police officers in comparison to other capital cities. However, they are also utterly ineffective. According to the same data, in 1994 there were 1,295 police officers for 100 criminals charged (Ruiz Harrell 1996, 29).

Another recent study (Zepeda Lecuona 1998) confirms Ruiz Harrell's main conclusions by showing how criminal investigations (*averiguaciones previas*) are handled by the public prosecutor's office in the Federal District. In 1995, of a total of 197,428 criminal investigations, a full 79 percent were sent to the "reserve"; in 3.66 percent of cases, an individual was arrested and charged before a judge; in 6.36 percent, charges were brought but no arrest was made; in 5 percent, no charges were brought. The "reserve" means that public prosecutors determine that they do not have enough elements or evidence to continue with the proceedings. In theory, any investigation "on the reserve" (*en reserva*) can be activated any time. In reality, the reserve means the final form of disposition for most criminal investigations.[22]

In sum, both studies find the main explanation of the high levels of impunity in the ineffective behavior of the police and the public prosecutor (*ministerio público*) and in their inability to investigate and prosecute a significant proportion of the reported crimes.

Environmental protection. A recent study (Canela Cacho, Cárdenas Suárez, and Guevara Sanginés 1998) on the *Procuraduría Federal de Protección al Ambiente* (PROFEPA), a federal agency established in 1993 and charged with the enforcement of national environmental laws and regulations, may shed some indirect light on law enforcement in this area.

The study analyzes the operation of the legal department (*Dirección General Jurídica*) of PROFEPA between 1993 and 1997, using data from *Sistema de Gestión de Litigios de Medio Ambiente* (SIGMA), a database on the litigation (comprising both administrative and judicial review proceedings) resulting from the inspections conducted by PROFEPA and the imposition of monetary fines (see also PROFEPA 2000). The data show the following trends:

The litigation rate has increased.

The average amount of the fines has diminished.

The percentage of administrative decisions confirmed by the Federal Fiscal Tribunal has decreased from 39 percent in 1992−93 to about 24 percent in 1996−97.

The overwhelming majority of decisions are challenged first before the legal department of PROFEPA.[23]

The Legal Department's success rate before the Fiscal Tribunal is considerably higher where the challenged decision was subject to a previous administrative review proceeding than where the decision was directly appealed to the Tribunal.

These findings demonstrate a number of interesting facts. First, in a sensitive area (environmental protection), law enforcement through a specialized administrative agency *does* exist in Mexico.[24] Second, the administrative agency in this area uses sophisticated information technology that may help improve its performance in law enforcement. Third, there are effective means for the internal quality control of decisions. And fourth, considering that litigation rates have grown and that a large proportion of decisions are invalidated by the Federal Fiscal Tribunal, there is reason to conclude that an effective and independent judicial review exists and that private parties find sufficient incentives to use it. Another factor that may help explain the high rate of litigation is the type of agents involved in these proceedings (mainly small and medium-size companies), which have access to legal resources (lawyers and courts) to defend their interests.

Employment disputes.   Another interesting area for the analysis of law enforcement relates to employment disputes. The so-called *juntas de conciliación y arbitraje*, which are essentially special bodies for the conciliation and adjudication of labor and employment disputes, consist of representatives of the government, the trade unions, and employers' associations. Formally, employment law grants individual workers a high level of protection.

Two different studies, one conducted in the late 1960s (Gessner 1984, 72–88) and the other in the early 1990s (Correas Vázquez 1997), provide some evidence on the main ways in which employment disputes are settled before the local juntas. In essence, they show that the most significant proportion of disputes refer to dismissals (*despido*). According to the law, in such cases workers have the option of seeking reinstatement in their jobs or monetary compensation. The amount of such compensation is regulated by the law. Data show that a large proportion of such disputes are settled and that workers normally accept compensation well below the amount established by the law. Workers accept this compensation because their economic situation compels them to settle, but also because attorneys' fees are contingent, for both parties, on the amount recovered or granted (Gessner 1984, 79).[25] This explains why the actual compensation is usually half the amount established by law. In most cases, the juntas do not adjudicate, but they establish an institutional framework for negotiations normally leading to extrajudicial settlement.

These examples indicate that law enforcement is highly differentiated between different areas of the law. The most visible factors that may explain variance between them include the socioeconomic level of the parties,[26] the relative costs for the parties to a proceeding, the quality and intensity of attorney intervention, and the independence or autonomy of the participating agency or court.

THE JUDICIARY AND OTHER JUSTICE INSTITUTIONS

This section will deal briefly with change and continuity processes in the Mexican judiciary and other justice institutions between 1970 and 2000 from a triple perspective: (1) it will analyze the growth processes experienced by the justice system; (2) it will present the most important changes in structure, organization, and jurisdiction of the judiciary; and (3) it will attempt to explain the general role and function of the judiciary in Mexico during the period considered. This overview will concentrate on the federal judiciary, and a cursory reference will be made to the judiciary of the Federal District.[27]

In very general terms, it can be said that the Mexican courts, both federal and state, have witnessed a steady process of growth in the number of cases filed each year during the period 1970–99. Whether this amounts to a "litigation explosion," as such a phenomenon has been termed in other countries, is quite uncertain. The reasons are that apart from their availability and reliability, Mexican judicial statistics have not been studied, and such growth does not seem to be exceptional when compared with other social growth processes (literacy, population, urbanization, and the like), which also have been notable during the same time period. Nevertheless, federal and state judges frequently complain that they have to face truly crushing caseloads and that only more resources for the courts may help resolve this problem. Such increases in litigation have not necessarily been accompanied by a comparable growth in the number of courts and in the size of judicial and other court personnel. This is especially true of state courts, although there may be some exceptions.

The federal judiciary. The federal judiciary is the most important court system in the country. It has jurisdiction in both ordinary federal matters and in amparo matters, which allow these courts to review the legality and constitutionality of any action or decision by any public authority, including all other federal and state courts and tribunals. In fact, the bulk of cases processed by the federal judiciary belong to its amparo jurisdiction, and it is in this sector that growth in caseloads has been most evident.

The federal judiciary is presently composed of the following courts: the Supreme Court of Justice (SCJ); the collegiate circuit courts (CCC); the unitary circuit courts (UCC); the district courts (DC); and the Electoral Court (EC).

The Supreme Court of Justice is the highest court in the country. Because of the jurisdictional breadth of the amparo suit, especially against judicial decisions, the SCJ most of the time has faced an "impossible task," as a distinguished legal scholar at the turn of the century put it. The majority of changes in its jurisdiction and composition since 1917 can be explained as attempts to help the court cope with its growing caseloads, but relief was always temporary.[28]

In 1987, a constitutional amendment sought to radically unburden the court of so-called legality amparos—that is, matters that did not involve strictly constitutional issues—thus furthering the goal of transforming the SCJ into a genuine constitutional court. In 1994, another constitutional amendment changed the court's composition by reducing the number of justices from twenty-six to eleven. It also enlarged the court's jurisdiction in constitutional matters, approximating the court to the European model of constitutional justice (Fix-Fierro 1998a, 6–7).

Most recently, another constitutional amendment was passed at the request of the SCJ itself. The amendment grants the court the power to transfer to the CCCs cases where it has already established a binding precedent (*jurisprudencia*) or cases it considers not important or relevant enough to warrant its intervention. The rationale behind this strategy is, according to the justices themselves, to allow the court to concentrate its efforts on the more relevant constitutional cases.

The Supreme Court's annual workload diminished almost steadily after 1970. In 1970, it disposed of 8,112 cases, and 6,481 were pending. In 1990, it disposed of 6,339 cases, and 2,739 were pending. The figures for 2000 were 6,869 and 1,286, respectively. This could be explained as an effect of the reform of 1968. The court's workload began to rise again after 1982 (the economic crisis that began that year may have played a role) and did so until 1987. For this reason, in those years, following amendments to the Organic Law of the federal judiciary, a substantial number of amparos were transferred to the court's chambers or to the CCCs.[29] The 1987 constitutional amendment was reflected in a marked decrease in the court's workload in the years thereafter. The 1994 and 1996 reforms did not alter the court's jurisdiction in amparo matters, so its workload did not change substantially for this reason. Despite the reduction in the number of justices, the SCJ has been able to reduce slightly the number of annual pending matters, and in March 1998, the justices approved a plan for eliminating backlog by the year 2000.[30] In 1999, a new constitutional amendment gave the court discretionary powers to send cases to the circuit courts for their final disposition.

The growth in the number of circuit and district courts was modest until the 1980s and evidently did not keep up with other social growth processes.[31] This is clearly shown by Table 9.4, which presents the number of circuit and district courts between 1930 and 1999, as compared with the country's population.

In relation to the population, the DCs and UCCs follow a similar pattern: their growth is very limited between 1930 and 1970, but the population and (as we will later see) workloads grow dramatically. In 1930, there was one DC and one UCC for 360,000 and 2,759,000 inhabitants, respectively. In 1970, the corresponding figures were 877,000 and 5,358,000. After 1970, a moderate growth begins, especially in the number of DCs, which accelerates in the 1970s and particularly in the 1990s. In 2000, there was one DC for 448,000 inhabitants, a proportion similar to that of the 1940s. By contrast, the relationship between the population and the UCCs began to decrease after 1980 to a level well below that of the 1930s.

The most dramatic development concerns the CCCs. In 1950, there was one CCC for more than 5 million inhabitants. After a slight increase, this proportion began to decline steadily to less than 1 million in 2000. If we con-

TABLE 9.4

Number of Circuit and District Courts
in Relation to Population, 1930–2000

Year	DC	CCC	UCC	Population (in thousands)	Population/court (in thousands)		
					DC	CCC	UCC
1930	46		6	16,552	360		2,759
1940	46		6	19,653	427		3,276
1950	46	5	6	25,791	561	5,158	4,299
1960	48	6	6	34,923	728	5,821	5,821
1970	55	13	9	48,225	877	3,710	5,358
1980	92	21	12	66,846	727	3,183	5,571
1990	148	66	30	81,249	549	1,231	2,708
1995	176	83	47	91,120	518	1,098	1,939
2000	217	138	56	97,400	448	705	1,739

SOURCES: Own calculation using data from the *Informes anuales de la Suprema Corte de Justicia de la Nación* (1970–2000); Cossío Díaz (1996); Banamex-Accival, *México Social 1997–1998*.
NOTE: DC (district court); CCC (collegiate circuit court); UCC (unitary circuit court); population for 2000 is taken from the preliminary results of the population census of that year.

sider that the CCCs have become the courts of last resort in many ordinary matters, their growing number means that the federal administration of justice has become more and more decentralized. At the same time, this creates a growing problem of inconsistent decisions among them, which must be resolved by the Supreme Court.

As demonstrated with respect to the DCs (CIDAC 1994, chap. 2; see also Magaloni and Negrete 2000), one important consequence of the limited growth in the number of courts was that, confronted with growing caseloads and wanting to keep backlogs manageable, the courts were forced to dismiss a high proportion of complaints on procedural grounds—that is, without examining their merits.[32] The proportion of amparos dismissed by DCs on procedural grounds (*improcedencia* and *sobreseimiento*) grew from 58 percent in 1940 to 70 percent in 1975, the time period when growth in the number of DCs was very limited or moderate at most. The rate of dismissals was 73 percent in 1993. It had apparently dropped to 54 percent in 2000.

It is interesting to note that such a high level of dismissals did not automatically diminish during the period when new DCs were being established at an accelerated pace. There are several possible reasons. First, the average workload levels are still high, similar to those prevailing in the 1970s (see following discussion). Second, the formalistic legal criteria developed for the dismissal on procedural grounds appear to have been incorporated into the judicial routines, regardless of other considerations. And third, there are no strong incentives to decide on the merits of cases, considering that a dismissal is also a mode of final disposition for the purposes of judicial statistics.

TABLE 9.5

Federal Judicial Budget, 1970–2000

Year	Nominal (new pesos)	Constant (new pesos, 1994)	Constant (USD, 1994)	Federal budget (%)	Per capita	Per federal judgeship
1970	109,736	141,161,035	36,665,204	0.15	2.9	1,094,272
1975	265,358	193,544,553	50,271,312	0.08	3.4	1,290,297
1980	1,000,017	237,623,021	61,720,265	0.06	3.6	1,231,207
1985	15,168,687	355,360,221	92,301,356	0.08	4.8	1,468,431
1990	257,000,000	427,476,548	111,032,869	0.13	5.3	994,131
1995	1,385,915,000	1,026,618,913	266,654,263	0.39	11.3	2,129,915
2000	6,723,350,703	2,076,389,963	539,322,068	0.56	21.3	2,974,771

SOURCES: Own calculation using data from Cossío Díaz (1996) and the *Diario Oficial de la Federación* (2000).
NOTE: The exchange rate in 1994 was 3.85 pesos for one dollar; the per capita and per judgeship budgets are expressed in constant new pesos for 1994; the number of judges results from the sum of all judges in the Supreme Court of Justice and circuit and district courts; the Electoral Court has not been included in the calculation for 2000.

Another interesting trend in the federal judiciary since 1970 is the growing proportion of courts that are specialized in civil, criminal, administrative, or labor matters.[33] The federal judiciary has received a substantial increase in financial resources since the mid-1980s and especially after 1990. This has allowed it not only to grow at an accelerated pace but also to modernize thoroughly.[34] Table 9.5 presents the evolution of the federal judicial budget in nominal and constant values per capita and per judgeship.

The table shows that the per capita budget grew steadily after 1970, but it increased substantially in the 1990s. The per-judgeship budget also increased between 1970 and 1985. It decreased between 1985 and 1990, as the number of judges and courts grew faster than the budget. The per capita budget in 2000 was almost seven times that of 1970.

Since their establishment in 1951, the circuit collegiate courts have exercised jurisdiction only in amparo matters, as an auxiliary to the Supreme Court's jurisdiction. The distribution of cases between the CCCs and the SCJ has varied over time, according to criteria of substantive, procedural, social, and economic relevance. Since 1987, the CCCs have had the final decision in the so-called legality amparos, the great bulk of which are amparos that challenge judicial decisions of state courts and the courts of the Federal District. Table 9.6 shows the evolution in the total and average number of matters before the CCCs between 1970 and 2000.

The table shows that the general trend has been toward a steady growth of workloads, but this growth has been compensated for by an increase in the number of CCCs. The average number of cases has greatly varied, oscillating between over two thousand and just over one thousand. The total workload of the CCCs more than doubled between 1995 and 2000. However, the growth in the number of courts and a rise in the average number of dispo-

TABLE 9.6

Cases Before the Collegiate Circuit Courts, 1970–2000

Year	Workload		Dispositions		Pending	
	Total	Average	Total	Average	Total	Average
1970	29,586	2,276	18,476	1,421	11,110	855
1975	26,008	1,530	19,897	1,170	6,111	360
1980	37,142	1,769	25,868	1,232	11,274	537
1985	64,633	2,084	41,119	1,326	23,514	758
1990	78,553	1,034	61,587	810	16,967	223
1995	112,684	1,358	96,981	1,168	15,703	189
2000	252,502	1,830	193,609	1,403	58,893	427

SOURCE: *Informes anuales de la Suprema Corte de Justicia de la Nación* (1970–2000).

sitions have kept the average number of pending cases below levels from the mid-1970s to the mid-1980s.

About two-thirds of the total number of cases are *amparos directos*—that is, amparos against final (mostly state) court and tribunal decisions.[35] Federal judges complain that the growth in this type of case has been extraordinary and that something must be done about it (for example, limiting the availability of this remedy). Local judges claim that the time has come for the devolution of the state court's autonomy, arguing that the conditions prevailing during the last century that led to the introduction of the amparo against court decisions no longer exist.[36] This is a very sensitive issue because any change in the present situation would mean a major transformation of the Mexican judiciary. So far, there has not been any serious public discussion of this issue nor have any studies been carried out to give it any support (Fix-Fierro 2001).

The unitary circuit courts are ordinary courts for appeals in federal civil and criminal cases. Criminal cases predominate: until 1995, the UCCs had to decide less than one thousand civil appeals. Table 9.7 shows the evolution of total and average workloads for the UCCs between 1970 and 2000.[37]

Once again, the general trend has been toward growing workloads. The average number of cases (which peaked in 1990) has had more variations, according to the growth in the number of UCCs. However, productivity has also risen, so the number of pending cases at the end of a year is, on average, lower in the 1990s than it was in the 1970s or 1980s.

District courts have jurisdiction in both amparo and ordinary federal matters. These two types of jurisdiction will be analyzed separately.

Table 9.8 shows the evolution of *amparos indirectos* (for example, challenges to actions by administrative authorities, including warrants for arrest and nonfinal judicial decisions).

TABLE 9.7

Civil and Criminal Appeals Before the Unitary Circuit Courts, 1970–2000

Year	Workload			Dispositions			Pending		
	Criminal	Civil	Average	Criminal	Civil	Average	Criminal	Civil	Average
1970	5,422	327	639	3,933	220	461	1,489	107	177
1975	9,761	239	1,000	7,078	144	722	2,683	95	278
1980	8,197	251	704	7,273	161	619	924	90	85
1985	11,006	377	632	9,222	284	528	1,784	93	104
1990	26,505	914	914	19,856	685	685	6,649	229	229
1995	30,129	641	655	27,777	591	604	2,352	50	51
2000	33,777	1,963	638	30,608	1,749	578	3,169	214	60

SOURCE: *Informes anuales de la Suprema Corte de Justicia de la Nación* (1970–2000).

TABLE 9.8

Amparos Indirectos Before the District Courts, 1970–2000

Year	Workload			Dispositions		Pending	
	Total	Average	Per 100,000 inhabitants	Total	Average	Total	Average
1970	62,849	1,143	111.1	58,823	1,070	4,026	73
1975	82,040	1,302	123.0	69,923	1,110	12,117	192
1980	114,668	1,246	149.5	98,906	1,075	15,762	171
1985	155,283	1,479	188.2	136,428	1,299	18,855	180
1990	249,589	1,686	271.1	227,608	1,538	21,981	149
1995	170,947	977	169.6	155,417	888	15,530	89
2000	209,630	966	187.6	180,222	831	9,408	136

SOURCE: *Informes anuales de la Suprema Corte de Justicia de la Nación* (1970–2000).
NOTE: The litigation rate per 100,000 inhabitants has been calculated on the basis of new filings only.

The growth in workloads is almost constant, with some jumps. In 1990, the total number of amparos was about four times the levels of 1970. The rise in the average number of amparos, dispositions, and pending matters is not so dramatic, because the number of new DCs also increases. Just as demand reaches its peak in 1990, the establishment of new courts accelerates. However, at the same time, an unusual decline in the workload begins, with a relative low point in 1994 and a gradual increase in the following years. In 2000, the average number of amparos entering DCs was below the levels of 1970.

If we consider their importance by subject matter, the most numerous cases are criminal amparos, followed by amparos in administrative, civil, and labor matters.[38] If we consider that the number of criminal prosecutions before state and Federal District courts is relatively low when compared with civil filings (see the following discussion on the Federal District), we come to the conclusion that the predominance of criminal amparos reflects the

TABLE 9.9

Federal Civil and Criminal Cases Before the District Courts, 1970–2000

	Workload				Dispositions			Pending		
			Per 100,000							
Year	Civil	Criminal	Average	inhabitants	Civil	Criminal	Average	Civil	Criminal	Average
1970	17,968	21,779	723	28.8	5,046	6,856	216	12,922	14,923	506
1975	10,377	35,512	728	29.3	4,527	12,411	269	5,850	23,101	460
1980	8,985	45,912	597	28.5	2,887	14,782	192	6,098	31,130	405
1985	6,575	41,622	459	20.7	1,588	11,154	121	4,987	30,668	340
1990	4,664	76,644	549	34.3	1,748	19,521	142	2,916	55,123	392
1995	4,175	108,077	641	25.8	1,506	35,481	211	2,669	72,596	430
2000	6,944	30,768	160	25.3	3,882	22,015	119	3,041	10,580	63

SOURCE: *Informes anuales de la Suprema Corte de Justicia de la Nación* (1970–2000).
NOTE: The litigation rate per 100,000 inhabitants has been calculated on the basis of new filings only.

higher personal and financial costs in criminal procedure, so the involved persons tend to resort more often to this remedy.

Table 9.9 shows the evolution of ordinary federal civil and criminal cases before the DCs between 1970 and 2000.

The evolution of workloads in federal civil and criminal cases seems to be somewhat different than in amparo matters. We can first observe a contrary development in the civil and criminal dockets. As criminal prosecutions and cases go up, civil cases (including commercial matters) go down (from 17,968 in 1970 to almost 4,000 in 1995). This means, on the one hand, that the ordinary jurisdiction of the DCs is "residual" in relation to their jurisdiction in amparo matters—that is, civil and criminal cases have to share a more or less fixed proportion of the DCs' resources. On the other hand, in federal commercial cases, plaintiffs have the choice of also filing before a local court, which they will more probably do if the DCs' workloads rise considerably, as is the case here. The pending prosecutions also rise at the end of each year, reaching more than 70,000 at the end of 1995. The number of criminal cases diminishes after 1994, probably reflecting a file cleanup of old cases.

The Electoral Court was incorporated into the federal judiciary in 1996. After an unsuccessful experiment in 1988, a federal Electoral Tribunal was first established in 1990 as an autonomous tribunal to review the legality of the federal electoral process. Successive changes in organization and jurisdiction of this tribunal after 1990 make it difficult to evaluate the development of workloads and dispositions, because remedies and cases are not comparable. Our impression is that the present EC has been quite effective in the settlement of electoral controversies, thus making a decisive contribution to the fairness of federal and state elections (Eisenstadt 1999; Melgar Adalid 1999).

The courts of the Federal District.   The prevalent image of the state and Federal District courts is that of an underfunded, overburdened, corrupt, and politically subordinated judiciary. Unfortunately, there are but a very few empirical studies on the reality of the state courts, which confirm some elements of the prevalent image (for example, Gessner 1984; Bustamante 1981; Zepeda Lecuona 1997). The state judiciaries, however, are very diverse and complex, and this makes it risky to provide any generalization.[39] Nevertheless, it is a fact that after 1995, almost all of them have started a significant process of change and reform. This process of change has translated into a considerable increase in financial resources and the establishment of new courts, in new and better methods for the selection of judges and other judicial officials, and in the creation of judicial schools (Concha and Caballero 2001).

At present, we do not have complete or systematic information to assess the evolution of the state and Federal District judiciaries for the whole period; therefore, this section will briefly discuss the judiciary of the Federal District for the period between 1992 and 1999.

The judiciary of the Federal District is composed of the High Court of the Federal District (*Tribunal Superior de Justicia del Distrito Federal*); first instance courts for civil, commercial, and criminal matters (*juzgados de primera instancia*); and the courts of the peace (*juzgados de paz*).[40] The High Court of the Federal District (HCFD) is, in turn, divided into several chambers, composed of three-judge panels, specializing in civil, criminal, and family matters. The first instance courts (CFI) and the courts of the peace (CP) are unitary courts. Tables 9.10, 9.11, and 9.12 show the evolution of total, as well

TABLE 9.10
Filings Before the Courts of the Federal District, 1992−1999

	Chambers of HCFD			First instance courts and courts of the peace			
Year	Filings	Dispositions	Difference	Filings	Per 100,000 inhabitants	Dispositions	Difference
1992	38,766	42,344	3,578	216,560	2,599	244,628	28,068
1993	39,375	n.a.	n.a.	205,554	2,325	n.a.	n.a.
1994	44,009	43,651	−358	237,905	2,708	256,609	18,704
1995	48,669	50,015	1,346	285,647	3,225	300,766	15,119
1996	58,209	57,424	−775	235,158	2,633	291,663	56,505
1997	57,346	55,525	−1,821	221,869	2,464	n.a.	n.a.
1998	58,770	56,111	−2,659	189,493	2,088	134,339	−55,154
1999	74,858	68,870	−5,988	199,482	2,185	n.a.	n.a.

SOURCE: *Informes anuales de labores del TSJDF* (1992−99); in some years there are more dispositions than filings, possibly reflecting efforts to reduce backlog.
NOTE: HCFD (High Court of the Federal District).

TABLE 9.11

Filings Before the Civil Courts and Civil Chambers
of the High Court of the Federal District, 1992–1999

Year	Civil chambers of HCFD Total	Civil courts of first instance Total	Per 100,000 inhabitants	Civil courts of the peace Total	Per 100,000 inhabitants
1992	31,623	86,476	1,037.6	15,422	185.0
1993	29,915	102,611	1,177.7	15,811	181.5
1994	33,555	115,405	1,313.6	15,362	174.9
1995	37,335	134,718	1,520.9	17,969	202.9
1996	n.a.	101,732	1,139.1	33,235★	372.2
1997	n.a.	n.a.	n.a.	n.a.	n.a.
1998	44,068	n.a.	n.a.	n.a.	n.a.
1999	56,113	131,129	1,436	33,570	368

SOURCE: *Informes anuales de labores del TSJDF* (1992–99).
★This jump in the number of filings with the civil CP is due to a change in their jurisdiction.

TABLE 9.12

Filings Before the Criminal Courts and Criminal Chambers
of the High Court of the Federal District, 1992–1999

Year	Criminal chambers of HCFD Total	Criminal courts of first instance Total	Per 100,000 inhabitants	Criminal courts of the peace Total	Per 100,000 inhabitants
1992	5,109	13,018	156.2	12,956	155.5
1993	5,073	11,824	135.7	13,710	157.4
1994	5,140	9,415	107.2	9,573	108.9
1995	5,912	12,304	138.9	10,149	114.6
1996	n.a.	14,011	156.9	10,481	117.4
1997	n.a.	n.a.	n.a.	n.a.	n.a.
1998	8,300	n.a.	n.a.	n.a.	n.a.
1999	8,350	16,493	180.6	18,290	200.3

SOURCE: *Informes anuales de labores del TSJDF* (1992–99).

as civil and criminal, filings before the courts and chambers of the HCFD for the period between 1992 and 1999.

These three tables reflect a huge disparity between civil and criminal filings. Filings before the chambers of the HCFD grow steadily, whereas the number of cases before the CP and the CFI do not seem to follow a constant pattern. Another aspect that can be observed is the more or less constant difference between filings and dispositions. The existence of a considerable backlog can be inferred only from Table 9.10, which also reflects periodic attempts to reduce it.

TABLE 9.13

*Filings Before the First Instance Courts
and Chambers of the High Court
of the Federal District, 1995*

Judicial organs (number)	Average annual filings
Chambers of HCFD	
Civil (7)	5,333
Family (2)	2,956
Criminal (5)	1,084
Criminal courts (66)	186
Civil courts (56)	2,405
Courts for renting matters (23)	1,473
Courts for urban property matters (4)	1,218
Family courts (40)	1,081
Bankruptcy courts (2)	185
Courts of the peace (36)	781

SOURCE: Own calculation using data from the *Informe anual de labores del TSJDF* (1995).

Unfortunately, the annual reports of the HCFD do not present enough information for calculating the average number of cases filed before the different types of courts and chambers of the local judiciary. However, the annual report for 1995 allows us to illustrate the great disparities between the average number of filings each year for different judicial organs, as shown in Table 9.13.

Finally, an interesting aspect of the operation of local courts is the proportion of their decisions challenged through the writ of amparo before the federal courts (see previous discussion). We provide here an example of a very rough estimate for a single year (1993) concerning the final decisions of the Federal District courts. In 1993, the HCFD issued 26,757 final decisions, about 3,400 of which were criminal sentences. In 1993, there were 6,693 civil amparos and 1,972 criminal amparos filed with the CCCs of the First Circuit (Federal District). This yields an approximate appeal rate of 28.7 percent in civil matters and of 37.1 percent in criminal matters. However, we have no information on the outcome of those amparos (Fix-Fierro 1998b, 197; 2001).[41]

The National Commission of Human Rights. Besides the growth processes in the judicial system, it is important to point out that a number of informal or alternative justice institutions have been established or reformed in the last thirty years. Some examples are the *Procuraduría Federal del Consumidor* (1976), the *Procuraduría de Defensa del Menor y la Familia* (1974), the *Procuraduría Federal*

TABLE 9.14

Complaints Before the National Commission of Human Rights
and Recommendations Issued, 1990–2000

| Period/Year | Complaints | | | Recommendations | |
	Filed	Dispositions during proceedings/advice or remand	Lack of jurisdiction	Issued	Total/partial compliance
1990–91	3,256	510	609	88	61
1991–92	6,988	2,091	2,915	185	148
1992–93	8,793	6,001	1,489	260	235
1993–94	8,804	7,942	1,183	267	235
1994–95	8,912	7,283	1,173	141	109
1995–96	8,357	6,929	846	116	101
1996–97	8,509	7,386	749	126	119
1997–98	8,716	6,816	487	136	117
1998	6,523	6,518	301	114	99
1999	5,414	4,763	151	104	97
2000	4,473	4,698	128	26	19

SOURCE: *Informes de actividades semestrales y anuales de la Comisión Nacional de Derechos Humanos* (1990–2000).

de Protección al Ambiente (1993), and the *Procuraduría Agraria* (1951/1992).[42] However, the most visible and influential institution of this kind is the *Comisión Nacional de Derechos Humanos* (CNDH), a national ombudsman first established by presidential decree in 1990. A 1992 amendment incorporated this National Commission of Human Rights (NCHR) into the constitution and provided that each state and the Federal District establish a similar institution.

The main field of activity of the NCHR consists of receiving complaints for private parties who claim that their constitutional rights have been violated by a public official or authority. The NCHR investigates the alleged violation, mediates or conciliates between the parties where possible, and if no solution is achieved, may issue a public and nonbinding "recommendation" addressed to the public official or authority. Table 9.14 gives an overview of its performance in this respect between 1990 and 2000.

Between June 1990 and the end of 1998, a total of 66,085 complaints had been filed with the NCHR, of which 65,079, or 98.4 percent, had been disposed of, and only 1,006 were still being processed (Informes CNDH 1998, 17). A total of 1,380 recommendations had been issued, of which 1,325 (96 percent) had been accepted by the officials or authorities concerned, with evidence of their total or partial compliance (Informes CNDH 1998, 580). At the end of 2000, ten years after the establishment of the NCHR, the total number of complaints filed was 75,972, of which 15,182 (20 percent) had been related to criminal cases. Of these complaints, 12,053 (79.4 percent) were filed by the victims of a crime, and the rest by the alleged criminal. This fact alone demonstrates, first, that human rights violations in Mexico are related to the most basic rights; second, the level of impunity in Mexico is so high that victims of crime have to resort to an ombudsman just to obtain any response from the criminal justice system. Also, against popular belief, it is clear that these ombudsmen for human rights have not been established for the sole protection of "criminals."

The most frequent complaints concern the following violations, mostly committed by law-enforcement officials: illegal detention, torture, homicide, abuse of authority, threats, physical injuries, false prosecution, delay in justice administration, denial of justice, infringement of prisoners' or indigenous populations' rights, medical malpractice, and deficient enforcement of judicial decisions.

The activities of the NCHR go well beyond the processing of individual and group complaints;[43] it has brought neglected issues or problems to public attention (prisoners' and migrant workers' rights, for example) and has made significant proposals that have been later adopted as public policy or legislation. It also demonstrates the growing importance of public opinion and civil society for the construction of the rule of law.

Furthermore, the NCHR has given access to groups of the population generally excluded from the court system. A voluntary survey of 1,857 persons appearing before the commission between October 1994 and February 1995 yielded the following results (Informes CNDH 1994–95, 556–65).

Thirty-four percent of appearing persons declared themselves to have no income,[44] 11.6 percent earned up to minimum wage,[45] 29.5 percent earned between one and three times the minimum wage, and 8.8 percent earned between five and ten times the minimum wage. Further, 30.2 percent declared themselves to be public servants or employees of a public company, 28.8 percent were independent workers, 17.8 percent worked at home, and 10.3 percent claimed to have no occupation. In addition, 6.3 percent lived in a rural area, 11.3 percent lived in a semiurban area, and 82.4 percent resided in urban areas. Finally, 32.7 percent had a primary education, 38 percent had a secondary education, and 22.6 percent had attended a university. These data clearly show that most persons appearing before the NCHR had lower incomes and education levels within Mexican society and lived predominantly in urban areas.

The role of the judiciary in Mexico, 1970–2000.   It is a difficult task indeed to attempt to assess the role of the judiciary in the Mexican legal system, as well as its contribution to Mexican society during the last thirty years. One of our informants told us that, despite the relative neglect in which the courts were being kept by the state, the judiciary was making a very important contribution to political stability and social peace. He saw the confirmation of this view in the fact that people were increasingly resorting to the courts, despite their traditional distrust of public institutions, and this was particularly significant during a period of recurrent economic crises and social change.

This official neglect of the courts began to change in the 1980s. The year 1987 was a significant turning point. An important constitutional amendment gave the Supreme Court and the federal judiciary more powers and incorporated into the constitution minimum guidelines for the local judiciaries and judges (Fix-Fierro 1998b). This trend continued in the 1990s. The establishment in 1995 of the Council of the Judiciary as the governance and disciplinary organ of the federal judiciary and of fifteen local judiciaries can be seen as a signal of a clear trend toward an increasing degree of professionalization, technification, and specialization of the courts (Fix-Fierro 1998b, 1999b).[46] At the same time, a growing public and media awareness of the judicial system took root. The courts themselves were called on more and more to resolve important public issues and scandalous cases. There are numerous recent examples, including official corruption and political assassinations.

The Supreme Court today plays an increasing role as a political and social arbitrator when adjudicating constitutional matters. Recent examples of the issues it has had to address include the constitutionality of local electoral laws, of single trade unions in public agencies, of NAFTA's (North American Free Trade Agreement) Chapter 19 binational panels, of financial and jurisdictional conflicts between different levels of government (mostly state and municipal governments), of extradition treaties, and of the intervention of the armed forces in public security aspects (for a discussion of some of the court's decisions on these matters, see Fix-Fierro 1998a).

The changes introduced into the judiciary and the examples just mentioned raise two questions of central importance: Has the judiciary improved or not? Is the judiciary up to the new tasks it is facing? We probed these important questions in our interviews and, not surprisingly, we received contradictory answers. We think that these contradictions are not only explained by the different backgrounds and outlooks of our informants but also reflect a situation where the "new" structures are still dependent on "old" mentalities and traditions. In fact, judicial reform cannot be accomplished without comparable transformations in legal education, the legal profession, and legal culture.

Many opinions expressed in the interviews point to the inadequate training and traditional mentality of judges as a major obstacle for a judiciary operating in a new environment. Following are some of the opinions we heard in this respect:

Supreme Court justices are clearly aware that the court has to play an enhanced role in Mexican public life, although they do not always agree
on the scope of this new role.[47] They are also groping for new ways of
thinking about the law that would help articulate the court's enhanced
role, but they do not seem to know very well where to look for the
appropriate answers.

Judges act in a very routine way. A formalistic mentality is still prevalent
among them, fostered by a lack of training, particularly in new, technically complex matters, and by antiquated procedural laws.

Judges have become proficient in the language of technique as a neutral-
izer of content. They do not seem willing to take responsibility for
framing their own decisions, and precedents help them in evading this
responsibility.

Judges still perceive their own role vis-à-vis justice and society in paternalistic terms. They think that they have to protect the "weak" and
prevent injustice, the letter or the spirit of law notwithstanding.

Other opinions point to structural problems that help explain judicial
mentality and behavior. For example, it can be argued that the full consequences of the judicial meritocratic culture that the new recruiting system
for federal judges should foster are not visible yet.[48] In any case, the high
turnover rate does not allow them to obtain enough training and experience.
High workloads, and not a formalistic approach alone, prevent judges from
examining cases properly.

Still other opinions stress the difficulties derived from incorporating foreign institutions and systems without sufficient consideration of their consequences for the Mexican legal system. We heard highly critical opinions in
this respect. Regarding the Supreme Court, we were told that it had become
a court too distant from the ordinary cases that mattered to citizens. Indeed,
the 1994 reform had not really enhanced the court's powers: it only gave it
the opportunity to get involved in politics, where it would probably do little
good. In this view, the social, political, and economic issues of the kind that
are now reaching the Supreme Court should be resolved instead by the political branches of government.

Similarly, the introduction of the Council of the Judiciary at the federal
and state levels had generated considerable conflict between this institution and the respective highest judicial body (Supreme Court or State High
Court). It had also reinforced the power of the chief justices in their capacity as presidents of the council, a power they used to share with their fellow
judges or justices.

These opinions suggest to us that the judiciary is affected both by the
transition from the old to the new (a situation that could be resolved in the

course of time) and by a disagreement about the convenience and the specific implementation of change. In other words, a significant sector of the legal profession has good reasons to believe that the problems lie in the type and direction of change, rather than in the old system. We assume that this consideration may lead to an attempt to make adjustments to the new structures, perhaps increasing the ambiguities and contradictions of the present situation.

LEGAL EDUCATION AND LEGAL SCHOLARSHIP

Legal training has been traditionally an important option for university students in Mexico. As explained earlier, until recently, many members of the country's political and bureaucratic elite came from the School of Law of the UNAM. Clearly, the study of the law has been much more than just university training with the aim of practicing the profession. It has been rather a specialized training in the language of the state and in the basic technology of social organization, as this was the main function expected from the law. Moreover, the study of law is still socially regarded as a privileged path to wealth, social prestige, and political power. Thus, the larger role played by the law in social life has impacted the organization of legal education and of the legal profession to this day. In this section, we attempt to identify changes and continuities in legal education since 1970.

Law students. The first important aspect to consider is the number of law students. Unfortunately, we do not have complete figures for the whole period. Instead, we can document some developments during the 1990s.

It should be noted first that the number and proportion of students in higher education increased sharply in the 1970s and 1980s. In 1970, there were 210,111 university students (about 0.45 percent of the population); this number had increased to 731,291 in 1980 (about 1.1 percent of the population) and to 1,583,379 in 2000 (about 1.6 percent of the population) (*Asociación Nacional de Universidades e Instituciones de Educación Superior* [ANUIES] 2000).

Law students have always represented a significant proportion of the total number of university students. In 1991, there were 111,025 law students, or about 10 percent of the 1,100,000 students enrolled in higher education (*licenciatura*). Accordingly, there were 132 law students per 100,000 inhabitants; 45,434 law students were women (41 percent). In 1990, a total of 12,781 students finished law school, but less than half of them (6,077) obtained a degree (*título*) recognized by the state, which enables them to practice the profession (ANUIES 1991).

In 2000, the total number of law students had increased to 188,422, or about 70 percent more within ten years. The study of law (*licenciatura en de-*

recho) was the most-demanded university discipline, just behind business administration (162,699) and public accounting (151,695 students) and well above medicine, with 69,464. The proportion of law students among all students in higher education had increased slightly to 11.9 percent, and the proportion of women had climbed to 48.3 percent (ANUIES 2000). There were consequently 193 law students per 100,000 inhabitants that year.

In 1999, there were 24,396 students who finished law school (46.5 percent were women), but only 14,682 or 60.2 percent (45.4 percent were women) obtained their degree. Although we do not presently have the figures to compare with other disciplines in previous years, it is interesting to note that a considerable number of law students do not graduate (between 35 and 40 percent).[49] In contrast, in medicine a higher proportion finish their studies and obtain their degree (about 80 percent in both cases, in 1996). Of those who finish their legal training, only about half satisfy all requirements to obtain their degree and practice law. It should be noted, however, that if a law student does not satisfy these requirements, he or she is not necessarily prevented from practicing law. In Mexico, lawyers do not have a monopoly over legal advice, and the degree is not required for representing clients in criminal and employment proceedings.

Law schools.   How many law schools are there in Mexico, and to what type of regime (public or private) do they belong? Once again, we do not have the figures for the whole period. However, it would be correct to say that until the 1980s, the great majority of law students attended public universities (the largest law school being undoubtedly the School of Law of the UNAM, with around 10,000 students), and only a small proportion of them attended private law schools (either independent law schools or law schools within private universities). The majority of the most prestigious or well-known private law schools were established from the 1960s onward. The explosion in the number of law students in private universities and in the number of private law schools occurred in the 1990s.

In 1991, of 1,091,324 students in higher education, 81.7 percent attended public universities, and 18.3 percent went to private universities. In 2000, the proportion of students in private schools had increased to 29.4 percent. Since we do not have specific data, we applied these proportions to law students. This would suggest some 90,707 students in public law schools and 20,318 in private law schools in 1991. In 2000, the corresponding figures would have been 133,026 law students in public universities and 55,396 in private law schools. This would mean that enrollment in public law schools grew about 30 percent, and enrollment in private law schools about 172 percent in less than ten years!

Not only have private law schools grown more rapidly than public law schools but their number has also multiplied in an explosive manner. In 1991, there were 119 law schools, and this number had increased to 326, an increase of about 174 percent in less than ten years (ANUIES 1991, 2000).[50] Almost all of these new schools were small private schools.

Legal specialization. Another important trend in legal education is the establishment of institutions for specialized and postgraduate legal training. As the degree for practicing law does not require specialized training for the different legal roles (judges, public prosecutors, attorneys), this function has been fulfilled by postgraduate studies (*posgrados*) in universities (*maestría* and *doctorado*—master's and doctorate degree, respectively) as part-time education.

Postgraduate legal studies have also experienced considerable growth. The oldest and most important postgraduate legal studies program belongs to the School of Law of the UNAM (since 1951). In 2000, this institution offered ten *especializaciones* (specializations such as constitutional, administrative, procedural, private, and criminal law).[51] Other public universities outside Mexico City have also established postgraduate studies, which are mainly taught during the weekend (Fridays and Saturdays) by local and nonlocal teachers.[52] Private universities have also opened postgraduate programs in Mexico City and elsewhere, with considerable success. Attendance is growing, and local judges and other public officials are among those enrolled in these programs. Because most of their students are already practicing lawyers, private universities (and to some extent, public universities) may charge considerable fees, and thus they are able to hire prestigious scholars and practitioners, both local and nonlocal, usually for individual weekend sessions. In 2000, according to data provided by ANUIES (2000), there were 7,325 students in postgraduate law programs (42.8 percent women), of whom 1,862 were studying an especialización, and 5,148 and 315 students, respectively, were pursuing a master's or doctoral degree.

Not only have university postgraduate studies expanded, but there has also been an identifiable trend toward the establishment of various institutes, centers, schools, and so forth for specialized legal training. Presently, courts and tribunals, both federal and state, have established their own judicial schools. In 1978, the federal judiciary created the *Instituto de Especialización Judicial*, which has offered an annual course since 1983. It changed its name to *Instituto de la Judicatura Federal* in 1995 and has expanded its courses, both in Mexico City and outside the capital.[53] In 2000, it started an intensive six-month training program for candidates for a district or circuit judgeship (Informes SCJN 2000, 326). The Electoral Court has its own *Centro de Documentación y Capacitación Electoral*, first established in 1990, and it recently opened an electoral judicial school. Other federal tribunals, such as the *Tri-*

bunal Federal de Justicia Fiscal y Administrativa and the *tribunales agrarios*, have also established their own specialized training centers.

The state judiciaries have followed suit. In 1997, of thirty-two local judiciaries, twenty-three had established an institute, center, or agency charged with judicial training and education (Fix-Fierro 1999b). In 2000, only four state judiciaries did not have their own training institute or center (Concha and Caballero 2001, 10). However, this does not mean that they all operate regularly or that they satisfy judicial training needs.

All these advancements notwithstanding, and with some local exceptions (and mostly for minor judges), in Mexico it is still not a legal requirement to obtain specialized training to become a judge, nor is it a requirement to attend continuing education courses in a periodic manner.

The Office of the Attorney General of the Republic (*Procuraduría General de la República*) established the *Instituto Nacional de Ciencias Penales* in 1976. This institute organizes, among other activities, mandatory courses for federal public prosecutors.

Legal scholarship.   A significant indicator of the growing relevance of legal scholarship in the last thirty years is the production of legal books and materials. The number of publishing houses, authors, and titles has grown considerably during this period, and especially in the last fifteen years. For example, we have identified at least ten important publishers who have started their own legal series since the 1970s.[54] These new series are added to those of the few older publishers, such as the UNAM and *Porrúa*, to the increasing publications by public institutions, such as the Supreme Court of Justice and the National Commission of Human Rights, and to the legal periodicals published by the most important law schools, both public and private. In one of the oldest and most important legal series of a private publishing house, *Biblioteca jurídica Porrúa*, there were 115 authors/coauthors and 175 titles in 1975; 196 and 354, respectively, in 1986; and 369 and 677, respectively, in 2000.

The Biblioteca jurídica Porrúa includes mostly Mexican authors, with occasional translations of foreign books. Most titles included in the series are meant for teaching. The series also comprises compilations and commentaries on legislation and judicial precedents. The legal series of other publishing houses have a similar profile.

More generally, we have identified the following categories of legal publications:

Compilations of legislation and judicial precedents (with or without commentaries)
Teaching manuals

Traditional legal doctrine (general treatises on civil, criminal, administrative law, and the like)

Translations of foreign legal books

Imported legal books (almost exclusively from Spain and Argentina)

Legal periodicals (journals, yearbooks, and the like)

Legal research (that is, production of "new" legal knowledge)

Our impression is that now, as before, the first two categories clearly predominate: most legal books with a strong doctrinal (as opposed to a practical) orientation are used in teaching.[55] It is also our impression that, despite the considerable growth in the number of authors and titles, the market for legal books is still small and insufficient. This is suggested by the lack of specialized legal libraries and bookstores outside Mexico City and by the fact that many of the publishing houses specialize in the publication of books produced by the professors of the major law schools.

Scope and quality.   For a long time, the School of Law of the UNAM has played a leading role in legal education. As the oldest and most prestigious law school in the country, it was the largest school and the most recognized center for political recruitment (Lomnitz and Salazar 2002). Private law schools adopted the UNAM's law curricula and even chose to have their degrees recognized by the UNAM. This leading role has diminished in recent times, as many private universities have gradually adopted their own curricula.

We were repeatedly told that legal education in public universities (UNAM, but also in some state universities with regional prestige, such as those in Guanajuato and San Luis Potosí) was good enough in the 1950s and 1960s. It began to decay with the "massification" of public universities in the 1970s.[56] This was an important reason for the growth of private universities. But lately, limits have been imposed on the growth of public law schools, and this means further opportunities for private law schools. These private schools have also become attractive because they offer a particular professional orientation (for example, in corporate lawyering) and the opportunity to forge significant personal relationships. However, other schools offer simpler and shorter curricula (three years instead of the customary five).

We asked our informants about the form, content, and quality of legal education. They did not paint a rosy picture. According to many of them, legal education is still very traditional. It has stagnated and transmits mostly legal-theoretical models of the past century. Teachers do not update their knowledge and are hardly familiar with modern teaching techniques. Many law students are more worried about their personal advancement than with the practice of a profession, and they express a degree of cynicism with respect to legal practice. The overall impression is that law graduates do not receive good or even sufficient legal training.[57]

In fact, it is quite difficult to assess the quality of legal education. There are no objective criteria, either formal or informal, for evaluating law schools and law graduates.[58] However, there are some visible elements, related to continuity rather than to change, that characterize legal education in Mexico:

> The majority of teachers in law schools are not full-time professors but practitioners who teach for a few hours a week. This makes it likely that they will reproduce traditional legal education and values.

> The number of available law books has increased. However, many of them also reproduce traditional legal ideas and models.[59] In fact, the classic Mexican law books of the 1950s and 1960s are still widely used by law students and teachers.

> Teaching methods rely heavily on theoretical presentations and are very rarely problem oriented. They tend to present a view of the law as a phenomenon isolated from both social reality and other social sciences.

> Technical legal skills are not, for the most part, the decisive criterion for evaluating a law graduate. Because the legal profession is still highly permeated by personal and social relationships, law schools play an important role as recruitment for law firms and the government. However, the skills expected from a law graduate are apparently so basic that the quality of education prior to law school may be much more a determinant for recruitment.

If the quality of legal education is generally poor and if legal technical skills are not decisive for practice, how can a more technically demanding legal system be sustained? It is quite obvious, as some of our informants suggested, that certain small sectors of the legal profession are capable of adapting quickly to the gap between legal education and the actual demands of legal practice, simply because their professional success or even survival depends on it. The question remains open, however, for the bulk of the legal profession.

THE LEGAL PROFESSION

This section examines data on the legal profession. As in other areas of the Mexican legal system, empirical research is almost nonexistent apart from the recent studies by Dezalay and Garth (1995, 1997) and Lomnitz and Salazar (2002).[60] We generally share these studies' main conclusions. For the purposes of this section, we characterize the legal profession as segmented, divided, and weakly organized. By a segmented profession we mean the

TABLE 9.15
Professionals in Mexico by Profession, 1990

Profession	Professionals		Distribution by gender (% by profession)	
	Total number	Per 100,000 inhabitants	M	F
Accounting	201,765 (10.6%)	248.3	135,732 (67.3%)	66,033 (32.7%)
Medicine	165,185 (8.7%)	203.3	118,648 (71.8%)	46,537 (28.2%)
Law	141,539 (7.5%)	174.2	106,557 (75.3%)	34,982 (24.7%)
Business administration	131,310 (6.9%)	161.6	91,123 (69.4%)	40,187 (30.6%)
Economics	35,695 (1.9%)	48.8	27,323 (76.5%)	8,372 (23.5%)
Social sciences	29,486 (1.6%)	36.3	8,648 (29.3%)	20,838 (70.7%)
Political science and public administration	15,166 (0.8%)	18.7	9,273 (61.1%)	5,893 (38.9%)

SOURCE: INEGI (1993).
NOTE: The table includes the first four professions with the most number of professionals and other areas close or related to the law.

considerable separation that exists between the different branches of the profession. The profession is also divided in the sense that there is a clear distinction between a small elite and the bulk of legal professionals. Finally, legal professionals are generally not organized and therefore lack influence as an identifiable group.

In general terms, in the last thirty years the number of Mexicans who received higher education increased significantly. In 1970, the total number of professionals was 267,012.[61] This figure increased to 1,897,377 in 1990. In other words, the percentage of professionals went from 1.6 to 5.9 percent of the population older than twenty-five years (INEGI 1993).

Unfortunately, there are no available comparative data on the proportion of lawyers in relation to the total number of professionals prior to 1990. Table 9.15 shows the composition of the professional population in 1990.[62]

The table indicates that although law is the third most important profession in absolute numbers, the number of lawyers is relatively small in relation to the total population. It is interesting to note that women represent only 24.7 percent of lawyers. However, the percentage of women studying law is significantly higher (41 percent in 1991 and 48.4 percent in 2000) (ANUIES 1991, 2000). Some available data indicate that the gap between male and female legal professionals may have been progressively reduced in the last ten years.

Of 141,539 legal professionals identified in the census of 1990, 84 percent had an occupation, but only 63.5 percent were likely to work in activities directly related to the law (professionals and government categories). Avail-

TABLE 9.16

Professionals in Mexico by Occupation Practice Setting, 1990

Profession	Occupied	Professionals	Technicians	Education	Government and executives	Office personnel
Accounting	168,480	64,520	12,116	4,126	39,551	28,462
	(83.5%)	(38.3%)	(7.2%)	(2.4%)	(23.5%)	(16.9%)
Medicine	135,703	108,406	2,467	3,781	6,195	8,516
	(82.2%)	(79.9%)	(1.8%)	(2.8%)	(4.6%)	(6.3%)
Law	118,964	61,048	1,880	7,993	14,550	20,335
	(84.0%)	(51.3%)	(1.6%)	(6.7%)	(12.2%)	(17.1%)
Business	109,576	12,329	4,384	4,617	39,802	26,529
administration	(83.4%)	(11.3%)	(4.0%)	(4.2%)	(36.3%)	(24.2%)
Economics	30,390	4,495	1,474	3,230	7,863	8,591
	(85.1%)	(14.8%)	(4.9%)	(10.6%)	(25.9%)	(28.3%)
Social sciences	22,092	2,866	3,407	7,345	1,824	4,587
	(74.9%)	(13.0%)	(15.4%)	(33.2%)	(8.3%)	(20.8%)
Political science and public	12,092	1,469	635	1,089	2,732	3,996
administration	(79.7%)	(12.1%)	(5.3%)	(9.0%)	(22.6%)	(33.0%)

SOURCES: XI Censo General de Población (1990); INEGI (1993).
NOTE: The table includes the four professions with most number of professionals, as well as other areas related to the law in Mexico; the percentage in the "occupied" column refers to the total number of professionals in that area; the percentages in the other columns refer to the total number of professionals who work in that area.

able data do not allow us to determine with more detail the real rates of practice setting for legal professionals in Mexico. Table 9.16 summarizes the situation for 1990.

We can compare these data with the number of legal professionals registered with the authorities charged with regulating the professions. According to data of the Federal Secretariat of Education (cited in Lomnitz and Salazar 2002), 142,774 law degrees were registered between 1945 and 1997. About half that number were registered after 1990. This would mean that by the end of the 1990s, there should have been more than 200,000 lawyers in Mexico. Of course, this is only a very rough estimate, and certainly not all of them would be involved specifically in legal professions.

The legal elite.   It is difficult to characterize the profile of the legal profession. Some lawyers work as middle- or low-level federal or state government officials. Others work solo in private practice or in small firms mainly concerned with local civil or criminal cases. A relatively small number occupy different positions as court officials or in other bureaucratic areas in the administration of justice. A significant number of lawyers are employed in various service sectors not directly related to legal practice. However, we can identify a legal elite well differentiated from the bulk of the legal professionals. We will briefly describe some of their main sectors, where significant changes have occurred in recent years.

Public officials. Until the 1980s, most top-level government officials, including the president of the republic, had a law degree. Numerous studies have shown the importance of legal training, particularly at the School of Law of the UNAM, as the main road to initiate and succeed in a political career (Smith 1979). However, it is important to note that technical skills were less important for political recruitment than the informal networks created among professors and classmates (Dezalay and Garth 1995, 9–10).

A significant change in the composition of the political elite in Mexico occurred after 1982. Economists and other professionals displaced lawyers from the top-level positions in government. In 1970–76, lawyers were 45 percent of these officials; economists, 17 percent (engineers, 14 percent; doctors, 8 percent). By 1989–91, lawyers and economists each had 23 percent; engineers, 19 percent (Camp 1995a, 1995b).

The changes in the composition of the elite have had several effects. Probably the most important is a more autonomous and technical role for law and lawyers in government. In contrast to the traditional elite, the new elite is characterized by the use of technical skills, mainly in economics and administration. From their point of view, lawyers lacked technical knowledge to "solve problems." At first, the new decision makers disregarded law as an instrument, but they rapidly learned that it was a necessary and decisive tool to implement the government's new policies (Dezalay and Garth 1995, 60). This opens the door for a more technical and less political role for lawyers in government, especially in some areas.[63] However, the number of lawyers trained in such matters is still relatively small, and traditional legal education does not provide these kinds of technical skills. It is not surprising then that the "new lawyers" in government are relatively young and come from private law schools rather than public universities.[64] Dezalay and Garth (1995) have shown precisely how and why lawyers possessing the new legal-technical skills required in government have begun to come from the private and academic sectors. They also explain that the new technical role of lawyers in certain areas, such as international trade, investment, human rights, and elections, has gone hand in hand with what they call the "international strategies" of lawyers—that is, the legitimacy they derive from the links they cultivate with the foreign centers of economic, political, and academic power.

Judges. There have also been significant changes in the recruitment process of judges. Until 1995, federal judges were appointed by the Supreme Court of Justice. There were no explicit rules, but an informal judicial career

TABLE 9.17

Biographical and Career Profiles of Circuit and District Judges, 1984

Biography and Career	District judges	Circuit judges
Clerks of Supreme Court	75 (78%)	65 (74.7%)
Average duration	3.4 years	3.7 years
Origin	20 states	23 states
Born in the Federal District	16 (16.6%)	9 (10.3%)
Assignment at place of origin	20 (20.8%)	11 (12.6%)
Number of assignments		
As district judges	1.8	1.9
As circuit judges	—	1.9
Seniority at federal judiciary	14.6 years	21.8 years
As district judges	4.3 years	5.5 years
As circuit judges	—	7.2 years
Age at entrance	29.7 years	29.2 years
Age at appointment		
As district judges	40.4 years	36.3 years
As circuit judges	—	43.7 years
Graduated from UNAM	32 (33.3%)	34 (39%)
Local judiciary	37 (38.5%)	39 (44.8%)
Teaching experience	49 (51%)	51 (58.6%)
Postgraduate studies	16 (16.6%)	16 (18.4%)

SOURCE: Own calculation using data from the *Diccionario Biográfico del Gobierno Mexicano* (1984).

had developed within the federal judiciary after 1944 (Cossío Díaz 1996). This career path usually moved from the lower posts of the district and circuit courts to the position of clerk (*secretario*) at the Supreme Court. From there, a Supreme Court clerk was likely to be appointed as a district judge at the proposal of one of the justices. Clerks remained in the Supreme Court for a period of three to six years, in close contact with one of the justices. During this time, they not only were trained in the way things were done but had the chance to "absorb," so to speak, the basic judicial philosophy of the federal judiciary, and they were also evaluated as to their personal qualifications for occupying a judicial post (Cossío Díaz 1996).

This recruitment system for federal judges was highly endogamic and hierarchical, as well as geographically diverse and mobile. Table 9.17 summarizes data published in 1984 taken from the biographical profiles of ninety-six district and eighty-seven circuit judges.

The table confirms that a great majority of district and circuit judges had been clerks at the Supreme Court for several years. They originated in more than twenty of the thirty-two federal entities, but almost half of all district and circuit judges had been born in only five states (Chiapas, Guanajuato, Jalisco, Michoacán, and Veracruz).[65] Surprisingly, not very many had been born in the Federal District, if we consider the very high degree of political and economic centralization in the country. The data also show that federal judges had spent practically all their professional career in the federal judiciary, and many worked, at one time or another, in a local judiciary. The system was highly hierarchical, because all judges had been clerks first, and almost all circuit judges (84 or 94.7 percent) had also been district judges. Finally, the table also shows the geographical mobility of the judges, because at that time only a minority were assigned to their place of birth, and they had been already assigned, on average, to two or more different locations.

After 1984, the federal judiciary began to grow rapidly, and the appointment of judges accelerated. The need to make ever more frequent appointments also reinforced the tendency toward internal "clientelism." According to an implicit, informal arrangement, justices would normally consent to the appointments proposed by their fellow justices (Cossío Díaz 1996, 65–66). This meant, for practical purposes, that judges would feel obligated to the justice who proposed their appointment. This, in turn, contributed to the formation of family-like groups of judicial officials headed by the Supreme Court justices themselves (Soberanes Fernández 1993, 453). The perception that this system no longer guaranteed the personal and professional qualifications of candidates to a judicial post was a major consideration for the 1994 judicial reform (Cossío Díaz 1996, 72–73). This reform established the Council of the Federal Judiciary as a body charged with administering a formal system for the selection and appointment of district and circuit judges through written and oral examinations (*concursos de oposición*).

Between 1995 and 2000, the Council of the Federal Judiciary appointed 276 circuit judges and 332 district judges.[66] This is a very high number of appointments when compared to the number of judgeships at the end of 2000: 470 circuit judges and 217 district judges.[67] It should be noted that not all appointments made during this period followed the procedures established by the law for carrying out concursos de oposición. Both in 1995 and 1999 —when the Council of the Federal Judiciary was initially established and after a constitutional amendment that altered its composition and powers was enacted—the "urgent" appointment of 71 circuit judges and 125 district judges was made.

Statistical data on the outcome of the first internal examinations in 1996 show a few new trends in the selection of federal judges. The most notable change is that examinations open up a greater opportunity for clerks working in nonspecialized district and circuit courts to become district judges. In other words, Supreme Court clerks do not have the same opportunity of becoming judges as they had with the old system, and, in fact, they are disadvantaged to some extent (as are clerks working in specialized, noncriminal courts) because the bulk of cases before the district courts of mixed jurisdiction are predominantly criminal in nature. The new appointment system may thus help reinforce the internal independence of judges, because they will not owe their appointment to anyone but themselves; it will also produce a greater diversity in their personal and professional backgrounds.

The first examinations for the appointment of federal judges carried out by the Council of the Federal Judiciary after the reform of 1999 seem to signal the intention of introducing a few adjustments to the appointment system. In particular, the post of clerk at the Supreme Court may again become a "natural" step in the judicial career. Furthermore, for the first time (at the beginning of 2000), the Council opened its examinations to professionals working outside the federal judiciary. All these changes make it difficult to assess the new trends in the composition of the judicial elite.

The state judiciaries have followed a similar pattern. Local judges were traditionally appointed, for limited periods of time, by the respective High Court (*Tribunal Superior*). After 1995, several states also established a Council of the Judiciary and a formal, albeit limited, judicial career path (Fix-Fierro 1999b). However, in 2000, twenty-five state judiciaries introduced a formal examination for the appointment of trial judges (Concha and Caballero 2001, 254). In most instances, the judicial career system does not include the level of appeals judges, who are still appointed at the discretion of the local executive and legislature.

Attorneys. We have stated elsewhere that in Mexico, to this day, it is sufficient to have a law degree to practice law as an attorney. There are no other requirements, and in particular, there is no need to be affiliated with a bar association. Several bar associations (*barras de abogados*) do exist. They organize conferences and seminars on legal problems, and they occasionally make public statements in the press and other media. However, even their members have the impression that they are social clubs rather than effective organizations of practicing attorneys. Some bar associations have their own code of ethics, but they do not enforce it. We find here that there is an absence of significant change and that change would certainly encounter strong resistance.[68]

A select number of law firms, most of them established in Mexico City, constitute the elite of the attorneys.[69] They have close ties to the business and industrial sector of the economy and more recently, also to the government.[70] It is interesting to note that the great majority of partners in these law firms did not graduate from the UNAM but come from other, mostly private, law schools—17 percent come from the UNAM and 83 percent from other schools.[71]

Legal scholars. In Mexico, the number of professional legal scholars is quite small. Universities employ only a few full-time law professors and researchers. The School of Law of the UNAM, for example, has around 800 part-time and relatively few full-time professors, who also have the obligation to do research. However, the system of professors-researchers has not worked very well because teaching duties absorb almost all the time available for research (see La investigación jurídica en México 1999, a panel debate on this topic). For this reason, the only effectively "professional-ized" research institution has been the *Instituto de Investigaciones Jurídicas* (IIJ) of the UNAM, although other efforts have been made to establish similar institutions[72]

However, full-time professors and researchers lead a rather precarious life as professional legal scholars. Material resources, such as libraries and other facilities, are usually less than adequate, and salaries are not very attractive, especially for young aspiring scholars. In fact, many full-time professors and researchers combine their duties as legal scholars with other professional ac-tivities, as private practitioners or legal advisers.

Nevertheless, legal scholars, especially those connected to the IIJ, form an influential elite. The IIJ's influence can be traced back to the cultivation of a more open and technical study of the law, which has permitted it and sev-eral of its members to participate in the design and operation of some of the new, modern legal institutions established since 1982, such as the national ombudsman for human rights established in 1990 (see Dezalay and Garth 1995; 1997; Lomnitz and Salazar 2002, 23–24).

Women in the legal profession. In general terms, we can identify a clear trend toward the growing participation of women in the legal profession, although with variations in different sectors. We have provided some data on this issue in previous sections of this chapter. Thus, we have shown that women make up almost half the number of law students (41 percent in 1991 and 48.3 per-cent in 2000), although not all of these women finish law school and receive their degree. Therefore, women will end up being underrepresented in the legal profession as a whole, even without considering other factors that may prevent them from joining the professional market and occupying posi-tions in it. This is confirmed by the data of the last population census (1990), which showed that only 24.7 percent of legal professionals were women. Nevertheless, there are also indications that women have been rapidly catch-ing up, as attested by the increasing percentage of women who graduate from law school.

We have some data on the number of women in certain elite sectors of the legal profession and institutions. In all of them, the percentage of women is considerably lower than that in the profession in general.

Women rapidly moved into new areas in the federal judiciary after 1975. There were less than 1 percent in 1975, 5.2 percent in 1980, and 17.5 percent in 1995. However, the data also show that their growing presence stagnated after 1995—that is, the examination system has not brought them any visible advantages in terms of chances for appointment.

Among the partners of ten major law firms in Mexico shown in Table 9.17, women constituted only 1 percent. Among legal scholars, the percentage is higher. For example, of seventy-three researchers of the *Instituto de Investigaciones Jurídicas de la UNAM* in 1999, twenty-one (29 percent) were women.

INTERNATIONAL FACTORS

This section explores the issue of how and to what extent international and foreign legal developments have affected legal change in Mexico during the last thirty years. As confirmed by the interviews, it is easy to determine that until the end of the 1980s, the Mexican legal system was relatively closed to outside influence and scrutiny.[73] This corresponded to the closed political and economic system that had prevailed for a long time. A relatively closed legal system also fostered, and was reinforced by, what could be called "Mexican legal nationalism," an attitude still encountered in some sectors of the legal profession today.

The reinsertion of Mexico into the international markets, as well as the growing outside scrutiny of its political and legal institutions, has spurred domestic legal change. As in past periods of its history, the Mexican legal system has modernized by adopting and adapting foreign or international legal models, becoming more open in the process. Of course, there are many vantage points for observing the impact of foreign legal institutions on the Mexican legal system: the number and type of international agreements entered into by the country; the internationalization of its legal profession; the contacts of judicial and other officials with their counterparts elsewhere; the membership in international organizations with potential influence on domestic law; the judicial precedents dealing with international legal issues, as well as domestic issues that concern or affect international institutions; and the authority of foreign legal ideas as acknowledged in legal research and literature.

The following discussion provides three examples of the increased influence of foreign legal elements on the domestic legal system.

International agreements.   The first is a comparison between the number and type of international agreements published in the *Diario Oficial de la Federación* during the six-year periods 1972–77 and 1990–95.[74] These two periods, which correspond roughly to the administrations of Presidents Echeverría and Salinas de Gortari,[75] were characterized by a high degree of

TABLE 9.18

International Agreements by Subject Matter,
1972–1977 and 1990–1995

Subject matter	Period	
	1972–77 (N = 116)	1990–95 (N = 227)
Cooperation	33 (28.4%)	49 (21.6%)
Criminal justice	9 (7.8%)	35 (15.4%)
Economy/trade	23 (19.8%)	18 (7.9%)
Environment	5 (4.3%)	32 (14.0%)
Human rights	1 (0.9%)	4 (1.8%)
Intellectual property	4 (3.4%)	2 (0.9%)
Labor	3 (2.6%)	10 (4.4%)
International organizations	14 (12.1%)	27 (11.9%)
Private law	1 (0.9%)	12 (5.3%)
Services	23 (19.8%)	28 (12.3%)
Taxation	0 (0.0%)	14 (6.2%)

SOURCE: Own calculation using the Index of the *Diario Oficial de la Federación* (1972–77; 1990–95).

international and domestic legislative "activism." In the first period, there were 116 such agreements and in the second, 227; 16 (13.8 percent) in the first period and 60 (26.4 percent) in the second period were likely to impact on the legal sphere of Mexican citizens; 61 (52.6 percent) in the first period and 120 (52.9 percent) in the second period were bilateral.[76]

There was a substantial increase in the number of international agreements published in the second period, almost double (227) the number of agreements published between 1972 and 1977 (116). The percentage of bilateral agreements remains practically the same. However, the number of agreements that potentially affect a citizen's legal sphere—that is, agreements that can be directly invoked by an individual in a judicial proceeding—grew considerably, both in absolute and relative terms.[77] This outcome was to be expected, if we take into account that international agreements (for example, in the area of human rights) are increasingly relevant for an individual's immediate legal rights and interests.

Table 9.18 shows a comparison between the two periods of the number and percentage of international agreements by subject matter.

Although any classification is arbitrary to some extent, the table clearly reflects a shift toward the adoption of international agreements more in consonance with an open legal system and a market-oriented economy. In the first period, no taxation agreement was published, reflecting the existence of a closed economy; however, Mexico signed numerous agreements to avoid double taxation in the second period. Environmental and human rights agreements also became more important, as did agreements related to private international and labor law.

Environmental and criminal justice agreements (mainly for cooperating in the fight against drug trafficking) became much more frequent. Although this could be more readily explained by international developments alone, such agreements would not be as frequent had the Mexican legal system remained closed. Finally, and against expectations, the percentage of economic/trade agreements and agreements related to services decreased in the second period. However, we should consider that the classification does not reflect the relative economic significance of those international agreements. In the first period, numerous agreements for cooperation were signed with Socialist and Third World countries, with which Mexico had tenuous economic relationships at best. Economic/trade agreements in the second period include NAFTA, the World Trade Organization (WTO) agreements, and several free-trade agreements with Latin American countries.

Another shift in the international priorities of Mexico between both periods is reflected in the number of bilateral agreements signed with the United States and Canada. In 1972–77, there were two agreements with the United States and two with Canada. In 1990–95, there were sixteen with the United States and eleven with Canada.

Judicial interpretations.   Another indicator of the growing importance of international elements in domestic legal life can be found in the interpretations issued by the federal courts. We analyzed the interpretations of the period between 1917 and 1998, contained in a CD-ROM published by the Supreme Court of Justice. Out of a total universe of about 200,000 interpretations (*tesis*), we selected 106 relevant interpretations (0.05 percent).[78] This figure is quite small and shows the limited relevance of international legal issues before the federal judiciary. But the number of interpretations increased significantly after 1988, precisely in the years in which the trend toward a more open legal system becomes visible. In the period 1977–88, there were 68, less than 1 per year; in 1988–98, there were 38—3.45 per year.

Other influences.   A study on NAFTA's binational panel process describes several avenues of external (American) influence on the domestic legal system (López-Ayllón and Fix-Fierro 1999):

> The strong influence of American procedures in the design and operation of the Mexican antidumping/countervailing duties system
>
> The influence of American "pragmatism" over Mexican "formalism" in some binational panel decisions
>
> The intensive communication and learning process among American and Mexican attorneys

LEGAL CULTURE

As stated previously, Mexican society and its legal system have undergone a process of deep change in the last thirty years. Therefore, it would be plausible to assume that legal culture has also changed.[79] However, it is quite difficult to prove that this has actually happened. We have found limited empirical data of the sort we want to consider. Existing indicators are scarce and mostly indirect. In fact, we have not found opinion polls and other surveys useful for the analysis of legal culture prior to 1990.

Existing data suggest a strong social ambivalence regarding the value of law and legality, a growing awareness of fundamental rights but a general ignorance of the constitution and other important laws, and the existence of a strong distrust of legal institutions and legal professionals, as discussed in the following examples.

A national survey conducted in the early 1990s (Beltrán, Castaños, and Flores 1996, 32–33) shows that a significant percentage of persons (65 percent) consider obedience to the law an important value. Of those surveyed, 36 percent thought that people must always obey the law, and 29 percent thought that they may change the laws if they do not like them. However, 35 percent answered that people may disobey the law if they find it to be unjust. Two other questions suggest a similar degree of ambivalence regarding the law as an institutional means for channeling and solving social problems. For example, 36 percent considered that the country's stability was affected if those who violate the law are not punished.[80] About 53 percent would totally or partially accept the legitimacy of noninstitutional means for the satisfaction of social demands.[81]

In 1995, the *Secretaría de Gobernación* (Secretariat of Interior) commissioned a national survey on the opinions and attitudes of the Mexican population toward the rule of law, legal values, and corruption. This survey (in *Este País* 92 [1998, 57]) received high levels of approval for the following statements:

"To violate the law is not that terrible; to be caught by the authorities is the bad thing about it" (62.2 percent).
"Where authorities cannot protect citizens, they have the right to take the law in their hands and make justice for themselves" (66.6 percent).
"It is acceptable to take advantage of official positions, provided they do not exaggerate and benefits are shared" (71 percent).
"We should only obey reasonable and just laws" (35 percent).

In response to another question ("What do you think would be better . . . "?), 7 percent responded that it would be better to manage by informal rules; 32 percent, to manage by written laws and rules; and 61 percent, to manage by both written laws and informal rules. It is interesting to note that the survey did not find significant differences between the various regions of the country and between the "traditional" and the "modern" sectors of the population.

The authors of this survey provided a general interpretation of data obtained in terms of the most basic attitudes of the Mexican population toward the law and conceived of as "stages of moral development" (Foro de discusión: "La corrupción. Entre la legalidad y las reglas no escritas," *Este País* 66 [1996]). They classified the population into three groups, each divided, in turn, into two categories.

The first group makes up about 48 percent of the population. They belong to the stage of "preconventional morality"—that is, they obey the law either because they fear punishment or because they want to maximize pleasure. The second group, characterized by a "conventional morality"—that is, the respect for the law is based on a social orientation—makes up another 35 percent of the population. The third group's attitudes, based on a "postconventional morality," are oriented by reason and universal values. Only 16 percent of the population belongs to this group. Within this last group, about 10 percent would be willing to violate the law if it conflicted with their values.

Other surveys show that social distrust of legal institutions and legal professionals runs very high. According to an opinion poll conducted in 1990 (in *Este País* 35 [1994, 10–15]), 15.6 percent of persons surveyed did not trust the legal system at all, 30.9 percent had "little," and 37.5 percent had "some" confidence in it.

This distrust is not limited to the general population. According to a survey of students at the UNAM (Ramos Gómez and Durand Ponte 1997), only 3.5 percent "fully" trusted judges and the justice system, 35.5 percent would trust them "to some extent," 30.1 percent would have "almost no" confidence in them, and 29 percent did not have any confidence at all.

Legal professionals and judicial proceedings generally command little respect. According to another opinion poll conducted only in Mexico City in 1996, a vast majority of persons believe that judicial proceedings are very slow, very expensive, and only moderately fair (in *Voz y voto* 41 [1996, 23–27]). A third or more of those persons polled regard judges, including Supreme Court justices, and attorneys as dishonest or very dishonest.

We believe that these and similar data more than reflect the traditionally bad opinion of the general public with respect to the law and legal institutions, a phenomenon that is also prevalent in many other societies. Despite the significant transformations of the legal system we have described in previous sections, opinion polls show rather that changes in the legal system have not yet permeated the level of external legal culture. Significant sectors of the population do not *perceive* changes or better conditions in the operation of the legal system.[82]

There does seem to be a growing, but not unanimous, social awareness of the value of fundamental rights and freedoms.[83] Asked if it would be acceptable for the police to torture a man accused of raping a woman to obtain his confession, 57 percent disagreed, 29 percent agreed, and 11 percent agreed partially (Beltrán, Castaños, and Flores 1996, 34). However, the constitution and some other important laws are largely unknown to the population. In a specific poll, 58 percent responded they did not know what was the "supreme law of the land"—that is, the constitution (in *Este País* 61 [1996, 7]).

Of course, poll data reveal opinions and attitudes, but not necessarily actual behavior. We have examined elsewhere recent events in Mexican public life (postelectoral conflicts in the early 1990s, the Chiapas rebellion in 1994, the student strike at the UNAM in 1999–2000, the bank creditors' movement after 1995) to show the existence of powerful social forces promoting a more intensive use of legal means and institutions, such as the courts, to settle conflicts that in previous years would have been naturally channeled to the political process. The increasing orientation of social expectations toward the law, and not away from it, seems to be a reality in many social fields. This can be interpreted as a sign of the growing autonomy of the legal system vis-à-vis the political system (Fix-Fierro and López-Ayllón 2001).

An important question concerns the sources of social knowledge about the law. We may find an indicator in a survey conducted in 1994–95 by the NCHR; 69.7 percent of the persons surveyed stated that they had some prior knowledge about the NCHR and its functions. Among these persons, 54.6 percent had obtained this knowledge through the media (38 percent, TV; 10.2 percent, radio; and 6.4 percent, newspapers); another 25.5 percent through friends and relatives; only 5.6 percent from lawyers; and 2.3 percent from a social organization. Questioned about the motivation for filing a complaint, 46.1 percent responded that they were complaining at their own initiative; 35.2 percent at the suggestion of friends and relatives; and less than 10 percent by a lawyer or a social organization (Informes CNDH 1994–95, 556–65).

Conclusion

A conclusion to the problem stated at the introduction of this chapter—that is, the issues posed by the emergence of a "new" rule of law in Mexico and its chances for success—is not possible without further research and, most important, without a deep reflection on the functions actually accomplished by the law in this country. No systematic effort of this kind exists at present. This chapter suggests, however, that there are several elements that should be taken into account.

Contrary to a widespread prejudice, Mexican law *does* perform a number of functions, because social and legal reality is highly heterogeneous, dynamic, and complex. Therefore, the question here is not only about what such functions may be but about their mutual articulation and their overall result. Contrary to a concept in which modernity is simply opposed to tradition, the complex reality of Mexican society admits the possibility of several levels of modernity, and their interplay in relation to law also becomes a relevant issue for analysis.

A second important aspect suggested by our research is that there are significant differences in the level of performance of legal institutions, both between areas of the law and between regions. The diversity between areas of the law and regions also suggests that, for purposes of comparison, it might not be completely appropriate to refer to the Mexican legal system as a whole. Instead, it might be more meaningful to make comparisons between specific, but similar legal areas and institutions of different countries. This sort of comparison may turn out to be more revealing of the functions accomplished by the law in a society.

Third, we think that the idea of the rule of law has broader dimensions than usually assumed. We find that the traditional, Western-type concept of the rule of law is insufficient for assessing the process of change in the Mexican legal system because the obvious implication would be that there has been no rule of law in Mexico. If, on the contrary, we use a broader concept, according to which the rule of law would mean that the law plays somehow an autonomous referential role for society, we must conclude that the rule of law exists in Mexico to the extent that at least a part of society responds to the basic coordinates of modernity. Consequently, what we are observing now is not the emergence of *the* rule of law, implying that there has been none before, but the extension of the possibilities already existing within the present rule of law and the transformation of the differential roles played by the legal system in society. In other words, legal institutions now seem capable of generating decision possibilities that would not have *existed* if conflicts were to be exclusively settled by the parties' political or economic power.

However, the present public discourse on the need of having an effective rule of law is used in various specific senses that express at least the following social expectations addressed to the legal system: equality (for example, in law enforcement), legitimacy (of public decisions), consensus (as the foundation of institutions), and arbitration and adjudication (under clear and predictable rules). We find that the social conditions for a better adjustment between these expectations and the responses of the legal system are close, but still faraway.

Finally, we would like to go back to the theoretical questions raised in our earlier discussion of the theoretical aspects of the Mexican legal system and try to define with more precision the circular relationship between social and legal change, in the light of the findings of our research. Our starting argument was that social change led to legal change, and this seemed to be sufficiently confirmed by the evolution of the Mexican legal system during the past thirty years. However, once the legal system has changed, we still have to identify the conditions under which the new legal norms and institutions will take hold in social practice, thereby leading to more social change. We think that institutions, in order to survive and consolidate themselves, are constrained to generate their own social legitimacy. This can be achieved on at least three levels: institutional design, organization, and communication. Regardless of their success, these institutional efforts will always have a social impact. Even if institutions fail, such failure is, paradoxically, a partial success, because, *by their very existence*, institutions change social expectations in a specific direction, and, in a sense, things will never be the same.

However, if we are concerned with the effectiveness of institutions—that is, they will be able to contribute to the construction of the rule of law—institutional design, organization, and communication should be directed, first, toward the production and selection of the human resources capable of operating in the new environment and second, toward the transformation of distrust or indifference among the population in both diffuse and specific support.[84] We find that the new institutions of the Mexican legal system are just now trying to do this, but much more needs to be done if their efforts are going to be successful.

Notes

1. This is not to say that the rule of law did not exist in Mexico prior to the period considered. At least in formal terms, the rule of law was consolidated during the second half of the nineteenth century.

2. Fernando Escalante Gonzalbo (1993) has shown how, during the nineteenth century, a modern legal system could not really work because the "imaginary" citizens of the time did not share or represent the values embodied in the law.

3. An interesting implication of this perception is that such change in direction was not determined only by ideology (neoliberalism), although the new ruling group

did not share the statist strategies, but also by the impossibility of keeping the same course.

4. For a different analysis of the relationship between social change and legal change, with special reference to Mexico and based on a critique of traditional legal ideas, see Cossío Díaz (2001, chaps. 3 and 4).

5. For an already classic study on the Mexican presidency and its wealth of legal and political powers, see Carpizo (1978).

6. Gessner's study (1984, 15–25) on social and legal conflicts in Mexico, conducted in the late1960s, offers some interesting insights on the attitudes of the population toward legal conflicts and the recourse to legal institutions.

7. Although it adopts a gender perspective, Varley (2000) provides numerous examples and cases of informal practices in the area of land tenure in urban Mexico.

8. There are different methodologies to count the number of constitutional amendments. We use the number of articles modified by a single amending decree.

9. We excluded all laws concerning the Federal District. Presently, the corresponding legislative powers are shared, depending on their subject matter, by the Federal Congress and the local Legislative Assembly.

10. A sector showing constant and frequent changes is that of criminal law and criminal procedure.

11. Most legal scholars share this perception, but their views differ as to the origins and depth of this gap. Some constitutional scholars situate the issue of the normative nature of the constitution completely in the political process. Therefore, their assessment in this respect depends directly on their judgment regarding the democratic qualities of Mexican politics. Other scholars, although acknowledging the regime's democratic deficiencies and the influence of extraconstitutional factors in constitutional life, postulate that the constitution has, in general terms, a normative value that has contributed to the stability and development of social and political life.

12. Examples include the president's reelection (1927–33), "socialist education" (1934–46), and tenure of federal judges (1934–44). The first date refers to the change of the original text of the 1917 constitution and the second, to the amendment's reversal.

13. Among other examples, we cite the recent case of a municipal president who was dismissed by the local Congress and later reinstated by the Supreme Court.

14. We have a firsthand account of this process by former president Miguel de la Madrid Hurtado (1982–88). See De la Madrid Hurtado (1998, 3–103).

15. The following explanation applies, mutatis mutandis, to the process of political change in the states.

16. In the 2000 election, no party achieved an absolute majority in any of the chambers of Congress.

17. For example, Raigosa (1995, 213–14) provides data on the amendment of federal criminal laws between 1982 and 1988. Thus, out of eighty-two legislative acts, seventy-six were legislative bills introduced by the executive, and the rest, by members of the legislature. Changes were introduced in the chamber of origin to sixty-three of the eighty-two bills, mostly by legislative committees. By contrast, the reviewing chamber introduced changes only on two occasions. There is another in-

teresting study (Díaz Cayeros and Magaloni 1998) that explores the changes introduced to the draft budget submitted annually by the president to the Chamber of Deputies in the period between 1960 and 1994. Not surprisingly, such changes become more frequent after 1982. On the operation of the Chamber of Deputies after 1997, see Casar (2000) and the essays compiled in Pérez and Martínez (2000, 85–103).

18. It should be noted that this phenomenon increases the likelihood that the executive will use his veto powers against legislation passed by Congress.

19. On the discussion in Congress on the Law of Telecommunications, see Berrueco García (1997).

20. Examples include antitrust, antidumping, environmental legislation, technical standards, etc.

21. This opinion was expressed to us in several interviews.

22. Another paper by Zepeda Lecuona (2002), "Ineficiencia al servicio de la impunidad: Las organizaciones de la procuración de justicia en México," estimates the overall effectiveness rate of all local prosecutors' offices (thirty-one states and the Federal District) for the year 1997 at 14.4 percent, which means that in only about fourteen of one hundred cases are prosecutors able to close the investigation and prosecution proceedings.

23. According to Mexican law, a private party affected by an administrative decision has the option of challenging it first before the agency itself or of resorting directly to the Fiscal Tribunal.

24. It is important to recall that during the NAFTA negotiations, one of the strongest arguments against the agreement was the alleged nonenforcement of environmental laws in Mexico. These arguments led to the negotiation of the North American Agreement on Environmental Cooperation and to the creation of the North American Environmental Commission.

25. Gessner argues that both attorneys have an incentive to help the parties reach a quick settlement because litigation would mean either the risk of losing everything or a compensation not worth the amount of work invested in the case, as most of the time the amount at stake is relatively small.

26. A study originally published in the late 1960s (Bustamante 1981) on the levels of corruption in different courts shows such levels vary depending on the socioeconomic level of the parties involved in a proceeding. Not surprisingly, the highest levels of corruption were found in criminal and labor courts, and the lowest in civil and administrative courts.

27. Besides the courts of the federal judiciary (*Poder Judicial de la Federación*), there are other federal tribunals that are judicial in nature and enjoy autonomy in rendering their decisions but are formally a part of the federal executive. Recently, there has been some discussion about formally incorporating these tribunals into the federal judiciary. These tribunals are the Federal Board for Conciliation and Arbitration (*Junta Federal de Conciliación y Arbitraje*), established in 1931 as the federal tribunal for resolving employment and labor disputes in the more important industrial branches subject to federal jurisdiction; the Federal Tribunal for Conciliation and Arbitration (*Tribunal Federal de Conciliación y Arbitraje*), which resolves labor disputes between the federal and Federal District governments and their employees; and the Federal Fiscal

Tribunal (*Tribunal Fiscal de la Federación*), first established in 1937 to settle tax controversies between taxpayers and federal authorities. The agrarian tribunals (*Tribunales Agrarios*) were established in 1992 to resolve all kinds of disputes related to landed property. For a recent evaluation of the agrarian tribunals, see Zepeda Lecuona (1999).

28. Under the original text of the 1917 constitution, the court was composed of eleven justices and worked only en banc. In 1928, the number of justices was increased to sixteen, and three specialized chambers were created. In 1934, the number of justices was again increased, to twenty-one, and a chamber for labor matters was established. In 1951, five more supernumerary justices were incorporated into the court, and the first CCCs were established with the aim of aiding the SCJ with its amparo backlog, which had by then assumed tremendous proportions. An important change in the distribution of cases between the SCJ and the CCCs was introduced in 1968. See Fix-Fierro (1998a, 1998b).

29. For example, there were 3,778 transfers in 1984 and 2,619 in 1985; for this reason, the number of court dispositions is not consistent with the number of pending matters at the end of the year.

30. "Acuerdo general número 2/1998, del Tribunal Pleno, del día diez de marzo de mil novecientos noventa y ocho, para llegar al año 2000 sin rezago," in *Semanario Judicial de la Federación y su Gaceta*, March 1998, 849–901.

31. Both DCs and UCCs are composed of a single judge. CCCs are composed of a panel of three judges.

32. CIDAC's study rejects the alternative explanation (i.e., that complaints are dismissed because attorneys are incompetent) by showing the close correlation between workloads, backlogs, and dismissal rates. However, it is a fact that attorneys sometimes file amparo complaints with the sole purpose of delaying other legal proceedings, and they therefore do not care if a final decision is issued at all.

33. It should be remembered that the UCCs are "specialized" in the sense that they hear appeals only in federal civil and criminal cases. In the SCJ's 2000 report, four UCCs are reported as specialized appeals courts in criminal matters; two others hear administrative and civil cases. All six reside in the Federal District. The Supreme Court also has specialized chambers (four between 1934 and 1994; presently, only two).

34. This included the modernization of the physical infrastructure (buildings), the introduction of information technologies, and the increase in the number of nonjudicial staff. Unfortunately, we do not have numbers for different years. In early 1998, the Council of the Federal Judiciary, which is the governing and disciplinary body of the federal judiciary, with the exception of the SCJ, had a staff of 14,716 persons (Consejo de la Judicatura Federal 1998, 5).

35. This was a constant proportion between 1987 and 1998.

36. The association of state high courts proposes, in effect, that most CCCs be transformed into state courts, with the existing judges and resources. See Patiño Rodríguez (1995).

37. Since 1995, the UCCs also have had a limited jurisdiction in amparo matters. In 1999, the total workload of the UCCs in amparo matters was 1,201 cases; dispositions were 1,038, and 163 cases were left pending.

38. The proportion is approximately four to one between criminal and civil amparos, and two to one between criminal and administrative amparos.

39. A document prepared by the *Instituto de Estudios Jurídicos del Poder Judicial* of the state of Quintana Roo on the basis of a questionnaire sent and responded to by the state judiciaries, confirms this view (1998). This document shows considerable differences between the states with respect to resources, salaries, judicial-training institutions, mechanisms for alternative dispute resolution, case assignment methods, and other services, workload, staff, etc.

40. Most state judiciaries follow this jurisdictional and organizational model.

41. We are adding 1,915 criminal sentences issued by the UCCs of the First Circuit to the estimate of the appeal rate.

42. Gessner (1984, v) contends that the reason for the proliferation of alternative dispute resolution (ADR) institutions in Mexico "lies in the structure of Mexican society, which favors and even requires that disputes be settled in the near social environment of the conflicting parties" (translation by Sergio López-Ayllón and Hector Fix-Fierro).

43. Besides this main function, the NCHR has developed special programs for the protection of the rights of vulnerable social groups, such as journalists, indigenous peoples, women, children and the family, disappeared persons, prisoners, and migrant workers.

44. It is important to note that not all persons who appear are the directly aggrieved individuals, because friends, relatives, and social organizations may file a complaint on their behalf.

45. Presently, the minimum wage is about 100 USD per month in Mexico City.

46. We should add that the 1990s witnessed the full judicialization of electoral and agrarian matters.

47. Some of the most controversial decisions of the new Supreme Court are clearly divided on the issue of the scope of the court's authority and intervention in particular issues. See Fix-Fierro (1998a).

48. In the federal judiciary, there existed close personal relationships between the Supreme Court justices and the lower judges (the selection process will be discussed later). The 1994 reform radically severed those links. As a consequence, we were told, judges felt "orphaned" and "unprotected." The 1999 reform, which gives the Supreme Court greater intervention into the composition and powers of the Council of the Federal Judiciary, can also be seen as an attempt to reestablish those links.

49. This is a rough estimate. The study of law lasts about five years, so we estimate that each year about a fifth of the total number of students enrolled in law school should graduate. We estimate then the difference between the "should graduate" and the "do graduate."

50. We counted the total number of "units." The same law school may have more than one unit in a particular state or the Federal District.

51. However, it was pointed out to us that, paradoxically, whereas the especializaciones at the School of Law of the UNAM were created with the aim of solving the problems of specialized training for the legal practice, they are often rejected in favor of more "academic" degrees for prestige reasons.

52. The Consejo Nacional de Ciencia y Tecnología (CONACyT) has a specific

program for giving support to postgraduate studies outside Mexico City, provided certain requirements are fulfilled.

53. On the history and activities of the *Instituto de la Judicatura Federal*, see Esquinca Muñoa (1999).

54. These publishers are ABZ, *Distribuciones Fontamara, Fondo de Cultura Económica*, Harla/Oxford University Press, McGraw-Hill, *Miguel Ángel Porrúa, Siglo XXI Editores*, Themis, *Trillas*, and *Universidad Autónoma Metropolitana*.

55. Many practitioners think that most legal books are not useful for solving the problems posed by professional practice.

56. However, some of our informants pointed out that they have the impression that although the numbers have decreased, the most capable and brightest students (and maybe also the worst) still come from the UNAM, perhaps because the training in this university is more "ecumenical": it transmits a more complete view of the law, and it is less directed to a specific market niche, as many private law schools are.

57. One of our informants believes that most graduates from public law schools are not capable of practicing any meaningful legal work because such schools were mainly created to solve an employment problem of middle-class groups. However, he attributed some "civilizational value" to such legal training, insofar as it transmitted the notion that there were other options besides violence for solving social problems. In his eyes, the study of law has been, at best, a higher course in "civic culture."

58. However, we are aware that an effort in this direction is being carried out by CENEVAL (*Centro Nacional de Evaluación*), an organization jointly established by universities and other institutions of higher education and the government. CENEVAL started a standard test for the evaluation of law graduates in the year 2000. On CENEVAL, see Gago Huguet (1999).

59. A preliminary analysis of the theoretical and methodological foundations of forty-three legal manuals by the most recognized authors involved in eleven areas of the law finds that, in general terms, Mexican legal doctrine does not take into account the contributions of the four most prominent legal theoreticians of the twentieth century (Kelsen, Ross, Hart, and Bobbio); only two authors explicitly based their doctrines on such contributions. However, other important legal scholars are frequently cited, such as Ihering, Jellinek, Duguit, Savigny, and Gény, and philosophers such as Kant, Bentham, St. Thomas of Aquinas, Locke, and Rousseau (note that they are older authors). Where theoretical elements can be found, they belong mostly to a particular area of the law, not to the general theory of law. The survey concludes, therefore, that Mexican legal scholars do not resort to the general theory of law as a theoretical and methodological foundation for their ideas, but rather to particular theories of the law. One of the consequences is that they lack a common language that would enable them to create more objective and rigorous legal doctrine. See Cossío Díaz and Raigosa Sotelo (1998).

60. These three studies describe the behavior of legal professionals in terms of a "relational" versus a "rule of law" model, "in that professional success depends to a large degree upon the lawyer's ability to construct and use personal social networks" (Lomnitz and Salazar 2002, 210).

61. The General Population Census defines a "professional" as a person older

than twenty-five years who claims to have completed at least four years of higher education. It is worth noting that these numbers have to be taken with caution, as they are not validated by other more reliable sources.

62. The corresponding figures for the 2000 population census have not been released yet.

63. According to one of our informants, when lawyers dominated the top governmental posts, decisions were made following either legal or political criteria, but legal forms and procedures were respected.

64. Dezalay and Garth (1995, 58) report that members of the lawyers' group that participated in the NAFTA (1991–93) negotiations were, on average, twenty-five to twenty-seven years old. Our data indicate that graduates from the UNAM represented 26 percent of the group. From the original group, only three lawyers remained in public service after 1994. The rest work either in major law firms or as counsel for private firms. Presently, the office of the legal counsel for international trade negotiations in *Secretaria de Comercio y Fomento Industrial* (SECOFI) is composed of lawyers averaging less than thirty years of age. Only one of them graduated from the School of Law of the UNAM.

65. In these states, we find public law schools with a long tradition and with regional prestige.

66. District and circuit judges are appointed for a period of six years, after which, if they are confirmed or promoted to a higher position, they may keep their posts until the mandatory retirement age (seventy-five years).

67. In a hierarchical judicial system, there are normally more trial judges than appeal judges. However, in Mexico, the federal judicial pyramid has been distorted by the fact that there are now many more circuit judges than district judges. If we consider that circuit judges are selected only from among district judges, then theoretically speaking, all district judges could be appointed as circuit judges without filling all the available posts and there would be no selection at all.

68. NAFTA opened the door to the possibility that "foreign legal consultants" could provide legal advice on foreign law in Mexico. It also permits the association of Mexican law firms with foreign law firms under some conditions and subject to the approval of Mexican, American, and Canadian bar associations. In Mexico, the organized bar has manifested its strong opposition to this possibility. See Nelson (1998, 76–79).

69. The bimonthly (now monthly) magazine *El mundo del abogado*, which has been published since May 1998, has included articles about several of these elite firms.

70. Dezalay and Garth (1995, 78) stated, "At present, Mexico's economic powers are served increasingly by legal intermediaries who can go between business and between business and the state, all the time building on their own social capital and a primarily 'made in USA' legal expertise."

71. Lomnitz and Salazar (2002) quote the following statement of the main partner of a large internationally oriented law firm: "We used to recruit students from the UNAM. Now the best ones come from ITAM (a private university). . . . The main problem we have in recruiting young lawyers is their training and education. We need intelligent, multilingual and transcultural lawyers. A purely Mexican law-

yer that doesn't understand what foreigners want is useless. And UNAM usually does not give that sort of education" (235).

72. In 1966, the IIJ had only four full-time researchers, and three of them were Spanish-born exiles. In 1999, the IIJ had seventy-three full-time researchers.

73. A former Supreme Court justice told us that until his retirement in 1989, the court very rarely had to deal with international cases, besides an occasional extradition case.

74. According to article 133 of the Mexican constitution, international agreements become domestic (federal) laws if they do not conflict with the constitution and are approved by the Senate and ratified by the executive, who must also promulgate and publish them in the *Diario Oficial*.

75. We started counting the international agreements published a little more than a year after the respective administration took office (December 1970 and 1988), assuming that new agreements took about a year to be negotiated, approved, ratified, and promulgated.

76. The Mexican Supreme Court has ruled that international agreements ratified in accordance with the constitution become ordinary domestic laws, and no implementing legislation is needed. This means that they can be directly invoked or enforced by private persons, if appropriate, in domestic legal (judicial) proceedings. However, this left open the question of their relationship to other federal laws. To avoid any conflict, international agreements with potential domestic legal impacts (for example, NAFTA) have been accompanied by changes in the relevant laws. A very recent interpretation by the court (1999) accords international agreements higher legal authority than ordinary federal laws.

77. This is a rough approximation because we judged these potential impacts by the name of the international agreement alone. For example, we considered that a bilateral agreement for cooperation in the area of tourism would not have such impact, but a bilateral agreement for the recognition of foreign degrees would.

78. *Internacional* or *internacionales* as keywords yielded 842 interpretations from which the relevant 106 were selected. They were related, for example, to the use of treaties for the interpretation of domestic laws or to the interpretation of the treaty itself. International cases included marriage abroad, recognition of powers of attorney, extradition, hierarchy of laws, jurisdiction of Mexican courts in international matters, trademarks, patents, etc.

79. We define legal culture here as "the set of cultural attitudes, deeply rooted and firmly held, that determine the way outsiders—people in society who play no regular legal system role—perceive and define the legal system and expect it to be (or not to be) used" (Merryman, Clark, and Friedman 1979, 27).

80. The other options were no agreement between workers and employers (17 percent); the loss of popular traditions (6 percent); poverty (33 percent).

81. The question was, "After waiting for a year for the government to bring water, the inhabitants of a village protested by blocking a road. Do you approve or disapprove of this attitude?" The results indicated that 40 percent approved, 13 percent approved partially, and 46 percent did not approve.

82. The 1996 survey just cited shows that no more than 7 percent of the popula-

tion had had contact with the justice system. Interestingly, the opinion of those who had had such contact was better regarding the honesty of judges, but worse with respect to delay in judicial proceedings.

83. This assertion was also made in several interviews.

84. We take this distinction from Gibson, Caldeira, and Baird (1998).

References

Asociación Nacional de Universidades e Instituciones de Educación Superior [ANUIES]. 1991. *Anuario estadístico 1991: Población escolar de licenciatura en universidades e institutos tecnológicos.* Mexico City: ANUIES.

———. 2000. *Anuario estadístico 1997: Población escolar de licenciatura en universidades e institutos tecnológicos.* Mexico City: ANUIES. Available: http://www.anuies.mx.

Banamex-Accival. 1998. *México social 1996–1998: Estadísticas seleccionadas.* 11th ed. Mexico City: Banamex.

Beltrán, Ulises, Fernando Castaños, Julia Isabel Flores, Yolanda Meyenberg, and Blanca Helena del Pozo. 1996. *Los mexicanos de los noventa.* Mexico City: Universidad Nacional Autónoma de México [UNAM]–Instituto de Investigaciones Sociales.

Berrueco García, Adriana. 1997. La reforma constitucional y la Ley Federal de Telecomunicaciones. Pp. 163–90 in *El uso y la práctica de la ley en México*, edited by Fernando Castañeda and Angélica Cuéllar. Mexico City: UNAM–Miguel Ángel Porrúa.

Bustamante, Jorge A. 1981. La justicia como variable dependiente. Pp. 13–44 in *Temas y problemas de la administración de justicia en México*, edited by José Ovalle Favela. Mexico City: UNAM.

Camp, Roderic Ai. 1995a. *Political recruitment across two centuries: Mexico 1884–1991.* Austin: University of Texas Press.

———. 1995b. El gabinete de Zedillo: Continuidad, cambio o revolución? *Este País* 51 (June):46–54.

Canela Cacho, José A., Héctor Cárdenas Suárez, and Alejandro Guevara Sanginés. 1998. Los sistemas de información computarizados como herramienta para mejorar la aplicación de la ley ambiental: El caso de la Dirección General Jurídica de la PROFEPA. Berkeley (a slightly abridged version of this unpublished paper appeared in *Comercio Exterior*, December 1998).

Carpizo, Jorge. 1978. *El presidencialismo mexicano.* Mexico City: Siglo XXI Editores.

Casar, María Amparo. 2000. Coaliciones y cohesión partidista en un congreso sin mayoría: La Cámara de Diputados de México, 1997–1999. *Política y Gobierno* 7 (1):183–202.

CIDAC (Centro de Investigación para el Desarrollo). 1994. *A la puerta de la ley: El estado de derecho en México.* Edited by Héctor Fix-Fierro. Mexico City: CIDAC–Cal y arena.

Comisión Nacional de Derechos Humanos. 1990–2000. *Informes de activadades de la Comisión Nacional de Derechos Humanos* [Informes CNDH]. Mexico City: CNDH.

Concha, Hugo, and José Antonio Caballero. 2001. *Diagnóstico sobre la administración de justicia en las entidades federativas: Un estudio institucional sobre la justicia local en México*. Mexico City: UNAM–National Center for State Courts.

Consejo de la Judicatura Federal. 1998. *Información básica: Febrero de 1995–Enero de 1998*. Mexico City: Consejo de la Judicatura Federal.

Correas Vázquez, Florencia. 1997. Alcances sociológicos de la justicia laboral. Pp. 215–29 in *El uso y la práctica de la ley en México*, edited by Fernando Castañeda and Angélica Cuéllar. Mexico City: UNAM–Miguel Ángel Porrúa.

Cossío Díaz, José Ramón. 1996. *Jurisdicción federal y carrera judicial en México*. Mexico City: UNAM.

———. 2001. *Cambio social y cambio jurídico*. Mexico City: Instituto Tecnológico Autónomo de México [ITAM]–Miguel Ángel Porrúa.

Cossío Díaz, José Ramón, and Luis Raigosa Sotelo. 1998. Teoría del derecho y dogmática jurídica mexicana: Un punto de vista. Pp. 319–28 in *Anuario de derecho público 1, 1997*. Mexico City: ITAM–McGraw-Hill.

De la Madrid Hurtado, Miguel. 1998. *El ejercicio de las facultades presidenciales*. Mexico City: Miguel Angel Porrúa.

De la Peza, José Luis. 1999. El juicio de revisión constitucional electoral como medio de control constitucional. Pp. 317–71 in *Estudios jurídicos en homenaje a Felipe Tena Ramírez*. Mexico City: Porrúa.

Dezalay, Yves, and Bryant G. Garth. 1995. Building the law and putting the state into play: International strategies among Mexico's divided elite. American Bar Foundation working paper 9509, Chicago.

———. 1997. Law, lawyers and social capital: 'Rule of law' versus relational capitalism. *Social & Legal Studies* 6 (1): 109–41.

Díaz Cayeros, Alberto, and Beatriz Magaloni. 1998. Autoridad presupuestal del poder legislativo en México: Una primera aproximación. *Política y Gobierno* 5 (2): 503–28.

Díaz y Díaz, Martín. 1999. La transición constitucional (notas sobre las condiciones de reemplazo). Pp. 167–90 in *Hacia una nueva constitucionalidad*. Mexico City: UNAM.

Eisenstadt, Todd. 1999. La justicia electoral en México: De contradicción en sí, a norma jurídica en una década: Un análisis de casos de la evolución de los tribunales federales electorales de México (1988–1997). Pp. 983–1050 in *Justicia electoral en el umbral del siglo XXI: Memoria del III Congreso Internacional de Derecho Electoral*, edited by José de Jesús Orozco Henríquez. Mexico City: Universidad Nacional Autónoma de México [UNAM]–Instituto Federal Electoral [IFE]–Tribunal Electoral del Poder Judicial de la Federación [TEPJF]–Universidad de Quintana Roo [UQRoo]–Programa de Naciones Unidas para el Desarrollo [PNUD].

Escalante Gonzalbo, Fernando. 1993. *Ciudadanos imaginarios*. Mexico City: El Colegio de México.

Esquinca Muñoa, César. 1999. El instituto de la judicatura federal. *Revista del Instituto de la Judicatura Federal* 4:61–92.

Fix-Fierro, Héctor. 1998a. Judicial reform and the Supreme Court of Mexico: The trajectory of three years. *United States–Mexico Law Journal* 6 (spring): 1–21.

———. 1998b. Poder judicial en la reforma del Distrito Federal. *Diálogo y Debate de Cultura Política* 2 (5–6): 176–202.

————. 1999a. Poder judicial. Pp. 157–221 in *Transiciones y diseños institucionales*, edited by Ma. del Refugio González and Sergio López-Ayllón. Mexico City: UNAM.

————. 1999b. El Consejo de la Judicatura en las entidades federativas: Una evaluación de su marco normativo y diseño institucional. *Diálogo y Debate de Cultura Política* 2 (7):123–61.

————. 2001. El futuro del amparo judicial. *Bien Común y Gobierno* 7 (81):5–16.

Fix-Fierro, Héctor, and Sergio López-Ayllón. 2001. Legalidad contra legitimidad: Los dilemas de la transición jurídica y el Estado de derecho en México. *Política y Gobierno* 8 (2):347–93.

Gago Huguet, Antonio. 1999. Las relaciones entre la UNAM y el CENEVAL. *Este País* 104 (November):58–63.

Gessner, Volkmar. 1984. *Los conflictos sociales y la administración de justicia en México.* Translated by Renate Marsiske. Mexico City: UNAM.

Gibson, James L., Gregory A. Caldeira, and Vanessa A. Baird. 1998. On the legitimacy of national high courts. *American Political Science Review* 92 (2):343–58.

González, María del Refugio. 1998. *Historia del derecho mexicano.* Mexico City: UNAM–McGraw-Hill.

————. 1999. Las transiciones jurídicas en México del siglo XIX a la revolución. Pp. 85–134 in *Transiciones y diseños institucionales*, edited by Ma. del Refugio González and Sergio López-Ayllón. Mexico City: UNAM.

INEGI. 1993. *Los profesionistas en México.* Aguascalientes, Mexico: Instituto Nacional de Estadística, Geografía e Informática.

La investigación jurídica en México (debate). 1999. *El Mundo del Abogado* 2 (7): 44–52.

Lomnitz, Larissa, and Rodrigo Salazar. 2002. Cultural elements in the practice of law in Mexico: Informal networks in a formal system. Pp. 209–48 in *Global prescriptions: The production, exportation, and importation of a new legal orthodoxy*, edited by Yves Dezalay and Bryant Garth. Ann Arbor: University of Michigan Press.

López-Ayllón, Sergio. 1995. Notes on Mexican legal culture. *Social & Legal Studies* 4 (4):477–92.

————. 1997. *Las transformaciones del sistema jurídico y los significados sociales del derecho en México: La encrucijada entre tradición y modernidad.* Mexico City: UNAM.

López-Ayllón, Sergio, and Héctor Fix-Fierro. 1999. Communication between legal cultures: The case of NAFTA's Chapter 19 binational panels. Pp. 3–48 in *The evolution of free trade in the Americas/L'évolution du libre échange dans les Amériques*, edited by L. Perret. Montréal: Wilson & Lafleur (Collection Bleue).

Magaloni, Ana Laura, and Layda Negrete. 2000. Desafueros del poder: La política de decidir sin resolver. *Trayectorias: Revista de Ciencias Sociales de la Universidad Autónoma de Nuevo León* 2 (2):54–68.

Medina Peña, Luis. 1995. *Hacia el nuevo estado: México 1920–1994.* 2d ed. Mexico City: Fondo de Cultura Econónuca [FCE].

Melgar Adalid, Mario. 1999. *La justicia electoral.* Mexico City: UNAM.

Merryman, John Henry, David S. Clark, and Lawrence M. Friedman. 1979. *Law and social change in Mediterranean Europe and Latin America: A handbook of legal and so-*

cial indicators for comparative study. Stanford, Calif.: Stanford Law School (Stanford Studies in Law and Development, SLADE).

Nelson, Steven C. 1998. Law practice of U.S. attorneys in Mexico and Mexican attorneys in the United States: A status report. *United States–Mexico Law Journal* 6 (spring):71–80.

Patiño Rodríguez, Julio. 1995. El federalismo judicial. Pp. 393–415 in *Memoria del Foro Nacional "Hacia un auténtico federalismo."* Mexico City: Comité organizador del Foro.

Pérez, Germán, and Antonia Martínez, eds. 2000. *La Cámara de Diputados en México.* Mexico City: Cámara de Diputados (LVII Legislatura)– Facultad Latinoamericana de Ciencias Sociales [FLACSO]–Miguel Ángel Porrúa.

Presidencia de la República. 1984. *Diccionario biográfico del gobierno mexicano 1984.* Mexico City: Presidencia de la República–Diana.

Procuraduría Federal de Protección al Medio Ambiente (PROFEPA). 2000. *El litigio ambiental en México y la Profepa: Reporte de desempeño jurisdiccional 1994–2000.* Mexico City: Semarnap-Profepa.

Raigosa, Luis. 1995. Algunas consideraciones sobre la creación de las leyes en México. *Isonomía* 3 (October):207–16.

Ramos Gómez, Federico, and Víctor Manuel Durand Ponte. 1997. Los universitarios y la confianza en las instituciones. *Este País* 77 (August):10–15.

Ruiz Harrell, Rafael. 1996. El saldo de la impunidad. *Revista Mexicana de Procuración de Justicia* 1 (2):15–30.

Sáenz Arroyo, José, comp. 1988. *La renovación nacional a través del derecho: La obra legislativa de Miguel de la Madrid.* Mexico City: Porrúa.

Schwarz, Carl. 1977. Jueces en la penumbra: La independencia del poder judicial en los Estados Unidos y en México. Translated by Fausto Rodríguez. *Anuario Jurídico* 2 (1975):143–219 (translated from Judicial independence in the United States and Mexico, *California Western International Law Journal* 3 [2]).

Secretaría de Hacienda y Crédito Público. 1995. *Plan Nacional de Desarrollo 1995–2000.* Mexico City: Secretaría de Hacienda y Crédito Público [SCHP].

Smith, Peter. 1979. *Labyrinth of power: Political recruitment in twentieth-century Mexico.* Princeton, N.J.: Princeton University Press.

Soberanes Fernández, José Luis. 1993. Informe sobre México. Pp. 425–69 in *Situación y políticas judiciales en América Latina,* edited by Jorge Correa Sutil. Santiago de Chile: Universidad Diego Portales.

Suprema Corte de Justicia de la Nación. 1970–2000. *Informes anuales de labores de la Suprema Corte de Justicia de la Nación* [Informes SCJN]. Mexico City: SCJN.

Valdez Abascal, Rubén. 1994. *La modernización jurídica nacional dentro del liberalismo social.* Mexico City: FCE.

Valdez Abascal, Rubén, and José E. Romero Apis, eds. 1994. *La modernización del derecho mexicano.* Mexico City: Porrúa.

Varley, Ann. 2000. De lo privado a lo público: Género, ilegalidad, y legalización de la tenencia de la tierra urbana. Pp. 59–93 in *Derecho, espacio urbano y medio ambiente,* edited by Edésio Fernandes. Madrid: Instituto Internacional de Sociología Jurídica de Oñati-Dykinson [IISJ]–Dykinson.

Vázquez Pando, Fernando Alejandro. 1978. La evolución general del derecho mexicano. *Jurídica* 10 (1):113–50.

Zepeda Lecuona, Guillermo. 1997. Análisis económico de los costos de acceso a la justicia en los ámbitos local y federal (Estado de Jalisco). Pp. 41–78 in *Justicia con eficiencia: Memoria del Primer Congreso Anual de la Asociación Mexicana de Derecho y Economía (Abril 1996)*. Mexico City: Asociación Mexicana de Derecho y Economía [AMDE].

———. 1998. Notas para un diagnóstico de la procuración de justicia en el fuero común. Pp. 1547–66 in *Liber ad honorem Sergio García Ramírez*, vol. 2. Mexico City: UNAM.

———. 1999. La disputa por la tierra: Los tribunales agrarios en México. *Estudios Agrarios* 11:9–49.

———. 2002. Inefficiency at the service of impunity: Criminal justice organization in Mexico. Pp. 61–107 in *Transnational crime and public security: Challenges in Mexico and the United States*, edited by John Bailey and Jorge Chabat. La Jolla: Center for U.S. Mexican Studies—University of California, San Diego.

CHAPTER 10

Citizens Running to the Courts: The Legal System in Puerto Rico and the Modernization Process

BLANCA G. SILVESTRINI

FOR DECADES, legal scholars have debated the nature of the legal system in Puerto Rico while attempting to understand the conflicting ways in which the civil law and common law traditions collided in a new colonial setting. The norms of the civil law system developed during the four centuries of Spanish colonialism came into apparent conflict, or at least tension, with the rules of the Anglo-Saxon common law after the U.S. invasion of Puerto Rico in 1898. Although the two systems have conflicted with each other in political rhetoric, in practice both systems have coexisted, although not always in normative harmony. Many of the tensions between these two legal traditions have not resulted directly from legal doctrines or theories. Rather, they are the result of the connection between legal matters and the socioeconomic processes that accompanied Puerto Rico's incorporation into the industrial and urban world. However, the colonial context in which these changes occurred complicate the understanding of what in itself is a complex process. How can we explain that at the inception of the twenty-first century, Puerto Rico has a "modern" legal system in place that responds to the socioeconomic and political challenges of the time and is trusted by a great majority of the population? The main thesis of this chapter is that in practice, the legal system has evolved to face the modernization processes and social changes Puerto Rico experienced in the twentieth century and has gradually gained the confidence of its clients. Actually the legal system has responded to the challenges by the citizens to make it work for their needs rather than according to the theoretical explanations provided by legal scholars.

Although in many Latin American countries, the legal system transformation accelerated in the final quarter of the twentieth century, the fundamental changes in Puerto Rico took place in two previous periods: the first in the early decades of the twentieth century when the United States enforced new judicial practices, and the second in relation to the constitutional reform in 1952. After the 1970s, the changes have been mostly in the organizational rather than in the structural and conceptual framework of the system. In addition, the colonial context in which these changes have taken place situates Puerto Rico in a peculiar position in relation to the rest of Latin America.

Precisely because of the colonial context, the law and legal system have been contested areas, for which scholars have claimed Puerto Rican national identity. The phrase "the defense of the Puerto Rican law" is used frequently in Puerto Rico's legal literature (see Trías Monge 1978, 1991; Delgado Cintrón 1978, 1982, 1988). For example, in his book on the Puerto Rican judicial system, José Trías Monge (1978), one of the most prolific scholars on the history of Puerto Rican law, summarizes his "defense" of Puerto Rican law by pointing out the still unresolved problem of "the creation for this country [Puerto Rico] of its own law, of a law that responds primarily to the needs and aspirations of our people, as conceived by them, of a law formed by Puerto Ricans or with their active and considered participation that is solely for Puerto Ricans" (255–56). Similarly Carmelo Delgado Cintrón (1978) has argued that "the institution of the judicial power, as part of the state, serves the American domination" and that even the legal system reform of the early 1950s is "not Puerto Rican law because its creator and promoter was an American judge" (148). A more recent study by Efrén Rivera Ramos (2001) looks carefully into the relationship of colonial law and Puerto Rican law to analyze the "inequality and disempowerment that colonialism entails" (248). Rivera Ramos concludes that "it is irrelevant whether those norms are deemed to be good or bad, detrimental or beneficial in some particular sense. The question is that they have been determined by others" (231).

In general, these viewpoints encompass profound sentiments of cultural and national identity to confront the Americanization or transculturation in legal matters resulting from a century of American colonial experience in Puerto Rico. But in spite of this theoretical questioning, after decades of legal practices, it is difficult to justify as foreign the product of the work of thousands of Puerto Rican men and women that in one way or another have labored to reconstruct and reconcile the legal system. Nor can the decision of thousands to use the system be disregarded. Therefore, while scholars were proposing the theory of a "defense" for the Puerto Rican law, common Puerto Ricans were beginning to use and trust the courts for resolving matters of all kinds, many of which earlier would have been resolved in alternative manners outside the courts. In the new courtrooms where thousands of Puerto Ricans work as functionaries of the courts, efforts are made to ease— not always successfully—commercial transactions, to interpret labor laws, and to address complaints of social and gender inequality, among others. The citizenry began to use the courts more and more frequently and effectively as the common method to resolve problems and controversies in a pragmatic form without considering criticisms about the legitimacy of the legal system. Some could argue that this is precisely a result of the colonial relationship with the United States. However, neither should the practice be discarded as irrelevant, nor should a dichotomy between practice and theory be proposed. Both legal practices and theoretical perspectives have coexisted and negotiated creative solutions in the contested world of modern Puerto Rico.

This chapter develops two central ideas. First, it presents how the models of modernization that developed in Puerto Rico throughout the century, but above all around the commonwealth constitution of 1952, involved a practical redefinition of the legal system. Second, it links this new legal system to the rise of a notion of participatory citizenship, which created a greater dependency on the courts for conflict resolution. The chapter is divided into two parts. The first part links the processes of formal modernization to the legal system. The second examines changes in the legal system's functioning after the 1970s and the significant increase in the use of the courts to solve conflicts of social and economic character. In the end, arguments of differentiation of Puerto Rican law vis-à-vis other systems, have not in practice precluded the continued use of the legal system by Puerto Ricans.

Modernization and the New Legal System

For over three decades, the Office of the Administration of the Courts has reported that the caseload, as well as the complexity, of the courts in Puerto Rico has increased. Requests to the legislature for a larger budget have been accompanied by claims of need for more specialized staff and better physical facilities in order to address the demands on the system. The legal system has struggled to reorganize its services in a more efficient way by establishing new levels of courts, changing the courts' competency, and adding a layer of professional services to alleviate the courts' duties (see, for example, Administración de los Tribunales 1973–74, 1988–89, 1992–93). One of the problems that the legal system faced was how to support its claim in a persuasive way. At first glance, the basic statistics compiled by the Administration of the Judicial System in Puerto Rico do not yield a significant increase in the rate of active cases in the courts per capita during the period 1974 to 1994. However, this does not mean that the courts are working less or that the citizens

TABLE 10.1

*Criminal and Civil Cases Resolved and Pending
in Superior Courts, 1965–1966 to 1995–1996*

| Period | Cases resolved | | Cases pending at end of year | |
	Criminal	Civil	Criminal	Civil
1965–66	20,231	62,995	7,083	28,089
1974–75	58,351	137,942	27,274	54,568
1985–86	48,702	123,730★	17,318★	42,756★
1995–96	61,390	144,063★	20,420★	36,805★

SOURCE: Administración de los Tribunales, *Informe anual Rama Judicial*, 1995–96.
★The numbers reflect a reorganization of the jurisdiction of the superior and district courts.

are not using the system. The superior court level can be used as an example of the difficulties faced with data gathering in a period of rapid change.

Table 10.1 shows an increase in the superior court caseload during a period of twenty years. After 1975, there is a decline in the civil cases resolved and pending. However, a reorganization of the jurisdictional competence of the court that increased the value of the damages claimed in superior court would account for much of the variance. The same is true for criminal cases, because the law removed most of the investigative and preliminary proceedings from the superior court level. In a similar way, the creation of numerous administrative agencies with adjudicative powers diverted initial court proceedings to other forums until they finally reached the superior court at a later time. Does it mean then that the figures do not support the idea of an increased trust of the citizens in the courts while the ongoing process of modernization of the legal system took place to face the changing socioeconomic conditions of Puerto Rico? Some of the explanations for the discrepancy in these figures can be accounted for in the experience of the legal system prior to the 1970s. Some are rooted in the reorganization of the system throughout the last quarter of the twentieth century to respond to the challenges and alleviate the increase in the number of cases and their complexity.

The annual report (*Informe anual*) of the Administración de los Tribunales for 1973–74 shows a significant increase in cases compared to the caseload in the previous decade. Although it is difficult to compare the exact courts' caseloads, of the three measures reported—new cases presented, cases resolved, and cases pending—the first seems to give the best idea of citizens' use of the courts. The other two categories are related more to the courts' efficiency in handling the cases than with clients' use of the system. Table 10.2 presents information on the new cases in the superior courts from 1965 to

TABLE 10.2

New Cases Presented in Superior Courts, 1965–1998

Type of case	1965–66	1970–71	1974–75	1988–89	1996–97[c]	1997–98[c]
Criminal cases	13,499	19,810	35,103	86,662	139,802	156,633
Civil cases	38,225	n.a.[a]	76,981	86,662[b]	139,802	156,633

SOURCE: Administración de los Tribunales, Informes anuales.
[a]The annual report does not provide data for this year but explains that "new cases continued increasing" (p. 75).
[b]Amount reflects the reorganization of the superior court competency in order to lower the number of cases.
[c]In January 1995 the new Law of the Judiciary approved on July 28, 1994, was enforced, consolidating the former superior, district, and municipal courts into a first instance court level.

1998. In the ten years between 1965 and 1975, there was a 98.6 percent increase in new civil cases. In the fiscal years between 1996–97 and 1997–98, there was an increase of 12 percent. Although the figures are not necessarily comparable because the courts changed their organization and jurisdictional competence through those decades, they provide a setting to begin asking questions about the Puerto Rican legal system. Each important change was faced with significant increases in the operating budget (which rose from just over $82 million in 1988–89 to more than $155 million ten years later) and with attempts to reorganize the court system, which were not always successful but which increased the complexity of the structure of the administration of justice and its budget. As such, this trend is not exceptional, as it was experienced in other countries.

In Puerto Rico, nevertheless, there is a special consideration that we must take into account. The increase in the use of the courts to resolve civil matters occurred in the midst of critiques by some sectors about the Puerto Rican "accommodation" to or even "assimilation" with (to borrow anthropological concepts) the U.S. legal system (Trías Monge 1978). Contrary to the criticisms, the system became even more complex and continuously adopted the American model without great dislocations in its practical functions. However, the credibility of the courts seemed not to be affected, as large numbers of citizens kept looking to the court for solutions to the controversies that affected them.

Although this new legal system had been part of the policy of the United States to incorporate Puerto Rico into the U.S. socioeconomic world since the beginning of the twentieth century, the system became a field both for affirming and questioning the new processes. After 1898, the U.S. government used the legal system to establish its power, legitimate it, and consolidate efficiently its permanence in Puerto Rico (Nazario Velasco 1999); however, the new system permitted and fomented the process of sociocultural change sought by diverse sections of the population (Rivera Ramos 2001, 21,

236). New norms and legal procedures were incorporated that in the long run increased the number of Puerto Ricans participating in some way or other in the legal system. New sectors of society, some from the elite and others from intermediate groups, became attorneys, judges, and personnel of the courts or were called for juries in criminal procedures. Furthermore, this same legal system that some jurists criticized as colonial and foreign created arenas for subordinated people to challenge the power of the urban interests. In the long run, the legal system was converted into an open forum for the creation and re-creation of new rights and judicial institutions in accordance with the times.[1]

There is no doubt that the modernization of the judicial system was one of the forms of control that the U.S. government implanted after the occupation, nor is there doubt that new doctrines, laws, and judicial theories were incorporated along with the new political system.[2] But what can be questioned is the effect these changes had on the way in which the people understood and used the new system that was established.

The Spanish legal system existing in 1898 in Puerto Rico had three levels. In the lowest level were the municipal courts, presided over by judges who were not attorneys, who charged tariffs from the litigants, and who were often criticized for their legal decisions (Nazario Velasco 1999). Then there were the courts of first instance or instruction with primary jurisdiction in civil cases and criminal investigations that were later carried to the higher-level tribunals for trial. At the appellate level, the San Juan Territorial Audience saw both criminal and civil cases that then could rise to the Supreme Court seated in Madrid. The substantive Spanish law had passed through an intensive process of reform precisely in the two decades before the Spanish-American War (Delgado Cintrón 1982; Nazario Velasco 1999). Therefore, many sectors of both Puerto Rican and American society thought that, at the time, the law was adequate for the new demands of a changing society. Nonetheless, both criticized the functioning of Spanish courts in Puerto Rico, the perceived partiality of the judges, and the lack of procedures to guarantee even the most elemental rights (Carroll 1899, 296–315). The long years of demanding reforms from Spain were not forgotten by significant Puerto Rican sectors that thought the United States was bringing the hoped for modernization of the legal system. The military government set up a judicial reform process to establish trial by jury, appellate procedures, habeas corpus, and injunctions and to restructure the administration of justice following the U.S. model (Nazario Velasco 1996). But the law also justified the U.S. presence and power in Puerto Rico, and it gave legitimacy to numerous instances of metropolitan repression (Rivera Ramos 2001, 236). Thus, some of the reforms were welcomed at the same time that significant opposition to the American government ensued. However, basic institutions for the "rule of law" developed, though flawed due to their colonial origin, and rapidly became part of the Puerto Rican legal values. They later served as the basis for the second stage of reforms that began around the 1952 constitution of the Commonwealth of Puerto Rico.

Together with the formal legal system reform, the creation of a law school at the University of Puerto Rico in 1913 became another important step in the implantation of the new model.[3] If the legal system was to respond to the new concepts and organizational structures, it had to train the lawyers. The Law Department, as it was initially called, was organized along the lines of American schools of law and was accredited by the Department of Education in New York in 1916. The program prescribed four years of specialized work, which meant previous university studies for admission, a significant divergence from other Latin American countries where the study of law started at the entry college level.[4] The law curriculum was a significant element in establishing the principles of the new legal system. Organized in the American way, the courses taught civil treatises at the same time that they emphasized case law. The American way of legal study was incorporated hand in hand with the civil law system, which little by little affected how cases were decided and how legal theory was defined. But even more important, the law as a field of study became science: "[I]t forced the rigorous analytical modes that the modern rationality required and helped to legitimize, as a science, the social organizational forms of capitalist nature and liberal thinking embodied in the codes" (Nazario Velasco 1996, 339; Delgado Cintrón 1980). Trías Monge (1978, 245) has explained how ideas from both legal systems were mixed through the process of training lawyers, in his opinion, in an erroneous way.

In practice, the process, even for attorneys, was complex. Although the Americanization of the law has been represented as a struggle between Puerto Rican and American groups, recent studies have shown that in the first years of government by the United States, the Puerto Rican legal profession also attempted to redefine the process to support their own agenda (see Nazario Velasco 1996, 401–8). One of these projects, possibly the most important for the survival and legitimization of the profession, was the legalization of conflict-resolution procedures—that is, the growing dependence on courts to resolve matters between citizens or between the state and its citizens. Access to the courts facilitated the acceptance of court proceedings by common citizens as the norm to solve a large part of their everyday circumstances.

It was not until the 1950s that, as a consequence of the recognition by the U.S. Congress that Puerto Rico could organize its own government, the restructuring of the legal system in Puerto Rico began to lead to its present form. The 1950 Organic Law of the Judiciary established a sole judicial district in Puerto Rico—that is, created a unified jurisdiction over the entire territory. This partially and temporarily solved some practical problems, such as the unequal work distribution in courts throughout the island, the inefficient use of public funds, and the congestion in the courts' calendars. Nonetheless, problems still existed, such as the unequal workload among municipal courts and the functioning of the justices of the peace, whose work depended on the population distribution and the complexity of the socioeconomic structures of each town. Although some courts were overburdened, the workload was much lighter in others.

The commonwealth constitution of 1952 completely reorganized the judicial branch. It created a Supreme Court with the responsibility for establishing an integrated judicial system. Prominent Puerto Rican attorneys, the majority of whom were educated at the University of Puerto Rico Law School, participated in drafting the constitution and other related laws. Abounding in their submitted proposals were references to the need for a "responsible administration" and the "efficient operations" the new system would use in its new scientific approach to a new legal culture. One of the revolutionary principles of the reform was judicial independence. This principle also included the power that the Supreme Court had to organize the lower courts. The other important constitutional principle was the integrated jurisdiction, functioning, and administration of the courts in Puerto Rico. An integrated system would be more efficient, would permit the equal distribution of the casework, and would give greater administrative flexibility (Informe de la Comisión de la Rama Judicial 1961, 2609). This broke with previous ideas about special courts by emphasizing judicial specialization rather than court specialization as a mode for reducing the constant need to increase the number of judges. As part of the guarantee for judicial independence, the Judicial Branch Commission recommended that the Legislative Assembly adopt various ways to prohibit political participation by judges.

In the Law of the Judiciary of 1952, the act that organized the new legal system under the commonwealth constitution, there were, among other novel elements, two that supported the above-mentioned scientific conception of the law. The first is the organization of judicial conferences. This program improved the administration of justice through critical evaluations of the courts (Report on the Judicial Administration Law of Puerto Rico [1952], cited in Trías Monge 1978, 141, 277). Judicial conferences also encouraged the professional development of judges and attorneys, as well as of the other technical personnel of the courts. Furthermore, they contributed to the expansion of the role of the courts with regard to social and economic aspects of society, because often the themes of the conferences bridged the gap between the judiciary and the rest of society by studying matters and problems of broad interest but with legal consequences.[5]

The second new element was the establishment of a legal services program for people of low economic means. Until then, pro bono attorneys were appointed by the court but did not have the resources to do their job adequately. The Puerto Rican low-income population could not turn to the courts, even to claim their fundamental rights, because they could not pay the cost of litigation. Under the Law of the Judiciary, the General Justice Court and the Office of the Administration of the Courts coordinated with the Bar Association and the University of Puerto Rico Law School to "stimulate the development of energetic and efficient methods for proportioning legal services to those who need them" (Trías Monge 1978, 141). These programs have had limited scope because of a lack of funding, but nonetheless have been important in the process of society's "legalization" by allowing people who previously did not have access to the courts to litigate their claims.

Both matters coincide with the reorganization of the curriculum in the Law School at the University of Puerto Rico and its expansion to include a legal services clinic. Therefore, the new government's objectives were in harmony with those of the university with regard to the legal system and the institutional help that the latter could offer as the only institution of higher education in the state. Furthermore, during the first fifteen years after the approval of the 1952 Law of the Judiciary, there were important studies carried out under the supervision of the Puerto Rican Supreme Court in collaboration with the University of Puerto Rico on problems such as the juvenile courts, the merit system in the courts, and judicial efficiency.[6]

With the profound reforms established in Puerto Rico by the constitution of 1952, the legal system expanded itself in ways similar to those described by legal scholars elsewhere (see Toharia in this volume). The legal system used this growth to gain credibility for the principle of judicial independence as well as for the rhetoric of efficiency and impartiality surrounding the new judicial branch. The system began to penetrate aspects of social life that were previously relegated to the private sphere and at the same time responded to the new challenges arising with the industrialization and urbanization processes.

In the period between 1952 and 1965, Puerto Rico experienced a series of profound socioeconomic changes. The economy transformed from predominantly agricultural to industrial. Hundreds of factories were established in the areas surrounding the cities, stimulating urban growth. Women entered the industrial and service markets in large numbers and in certain sectors displaced male labor (Silvestrini 1980). Many of these new forms of social structure had direct legal repercussions in statutes, administrative law, and labor and business issues. The larger number of torts, family relations matters, and probate claims were also related to the new urban and industrial surrounding. The legal system had to be modified to attend to the pressures produced by these changes and to ease the process in accord with the times.

The 1952 restructuring of the legal system had two direct consequences. First, it significantly increased the number of judges and attorneys. Second, it created a series of allied and supporting programs that increased the professional personnel and staff of the courts. The number of superior court judges grew from thirty in 1952 to eighty-nine in 1976 (Administración de los Tribunales 1974–75, table B-1). The number of law school students increased rapidly as two private law schools were organized following the curriculum model of the University of Puerto Rico. By the end of the 1990s, Puerto Rico had three accredited law schools and more than fifteen thousand attorneys (Colegio de Abogados de Puerto Rico 1998).

The increase in the number of judges was accompanied by an expansion in the number and function of the professional and technical court personnel. Professional and technical employees were recruited for family relations units and juvenile court services. Some were attorneys, and others acted in investigative and professional support roles. The courts began to use health professionals more frequently, especially psychologists and therapists, whose expert opinions increasingly gained influence in judicial decisions. In criminal cases, parole officers, counselors, and alternative justice programs acquired a central role. In practice, though, the new judicial framework created some contradictory results. At the same time that the administration of justice became more professional in its services and citizens' needs were more often taken into consideration, the court proceedings became more complex, the wait for resolution of the cases longer, and the dissatisfaction more widespread among the citizens who were dealing with a system that did not always promptly resolve their disputes.

Although it is difficult to measure with precision the effects of the reorganization of the legal system in terms of the relationship of courts and their clients, or the improvement in the resolution of cases, there are some indicators showing that the courts became more efficient even though the new structure still had some areas that needed attention. Table 10.3 shows that the number of cases pending at the end of the fiscal year (see column 10) and the total active cases (column 6) increased each year between 1965 and 1975. Some of the rise can be accounted for by the near duplication of the new cases with original jurisdiction in the superior court (see column 3), which indicates a higher rate of clients. However, in terms of the case resolution,

TABLE 10.3

Civil Cases in the Superior Court, Fiscal Years 1965–1966 to 1974–1975

Year	Cases at beginning of fiscal year	Original jurisdiction	New cases Other[a]	New cases Total	Total active cases	Cases resolved On the merits	Cases resolved Other[b]	Cases resolved Total	Cases pending end of year
1965–66	24,770	36,869	1,356	38,335	62,995	17,165	17,741	34,906	28,089
1966–67	26,966	38,273	1,376	39,649	66,615	18,930	20,542	39,472	27,143
1967–68	26,134	42,278	1,453	43,731	69,865	19,623	21,475	41,098	28,767
1968–69	27,285	45,929	1,303	47,232	74,517	20,765	19,781	40,546	33,971
1969–70	31,824	47,424	1,724	49,148	80,972	23,862	20,311	44,173	36,799
1970–71	35,260	51,339	1,605	52,944	88,204	26,146	20,353	46,499	41,705
1971–72	40,691	59,461	1,891	61,352	102,043	31,279	21,670	52,949	49,094
1972–73	47,786	65,455	2,412	67,867	115,653	34,072	24,793	58,865	56,788
1973–74	54,128	71,885	2,120	74,005	128,133	39,455	25,808	65,263	62,870
1974–75	60,961	75,548	1,433	76,981	137,942	45,190	38,184	83,374	54,568

SOURCE: Administración de Tribunales, *Informe anual,* 1974–75.
NOTE: Figures from *Informe anual* do not indicate that cases pending at the end of one year equal the cases pending at the beginning of the next year.
[a] Other new cases include those transferred to the superior court, appeals from the district court, and cases reinstated.
[b] Other cases resolved include those filed without action, transactions, *desestimados (traduccion),* and appealed to Supreme Court.

the increase in new cases was over 100 percent, with the noncontentious cases increasing 3.7 times between 1965 and 1975. In general, the courts were able to deal with more cases but still had a large caseload unattended.

Figure 10.1 (case distribution by topic) shows that 33 percent of the civil cases handled in the superior court pertained to family law. This fact is interesting because the family was an area traditionally understood to be in the private arena in which the legal system had a relatively small part. Nonetheless, with the incorporation of a larger number of women in professional and industrial sectors of the economy and the corresponding feminist mobilization in the 1970s, many groups began to demand a legislative recognition of gender equality. In spite of the fact that the commonwealth constitution prohibited sexual discrimination, there remained in the 1970s innumerable legal statutes discriminating against and subordinating women, many related to family law. The civil code of 1902, revised in 1930, echoed social practices that kept women, particularly married women, in a state of subordination to their husbands. Thanks to the work of diverse feminist groups, many new theories in labor and family law rose to prominence. In 1976, changes in family law, such as the coadministration of the *sociedad legal de gananciales* (community property) and the shared roles in child custody, were approved. These legislative changes, together with the restructuring of the legal administration, opened the doors for a greater number of women to claim rights for themselves and for their children in the courts. In spite of the ap-

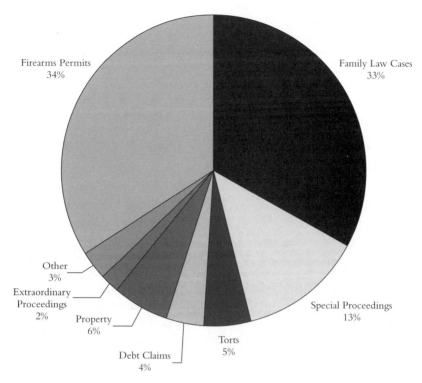

FIGURE 10.1 Case Distribution in the Superior Court, 1974–1975

parent legal equality of women and their easier access to the courts, these systemic reforms did not always benefit women equally. In reality, the system resulted in an excessive dependence by women, especially those of lower income levels, on judicial proceedings, even when they were costly and not efficient in practice. Delays continued to be the norm in the courts, and preconceived ideas about gender roles and the lack of direct and effective ways to make decisions over family relations still persist. In the long run, even though the legal system has improved, there are still tensions and incongruity caused by excessive complexity both in formal proceedings and in court-related professional services.

Changes in the practice of family law and the way in which the Puerto Rican legal system faces increasing demand in this area returns us to the themes discussed at the beginning of this chapter. Is there a contradiction or tension in a legal system when the courts oversee child support by establishing a program to regulate parent's compliance with these obligations? Should the courts become active in developing new concepts, such as no-fault or mutual-consent divorce, or intervene to resolve new controversies that reflect the interaction of insurance law and family law, because it would incorporate elements that were not present in the civil code before 1900? Are those new legal developments to be considered "foreign" law because of the political status of Puerto Rico? The increase in citizens' use of the courts to resolve everyday controversies reflects the legal system's transformation to connect with the changes the people have experienced in Puerto Rico throughout this century. In many significant ways, the courts changed as Puerto Rico did, becoming part of trends that are found in other Latin American countries.

The Legal System Since the 1970s

By the end of the 1960s and the beginning of the 1970s, the consequences of the rapid modernization process in Puerto Rico began to show. The population continued to grow, with 50 percent under twenty-one years old, in spite of the widespread migration to the United States. Industrialization increased while agriculture deteriorated. The new industries did not provide enough job opportunities. Although industrial development policies were promoted by the government, unemployment continued to be an acute problem. The rural population experienced an excessive displacement into the urban regions of the island and the large cities of the eastern United States, while diverse sectors saw changes in their living conditions. The increase in random violence was one of the qualitative changes of this period (Silvestrini 1980, 115). Interpersonal and communal tensions multiplied with the disappearance of the most traditional means of resolving conflicts. Violent crimes, thefts, and car thefts increased in such magnitude that everyday life became difficult. Little by little, the criminal courts and the civil courts became the preferred methods for people to resolve their new urban problems: contractual disagreements, disruption of family relations, labor disputes, and control of criminality.

The government's answer to the people's demand was to expand the courts, create more positions for judges, and appropriate more funds for attending to the increase in the number and complexity of cases.[7] For example, at the beginning of fiscal year 1974, the unified court system had a total of 137,413 civil, criminal, and transit cases pending from the previous year. During the year 1974–75, 566,168 new cases were presented to the court for a total workload of 703,581 cases. The annual report of the Administración de los Tribunales (1974–75, 13) shows that in this year the courts resolved 556,009 cases, leaving some 147,572 without resolution at the end of the year. The absolute number of cases is significant because if we consider the total population of Puerto Rico at the time (2,721,754 persons in 1970), at least in theory, one of every four persons could have had a case before the court.

The increase in cases reflects again an expansion of the process of legalization. There was an increased sense that people with claims could go all the way to the Supreme Court to obtain a remedy. A glance at the distribution of cases within the Supreme Court in 1974–75, for example, shows that 41.46 percent of the cases were civil revisions and 37.4 percent were certiorari (which were predominantly of civil nature), and only 4.4 percent were criminal appeals. When the nature of the cases decided by the Supreme Court in 1974–75 is examined, actions in civil cases are predominantly of tort nature instead of a constitutional character as would be expected. Likewise, the majority of criminal cases are related to drug laws, a social problem that by the 1970s was becoming widespread. Therefore, these trends further support the thesis that a greater dependence on the courts to resolve social matters was slowly emerging.

In the annual report for 1974–75, the judiciary considered that one of the most striking problems was the increase in the number of cases presented in the Supreme Court and the consequent delay in their disposition (Administración de los Tribunales 1974–75, 5). In accordance, the Puerto Rican legislature amended the Law of the Judiciary in August 1974 to create the Appellate Division of the Superior Court. The division would function in sections with at least three judges for consideration of each case in appeal.[8] If we consider that criminal appeals constituted only 4.4 percent of the cases before the Supreme Court, this measure by itself could not have succeeded in alleviating the court's calendar. In spite of this measure, the appeals continued to grow and the Supreme Court continued to have an overloaded case calendar, supporting again the thesis of society's overlegalization.

Another significant reform was approved by the Puerto Rican legislature in 1974—the requirement that municipal judges must be lawyers who are admitted to the bar.[9] This new requirement responded to criticisms as early as the beginning of the twentieth century that justices of the peace did not have to have a legal education. With this step, the process of professionalizing the system advanced because it would mandate a common basis of training for all judges. Through the bar examinations, the Supreme Court also had control over the formal education and training standards of the legal profession.

The goal to organize the legal system scientifically as a foundation for modernization defined the Supreme Court's efforts to reform the legal system in the 1970s. In 1973, the Puerto Rican legislature approved a law authorizing the judicial branch to establish and regulate an independent system of personnel. It also legislated the establishment of an autonomous budget for the judicial branch that would not depend on the executive but would be directly approved by the legislature. Two years later, the Office of the Administration of the Courts was restructured with the responsibility of establishing a "scientific" personnel system, a more efficient method of handling the caseload, and the collection of effective statistics about the system. The office was also charged with developing effective budget management practices. This scientific reform, as it was called at the time, became the practical framework of the legal system but did not necessarily solve its problem. Overall, these measures affirmed the principle of a judiciary autonomous from the rest of the Puerto Rican government but added complicated, sometimes more bureaucratic, obligations.[10] The judicial branch then had to develop job descriptions, create administrative norms, and administer its own budget.[11] The 1975 annual report of the judicial branch incorporated the concept of modernization when it explained that the changes it had made "accorded with the requirements of our time" (p. 38). As part of the reorganization, more reliable judicial statistics and the introduction of computers were considered indispensable, not only to maintain up-to-date information but also to better serve the lawyers and citizens.[12]

Part of the reorganization of the legal system was the creation of direct service programs for the users. These services were not legal in nature but social and extended the work of the courts even farther from the judicial. The Diagnostic and Treatment Clinic for Juveniles, for example, had as its goal to respond "to the need for studying the juvenile in all that could explain the antisocial conduct that occasions his appearance at the Court" (Administración de los Tribunales 1974–75, 45). To this effect, the services of social workers, psychologists, psychiatrists, and neurologists were recruited. Juveniles with charges before the superior court were referred to judges or court social services personnel to receive direct help. Definitively, this was a novel expansion of the court's roles and its entrance to the new world of sociomedical and social science research. Beyond referring people to the services of the independent professionals, the court contracted with counselors and psychologists who provided assistance in direct programs under the auspices of the courts. These initiatives strengthen the courts' participation in the welfare state, as the legal system serves as intermediary in interpersonal and community relations.

As part of these new court functions, the family relations division expanded. In this sphere, the legal system also went beyond its traditional responsibilities and undertook a social function as keeper of the "principle that the family is the primary base of society and a source of great security and well-being for the individual." The courts organized direct services "to guide the strengthening of the family to avoid its disintegration, taking into account the self-determination of the individual in relation to the cultural and social values existing and in the process of change" (Administración de los Tribunales 1974–75, 51). This social rhetoric, in line with the social and civil rights reform that characterized the times, made the legal system's new social responsibility stand out—that of counteracting the other paths or the undesirable results of the modernization policy promoted by the government. The cited annual report from 1975 concludes on this particular point: "The familial disintegration could result in the abandonment of children, the deterioration of conjugal and paternal relations, the maladjusted and delinquent juvenile and adult" (51). Therefore, the legal system would acquire a much more proactive role in social reform—that is, the task of avoiding possible deterioration resulting from the modernization. Thus, it offered direct services to those whom the system touched in one way or another.

These trends continued throughout the 1980s. Year after year the Office of the Administration of the Courts complained of overloaded calendars, lack of funds for administering the courts, and the need for more personnel. But there was little realization that the legal system had become increasingly complex, not necessarily because it handled more cases per capita, but because the courts had acquired additional functions. A decade later, the superior court had one hundred judges and a budget of more than $82 million to attend to 172,432 criminal and civil cases.[13] The family relations cases took up the largest percentage of the volume of unresolved cases (Rama Judicial de Puerto Rico 1988–89, 19).

Judicial reform was not again considered until the 1990s, even though some of the problems of the system had existed since the 1970s. Among the issues raised in the public debate was the recognition of the right to appeals in civil cases. Also included were the workload of the Supreme Court and the inequality of work among judges, where some courtrooms had overburdened calendars and others had significantly fewer cases. The Law of the Judiciary was amended in 1991 to include the municipal court in the court of first instance, therefore changing its character to an adjudicative court. Although the position of municipal judge had been created in 1974 when the law provided for the gradual elimination of the justice of the peace post, the old municipal court had only investigative functions and issued bail, arrest, and search orders. The municipal court remained as a separate level of courts and without any adjudicative responsibilities until 1991 (Rama Judicial de Puerto Rico 1988–89, 19; 1992–93, 5). This change was the final step in the creation of a unified legal system for the jurisdiction of Puerto Rico as it had been intended since the constitution was enacted (see Figure 10.2).

Nonetheless, the principal debate for reform was over the need to create an appellate level in the court system. The commonwealth constitution created the Supreme Court as the final appeal level, establishing its competency in a limited number of actions and giving it the power to review judgments handed down by the courts of first instance.[14] For many years, different

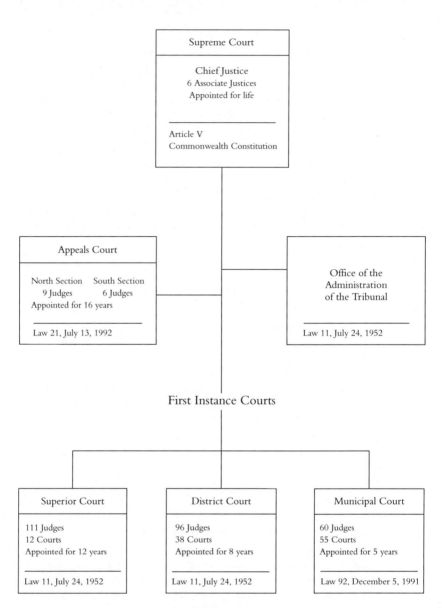

FIGURE 10.2 Organization of the Judicial Branch, 1995

studies of the Puerto Rican judicial branch suggested creating an intermediate forum for appeals, but the idea was rejected because of its high cost and potential for lengthy delay of any final resolution of the cases, creating another step in the legal system.[15] It was not until 1987 that the creation of an appellate division was considered in a positive way, a court "with competency to oversee civil, criminal, and administrative cases accompanied by the proposal of reestablishing the right to appeal in civil cases resolved by the Superior Court" (Informe de la Comisión Asesora del Juez Presidente sobre la Estructura y Funcionamiento del Tribunal de Primera Instancia 1987, 5.) The justification for this new court was predicated on two principles. First, the structure favored the idea of appellate justice as collegial, where a decision made by a panel of judges was better than one made by an individual. Second, it tried to resolve the inequality presented by the civil cases that were decided in first instance by the superior court. Beginning in 1974, the district and municipal court decisions could be appealed in a collegial forum at the superior court, but the civil cases presented in first instance in the superior court, except those accepted in revision by the Supreme Court, did not have anywhere to go on appeal.

Accordingly, a bill for the creation of the appellate court was proposed in 1992.[16] The bill tried to address the inequality of opportunities for litigation, stating that "it would give to all litigants a real opportunity, at present unavailable, for the decisions of one judge in the court of first instance to be reviewed by several judges of a superior level. Through this forum, we can answer the demand for a social democratic conscience dedicated to the goal of equal justice for all" (Departamento de Justicia 1992). A new law was passed that created the Puerto Rican appellate court as a court of intermediate record between the Supreme Court and the court of first instance.[17] Furthermore, the law gave the right of appeal in civil cases; the right of appeal had not previously existed as such and was available only through discretionary review. In its first year of operation, the Supreme Court referred 526 cases to the appeals court, reducing almost by half the number of cases pending before the Supreme Court (Rama Judicial de Puerto Rico 1993, 14). The life of this appeals court, nonetheless, was not long. It became entangled in a political polemic and was dissolved within a year (Alvarez González 1996; Comentario 1994).

Although the 1992 law was repealed in 1993, the idea of an appellate court still had support, and a new Law of the Judiciary in 1994, as amended by Law Number 248 on December 25, 1995, created the circuit court of appeals.[18] This court serves as an intermediate court between the court of first instance and the Supreme Court, constituting a single section seated in San Juan.[19] The principal goal of this reform was to lessen the Supreme Court's workload by providing an appellate level to attend to a large part of the pending cases. Although there still has not been a complete evaluation of this court's operations, the director of the courts administration reported that the cost of the judicial reform as of March 1999 surpassed $37,915,708. Between 1995 and 1999, 23 new appeals judges and 182 new judges of first instance have been named (Bauermeister 1999, 941, 947).[20]

The new layer in the legal system, like the increase in the number of judges and the budget, supports the thesis of this chapter. In the 1990s, the legal system expanded even more. The number and the complexity of the cases increased, more judges were appointed, and the number of court functionaries grew, along with the operational budget for the system. Unfortunately for Puerto Rico, legal issues are only resolved by the "highway to the courts." Public policy efforts to develop alternative dispute-resolution methods have been limited and have not gained sufficient credibility to substantially relieve the courts' calendars. Neither the bar association nor the law schools have incorporated this agenda as part of the solution to the problem of excessive legalization of society, perhaps because the profession sees itself as directed toward litigation. Over time, in spite of the intense criticism by academics and jurists, the legal system has maintained the trust of the thousands of citizens that resort to its courtrooms in search of solutions to their claims.

Conclusion

A century after the American occupation of Puerto Rico and after various judicial reforms, prominent Puerto Rican attorneys and jurists continue protesting that "our law [referring to the Puerto Rican legal system] is in good measure the law of others. Vast zones of judicial order are governed by laws in whose creation our people did not participate or, when they did, their participation was for the great part symbolic" (Trías Monge 1978, 242). According to José Trías Monge, even when the judicial reforms created their own models, the judicial system was a victim "of a defective vision" and adopted "basic premises of the old law . . . in bewildering and inconsistent form[s]. . . . We altered the roles of case-law, legislation and doctrine, though court decisions still reflect a marked ambivalence about these extremes. Our view of the law is closer to the Anglo-Saxon tradition than to that of civil law countries" (245). Trías Monge concludes that "it is vital that Puerto Rico finally formulate its own law" (249).

We have seen, nonetheless, how the practice of law has forged the legal system, how it has tried to respond to the problems that Puerto Ricans confront in their daily lives. We have also documented how citizens, in spite of the delays and limitations of the legal system, trust it by using it. The contrary would be to assert that the clients of the legal system are mistaken because they increasingly use a system to which they object. The legal systems are continuously changing, because they are part of historical processes that are continuously changing (Friedman 1975). These transformations adapt to and adopt new styles, approaches, and practices. They are validated or not in their acceptance and use, and some are even contradictory (Munger 1990; Stookey 1990). Legal systems are not complete nor is their structure set in a straight line, because they respond to and form part of the historical processes of a country (Friedman 1975). The theoretical analysis of why and how the legal system in Puerto Rico became institutionalized, in spite of the colonial context in which it was organized, goes beyond the scope of this chapter. But it is valuable to mention the intricate ties between the processes of giving credibility to the system and the transformations that have been occurring in society. Although some scholars have explained the process as a form of support and sanction to the exercise of power, it seems that in the case of Puerto Rico, the legal system has also helped to mold those power relations. This double bind has possibly facilitated the recognition of the notion of the rule of law as a social value in spite of the internal and political contradictions the legal system has faced (Sugarman 1981; Rivera Ramos 2001). Furthermore, as Gordon (1984) argues, a good part of the system provides the ideological and linguistic tools for those who exercise power, as well as for those who resist the power, by marking off the boundaries between the camps that fight for it.

In Puerto Rico, once the legal system was rooted in the rule of law by the constitutional reform of 1952, a certain critical trust grew that promoted its growth. The legal system legitimated at the same time that it created the categories through which it would function and be evaluated in the social realm. In this way, it formed a strong knot between legal and social processes (Bordieu 1987). Even further, this popular legitimation of the process is related in part to the understanding by its clients that the legal system provides a "scientific manner" by which to solve controversies. Part of the credibility ascribed to the system comes from the belief that using scientific methods in the practice of law and in the courts would guarantee "the infallibility of knowledge and articulation of the social reality in the laws" (Nazario Velasco 1999, 29).

Through this chapter, I am hoping to open an area of debate and research that explores the diverse issues raised by the legal system's transformation as the century progressed—and its relation to the social and economic changes in Puerto Rico. These issues include the establishment and use of the new juvenile courts, the bureaucratization of the relationship between the citizen and the state, the surge of hundreds of administrative law cases, and, most important, the structure of criminal justice. A study of the new legal culture accompanying these changes, although difficult, could illuminate the apparent gap between the assertions of the powerful groups in the judicial profession and the way in which other sectors of the profession have understood, used, and criticized the legal system. Finally, it would be interesting to explore "the reform spirit" that dominated through distinct manifestations and stages the work of the government and civil society and the results of these reforms that continue to infuse the courts. After all, as Lawrence Friedman (1975) has stated in his book *The Legal System*: "Social theories of law suggest that at any given time existing rules reflect with rough accuracy those social forces actually bearing on the subject of the rules. . . . [Therefore] the legal system will probably reflect *all* social forces in proportion to their influence and power" (307). Because of this, we should not consider it strange that when confronting the critical theories about the collision of legal systems in Puerto Rico, we find the citizens using the system as a contemporary adaptation in their own process of historical and cultural creation.

Notes

1. Starting with the reforms of 1952, the legal system became "Puerto Ricanized" —that is, it began to respond more directly to the Puerto Ricans' way of thinking and to the needs of the country. The theorists continued to question its legitimacy, but its users, much less so. The question of how the legal system won legitimacy in the minds of much of the legal profession and the public is still open. This chapter will present the general trends, but more detailed studies of this issue have yet to be developed.

2. Immediately after a military government of the United States was established in 1898, the U.S. Congress began to study conditions in its newly acquired territory. One of the factors it watched carefully was the legal system, which it considered to be a fundamental piece in the process of Americanization and cultural change. This idea was planted by Governor Davis in congressional hearings in 1900, when he stated: "One subject of great importance, concerning which almost all Americans wish to ask questions, is the judiciary. A complicated system of procedure existed, one which we could not understand or could not master with facility. After long consultation and the preparation of drafts or projects outlining changes, the leading lawyers of the island and the leading judges, speaking through a judicial board, recommended a revision of the system of procedure. . . . These changes were recommended by native Puerto Ricans, and they were implanted by me as military commander, and much improvement has resulted" (U.S. Congress 1900, 5).

3. The founding of the University of Puerto Rico in 1903 was part of this initial

process of modernization, as much for its organization as for its training of a large proportion of the professionals who embarked on the work to realize the changes.

4. In 1938, the law program established a bachelor's degree as a requirement for admission. In 1944, the Law School of the University of Puerto Rico joined the Association of American Law Schools and in 1945 was accredited by the American Bar Association.

5. Some of the most recent studies of the judicial conference, such as the report on gender discrimination in the courts, are good examples of this trend (Tribunal Supremo de Puerto Rico 1995).

6. It is interesting to note that both measures used the American legal system as a model. At both the federal and state levels, there were legal services available to the poor. The measures also promoted the professional development of court personnel beyond the law school arenas.

7. Furthermore, in criminal cases there was an increase in the number of police, crime control agencies, and prisons (Silvestrini 1980).

8. This would serve appeals in the criminal cases processed in the superior court through certiorari to review final sentences of the superior court in those cases generally initiated in the district court and in other criminal matters that the superior court disposed of (Law Number 11, August 8, 1974).

9. Law Number 7, August 8, 1974.

10. The organization of the Office of the Administration of the Courts in 1975 is complex: three departments, each with at least three divisions, and four other divisions related to each other through planning, auditing information, organization, methods, and legal issues. There were two administrative divisions (auxiliary services and personnel). The most interesting was the social services division, which attended to family matters, juveniles, and child support. It provided direct services to the users and their attorneys (Administración de los Tribunales 1974–75, 30).

11. For example, in 1975 the administration of justice system had 2,791 employees: 167 in the Supreme Court; 258 in court administration; 1,438 in the superior courts; 786 in the district courts; 15 municipal judges; and 127 justices of the peace (Administración de los Tribunales 1974–75, 37).

12. The Office of the Administration of the Courts also developed a mechanism to collect child support payments and to provide statistical information on criminal offenses to other government agencies. It planned to collect computerized information on the criminal files of people, vehicles and stolen articles, arms registries, missing persons, persons on bail, fugitives, case calendars, criminal statistics, and other data (Administración de los Tribunales 1974–75, 38, 39).

13. In 1988–89, there were 118,999 criminal and civil cases presented, adding to the 53,433 pending. Of these, 112,358 were resolved, leaving 60,074 pending (Rama Judicial de Puerto Rico 1988–89, 19).

14. Law of the Judiciary, sec. 31. The superior court has by law the responsibility to attend to the appeals proceeding from the district court and municipal court decisions (secs. 221–22).

15. This point of view had been expressed since the discussion of Law Number 115 on June 26, 1958. On this occasion, José Trías Monge proposed that instead

of creating a new appeals level, the positions of superior and district court judges should be strengthened (Diario de Sesiones la Asamblea Legislativa de Puerto Rico [Diary of the Legislative Assembly Sessions] 1958, 10, 66, 1565–66). Later studies concurred with this position, showing that in addition to raising the cost, it delayed the final resolution of the cases. For a complete summary, see Comentario en torno al Tribunal de Apelaciones (1994, 143).

16. For details, see P. del S. 1313 (Departamento de Justicia 1992).

17. Law Number 21, July 13, 1992.

18. Law Number 11, June 2, 1993, repealed the appeals court law. Immediately, the judges named to the court appealed the decision to the Supreme Court, but the issue became moot with the approval of the next Law of the Judiciary.

19. The circuit court of appeals is composed of thirty-three judges. The judges are appointed by the governor of Puerto Rico with the advice and consent of the Senate and perform their duties for sixteen years. The court is divided into eleven panels, each one with three judges, distributed territorially. The circuit court of appeals reviews through the appeals system all the final sentences, civil or criminal, dictated by the court of first instance (Law Number 248, December 25, 1995).

20. In addition to the new judges, others were promoted to create a total of 355 judges in Puerto Rico. These are divided as follows: 7 Supreme Court judges, 33 circuit court of appeals judges, and 315 court of first instance judges.

References

Administración de los Tribunales. 1951–96. *Informe anual.* San Juan, P.R. Mimeographed.

———. 1995–96. *Informe anual Rama Judicial.* San Juan, P.R.

Alvarez González, José Julián. 1996. La nueva ley de la Judicatura y la competencia obligatoria del Tribunal Supremo: Algunas jorobas de un solo camello. *Revista Jurídica de la Universidad de Puerto Rico* 65:1–82.

Bauermeister, Mercedes M. 1999. Ponencia en el Foro La Ley de la Judicatura de 1994: Un análisis crítico de sus efectos. *Revista Jurídica de la Universidad de Puerto Rico* 68:941–49.

Bordieu, Pierre. 1987. The force of law: Toward a sociology of the juridical field. *The Hastings Law Journal* 38:805–50.

Carroll, Henry K. 1899. *Report on the Island of Porto Rico.* Washington, D.C.: U.S. Government Printing Office.

Colegio de Abogados de Puerto Rico. 1998. *Informe anual.* San Juan, P.R.

Comentario en torno al Tribunal de Apelaciones. 1994. *Revista Jurídica de la Universidad de Puerto Rico* 63:143–48.

Delgado Cintrón, Carmelo. 1978. Cuestiones ideológicas del Poder Judicial en Puerto Rico. *Revista Jurídica de la Universidad de Puerto Rico* 47:107.

———. 1980. La administración de justicia en Puerto Rico durante el gobierno militar de Estados Unidos, 1898–1900. *Revista Jurídica de la Universidad de Puerto Rico* 49:333.

———. 1982. La organización judicial de Puerto Rico, 1800–1898. *Revista Jurídica de la Universidad de Puerto Rico* 51:381–402.

————. 1988. *Derecho y colonialismo: La trayectoria histórica del derecho puertorriqueño.* Río Piedras, P.R.: Editorial Edil.

Departamento de Justicia. 1992. Informe sobre el P. del S. 1313 a las Comisiones de los Jurídico y de Hacienda, 8 de mayo. Cited in Comentario en torno al Tribunal de Apelaciones, *Revista Jurídica de la Universidad de Puerto Rico* 63 (1994):144–99.

Diario de Sesiones la Asamblea Legislativa de Puerto Rico [Diary of the Legislative Assembly Sessions]. 1958. Vol. 10, no. 66, pp. 1565–66.

Friedman, Lawrence M. 1975. *The legal system: A social science perspective.* New York: Russell Sage.

Gordon, Robert. 1984. Critical legal histories. *Stanford Law Review* 36:57–125.

Informe de la Comisión Asesora del Juez Presidente sobre la Estructura y Funcionamiento del Tribunal de Primera Instancia. 1987. *Revista del Colegio de Abogados de Puerto Rico* 48.2.

Informe de la Comisión de la Rama Judicial. 1966. *Diario de Sesiones de la Convención Constituyente de Puerto Rico* 4:2609.

Informe sobre la Ley de la Judicatura de Puerto Rico. 1952. En Archivo, Secretaría del Tribunal Supremo. In *El sistema judicial de Puerto Rico,* by José Trías Monge. San Juan, P.R.: Editorial de la Universidad de Puerto Rico.

Merryman, John H., David S. Clark, and Lawrence M. Friedman. 1979. *Law and social change in Mediterranean Europe and Latin America: A handbook of legal and social indicators for comparative study.* New York: Dobbs Ferry.

Munger, F. 1990. Trial courts and social change: The evolution of the field of study. *Law and Society Review* 24:217–26.

Nazario Velasco, Rubén. 1996. Negociación en la tradición legal: Los abogados y el estado colonial en Puerto Rico, 1898–1905. Ph.D. diss., University of Puerto Rico.

————. 1999. *Discurso legal y orden poscolonial: Los abogados de Puerto Rico ante el 1898.* Hato Rey, P.R.: Publicaciones Puertorriqueñas.

Rama Judicial de Puerto Rico. 1988–98. *Informe anual.* San Juan: P.R. Mimeographed.

Rivera Ramos, Efrén. 2001. The legal construction of identity: The judicial and social legacy of American colonialism in Puerto Rico. Washington, D.C.: American Psychological Association.

Silvestrini, Blanca G. 1980. *Violencia y criminalidad en Puerto Rico (1898–1973).* San Juan, P.R.: Editorial de la Universidad de Puerto Rico.

Stookey, John A. 1990. Trials and tribulations: Crises, litigation, and legal change. *Law and Society Review* 24:497–520.

Sugarman, David. 1981. Theory and practice in law and history: A prologue to the study of the relationship between law and economics from the socio-historical perspective. In *Law, State and Society,* edited by Robert Fryer. London: Croom Helm.

Trías Monge, José. 1978. *El sistema judicial de Puerto Rico.* San Juan, P.R.: Editorial de la Universidad de Puerto Rico.

————. 1991. *El choque de dos culturas jurídicas en Puerto Rico: El caso de la responsabilidad extracontractual.* San Juan: Equity Publishing.

Tribunal Supremo de Puerto Rico. 1995. *Informe anual, 1995–96.* San Juan, P.R. Mimeographed.

U.S. Congress. 1900. *Hearings before the United States Senate Committee on Pacific Islands and Porto Rico, on Senate Bill 2264.* 56th Cong., 2d sess., S. Doc. 147. Washington, D.C.: U.S. Government Printing Office.

CHAPTER 11

The Organization, Functioning, and Evaluation of the Spanish Judicial System, 1975–2000: A Case Study in Legal Culture

JOSÉ JUAN TOHARIA

OVER THE LAST quarter of the twentieth century, Spain has experienced a dramatic transformation as a result of three basic and interlocking processes of change. Since the mid-1960s and in the wake of the postwar economic recovery of Western Europe, Spain has experienced an intense process of economic growth that ultimately placed it among the most developed countries in the world.[1] On the other hand, in the second half of the 1970s, Spain returned to democratic rule under the form of a parliamentary monarchy,[2] with free elections in 1977 and the enactment in 1978 of the current constitution.[3] Finally, in the mid-1980s, Spain formally became a member of the European Community—now the European Union (EU). By the end of the 1990s, Spain became one of the eleven EU members that agreed to have their national currencies replaced by a common new currency (the euro) as of March 2002: apparently a merely economic measure, but in fact a decision full of symbolic meaning in terms of national sovereignty and supranational integration. (For a political chronology, see Table 11.10 at the end of the chapter.)

Economic development, democratic recovery, and European integration are thus the elements that have marked Spanish life in a radical way over the last three decades. The aim of this chapter is to analyze the degree to which these deep processes of change may have influenced Spanish legal culture.[4] The way in which a system of justice is organized, the way in which it performs its functions in everyday practice, and the way in which it is perceived and evaluated by the citizenry represent instances in which legal cultural factors can be said to be at work. Thus the organization, the functioning, and the social image of the Spanish system of justice will be treated here as telling indicators of the complex set of values and cultural patterns usually referred to as legal culture.

This chapter is organized in three sections, each one attempting to answer a basic question:

1. **The organization of justice**: What legal-cultural elements can be said to lie behind the Spanish system of justice as it now appears to be organized?
2. **The use of justice**: To what extent has the new social, economic, and political context affected the way in which courts are used by the citizenry? The recourse to courts has been traditionally very low in Spain: Have litigation rates varied perceptibly during the period we are considering (1975–2000)?
3. **The image of justice**: What is the prevailing image of the system of justice within Spanish society? How do the citizens evaluate the way in which it performs its functions?

The Organization of the Spanish System of Justice: A Few Relevant Features

The restitution of democracy in Spain was not followed by the establishment of a brand-new system of justice.[5] Spain belongs to the civil law tradition (and to be more specific, to the Romanistic or Napoleonic variant within it),[6] and civil law systems have shown a remarkable ability to float past social and political upheavals.[7]

As a result, the present system of justice combines a basic structure, two centuries old, with implants of new mechanisms and institutions brought about by the return to democracy and the integration into a supranational entity (the European Union). A formal portrait of the present Spanish system of justice might read as follows:

Justice emanates from the people and is administered in the name of the king by a self-governing body of independent, responsible, and professional judges,[8] in accordance with certain principles and criteria (such as absence of judicial creativity, subjection to a specific set of "sources of the law," appeals, written opinions expressing reasons, popular participation in some criminal cases, free access, publicity, and, in the penal area, the inquisitorial system) within a system of courts comprising four specialized areas (civil, criminal, labor, and administrative) and subject to review in matters concerning basic individual rights by the *Tribunal Constitucional* (Constitutional Court).

Three additional features should also be mentioned. Over the last two decades, the Spanish judiciary has been strongly rejuvenated, it has experienced a deep and rapid process of feminization, and it has achieved a substantial degree of internal ideological pluralism.

On the whole, this global description seems to contain hardly any truly original feature: with minor adaptations it could be said to describe the system of justice in most of the EU countries (or, for that matter, in any democratic civil law country). What is remarkable is that it can now be fully applied to the case of Spain—for long a deviant case within the European civil law family. The Spanish system of justice has moved away from its configuration in 1975, and in the process of adapting itself to the new democratic institutional setting, developments of an unexpected and far-reaching significance became possible.[9]

JUDICIAL INDEPENDENCE

No authoritarian regime can be really expected to have a reasonably independent judiciary, and Franco's Spain (1939–75) was far from being an exception. Consequently, the topic of judicial independence became a pressing issue as soon as democracy was established. The scheme provided in this respect by the 1978 constitution can be summarized in just three words: "independence through self-government." The General Council of the Judiciary (*Consejo General del Poder Judicial*; henceforth CGPJ), basically modeled along the lines of the Italian *Consiglio della Magistratura*, was created to act both as guardian of judicial independence and as governing board of the judicial system. The Ministry of Justice still exists but is completely deprived of its traditional powers with respect to the selection, promotion, and supervision of the judiciary. The CGPJ is composed of twenty members plus a president elected by its members.[10] The president may be one of the members, or an outsider. The president of the CGPJ automatically becomes president of the Supreme Court as well.[11] Neither the public prosecutors (*ministerio fiscal*) nor the auxiliary personnel of justice (clerks, officials, assistants, and agents) fall under the authority of the CGPJ because, strictly speaking, they are not defined as part of the judicial profession. The management of what may be called the "logistics of justice" (that is, auxiliary personnel, facilities, work conditions) falls to the Ministry of Justice except in those regions (*comunidades autónomas*) where such a responsibility has already been transferred to the respective regional governments.[12]

Under the present constitution, the concept "judicial independence" means in fact "personal independence of each individual judge": in the application of the law to particular cases, judges are indeed required to be subject only "to the authority of the law" (art. 117.1 of the SC). That is, they have to make personal decisions without outside interference of any kind. For instance, they are not allowed to address themselves to superior courts for advice or guidance, nor can superior courts make indications or suggestions concerning the resolution of specific cases.[13] As for the supervisory powers attributed to the CGPJ over the functioning of the judicial machinery, in no instance can they be extended to the way in which judges have interpreted and applied the law in their decisions.[14] A corollary of judicial independence is that it is legally impossible for judges to belong to political parties or unions.[15]

As a result of the way in which they perform their duties, judges can incur civil, penal, or disciplinary liability. Civil and penal liabilities are assessed by the ordinary courts, as would be the case with any other citizen, whereas disciplinary sanctions for judicial misconduct fall exclusively to the CGPJ.

A UNIFIED SYSTEM OF COURTS

The mention of a unified system of courts as a remarkable novelty is bound to seem surprising to any outside observer. However, in the Spanish historical context the establishment of a unified system of courts has represented a change full of symbolic significance. Under Francoism (1939–75), the Administration of Justice was articulated, in practice, in two parallel and differentiated systems: on the one side, ordinary justice, substantially independent from political power but strongly limited in its field of action; on the other, a broad and complex set of special courts, which were entrusted with all matters with some degree of political relevance and which were closely controlled by the government.[16] The system of justice could thus be described as both basically independent and narrowly controlled, depending on the dimension of law under consideration.[17] The constitution of 1978 (art. 117.5) established the principle of jurisdictional unity, with the abolition and prohibition of all special courts. As a result, the system of justice was clearly strengthened, overcoming the "independent as long as powerless" type of situation it had experienced under Francoism (Toharia 1975, chap. 11).

This unified system of courts is nevertheless compatible with the functional specialization of courts. Spanish justice, at present, covers four large and differentiated areas: civil, penal, labor (technically referred to as "social"), and administrative.[18] These four areas already existed in 1975 at the end of Franco Spain, but with important differences in status and internal organization.[19] The democratic regime has redefined them as specialties within a single and unified system of ordinary justice—that is, currently they are all served by the same body of judges who can travel freely from courts in one area to courts in another (provided they have previously acquired the corresponding specialization).

THE SOURCES OF THE LAW AND JUDICIAL CREATIVITY

In their decisions, judges must limit themselves to the application of "law, custom, and the general principles of the law" (art. 1, para. 1 and 7 of the civil code; henceforth CC).[20] This means that, in principle, judges cannot create law nor base their decisions on "sources of law" other than the three just mentioned (although as will be seen, the existence of a constitution and membership within the European Union have now contributed to the complexity of this issue).[21]

Also according to article 1 of the CC, primacy among the three cited sources belongs in all cases to statutory law.[22] Custom will be taken into account only in the absence of applicable statutes and "as long as it is not contrary to morality or public order and can adequately be proved to be in existence."[23] The general principles of the law apply only in the absence of appropriate statutory law or custom.

This officially established hierarchy of sources of the law represents a combination of highly formalized norms (statutory law), with mere customary practices and folkways (custom) and with highly generic, abstract, and value-laden formulations (the general principles of the law).[24]

The rulings of the Supreme Court—that is, judicial precedents (whose official name in most civil law countries—*jurisprudencia, jurisprudence, giurisprudenza*—may cause confusion to persons trained in the common law tradition)—are given a somewhat ambiguous status in the recently revised article 1.6 of the CC, which states that the body of norms in force is to be complemented with the "precedents established in a repeated way by the Supreme Court when interpreting statutes, customs and general principles."[25] Should this complementary nature be taken to mean that Supreme Court rulings must be granted the same binding power as the three classical sources of law? The dominant interpretation is that the jurisprudencia coming from the Supreme Court does not constitute a source of the law and consequently lacks any real binding power. However, the Supreme Court itself has established that its rulings should guide the decisions of the lower courts: a decision going against Supreme Court precedent may be subject to appeal on that ground alone. But this is just meant as a ground offered to the losing party, not as a compulsory mandate with automatically invalidating effects.[26]

A recent revision of the CC introduced an interesting innovation: judges are now required to interpret the sources of the law "according to the social reality of the time in which they are to be applied" (art. 3.1). Traditionally, judicial interpretation of the law attempted basically to ascertain what might have been the intended purpose of the legislative body when enacting the statute under consideration. This new form of article 3.1 of the CC introduces a totally different perspective: judicial application of the legal norms is now required to be undertaken with a sense of relevancy and adjustment to current social conditions irrespective of the original purpose behind the norm. It would certainly be an exaggeration to conclude that this new requirement fully opens the door to judicial creativity, but it certainly seems to grant judges a remarkable and unprecedented margin of interpretive flexibility.

Finally, the existence of a constitution and the integration within the European Union has implied a de facto but obvious enlargement of the three-fold list of sources of the law. In fact, the constitution does not represent just a new, additional source of the law but "the supreme source of legality" (Diez-Picazo and Gullón 1997, 95). In turn, the rulings of the Constitutional Court, as the only authorized interpreter of the constitution, rank even higher than those of the Supreme Court.[27] Insofar as they establish how constitutional norms must be understood and applied, they represent an obvious and basic source of law.[28]

However, the legislation enacted by the European Union is directly applicable in all member countries and ranks above national legislation; that is, in the event of a contradiction between a national norm and an EU statute, the latter prevails.[29] And the same can be said with regard to the rulings of the Court of Justice of the European Communities, which are directly binding on the member states as well as on their courts of justice.[30]

THE *AUDIENCIA NACIONAL* WITHIN THE HIERARCHY OF COURTS

The hierarchy of courts within the Spanish system of justice is organized basically along the usual scheme of two instances—trial and appeal. First instance courts (*juzgados*) give a first ruling in civil, labor, and in some administrative and criminal cases.[31] Courts of appeal act as second instance courts.[32] The increasingly controversial and debated persistence of the "instructing judge" (*juez de instrucción*) for major criminal cases accounts for the extant differences in the case of penal justice. The instructing judge (not the public prosecutor) is charged with conducting the investigation of major criminal cases and has the power to decide whether prosecution is to be upheld or dropped. If the decision is to formally file and indict, the judge must pass all the materials gathered (presented in written form, the *sumario*) to the *audiencia provincial* for hearings and sentencing.[33] In the audiencia, the public interest will no longer be represented by the instructing judge but by the public prosecutor.

The Supreme Court, sitting in Madrid, has final authority or *casación* (to reverse in those cases where an appeal is possible). The purpose of casación is to guarantee the uniform interpretation of norms by all inferior courts and should not be understood as some kind of third instance.[34] A cassation appeal has to be based either on an alleged *infraction of law* (when the appealed decision is considered not to have correctly applied the substantive legal norms in force, including Supreme Court jurisprudencia, as noted before) or on alleged *violation of form* (when the appealed decision is considered not to have observed the appropriate procedural rules). In the case of appeals for infraction of the law, the Supreme Court does not limit itself to reversing the appealed decision,[35] but proceeds as well to make a new—and final—decision. In fact, in so doing the Supreme Court can be said to be issuing two decisions at the same time: one that rescinds the appealed decision and another in which the matter is definitively resolved. In appeals for violation of form, the acceptance of the claim means that the case will be remanded to the trial court.

So far, little is particularly peculiar or innovative in the Spanish pyramid of courts (other than the oddity of the persistence of the figure of the instructing judge).[36] What really represented a novelty of unexpected and far-reaching consequences was the introduction within the Spanish judicial landscape of such an institution as the *Audiencia Nacional* (National Court; henceforth AN). The LOPJ typified the AN as some sort of "federal" court competent in what could be considered federal crimes, such as drug trafficking or terrorism.[37] But through a bold and imaginative application of the existing legislation, the AN has made a remarkable breakthrough in the field of international criminal justice.

Article 23 of the LOPJ states that Spanish justice (namely, the AN) is competent to try crimes committed outside Spanish territory, either by Spaniards or foreigners, having to do with genocide, terrorism, piracy, money forgery, prostitution, drug trafficking, and "any other matter that according to international treaties ought to be prosecuted in Spain," on just one condition: the accused person had not already been tried elsewhere for the same crimes.

The innovative step undertaken by the AN was to use such a legal provision to put into practice the contents of the international treaties signed by Spain, as well as by many other democratic countries.[38] A new path was thus opened in the search for viable mechanisms to turn the longed-for ideal of "universal justice" into a tangible reality. In this sense, it can be said that *Operación Condor* and the Pinochet case (to name the two that have made the most headlines worldwide) have represented a decisive turning point in the international judicial treatment of crimes against humanity.[39] In fact, an unexpected new judicial scheme can be said to have emerged under the lead of the AN and independently of the will and controlling influence of national governments. An informal, but nonetheless highly effective, international community of judges can be considered to be in the making.[40] What in 1997 seemed a total fantasy has become a fact: Argentinean torturers, after years of impunity, have finally been tried and imprisoned either in Argentina or in

Spain, and in February 2001, the former Chilean dictator General Pinochet was formally indicted and put under arrest in his own country, to await trial on a constantly increasing number of charges.[41] In a sense, it can paradoxically be said that it was fortunate that the investigation of cases with such a potential for international pressures and diplomatic under-the-table arrangements fell on the hands of the otherwise-questioned figure of an instructing judge, rather than on those of a public prosecutor (whose dependence, however indirect, on the government might have made the prosecutor more receptive to arguments of convenience and of "raison d'état").

THE REINTRODUCTION OF JURY TRIAL

In the field of criminal law, the 1978 constitution introduced two basic changes: the death penalty was formally abolished, and jury trial was reintroduced for some specific criminal cases.[42] Both measures were meant to symbolize a sharp break from the criminal justice system of the previous regime.[43]

In the case of trial by jury, the climate of opinion has been far from stable.[44] Since 1978, several opinion polls had shown the existence among the Spanish population of a substantial, although reticent, support for it. Spaniards declared themselves in favor of the existence of jury trial—as long as they personally would not be called to form part of it! (see Toharia 1987). In any case, by 1995 when the law establishing jury trial was finally passed, its popularity seemed quite solid. At that time, the dominant idea in Spanish society was that jurors would be more likely than professional judges to make fair decisions; and the majority of Spaniards expressed a preference to be tried, if ever put to trial, by a jury rather than by a professional judge (see Table 11.1). However, just two years later, in 1997, the climate of opinion experienced a spectacular turnaround; professional judges came to be clearly preferred over juries. In all likelihood, a single, highly publicized case in 1997 (the Otegui case), seems to have undermined the seemingly strong support for the jury

TABLE 11.1

"In your opinion, who is in a better position to give a fair decision: professional judges or lay jurors?"

Year	Professional judges (%)	Lay jurors (%)
1987	28	46
1992	30	54
1996	41	48
1997	55	34
2000	50	39

SOURCE: Toharia (2001a).
NOTE: "DK/NA" (don't know/not applicable) not included.

TABLE 11.2

*"If you were the defendant in a criminal case,
would you rather be tried by professional judges
or by lay jurors?"*

Year	Professional judges (%)	Lay jurors (%)
1983	32	44
1985	31	45
1986	32	43
1987	26	47
1990	29	45
1992	29	50
1996	37	49
1997	54	32
2000	38	49

SOURCE: Toharia (2001a).
NOTE: "DK/NA" (don't know/not applicable) not included.

system and its credibility. More recent opinion data in 2000 show a slight, partial recovery of the image of jury trial.[45] A small majority of Spaniards once more hold the view that they would prefer to be tried by a jury rather than by a professional judge, but a large absolute majority still think that judges are likelier than juries to reach a fair, legally coherent decision (see Table 11.2).[46] In any case, and whatever its symbolic value and public support, the fact is that the role of jury trial within the system of criminal justice is marginal: in 1998, only 290 jury trials were held in all Spain.[47]

"JUDGE AND CO.": THE PERSONNEL OF JUSTICE

Judges. Justice is administered by professional judges, "independent, irremovable, accountable for their actions, and subject only to the authority of the law" (art. 117.1 of the SC).[48] As is common in most countries within the European Union (or, for that matter, in countries with civil law systems), judges in Spain form a professional bureaucratic body (the "judicial career"). The average entrance age is usually quite young (around twenty-five years of age).

The selection of new judges is basically made through a fairly demanding examination granting entrance to the Judicial School.[49] Since 1985, judges and public prosecutors have become totally separated professions, with completely differentiated organizations in terms of selection, training, and promotion.[50]

Judges: How many are there? In 1998, there were 3,718 judges in all Spain (versus 1,842 in 1975; 2,328 in 1985; and 3,132 in 1990). Other court personnel increased from 10,677 in 1975 to 33,213 in 1995. Even though the total number of judges has experienced a sizable increase over the last years, the judge/population rate is still considerably lower in Spain than in most European countries. In 1995, Spain had 8.5 judges per 100,000 inhabitants, compared to a rate of 10.2 in France, 11.9 in Italy, 20.5 in Austria, and a remarkable 27.1 in Germany (Contini 2000).

Judges: Who are they? The increase in the total number of judges has been accompanied by a substantial process of renovation of the judiciary. The social characteristics of judges have become increasingly attuned to the global profile of the current Spanish social structure. Judges no longer represent an isolated, socially unrepresentative stratum within an ivory tower— though the process toward making them more socially representative is far from completed.

On the one hand, women already make up a third (34 percent in 1999) of the total judicial staff. This is still a long way from the 52 percent that women represent in the global Spanish population, but also a long way from the mere 4 percent that they represented among all judges who had entered the career before 1977. This trend toward the equalization of the gender composition of the judiciary is proceeding at considerable speed. Eighteen percent of all judges who entered the judiciary between 1978 and 1985 were women. Since that date, the proportion of women in each new cohort of judges has continued to rise: 32 percent among those who entered in 1985; 47 percent, in 1987; 54 percent, in 1997; and 62 percent among the would-be judges who began their two-year training period in the Judicial School in September 2000.[51]

As for the age composition of the judiciary, today something more that half of the judges are under forty years of age; in 1972, only 14 percent were below that age.[52]

The Spanish judiciary has also changed in recent years in terms of its social origin. Traditionally, there has been an overrepresentation within the judicial career of the less developed areas of the country. In 1972, 81 percent of all judges were born either in Madrid or in the less developed regions (Galicia, Castilla, Andalucia, and Extremadura) (see Toharia 1975). There were, in sharp contrast, scarcely any judges born in the more industrialized and affluent zones (such as Catalonia or the Basque Country). The geographical origin of judges has been gradually converging, in recent years, with the actual spatial distribution of the Spanish population. Today, judges born in the less developed parts of Spain have come to represent 57 percent of the total staff (the population combined of those regions represented around 50 percent of the total Spanish population in the late 1960s, the average year of birth for the members of the current judiciary). By contrast, the percentage of judges born in the wealthier parts of Spain (Madrid included) has increased from 17 percent to 32 percent.

With respect to social origin, slight but significant variations have taken place. The majority of the judges still come from middle-class or upper-middle-class sectors: 27 percent are sons (or daughters) of legal professionals, 18 percent of civil servants, and 14 percent of liberal professionals. At present, 8 percent come from working-class families (a sector totally unrepresented twenty years ago). In sum, the traditionally predominant rural, middle-class origin of the judiciary is gradually fading, giving way to a more balanced representation of the prevailing social structure.

Judges: What are they?   The available data on the ideological and attitudinal profile of Spanish judges show a remarkable parallelism with the corresponding patterns prevailing in Spanish society. In their ideas, values, and attitudes, judges can thus be said to be, on the whole, reasonably representative of their society (see Toharia 1987). In any case, this is also the predominant perception among the Spanish population. A large majority perceive the existence within the judiciary of a proportion of conservative- or progressive-oriented persons basically parallel to the proportion of conservative or progressive persons in the society as a whole; and the existence of such an ideological pluralism within the judiciary is valued as a positive asset by a large majority of Spaniards (see Toharia 2001a).

Other personnel within the system of justice.   In addition to judges, there is an entire constellation of occupations connected with the judicial system. There are occupations that may be described as "intrajudicial" in the sense that they form part of the daily routine of courts: court clerks (*secretarios de tribunales*), administrative staff of various kinds (officials, auxiliaries, agents), and forensic specialists.[53] None of these court-related professionals are hierarchically subordinated to the judge or the court clerk. Public prosecutors (who in Spain still use the somewhat disorienting name *fiscales* or *ministerio fiscal*) represent a special case:[54] they both represent the government within the judicial sphere and are charged with the impartial protection and promotion of the public interest. At the same time, they are expected to act as active protectors of judicial independence, promoting legal actions against any person or institution threatening the normal functioning of courts. No doubt, too many—and too self-contradictory—strings for a single violin. In its present configuration, the figure of the public prosecutor is certainly in urgent need of reshaping, of having its institutional profile clarified.[55]

There are also "extrajudicial" professions, which interact in a regular way with the judicial system but do not form part of its institutional framework: attorneys, *procuradores* (roughly the Spanish equivalent of British solicitors), and notaries.[56]

The Use of Justice

The quest for "total justice" (Friedman 1994)—that is, the search for remedies to all (or the majority of) problems through the use of laws and the courts, which Friedman finds characteristic of contemporary civic culture —has also pervaded the legal and political culture of democratic Spain. The use of legal mechanisms is constantly increasing, with the resulting *extension* of the legal system.[57]

THE EXTENSION OF THE LEGAL SYSTEM

The extension of the Spanish legal system is not easily measurable or quantifiable, as there is not a single, indisputable set of indicators available for that purpose. But indirect appraisals may be attempted through the accumulation and juxtaposition of different types of data, such as the ones considered in the following sections.

Legal rules.   The number of laws and rules of all types enacted and in force, as well as the total number of decisions taken by the different branches and agencies of government, can be said to be data that reflect the extension of the legal system. Spain has not escaped what seems to be the fate of the majority of industrialized countries, with almost an orgy of new rules, only partially explainable by the need to adapt the legal system to the new democratic situation.

In any case, this first indicator reflects only what, in the terminology of Roscoe Pound, can be called "law in the books." A second, and more telling, dimension in the process of extension of the legal system has to do with the degree to which such laws in the books become "laws in use." Do more people become actually integrated into the legal system? Do they make more use of the legal instruments available? Do legal relations of all kinds increase in number?

Integration.   Integration into the legal system can be measured, first, by considering the proportion of the population that has had contact with it. Among the Spanish population, 41 percent now say that they have received professional legal counsel from a lawyer—double the percentage obtained just two decades ago—a fact that certainly helps to explain the impressive growth experienced by the total number of practicing attorneys, as will be seen. Additionally, 56 percent indicate they have used the services of notaries for some legal transaction, and as many as 35 percent claim to have had contact (of whatever kind) with the courts of justice. These data seem to reflect an increasing familiarity with the legal world, which is reflected by the fact that in opinion polls on legal matters, the percentage of respondents

TABLE 11.3

Contact with the Legal System, 1997

Percentage of Spaniards over 18 years of age who said that	
they have had some personal contact with courts	35
they have received professional counsel from a lawyer	41
they have ever gone to a notary for a legal transaction	56
they have ever been victim of any type of crime	46
they have been victims of any type of crime during the previous year	9
Average percentage of interviewees who answered questions in survey on the courts	90

is usually around 90 percent (see Table 11.3). To put it in other terms, only 10 percent of Spaniards now consider themselves unable to answer such questions.

Additionally, the global level of integration within the legal system can be estimated from the observable prevalence in society of what can be labeled a "culture of claiming"—that is, the predisposition among the population to make claims rather than to give up when suffering damage of some kind. In this respect, the change is dramatic. At the beginning of the 1970s, 68 percent of all Spaniards declared that, even though they might consider themselves to have been harmed unduly, they would rather let things go without "stirring up a fuss" (see López Pintor and Buceta 1975, 120). In sharp contrast, in 1996 two out of three citizens who had a problem with a public agency would instead proceed to file a claim: a total reversal of the previously predominant attitude (cited in García de la Cruz 1997, 31). Even if, as García de la Cruz (1999) notes, "globally speaking, Spaniards are still clumsy claimers, as quite a few do not file their request through the appropriate channels, or do not provide the required data, or do not meet deadlines, or do not ask for the proper professional advice, or are simply unable to clearly state their demands," the fact remains that a new cultural pattern encouraging the search for compensation for damages seems to have clearly developed.

An additional obvious, though indirect, indicator of the level of legal integration is the evolution in the number of practicing lawyers (see Table 11.4). As legal experts, lawyers play a key role in shaping legal relations and in facilitating the claiming process. A basic correlation can thus be hypothesized to exist between the total number of lawyers, the global social demand for their services, and the social use of the legal system. In 1998, the total number of practicing lawyers in Spain came close to ninety-six thousand[58]—a far cry from the thirty-eight thousand registered in 1980. A recent study of the lawyers practicing in Madrid revealed the following:[59]

TABLE 11.4

Practicing Lawyers in Spain, 1980–1998

Year	Total number★	Rate per 100,000 inhabitants	Index (1980 = 100)
1980	27,983	75	100
1985	38,730	101	138
1990	55,076	138	197
1994	74,990	188	267
1998	96,000	240	343

SOURCE: Secretaria Tecnica del Consejo General de la Abogada Española.

NOTE: Data for 1998 are estimates.

★ Figures refer to *abogados ejercientes residentes*; a lawyer may join the bar with a nonpracticing status and is entitled to some benefits but is not actually engaged in the profession: only practicing lawyers (*ejercientes*) are taken into account; lawyers have to be members of the different bars in order to practice within their territories, which implies a certain amount of multiple affiliation that has not been controlled for in the data included.

1. Only 38 percent of all lawyers could be considered regular litigators (meaning that they bring a minimum of twenty cases a year before the courts).

2. The remaining two-thirds (62 percent), do just occasional or no litigation at all, devoting themselves mainly to counsel and advisory functions.[60]

3. Most of the litigating lawyers (59 percent) devote themselves primarily, or exclusively, to civil cases (including commercial cases); 19 percent specialize in criminal cases, 15 percent in labor cases, and 7 percent in administrative cases. This pattern of professional specialization can be compared with the distribution of all incoming cases by legal area.

4. In 1999, distribution of the litigating lawyers in Madrid by area of specialization was as follows: civil (59 percent); criminal (19 percent); labor (15 percent); and administrative (7 percent).

5. In 1998, distribution by legal area of all cases entered in the Spanish courts was as follows: civil (30 percent); criminal (50 percent); labor (14 percent); and administrative (6 percent).

As can be seen, there is a close relationship between the percentage of lawyers devoted to labor and administrative litigation and the number of cases filed in those two areas. Lawyers specialized in labor law represent 15 percent of all lawyers, and labor cases represent 14 percent of all cases; and a similar close correspondence appears to exist in the administrative area. Things are different in civil and criminal matters. Civil cases, which on the whole represent 30 percent of all cases, attract the professional attention of 59 percent of all litigating lawyers; criminal cases represent 50 percent of all cases, but only 19 percent of all lawyers specialize in them. This pattern seems to suggest that civil cases, on average, are likely to be "big cases." As such, they require from lawyers a higher level of differentiated attention, which prevents the concentration of cases in just a few hands. Criminal litigation, on the contrary, seems more likely to be composed of a myriad "little cases," allowing for their accumulation in a relatively few expert hands.

Legal relations. In civil law systems, notarial activity can provide a reasonably reliable indication of the global volume of legal transactions in society. Unlike its common law counterpart, the civil law notary plays a key role in the legal system by giving official validity to transactions. A notarized contract (or will, or declaration) is unlikely ever to be successfully challenged in court. Notarial intervention guarantees the full legal validity of the transaction. Consequently, no substantial legal transaction of any kind escapes its control. In this sense, the volume of notarial activity may be taken to express the global level of legal activity in society.

Over the past twenty-five years, notarial activity has kept growing in Spain at a pace similar to that in previous decades (see Toharia 1974a, 1974b). In 1998, the total number of notarized legal transactions was more than 5.5 million, in contrast with less than 4 million in 1990 and more than 2 million in 1975 (see Table 11.5).

TABLE 11.5

Incoming Civil Cases in All First Instance Courts and Legal Transactions Supervised by Notaries, 1975–1998

Year	Total number, incoming civil cases (A)	Total number, notarized transactions (B)	A as % of B
1975	290,007	2,158,635	9.9
1978	251,698	2,550,437	9.9
1979	249,492	2,735,088	9.1
1983	358,077	2,995,094	12.0
1984	360,632	3,022,786	11.9
1985	353,592	3,525,035	10.0
1987	361,596	3,956,166	9.1
1989	379,756	4,238,204	9.0
1990	488,876	3,987,055	12.3
1992	606,697	4,418,085	13.7
1994	673,730	4,726,656	14.3
1998	515,698	5,652,200	9.1

SOURCES: Instituto Nacional de Estadístico (INE) and General Council of the Judiciary.

TABLE 11.6

Incoming Cases in the Spanish Courts, 1975–1998

| | 1975 | | 1998 | |
Legal area	Total number	%	Total number	%
Civil	290,007	22	515,698	10
Criminal	828,213	63	4,405,157	83
Labor	192,838	14	241,733	5
Administrative	7,220	1	134,684	2
Total	1,318,278	100	5,297,272	100

THE EXPANSION OF THE JUDICIAL SYSTEM:
A LITIGATION EXPLOSION?

Over the last twenty-five years, the Spanish judicial system can be said to have experienced two quite different kinds of expansion: one of a qualitative nature (the "judicialization" of public life, with the entrance into the judicial arena of matters formerly processed by the political system), and the other of a quantitative nature (the increase in the global flow of litigation). Only this second type of expansion will be considered here. The data contained in Table 11.6 seem to suggest that the total volume of litigation has quadrupled between 1975 and 1998, an impressive litigation explosion.

In other words, the pattern of a low level of litigation traditionally characteristic of the Spanish legal system would seem to have been broken, and at the same time a real avalanche of criminal cases has occurred (see Toharia 1974a, 1974b). But is this really the case, or is there more in the picture than meets the eye? The first qualification is that in relative terms, this apparent increase in the resort to courts is far from equal in all four legal areas. Between 1975 and 1999, incoming civil cases appear to have multiplied by 2, incoming criminal cases by 5, incoming labor cases by only 1.2, but incoming administrative cases by almost 20. That is, the arrival and consolidation of democracy seem to coincide with a blooming of litigation against the different branches and levels of public administration.

A closer look at the data in Table 11.5 on the evolution of the total volume of incoming civil cases reveals a three-stage pattern.[61] First, in the 1970s, the total never reached 300,000 new cases per year (a rate of some 80 cases per 100,000 inhabitants). Second, in the 1980s, there was a slight increase in the influx of civil cases: the total fluctuates between a maximum of almost 380,000 and a minimum of something less than 350,000 (an average rate of approximately 90 cases per 100,000 inhabitants). Third, in 1989, misdemeanors relating to traffic accidents were transferred from criminal to civil courts, representing an additional influx of cases (Pastor 1993, 72). During the next five years, the total number of incoming civil cases increased gradually, reaching a maximum of some 680,000 cases in 1993 (which represents a rate of 172 cases per 100,000 inhabitants). However, after 1993, the number of incoming civil cases tended to decrease gradually, and by 1998 the total number of incoming cases (little more than 500,000, a rate of 129 cases per 100,000 inhabitants) was equivalent to the total registered in 1990. After a short period of expansion (caused mainly by the net addition of new types of cases), civil litigation seems to have stabilized.

An additional and more sophisticated way of analyzing the evolution of civil litigation would be to correlate it with the global volume of legal activity registered each year, as measured by the legal transactions legalized by notaries. The hypothesis behind such an exercise is that an increase in the number of civil cases can be said to reflect a real increase of civil litigiousness only if at the same time all other factors (and primarily the volume of legal activity) remain constant. But if an increase of legal activity takes place, it can be safely assumed that a more or less proportional increase in the volume of civil litigation will result. The data in Table 11.5 indicate that in 1975, incoming civil cases totaled an amount roughly equivalent to 10 percent of the total legal transactions handled by notaries. This proportion remained basically the same in the 1980s. For a short period (1990–93), when civil courts begin to receive cases formerly dealt with by criminal courts, this percentage increased, reaching its peak of 16 percent in 1993. However, immediately afterward, the figure returned to previously registered levels: by 1998, incoming civil cases represented just about 9 percent of all notary-assisted transactions. The conclusion that can be reached is that, on the whole, the volume of civil (and commercial) litigation in Spain seems to be equivalent, in a remarkably stable way, to about 10 percent of all legal transactions established. In relative terms, civil litigation seems to remain substantially stable. The truth behind the apparent fact is that no litigation "explosion" has taken place.

Labor litigation has been gradually declining in recent years (see Table 11.7). After a short period of increase in the second half of the 1970s (coinciding with the end of the Franco dictatorship), the creation in the early 1980s of the Institute of Mediation, Arbitration, and Conciliation (IMAC) may be credited with the gradual decrease in labor litigation.[62] The total of incoming labor cases in 1998 was the lowest ever. Obviously, the institutions and mechanisms set up to filter out cases before they reach court have proved effective.[63] Labor litigation appears to have been contracting rather than expanding.

Administrative litigation, on the contrary, has experienced a tremendous growth since 1975 (see Table 11.7). The flow of cases in this area has become twenty times larger in the last twenty-five years. However, the tremendous expansion of this type of litigation does not become as immediately apparent

TABLE 11.7

Incoming Administrative and Labor Cases, ★

1975–1998

Year	Total number, administrative cases	Total number, labor cases
1975	7,220	192,838
1976	11,864	259,306
1977	12,924	291,909
1978	12,566	385,219
1979	14,023	428,913
1980	14,513	270,002
1981	13,725	300,158
1982	14,495	286,158
1983	17,888	357,996
1984	21,515	370,846
1985	25,603	322,190
1986	33,903	298,066
1987	39,935	305,584
1988	42,259	306,846
1989	48,266	291,113
1990	53,181	316,850
1991	61,207	
1992	72,041	
1993	90,153	
1994	105,688	270,543
1995	113,004	261,398
1996	117,253	261,140
1997	134,691	253,459
1998	134,684	241,733

★ *Tribunales Superiores de Justicia* and *Juzgados de lo Social*, respectively; until 1985, these courts were officially named *Audiencias Territoriales* and *Magistraturas de Trabajo*, respectively; administrative cases get access to court after they have completed an internal round of appeals inside the very administrative body that produced the contested decision; until 1999, when first instance administrative courts were created, all incoming cases in this area were handled by the courts of appeals.

as it should be. Until 1998, all administrative litigation took place exclusively in second-level courts (courts of appeal). The total number of incoming cases (117,253 in 1996; 134,691 in 1997; 134,684 in 1998) seemed relatively modest when compared to incoming civil, labor, or criminal cases, which are filed at first instance courts. But the fact is, as Pastor (1993) has remarked, that in second-level courts—through which administrative cases make their entrance into the judicial arena—administrative cases challenging some administrative agency are by far the predominant type of case (55 percent of all cases filed with the Supreme Court, 92 percent of those filed with the AN, and 58 percent of those filed with the superior courts of justice). That is, from the perspective of second-level courts, administrative litigation certainly has a starring role. This may be taken to express the gradual consolidation and generalization of the new "culture of claiming" with respect to public administration.[64]

When the average citizen hears the word *justice*, it is usually taken to mean "criminal justice"—understandably, as 83 percent of all incoming cases in the courts are criminal cases. The public perception of the existence of other types of cases is thus overshadowed by the apparent formidable volume of criminal justice. In fact, this is something of a mirage: an artificial inflation resulting from the procedural peculiarities of criminal cases, rather than a faithful reflection of reality. Under an inquisitorial system of criminal law, such as the one presently in force in Spain, all potentially criminal cases are subject to a judicial screening process. This preliminary phase of judicial intervention is exclusively oriented to elucidate if the cases under consideration provide enough grounds for a formal indictment. Obviously, such a system imposes a gigantic workload on the investigating courts: in 1998, 85 percent of all preliminary judicial inquiries in criminal cases resulted in the dropping of the case. In other words, criminal courts had to examine one hundred potential cases in order to finally find just fifteen potential real cases of crime.[65] This ratio (85 percent to 15 percent) graphically points both to the waste of judicial energy generated by the present system and to the resulting inflation of the statistics on the activity of criminal courts.

A more reliable indicator of the actual volume of criminality and criminal judicial activity can be obtained from other more refined sources. For instance, over the last decade the juzgados penales (first instance criminal courts dealing with relatively minor crimes) produced an annual average of some 130,000 decisions. On the other hand, in 1998, the total number of decisions given out by the *audiencias principales* (which consider major criminal cases) was 77,000. An additional figure worth keeping in mind is the total number of prison inmates: around 40,000, on average, over the last decade.[66] And, finally, the number of reported acts of violence against persons ranks annually on the order of 10,000 (exactly 13,830 in 1997, the last date with available information), a rate of scarcely 0.3 per 1,000 inhabitants. All this invites the conclusion that the actual flow of criminal cases is well below what a first look at global statistics might suggest.[67] It can be safely hypothesized that if the Spanish criminal justice system were reorganized around the accusatory principle, freeing the courts from their present burden of preliminary investigations, the total number of incoming cases would drop to a figure around 500,000 per year (a figure representing approximately 15 percent of the current volume of preliminary inquiries). Automatically, the impact of criminal justice on the overall image of the judicial system would be enormously reduced.

TABLE II.8

*"Globally, how would you rate the way
in which courts operate in Spain?"*

Year	Very well or well	So-so	Poorly or very poorly	DK/NA*
1987	20	31	28	21
1990	22	33	33	12
1992	18	26	38	18
1995	15	36	46	3
1997	16	28	51	5
2000	19	30	46	5

SOURCE: Toharia (2001a).
*DK/NA (don't know/not applicable).

The Evaluation of the Functioning of the Judicial System

Systems of justice have almost universally a bad image: both experts and the general population complain—sometimes quite bitterly—about the way in which the systems perform their functions. This probably explains the current universal interest in judicial reform, a topic so popular nowadays as to give the impression that judicial systems are on the verge of collapsing everywhere.[68] Or almost everywhere: there are indeed a few, exceptional countries where the citizenry surprisingly turns out to be fairly satisfied with the operation of their judicial system, as we shall see.

Before proceeding any further, an important preliminary point needs to be clarified. The legal world is indeed a highly technical and sophisticated world, unlikely to be known even approximately—much less understood —by the average citizen. If so, why bother to consider the way in which people evaluate the performance of the judicial system? What can they possibly know? What could be the value of investigating the state of public opinion? The simplest possible answer to such questions is that the citizens' response to institutional performance cannot be ignored within a democratic system, a system in which, in the end, all legitimacy stems from popular support. Citizens do not need to be legal experts to express a valid global opinion about their judicial system, just as they are not required to be experts in fiscal, military, educational, or international matters when called to vote for candidates offering various alternative views on such issues. Democracy rests on opinion (not on technical knowledge or expertise) because opinion represents the main mechanism through which social legitimacy is granted. It is certainly within the province of legal experts to determine whether a system of justice has the appropriate organization, functionality, or procedural mechanisms. Regardless of the expert evaluation, a judicial system (as is true of any other politically relevant institution) will be seriously impaired in its social legitimacy if the population it is supposed to serve holds a negative opinion about the way it operates. And institutions with weak social legitimacy can hardly be expected to perform properly in a context where popular support is a prerequisite for their effective influence and moral leadership over society. In this sense, the exploration of the prevailing states of opinion with respect to the judicial system becomes an invaluable additional tool when attempting to diagnose the quality of its operation. Public opinion cannot be expected to provide cures, but it certainly expresses symptoms. Patients do not need to know medicine to indicate where they are experiencing pain: it is for the expert to interpret and make sense of the information thus provided.[69]

In contemporary Spanish society, the overall performance of the system of justice is considered to be bad or very bad by one out of every two citizens (see Table 11.8).[70] Within the European context, this is far from exceptional: in fact, it rather tends to be the usual pattern of answer, at least in all southern European countries that share a similar type of legal and judicial system. Table 11.9 contains the results of a 1997 survey on the performance of courts in all fifteen countries of the European Union. As can be seen, the lowest percentages of satisfaction with court operation were found in Italy (8 percent), Portugal (13 percent), France (14 percent), Belgium (17 percent), Spain (17 percent), and Greece (23 percent). In contrast, 61 percent of the

TABLE 11.9

*Percentage of Interviewees That Rate as "Good"
the Operation of Courts in Their Own Country*

Finland	61
Denmark	54
Austria	52
Netherlands	45
Luxembourg	41
Germany	39
Sweden	38
Ireland	33
United Kingdom	33
Greece	23
Spain	17
Belgium	17
France	14
Portugal	13
Italy	8

SOURCE: Eurobaromètre (1997).

total population in Finland (54 percent in Denmark and 52 percent in Austria) rated positively the overall performance of their courts.

Data in Table 11.9 are interesting on two accounts. On the one hand, they call into question the idea that it is impossible for any system of courts to achieve a good, positive social image. As the case of Finland seems to prove, there do exist systems of courts that receive a highly positive social evaluation for their performance. There may not be many, but they exist (in fact, in the EU, just three countries—20 percent of all member countries—have their courts positively rated by a majority of the citizenship). On the other hand, data in Table 11.9 make remarkably clear that the worst-rated systems of courts belong to the same legal family: the "Napoleonic" variant of the civil law branch. This seems to suggest that some common, structural component may be at work, causing similar functional deficiencies and similar levels of frustration among the respective populations. A detailed, systematic comparison of the two extreme cases (Finland and Italy, the best and worst rated) could certainly be highly illuminating in this respect. But in the absence of such a comparative study, a sound guess can be made about the most likely cause for such widely differing social evaluations: the average length of judicial proceedings. In Finland, an average civil case (first instance plus appeal) will take some six months in court, as compared with seven to eight years in Italy![71] The procedural complexities common to all southern European civil law countries do indeed cause an extremely slow pace of court proceedings. And this generalized judicial slow motion, which would simply be intolerable for any other public service within countries so highly developed socially and economically, is certainly likely to be strongly resented by citizens—hence the harsh social evaluation of the performance of courts.

In the specific case of Spain, this explanatory hypothesis seems to be clearly upheld by survey data recently available.[72] A detailed scrutiny of the public mind with respect to courts has shown that among the Spanish population, courts are reasonably well rated for the professional competence of their members, their empathy with prevailing cultural and social patterns, their level of independence with respect to the government and interest groups, and the fairness of their rulings: not so bad an image for a system of justice emerging from a forty-year dictatorship. However, courts are poorly rated with respect to their accessibility and, particularly, with respect to the length of their proceedings. And these two negative features seem to weigh so strongly in the respondents' minds that they overshadow all other positive considerations. As a result, the global evaluation expressed turns out to be almost unqualifiedly critical (in fact, the evaluation of the operation of courts expressed by the average Spanish citizen turns out to be closely parallel to the evaluation made by legal experts; see Toharia 2001a). In a sense, this would

TABLE 11.10

Political Chronology, 1975–2000

1975	General Franco dies; Juan Carlos I proclaimed king
1976	Adolfo Suárez appointed head of government by King Juan Carlos
1976	Enactment of the Law for Political Reform, approved by a referendum in December; the law creates the legal mechanisms to allow the transition from Francoism to full democracy without any breach in prevailing legality
1977	June: first fully democratic elections since 1936; Suarez's UCD wins a plurality and forms the first democratic government
1978	December 6: a new constitution is approved in a national referendum
1979	Second general elections: Suarez's UCD remains in power
1980	*Ley Orgánica del Consejo General del Poder Judicial* (organic law creating the Council of the Judiciary)
1981	February 23: attempted coup, with government and parliamentarians held hostages within Parliament; the king's intervention as commander in chief made possible the arrest of the rebel officers and their accomplices
1981	Civil code reform: divorce is introduced, and legal distinction between children born to married or unmarried is abolished
1981	Spain enters NATO
1982	The PSOE (Socialist Party), led by Felipe González, wins an absolute majority in Parliament, beginning an uninterrupted period of fourteen years in power
1984	Full integration of labor courts within the regular system of justice
1985	Spain admitted as a full member within the European Community
1985	*Ley Orgánica del Poder Judicial* (Organic Law of the Judiciary establishing the new organizational scheme of courts)
1985	*Estatuto del Ministerio Fiscal* (law regulating the organization of public prosecution; prosecutors organized as a career differentiated from the judiciary)
1985	*Ley de planta y demarcación judicial* (law establishing the new map of court jurisdictions and reorganizing the internal composition of the judiciary)
1988	*Juzgados de lo penal* (first instance criminal courts) are created to deal with minor crimes, with purely oral and simpler proceedings
1992	A new type of faster criminal court proceeding is set up for cases well established and not requiring further investigations
1995	Jury trial is reintroduced (after having been suspended in 1936)
1995	New criminal code is enacted (the criminal code of democracy, as described by the media)
1996	The center-right Popular Party wins the election and forms a government
1997	*Libro Blanco de la Justicia* (White Book on the State of Justice) elaborated by the CGPJ
1997	Spain joins the eleven EU member countries that accept the replacement as of January 2002 of their national currencies by a new common currency (the euro)
1998	The terrorist ETA group announces an "indefinite cease-fire"
1998	*Ley reguladora de la Jurisdicción Contencioso-Administrativa* (law reorganizing administrative courts)
1999	First-instance administrative courts begin to operate
1999	ETA decides to put an end to its cease-fire and returns to its terrorist activities
2001	The new *Ley de Enjuiciamiento civil* passed in 2000 (law reorganizing civil cases, with simpler and faster proceedings) becomes fully effective

seem somewhat unfair. However, in a modern, democratic society, the citizens certainly tend to take for granted good features of public institutions and services: these, as a consequence, usually pass unnoticed, with the functional invisibility characteristic of things that *could not possibly not be there*. At the same time, public attention tends to concentrate instead on all that does not meet the expected high level of quality: the things that *ought not to be there*. The performance of public services and institutions is thus routinely measured by the citizenry not so much against what they achieve as against what they fail to provide. And this is probably what explains why the overall, global image of the performance of courts turns out to be so intensely negative, despite the good ratings accorded to several basic aspects of the way in which they operate, which might seem to call for a more balanced appraisal. It is not that everything in the system of justice is perceived to be functioning poorly, but what is evaluated as operating unsatisfactorily has an impact strong enough to tip the balance of the final verdict decisively toward the negative end.

Notes

1. In the late 1950s, more than half of the Spanish active population was employed in agriculture, and it was only in 1953 that the country managed to recover the per capita income that it had enjoyed in 1935 (that is, on the eve of the three-year civil war). By contrast, in the 1990s Spain ranked tenth in terms of gross national product (GNP) and twenty-second in terms of GNP per capita among all countries. This remarkable economic success is only marginally attributable to Franco's regime. An unprecedented prosperity in countries such as Germany, France, and Belgium (which allowed for a massive migration of workers from rural Spain, with the ensuing beneficial effect on the country's rate of unemployment); the resulting massive influx of foreign currency in the form of savings sent back home by these migrant workers; and the growing popularity of the Spanish Mediterranean coast as a vacation spot for Western Europeans, which meant the takeoff of the Spanish tourism industry (in the 1970s Spain had 35 million inhabitants and received 35 million tourists yearly—this last figure more than doubled by the end of the 1990s, reaching more than 80 million), were the real factors that made possible what at the time was labeled "the Spanish economic miracle."

2. This occurred after almost forty years (1939–75) of autocracy under General Franco.

3. During the three-year period between Franco's death (November 1975) and the formal enactment of the present democratic constitution (December 1978), Prime Minister Adolfo Suárez, under the guidance of King Juan Carlos, undertook what is now referred to by historians as "La Reforma" (the Reform), a gradual process of

legal and political change leading to full democracy, overcoming the provisions of the *Leyes Fundamentales* (Fundamental Laws)—the Francoist "constitution." This set of so-called fundamental laws was meant to institutionalize an "organic democracy" (a Fascist-type attempt to supersede "party democracy"). The king, as Franco's appointed successor, was expected to preside over such a system and keep it unchanged. Juan Carlos's determination to turn Spain into a democracy required a highly skillful and risky—but finally remarkably successful—process of legal engineering: the Francoist Parliament itself was made to enact an additional fundamental law that made possible a referendum on the establishment of a democratic system. The Francoist regime hard-liners were thus forced to accept as fully "legal," in their own terms, what in fact opened the door to the total subversion of the political system. The fact is that transition to democracy in Spain did not result from a revolution, from a coup, from a collapse of the former regime, or from some kind of void in power (as in Portugal in 1974, in Eastern European countries, and in most Latin American countries in the late 1980s and 1990s) but from a gradual change of the laws in force, within the prevailing institutions, and through the existing procedures (in a sense, an antecedent of what happened in the next decade in Uruguay or Chile, or if one wishes to stretch somehow the analogy, in Mexico in the July 2000 election). This emphasis on the preservation of legality and on change through purely legalistic means and procedures that characterizes the process of *reforma* (as opposed to the *ruptura*, or "breaking up," strategy favored by some opposition groups immediately after Franco's death) can be safely hypothesized to have marked the legal culture of contemporary Spaniards.

4. I use the term "legal culture" in the sense in which it was originally coined by Friedman (1969) and put in use in the seminal Stanford Studies in Law and Development (SLADE) project in 1974.

5. There never was such a thing as a total reorganization of justice over the last two hundred years as the country moved from absolutist to parliamentarian monarchy, or from monarchy to republic, or from a republic to a Fascist dictatorship under General Franco. This peculiar stability of the system of justice is also found in countries such as France, Italy, and Germany—that is, in countries sharing a basic common model of a civil law system.

6. This is the terminology used by Zweigert and Kötz (1998), who within the European system distinguish three subvariants of "civil" systems: Romanistic (France, and in its wake, countries such as Italy or Spain), Germanic (Germany, Austria, Switzerland), and Nordic (the Scandinavian countries).

7. For a more detailed discussion of this point, see Toharia (2001a, 2001b).

8. "Justice emanates from the people and is administered in the name of the King" (art. 117.1 of the Spanish constitution; henceforth cited as SC).

9. The reform of the system of justice was undertaken under what can be described as a "democratic deficit syndrome," a particular frame of mind not uncommon to countries that are newcomers to democratic rule. After four decades of dictatorship, Spain was more than eager to go to extremes in terms of democratization and modernization in order to "keep up with the Joneses" (the "Joneses" being, in this particular instance, the political and judicial systems of Western Europe, with France and Italy as favored reference models). In turn, the Spanish case may be said

to have served as a reference for a number of Latin American countries that regained democracy during the 1980s and 1990s. It has to be kept in mind that by the late 1970s, most Latin American countries, with just a few exceptions, were under autocratic rule; by the turn of this century, the situation had changed dramatically, and democracy is now the general rule in the area (with Cuba the only clear exception).

10. The constitution of 1978 established that the twenty members of the CGPJ will be elected in the following way: twelve to be judges and the other eight to be jurists of recognized prestige. But it says nothing about how to carry out that election. A law enacted in 1980 established that the twelve members of judicial origin would be elected *by the members of the judiciary themselves*. A new law passed in 1985 by the Socialist government of Felipe González and still in force established instead that the twelve members of judicial origin, as well as the remaining eight coming from judicial professions, should all be elected by Parliament with a qualified majority (three-fifths of its members, in order to force negotiations and compromises between the different parties). This change was received with basic displeasure by the majority of judges as well as by the conservative Popular Party (then in opposition, but in power since 1996). In spite of the repeated pledge by the Popular Party to return to the previous system, the system of election of the members of the CGPJ remains unchanged in the early 21st century. At the root of this dispute lie two opposing forms of understanding the place of courts of justice in a democratic society. The recognition of judicial corporatism (only judges can elect judges to rule over matters concerning judges) implies granting a free-floating status to the judiciary, above any outside mechanism of control and accountability. Conversely, leaving the election to members of Parliament alone implies the risk of politicization of the whole process with the eventual establishment of a de facto system of political quotas (the well-known Italian system of *lottizzazione*)—as has in fact happened both in Italy and in Spain. Even so, and despite its obvious risks and deficiencies, this second alternative seems more attuned to the basic principles of parliamentary democracy. However, it badly needs some reforms in order to fully depoliticize an organ originally meant to keep politics out of the judicial arena! (see Toharia 1999b).

11. As a result, the same person presides at the same time over the highest court and the governing board of the judiciary; but this is the only point of connection between the two institutions, which at times get tangled in disputes of competence on specific points. For instance, when the CGPJ applies a disciplinary measure against a given judge and this judge appeals the sanction to the Supreme Court, who will have the final word on the matter? Probably the idea of having a shared presidency was meant to smooth out such potential frictions between the two institutions, creating some sense of continuity between them.

12. One of the biggest innovations of the 1978 constitution was the reorganization of the Spanish state into seventeen autonomous communities: an end to the secular tradition of a highly centralized state. In practice (though not in legal terminology), the autonomous system has meant the federalization of the country: each autonomous community has a flag, an anthem, a Parliament, a government, its own taxes and police force, and in some cases its own official language (along with Spanish). So far, the judiciary has remained "federal."

13. Art. 12.1 of the *Ley Orgánica del Poder Judicial* (the statute regulating the organization and competences of the judicial system; henceforth LOPJ). This applies as well to the precedents set by the Supreme Court, as will be discussed later. For the difference between an ordinary and an "organic" law, see note 23.

14. Art. 176.2 of the LOPJ. Such control would correspond exclusively to the appropriate superior court, if and when an appeal is filed.

15. Judges can, nonetheless, temporarily leave the judicial profession in order to serve a political post or to run for a seat in Parliament, with the possibility of returning to the bench at any time (after quitting their political assignment). Although union affiliation is strictly prohibited, judges can nonetheless join "judicial associations" (in practice, a euphemism for unions of judges). At present, about 50 percent of all judges belong to one of the four existing associations. The more conservatively oriented association, the *Asociación Profesional de la Magistratura* (Professional Association of the Judiciary), has the largest affiliation, with about 25 percent of all judges; the membership of the more progressively oriented *Jueces para la democracia* (Judges for Democratic Action) represents 11 percent of all judges, closely followed by the *Asociación Francisco de Vitoria* (Association Francisco de Vitoria, named after the sixteenth-century theologian and legal scholar considered to be one of the founders of international law), with a centrist orientation and about 10 percent of all judges as members. The membership in the newly formed *Unión Judicial Independiente* (Independent Judicial Union), a splinter from the right of the Professional Association of the Judiciary, so far barely represents 1 percent of all existing judges. See *El País*, 2 Feb. 2001, p. 18.

16. By 1974, the Franco regime had a total of twenty-two special courts (Toharia 1974, 1975, chap. 11).

17. For a more detailed analysis, see Toharia (1975). Tocqueville describes in his *L'Ancien regime et la Revolution* (chap. 4) a not too different situation when analyzing the birth of administrative justice in pre-Revolutionary France: *"Il n'y avait pas de pays en Europe où les tribunaux ordinaires dependissent moins du gouvernement qu'en France, mais il n'y en avait guère non plus où les tribunaux exceptionnels fussent plus en usage"* [There was no country in Europe where ordinary courts were less dependent on the government than in France, but there was also no country where exceptional courts were more in use].

18. The administrative courts (*contencioso-administrativo*) were first introduced in the Spanish judicial system in 1845 and are staffed with ordinary judges—a clear departure from the original French model. The French judicial administrative order is composed in the first instance of the *tribunaux administratifs* and in the second by the *Cour Administrative d'Appel*, with the *Conseil d'État* as the last instance of *cassation*. Labor courts (now renamed "social") were created in 1908 (called "industrial courts") and are also staffed with ordinary judges—another difference from French labor courts (*conseils de prud'hommes*), which are staffed with representatives of both employers and laborers. Commercial cases (which in France are dealt with by the *tribunaux de commerce*, served by representatives of the business community) are dealt with in Spain by regular civil courts. Consequently, whereas in France the courts of justice concern themselves exclusively with civil (in the strict technical sense of the

term—that is, excluding mercantile matters) and penal cases, Spanish courts have competence as well over commercial, labor, and administrative cases.

19. Military justice, which had large powers under Francoism (any dispute of whatever kind in which the army or any of its members was implicated was under the exclusive jurisdiction of the military courts), has been reduced by article 117.5 of the SC exclusively to military matters in the event of a state of siege or under martial law. All appeals against the decisions of military courts are examined by the Supreme Court.

20. This is in fact the standard formulation, with slight variants, in practically all civil law European countries. See Zweigert and Kötz (1998, 18).

21. The expression "sources of the law" (*fuentes de la ley*) refers to the different repertoires of legal norms (whether formal or informal) to which the judge has to turn when looking for the appropriate rule to solve a case. The expression is obviously ambiguous as it could also be taken to designate the authority from which all legal norms emanate (that is, usually the legislative power). See Diez-Picazo and Gullón (1997, 94–95).

22. The preponderant role of statutes in civil law systems is vividly expressed in Von Kirchmann's famous dictum: "Three rectifying words of the legislator and entire libraries become garbage" (cited in O'Callaghan 1997, 170).

23. A distinction has to be made between "ordinary" laws, which require only a majority in Parliament for passage, and "organic" laws, which require a qualified majority (absolute majority in a global final vote over the entire text). This is meant to grant a stronger stability to organic laws (granting them de facto a quasi-constitutional status). Laws referring to basic rights and freedoms, to the electoral system, or to some other particularly important matters are required by article 81 of the SC to be passed as organic laws. With respect to custom as a legally binding source, it has to be noted that should one of the parties allege a given custom as a legal basis for the claim, the party must provide adequate proofs of its existence in order for the judge to give it consideration. This implies an interesting breach of the principle *iuria novit curia* (which can be translated as "the court is supposed to know the legal norms in force"), a basic feature of most civil law systems of justice, which means that the litigants do not have the burden of proving the existence of the body of laws in force. The litigants simply have to provide the facts; it is up to the courts to find out the law (as expressed in the principle *da mihi factum dabo tibi ius*).

24. What should specifically be understood by "general principles of the law" is something that the CC does not clarify, thus contributing to the basically confusing nature of this third possible source of the law. The concept of legal "general principles" appeared first as "natural legal principles" in the Austrian Civil Code of 1811. The now common and well-established term "general principles of law" appeared in the Italian Civil Code of 1865. At present, the term can even be found in article 38 of the Statute of the United Nations [UN] International Court of Justice, seated in The Hague, which states that the court will apply international conventions, international customs, and "the general principles of law recognized by civilized nations" (see Diez-Picazo and Gullón 1997, 138). General principles of the law should not be confused with related concepts such as equity, analogy, or judicial maxims. Analogy

and equity represent means for the application of the general principles of the law. Juridical maxims, or *regulae juris*, are no more than juridical refrains or proverbs (such as *pacta sunt servanda* or *non bis in idem*). As examples of general principles, Diez-Picazo and Gullón (1997, 141–42) point to statements included in the Spanish constitution (for example, laws must be inspired by the values of liberty, equality, and political pluralism) or in different articles of the CC (for example, the requisite of total autonomy and free will when signing a contract or the obligation to remedy damages caused by fault or negligence).

25. The Supreme Court itself has interpreted this requisite of reiteration in the most minimal possible way: two opinions suffice to establish a precedent.

26. As Albaladejo (1996) points out, in fact "*jurisprudencia* is not even binding on the Supreme Court itself, which . . . can change its doctrine in successive cases" (144).

27. As López-Guerra (1998) points out, the appearance of the continental model of the Constitutional Court in the 1920s under the powerful personal influence of Hans Kelsen responds "to the desire to guarantee the stability of democratic institutions . . . against their potential erosion or gradual suppression by a (momentary) anti-constitutional majority in Parliament" (95). The Spanish Constitutional Court, established by the constitution in 1978, began to function in 1979. It is made up of twelve magistrates: four elected by the Congress of Deputies (by a majority of three-fifths of its members), four elected by the Senate (with the same qualified majority), two named by the CGPJ, and two named by the government. The mandate of the magistrates lasts nine years, renewing itself by one-third every three years.

28. Article 5.1 of the LOPJ states that judges are bound to apply the legal norms in the way in which these may happen to have been interpreted by the Constitutional Court.

29. EU legislation does not need ratification to become incorporated fully into the national body of laws in force—as is the case with international treaties. EU law defines itself as a "law passed for the European citizens," not for the member states.

30. The plural in the name of this court (which has its seat in Luxembourg) may be surprising nowadays but results from its historical origin. The court was indeed created at a time when three different entities coexisted: the European Community of Coal and Steel, Euratom, and the European Economic Community. The court was established to serve all three. Later, as these three original communities merged into the European Community (which eventually gave way to the current European Union), the court retained its original name. In fact, it could now be more aptly labeled as the "Court of Justice of the European Union." It is composed of fifteen magistrates, one from each of the member states.

31. The effort to homogenize the organization and procedural functioning of the different specialized areas, as required by the constitution, has led to the creation of first instance courts in areas where they had never existed before. In 1988, the *juzgados penales* (first instance criminal courts) were created to sentence some relatively minor criminal cases through a mainly oral, abbreviated procedure. It is interesting to note that in these criminal cases, investigation and accusation are duties of the public prosecutor, a novelty that implies a promising break in the centuries-old tradition of inquisitorial justice carried out by "instructing judges." In 1998, first instance

courts (*juzgados de lo contencioso-administrativo*) were established for some administrative cases (normally, claims against second-level administrative agencies). Claims against higher levels of public administration fall normally under the direct competence of courts of appeals (*tribunales superiores de justicia* or *audiencia nacional*). In 1985, first instance labor courts had their name changed from *magistraturas de trabajo* to *juzgados de lo social* as a result of this very emphasis on homogenization (merely terminological in this case).

32. The tribunales superiores de justicia (one in each of the seventeen autonomous regions) are the prototypical second instance courts in most cases. Normally, cases are heard by three judges.

33. As their very name indicates, there is an audiencia in each of the fifty provinces.

34. The term is an obvious gallicism, borrowed from the French verb *casser*, meaning "to break."

35. This is unlike the French *Cour de Cassation*, originally taken as a model.

36. Spain is the only country within the European Union where such a figure still exists in full: even in France, where the figure originated, *juges d'instruction* have lost, as of January 2001, the power to decree the imprisonment of persons under investigation, now transferred to the newly created "judge of freedoms and detentions"; a severe blow to the "most powerful man in France," as Napoleon is credited to have defined the instructing judge.

37. The powers of all other courts (with the obvious exception of the Supreme Court and the Constitutional Court) are limited to a specific territory: the judicial district (*partido judicial*) in the case of first instance court, the province in the case of the audiencias provinciales, the region (or comunidad autónoma) in the case of the *tribunales de justicia*, and the municipality in the case of the *jueces de paz* (lay judges dealing with minor cases). By contrast, the competence of the AN extends to all the Spanish territory—and beyond, as will be seen.

38. The proceedings within the AN were undertaken originally by Carlos Castresana, a member of the Public Prosecutor Office at the AN, and then, and most conspicuously, by Judge Baltasar Garzón, instructing judge in charge of *Juzgado de Instrucción* (Instructing Court) Number 5 within the AN. See Urbano (2000, 491). The mentioned international agreements include articles 4 and 5.1.c of the United Nations Convention Against Torture and Other Cruel, Inhuman or Degrading Forms of Treatment (December 1984); article 6c of the Statute of the International Court for the former Yugoslavia (1995); the four Geneva Conventions (July 1949); and article 3 of the Statute of the Nuremberg Court, still in force. All of these had been ratified by Spain.

39. *Operación Cóndor* was the code name given at the time to a coordinated, and particularly ferocious, repressive action jointly undertaken by the Argentinean and Chilean military juntas against leftist political opponents. The AN has also extended its competences to cases of international arms trafficking (such as the Al-Kasser case), drug trafficking, and money laundering (such as the so-called Yomagate, a case in which close relatives of Menem [president of Argentina at the time] were implicated), which have received lesser media coverage.

40. This refers to independent judges within democratic systems subject to the rule of law. Were this pattern to consolidate, the International Criminal Court (still to be created, pending ratification by all major world powers—something not in the immediately foreseeable future) would automatically find itself to be obsolete and superseded! The Gordian knot of how to make universal criminal justice possible might find itself cut by Garzón's initiative and the ensuing acceptance and adherence of judges from other countries.

41. The Pinochet case will not be easily forgotten. As of December 2000, there were already about fifty known Ph.D. dissertations being written on the topic (Urbano, 2000). The story, which just a short time ago would have seemed to be science fiction, can be summarized as follows:

October 16, 1998: Judge Garzón issued an order of arrest against General Pinochet on charges of torture, genocide, and terrorism. Pinochet was then at a London clinic recovering from minor discal hernia surgery.

October 27, 1998: Following Garzón's request, additional petitions for extradition piled up from Switzerland, France, Sweden, Norway, Canada, Italy, Belgium, Luxembourg, Germany, and the U.S. Attorney General.

October 28, 1998: In a plenary session, the Spanish AN unanimously confirmed the competence of Judge Garzón to prosecute Pinochet, upholding the full applicability of the principle of "universal criminal justice" in crimes against human rights.

November 4, 1998: In London, the law lords chamber in the British House of Lords ruled (three to two) that Pinochet lacked diplomatic immunity and as such was extraditable to Spain, fully recognizing the legal validity of Garzón's initiative.

December 9, 1998: British Home Minister Jack Straw granted Pinochet's extradition. However, at this point, Pinochet's legal counsel filed the request for a revision of the November 1998 ruling by the House of Lords, on grounds that one of the lords who voted for extradition (Lord Hoffman) was a member of a charitable organization linked with Amnesty International (AI had endorsed the accusation filed by Garzón). In spite of the fact that such an affiliation was publicly known before the trial and that the defendants had not found at the time any fault with it, the lord chancellor granted a revision of the case in order to preserve the image of full impartiality of British justice.

March 24, 1999: The case was reviewed by a new, seven-member panel of law lords, and Pinochet's claim was rejected (this time by an uncontroversial six-to-one majority). However, the new decision approached the case from a somewhat more restrictive angle and stated that Pinochet could be tried in Spain only for crimes committed after 1988, the year when the United Kingdom ratified the 1984 UN treaty against torture. This automatically restricted Garzón's indictment to just a small number of cases of torture, out of the original thousands he had documented (by 1988, the apex of the repression undertaken by the Pinochet regime had long passed).

April 14, 1999: For the second time, Straw granted the extradition, and Pinochet's counsel filed a new petition for revision of his decision, this time on purely "humanitarian terms," alleging the old age and apparently poor health of the former dictator. Minister Straw ordered a medical examination and, in spite of the rather inconclusive results, finally accepted the "humanitarian" petition and allowed Pinochet to return home.

March 2, 2000: Pinochet left Great Britain for Chile, but hardly an hour after his plane had taken off, Judge Juan Guzman from the Chilean court of appeals in Santiago filed a formal request to the Chilean Supreme Court to have Pinochet's senatorial immunity lifted, charging him with sixty crimes. Judge Guzman had been regularly informed by Garzón of the proceedings. His request relied on much of the material that Garzón had gathered and sent him.

August 8, 2000: The Chilean Supreme Court (in a landmark fourteen-to-six vote) agreed to lift the lifelong political immunity Pinochet had granted himself, making him prosecutable. By then, the number of charges against him had risen to 157.

February 2001: After new medical examinations and a preliminary judicial interrogation, General Pinochet was formally indicted by Judge Guzman and put under house arrest (in consideration of his old age and ailing condition) awaiting trial. He nonetheless was fingerprinted and photographed (front and profile)—the usual routine for indicted people.

For a more detailed account from Judge Garzón's perspective of how what had long seemed totally out of the question finally came true, see Urbano (2000, esp. chap. 10, pointedly titled "The English Patient"). In Spain, Garzón's investigations of crimes committed by the Argentinean junta still proceed: In January 2001, the new Mexican government granted the extradition to Spain of the former Argentinean captain Cavallo, formally accused by Garzón of the kidnapping, torture, and final disappearance of 227 persons in the late 1970s. In the meantime, in Argentina, and relying basically on Garzón's investigations, the federal court has reopened the cases against twelve torturers (four of them former junta members), accepting the argument that there is no statute of limitations on crimes against humanity, nor can they be pardoned; a decisive blow to the validity of the "Final Point" laws (hastily passed by the Argentinean government on the return to democracy as the result of a forced compromise with influential sectors of the armed forces). Indeed, all "final points" seem to have been erased by this new development in international criminal justice, which will undoubtedly continue.

42. Abolition of the death penalty is now a prerequisite for any country applying for membership into the European Union. The abolition of the death penalty took effect as soon as the constitution was enacted (December 1978), but it took eighteen more years before jury trial became law (the Law on Jury Trials was passed in 1995, and it began to operate in 1996).

43. With respect to the death penalty, the climate of opinion has been fairly stable since 1978: an absolute, clear majority of the Spanish population agrees with its abolition. Even in periods of particular intensity of ETA terrorist activity, the opponents of the death penalty have outnumbered those favoring it.

44. In Spain, the jury is made up of nine members, randomly selected from the citizenry, and is presided over by a judge. It is the judge's responsibility to prepare in an easy, understandable way the list of questions referring to the facts on which the jury must pronounce a verdict. The judge can also assist the jury in its deliberations.

The final decision is made by the judge after the jury has given a verdict. The jury must express a vote for each of the facts submitted for its consideration: in order to declare the facts proven, at least seven votes are required if the facts are against the accused, but only five if they are favorable. Only when such a detailed vote has taken place does the jury proceed to vote on innocence or guilt (similarly, at least seven votes are needed for a declaration of guilt, but only five for innocence). The consequence of such an elaborate system (the constitution requires that all decisions must be supported by reasons) is that on occasion, final decisions on innocence or guilt may not follow logically from the facts previously voted as proven (as was conspicuously the case in the notorious Otegui case of 1997; see note 45). Should this happen, the judge can return the verdict to the jury, indicating the points of contradiction and requesting their review. Decisions after trial by jury can be appealed only with respect to the points of law involved; facts considered as established are undisputable.

45. In 1996, in the Basque Country, a jury considered not guilty a militant from the radical separatist group HB in the killing in cold blood of two agents of the Basque autonomous police who had approached his home unarmed on a routine inspection. The decision of the jury caused an enormous scandal in the Basque Country (as in the rest of Spain), amid a strong suspicion that the terrorist organization ETA (to which HB is directly linked) had intimidated the jurors. The case was considered an ordinary case of homicide (rather than a terrorist act) and assigned to local jury trial rather than falling under the competence of the Madrid-based AN.

46. See Toharia (2001a). The pattern of opinion can be interpreted as expressing a perception of juries as weak and easy to manipulate, something that could represent an advantage for the accused person but be deleterious to the public interest.

47. The competence of the jury extends only to cases of homicide (excluding those referred to as terrorist acts), threats, trespassing, forest arson, misuse or improper care of documents, perjury, influence peddling, and misappropriation of public funds. Of the 290 jury trials, 85 percent ended with a condemnatory verdict (see *Memoria del Fiscal General del Estado*, Madrid, 1999). In any case, this meager figure cannot compare with the 121,801 penal cases resolved by the juzgados penales, or the 105,840 resolved by the audiencias provinciales in nonjury cases in that same year.

48. "Judge and Co." is Jeremy Bentham's gently ironical expression to refer to the judicial system as a whole.

49. All Spanish adults with a law degree can apply to take such an examination. The examination consists of a series of tests on juridical knowledge. The examining board is composed of three senior judges (one of whom acts as president), one public prosecutor, two law professors in juridical disciplines, a practicing lawyer with more than ten years' experience, and a high-ranking civil servant (art. 304 of the LOPJ). In addition to this traditional system, the LOPJ of 1985 (arts. 301 and 311) has made possible two new ways of accessing the judicial career: (1) lawyers with at least six years of professional experience can apply for direct admission into the Judicial School, without any entrance examination (the stay in the Judicial School will last two years, as with candidates admitted through competitive examination); (2) lawyers with recognized experience and prestige and more than ten years of practice can apply for direct admission into the judiciary.

50. This is unlike the situation in Italy or France, where judges and prosecutors belong to the same bureaucratic career and consequently have the possibility of moving from one role to the other at any time.

51. This pattern is common to most civil law countries where the process of feminization of the judiciary is bound to go well beyond the 52 percent level that could be expected under strict demographic proportionality, which raises the interesting perspective of a traditionally all-male profession becoming predominantly female-staffed in countries such as France, Italy, Spain, or Brazil.

52. Slightly over 55 percent of the total Spanish population is now under forty years of age.

53. "Court clerks act as notaries in judicial matters, and assist judges in the exercise of their functions" (art. 472 of the LOPJ); officials and auxiliaries make up the bureaucratic personnel of the judicial system; and agents act as a kind of judicial police within the strict limits of the court premises. Forensic specialists are physicians in the service of the administration of justice; they form a bureaucratic corps entered through competitive examination. They function as technical assistants to the courts (arts. 497 and 498 of the LOPJ). The LOPJ (art. 473) confers on the court clerk the coordination of all the personnel attached to the court, under the supervision of the judge. However, neither court clerks nor judges have any disciplinary powers over their personnel.

54. Historically, the royal functionaries charged with the legal protection of the public interest were at the same time supervisors of tax collection, hence their name, which has managed to remain even after the loss of this function in the nineteenth century.

55. Even the Council of the Judiciary has recently (September 2000) urged the substitution of instructing judges for fiscales, with the subsequent redefinition of their respective functions.

56. "Representation of the parties in all types of procedures is the exclusive responsibility of the *Procurador*" (art. 438 of the LOPJ). Except in some specific cases, the procurador is the unavoidable link with the court, which cannot be addressed directly by the claimants or the attorneys. Procuradores represent an old profession designed to facilitate physical communications between courts and parties; their existence is now being strongly questioned.

57. As Merryman points out, *extension* of a legal system must be understood to mean "the social reach of the legal system, the area of social activity to which it attempts or purports to apply" (in Legrand 1999, 63).

58. A figure three times larger than the corresponding figure for France in 1995! (The total Spanish population is about two-thirds the size of the French population.)

59. Toharia and García de la Cruz (1999); fieldwork of this study used a total sample of 1,500 randomly selected practicing lawyers out of the 24,596 registered in the Madrid Bar Association in May 1999 and was carried out between June 30 and July 15, 1999. Madrid lawyers represent more than a fourth of all Spanish lawyers: the results obtained can thus be reasonably extrapolated to the entire profession.

60. In 1972, 44 percent of all Madrid lawyers could be considered to be regular litigators and 50 percent as nonlitigators (see Toharia 1976). The difference between

the two sets of percentages indicates the growing dedication to non-court-related activities.

61. The figures do not include cases related to family matters. Family cases appear as a differentiated category in 1983 and represented a total of 57,818 cases in 1989; 67,061 in 1990, and 93,024 in 1998.

62. All labor cases are required to attempt a negotiated solution within the IMAC before being allowed to go to court.

63. The rate of incoming labor cases per 1,000 persons within the active population has decreased from 19 in 1975 to 16 in 1998.

64. It must be noted, however, that under Spanish law, public administration is not allowed to seek negotiated solutions in a certain number of situations. Litigation then becomes unavoidable. Also, in some instances, administrative bodies defer their decision until a judicial decision forces them to act in a given way, as a way of covering themselves from political responsibility for their actions.

65. Indictment only means the opening of the trial phase.

66. There were 33,911 in 1990 and 42,636 in 1997 (31,793 convicted; 10,843 on remand). In 1990, the total detention rate (convicted plus prisoners on remand) in Spain was 86 per 100,000 inhabitants, as compared with 132 in Austria, 93 in Portugal, 90 in England and Wales, 82 in France, 78 in Germany, 57 in Italy, and 44 in the Netherlands (information from Contini 2000).

67. Also, if things were otherwise, it would be difficult to explain why only 19 percent of all litigating lawyers specialize in criminal cases.

68. The recently published account of the situation of civil justice in different countries edited by A. Zuckerman (1999) is significantly titled *Civil Justice in Crisis*. Literature on judicial reform is growing at a fast pace. For a sound and useful introductory annotated bibliography, see Stephenson (1999). Messick (1999) and Messick and Hammergren (1998) provide a careful account of the results of judicial reform projects in several areas of the world.

69. For a more detailed discussion of the case in favor of the use of opinion polls in the evaluation of systems of justice, see Toharia (2001a).

70. Data in Table 11.8 seem to reflect a gradual increase in this negative evaluation over the last two decades. In fact, what seems to have happened is that as the number of persons in the "DK/NA" category decreased, the percentage of interviewees expressing a negative opinion experienced a correlative growth. Data seem thus to suggest not so much a collapse of the social image of justice as an expansion of the percentage of persons who express an opinion: the percentage considering the performance of justice "well"/"very well" or "so-so" has tended to remain stable.

71. The case would take two years in Spain and two and a half years in France.

72. The data are systematically analyzed in Toharia (2001a).

References

Albaladejo, M. 1996. *Derecho civil: Introducción y parte general*. Barcelona: Bosch.

Contini, F., ed. 2000. *European data base on judicial systems*. Bologna: IRSG.

Diez-Picazo, L., and A. Gullón. 1997. *Sistema de derecho civil: Volumen I.* Madrid: Tecnos.

Friedman, L. M. 1969. Legal culture and social development. *Law and Society Review* 4:29.

———. 1994. *Total justice.* New York: Russell Sage, 1985. Reprint.

García de la Cruz, J. J. 1997. Cultura cívica de la reclamación. In *Fundación Encuentro, Informe España 1996.* Madrid: Fundación Encuentro.

———. 1999. La cultura de la reclamación como indicador de desarrollo democrático: Tres perspectivas de análisis. *Politeia* 22:7–28.

Jacob, H., E. Blankenburg, H. M. Kritzer, D. Provine, and J. Sanders, eds. 1996. *Courts, law and politics in comparative perspective.* New Haven, Conn.: Yale University Press.

Legrand, P. 1999. John Henry Merryman and comparative legal studies: A dialogue. *The American Journal of Comparative Law* 47 (1):3–66.

López-Guerra, Luis, ed. 1998. *Las sentencias básicas del Tribunal Constitucional.* Madrid: Boletín Oficial del Estado.

López Pintor, R., and R. Buceta. 1975. *Los españoles de los años setenta.* Madrid: Tecnos.

Messick, R. E. 1999. Judicial reform and economic development: A survey of issues. *World Bank Research Observer* 14 (1):7–28.

Messick, R. E., and L. Hammergren. 1998. The challenge of judicial reform. Chap. 6 in *Beyond the Washington Consensus: Institutions matter,* edited by Shahid Burki Javed and Guillermo E. Perry. Washington, D.C.: The World Bank.

O'Callaghan, X. 1997. *Compendio de derecho civil: Parte general.* Madrid: Editoriales de Derecho Reunidas, S.A. (EDRESA).

Pastor, S. 1993. *¡Ah de la justicia!* Madrid: Civitas.

Stephenson, M. 1999. *Annotated bibliography on judicial and legal reform.* World Bank, Washington, D.C. Mimeographed. Available on the Legal Institutions Thematic Group Web site: www1.worldbank.org/publicsector/legal/annotated.html.

Toharia, J. J. 1974a. *Cambio social y vida jurídica en España, 1900–1975.* Madrid: Editorial Cuadernos para el Diálogo.

———. 1974b. *Modernización, autoritarismo y administración de justicia en España.* Madrid: Editorial Cuadernos para el Diálogo.

———. 1975. *El juez español: Un análisis sociológico.* Madrid: Tecnos.

———. 1976. Economic development and litigation: The case of Spain. In *Zur Soziologie des Gerichtsverfahrens,* edited by L. M. Friedman and M. Rehbinder. Jahrbuch für Rechtssoziologie und Rechtstheorie. Band 4. Opladen: Westdeutscher Verlag.

———. 1987. *¡Pleitos tengas! Introducción a la cultura legal española.* Madrid: Centro de Investigaciones Sociológicas.

———. 1989. *Cambios recientes en la sociedad española.* Madrid: Instituto de Estudios Económicos.

———. 1998. *Insuficiencias, deficiencias y disfunciones del sistema jurídico-judicial y sus consecuencias sobre la actividad económica y empresarial: La Administración de Justicia vista por el empresariado español.* Madrid: Fundación ICO.

———. 1999a. La buena justicia y la independencia judicial. *Justicia y Sociedad* 3 (October):11–32.

————. 1999b. La justicia. Pp. 97–114 in *El gobierno de Aznar*, edited by J. Tusell. Barcelona: Crítica.

————. 2001a. *Opinión pública y justicia*. Madrid: CGPJ.

————. 2001b. Judges. Entry in the new edition of *The international encyclopaedia of social and behavioral sciences*. London: Elsevier.

Toharia, J. J., and J. J. García de la Cruz. 1999. Evaluación del funcionamiento de los tribunales de justicia de la comunidad de Madrid: Encuesta a una muestra de abogados del Ilustre Colegio de Abogados de Madrid. *Otrosí* 9 (November): 18–38.

Urbano, P. 2000. *Garzón, el hombre que veía amanecer*. Barcelona: Plaza y Janés.

Zuckerman, A., ed. 1999. *Civil justice in crisis: Comparative perspective of civil procedure*. New York: Oxford University Press.

Zweigert, K., and H. Kötz. 1998. *An introduction to comparative law*. Oxford: Clarendon Press.

CHAPTER 12

Venezuela, 1958–1999:
The Legal System in an Impaired Democracy

ROGELIO PÉREZ-PERDOMO

THE YEAR 1958 is generally taken as the starting point of the most recent period in the political history of twentieth-century Venezuela. The event that marked this beginning was the exit from power and from the country of General Marcos Pérez Jiménez, a military leader who was fraudulently elected in 1952 and who tried to legitimate his power in the election of 1957. The provisional government of 1958 organized free and democratic elections in December of that year. In the forty years that followed, a political system developed that was considered a stable democracy, with political parties as central actors (Njaim et al. 1975; Levine 1978; Martz and Myers 1977; Karl 1986; Rey 1980, 1989, 249–311). The political system has shown signs of crisis and rapid transformation in the last decade (Álvarez 1996; Kornblith 1998; Njaim 1997; Rey 1991), and it is likely that we can consider 1999 to be the end of the period.

A document that marks the beginning of the period was the pact of governability of 1958 (called *Pacto de Punto Fijo*). In recent years, the expression *democracia punto fijista* came to mean a government run by the inner circles of political parties, with a minimal role for citizen participation. It is also generally agreed that neither the rule of law nor a genuine welfare state was implemented for the majority of the population during this period. These limitations made the functioning of the state defective, reduced the legitimacy of

I thank C. L. Roche, H. Njaim, and Rafael Pérez-Perdomo for information and guidance in various aspects of this work. C. Alguídegui and B. Piña Montes helped me locate recent unpublished information. Alinson Bidwell and Melissa Jones were very important in the English translation. I thank especially Lawrence Friedman for his thorough revision.

the political system, and generated the present crisis. This chapter proposes to analyze the functioning of the legal system and the relationships between law and politics during the period 1958–99.

Not only was the political system widely criticized, but the constitution itself (passed in 1961) was also brought into question. People felt that the judiciary was utterly corrupt and inefficient, considering it one of the worst features of the Venezuelan state. In a 1999 referendum, the public overwhelmingly approved the convocation of a constituent assembly to change the political system and to draft a proposed constitution, which was later approved in a referendum in December 1999. We do not yet know what type of political system will result from these changes, but the perception that a period has ended seems justified.

Table 12.1 offers a brief chronology of the period with some political changes and important legislation. This section will outline the principal stages of the period under analysis.

Venezuelan political life during the period we are studying is generally divided into five-year periods, corresponding to the terms of the president of the republic and the Congress (hence, generally called *constitutional periods*). Nevertheless, we prefer to divide the period into ten-year periods, not only for convenience, but also because these periods have a certain coherence.

The decade 1958–68 can be considered a period of political stabilization and definition of the rules of the game. The Pacto de Punto Fijo was signed by the principal democratic parties that existed in 1958 (*Acción Democrática* [AD], *Copei*, and *Unión Republicana Democrática* [URD]), but not by the Communist Party, which had played an important role in the overthrow of the military dictatorship. The stage was marked first by various attempts at military coups and later by rebellions of guerrilla groups sponsored by the Communist Party and other self-proclaimed Marxist revolutionary groups. The administrations of the time period were coalitions (AD-Copei in 1959–64; AD-URD and other groups in the next five-year period) that achieved control of the subversives, and there was undeniable popular support for the political system. The characteristics of the system were expansion of education and health services, agrarian and urban reform, and the strengthening of the two principal political parties, AD and Copei, with policies of clientelism.

The second decade is the 1970s. By now we can consider partisan democracy to be consolidated. In December 1968 voters elected an opposition leader for the first time in Venezuela, and in 1973 and 1983 the political parties in power switched again without causing any unrest in the country. The rise in oil prices in 1973 (the boom that corresponds to the crisis in consumer countries) enriched the state. Several important industries were nationalized, among them the oil companies. The state made enormous investments in big industrial complexes, barriers were erected to foreign investment, and

Political Chronology, 1958–1999

1958	January 23: exile of General Pérez Jiménez; establishment of the *Junta de Gobierno*
	October: *Pacto de Punto Fijo*
	December: general elections; Rómulo Betancourt (AD) elected president
1959	Coalition government is established (AD, URD, COPEI)
1961	New national constitution comes into force
1963	December: Raúl Leoni (AD) elected president
1964	Coalition government is established (AD, FND)
1968	December: Rafael Caldera (Copei) elected president
1969	Government established with minority in the Congress
	Reform of the *Ley Orgánica del Poder Judicial* and creation of the Judiciary Council
1971	Legalization of Communist Party and MIR; end of guerrilla activities (*pacificación*)
1973	Petroleum price increase begins
	December: Carlos Andrés Pérez (AD) elected president
1974	New government with enormous fiscal resources; large investments in public enterprises announced (*la gran Venezuela*)
1975	Nationalization of petroleum
1978	Serious corruption scandals
	December: Luis Herrera Campins (Copei) elected president
1979	New government begins; President Herrera mentions the enormous external debt in his inauguration speech
	Congress declares President Pérez politically responsible in the Sierra Nevada case; attorney general decides not to press criminal charges
1983	February ("Black Friday"); control over exchange rates established and continuing currency devaluation begins
	Corruption scandals involving various ministers
	December: Jaime Lusinchi (AD) elected president
1984	New government begins, with majority in Congress; mismanagement of the economy continues
1988	Shortage of foodstuffs and other products; frequent corruption scandals
	December: Carlos Andrés Pérez (AD) elected president; campaigns with reciprocal accusations of corruption against AD and Copei
1989	February: New government begins; agreement with FMI signed; radical changes in the political economy (*el gran viraje*)
	February 27: Popular protests and looting (*caracazo*)
	December: Law of Decentralization of Public Power
1992	Attempted coups d'etat in February and November
1993	President Pérez is accused of corruption and impeached by Congress
	December: Rafael Caldera (*Convergencia*) elected president
1994	Minority government formed and populist measures announced
1996	Government changes to a more liberal political economy (*Agenda Venezuela*); agreement with FMI announced
1998	December: Hugo Chávez (MVR) elected president
1999	Convocation of constituent assembly approved in referendum; new constitution approved in December referendum

national industries were intensely protected. The state became a pervasive regulator of the economy.

In the 1980s difficulties were perceived with this system. In 1979 the new government made the magnitude of the public debt known. In 1982 the government established control of exchange rates, and a period of successive devaluation of the currency and acceleration of inflation began. Economic growth was very weak, when it was not negative. State intervention in the economy increased, but no longer for the purpose of *development* (the declared objective until then) but to avoid the effects of a confused political economy that had practically halted private investment in the country. Accusations of corruption among politicians became more and more serious and frequent. Corruption was used as the most powerful argument against political enemies. The political parties weakened to the point of becoming federations of groups in permanent conflict. The weakening of the political system was gradual, and the democratic system seemed in fact more consolidated: the presidential candidates of the two main parties gained nearly 90 percent of the votes in the general elections of 1983 and 1988. They clearly remained the two main forces in Congress up to 1993.

The most recent decade was marked by clear deterioration of the political system. In 1989 the government attempted a radical change in economic policy (*el gran viraje*) and signed a letter of intention with the International Monetary Fund to liberalize commerce and the economy. In February 1989 Caracas experienced violent protests and lootings, requiring the army to reestablish order (*el caracazo*). No well-known political group seemed to be behind these events, a fact that demonstrated the gap between the political parties and the general public.

That same year an attempt was made to bring the political system closer to local problems and regional necessities by separating these elections from the national ones and organizing the first direct elections for mayors and governors. In 1992 there were two failed attempts at military coups, but there was demonstration of popular support for the democratic system.

The coup attempts were preceded in 1991 by a public manifesto called the *Carta de los Notables* that highlighted the corruption of the political system and the ineffectiveness of the judges, including the Supreme Court of Justice. The attempted coup of February 1992 was a military failure but evidenced the magnitude of the political crisis. One of its effects was to increase debate about the appointment of Supreme Court justices that year, which resulted in a more independent Supreme Court. In 1993 President Pérez was tried before the Supreme Court and dismissed from office on charges of corruption. In December of that year, Rafael Caldera, who was the founder of Copei but was later thrown out of that party, was elected president. He governed with the help of old leftist groups and with dissidents from Copei. In

December 1998 Lieutenant Colonel Hugo Chávez, leader of the first coup attempt in 1992, was elected on a platform that promised to prosecute corrupt politicians and reform the constitution and political system (*refundar la República*). It should be noted that the parties that signed the Pacto de Punto Fijo and that dominated Venezuelan politics until 1998 did not have any importance in the presidential election of 1998, or even in the elections that followed.

If we look back at the decade, we see that the political elite had a clear awareness of a looming crisis. Attempts at reform were made too late and did not achieve the hoped-for effects. One example to consider was constitutional reform. In 1989 a bicameral commission was appointed, presided over by Senator Caldera, to study a revision of the constitution of 1961. The commission decided to proceed by way of amendment. In 1992, when crisis was evident, the commission—whose work had received no attention from Congress or the public—moved to center stage. It made the decision to go by way of *reform*, a fundamental change that required approval by referendum. But serious obstacles arose, not only because of a general lack of agreement among Congress members, and among the public at large, but also because of disagreement on the role that Congress should play. Because Congress seemed to be a mere instrument of the traditional parties, various groups called for a constituent assembly, following the example of political reforms in Colombia (1991) and Brazil (1988) (Combellas 1993). The constitution of 1961 did not provide for any such reform procedure. The call for such an assembly was among Chavez's proposals as presidential candidate, and in January 1999 the Supreme Court declared it was constitutional and acceptable for the president to hold a referendum to decide if a constituent assembly should be convoked for constitutional change and reform of the political system. The referendum was held in 1999, the assembly was elected, and this resulted in a draft constitution that was approved in a new referendum in December of that same year.

In summary, the 1990s can be seen as a time of intense crisis that brought about the events described and substantial changes in the cast of political characters. The democratic political system in place since 1958 (the democracia puntofijista, in Venezuelan political jargon) clearly came to an end. The manner in which the crisis ended can be considered a consolidation of the democratic and institutional system, because all of the changes occurred through elections, and attempts at change through violence failed. However, it is too early to know how democratic and how respectful of the rule of law the renovated political system will be. The constitution of 1999 and the political changes of that year appear to be oriented toward minimizing the importance of the political parties and centralizing the system in the person of the president of the republic. In this sense it seems to correspond more

FIGURE 12.1 Workers' Real Wages, 1950–1997
Baptista (1999).

to the Latin American tradition of *political personalism* (Soriano de García-Pelayo 1996) or a Caesarian democracy.

In political-economic terms, the most important fact of the whole period was the vast influence on oil prices. Oil generated an income that permitted the state to consolidate from the 1930s on. At the beginning of the period that we are analyzing, the income per capita of Venezuela was double the average of that of the rest of the Latin American countries. Much of the national well-being was due to the distribution of petroleum income (Baptista 1989, 1999), and the state, or more accurately, the network of clients that formed the political parties, was the major instrument of distribution for all sectors of society. Starting in 1978, the situation changed dramatically. The waste of enormous oil revenues during that decade, together with subsequent indebtedness and economic mismanagement, progressively reduced both net private investment and real wages. Figures 12.1 and 12.2 graphically depict the economic situation. Baptista (1989, 1999) maintains that the crisis is extremely serious, which implies that the Venezuelan economy has lost vitality and that recuperation in the immediate future cannot be hoped for.

The gravity of the political and economic crisis of the 1990s makes it easy to forget that the process of change accelerated in the last forty years of the century and that not all of the changes can be considered negative. Educa-

FIGURE I2.2 Relative Size of Private Investment in Relation to GNP, 1950–1998
Baptista (1999).

tion was more widely provided, and illiteracy was reduced in the population
over fifteen years of age from more than 35 percent in the beginning of the
period to less than 10 percent in 1995. Sanitary conditions improved, increasing the life expectancy at birth from sixty-four to seventy-three years. Communication media, especially television and radio, grew dramatically and became more widely available. Table 12.2 shows some important indicators of
change during the time period.

In summary, the Venezuelan political system since 1958 has been considered democratic in the sense that, generally speaking, freedom of expression
and of the press was respected, elections were held, and the results were honored. Those who dissented were accepted as opposition, in a clearly plural
system. The various organs of the state respected constitutional limits in their
relations with each other. But the political parties played an important role
in the operation of the state, beyond what is typical in modern democracies.
Not only were positions within the state treated as a vast stock or booty to
be parceled out, but the client networks that made up the parties were instruments for the distribution of enormous wealth, derived in great measure
from oil income. Each social group gained privileges and advantages. For the

business owners the state acted as *estado de fomento* (promotion) to protect, finance, and facilitate private economic activity (Pérez-Perdomo 1999). For other groups it acted as dispenser of jobs (and fake jobs) in a growing bureaucracy. For the less advantaged groups the state acted as *estado de beneficencia*, distributing free services of all kinds, including health, housing, education, and training. The system had a certain legitimacy, as membership in a client network could lead to a rather rapid social ascent if the head of the network was sufficiently powerful to benefit the members and if the clients, by education or initiative, could take advantage of the privileges that the system was offering.

The central thesis here is that a client-based state, to the degree that it existed in Venezuela, is incompatible with norms that characterize the rule of law.[1] In order for a client-based state to function, laws must be flexible (to the point where they are perverted), if not simply ignored. Only in this way can the system of favors and privileges function without major obstacles.

We know that the assertions we have made are controversial and should be further nuanced. There are those who maintain that the Venezuelan institutional system under the constitution of 1961 was an *estado social de derecho* (welfare state and rule of law) (Brewer Carías 1975; Combellas, 1979). The constitutional design of 1961, the rights it declared, and the state organisms it assigned to watch over or guarantee the enjoyment of these rights are the basis for this characterization. Apart from the legal basis, people felt that the democratic regime in which the press was free and public demonstrations permitted, in which political parties were easily formed, and in which civilians held power, was a regime of freedom. For example, Carrera Damas (1980) asserted that Venezuela in the period 1958–74 had achieved freedom but still needed to achieve development. In other words, it was a democratic rule of law, though plagued by poverty and lack of services for a substantial part of the population. This view was very common during the period: what was lacking in Venezuela was development, sustainable material progress. But

TABLE 12.2

Principal Socioeconomic Indicators

Socioeconomic indicators	1961	1971	1981	1990	1999
Population per 1,000 inhabitants	7,869	11,094	15,515	19,602	23,707
Rural population (%)	41	30.7	22.2	16	14
Life expectancy at birth	63.8	66.1	68.8	71.8	73
TV sets per 1,000 inhabitants	37	82	113	159	165
Illiterate population (15+ years) (%)	36.7	23.5		10.0	8.9

SOURCE: United Nations, *Statistical Yearbook*; UNESCO, *Statistical Yearbook*, respective years (1999 or closest year available).

this vision does not recognize the significance of uncertainty in legal process and human rights abuses against a substantial part of the population that not only inhibited investments but also delegitimized the political system and brought it to a breaking point.

In Latin America the absence of the rule of law is generally associated with indiscriminate repression against whole social or political groups. In the case of the Venezuelan democratic regime, the repression was relatively moderate, although this assertion is also controversial. There was considerable political repression in the first ten years of the period: rebellions, first by rightist military officials and later by leftist guerrillas, justified the repression. It cannot be said that human rights were scrupulously respected at this time. Torture and extrajudicial executions were carried out with impunity, although not on a large scale. Relatively few people and groups were mistreated. Once the country was pacified, police continued to detain and torture low-income persons whom they suspected of having committed crimes (Torres 1987). The different branches of the police and military forces practiced with growing frequency violent procedures and abuses of human rights and also extorted small bribes and committed other crimes, all with considerable impunity (Navarro and Pérez-Perdomo 1991).[2]

The political system, the public administration, and the judiciary all functioned with high levels of corruption (Quintero 1988; Pérez-Perdomo 1995, 1996b; Njaim 1995; Capriles 1991). The police were especially corrupt. The corruption could act as a cause of violent abuses or as a moderator of such abuses.[3] In some cases, the massive violation of human rights was part of a system of exploitation of certain groups, such as prisoners (Pérez-Perdomo and Rosales 1999). In general, the control of power through elections limited the worst abuses but could not assure that the institutional system would serve to guarantee human rights or legality, or that it would have the willingness and capability to correct police abuses and corruption. The situation became worse in the 1980s and 1990s as a consequence of the deteriorated economic situation and the increasing publicity of corruption cases.

The flaws of the Venezuelan institutional system lead us to question whether there has truly been a rule of law, even though we have had separation of powers, constitutional and legal control of laws and administrative acts, and formal guarantees (protection) of constitutional rights. Those who have looked closer at the actions of the political bodies and the real situation of people, especially of low-income people, have shown that the formal guarantees were not effective. It cannot be considered that there was a rule of law when abuses of power were part of public policy and the rights of a substantial part of the population were not secured (Hernández 1977; Pérez-Perdomo 1995; Quintero 1988). Impunity for violation of human rights was the general rule (Faúndez and Cornieles 1994).

One cannot speak of a "welfare state" when the state did not provide welfare nor did any such thing exist for the majority of the population. For these reasons we assert that the qualification (welfare state) is wrongly applied to Venezuela for the period that we are analyzing. The Venezuelan state during this period, like the Western European democracies that were its models, was very active intervening in the economy and sustaining or regulating private initiatives. But because of the political and legal culture, property rights and freedom of contract were not guaranteed. As we will see later, regulation of rents, of prices, of labor relations, and of urban reform, as well as protection of major industrial activities, distanced Venezuela from the market economy model perhaps to a much larger degree than the European countries that served as examples. The unruly functioning of the state gave still more discretion to politicians and functionaries.

Consideration of how much democracy or liberty actually existed in Venezuela during the period under analysis and to what extent a rule of law or respect for laws and rights existed calls attention to the central problem of the relationship between democracy and the rule of law. The two ideas have different historical origins. In this work we postulate that in modern society, liberal democracy—which implies respect for the rights of citizens and, in general, all the residents of the state—and rule of law are complementary. This does not imply that certain basic aspects of democracy cannot exist in countries where there is not a consolidated rule of law. Some have called this type of political regime *disjunctive democracies* (Holston and Caldeira 1998) or *illiberal democracies* (Zakaria 1997). The case of Venezuela, like other Latin American countries, suggests that democracy can exist with a weak rule of law and without market-based economic relations. The central argument of this work is that such a democracy did not turn out to be stable in Venezuela.

This chapter analyzes thoroughly the relationship between law and social practices in Venezuela and the people's implicit attitudes toward the law. We begin with a brief description of changes in the legislative process and legislation and their sociopolitical significance. Afterward, we analyze the judges and the workings of the judiciary. The third part of this chapter discusses legal education and the legal profession. The final section discusses some defining characteristics of Venezuelan legal culture in the period that we are analyzing and the relationship between the rule of law and democracy.

Legislation and Social Change

With the fall of General Pérez Jiménez, several government juntas formed, and ultimately Edgar Sanabria, a respected professor of Roman law, became provisional president. These provisional governments had as their mission the organization of general elections. They did little by way of legislation, despite the general accepted theory of de facto governments that said that the government would assume all the powers of the state. Notable among the measures of the provisional governments was the dissolution of the National Congress, considered illegitimate because of the electoral fraud that brought Pérez Jiménez to the presidency in 1952. The police force, known for its systematic use of torture, was likewise dissolved. In the legislative plan, the de facto government approved a new *Ley de Universidades* (Law of Universities) and modified the income tax to place more of a burden on large businesses (mostly the multinational oil companies). Of greater interest is the legislation passed later by the democratic regime once it was constituted. We will discuss it by traditional legal subject matter.

THE CONSTITUTION OF 1961 AND THE STRUCTURE OF THE STATE

The Congress, elected in December 1958, assumed drafting a new constitution as one of its important tasks. The main political groups engaged in continuous consultation with the political and business elite (not including the general population), and they did extensive technical work. This political consensus and technical and legal elaboration produced the national constitution, which, approved by Congress, went into effect January 23, 1961 (Oropeza 1986).

In order to understand the importance of this constitution, some historical context must be given. Venezuela had formally been a federal country since 1863, the year in which the federalists (whose opponents were the conservatives) won the war. In practice, Venezuela was so fragmented during the nineteenth century that it could scarcely be considered a nation-state, in spite of all the efforts to organize it in that way (Pérez-Perdomo 1990). During the first half of the twentieth century, a very centralized system was constructed, although—for historical reasons—it kept the form of a federal state. In 1958, when democracy was reestablished in Venezuela, the centralist character was accentuated because the political parties were centrally organized under the strong leadership of their founders.

The constitution of 1961 provided for a balanced distribution of power, with a certain predominance of Congress over the president of the republic and a relatively modest position for the judiciary. The National Congress elected, without input from the president, the Supreme Court, the *fiscal general*, and the general comptroller.[4] The president could not veto legislation but only ask Congress to reconsider it. Congress could dismiss ministers with a majority vote. To appoint the *procurador general* (attorney general for noncriminal matters), ambassadors, and high-ranking military officials, the president needed authorization from the Senate. The Supreme Court could annul legislation as unconstitutional and could review and reverse administrative acts that violated the constitution or other laws (*Estudios sobre la constitución*, 1979).

Both the president and the Congress were elected for terms of five years. The president could not dissolve the Congress, nor could the Congress dismiss the president if it disapproved of his administration. Presidential re-election was prohibited for the next two terms. The president could be tried only if he committed a crime. Only the fiscal general could accuse him, and the acceptance of the Supreme Court and the Congress was necessary for a trial in the Supreme Court.

The system was representative democracy with proportional representation. By tradition, each party was identified with a color (or combination of colors). The system of closed lists guaranteed that parties would have an absolutely key role in controlling who was elected. Basically, citizens voted for a party every five years, and this was the extent of their political participation. What they could expect was that the party — or their friends within the party — would repay their loyalty with some type of advantage or favor.

Congress was the arena of debate between the political parties and the place where they negotiated. Relations between the president and Congress were harmonious if a majority party or coalition supported the president. When the president did not have this support, relations with Congress were tense. The highest point of conflict was the removal from office of President Carlos Andrés Pérez in 1993; he had lost the support of his own party and was dismissed and found guilty of misappropriation of funds by the Supreme Court.

The constitution was very generous in granting rights. Besides traditional individual and political rights, the constitution enumerated *social rights* such as protection of health, education, work, and social security. It also declared *economic rights*, including the promotion of development as an obligation of the state, the grant of land and credits to farmers and rural workers, and the defense and conservation of natural resources. In practice, this meant that the state would establish programs but that the citizen would have to find some patron to gain the benefit or advantage, making it more like a gift from friends or political allies than a genuine civil right (Acedo Machado 1987; Capriles 1996). What was established was not a culture of rights, but rather one of favors.

Rights and favors can collide, and frequently do. For example, an appointment as a police officer is a favor that someone does for the appointee. Because it is a favor, the new police officer does not understand his obligation to be the provision of a service, but rather the exercise of a power. Naturally, this can lead to abuse of another citizen's rights, who, in turn, has no other defense but to find a more powerful friend who can protect him from abuse, including punishing the police officer. The judiciary follows the same logic, and therefore truly disinterested protection of rights cannot be hoped for. In this context, the constitution and the legal system itself had limited importance.

Nevertheless, it cannot be said that the legal system was purely declarative or formal. The laws were general guidelines for relations among citizens and between citizens and the state. As we will see later, the number of lawyers grew substantially in this period; this occurred because they were consulted, prepared contracts, processed claims, and performed other typical legal tasks, even though recourse to adjudication was not considered ethically appropriate (Pérez-Perdomo 1996a, 1996b).

The constitution, in particular, played an important role in the definition of political roles. High functionaries clashed on the limits of their powers. When the conflict could not be resolved by political negotiation, the Supreme Court began to be used. The organic part of the constitution and the court itself had undeniable importance.

In the 1980s, when the system was discredited, there were pressures for change, and the elite itself embarked on a policy of state reform. Among the central aspects of political reform achieved at the end of the decade and the beginning of the 1990s were decentralization and the direct election of governors and mayors. There was a change in the electoral system, too: proportional representation was weakened, and a referendum system was institutionalized. These changes weakened the power of the political parties and led the way to the radical changes of the late 1990s.

The constitution of 1961 provided for amendment and reform as means of change. In both processes Congress played a central role. In 1999 the Supreme Court decided that, by virtue of the electoral legislation and the principles of democratic government, an advisory referendum could be called to determine if the public wished a constituent assembly to be convoked. This decision allowed radical changes to take place in a way that technically did not imply rebellion against the state and that, at least in its broad outlines, respected institutional order.

THE LEGISLATIVE PROCESS

The constitution put power to initiate legislation in the hands of Congress itself (its commissions or at least three members) and in the executive branch (the ministers). The Supreme Court held this power on matters that concerned judicial organization and procedure. The public also had a role: twenty thousand or more voters could propose legislation (Constitution 1961, art. 165). This last possibility was rarely used, typically only when there was a desire to highlight popular support for a legal change. There were two types of legislative procedure. Normally, a bill was discussed twice in each chamber and, if there was agreement, sent to the executive branch for promulgation and publication. The constitution provided mechanisms for resolving disagreements between the chambers. Each chamber had permanent commissions in which the different political forces were represented.

As is the case under various constitutional systems, Congress had other functions besides legislative ones: it was an arena of political debate and a center of control of executive power (Instituto de Estudios Políticos 1971). Congress was quickly criticized for not legislating adequately. It was seen as a place for rhetorical discussions. Deputies and senators were criticized for not working hard on their main job, legislation. It was pointed out that the work of Congress was technically deficient. Political clients of each party, rather than people ready to work with seriousness and efficiency in legislative tasks, filled commissions. It is not important whether this vision of Congress was correct. The criticism was important enough to make the leaders in Congress worry and to lead them to propose reforms in the legislative process and in Congress itself. This led to two important reforms.

The first and most important reform, from the constitutional point of view, was the creation of the Legislative Commission. This reform, embodied in Amendment 2 (1983), modified legislative procedure to open a new path of discussion of a proposal: discussion in the Legislative Commission.[5] Once approved there, it passed to Congress to be discussed in a joint session of both chambers. It was thought that this procedure was more appropriate for discussion of major legislative texts, such as codes. In practice, the Legislative Commission worked only for discussion and approval of the reform of the Code of Civil Procedure (1987) and the Organic Code of Penal Process (1998). For long periods it was inactive.

The second reform was organizational, but proved to be more important for the work of Congress. We will not enter here into the details of the regulation (Gabaldón and Oberto 1985; Oberto 1995) that gave deputies and senators important incentives to attend sessions of the chambers and meetings of the commissions. These organizational reforms first created the Office of Legal Advice, and much more recently, a similar office for economic advice. A public competition was held for selecting legal advisers, and substantially higher salaries than those of the regular civil service were offered. Legal scholars generally felt that this reform increased the technical quality of legislation, but it did not have a major impact on the public image of Congress. The economic advice office was more recent (1998). Its influence on the legislative process has not been evaluated.

The executive branch played an important role, generally overlooked, in the legislative process. Most legislative proposals were prepared by the executive and presented by cabinet ministers. The executive was also charged with publication and enforcement of the law. It was the job of the executive to make the organizational changes and take the necessary actions for the laws to be carried out and their objectives realized (Njaim 1996). A fuller and more realistic view of the legislative process would include the preparation of the legislation and its enforcement and evaluation (Njaim and Pérez-Perdomo 1995). The executive could also legislate when empowered by congressional delegation (Constitution 1961, art. 190, 8) in situations of economic or financial emergency, and in relation to these areas. The time of this delegation was strictly limited. In general, presidents obtained such authorizations once each and made important modifications to legislation via legislative decrees (or delegated legislation).

The executive also used suspension of the so-called economic guarantee (Constitution 1961, art. 96) in order to have a free hand in regulating the economy; but the president used this power with considerable moderation (Planchart, Lovera, and Toro 1985; Njaim 1995). The guarantee was reinstated in 1991 because of the change in the political economy that began in 1989. The governments were relatively moderate in their use of discretionary powers, but they seemed unaware of the spirit of the constitutional guarantees and of the fact that suspension of guarantees should be exceptional.

A general evaluation of legislative activity during the forty years of democratic legislation would take a whole book; here we analyze only a few areas. Some general observations can be made concerning the volume of legislation. Table 12.3 shows the number of laws approved or modifications made in each five-year period.

The total is 1,317 legislative acts, of which 1,257 were laws passed by Congress and 160 decreed by the executive power through legislative delegation. If we take the sum of all laws (including decrees) effective in December 1999, the total is 344 (276 laws and 68 decrees); it can thus be inferred that legislation was frequently amended. This is confirmed by the fact that only 19 percent of the legislation effective on December 31, 1999, had been elaborated or modified prior to 1958, and 44 percent was approved (or modified) in the 1990s (*Servicio Autónomo de Información Legislativa* [SAIL], *Índice de Legislación Vigente* [legislative database]; our calculation). The only area subject to legislative delegation was the economic-financial one, which is also the area most subject to variation. It certainly cannot be said that Congress and the executive abandoned legislation or that they failed to use legislation to respond to social needs or promote social change. However, this assertion says nothing about the quality of the legislation. Needs and changes were seen through the eyes of certain social groups and certain economic and political interests. In the following pages, we will analyze some areas of legislation in terms of their quality or the interests they respond to.

TABLE 12.3

Legislation Approved or Modified
per Five-Year Period

Period	Ordinary legislation	Decrees
1959–63	96	8
1964–68	135	0
1969–73	134	0
1974–78	140	35
1979–83	162	0
1984–88	180	33
1989–93	93	15[a]
1994–98	216	15
1999[b]	1	54

SOURCE: Servicio Autónomo de Información Legislativa (SAIL), quantification by Berta Piña Montes.
[a] In the last year of this period, President Carlos Andrés Pérez was removed from office by Congress; Provisional President R. J. Velázquez issued the decrees.
[b] In 1999, President Chávez called a referendum, and convocation of the National Constituent Assembly was approved, which does not appear in this table; the only law of 1999 is the one that allowed government by decree.

ON CRIMES AND PENALTIES

The penal code is the basic penal law. The code of 1873 closely followed the Spanish model. The reform of 1897 was influenced by the Italian code of 1889 (Jiménez de Asúa 1950, 1:954). Despite various later reforms, the penal code remains faithful to this model. The last important reform was in 1926. In 1964 there was a minor reform, increasing punishment for crimes related to the rebellions at that time. The penal code has had enormous stability in the period we are analyzing, but this does not imply that penal legislation has not had important modifications, just that this has been done through special laws. Among these should be noted the Organic Law on Abuse of Stupefacient and Psychotropic Substances (generally known as the Anti-Drug Law, 1993, amending the law of 1984) and the Organic Law of Protection of the Public Patrimony (1982). The Penal Law of the Environment (1992) also shows the trend to criminalize behavior, but the social impact has been small.

First, one should analyze the meaning of the stability of the penal code in this period. The penal code is a catalogue of behaviors that are carefully defined and for which minimum and maximum punishments are established. The context is a basic principle for interpreting the code; thus, its arrangement into books and chapters is very important. The penal code distinguishes between crimes committed against persons, against property, against good manners and family order, against the conservation of public and private interests, against the public patrimony, and against public order. Significantly, rape and other sexual crimes are not defined as crimes against persons or against sexual freedom but are situated together with crimes against good manners and family order. Although the victims of these crimes can be of either sex, the main victims are women. In the perspective of the code, they are important more as members of a family than as individuals.

The perception of a woman as someone whose value lies in her relationship with a family or a man is quite explicit in the code. For example, Article 428 of the penal code substantially reduced the penalty of a husband, father, or grandfather who killed or wounded a woman or her lover surprised in the sexual act. The Supreme Court declared this law unconstitutional on March 5, 1980 (*CS, Sala Plena*), as contrary to the equality of men and women. Honor, as it was understood in the nineteenth century, came before the right to life. Under Article 424 a duel is an extenuating circumstance for one charged with homicide or injury, unless the duel was dishonorable (which would aggravate the charge). When homicide or injury has been provoked by offenses against someone's honor, the punishment would also be reduced. The language of the penal code here brings us back to the nineteenth century.

Venezuelan society during the period under analysis had left completely behind these old notions of women and of honor that appear in the penal code. Women had growing access to university education and to the most important social and political positions to the point that, as we will later see, there were more women than men among judges themselves. The fact that the penal code has not been reformed shows negligence on the part of those responsible for legislative politics—a failure to reflect social change in the laws or possibly even to guide social change in this important area.

The legislators did pay attention to drugs and to corruption. In 1984 the Law of Undue Use of Stupefacient and Psychotropic Substances was promulgated, and in the same law the National Commission Against the Illicit Use of Drugs was created. The law became controversial, and there were considerable practical difficulties in applying it (Borrego and Rosales 1992). It was amended in 1993. The Law of Protection of the Public Patrimony was promulgated in 1982 as a consequence of serious corruption scandals that had shaken the country from 1978 on. Both laws are repressive; both established special judges and procedures.

The Anti-Drug Law of 1984 does not treat *use* as a crime; users are subject to treatment and rehabilitation. Conversely, those involved in production, sale, and distribution are severely punished. In practice, due mostly to the absence of treatment centers and infrastructure for effective rehabilitation measures, users were treated as criminals and sent to prison. At the same time, the law ordered the preventive detention, without the possibility of bail, of those prosecuted for crimes related to drugs. The law also made it obligatory to consult with judges of higher courts. The Supreme Court could review the decisions if the district attorney requested it. This guaranteed lengthy process. Borrego and Rosales (1992, 44) analyzed the cases brought to the criminal courts in Caracas between 1984 and 1988 and found that 72 percent of the defendants were prosecuted for use and 19 percent, for possession. Possession usually implied quantities difficult to distinguish from personal doses. The 1993 reform corrected the worst abuses in this law.

The *Ley de Salvaguarda del Patrimonio Público* (Protection of the Public Patrimony) was also characterized by its repressiveness. It defined various traditional crimes so broadly that, if taken literally, it would be practically impossible to exercise any public function without committing a crime. For example, an official who called home from his office to inquire about the health of his son would be guilty of *graft*. If accused of unjustified enrichment, the defendant had to prove his or her innocence. Bail was also excluded for those prosecuted for these crimes. These extremely repressive measures were balanced by a rather short statute of limitations—five years; for ordinary penal legislation, the statute varies according to the seriousness of the crime.

Criminal procedure was another neglected area of penal legislation almost until the end of the period. The law in force until 1998 was the *Código de Enjuiciamiento Criminal* (Code of Criminal Procedure) of 1926. This code, like similar ones in Latin America, can be considered "backward" in comparison with those of Europe. Latin America codified the old Spanish process from the colonial period and ignored the modernizing impact of English process and the liberal ideas of the French Revolution, which led to reforms in European legislation in the nineteenth century. The Latin American penal process included a long phase of secret investigation—secret from the defendant's standpoint—and conducted by the same judges who would then decide the case. The process could be delayed by appeals at each stage. The general rule was detention of the suspect for the duration of the process. The reason given for the maintenance of such an archaic system, contrary to human rights and to the principles recognized in the constitution and international treaties, was mistrust of social groups that were considered dangerous. The guarantees of due process were perceived as a risk in the face of the possibility that a substantial portion of the population might commit crime. Therefore, it seemed more fitting to give discretionary powers to the police and the judges and to control through appeal any deviation from due process on the part of these authorities (Duce and Pérez-Perdomo 2000). In Venezuela the decision to reform the process took place after criticism from all sectors and international pressure, but a coalition between reformists who want more respect for human rights and those who want a more efficient system that provides quick punishment of criminals is probably unstable.

The attention given to certain aspects of penal legislation—partly due to pressure from the United States (mainly related to drugs) and from international organizations (concerning procedure) and the general clamor for punishment of corrupt officials—shows that those responsible for legislation in this matter merely react to outside influences. In this regard, we include not only the political elite who controlled Congress and the executive but also legal scholars, who were too caught up in the formal aspects of law to think in a general way about the political and social significance of legislation.

CIVIL AND UNCIVIL REFORMS

The sphere of civil law is ill-defined. Often it is simply described in terms of what it is not—religious, military, political, or commercial. Here we deal with two examples of civil law in the strict sense: family and property, both regulated in the civil code.

The first Venezuelan civil code dates from 1862, but the code of 1873 is the basis of modern legislation. There were later points of reform, such as the introduction of divorce in 1904. In 1942 the drafters consciously decided to maintain the 1873 version, based on the Italian civil code of 1865, despite the modernization of codes in Europe and other Latin American countries during the late nineteenth century and beginning of the twentieth. Only the chapter corresponding to *obligations* was modernized, following the Franco-Italian unification project of 1927, which actually had not been well received in the countries of origin.

In the 1970s it was obvious that the part of the code relating to family and to divorce did not correspond with the customs and aspirations of a growing number of Venezuelans, especially Venezuelan women. A dozen proposals were presented to Congress, but they died either because of disagreement among the interested parties or because of the inertia of Congress. In 1979 women from different political sectors attempted a revision of the code. They followed a very intelligent strategy of popular mobilization and political lobbying, overcoming the opposition of the Catholic Church and of various other conservative sectors, including the president of the republic. In 1982 Congress approved a partial reform of the civil code that recognized equality of women inside the family and the equality of natural and legitimate children. It liberalized divorce, too. This reform was a popular proposal and generated intense public discussion. The new code ended the primacy of the husband or father in the distribution of goods and in the education of children and established joint custody between father and mother. In cases of disagreement between married couples, the judge would decide. Several jurists made technical objections on the grounds that the reform destroyed the logical architecture of the civil code. The Catholic Church protested against the liberalization of divorce. Others perceived the reform as an unacceptable intervention by the state into internal family affairs and as an incentive for litigation (Prince de Kew 1990). In practice, no explosion of litigation has occurred. If any trend is perceivable, it is the greater use of the courts by men who wish to keep custody of their children in cases of divorce (for the reform in general and its impact, see Reyna de Roche 1991; San Juan 1991; Roche and San Juan 1993). The latter studies showed that the new regulation did not increase litigation or conflict inside families.

We now consider the law of real property. Between 1958 and 1999 the urban population in Venezuela grew from 50 percent to 86 percent. Even though the population of the country increased from 7 million to 23 million, the rural population only grew from 3.5 million to 4.8 million. What changes in legislation accompanied this immense social change?

In the beginning of the period, much importance was placed on the Law of Agrarian Reform (1960) that briefly preceded the constitution. The central idea of the reform was to expropriate the unproductive *latifundios* (large estates) and endow poor peasants with lands and credit. For various reasons, this did not have the hoped-for result of making residence in rural areas attractive or of augmenting rural production (Torrealba 1983; Suárez, Torrealba, and Vessuri 1983).

The greatest changes occurred in the cities, especially in Caracas and other urban areas such as Maracaibo, Puerto La Cruz-Barcelona, Barquisimeto, Valencia, and San Cristóbal. It is important to note that the construction industry was very significant economically during the 1950s (Machado de Acedo 1981) and continued to be until the 1980s. The most important legislation affecting the urban areas was the Law of Regulation of Rents (1960), reformed in 1986, and the *Ley de Propiedad Horizontal* (property in a condominium), promulgated as a legislative decree in September 1958 and amended in 1983. Naturally, there was other legislation, such as laws that regulated mortgage rates and the financing and distribution of public housing. The most notable change was, nevertheless, the emergence of an informal sector: self-made houses, generally constructed on abandoned or municipal land, in violation of urban regulations.

There is a huge literature on the subject, but, in brief, the regulation of rents destroyed the market in rental housing. Rental housing construction, frequent in the 1950s, simply ceased. Tenants could remain in rental housing practically indefinitely, paying rents that increased only insignificantly. An illegal and limited market of transfer of rental housing developed, with an initial cost that did not benefit the owner. The state created an office of rental regulation, and there was a moderate amount of litigation. The owners who wanted to reclaim their houses had to involve themselves in endless lawsuits or pay the tenants to vacate. In general, regulation mostly functioned to benefit a small and illegal market in rental housing.

The alternative to renting was to buy a house. Until the middle of the 1970s, this was an alternative accessible to a relatively numerous sector of the population, given the relatively low interest rates and growing real wages. A good part of the construction in the main cities consisted of condominiums; this proceeded without many legal or other difficulties. This market had narrowed by the two last decades of the period until it was only within reach of the most privileged.

The official or noncommercial housing sector was relatively narrow. The granting of housing by the *Instituto Nacional de la Vivienda* (formerly the *Banco Obrero*), was always associated with political clientelism. Only people of a certain income level (certainly not the poorest) and with political connections (*palanca*), could obtain such a privilege (Sánchez 1974).

A large and growing sector of the population was excluded from the official and commercial market and could obtain housing only in the informal sector, or *barrios*. Housing in barrios is characteristically constructed without any previous study or municipal permits, generally on invaded lands. The government selectively tolerated these invasions. In fact, the tolerated invasions were organized by political activists of the government's own party or a party with good local and national representation. Squatting was organized with considerable care, in places where a reaction from the government or a private property owner was improbable. Once a barrio was established, the houses built, and a large group of people assembled who were willing to resist any attempt at evacuation, it would be considered permanent. Public policies have varied on this issue over time. Until the 1980s some official agencies distributed construction materials free of charge so that tenants of ramshackle houses could improve them and make them more solid. The barrios were gradually granted services, and schools and clinics were built in adjacent areas. People spoke of the "consolidation" of the barrios.

The notable fact about this policy was its own political success. Toleration of invasion of public land, and the later services provided in barrios, were other ways people could benefit from the client networks of the main parties. In fact, the latter policy began with explicit support and money from the United States in order to counteract the enormous communist influence in the Caracas barrios at the beginning of the period (Ray 1969). The barrios became clients of the democratic parties, although loyalty could change from one group to another according to the quality of the local activists' client network.

All of these changes were made without changing the civil code's traditional property rules, which remained more appropriate for a rural society or for cities with very slow growth. These rules are entirely favorable to landowners but are also ineffective because of procedural and political difficulties arising from massive invasions (Pérez-Perdomo and Nikken 1979). Urban planning was the responsibility of municipal authorities who kept to the illusion of a unified urban space and did not foresee different rules for different social sectors. Some jurists called for more comprehensive urban regulation (Brewer 1983), but this did not occur until 1987.

From the legal perspective, the barrios present a peculiar situation. Because they are not included in urban plans, the houses of the barrios could be destroyed by order of the municipal engineer, or property owners could force evacuations and reclaim their land if they sued successfully. Construction on another person's property cannot be registered without permission from the owner, according to a Supreme Court decision, and the Law of Rental Properties prohibits renting a dwelling considered a *rancho*. These dwellings are truly unmarketable. Yet, their inhabitants made important investments in them (especially considering their income level) and had considerable security in their tenancy (Karst, Schwartz, and Schwartz 1973). Informal political networks lent security to transactions in the barrios (Camacho and Tarhan 1991). The municipal government also invented an extralegal system for the regulation of conflicts (Pérez-Perdomo and Nikken 1979). A parallel and informal system that resolved the major problems of absence of formal law was created. This did not, however, resolve other problems such as the greater vulnerability of their dwellings to collapse and fires due to the topography of the barrios and the labyrinthine character of their construction (Pérez-Perdomo and Bolivar 1998).

From the beginning of the 1990s, much of the clientelism in the barrios seemed to decay. In 1989 there was a true change in policy. The authorities decided to end widespread subsidies and to act more in accord with the rules of a liberal state. Food and transportation costs skyrocketed, which particularly affected the population of the barrios. Local gangs lost respect for traditional rules, and relations became very violent. Given the topography and tradition, the police did not usually intervene in the barrios. When they did, it was in short raids of great violence and abuse against the people in the barrios, who lacked protection. Violent crime began to increase sharply, aggravated by a crisis that frequently paralyzed the public hospitals or made them function with a minimum of supplies (Pérez-Perdomo, Malpica, and González 1997).

In sum, Venezuela experienced an accelerated process of urbanization without changing its antiquated laws. Much of the process of urbanization was done while the law turned its back, or in direct violation of law. The results were not "civil." Recent proposals typically call for *regularization*. This implies incorporating the barrios into the mainstream urban fabric through urban regulation, as well as the granting of legitimate title to properties in these areas (Fundación de la Vivienda Popular 1991).

THE CIVIL PROCESS

In contrast to the civil code reform (1982), a revision of the Code of Civil Procedure was promulgated in January 1986 and made effective in March 1987. Until 1987 the code of 1916 was in effect. It was generally considered good technically, but inappropriate for the more complex society of the second half of the century. We will not analyze the technical aspects of the reform but the legislative process itself.

Fuenmayor (1997), one of the code drafters, wrote an account of the reform process. In 1969 the Commission for Reform of the Code of Civil Procedure was formed, made up of a number of lawyers and judges; the number, in time, was reduced to four people. In 1975 the commission submitted the draft code to the president, who sent it to Congress where it was ignored. *Engavetamiento* (to put something in a drawer and forget it) is the name used in Venezuela for this type of inaction. Ten years later, the president of the Legislative Commission decided to resuscitate the proposal. He called the drafters in to meet with the commission members, and in a few months the proposal was approved with modifications, some of which were unfortunate, in Fuenmayor's opinion.

In this case, the preparation of the legislative proposal lacked study and consultation. Ten years after the reform, a professor in this field still complains of these faults and points out the lawyers' rejection of the reforms (Molina Galicia 1996). Another of the drafters (Rengel Romberg 1996) complains that judges and lawyers have not understood some important aspects of the new code, such as the distinction between lack of jurisdiction and competence, which have radically different consequences. The Supreme Court itself interpreted some rules in such a manner as to pervert the reform.

The closed character of the legislative process was the problem here. There was no diagnosis of what reform was needed or what alternatives were available to the drafters. It is also clear that before 1985, not only were there few opportunities for the public to be truly informed of the purpose and content of the revision, but there was also no reason to take revision seriously nor incentives to participate in the legislative process. When the Legislative Commission took over the process, they proceeded in a great hurry. One might think that the sixteen years that transpired between the designation of a reform commission and the approval of the law would be sufficient to produce a well-studied reform. But considering the large periods of hibernation that the project experienced and the final rush to approve it, the resistance of those affected by the reform is understandable, and we can see the effect of a lack of democratic or participatory aspects in the legislative process.

This type of closed legislative process, with many elements of improvisation, as was the case with the Code of Civil Procedure, was much more common than the more public and consultative one for the civil code. Given this history, it is natural that the legislative process has been perceived by many Venezuelans—including law scholars—as a hazardous process of political imposition, a situation that does not lead the citizens to identify themselves with the laws or with the political processes that produced them.

The Judiciary and Judicial Activity

Judges have played a minor role in the twentieth-century history of Venezuela. With a clearly personal (or dictatorial) political system until 1935, one could not imagine that courts enjoyed much independence from the political powers or had any important role. Formally, the appointment of the judges and the administration of the judicial budget depended on the executive power or on a collaboration between this body and Congress. In practice, there was very little judicial independence. Only the political stability between 1915 and 1945 and the personal respectability of some judges limited the intrusion of political powers into judicial decisions. Various studies show that such dependence continued or increased in the period from 1958 to 1998 (Quintero 1988; Pérez-Perdomo 1995), but the mechanisms of dependence varied considerably during the period.

Dependence or responsibility of judges is not the only, and perhaps not the most important, theme in the relationship between the judicial system and society. This section analyzes how the system operated and what functions it served. We begin with these aspects and then turn to practices and policies already mentioned. Finally, we examine the central ideas of the judicial reforms initiated in the last years of the period.

STRUCTURE AND FUNCTIONING OF THE SYSTEM

Under the constitution of 1961, the judiciary consists of the Supreme Court and the other courts of the country. However, the *Ministerio Público* (headed by the fiscal general), and the Ministry of Justice also had important functions in the operation of the justice system. The Ministerio Público, independent from the other organs of the state, functioned both as a prosecutor and as an ombudsman. The Ministry of Justice, as part of the executive power, had responsibility for the judicial police, the prisons, and other units

TABLE 12.4

Number of Courts, 1962–1997

Court	1962	1971	1981	1990	1997
Superior (appellate)	41	55	96	148	181
Primera instancia	143[d]	200[b]	289[c]	326	368
Municipal[d]	173	169	200	208	219
Parroquia[d]	359	359	356	354	343
Total	716	783	941	1,036	1,111
Per 100,000 inhabitants	9.5	7.30	6.48	5.23	4.88

SOURCES: Court figures for 1962, *Memoria y Cuenta del Ministerio de Justicia* (1962, 163); for 1971, 1981, 1990, and 1997, *Anuario Estadístico de Venezuela*, OCEI, respective years; population figures, OCEI.

[a] Includes 32 *juzgados de instrucción* (courts for criminal investigation).

[b] Includes 53 *juzgados de instrucción.*

[c] Includes 77 *juzgados de instrucción.*

[d] As a consequence of reorganization of the political divisions in the state, beginning in 1996 the former district courts (for the whole country) and department courts (in the Federal District) were renamed municipal courts; the former municipal courts (for the whole country) became *parroquia* courts.

charged with the execution of punishments. We will focus here exclusively on the judges and courts.

The Supreme Court maintained its basic structure during the entire period. The constitution of 1961 did not regulate the number of magistrates or the internal organization of the court, which was done by the Organic Law of the Supreme Court of Justice. During the entire period, the court consisted of fifteen magistrates organized in four *salas* (chambers). The *Sala Plena* (the meeting of all the magistrates) was charged with the most important constitutional functions. For usual cases, the magistrates were divided into three chambers: *Sala Político-Administrativa, Sala de Casación Civil,* and *Sala de Casación Penal.* Each chamber had a certain number of substitute magistrates at its disposal. In the first years of the period, the court consisted basically only of these. But the growing number of cases required the recruitment of support personnel. These lawyers (clerks) were engaged to help in the elaboration of decisions. The court created a Court of Substantiation to manage all the steps prior to decisions and an Auxiliary Chamber for fiscal matters (both as part of the Administrative Chamber). All of this implied a substantial augmentation of the personnel of the court during the period. By the end of the period, the court had nearly two hundred lawyers working full-time in distinct jurisdictional capacities.

The top level of the Venezuelan judicial system (the Supreme Court and the superior courts) grew during the period. Table 12.4 shows the changes in the number of courts, arranged hierarchically. We have chosen the national census years, or the nearest possible for which data are available.

According to the *Memoria y Cuenta del Ministerio de Justicia* of 1962 (Report on the Activities and Outcomes of the Ministry of Justice, p. 159), the dictatorship of Pérez Jiménez eliminated 224 courts. In 1958 there were 543 courts, of which 256 were municipal courts, 163 were district (now municipal), 88 were *primera instancia* (first instance), and 36 were superior. As most superior courts sat in panels of 3 judges, there was a total of 591 judges. Only 211 of these had a law degree. There were 8.44 judges per 100,000 inhabitants. The democratic government's policy was to increase the number of courts and to put people trained in law at the head of them. The number of courts sitting in panels was also drastically reduced. By 1962 the number of courts had substantially increased. It can be seen that the greatest increases were at the level of municipal courts. The figure shows a later moderate increase in the absolute number of courts, which reflects a decrease by half in proportion to the population of the country. Growth was concentrated in superior courts and first instance courts, which hear the most important cases. On the other hand, municipal and parochial courts remained stable in absolute numbers. These courts were extensively distributed throughout the territory and heard small claims cases, whereas the first instance courts and superior courts were concentrated in the state capitals and, above all, in Caracas. We will analyze the significance of this concentration when we analyze the efficiency of, and the citizens' access to, the justice system.

The number of courts is a good indicator of the total number of judges. By law, each court must have a judge. But the *Corte Primera de lo Contencioso Administrativo* (High Administrative Court) and the *Tribunal Superior de Salvaguarda* (High Court for Corruption Cases) have panels with three judges each. Between 1990 and 1999 there were fifty judges who went from court to court to clear up backlogs in first instance and superior criminal courts. Thus, to calculate the number of judges, we take the number of courts and add fifty-four. This brings the figure for judges per 100,000 inhabitants in 1998 to approximately five. Consequently, despite an initial increase in the number of judges during the period—produced above all in the lower levels of the judiciary—the number of judges substantially decreased, relatively speaking, during the forty years of democracy.

In addition to a judge, each court has a secretary, an *alguacil* (sheriff), and an indeterminate number of auxiliary personnel for office work. The number of auxiliary personnel can vary greatly from one court to another. Some courts with low workload have none. In those that manage a large volume of cases, auxiliary personnel can amount to as many as twenty people. By the end of the period, the total number of employees of the *Consejo de la Judicatura* (Judiciary Council), which excluded the Supreme Court, came to twelve thousand. Unfortunately, we have not been able to find information about the total number of court employees at the beginning of the period,

TABLE 12.5

Change in Distribution of Matters Heard in
Primera Instancia *and Superior Courts*

Cases	1962	1998
Superior (criminal matters only)	8	91
Primera instancia (criminal matters only)	67	175
Superior (criminal and other matters)	20	5
Primera instancia (criminal and other matters)	2	6
Superior (noncriminal only)	13	85
Primera instancia (noncriminal only)	74	187

SOURCES: For 1962, *Memoria y Cuenta del Ministro de Justicia* (1962, 161); for 1998, *Memoria y Cuenta del Consejo de la Judicatura* (1998, 107).
NOTE: The courts that specialize in cases of *salvaguarda* (corruption) and bank crimes are included as criminal courts.

nor were we able to build a historical series. But it can be concluded that while the top layers of the judicial system grew, the rest of the system suffered a reduction.

Changes in the subject matter of cases heard are another important aspect to be considered. For this, see Table 12.5, which refers only to the superior and first instance courts. Cases in the municipal courts will be discussed later.

There has clearly been a trend to specialization in the courts, mostly with regard to criminal cases, and a very substantial increase in the number of courts that hear criminal cases only. Half of the superior courts specialize in criminal cases. Only a few courts hear criminal cases together with other cases. The fifty itinerant judges also hear criminal cases only. The courts that hear noncriminal cases are less specialized. Perhaps labor is the only other type of case that produces similar specialization; seven superior courts and twenty-five first instance courts hear these cases exclusively. In other words, during the period under study, the criminal area became considerably specialized and acquired great importance in the system.

There is a military justice system, regulated in the Code of Military Justice, parallel to the system just described. This parallel system is smaller and has been little studied. It had considerable importance in the first part of the period under analysis, when it prosecuted military and guerrilla rebels, and again in 1992–93 after the coup of 1992. Regrettably, we lack data, and no study exists to which we can refer.[6]

In summary, the Venezuelan judicial apparatus is small and became smaller during the period that we are studying, but has become increasingly concerned with criminal cases. How do the cases heard by the courts relate to the social and economic life of the country? We will discuss two aspects of the justice system: criminal and business cases.

CRIME AND PUNISHMENT

We first concentrate our analysis on police activity. The statistics do not always report this activity in the same way; therefore, we have chosen the earliest year (1983) and the most recent (1997) for which the data are homogeneous, as shown in Table 12.6.

The category "handled by the police" refers to crimes that are reported to the police or that the police uncover through their own investigations. It should be noted that this is not an indicator of levels of delinquency but of reporting rates or investigative activity, especially for cases such as those related to drugs, in which citizens frequently do not make accusations.[7] Note that the number of cases handled also increased significantly in relative terms. "Cases resolved by the police" are those in which the police believe they have identified the perpetrator. It is naturally a smaller figure, and it declines in this period, going from 57 to 45 percent of cases handled. In the final years, the number of people detained by the police surpassed the number of cases resolved and continued to increase, also relative to 100,000 inhabitants. That there could be more arrests than cases resolved is easily explained: there could be more than one arrest per case, and some arrests do not result in any charges, because the police free the suspect before informing the courts. The constitution of 1961 authorized police detention for seventy-two hours, the maximum time for which a person could be detained before a writ of arrest must be made.

The police with investigative function (*instrucción*)—in this period these were the *Policía Técnica Judicial* and the *Fuerzas Armadas de Cooperación* or *Guardia Nacional*—and the judges of first instance in criminal courts could open and close investigations. We are interested in the number of judicially closed investigations. There the judge in charge of investigation determines

TABLE 12.6
Judicial and Police Activity

Cases	1983	1997
Number of cases handled by the police	143,324 (874)	236,742 (999)
Number of cases resolved by the police	81,798	105,933
Number of arrests made	70,798 (432)	119,799 (506)
Number of cases closed in the courts	18,716	48,432

SOURCE: *Anuario Estadístico de Venezuela*, OCEI, 1983, 1997 (1984, 1998).
NOTE: The figures in parentheses are relative to 100,000 inhabitants.

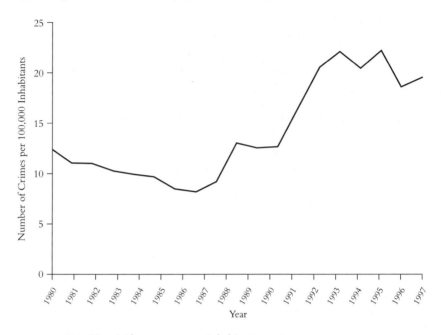

FIGURE 12.3 Homicides per 100,000 Inhabitants, 1980–1997
Anuario Estadístico de Venzuela, OCEI, respective years.

that a crime has not been committed, the statute of limitations has barred the investigation, or the suspect has died. The number of investigations closed by the courts increases proportionally during the period in relation to the number of cases that the police claim to have resolved.

The figures do not reflect the way the public experienced criminal activity. In the 1980s a perception of insecurity grew, due mostly to the increase in crimes against property (Navarro and Pérez-Perdomo 1991). The official policy was to relax the restrictions on weapons possession and to authorize merchants and "heads of good families" to carry personal weapons. Through burglaries or other means, the weapons ended up in the hands of criminals, which resulted in a substantial increase in lethal violent crimes. This can be seen in the increase in homicides from 1989 onward, especially affecting the capital region (Caracas and its surrounding areas) (Pérez-Perdomo, Malpica, and González 1997). Figure 12.3 shows the number of homicides. The situation in the capital region was worse than the national picture: in 1994 it reached 58 homicides per 100,000 inhabitants, though it dropped to 38 in 1997. The creation of municipal police bodies, who adopted a more communitarian and civilized model for exercising the police function (Márquez and Castillo 1999), could have had an influence.

As a response to the perception of increased criminal activity, the government increased the number of police officials and instructed them in *mano dura* (iron-fisted) policies. In practice, this resulted in a much more abusive police force: massive arrests were based on stereotyping, and suspects were systematically mistreated. Police forces themselves began to commit crimes. A study done at the beginning of the 1990s (Navarro and Pérez-Perdomo 1991) found that people feared that muggers might actually be police officers (or police officers actually muggers). In a later study of victimization in the area of Caracas (Briceño-León et al. 1997), 13 percent said that the police had extracted *peaje* from them that year (small bribes to allow a person to continue walking along). As only 6 percent reported being asked by criminals for peaje, the police much more frequently committed the extortion.

It is not surprising, then, that global reports on human rights abuses began to include critical chapters about Venezuela, and that at the end of the period the new Organic Code of Criminal Procedure (1998) substantially decreased the power of the police.[8] This code prohibited arrests without writs of arrest (or allowed them only when *in flagrante delicto*). The code also placed the police under the supervision of the Public Ministry.

What happened when crimes were brought before the courts? According to the written law, the judge received the documents from the police and decided whether to close the case or produce a writ of arrest or an order to put the defendant on trial (the latter for less serious crimes). If the process continued, time was allowed for the interrogation of the suspect, for the district attorney to formulate charges, and for the suspect to prepare a defense. The trial followed, at the end of which the lawyers were given the opportunity to present their written reports, and the judge made a written decision. Procedural decisions could be appealed and ruled on by a higher-court judge, who would then return the case to the first instance judge. In case of procedural mistakes, the case could be returned to a previous stage. There were also ways for the process to become paralyzed. Trials tended to be very slow, unless one of the lawyers (generally the defense attorney) persisted in demanding that the case be resolved. This generally occurred with people who could pay for a good and committed lawyer. For low-income people, the process tended to be very slow, and neglect was routine (Van Groningen 1980).

The Judiciary Council was in charge of evaluating the judges. Nevertheless, it never designed technical means to measure the actual duration of processes, despite being obliged to do so, since it was an element of evaluation of judges according to the Law of Judicial Careers. In fact, the duration of trials was never investigated. In practice, trials moved with irregular speed, with a tendency toward slowness. One study found that a sample of homicide trials around 1980 in the jurisdiction of Caracas dragged on for more

TABLE 12.7

Criminal Trials Initiated and Concluded
in Primera Instancia

Writs and verdicts	1983	1997
Writs of arrest	11,408	20,343
Writs of subjection to trial	2,395	8,665
Writs of dismissal	3,010	4,573
Verdicts★ of dismissal	2,295	1,200
Not guilty verdicts	1,212	2,002
Guilty verdicts	6,500	11,000

SOURCE: *Anuario Estadístico de Venezuela*, OCEI, respective years.
★We have translated *sentencia* as *verdict*, but note that there were never
any juries, and the verdict was the judge's final decision in the case.

than four years (Van Groningen 1980). Various interviewees indicated that
trials became even slower in the 1980s and 1990s.

Table 12.7 shows the two principal ways that a trial could be initiated
when there was a suspect (writ of arrest or writ of subjection to trial) and its
possible conclusions. The years chosen were 1997, the last one for which relevant statistics have been published, and 1983, the earliest for which we have
equivalent statistics. In both years the previous Code of Criminal Procedure
(of 1926) was in effect.

It should be noted that the number of writs of arrest and of subjection to
trial cannot be added together to arrive at the total number of cases initiated,
because judges can change a writ of arrest to one of subjection to trial, or vice
versa, according to the circumstances. Therefore, the total of the two would
be much greater than the true number of trials initiated.

Note that there are many ways in which a criminal trial can end. The
normal form of conclusion is a verdict (*sentencia*). A verdict can be guilty
or innocent. There can also be verdicts of dismissal, which are pronounced
when the judge considers that there was not enough evidence for a decision,
no crime was committed, or the case becomes barred by the statute of limitations during the course of the trial. A judge can dismiss a case before the
verdict (writ of dismissal) if the judge considers that any of these situations
has occurred. If we look at all the ways in which criminal cases can end, it
is noteworthy that in 1983 approximately half of the trials ended in a guilty
verdict, whereas the proportion had increased to 59 percent by 1997. But
perhaps the most relevant figure is that only 9.2 percent of police arrests
ended as guilty verdicts. The high number of dismissals (44 percent of all decisions that ended trials in 1997) suggests that many cases never should have
been initiated. Even more frequently, the process went on for so long that it

TABLE 12.8

Inmates in Venezuelan Prisons

Inmates	1962	1977	1987	1997
Prisoner population	8,217	15,357	28,972	25,575
Prisoners per 100,000 inhabitants	102	118	160	111
% of sentenced/total prisoners	32	39	33	31

SOURCES: For 1962, *Memoria y Cuenta del Ministro de Justicia* (1963); for other years, *Anuario Estadístico de Venezuela*, OCEI, respective years.

no longer made sense to continue because the defendant had already served a full term before ever having been sentenced.

The prison population is another indicator of the problems with Venezuelan justice. The population increased during the period, until 1991, when it reached 31,100 prisoners (156 per 100,000 inhabitants). Policies of both the judiciary and the minister of justice lowered the number to 25,575 prisoners in 1997 (111 per 100,000 inhabitants). Table 12.8 depicts the prison population for selected years.

In general terms, it cannot be said that Venezuelan democracy was especially repressive, in the sense of maintaining a high number of citizens in the prisons. The number was comparable to that of Spain or Costa Rica, countries with substantially lower rates of criminality (Pérez-Perdomo and Rosales 1999). The distinguishing feature in Venezuela during the period was that the number of prisoners awaiting verdict was very high. It can be said, then, that the judicial system was not especially repressive but that a repressive political system existed that was not adequately controlled by the judicial system. Further, the criminal process could not distinguish between guilty and innocent persons within a reasonable time period. In fact, close to half of the people who were tried in the courts were freed due to insufficient cause to continue the trial. If we add to this that the overwhelming majority of prisoners were low-income people who had enormous cultural and economic difficulty in defending themselves, the result was a Kafkaesque machine that punished without distinguishing between guilty and innocent but that tended to choose people for punishment from within the same social class (Van Groningen 1980; Pérez-Perdomo 1987). It is not surprising, therefore, that the judicial system was perceived as a tool of class oppression.

The new Organic Code of Criminal Procedure (1998) radically changes criminal procedure. It embraces the accusatory model, gives a very important role to the Public Ministry, permits and regulates plea bargaining, drastically reduces the power of the police, and severely limits preventive imprisonment. This code became fully effective on July 1, 1999, at the end of

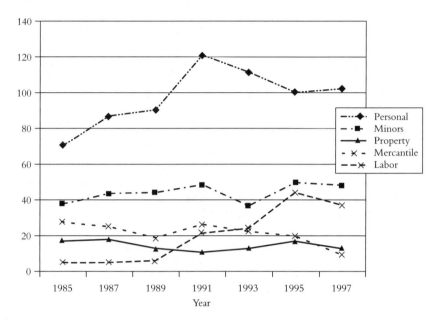

FIGURE 12.4 Number of *Asuntos Ingresados* in Noncriminal Matters in *Primera Instancia* Courts, 1985–1997
Source: Anuario Estadístico de Venezuela, OCEI, respective years.

the period under study. It is too soon to analyze its impact, but a first look shows a substantial impact on the imprisoned population, which was reduced by half six months after the code came into effect (13,352 prisoners on December 16, 1999; information from Ministries of the Interior and of Justice based on daily reports of prison population). The proportion of sentenced prisoners to total prisoners rose to 53 percent. Even though the practical problems of application seem enormous, the impression of some insiders is that the procedures have been greatly accelerated (informal interviews in Caracas in December 1999).

Police chiefs and a certain sector of the public feared greatly that the new criminal process would cause a substantial increase in crime rates, especially violent crimes, which were already very high in the country, particularly in Caracas (Pérez-Perdomo 1998; Duce and Pérez-Perdomo 2001). It has not been possible to locate statistics on this subject, reflecting the fact that the authorities have little interest in providing reliable information that would permit a rational discussion based on data rather than anecdotes.

LITIGATION AND JUDICIAL ACTIVITY

The statistical data on noncriminal matters is even less detailed. Figure 12.4 gives an idea of the change in number of *asuntos ingresados* (cases filed) in each of five principal legal areas. The meaning of this category is not clear, but lacking better data it can be taken as an indicator of judicial activity, although it does not necessarily imply the number of lawsuits.

The figures are absolute. It can be seen that "personal" matters have grown substantially, with a peak in 1991. Personal cases or, more appropriately, cases of personal civil rights, basically refer to divorces and suits to correct mistakes made by the civil registry. In general, there is no actual litigation in these cases; the "trials" ratify agreements already made between the parties. Recourse to the court is prescribed by legislation in these cases. In practice, all these could be described as quasi-notarial activity. There are separate statistics on divorces: there were 16,979 in 1993 and 14,282 in 1995. Because divorces account for the majority of personal cases, it is doubtful that asuntos ingresados represent cases that the courts actually handled.

The category "minors" covers two types of courts: correctional juvenile courts, with jurisdiction in criminal matters, and civil courts, which mostly deal with custody and child support issues. Unfortunately, the available statistics do not distinguish between these two categories of cases.

From the perspective of studying the relationship between litigation and society, the most important cases are those that deal with commercial rights and property. These are most directly related to economic activity. Resorting to the judicial system is not obligatory, as it is in personal cases. If we look at this activity, we find a substantial increase, due both to demographic and economic growth. An appropriate indicator of the growth both in businesses and in the legalization of business activity is the increase in the number of documents that have to be registered or notarized and that, in consequence, require the intervention of a lawyer for their writing or authorization. Table 12.9 shows the number of documents for selected years.

TABLE 12.9

Registered and Notarized Documents, Selected Years

Documents	1971	1981	1991
In property registries	96,093	408,933	1,272,529
In mercantile registries	23,062	119,360	368,978
With notaries	226,690	1,044,065	3,183,924
Total	345,845	1,572,358	4,825,431
Documents per 100,000 inhabitants	3,118	10,134	24,161

SOURCE: Pérez-Perdomo (1996b, 135).

TABLE I2.IO

Traffic and Cases Introduced Related to Traffic, 1992–1996

Facts	1992	1993	1994	1995	1996
Total number of cars	2,002,297	2,039,373	2,056,595	2,052,798	2,069,532
Traffic accidents	82,170	84,257	84,088	77,538	78,411
Traffic accidents with fatalities	2,215	2,372	2,920	2,087	2,439
Cases brought in traffic courts	2,048	2,048	2,433	2,874	1,654

SOURCE: *Anuario Estadístico de Venezuela*, OCEI, respective years.

The remarkable thing is that in spite of the increase in number of documents written by lawyers—a measure of "legalization"—the number of cases heard by the courts has remained stable in absolute numbers. Relative to 100,000 inhabitants, there has been a clear decrease. A visit to the courts shows that the cases are mostly related to collection of debts and, by a large majority, initiated by banks and other credit institutions that are trying to collect debts for which they have security interests. The debtors are generally individual citizens or small businesses. Conflicts between medium-size or large businesses are not generally brought to court. In a previous investigation (Pérez-Perdomo 1996b), we failed to find disputes between companies in the courts because there were so few. We had to seek business lawyers and ask them about cases in which two or more businesses were in conflict.

The increase in labor-related cases is not necessarily due to an increase in labor conflict in Venezuela but to two concomitant factors. The immediate one was the promulgation of the Organic Labor Law in December 1990, which eliminated tripartite commissions and gave their responsibilities to the labor courts. The tripartite commissions had resolved cases of firing. Until June 1997 Venezuelan legislation had established double payment of benefits in the event of unjustified dismissal of employees. Benefits were calculated according to the last wage. This created a very important distinction between justified and unjustified dismissal and was, consequently, an incentive to litigate about the matter. The reform of 1997 permitted annual payment of benefits, which diminished an important part of the incentive for litigation. These legislative changes explain the increase during 1991 and the decrease during 1997.

To understand the relationship between a business and the courts, we have studied PDVSA (Petróleos de Venezuela S.A.), the largest Venezuelan corporation. In December 1998 PDVSA was being sued in 675 cases. Seventy-five percent of these were labor cases, and 12 percent were tax cases. For its part PDVSA was the claimant in 38 cases, generally for nonfulfillment or breach of contract (Pérez-Perdomo 2000).

Traffic-related cases are also important for our analysis. Table 12.10 shows the number of traffic cases in relation to the number of accidents, the number of accidents with fatalities, and the total number of vehicles involved.

It is worth noting that in Venezuela many traffic accidents are not reported because the police frequently arrive late to the scene of the accident. If the accident is minor, the parties generally negotiate, and each one— or the insurance of each one—pays the damages sustained. In any case it is noteworthy that the cases filed in the traffic courts represent between 2 and 4 percent of all accidents. It is probable that the number of trials begun is even lower, as we have already seen that asuntos ingresados are not the same as actual trials.

In summary, few people are motivated to litigate in Venezuela except in labor cases in which the fired worker has nothing to lose and much to gain through litigation, and in cases such as divorce, in which litigation is the form that must be adopted to obtain a desired result. This conclusion is not surprising for Venezuelans, who feel that the judicial system functions very poorly and who do not trust judges and courts. We shall see why this is so.

DEPENDENCE AND CORRUPTION

The constitutions of 1936 and 1953 provided that Congress would elect the magistrates (called at the time *vocales*) of the then-called *Corte Federal y de Casación* for a constitutional period (five years). The Organic Judiciary Law of 1956 kept the traditional rule of appointing the judges for five years. It provided also that they would be appointed by the Corte Federal y de Casación (later called the *Corte Suprema de Justicia*) from a group of three for each judgeship proposed by the minister of justice.

The constitution of 1961 attempted to modify the system. It established a nine-year term for the justices of the Supreme Court—a term clearly longer than the five-year constitutional period. Reelection, although prohibited for the president, was permitted for the justices. Congress appointed the justices, and the court was replaced in thirds every three years. The constitution stated that "the law will provide what is conducive to the establishment of the judicial career and what is conducive to assure the capacity, stability and independence of the judges" (art. 207). It also provided for a judiciary council "to assure the independence, effectiveness, discipline and decency of the courts and to guarantee to the judges the benefits of the judicial career" (art. 217).

Despite whatever was provided in the constitution, Congress (or the political parties that made up Congress) were in no hurry to guarantee the judicial career by law or to create the Judiciary Council, and the Organic Law of the Judiciary of 1956 continued to be applied. The election of a new president, the leader of the main opposition party at the time, set in motion forces that led to the change. In 1969 there were rumors that the minister of justice had a list of judges of the Acción Democrática party who were to be dismissed and replaced by judges from Copei. As Acción Democrática was the main party in Congress, it formed a coalition with other parties to modify the Organic Law of the Judiciary and to create the Judiciary Council (1969). The council consisted of nine magistrates: five appointed by the Sala Político-Administrativa of the Supreme Court (controlled by Acción Democrática), two by the Congress, and two by the executive. The president used all his constitutional resources to stop the reform, including charging that it was unconstitutional. The Supreme Court of Justice, in an eight-to-seven vote (along straight party lines) rejected the argument.

Brito González (1978) has shown, using public statements by persons involved, that there was a conscious struggle for political control of the judiciary. To counteract this image, Rafael Pizani, an independent and very well known lawyer-scholar, was appointed as first president. He soon publicly resigned because the parties were dividing up the judicial positions and using the council to legitimate that division. Pizani made this point clear both in his letter of resignation and in many later declarations. Other authors, themselves members of the high judiciary (Rodríguez Corro 1984; Calcaño de Temeltas 1982), present the Judiciary Council as the great achievement of Venezuelan democracy in guaranteeing the independence of judges. Reciprocal accusations among the magistrates of fraud in the selection of judges, or of use of the council for political clientelism, caused public opinion to identify the judiciary with the worst characteristics of the Venezuelan political system (Pérez-Perdomo 1996b). This led to the abandonment of the council in the constitution of 1999.

An analysis of Venezuelan legislation on judicial matters from the 1980s shows a legislative effort to establish a judicial career and to create incentives and sanctions to assure the proper functioning of justice. The Law on the Judicial Career (1980) probably best exemplifies this effort. This law regulated entrance competitions as well as the criteria for evaluating and sanctioning the judges. This is not the place to evaluate the ideology behind this legislation, except to observe that it was a dead letter in the matter of selection of the judges and control of deviant behavior. The reasons were twofold: the Judiciary Council—an organism penetrated by political clientelism—was responsible for applying it, and an absolutely archaic system of administration made it impossible to implement the criteria provided for in the law. For example, complying with deadlines is considered by law to be an important element in the evaluation of the work of the judges, but neither the council nor any other entity ever had any information about the duration of trials. Even so, the judicial career was protected by the permanence of judges in their positions. The procedures for sanction, and especially for dismissal, became complex and, in practice, relatively few judges were dismissed. As we will see later, legal protection was especially effective when judges had protectors in the Judiciary Council or in the political system.

A common criticism of the judiciary was that judges and judicial officials were corrupt. Any judicial task had a cost, which anyone interested in moving the judicial apparatus had to pay. This charge was a kind of judicial surtax, but the system allowed for many abuses and for overcharging (Santana Mujica 1971; Quintero 1988). Corruption covered the entire field of justice, not just the courts. For example, in order for prisoners to appear before court and to avoid a kind of procedural paralysis, they had to pay a bribe to get themselves transported to the court. Any service in prison meant bribing the guards or paying other prisoners (Pérez-Perdomo and Rosales 1999). The corruption of the judges themselves was even more serious. Payments to judges were of a considerable magnitude that varied according to the type of case and client. The perception was that justice could be bought and that many judges had no interest in changing the system because they were the main beneficiaries.

A well-known form of corruption was the system of *tribus* (tribes). A tribe was an informal network at whose head could be a lawyer-politician, a judge, or a magistrate. The name derives from the most important network during a good part of the period, the *Tribe of David*. Of course, everybody knew who David was (an important lawyer-politician). This tribe was well connected to the Democratic Action Party (Acción Democrática), and some of its members became justices on the Supreme Court and magistrates on the Judiciary Council. Other groups were not called tribes—for example, the so-called *Borsalino Clan* (from Copei and somewhat less important). There were numerous reports and scandals in the press about tribes and other forms of corruption,[9] including the publication of books filled with information— generally gossip—about shameful acts (Rangel 1985; Ojeda 1995). None of these scandals seemed to make a dent in the system (Quintero 1988; Pérez-Perdomo 1995).

The Judiciary Council was the entity charged with the sanctioning of judges. As it was deeply penetrated by client networks, it did not appropriately exercise this function. In its first years of existence, it sanctioned very few judges. Between 1971 and 1982 it dismissed fourteen, which reveals, according to Calcaño de Temeltas (1982), that "contrary to the generally unfavorable opinion of the service of administration of justice in Venezuela, our judiciary presents a general picture that reflects a high index of honesty and efficiency" (181). Calcaño de Temeltas was a council magistrate and later a justice on the Supreme Court. From 1983–85 and in more recent years, the council was more active in sanctioning. In its *Memoria y Cuenta* of 1998 (p. 36), the Judiciary Council highlights the increase in its disciplinary activity: in that year forty-seven judges were dismissed and a similar number suspended (versus fifteen and seventeen in the previous year). Journalists have noted (Rangel 1985, 23) that only those judges who did not have a connection (who were not part of a network) in the Judiciary Council were sanctioned. Several judges in personal interviews confirmed to me the accuracy of this perception.

Of course, corruption was not a characteristic exclusive to the judiciary. The entire political economic system operated with corrupt money: there were people who received soft loans, import licenses, and favorable regulation of prices in return for financing the political activity and the personal well-being of politicians and officials (Capriles 1991, 1996; Pérez-Perdomo 1991, 1996c). Nevertheless, corruption in the judiciary was particularly serious because this was the state organization charged with punishing corruption.

The Ley de Salvaguarda del Patrimonio Público (1983) established severe penalties: it set up the Higher Court of Salvaguarda, a special appellate court. This could act as a trial court in cases of ministers and other high-ranking officials charged with corruption. The appointment of salvaguarda judges was in the hands of the Supreme Court. In practice, one judge was always from Democratic Action, another from Copei, and one independent or a member of the Socialist Party. Conflicts inside the court were so intense that on various occasions they paralyzed the court.

The fact is that the penetration of the judiciary by client networks and the venality of many judges kept the judiciary from acting as a reliable forum where the crimes of the powerful, including corruption, could be punished. Furthermore, the inefficiency and inaccessibility of the courts prevented them from acting as a valid instrument guaranteeing respect for human rights. We now look at this other aspect of the working of the judicial system.

ACCESS

A corrupt, disorganized, and slow judicial system, such as the one described, implies a serious barrier to justice. This barrier is much higher for those people who do not have the economic means and the social capital to move the heavy machinery of the administration of justice. Conversely, those who have these means and the willingness to use them to obtain a decision can use those advantages as tools.

An analysis of the problems of access can be made from two perspectives. The first considers the supply of the justice system, and the second considers the user and the mechanisms available to operate the system. We will discuss these two perspectives in that order.

The courts that hear small claims cases, the municipal courts, are those that would be more frequented by low-income people, as these courts generally deal with transactions of small sums. Nevertheless, it is noteworthy that

TABLE 12.11
Cases Introduced in Parroquia Courts

Cases	1987 (%)	1997 (%)
Civil and commercial matters	7.4	13.1
Criminal matters	11.9	13.2
Civil and commercial remands	12.2	5.2
Criminal remands	4.5	1.8
Noncontentious matters	29.8	66.6
Notarial matters	34.2	—
Total	100	100
	(165,015)	(182,237)

SOURCE: *Anuario Estadístico de Venezuela*, OCEI, respective years.
NOTE: Numbers in parentheses are absolute.

these cases do not dominate the dockets of these courts. Table 12.11 shows the cases that the *parroquia* courts (now, municipal courts) heard for two selected years.[10]

It can be seen that quasi-notarial cases (especially marriage ceremonies) make up the greatest volume of cases, although notarial activity disappeared in 1997 (when judges ceased to be notaries). To a large degree the parroquia courts act as auxiliaries to other courts (remands, or *comisiones*, in Venezuelan judicial language), although such activity has decreased in recent years. The criminal matters are inquiries into crimes in rural areas or in very small cities where there is no first instance judge or an office of judicial police. In this sense the parroquia judges are auxiliaries to criminal judges, as they prepare the case for the preliminary decisions. It would also be within their purview to hear misdemeanor cases as prescribed in the penal code. Nevertheless, in various parroquia courts we observed that these cases were not brought before judges but were directly resolved by prefects or municipal officials.

Only civil and commercial matters come to actual trial. The number of these cases has substantially increased in absolute figures but is still very low in relation to the total number of cases. Remember, too, that the table presents absolute figures, not indicators per 100,000 inhabitants. In the courts that we visited, low-income people do not initiate these cases; they are debt collections generally initiated by merchants who have sold goods that the buyer has not paid for in full. In other words, unless they are obligated to do so because they are being sued, low-income people do not go to the courts.

Why not? The municipal judges are trained in the law. Procedure is formal, and the parties need to be represented by lawyers. Legal representation is a significant economic barrier, especially when the amount to be reclaimed is not very high. There is also an important cultural barrier: low-income people are not generally familiar with the legal rules or language. To make a claim in court, they would, in a sense, have to let go the claim and entrust it to their lawyer, because they know that they would not understand what would happen in court. It is not surprising, then, that they tend not to use the courts.

The traditional remedy with which the state responded to the difficulty of access was to hire full-time lawyers and to offer their legal services free of charge to low-income people. This policy is generally expressed in distinct legal service programs: for prisoners, minors, workers, and peasants. General legal-aid offices are few and poorly staffed. An evaluation made at the beginning of the 1980s showed that legal-aid lawyers did not feel any identification with their "clients" (Pérez-Perdomo 1987). It was a high cost to clients in time and in personal dignity to try to get legal services that, in addition, were of very low quality. Only in labor issues were claims advanced because the unions took on much of the consulting work and because, due to the nature of the claims, lawyers worked on a contingency basis. Contingency fees are prohibited by the Lawyers' Code of Ethics and considered invalid under the civil code. The *procuradores de trabajadores* (labor procurators, or lawyers paid by the Labor Ministry to represent workers) were used by very few workers, and generally with very unfavorable results.

Low-income people did not voluntarily use the judicial system and were also unprotected when they were brought before it in criminal cases or in situations of debt collection. For conflicts that involved people at their level, such as neighborhood problems or disputes related to property or contracts in urban barrios or in rural areas, distinct mechanisms of mediation existed that functioned relatively well, despite their extralegal character (Pérez-Perdomo and Nikken 1979). In 1993 the *Asociación Civil Primero Justicia* (a nongovernmental organization, or NGO) drafted legislation on the justice of the peace, proposed later by a group of Parliament members and approved by Congress. As often occurs, the draft was not publicly debated until after the law was approved. This law completely ignores the existing mechanisms of mediation and establishes another: justices of the peace. They are elected by the municipal population; they do not have to be trained in law; and their mission is not to judge according to law but to mediate or conciliate. They work in the late afternoon and early evening. Implementation is left up to each municipality, and there are several municipalities in which justices of peace are working. Studies evaluating the impact of the justices of the peace are in progress. The establishment of justices of the peace can be considered a step in the direction of judicial reform, which is discussed in the following section.

JUDICIAL REFORM

Complaints about poor functioning of the judicial system and about abusive interventions by the political parties in the appointment of judges and justices began in the very first years of Venezuelan democracy (Lepervanche Parpacén 1965). Yet it is only much later that the administration of justice became a focus of political attention. Naim and Piñango (1984) and Naim (1989) note that businesses in Venezuela encounter serious difficulties due to the lack of a judicial system worthy of the name. Rangel (1985), Ojeda (1995), and many other journalists emphasize the corruption in the system and the influence of financially oriented political networks. The *Carta de los Notables* in 1991, mentioned at the beginning of this chapter, became a landmark of the political centrality of judicial reform. This letter described the profound corruption of the political system, observed that the judicial system was incapable of taking corrective action because of its own corruption, and called for the resignation of the Supreme Court justices and the Judiciary Council magistrates. As a consequence of these events and criticisms, the Venezuelan government solicited a loan from the World Bank and initiated various reform projects.

It is worth pointing out that *judicial reform* has a plurality of meanings in Venezuela, both for the general public and for the judges themselves. A common meaning is the dismissal of corrupt judges. For some people this appears to be the key goal: if honest and hardworking judges are appointed, the problems would also be resolved. Other people seem to pay more attention to the norms of judicial procedure. For example, the Law on Justice of the Peace and the Organic Code of Criminal Procedure were presented as important steps toward reform. Finally, more specialized people identify reform with changes in micro- and macrostructural aspects of the system. It is likely that judicial reform would not be a coherent whole.

The Judiciary Council was one focus of attention. Because it was itself penetrated by client networks, the disciplinary procedures that it followed were seen as selectively directed against those who did not have the support of these networks. Various constitutional reform proposals in the 1990s included the creation of a High Commission of Justice (or equivalent body) that would be in charge of the purge and would guide and coordinate policies in the system of justice. These proposals encountered strong resistance because, on the one hand, they would destroy judicial tenure and, on the other hand, they would put at the head of the judiciary an entity made up of the representatives of traditional political power.

In 1999 one of the first acts of the National Constituent Assembly was the Decree of Reorganization of the Judiciary (August 18, 1999). This decree ordered the suspension and immediate dismissal of judges and judicial functionaries in certain cases. Execution of the decree was given to the Commission of Judicial Emergency. The creation of this commission was very important for giving teeth to the work of the inspector general of courts, a position reinvigorated by the legal reforms generated by the process of judicial reform, headed by an official appointed by the Supreme Court of Justice. The work of the inspector general and the Commission of Judicial Emergency revealed the magnitude of the decay and took important corrective measures. Twenty-eight judges were dismissed because the outward signs of wealth were far beyond the means of a judge's salary (illegal enrichment). One judge was dismissed because he had a writ of arrest against him for extortion. One hundred judges were suspended for having accumulated seven or more accusations against them, sixty-seven for very serious accusations. Twenty-three judges were dismissed for having extremely poor performance. Thirty more people were dismissed for nepotism (for being direct relatives of judges in the same court) (*Quinto Día*, December 17–24, 1999, 3–35). In total, about 15 percent of the judges were subjected to serious disciplinary measures during the final three months of 1999.

The main idea of reorganizing the courts was to convert the one-person courts, which are small administrative units, into larger administrative units that allowed the judges to concentrate on their jurisdictional functions and give them more efficient administrative support. This seems to have progressed much more slowly. Serious conflicts between the magistrates of the Judiciary Council and the lack of managerial capacity in this council impaired this aspect of the reform. According to the *Informe de Gestión del Proyecto* of May 25, 1999, the "implementation of the organization model of the integrated system of administration, decisions and documentation" (whatever this means) took up much of the decade.[11] Pilot courts in Anzoátegui and Lara were not established until March 1999, and with extreme difficulty.

The elaboration of laws such as the Law of the Justices of the Peace and the Organic Code of Criminal Procedure, as well as the laws concerning the Supreme Court and the Ministerio Público, has been the easiest part of judicial reform to accomplish, but we do not yet know the practical results. The diagnostic studies that were prepared—if any were—remain confidential. This makes it difficult to evaluate the effect of the reforms.

Legal Studies and Transformations of the Legal Professions

Students and university professors were very important in the resistance to dictatorship. In 1952 the Central University of Venezuela was closed as a consequence of student protests. The rector and other prominent faculty members had to go into exile. As a consequence, the university's autonomy was suppressed, and a fee system was established, ending the tradition of free education. In 1957 new protests against the dictatorship again led to a closing of the universities. In the events immediately following the fall of the dictatorship, students were the segment of the population most mobilized to resist the attempts at restoring military rule at that time. Because of this, the universities attracted much political attention in 1958.

It is not surprising then that the Universities Act of 1952 was modified by decree of the de facto government in 1958 and that rules and policies considered progressive were adopted. The general sense of the new regulation was *democratization*: access to the university was facilitated and made free. The faculty elected the university authorities with input from representatives of the student body. Each *facultad* also chose its dean, and, in practice, the university became a federation of *facultades* with certain common programs and services. This implied a high degree of *corporatism*: the professions controlled the faculties whose curriculums and programs tended toward fossilization. The 1958 legislation opened the possibility of creating research institutes inside the universities and required research for the advancement of professors. These policies were not very consistent, in the sense that the enormous student pressure that could be expected was not compatible with the conversion of the university into a large research center. This section of the chapter looks at the results of these policies in practice and analyzes the transformation of the legal professions, especially of lawyers.

NUMBER OF STUDENTS AND QUALITY OF TEACHING

In the nineteenth century, Venezuela had two universities with law schools: the Central University of Venezuela (Caracas) and the University of the Andes (Mérida). In the first half of the twentieth century, the University of Zulia (Maracaibo) was founded. In the 1950s two private universities were created, the Andrés Bello Catholic University and the Santa María University (both in Caracas), and in 1958 the University of Carabobo, a public university. All had law schools. For the main part of the period that we are analyzing, only these six law schools existed, as it was official policy not to authorize the creation of others, although many other public and private universities were created. Only in the 1990s did the National Council of Universities authorize other law schools, all of them private. In 1999 there were four law schools in public universities and twelve in private universities.

In 1957 the country had 1,500 law students. The open-door policy of the university brought about a rapid increase in the number of students in subsequent years until it stabilized between 6,000 and 7,000 in the 1960s. During the following decade, enrollment again accelerated, and in 1980 the number reached 15,000 (Pérez-Perdomo 1981, 182). In 1999 there were 37,650 law students, with 72 percent of them in private universities (Consejo Nacional de Universidades, Oficina de Planificación del Sector Universitario, *Boletín Estadístico*, no. 19).

The law schools of the public universities were the first to grow. In the mid-1970s the universities limited access to a variety of careers, including law, and established a system of selection for the public universities managed by the National Council of Universities. Students could choose between three career or university options, and, according to the results of entrance exams, would be admitted to one. The system did not function well for the law schools of the public universities. The better-prepared students and those able to pay began to prefer the Catholic University, which had its own entrance exams. An increasing number began to go to the Santa María University, which followed an open-door policy. In 1987 the Central University decided to institute its own system of selection and admission, partially independent from the national system of selection, with results that were considered satisfactory (Torres Arends 1997, 12). The other public universities rapidly followed the example of the Central University, and the growth of the law schools stopped, while the Santa María University became enormous. In the 1990s the National Council of Universities authorized the creation of law schools in various private universities distributed geographically throughout the entire country. All of this was done with considerable disorder.

The law schools differ greatly in prestige. The Law School of the Andrés Bello Catholic University with headquarters in Caracas and the Law School of the Central University have a good reputation. The University of Zulia (Maracaibo) and the University of the Andes (Mérida) also have considerable prestige. Until 1999 other schools had negative reputations or were unknown. No formal system of ranking of the different law schools exists; therefore, evaluation is strictly on an informal basis.

The law curricula can vary from one school to another. There is a basic list of subject areas, approved by the National Council of Universities; it includes subjects related to important codes or laws (constitutional law, civil, criminal, mercantile, civil procedure, criminal procedure, and labor). Other subjects such as Roman law, sociology, and philosophy of law are also considered important. Some universities include legal practice, legal logic, professional ethics, history of law and institutions, and comparative law. Some schools have legal clinics that generally give credits for legal practice. The curricula tend to be rigid, and students have little opportunity to take elective subjects.

Each subject has a syllabus (*programa*), which is usually a list of topics, and a text. The text is the written version of the explanations that the professor makes of the principles, concepts, and rules of the subject. Frequently, the text is made up of the professor's own notes. The students are not expected to construct and solve problems, find and analyze information, negotiate, argue, or develop some other ability, let alone develop skills of deductive inference from principles (Torres Arends 1997). It is not surprising that the methodology has been much criticized; but there has been no systematic effort to change it. This inertia is due in large part to the fact that professors are mostly lawyers or judges who dedicate only a few hours a week to their university activity.

Cornieles et al. (1997) analyzed the content of courses as they appear in syllabi and manuals. They were interested in determining if the modern approach of the Convention on Children's Rights, signed by Venezuela in 1990 and elaborated later in an extensive Law of the Rights of Children and Adolescents (1998), had been incorporated into subjects such as civil, labor, and criminal law. The analysis presents a desolate picture of outdated and archaic teaching, even in the law schools that enjoy the highest prestige.

The enormous deficiencies of legal education have necessitated the development of postgraduate courses. These courses tend to be conceived as specializations—that is, more recent and detailed information in a certain field of law—and only exceptionally as preparation for an activity. It is not surprising that graduates in law perceive that their chances of employment would be improved if they obtained a masters' degree from a good North American university (Pérez-Perdomo 2001).

PROFESSORS, SCHOLARSHIP, AND PUBLICATIONS

The tradition in Venezuela, as in other Latin American countries, is that the occupation of law professor is only an appendix to another professional activity. As previously mentioned, some lawyers and judges tend to offer a few hours of class as professors. Appointment as a university professor tends to add prestige to a professional practice, which is why the position of professor who works by the hour was (and perhaps still is) sought even when remuneration is low.

Some legal professionals who doubled as scholars, or aspired to achieve an academic position, published in law reviews or books. It is not surprising that many of these publications had a close relationship with practice. For example, they might address the theoretical problems created by the practical application of certain rules. They might also publish guides for better comprehension of certain legal texts, or critiques of certain interpretations that the courts or other authors were making of legal texts. In some cases, the research that these analyses reflect is surprisingly sophisticated: the footnotes make reference to a voluminous bibliography in various languages, but the general tendency has been that the research is poor, listing references to sources mainly in Spanish, and very much inclined toward problems of legal practice.[12]

Legal scholarship, or the *science of law* that we have described, can be characterized as an activity performed by *honoratiores*, by people whose gratification is the honor that can be derived from being among the people who publish books and legal articles. The institutional expression of this model of activity is the Academy of Political and Social Sciences, created in 1924. The name may seem today rather unrelated to law, but the law school it-self was called *Facultad de Ciencias Políticas y Sociales* until 1950. In practice, lawyers have always dominated the academy. Sociologists, anthropologists, geographers, and political scientists still have not been admitted. Academi-cians are recruited from within their own ranks and do not have any duties besides attending periodic meetings. They are paid a small amount for at-tending these meetings. The academy does have significance: it publishes a quarterly bulletin of academics' works and books and gives opinions about legislative reforms, but it is clear that its principal mission is to distinguish or honor those chosen to be members.

During this period, there was an effort to professionalize legal research and the job of professor. In 1950, during the government of Pérez Jiménez, Dean Muci Abraham established the *Revista de la Facultad de Derecho de la Universi-dad Central de Venezuela*, whose first issue was paid for from his own pocket (interview with Muci Abraham). The university sent various students to Eu-rope with scholarships to broaden their legal studies, and on their return hired them as full-time professors. In 1958 the university created the four re-search institutes that the facultad has maintained since then: Public Law, Pri-vate Law, Political Studies, and Penal and Criminological Sciences.

The limitations of research and scholarship in Venezuela during the pe-riod are evident in the fact that three of four research institutes felt the need to hire foreign scholars to lead them. At the beginning of the 1960s the Insti-tute of Public Law hired A. R. Brewer-Carías, a law student at the time, as a research assistant. The institute was a room with one table and two pro-fessors. Brewer, as an assistant, did not have any specific task and so began to work on his own (interview with A. R. Brewer). The data of M. Roche (1965) shows that for 1963 there were six institutes for legal and political sci-ences in the whole country, with a total of only ten researchers. Clearly, this is a period in which scholarship as a career was still an aspiration.

The 1958 Law of Universities established councils of scientific and hu-manistic development in each university as tools to support research and scholarship. These councils developed fellowship programs to train profes-sors and scholars, and grants to support research and trips to give papers at scholarly meetings. During the first period, law professors used few of these resources to finance research projects or attend meetings. From its creation until 1982, the Council of Development had ninety-eight scholarship recip-ients in the areas of law and political science. Fifty-seven of these had edu-cational careers, and forty also had careers as scholars. Of the twenty-nine fellowship recipients before 1963, only eight (25 percent) became scholars; of the sixty-nine after 1963, thirty-two (46 percent) had careers as researchers. This shows that the former scholarship holders, who had an obligation to

TABLE 12.12

Activity of Researchers of the Faculty of Legal and Political Sciences of the Central University of Venezuela

Researchers according to productivity	Articles per year	Years of study abroad	Teaching hours (undergraduate) per week	Career delayed (in years)	Time dedicated to compilation (%)
3 most productive	3.54	3.66	3	0	0
7 following	.75	2.14	4	8	0
10 least productive	.12	1.2	5.5	13	50

SOURCES: Archivo de la Facultad de Ciencias Jurídicas y Políticas de la Universidad Central de Venezuela; Pérez-Perdomo (1985a).

work for the university for twice the time of the scholarship, did not at first see research as an attractive type of work. This happened even if at the time the universities offered better salaries to those who worked exclusively for them than did the judiciary or the state bureaucracy.

In January 1984 there were sixty people who formally occupied research positions at the Facultad de Ciencias Jurídicas y Políticas at the Central University. There were also legal research institutes, a number of researchers in the other three national universities, and a small legal research center in the Andrés Bello Catholic University, which basically did contract research and did not have a corps of researchers. Pérez-Perdomo (1985a) showed that only a small group of researchers at the Central University had internalized the ethos of research. Table 12.12 illustrates this by quantifying data taken from the resumés of researchers:

The table shows that at the beginning of the 1980s there were two very different groups: the ten most productive researchers had done postgraduate study for a longer time abroad, had a limited teaching load, and tended not to delay their career very much.[13] These people clearly dedicated themselves to research and avoided the work of mere compilation of teaching materials that the institutes deemed important at the time. The most ambitious example of a compilation in Venezuela is the civil code edited by the *Instituto de Derecho Privado* at the Universidad Central de Venezuela. The publication started in 1969 (in many volumes), and it is still under way. The characteristics of the people who really internalized the ethos of research appear much more accentuated in the three most productive researchers. The ten least productive researchers can scarcely be called researchers, as they published very little and did not pursue a research career assiduously. This line is not necessarily between people who work hard and those who do not. The table does not show the production of teaching materials, which is nearly equal for the groups. It is clear that those who did not internalize the role of researcher accepted compilation projects more easily, or even preferred them. They devoted half of their career predominantly to putting together materials.

When institutes were the center point of university research, social or interdisciplinary scholarship in law began to emerge (Pérez-Perdomo 1984). The social approach to law appeared in Venezuela as early as the end of the nineteenth century, influenced above all by the diffusion of the ideas of Spencer, Tarde, and Durkheim, among others. Sociology was taught in law schools (or political science schools, as they were called at the time) from the beginning of the twentieth century in Caracas and Mérida. Authors such as José Gil Fortoul, Laureano Vallenilla Lanz (Plaza de Palacios 1985, 1996), and Julio César Sala (Strozzi 1986) wrote about the law and are among those who introduced sociological thought in Venezuela. Toward the middle of the century, authors in the areas of labor law (Caldera 1939) and family law (Abouhamad 1977) reacted against the prevalence of formalism and discussed the law in ways that took social elements into consideration.

However, it was in the institutes of the Central University that some researchers began to systematically apply the contemporary social sciences to law. Proximity, cordial relations, and common projects among the researchers of the various institutes encouraged the movement. In the 1970s the Institute of Political Studies and the Institute of Penal Sciences and Criminology (which systematically employed nonlawyers) spurred the emergence of studies that could clearly be considered within the tradition of law and society. This was the beginning of the application of methodologies and concepts from the modern social sciences (Pérez-Perdomo 1984). In the second half of the 1970s, the Doctorate of Law, which was begun along with a doctorate in political science, was an important source of studies and doctoral theses with this orientation. Significant interdisciplinary research was also done in other universities, especially at the Institute of Criminology of the University of Zulia (Maracaibo).

Recent years have brought very interesting developments that have not yet been studied. The university research institutes have seen a reduction in their staff. Scholarship as a profession has become much less attractive, due to low university salaries and a decrease in the importance placed on research within the universities. Programs were instituted to counteract this decline. The best known of these was the Program for Promotion of Researchers (PPI), created in 1990. The government established a fund, linked to the National Council of Scientific Research, which gives financial rewards to scholars associated with research institutes if they are productive. The goal of the program was to ensure the survival of research at a time when university salaries were decreasing at an alarming rate in real terms, because the universities could not increase salaries to take inflation into account. It is interesting to note that the number of people in legal scholarship who could be incorporated into the program was very small, clearly outnumbered by people in political sciences and other social sciences. By tradition, political science and law are part of the same university faculty, and legal scholarship looks weak in comparison with other social sciences, including political science.[14] The difficult situation in the university or the economy cannot account by itself for the sorry situation of legal scholarship. The market for highly qualified lawyers and the exhaustion of the formalist paradigm of legal scholarship could be a better explanation.

Where is legal research done in Venezuela today? What type of research is done? The university institutes have certainly decayed, and the number of active researchers in those institutes has decreased, but a number of university researchers have remained active. It should be noted that the faculties of legal and political sciences continue to publish journals regularly. University and nonuniversity publishers, specialized (*Editorial Jurídica Venezolana*, for example) and nonspecialized (*Monte Ávila, Vadell Hermanos*), continue to publish law-related books. If we analyzed the authorship of these books and articles, we could find out which scholars are active, and an analysis of their work would show what paradigms are dominant in legal research. Such analyses have not been systematically made, but a tentative classification can be offered.

One group of books and articles is written by jurists who work as lawyers or judges and who are frequently also university professors. This group is within a tradition of academic publishing in law that has existed since the beginning of the century. In general, this publishing is intended to help the reader interpret legal texts or discuss important legal concepts. This literature generally does not make reference to cases or social problems but solely concerns the rules of law, except for a few references to practical problems from the authors' experiences and the analysis of a few judicial decisions. Highly conceptual and learned research, which could be considered the most elevated in the mid-twentieth century, seems to have disappeared.

The second group is much more diverse. It includes the publications of the university research institutes, reflecting a growing interest in law among social and political science scholars. The Central University and the Zulia University are the most prolific. There are also publications generated by the research centers, under contract with other institutions. Research centers may be affiliated with universities. The best known of these centers is the Center of Legal Research of the Andrés Bello Catholic University (Caracas); it has produced publications of this type since the 1970s and substantially increased its output in the 1990s. Another relatively important center is the *Instituto de Estudios Superiores de Administración* (IESA) (Caracas), a teaching and research center in business and public politics, which has been interested in the working of the legal system since 1990. Some of the work of these cen-

TABLE 12.13
Lawyers in Venezuela

Year	Number	Number per 100,000 inhabitants
1961	4,256	57
1971	8,102	76
1981	16,045	111
1990	31,350	159
1995	50,000	229
2001	82,939	337

SOURCES: Pérez-Perdomo (1981, 1996b); for 2001, estimate based on information from Inpreabogado.

ters is published in journals and books, but another part consists of reports that have a limited circulation. Organizations dedicated to consulting or to promoting certain policies, such as *Primero Justicia* (now *Consorcio Justicia*), which is very active in problems related to judicial reform, should also be included in this group. Other groups are much more specialized. For example, *Programa Venezolana de Educación-Acción en Derechos Humanos* (PROVEA) is a human rights program that publishes an annual report on the subject. The publications of these centers and groups are varied and unequal. The publications cannot all be considered academic research, and, in fact, the goal is to contribute to public debate, unlike the more disinterested scholarship that is found in journals of First World countries. These publications frequently make reference to social problems, statistical figures, or cases. For this reason, the research in these publications is closer to law and society research.

CHANGES IN THE LEGAL PROFESSION

In Venezuela since the middle of the 1950s, graduates in law receive the title of *abogado* (lawyer) and are authorized to practice the profession if they complete certain bureaucratic requirements. No other exam or period of practice is necessary.

The first thing that strikes us when we analyze this period is the very rapid growth in the number of lawyers, as can be seen in Table 12.13.

The years selected correspond to those of the national census, except 1995, which is the most recent year for which we have figures. It can be seen that the figure doubles every decade in absolute numbers, and in relative numbers the figure has increased fivefold over the entire period. At the beginning of the period, lawyers were concentrated in Caracas and the other important cities. We do not have figures for the end of the period, but a greater geographic dispersion is evident; advertisements of lawyers can be seen even in small cities.

In 1958 lawyers typically worked in individual practices or small firms. Only the most important businesses hired a lawyer full-time, and only exceptionally, more than one. In 1980 a comprehensive study found only ten law firms with between 10 and 20 lawyers (Pérez-Perdomo 1981). In 1999 the publication *Latin Lawyer* included thirteen Venezuelan firms with more than 20 lawyers among those one hundred recommended Latin American firms. The largest of these firms had 76 lawyers, and four other firms had more than 40. Legal departments of businesses have grown even more. PDVSA, the state oil company and the largest Venezuelan industrial enterprise, has 143 full-time lawyers (Pérez-Perdomo 2001).[15] Predominantly financial companies use lawyers more extensively. The large banking groups have more than 200 lawyers each. Nevertheless, the state continues to be the largest employer of lawyers, and small firms with only a few lawyers are very common.

At the beginning of the period, the legal profession was quite undifferentiated. A lawyer could be successively a practicing lawyer, a professor, a judge, and a state official. This situation began to move rapidly toward greater differentiation and specialization of functions. Judges tended to stay in their career, as did public officials. The occupation of lawyer also became a career, and it is no longer common for lawyers to leave the profession temporarily to perform other functions. Only scholars have not become professionals: professors of law frequently serve other functions, from which they derive the major part of their income.

By the end of the period, the legal profession had become very stratified. The social background of a person, the university in which she or he studied, and her or his postgraduate education, all matter a great deal. Social background has a lot to do with the importance of social networks in Venezuela. People of modest social origin tend to belong to networks in which the members have equally modest social positions and incomes. Their professional practice will be linked to these groups. Students who go to more prestigious universities have a better chance of obtaining good jobs. Postgraduate work can also help an individual obtain a better position. For the highest positions, such as following a career in a corporate firm or obtaining an in-house counsel position in an important company, postgraduate study in a good North American university and knowledge of English are very important, if not indispensable, credentials.

In their time, the political parties were important ladders of social and professional mobility for lawyers who did not have other support networks. Active membership in a party facilitated entrance into the state bureaucracy, which, in turn, facilitated the acquisition of knowledge, professional contacts, and possibly the opportunity to study abroad. In other cases, knowledge did not turn out to be so necessary, and the cultivation of relationships within a political network could mean very rapid ascent, at times beyond the capacity and knowledge of the professional. It could also mean rapid wealth, as work in the political networks could allow one to get decisions that were very favorable to oneself or to one's clients.[16] This form of decision granting and wealth accumulation is what has been called corruption.

The struggle against corruption has various ethical and social elements. One of these is related to these distinct professional strata. Business lawyers tend to come out of upper or upper-middle social groups, to have studied law in good universities, and perhaps to have done postgraduate study abroad. On the contrary, many judges and public decision makers come from modest social backgrounds, have done worse in their university studies, and have less legal knowledge. The struggle for the cleansing of the judiciary and of public functionaries contains an element of reaction against the power that these *parvenus* have achieved. Of course, this does not discount the very sincere moral indignation against shamelessly corrupt judges and public officials, some of whom did not come from the lower strata of society or of the profession.

Legal Culture, the Rule of Law, and Democracy

This chapter has described the functioning of the legal system in Venezuela in the period 1958–99. As structured, there was the appearance of the rule of law, but the system failed to protect the rights of a majority of the population or guarantee legal certainty to businesspeople. These failures were not accidental. We have shown that corruption and official abuse were tied to the way the political system functioned. The state was a system for the distribution of favors, and the predominant form of legitimization was clientelism. When, for different reasons, the economic system failed to provide means to satisfy the majority of the population with this distributive arrangement, the abuses of the system became evident and unbearable. Corruption appeared like a stain, and the general system entered into crisis. The reforms attempted in the early 1990s could not save the system.

In this final section, we return to a few of the basic concepts that underlie this work and restate them in light of recent events and of the immediate future that we can expect for the current Bolivarian Republic of Venezuela.

Two basic concepts used here are those of *democracy* and *rule of law*. We have made a traditional distinction between them. Democracy, in one sense, refers to government by the majority, regularly expressed in elections. The Venezuelan political system during the period was democratic. Here we follow the consensus of political scientists who have studied the system. But it is also true that for a good part of the period, the tendency was to concentrate political decisions at the apex of the national parties, limiting general and local participation (Rey 1989, 249–323). In the 1990s these criticisms led to decentralization, and the political system became more open. However, as it was observed, democracy in Venezuela was purely political and not social, as poverty and unequal distribution of income were never overcome. In the 1990s these traits became even more accentuated. Democracy is a complex concept, and we chose to define it as a political concept.

The concept of the rule of law means that the power of the state is limited by rules and by the fundamental rights of citizens.[17] As we observed in first part of the chapter, Venezuela appeared to be a state subject to the rule of law. To a certain degree, the power of the regime was limited by the presence of several political groups in the various organs of the state or with the ability to mobilize within society. An important feature of the political system was compromises among groups of the elite, because the government had to consult not only the opposition about its most important decisions but also organizations of businesspeople, organizations of workers, the high military authority, and the Catholic hierarchy. Conversely, the state never could guarantee the rights of citizens because of the corruption and inefficiency of the system of justice, among other reasons.

The concepts of democracy and the rule of law have generated entire libraries of discussion, and the definitions that we have advanced are merely instrumental. In contemporary theory both concepts are related, and the rule of law is thought to be a characteristic of any stable democracy (Dahl 1989; Held 1987; Weingast 1997; Ely 1980). We are not opposed to this idea; on the contrary, we argue that in Venezuela the rule of law was not realized in practice, and that this—together with economic circumstances that are irrelevant to the present analysis[18]—made the entire system unstable.

We have hardly made direct reference to legal culture at all. This is a concept that refers to people's attitudes and opinions in relation with the legal system (Friedman 1975, 1997). In this concluding section we will direct our attention briefly to the legal culture of the time, limiting ourselves to what Friedman calls the external legal culture—that is, the attitudes and opinions on law of the population in general.

Legal culture can be expressed directly in opinions (obtained, for example, in opinion polls), in popular messages as revealed by the media, and in behavior—obeying the law or using the courts, for example. This chapter has illustrated some apparently inconsistent behaviors that have characterized the functioning of legal order, such as the increasing use of lawyers for advice in business and drafting of documents and the avoidance of courts as forums to resolve conflicts. In another work, we showed that those who make instrumental use of the judicial system—that is, use its weaknesses to obtain advantages in business—receive moral condemnation (Pérez-Perdomo 1996b, 144–58). This condemnation extends, too, to those who use the courts, unless they are *functional* litigants—that is, they do it as part of their sphere of business, as banks do—or *expressive* litigants. In this last case one goes to the courts, despite their imperfections, to make a public statement about a conflict that the public is interested in or to clear one's reputation. In other words, litigation should be avoided as morally suspicious, except when social norms authorize it.

The opinions of Venezuelan citizens about their laws, legislators, and judges have not been systematically gathered. We know that the normative image of judges as protectors of legality and of the rights of citizens does not resemble the popular image, well represented in the journalistic literature, of a corrupt judiciary penetrated by client networks (Pérez-Perdomo 1996c). The fact that the Supreme Court and the Judiciary Council never bothered to collect opinions on the working of the judicial system—or that they never published such opinions if they did—indicates the imperial attitude of the high judiciary. Their relationship with citizens was that of a power that did not feel obliged to take the opinion of the citizenry into account, nor to improve its services. This is an indicator of legal culture and of the weakness of the judiciary.[19]

The dissatisfaction of Venezuelans with the judiciary and the political implications of this dissatisfaction were highly visible in the early 1990s. An example is the *Carta de los Notables* (1991), a public manifesto that called for the resignation of the Supreme Court justices who, around the middle of 1991, had exonerated various people accused of corruption, using purely formalist arguments. The open intervention of the heads of the political parties in the selection of magistrates meant that they could not be seen as impartial or independent.

The attempted coup of February 1992 and the political instability that resulted from the lack of public support for the constituted government caused Congress—for the first time—to consult broadly before partially replacing the magistrates of the Supreme Court whose terms had expired. This reform, together with the enormous unpopularity of the president and the weakening of his support, allowed the court to try President Carlos Andrés Pérez in 1993 and to find him guilty of misuse of funds.[20] In 1999 the court was called on to decide if the recently elected President Chávez could convoke a constituent assembly, a path of reform that the constitution of 1961 did not provide for. In a series of decisions, the court decided in favor of convocation of the assembly and later obliged Chávez to change the terms of his original proposal. When the National Constituent Assembly declared the reorganization of the judiciary in August 1999 and designated a Commission of Judicial Emergency (one of whose members would be a Supreme Court justice), the court decided that such a commission did not exceed the powers of the constituent assembly. The chief justice was in the minority and decided to resign, saying that the court "had committed suicide in order not to be assassinated." The court later held that, because of the nature of the constituent assembly, its acts could not be reviewed for unconstitutionality.

In short, the court regulated political change and allowed a peaceful political transition, perhaps flexibly interpreting the terms of the constitution of 1961 in order to avoid conflict with the National Constituent Assembly. The change has also been of a democratic nature, since in 1999 the populace expressed its wishes in three national elections: in a referendum to decide if a constituent assembly should be convoked, in the elections to select that assembly, and in a referendum to approve the constitution.

The constitution that was approved in December 1999 eliminated the Judiciary Council, which as we have seen, was the center of political clientelism. The new constitution gives the court—which is now called the Tribunal Supremo de Justicia—the powers to administer the judicial system and to evaluate and sanction judges, a power that previously belonged to the Judiciary Council. The Supreme Court has a new structure. In large part, studies that the court had made or commissioned in recent years paved the way. Among the changes is the creation of a Constitutional Chamber that would have attributes similar to constitutional courts of other countries, with considerable powers to control the constitutionality of actions of Congress and the president. The constitution sets up a relatively complex system for the selection of magistrates, under rules to be established by the National Assembly (which replaced Congress). In December 1999 the constituent assembly appointed provisional magistrates, selecting prestigious and independent jurists, but packing the court with Chavez's sympathizers. As we have said, all of this has occurred in the context of judicial reform that is still proceeding and a political transformation whose results are not yet clear.

Can it be said that the changes permit a stronger, more modern, more participative democracy, and one more respectful of the fundamental premises of the rule of law? Of course, it is too soon to know. The constitution also adds to the powers of the president, diminishes those of Congress, and permits the military greater political participation. The traditional political parties have practically disappeared, and for the moment what we have is a leader who values direct communication with the public. Those who express disagreement are dismissed as bedfellows of the corrupt, if not corrupt themselves. The political system that appears to be emerging does not claim to be a liberal democracy. We do not know how independent of political power the Supreme Court and those who wield moral power (general comptroller, attorney general, *defensor del pueblo*—or ombudsman) will be, although they enjoy complete autonomy from political power according to the constitutional text. There are people who think that Venezuela is on the way to losing democracy, without gaining the rule of law. But the social sciences, like Minerva's owl, in Hegel's words, only take flight at dusk.

Notes

1. Clientelism is a common characteristic of political systems. Our thesis implies that it became the most important feature of the Venezuelan system and that, as a system of legitimization, it smothered any other type of legitimate political power.

2. In most contemporary political systems the police commit abuses against vulnerable people (poor, immigrants, people of African or indigenous origin). In Venezuela and other Latin American countries these groups are majorities. What the disfavored groups hoped for, and generally still hope for, is charity from the state or protection from client networks. The client networks are also very important for the strata of the population included in the distribution of wealth as a means of obtaining privileges. A political system based on client networks produces a culture more of privileges than of rights.

3. The relationship between police violence and corruption was very suggestively presented in the film *Disparen a matar!* (Shoot to Kill!), but we are not aware of any scholarly analysis of the topic.

4. The *fiscal general* is ombudsman and, at the same time, head of prosecutors.

5. Amendment 1 (1973) excluded from public functions those who had been convicted of corruption crimes with prison terms of more than three years. Amendment 2 (1983) was more extensive and, among other things, established the legislative procedure by way of the Legislative Commission.

6. It is interesting to observe that in the *justice* section of the Annual Statistics for Venezuela, data about military courts are not published.

7. For figures on violent crime in Venezuela, see Pérez-Perdomo, Malpica, and González 1997.

8. The new Organic Code of Criminal Procedure was promulgated January 23, 1998, but did not become fully effective until July 1, 1999.

9. Among the various scandals of judicial corruption was the case of *petro-espías* —employees of the state oil business who transmitted confidential information on prices for their personal benefit (and that damaged the company). In that case, a judge signed orders releasing the prisoners before the hour when the court opened, and a small plane waited for the defendants to remove them from the country. The press later divulged information about how much these oil spies paid to the Borsalino Clan and how much the judge had received. In the case of the *Miracle Rain*, a criminal judge being investigated for extortion threw a large quantity of bank notes from her window when the police were about to search her house. In her defense she claimed mental illness. In another case a judge was removed for giving cars that had been recovered by the police but not reclaimed (because the owners were never notified) to his relatives and friends. In his defense he claimed that it was a common practice.

10. Even though it occurred after our period of analysis, in 1999, as a result of a transformation within the Venezuelan judiciary, all existing parroquia courts were renamed *Juzgados de Municipio* (municipal courts), which currently form the lowest level within the judicial structure. Some of these municipal courts, *Juzgados Ejecutores de Medidas*, were given the single task of enforcing judgments from other courts.

11. This is an internal document of Consejo de la Judicatura, Proyecto de Infraestructura de Apoyo al Poder Judicial.

12. The tradition since the nineteenth century has been to cite books in French or Italian. In the twentieth century, with the introduction of the so-called jurisprudence of concepts, various authors (especially L. Loreto and J. Melich) began to cite books in German. More recently, authors are paying more attention to a bibliography in English. Of course, the bulk of the bibliography has always been in Spanish.

13. Professors and researchers have a career, which is called *escalafón* in Venezuela. To begin the process, one must enter into a competition that is open to the public. A successful candidate becomes an instructor for a two-year evaluative period. The stages that follow—assistant, *agregado*, *asociado*, and *titular* (full) professor—each have a time requirement and a publishing requirement. To reach the level of associate professor, a doctoral degree is required, and to become a full professor, the published work must be an important book. In sum, to become a full professor, a minimum of fifteen years and four research publications is required.

14. The source is personal information. The author was a member of the Committee on Social Sciences within the program.

15. The figure does not include lawyers who are paid a retainer fee but who work in their own offices or graduates in law who have nonlegal jobs within PDVSA.

16. Venezuelan political jargon never invented a word for this type of rapid and illegal (or at the limits of legality) gaining of wealth, but in Spain it is known as *pelotazo*.

17. For a brief historical introduction to the idea of rule of law (*estado de derecho*), see García-Pelayo (1986). For recent polemics about the concept, see Fernández (1997) and Pisarello (1998). For an analysis from a completely different perspective, see Carothers (1998).

18. Analyses of the relationship between democracy and the economic regime in Venezuela have varied greatly. In the early literature of the period, there is an insistence that political democracy could not be consolidated without social democracy —that is, disappearance of poverty and more equal distribution of wealth. The major work in this direction is that of Silva Michelena (1970), who sees democracy in crisis because only socialism could produce such a result, and relationships of dependency impeded Venezuela from following the road of socialism. The predominant thesis today among academic economists attributes the stagnation of the Venezuelan economy to the lack of a market economy and a more intense integration with the capitalist system.

19. According to a 1977 opinion poll, 47 percent of the population thought that the courts would not protect their rights if they were in conflict with certain powerful people. In 1984 this proportion was 75 percent (Pérez-Perdomo 1985b, 72). In a recent study (Programa de Naciones Unidas para el Desarrollo [PNUD] 1998), the judiciary appears in the last place in the confidence of the population. Only 0.8 percent had confidence in the institution, 95 percent thought that the justice system favors the wealthy, and 60 percent expressed the view that corruption was the main problem to be solved to improve the judiciary in Venezuela.

20. President Pérez ordered 250 million bolivars (approximately US$17 million at the time) to be changed at a preferential rate of exchange one day before eliminating

the preferential rate of exchange. The investigation showed that he had used a large quantity of dollars to send Venezuelan police to Nicaragua to protect the recently elected President Chamorro. The fiscal general accused him of embezzlement and misuse of public funds. Later, the Higher Court of Salvaguarda opened another procedure for illegal enrichment because President Pérez's notorious lover maintained a lifestyle in New York that was far beyond her means (and those of the president). This second trial began much later and became paralyzed for different procedural reasons (among them the election of President Pérez as senator in 1998). What this case reveals is that the most serious accusation was never acted on, and condemnation was produced by behavior that could be considered politically unwise but not perhaps grounds for a judicial procedure. More than the acts themselves, what seems to have condemned President Pérez was his enormous unpopularity and the perception that the system needed to be relegitimated. In a theory of corruption (Klitgaard 1988) widespread in Venezuela at the time, it is asserted that the punishment of a big fish is very important in order for the public to believe that the struggle against corruption is seriously under way.

References

Abouhamad Hobaica, Chibly. 1977. *Nuevo enfoque del derecho de familia.* Caracas: Sucre.

Acedo Machado, Clementina. 1987. Necesidades jurídicas y acceso a la justicia de un nuevo sector: Beneficiarios del seguro social. Pp. 219–48 in *Justicia y pobreza en Venezuela,* edited by R. Pérez-Perdomo. Caracas: Monte Ávila.

Álvarez, Angel, ed. 1996. *El sistema político venezolano: Crisis y transformaciones.* Caracas: Universidad Central de Venezuela.

Baptista, Asdrúbal. 1989. Tiempos de mengua: Los años finales de una estructura económica. Pp. 105–56 in *Venezuela contemporánea 1974–1989,* edited by Fundación Eugenio Mendoza. Caracas: Fundación Eugenio Mendoza.

———. 1997. *Teoría económica del capitalismo rentístico: Economía, petróleo y renta.* Caracas: Ediciones Instituto de Estudios Superiores de Administración (IESA).

———. 1999. *Venezuela: Constitution and economic order.* Paper presented at the workshop on Venezuela, 29 November, University of Cambridge, Cambridge, England.

Bolívar, Teolinda, and J. Baldó, eds. 1996. *La cuestión de los barrios.* Caracas: Monte Ávila.

Borrego, Carmelo, and E. Rosales. 1992. *Drogas y justicia penal: Interpretación jurídica y realidad judicial.* Caracas: Livrosca.

Brewer Carías, Allan Randolph. 1975. *Cambio político y reforma del estado en Venezuela.* Madrid: Tecnos.

———. 1983. La urbanización en Venezuela y la ausencia de derecho urbanístico. Pp. 15–29 in *Derecho urbanístico,* edited by Instituto de Derecho Público. Caracas: Universidad Central de Venezuela.

Briceño-León, R., A. Camardiel, O. Avila, E. De Armas, and V. Zubillaga. 1997. La cultura emergente de la violencia en Caracas. *Revista Venezolana de Economía y Ciencias Sociales* 3 (2–3):195–214.

Brito González, José. 1978. Consideraciones acerca de la idea y concreción del Consejo de la Judicatura en el marco del estado contemporáneo. *Politeia* 7:215–81.

Calcaño de Temeltas, Josefina. 1982. La responsabilidad de los jueces en Venezuela. Pp. 146–97 in *El derecho venezolano en 1982,* edited by Facultad de Ciencias Jurídicas y Politicas. Caracas: Universidad Central de Venezuela.

Caldera, Rafael. 1939. *Derecho del trabajo.* Caracas: Tipografía La Nación.

Camacho, Oscar Olinto, and A. Tarhan. 1991. *Alquiler y propiedad en barrios de Caracas.* Ottawa: International Development Research Centre; Caracas: Universidad Central de Venezuela.

Capriles, Ruth. 1991. La corrupción al servicio de un proyecto político económico. Pp. 29–47 in *Corrupción y control: Una perspectiva comparada,* edited by R. Pérez-Perdomo and R. Capriles. Caracas: Ediciones IESA.

———. 1996. La ética pública de la democracia venezolana. Pp. 203–51 in *Lo público y lo privado: Redefinición de los ámbitos del estado y de la sociedad,* edited by G. Soriano and H. Njaim. Caracas: Fundación Manuel García-Pelayo.

Carothers, Thomas. 1998. The rule of law revival. *Foreign Affairs* 77 (2):95–107.

Carrera Damas, Germán. 1980. *Una nación llamada Venezuela.* Caracas: Universidad Central de Venezuela.

Combellas, Ricardo. 1979. El concepto de estado social de derecho y la constitución Venezolana de 1961. Pp. 791–807 in *Estudios sobre la constitución: Libro homenaje a Rafael Caldera.* Caracas: Universidad Central de Venezuela.

———. 1993. La reforma constitucional en Venezuela: Retrospectiva de una experiencia frustrada. Pp. 9–29 in *Venezuela: Crisis política y reforma constitucional,* edited by R. Combellas. Caracas: Universidad Central de Venezuela.

Cornieles, Cristóbal, C. L. Roche, M. J. Ferrer, and L. M. Toro. 1997. *La Convención de los Derechos del Niño y los pensa de estudio de derecho en Venezuela.* Caracas: UNICEF.

Dahl, Robert. 1989. *Democracy and its critics.* New Haven, Conn.: Yale University Press.

Duce, Mauricio, and R. Pérez-Perdomo. 2001. Seguridad ciudadana y reforma de la justicia penal en América Latina. *Boletin Mexicano de Derecho Comparado* 102: 755–87.

Ely, John Hart. 1980. *Democracy and distrust: A theory of jucidial review.* Cambridge, Mass.: Harvard University Press.

Estudios sobre la constitución. 1979. *Estudios sobre la constitución: Libro homenaje a Rafael Caldera.* Caracas: Universidad Central de Venezuela.

Faúndez Ledesma, Héctor, and C. Cornieles. 1994. Violación de derechos humanos e impunidad: El caso de Venezuela. Unpublished research report. Caracas: Centro de Investigaciones Jurídica, Universidad Católica Andrés Bello.

Fernández, Eusebio. 1997. Hacia un concepto restringido de estado de derecho. *Sistema* 138: 101–14.

Friedman, Lawrence M. 1975. *The legal system: A social science perspective.* New York: Russell Sage Foundation.

———. 1997. The concept of legal culture: A reply. Pp. 33–40 in *Comparing legal cultures,* edited by D. Nelken. Aldershot, England: Dartmouth.

Fuenmayor, José Andrés. 1997. Antecedentes históricos del Código de Proce-

dimiento Civil de 1987. Pp. 13–27 in *Jornadas de Derecho Procesal Civil*, edited by
J. A. Fuenmayor, A. Abreu Burelli, L. I. Zerpa, A. Rengel Romberg, J. E. Ca-
brero, R. Escovar León, and A. Febres Cordero. Valencia, Venezuela: Vadell Hermanos Editores.

Fundación de la Vivienda Popular. 1991. *Tenencia de la tierra en los barrios: Regulariza-
ción*. Caracas: Fundación de la Vivienda Popular.

Gabaldón, Arnoldo, and L. E. Oberto. 1985. *La reforma parlamentaria: Necesidades y alternativas de modernización de la acción legislativa*. Caracas: Congreso de la República.

García-Pelayo, Manuel. 1986. El estado de derecho y los tribunales constitucionales.
Pp. 21–67 in *El tribunal de garantías constitucionales en debate*, edited by M. García-
Pelayo, Ana M. Vidal, C. Marcial Rubio, and B. Domingo Garcia. Lima: Con-
sejo Latinoamericano de Derecho y Desarrollo.

Held, David. 1987. *Models of democracy*. Stanford, Calif.: Stanford University Press.

Hernández, Tosca. 1977. *La ideologización del delito y de la pena*. Caracas: Universidad
Central de Venezuela.

Holston, James, and T. P. R. Caldeira. 1998. Democracy, law and violence: Dis-
junctions of Brazilian citizenship. Pp. 263–96 in *Fault lines of democracy in post-
transition Latin America*, edited by F. Aguero and J. Stark. Miami: North-South
Center Press.

Instituto de Estudios Políticos, Universidad Central de Venezuela. 1971. *Parlamentos
bicamerales*. Caracas: Ediciones del Congreso de la República.

Jiménez de Asúa, Luis. 1950. *Tratado de derecho penal*. Buenos Aires: Losada.

Karl, Terry. 1986. Petroleum and political pacts: The transition to democracy in Venezuela. In *Transitions from authoritarian rule/Latin America*, edited by G. O'Donnell,
P. Schmitter, and L. Whitehead. Baltimore, Md.: Johns Hopkins University Press.

Karst, Kenneth, Murray L. Schwartz, and Audrey J. Schwartz. 1973. *The evolution of
law in the barrios of Caracas*. Los Angeles: University of California Press.

Klitgaard, Robert. 1988. *Controlling corruption*. Berkeley: University of California
Press.

Kornblith, Miriam. 1998. *Venezuela en los 90: Las crisis de la democracia*. Caracas: Universidad Central de Venezuela y Ediciones IESA.

Latin Lawyer. 1999. *Latin lawyer: A who's who of Latin American law firms*. London: Law
Business Research Ltd.

Lepervanche Parpacén, René. 1965. *El poder judicial ante la opinión pública*. Caracas:
Bolsa de Comercio.

Levine, Daniel. 1978. Venezuela since 1958: The consolidation of democratic politics. Pp. 82–109 in *The breakdown of democratic regimes: Latin America*, edited by
J. Linz and A. Stepan. Baltimore, Md.: Johns Hopkins University Press.

Machado de Acedo, Clemy. 1981. La industria de la construcción entre 1944 y 1959.
Pp. 95–173 in *Estado y grupos económicos en Venezuela*, edited by C. Machado de
Acedo, E. Plaza, and E. Pacheco. Caracas: Editorial Ateneo de Caracas.

Márquez, Patricia, and A. Castillo. 1999. Las policías municipales del área metropolitana de Caracas. *Fermentum* 26:355–82.

Martz, John, and D. Myers, eds. 1977. *Venezuela: The democratic experience*. New York:
Praeger.

Molina Galicia, René. 1996. Perspectiva y prospectiva de la reforma procesal venezolana. Pp. 31–91 in *Derecho Procesal Civil: El Código de Procedimiento Civil diez años después*, edited by Instituto de Estudios Jurídicos del Estado Lara. Barquisimeto, Venezuela: IESA.

Naim, Moisés. 1989. Viejas costumbres y nuevas realidades en la gerencia venezolana. Pp. 493–520 in *Las empresas venezolanas: Su gerencia*, edited by M. Naim. Caracas: Ediciones IESA.

Naim, Moisés, and R. Piñango. 1984. El caso Venezuela: Una ilusión de armonía. Pp. 538–79 in *El caso Venezuela: Una ilusión de armonía*, edited by M. Naim and R. Piñango. Caracas: Ediciones IESA.

Navarro, Juan Carlos, and R. Pérez-Perdomo. 1991. Seguridad personal: Percepciones y realidades. Pp. 27–79 in *Seguridad personal, un asalto al tema*, edited by J. C. Navarro and R. Pérez-Perdomo. Caracas: Ediciones IESA.

Njaim, Humberto. 1995. *La corrupción, un problema de estado*. Caracas: Universidad Central de Venezuela.

———. 1996. La seguridad jurídica en el contexto político venezolano. Pp. 53–100 in *Seguridad jurídica y competitividad*, edited by M. E. Boza and R. Pérez-Perdomo. Caracas: Ediciones IESA.

———. 1997. Estado y partidos ante el desafío de la sociedad civil. Pp. 199–225 in *Vigencia hoy de estado y sociedad*, edited by G. Soriano de García-Pelayo and H. Njaim. Caracas: Fundación Manuel García-Pelayo.

Njaim, Humberto, R. Combellas, E. Josko de Guerón, and A. Stambouli. 1975. *El sistema político venezolano*. Caracas: Universidad Central de Venezuela.

Njaim, Humberto, and R. Pérez-Perdomo. 1995. La función legislativa en Venezuela: Análisis y proposiciones. Pp. 121–57 in *La reforma parlamentaria para la Venezuela del siglo XXI*. Caracas: Konrad Adenauer Stiftung & Comisión Presidencial para la Reforma del Estado (COPRE).

Oberto, Luis Enrique. 1995. La modernización del parlamento y la reforma del estado. In *La reforma parlamentaria para la Venezuela del siglo XXI*. Caracas: Konrad Adenauer Stiftung & COPRE.

Ojeda, William. 1995. *Cuánto vale un juez?* Valencia, Venezuela: Badell Hermanos Editores.

Oropeza, Angel. 1986. *La nueva constitución venezolana de 1961*. Caracas: Academia Nacional de la Historia.

Pérez-Perdomo, Rogelio. 1981. *Los abogados en Venezuela: Estudio de una elite intelectual y política 1780–1980*. Caracas: Monte Ávila.

———. 1984. La investigación jurídica en Venezuela contemporánea. Pp. 279–304 in *Ciencia académica en la Venezuela moderna: Historia reciente y perspectivas de las disciplinas jurídicas*, edited by H. Vessuri. Caracas: Fondo Editorial Acta Científica.

———. 1985a. La producción de los investigadores de la Facultad de Ciencias Jurídicas y Políticas de la Universidad Central de Venezuela. *Archivos Latinoamericanos de Metodología y Filosofía del Derecho* 2:73–85.

———. 1985b. La administración de justicia en Venezuela: Evaluación y alternativas. *Revista de Derecho Privado* 2 (4):49–80.

———. 1987. Asistencia jurídica y acceso a la justicia en Venezuela. Pp. 13–48 in

Justicia y pobreza en Venezuela, edited by Rogelio Pérez-Perdomo. Caracas: Monte Ávila.

————. 1990. La organización del estado en el siglo XIX (1830–1999). *Politeia* 14: 349–404.

————. 1991. Corrupción y ambiente de los negocios en Venezuela. Pp. 1–28 in *Corrupción y control: Una perspectiva comparada*, edited by R. Pérez-Perdomo and R. Capriles. Caracas: Ediciones IESA.

————. 1995. *Políticas judiciales en Venezuela*. Caracas: Ediciones IESA.

————. 1996a. Seguridad jurídica y competitividad: Coordenadas para una investigación. Pp. 1–24 in *Seguridad jurídica y competitividad*, edited by M. E. Boza and R. Pérez-Perdomo. Caracas: Ediciones IESA.

————. 1996b. De la justicia y otros demonios. Pp. 117–73 in *Seguridad jurídica y competitividad*, edited by M. E. Boza and R. Pérez-Perdomo. Caracas: Ediciones IESA.

————. 1996c. Corrupción: La difícil relación entre política y derecho. *Politeia* 19: 335–70.

————. 1998. El Código Orgánico Procesal Penal y el funcionamiento de la administración de justicia. *Capítulo Criminológico* 26 (1):19–43.

————. 1999. *Requiem para Fomento*. Caracas: Ediciones IESA.

————. 2001. Oil lawyers and the globalization of the Venezuelan oil industry. In *Rules and networks: The legal culture of global business transactions*, edited by R. Appelbaum, W. Felstiner, and V. Gessner. Oxford, England: Hart.

Pérez-Perdomo, Rogelio, and T. Bolívar. 1998. Legal pluralism in Caracas, Venezuela. Pp. 123–39 in *Illegal cities*, edited by E. Fernandes and A. Varley. London: Zed Books.

Pérez-Perdomo, Rogelio, C. Malpica, and N. González. 1997. Magnitud de la violencia delictiva en Venezuela. *Espacio Abierto: Cuaderno Venezolano de Sociología* 6 (1).

Pérez-Perdomo, Rogelio, and P. Nikken. 1979. *Derecho y propiedad de la vivienda en los barrios de Caracas*. Caracas: Fondo de Cultura Económica y Universidad Central de Venezuela.

Pérez-Perdomo, Rogelio, and E. Rosales. 1999. La violencia en el espacio carcelario venezolano. *Revista de Derecho Penal y Criminología*, 2d ser., no. 3. Madrid.

Pisarello, Gerardo. 1998. Por un concepto exigente de estado de derecho. *Sistema* 144:97–106.

Planchart, Gustavo, M. Lovera, and R. Toro. 1985. *Evolución de la restricción de la garantía económica de 1960 a 1985*. Caracas: Cámara de Comercio.

Plaza de Palacios, Elena. 1985. *José Gil Fortoul*. Caracas: Congreso de la República.

————. 1996. *La tragedia de una amarga convicción*. Caracas: Universidad Central de Venezuela.

Prince de Kew, Carmen. 1990. *Reforma parcial del Código Civil: Análisis de una política pública*. Caracas: Universidad Simón Bolivar y Congreso de la República.

Programa de las Naciones Unidas para el Desarrollo (PNUD). 1987. *Justicia y gobernabilidad: Venezuela: Una reforma judicial en marcha*. Caracas: Nueva Sociedad.

Quintero, Mariolga. 1988. *Justicia y realidad*. Caracas: Universidad Central de Venezuela.

Rangel, José Vicente. 1985. *El poder de juzgar en Venezuela: Jueces, moral y democracia.* Caracas: Ediciones Centauro.

Ray, Talton. 1969. *The politics of the barrios of Venezuela.* Berkeley: University of California Press.

Rengel Romberg, Arístides. 1996. Los diez años del nuevo Código de Procedimiento Civil y la jurisprudencia de la Corte Suprema de Justicia. Pp. 95–155 in *Derecho procesal civil: El Código de Procedimiento Civil diez años después,* edited by Instituto de Estudios Jurídicos del Estado Lara. Barquisimeto, Venezuela: IESA.

Rey, Juan Carlos. 1980. *Problemas sociopolíticos de América Latina.* Caracas: Editorial Ateneo.

———. 1989. *El futuro de la democracia en Venezuela.* Caracas: Instituto Internacional de Estudios Avanzados.

———. 1991. La democracia venezolana y la crisis del sistema político de conciliación. *Revista de Estudios Políticos* 74.

Reyes, Pedro M. 1988. Venezuela y su experiencia en los programas de reforma judicial. Paper presented at Banco Mundial's *Conferencia sobre Reforma Judicial en América Latina y el Caribe,* Washington, D.C.

Reyna de Roche, Carmen Luisa. 1991. *Patria potestad y matricentrismo en Venezuela.* Caracas: Universidad Central de Venezuela.

Roche, Carmen L., and M. San Juan. 1993. Papel del derecho en los conflictos entre padres después de la separación o el divorcio: Efectos de la reforma del Código Civil Venezolano de 1982. *Revista de la Facultad de Ciencias Jurídicas y Políticas* 88: 133–53.

Roche, Marcel, ed. 1965. *La ciencia base de nuestro progreso: Fundamento para la creación de un Consejo Nacional de Investigaciones Científicas y Tecnológicas en Venezuela.* Caracas: Ediciones IVIC.

Rodríguez Corro, Gonzalo. 1984. Reforma de la administración de justicia: Breve análisis de la experiencia venezolana a raíz de la creación del Consejo de la Judicatura. In *La administración de justicia en América Latina,* edited by J. de Belaunde. Lima, Peru: Consejo Latinoamericano de Derecho y Desarrollo.

Sanchez, Magaly. 1974. Estructura social y política de la vivienda en los barrios de Caracas. In *Estructura de clases y política urbana en América Latina,* edited by M. Castells. Argentina: SIAP.

San Juan, Miriam. 1991. *Familia, potestades parentales y sistema jurídico.* Caracas: Universidad Central de Venezuela.

Santana Mujica, Miguel. 1971. *Costo del proceso.* Caracas: La Torre.

Silva Michelena, José A. 1970. *Crisis de la democracia.* Caracas: Universidad Central de Venezuela.

Soriano de García Pelayo, Graciela. 1996. *El personalismo político hispanoamericano del siglo XIX.* Caracas: Monte Ávila.

Strozzi, Susana. 1986. *Julio C. Salas.* Caracas: Fondo Editorial Lola Fuenmayor.

Suárez, María M., R. Torrealba, and H. Vessuri, eds. 1983. *Cambio social y urbanización en Venezela.* Caracas: Monte Ávila.

Torrealba, Ricardo. 1983. La migración rural-urbana y los cambios en la estructura del empleo: El caso venezolano. Pp. 109–40 in *Cambio social y urbanización en Venezuela,* edited by M. M. Suárez, R. Torrealba, and H. Vessuri. Caracas: Monte Ávila.

Torres, Arístides. 1987. Los pobres y la justicia penal. Pp. 79–101 in *Justicia y pobreza en Venezuela*, edited by R. Pérez-Perdomo. Caracas: Monte Ávila.

Torres Arends, Irene. 1997. *Educación jurídica y razonamiento*. Caracas: Universidad Central de Venezuela.

Van Groningen, Karin. 1980. *Desigualdad social y aplicación de la ley penal*. Caracas: Editorial Jurídica Venezolana.

Weingast, Barry. 1997. The political foundations of democracy and rule of law. *American Political Science Review* 91 (2).

Zakaria, Fareed. 1997. The rise of illiberal democracy. *Foreign Affairs* 76 (6).

CHAPTER 13

Patterns of Foreign Legal Investment and State Transformation in Latin America

YVES DEZALAY AND BRYANT GARTH

THE TRANSFORMATIONS that can be seen in the civil law world over the past three or four decades have begun to change the position of law in several respects. First, the position of law and lawyers has in fact regained some strength from the relative marginality and defensiveness characteristic of the 1960s and evident both from the fact of the law and development movement and its generally acknowledged failures. The new strength, however, comes with a different orientation. The civil and common law worlds became much more blurred in Latin America. Rather than deriving legitimacy from the civilian centers in France, Germany, Italy, or Spain, a new generation of law and lawyers takes its legitimacy from the authority of law in the United States. Advanced degrees in the United States, indeed, have become essential to success in the world of business law in the south, and they have increasingly become essential in the world of human rights and environmental protection.[1]

Our own research, which focuses on Argentina, Brazil, Chile, and Mexico, traces these changes by exploring developments both in North and South America (Dezalay and Garth 2002). The change in orientation, which is characteristic of transnational law more generally (Dezalay and Garth 1996), makes it tempting to see a convergence toward a U.S. model of law and state. The so-called Washington Consensus, built on relatively open elections and neoliberal economic policies, is another way to describe what is promoted by those who celebrate a convergence (Williamson 1990). The latest evidence is the new emphasis of the World Bank and other developmental agencies on promoting legal reform and a more important role for the courts in the government (see especially World Bank 1998; Dakolias 1995).

We recognize these activities and forces promoting a kind of convergence, but our research strategy seeks to examine the place of the activities in local structures of power. Rather than falling into the trap of promoting a convergence by highlighting converging features, our approach seeks to gain a more balanced understanding of the processes that generate change in particular domestic settings. This analysis, which is organized around the theoretical concept of the field, links the north and the south by focusing on "international strategies" and "palace wars" (on palace wars, see Bourdieu 1996). The processes that produce the change are set in motion and generate their results through the particular features of local palace wars for power and influence in the field of state power. One way to gain resources to fight in local palace wars is to invest in international capital that can then be reoriented back home. The changes in law can be traced through these international strategies and local palace wars.

The theoretical concept of the field refers to a semiautonomous space of conflict within which actors and groups compete in relation to each other on the basis of the capital that they possess—including material resources, expertise, social connections, and the symbolic capital of degrees, professional identities, and the like (Bourdieu and Wacquant 1992). The power of symbolic capital derives from the collective beliefs of others in the worth of the various forms of capital, and the value can change over time. Part of the competition in the field is about the value of particular kinds of capital. Most obviously, the relative value of U.S. law degrees in comparison to European law degrees in Latin America has changed dramatically over the past thirty years. Similarly, the relative value of degrees and expertise in economics in comparison to law changed significantly in favor of economics (see Yergin and Stanislaw 1998). Events and circumstances outside the field of law can also have a strong impact on the relative values. Economic crises first in the 1930s and then again in the 1970s, for example, helped produce the increase in the relative value of economic expertise. This competition is especially important because knowledge about the state, or "state knowledge" (such as law or macroeconomics), provides key weapons in the competition in the field of state power. This knowledge is self-legitimating and helps to produce the collective beliefs that the possessors of this knowledge deserve to manage the state.

Analyses organized around the concept of the field, in sum, bring several theoretical advantages that we hope this chapter will illustrate. The flexibility of this structural approach helps to avoid imposing a predetermined (and parochial or even imperialistic) representation on complex and ever changing social dynamics. It avoids the natural tendency to try to read the experiences we examine in terms of a theory of the professions and their supposed social role that derives mainly from the experience of the United States (or elsewhere). In particular, this approach—a variation of the "law in context" approach identified with Lawrence Friedman—allows us to pay more attention to the central role of the field of state power. The major turning points in the stories of professions (and the field of state power) relate not to changes in professional ideology or professional organization but rather to such "external" events as military coups, denunciations of torture, problems of international debt, and economic restructuring. The focus on the actors in the field of state power makes clear the forms of competition for state power and the changing role of foreign and domestic degrees, contacts, and expertise in that competition. We define the field not only to include the positions within the state itself but also those that are around the state and that help set the policies and rules that define state governance.

Similarly, analyses in terms of the field permit analyses of the interaction between different national fields of state expertise. This approach challenges theoretical approaches that seek to read recent developments as contests characterized simplistically as between "reformers" and "traditionalists," or even between the "progressive" legal activities of cause lawyers on one side and the "regulatory" activities of lawyers working on behalf of neoliberal economic policies on the other. Our approach brings to the surface the ideological content of the traditionalist versus reformist dichotomy and shows how both sides in the latter contest often relate to a U.S.-oriented view of law and politics associated with a particular export in state expertise. U.S.-oriented readings—which are quite tempting given the power of U.S. representations—unthinkingly promote the import of that expertise by framing the contest precisely in U.S. terms.

Analyses built on the field also offer a way to explain how the "preferences" of state elites are shaped (Haggard 1985). Instead of simply wondering why some elites in Latin America enthusiastically embraced neoliberalism, human rights, or the rule of law and others did not, for example, or worse, celebrating the good judgment of those on our side uncritically, we can learn much from a focus on the structural positions of professional elites in the field of state power. In particular, we can move toward more theoretical explanations that relate to different models of segmentation and stratification. Preferences are formed according to what opportunities are available at a particular time and how individuals and groups assess the potential value of investment in different strategies—buying international recipes, for example, versus playing by traditional state rules in order to gain power or make a career according to a traditional manner.

One general task of the work summarized in part here is to try to see why, how, and with what success actors import particular ideas, approaches, and institutions, including U.S.-style law. For present purposes, however, this chapter will seek mainly to provide a perspective that is complementary to those found in the other chapters of this volume. Most of the chapters focus

on change and stability in the way that law is used in the particular countries that are the subject of this volume. They raise questions, for example,
about how economic and political change affects the use of the courts and
the structure of the legal profession. We try to highlight structural factors in
the four countries that we studied that have produced differences in the way
that international investment in law has been received and used. That is, we
locate the changes not specifically according to "requirements" of a modern
economy or demands for more human rights or democracy. We try to explain how particular social constructions emerge to manage the economy
or the state, and how the activities of individuals and groups produce those
constructions. The purpose here is not to repeat the microstories of the four
countries, which we have reported in detailed case studies available as working papers (summarized in Dezalay and Garth 2002). The purpose is to show
that the different positions of law in the four countries lead to different outcomes of foreign legal investment. Thus, to return to our two organizing
themes, we wish to show that international strategies in the north and the
south have been quite important in changing the position of law in the state
and economy; and that both the strategies and the results are in large part determined by the different structures of state power.

As a general matter, international strategies can offer an opportunity for
an excluded elite (or aspiring elite) to mount a counteroffensive to gain a
stronger position in the field of state power. We recognize that our explanation in terms of strategic investments and counteroffensives can be misleading. This explanation is a sociological construction that we are applying after the fact. For most of the individuals whose activities we explain in these
terms, the individual choices that they make seem to be natural and normal
given the circumstances in which they find themselves. They choose to do
it because of the familial and professional trajectories that determine what
Bourdieu terms their habitus.[2]

How what we term as counteroffensives play out depends on the particular histories of each country and the structures of state power produced by
those histories. The structural approach reveals the patterns of change in the
state and also helps to explain why some "transplants" succeed or fail—more
accurately, are reinterpreted by the importers very differently from what the
exporters had in mind. This account of transplants helps to explain the impact of the law and development movement and the new efforts at court
reform.

In order to see the different patterns, we examine transformations in the
period roughly in the period since World War II. Each country, of course,
has a different history leading to different patterns of investment and growth,
but it is instructive to group the four countries into two pairs. Brazil and
Chile provide variations on what is essentially the classic pattern in Latin

America (Lynch 1981; Pérez-Perdomo 1988). Events in Argentina and Mexico, in contrast, had already destroyed or radically altered that pattern prior to World War II.

Chile and Brazil were characterized by the hegemony—always relatively fragile and threatened—of a relatively small group, which managed the assets of the state, the private sector, and the learned academy. The broad combination of institutions under their control made it easy to characterize these elites as an "establishment," and law played a major role in legitimating and holding together the compromises among elite groups that allowed this establishment to maintain its power over time. This establishment occupied a role with many similarities to that occupied by the Eastern establishment of the United States. We term the law graduates that played a crucial role in this establishment the "gentlemen lawyers of the state," and they served as representatives both of the state and the leading families of the aristocratic elite. Typically, they were educated in and built their political networks at the famous faculties of law—the University of Recife or Sao Paulo in Brazil and the University of Chile in Santiago. They often added to that local credential the further legitimacy of education abroad at the University of Coimbra in Portugal or one of the other leading civil law faculties in Europe. The part-time professors of the leading universities in Brazil and Chile participated actively in politics and in the economy. Indeed, the faculties of law served as crossroads for the fields of state power. For the most part the members of these relatively small elites were able to practice a politics of compromise that combined intense competition for state power with maintenance of the dominant position of the well-connected legal elites.

These gentlemen lawyers of the state often had their role and legitimacy challenged by groups excluded from power. One such challenge took place in the 1930s at the time of the Great Depression. In particular, internationally legitimate economics, centered in Cambridge, England, and later in such institutions as Comisión Económica para América Latina y el Caribe (CEPAL) in Santiago, Chile, gained prestige over the generalist knowledge of the lawyers who controlled the state and the institutions around the state. In the 1930s and 1940s, this investment in economic expertise served to promote a strong state, import substitution, and state ownership of major enterprises and industries—policies that came to be identified with "developmentalism." This form of developmentalism posed a challenge to the traditional elites, but the challenge was met in both Brazil and Chile by absorbing the newcomers from economics into the prevailing structures of state power. The legal elite was able to maintain its dominant position by making space for a new activist state and new actors and expertise. This challenge was only the beginning, however, with the more recent confrontations exacerbated by the politics of the cold war and what has been called the "intellectual cold war."

Challengers to the relatively small group of lawyer-statesmen in Brazil and Chile gradually gained strength and intensity. Individuals from groups who could not find places in the traditional elite could develop a new state knowledge—economics and sociology in Chile, mainly economics and political science in Brazil—that could challenge the hegemony of European-oriented politicians of the law. This potential supply side of challengers to the traditional elite found opportunities to advance their position through international strategies that became available in the post–World War II period. The international strategies could both strengthen the position of aspiring elites and add intensity to the challenge to the common target and point of reference—the legal establishment.

Governmental and private organizations in the United States, in particular, invested heavily in the reform of education in Latin America in the postwar period. These efforts concentrated on upgrading the quality not only of economics but also of other disciplines, including anthropology, political science, and sociology—all in the name of modernization and economic development. The emphasis was on developing specialized disciplines, on scholarly research and publication, on doctoral degrees, and on study abroad. Potential challengers to the generalist lawyers could take advantage of these new opportunities. From the perspective of the United States, especially after Castro came to power, these programs could make friends and fight communism by the introduction of ideas and technologies that would lead to economic development without promoting the left (Smith 1996). In this respect the Ford Foundation and the government were completely in accord.

Not all law graduates or members of the legal elite resisted proposed changes and reforms. Lawyers who sought to preserve their position by promoting the development programs formed partnerships with governmental entities and foundations to make the case that law was a tool that also could be modern and helpful to development. They feared that economics was displacing their expertise from the center of state power. The idea of the resultant law and development program—which originated in both the north and the south—was that reforms in legal education or in the relationship between the law and the business world would turn traditional lawyers—deemed obstacles to development—into progressive actors in the service of economic progress. As with respect to the programs in economics, political science, and sociology, the programs in law and development promoted especially the expertise that came from the United States. The law and development programs in Brazil thus targeted business law as well as legal education, while that in Chile aimed to reform legal education. Pragmatic legal practices, full-time professors, and the case method were promoted in both places, with exchanges designed to gain supporters for the new approaches. Neither program, however, could claim the kind of academic successes that counterpart programs in economics and social science produced. The effort to promote full-time professors, for example, made no progress, and the case method of instruction found only brief periods of success. The programs never received very favorable evaluations, and indeed it is instructive that many of the leading actors in promoting law and development pronounced the effort a failure (Trubek and Galanter 1974; Merryman 1977). James Gardner (1980), reflecting the changing balance of power in the Ford Foundation, which was heavily involved in Brazil and Chile, pronounced the movement not only dead but a form of imperialism. In contrast, the more successful exports in economics, political science, and sociology were able to escape that moniker. The consensus of failure in the programs of law and development contributed to make law become even more discredited in the 1960s and 1970s.[3] Law was seen to offer very little to resolve the major crises that were provoked by the cold war and by the growing economic problems that these countries faced.

International strategies in the context of the cold war served to ignite major state crises. The military in Brazil, which came to power in 1964, hardened its position against those identified with the left in 1969. This toughening served to exclude a large portion of the descendants of the elite from state power, as many had flirted with leftist movements in the more reformist-oriented periods. The increasingly violent suppression of dissent was in part a reflection of the lack of faith in law. In Chile, the Pinochet dictatorship, which came to power in 1973, exiled or killed many of those who had been in power in the reformist governments that preceded the military intervention. Both military interventions were made in the name of the cold war and strongly defended the private property of the old elites. They might have been expected to bring back the power and influence of the old elites and the politicians of the law that supported them. In fact, however, the new groups in power had very little respect for the oligarchies that had ruled the state in the name of the law. Not only were they quick to persecute the reformists from the old elite who had embraced leftist ideologies, but they also did not look to the legal establishment to provide the leadership of the new governments. Pinochet reportedly gave the Chilean Supreme Court cars and chauffeurs to win their affection, but law did not play a central role in the Pinochet administration until much later.

In Chile, the military formed an alliance with neoliberal economists— the Chicago Boys—produced by the remarkably successful Chile Project (which can be contrasted with the Chile Law Project). The economists obliged with an agenda that put law and lawyers in a relatively marginal position. The military and the economists, indeed, could unite against the politics of the old legal elite. In Brazil, the situation was more complicated, but economists generally—and especially Antonio Delfim Netto, who dominated the economic policymaking in the 1970s—emerged to play the leading roles in the military governments and their successors.[4]

The position of core legal institutions in Brazil and Chile, in particular the courts and the faculties of law, was substantially weakened through these successive challenges. Both had gained their prestige and legitimacy in part through their connections to the old families on the one hand, and to European legal authority on the other. The prestige of the judiciary and the law professors—many of whom were also judges—declined as they came increasingly to seem anachronistic and out of touch with the expertise necessary to promote economic progress. Law professors appeared as dilettantes, not real scholars or systematic researchers, and courts were practically irrelevant to the major issues of governance. The position of law in the institutions of the state therefore declined, despite the efforts of the promoters of law and development. The military coups encountered very little resistance from the courts or the law faculties in Brazil or in Chile, and the courts and law faculties played relatively minor roles after the coups. The success of the challenges to this elite in the 1970s and 1980s was evident from the fact that the action was simply elsewhere. The picture, in short, is one of a series of attacks that weakened and discredited the traditional legal elite—the gentlemen politicians of the law. The courts and the legal academies offered little resistance to the military coups and to the economists who came with them to power, nor did they have much expertise to offer toward the state transformations that the military regimes facilitated.

The starting points were very different in Mexico and Argentina, and therefore the impact of comparable international strategies was also very different. The strategy of the traditional legal elite—cosmopolitan scholars, statesmen, and inheritors of the landed aristocracy—had largely been eliminated as a source of governmental power and legitimacy prior to the depression of the 1930s. Earlier challenges to the comparable elite groups—with comparable origins in colonial policies—in Argentina and Mexico had already deeply changed the landscape of power. The Porfirian elite in Mexico —the historical counterpart to what was seen in Brazil and Chile—was defeated in the Mexican Revolution early in this century, creating a durable division in Mexico's elite. The traditional elite was not eliminated, despite the rhetoric of land reform and the policies connected to the revolution, but it was formally discredited and pushed outside the governing alliance. Still, as a political compromise that has lasted more or less to the present, the elite was permitted to rebuild and indeed thrive. With the exception of Monterrey, which preserved the political power of the old families, the descendants of the Porfirian elite essentially stayed outside the state and concentrated on building and maintaining their family landholdings and enterprises. They did not participate directly in state governance.

The new state elite, in contrast, was made up of a new, legally educated group who descended from the winning side in the Mexican Revolution. They built their base in the Partido Revolucionario Institucional (PRI), Mexico's long dominant political party, and built political families that dominated the leadership of the PRI. While largely the product of the same educational institutions that had produced the prerevolutionary state elite, especially the faculty of law of the National University in Mexico City (UNAM), the new ruling elite in Mexico did not connect to private power in the same way that the gentlemen lawyers of Brazil and Chile did. Indeed, the separation of the elites became evident even in the law schools that they attended. Those from the private side who sought a legal education—usually relatively poor cousins who did not have a business to inherit—tended to obtain their degrees from private schools such as Escuela Libre—not the UNAM. The two sides of the law thus barely touched, showing quite clearly that there was nothing that could be characterized as a general legal elite.

In Mexico, as part of the public side, the courts and even the faculties of law were folded closely into the PRI and the structure of incentives it provided. Graduates of UNAM who did not gain strong positions in the party hierarchy but were able to participate in lower-status political networks moved into the judiciary. They owed their existence to the PRI and its patronage. Law professors gained prestige and power mainly through connections to the PRI. Many of course went into politics with their classmates or even their students. Scholarship could gain attention, but the way to advance professionally was through the PRI and political loyalty. Similarly, on the private side, law graduates might try to show their legal skills, but most of them aspired not to stay in the relatively marginal position of practicing lawyer. They sought to be given a role in the family enterprises that they served. In Mexico, therefore, the judiciary and legal scholarship played an even more marginal role in the governance and legitimacy of the state than they did in Brazil and Chile. Instead of a seamless relationship between old families, courts, and the faculties of law, each reinforcing the stability and legitimacy of the state, the courts and the law were much less integral to the PRI-dominated Mexican state.

Argentina's history led to similarly weak positions of the judiciary and the faculties of law, but the source of this weakness was very different. Frequent crises—including more than twenty coups in the twentieth century—provided a legacy that severely limited the extent of learned and professional investment in the construction of any state institutions, including legal ones. Professional groups who were willing to invest in a particular regime were typically thrown out of the state (even the country) when the regime—whether populist or military—changed. Each time regimes changed power, they changed completely the identity not only of those managing the state but also of the judiciary and even the faculties of law. State institutions were weak because of the repeated purges and what it meant for professional investment in those institutions. Professionals understandably tended to invest elsewhere, including abroad, rather than run the risk of investment in the highly unstable Argentine state. Lawyers and professors of law, therefore, had no special connection to the state as such, either through their families or their expertise. They occupied no dominant position akin to what was found in Brazil or Chile, or even in the state elite in Mexico. The institutions associated with the law—the faculties of law and the courts—were extremely weak and marginal in the violent struggles for state power.

The stories in Mexico and Argentina therefore do not have the battle lines seen in Brazil and Chile. The former professional elites were divided and fragmented, and the forms of accumulation of foreign capital were therefore bound to be different. In particular, we find parallel international strategies that, in contrast to the situation in Brazil and Chile, could practically ignore each other. Lacking a common enemy, the different groups would use other factors to determine the specifics of their professional strategies.

It is almost axiomatic, in addition, that elite investment in cosmopolitan strategies tends to relate inversely to the strength of the elite's connection to local state institutions. In other words, relatively privileged elites—capable of international strategies—who have weak and fragile positions in the state will typically be far more cosmopolitan than counterparts who are well connected in the state. The latter will of course invest more in their own states. Accordingly, strategies of cosmopolitanism in Argentina and Mexico were products of a local demand by relatively prosperous and privileged elites excluded from state power. In Brazil and Chile, in contrast, the relatively privileged elites were well connected to state institutions and less needy of cosmopolitan strategies. Interestingly, these differences were evidently taken into account in the U.S. programs directed toward Latin America. In Brazil and Chile, there was a heavy emphasis on the supply from abroad into the countries, reflected especially in the quite visible U.S. investment in education and knowledge. It was almost necessary to persuade local elites that they should invest in foreign education and knowledge. That active foreign investment was not necessary for the Mexican private elite—excluded from state power —or for Argentine professional elites to gain familiarity with U.S. ideas and technologies—including legal ones. It is similarly instructive that the Ford Foundation in Argentina did not need to create anything new when it began to invest there. It could simply step into the shoes of the Di Tella Foundation. A good portion of the elite had already been "Americanized" and built institutions around that state that resembled those in the United States. Think tanks and private law firms, as well as the notable foundation, provided places where Argentine professionals could both invest their foreign know-how and replicate institutions they saw abroad.

Mexico, as previously noted, was characterized by one basic divide, with different worlds of public and private translating also into two very different legal worlds—with separate family backgrounds, law schools, and potential career trajectories. The strategies of each side of that basic divide were therefore very different. Within the public side, cosmopolitan investment was very slow to gain any influence in the state. Indeed, cosmopolitan investment from the public side in the field of law began with a low-profile investment in pure law by individuals in the UNAM faculty's Instituto des Investigaciones Jurídicas, and not until the late 1980s did this investment really translate into state politics. The international strategy of this group of relatively dominated scholars found a place in the field of human rights, but only much later was this investment turned into strategies directed toward state power.

On the side of the private bourgeoisie and the groups descended from the traditional prerevolutionary elite in Mexico, cosmopolitan legal strategies tended for a small fraction of the elite to create a foreign legal enclave providing services to foreign businesses. This group had very little spillover into the state, except in very technical areas of the law, such as with respect to patents, where the state counterparts in negotiations with business needed more technical skill than clientelistic connections. This group of private lawyers connected at least initially to law firms in the United States, maintained a very different legal world than the lawyers from the public side, but, despite links abroad, did not invest substantially in technical legal expertise. While outside the state elite, they also operated in a world dominated by personal relations. In the words of one of the Mexican lawyers, they provided the "know-who" that combined with the foreign lawyers' "know-how."

The divide between the two legal sectors has begun to change in Mexico, but it continues to exist. International strategies in the Mexican context have served to challenge the divide rather than the position of any particular elite. Economists, as relative newcomers to state governance in Mexico, were initially dominated by the state elite that was built largely on personal relationships formed in the faculty of law at UNAM. They needed to build some stature and autonomy with respect to the lawyers in the state. They invested relatively early in technical knowledge, which led them to the United States —following the relative prestige of economics internationally. They used this expertise to gain a foothold in state institutions, but they tended to serve mainly as technocrats cut off from the chief sources of political power. The growing importance of this technocratic state knowledge, which was made especially salient with the economic crises of the 1970s and the debt crisis of the 1980s, prompted a certain number of the children of the political elite to invest in legitimate economics. Their international strategy within the PRI allowed them to join with economists who came from the private side and were produced from the private schools, especially Instituto Tecnológico Autónomo de Mexico (ITAM). They had followed a cosmopolitan strategy to gain credentials that counted in the private business sphere in Mexico (and also brought some of them into technocratic positions in the government). Linked through their educations abroad and shared expertise, the economists from both sides of the divide became the "technopols" of the Salinas and Zedillo administrations. They not only gained the dominant position in matters of economic policy but also gained control of the state. Salinas, who was the president from 1988 to 1994, engineered the North American Free Trade Agreement (NAFTA) with the United States and Canada, and both administrations moved to follow the economic recipes of the Washington Consensus.

As a counterpart to the rise to power of the technopols, Salinas and his administration decided also to increase their investment in new forms of political legitimacy. Increasing pressures from abroad, including the then-thriving international human rights community, brought the Salinas government to draw on those who had invested in the international strategy of developing human rights expertise at UNAM. Salinas therefore brought Jorge Carpizo, one of the key individuals at the Instituto des Investigaciones Jurídicas, and his progeny into the state. The investment began with the National Commission of Human Rights (NCHR)—a Mexican ombudsman-like institution whose first leader was Carpizo. These activities—along with those of the economists—undermined the traditional PRI clientelism in which it also participated. NAFTA, election reform, human rights policies that undermine local police discretion and power, and the anticorruption and antidrug campaigns have further accelerated this investment in new forms of international legal legitimacy. Those who invested in human rights, including Jorge Carpizo and Jorge Madrazo, his successor at the NCHR, have made very prominent political careers within the PRI through the NCHR and then the Office of Attorney General. The same is also true for those lawyers who invested in economics expertise, whether through NAFTA negotiations or work in the government's more U.S.-oriented and technical departments. International strategies on the public side have gradually had an impact on the clientelism of the PRI. Elections are now more open, and some traditional forms of political power have been undermined. Economists and then lawyers drew on international strategies both to gain power and to invest their new expertise in the state.

On the other side, the private law firms, which have long connected lawyers from the old elite families with foreign businesses, have also moved more deeply into technical law made in the United States. They gained considerable expertise and foreign know-how in the negotiations and events that followed the debt crisis of the early 1980s, and they have used this technical legitimacy to connect to human rights issues such as fair elections. Building on new legal expertise from the United States, they have moved much closer to the government and state power. For example, Santiago Creel—a descendant of the old elite—used his graduate degree from abroad, success in private international law firms, activity in regulating elections, and U.S. contacts to move into the state as a member of a reinvigorated legislature on the side of the National Action Party (PAN). Within the Mexican landscape, therefore, international strategies have helped to bring the old private elite back into the state—first through economics and later through law. More generally, international legal investment has helped to bridge the divide between the two elites now converging around U.S.-minted expertise, including economic law and human rights.

Argentina shares a similar logic to Mexico, but the situation is more complex. There has been no simple divide that international strategies might seek to overcome. Foreign capital has long been readily available and usable in Argentina. There was also relatively early access in Argentina to the United States by lawyers and other professionals. In contrast to the elite in Mexico, for example, the Argentine elite, exemplified by such individuals as Raul Prebisch, the economist famous especially for his work at the CEPAL in Santiago, Chile, and with the United Nations Committee on Trade and Development (UNCTAD), has long invested quite substantially in international institutions. For related reasons, Argentine elite professionals have also invested in hybrid institutions located around the state.

The two main hybrid vehicles found in Argentina are both very U.S. oriented, but that orientation did not require aggressive export policies akin to what was seen in Brazil and Chile. They are home produced—then reinforced by foreign connections and investment. The first such hybrid institution is the corporate law firm, representing an institutionalization of the role of *comprador* in Argentina. The stability of the corporate law firm sector stems from an ability to bring together foreign capital, the Argentine business community, and the Argentine state—even while the state changed very dramatically from one regime to another. The family structure of the firms enabled them to accumulate wealth and reproduce themselves over time.

Cosmopolitan gentlemen lawyers generally stayed out of the state in Argentina. As the value of U.S. expertise ascended, these lawyers increasingly sent their children to the United States to purchase a degree, gain expertise, and build connections, all of which could be used to sustain this privileged professional sector in Argentina.

The family organization of the law firms has been quite successful, even if it is always somewhat fragile (and gradually changing). The relative lack of possibilities for new entry might lead to professional tensions. Another danger is family feuds, which cause some firms to divide. Finally, when lawyers from this sector have succumbed to a temptation to move into the state, such as was the case for Martinez de Hoz, who became the minister of finance under the military regime in the late 1970s, and Guillermo Walter Klein, a lawyer who assisted him, their family firms can be hurt by the next regime's politics of revenge. Still, with the strong incentives among this elite sector not to invest directly in the state, or even the courts or the faculties of law, the family firms have for the most part thrived. International strategies have helped to maintain and build these firms outside the state.

The potential competition to the quite powerful corporate law firms in Argentina was typically not even seen as competition. Lacking the legal hegemony that existed in Brazil or Chile, law was not a particular target for aspiring elites. Also, because the legal elite in Argentina already depended for its legitimacy on foreign ties and expertise, potential competitors were already in the same boat as corporate lawyers. The problem for the potential new competition in Argentina was therefore the same problem that law faced —where to invest international strategies locally. The problem of the weak autonomy of the law faculties extended to the universities generally, making it difficult to invest either in the universities or the state. As a result, the other dominant institutional form for this kind of international investment in Argentina was the private think tank, again a typically American form but also a clearly local product. Since the Di Tella family acted very much like the Rockefeller family in the United States at the turn of the century, investing in legitimacy through statelike institutions, there was almost a predetermined convergence. The result for the newer social sciences was therefore quite similar to that seen in the corporate law firm sector. The think tanks could keep open the channels of communication between foreign expertise and capital on the one side and whatever form of state existed on the other. Although the think tanks and the law firms both existed outside the state, they constituted sectors that could provide brokers with whoever was in power at a particular moment.

This arrangement meant, however, that the new disciplines still had no state institutions to take over. The historically weak status of law, constantly purged by new governments destroying any residue of previous ones, meant that there was no strong state to reform according to new state expertise. There was nothing in Argentina to seize except political power. Entry into the state, therefore, came only from playing politics and becoming sources of patronage for Argentine-style political networks. Family connections might serve to limit individual risk, but there were severe costs to political strategies when power changed hands. In the Argentine context, therefore, the new technologies of power, like the old ones, were employed only as instrumental political tools. The rhetoric might be state of the art internationally, but the point was only to knock off the opposition. Unlike the case of the United States, in particular, it was simply not possible in Argentina to combine scientific credibility and political advocacy without killing scientific credibility. The result was that the Argentine state was repeatedly torn apart, and new expertise did not lead to any lasting institutional change.

It is instructive that in Argentina, unlike in Mexico, we can focus on a clear dividing line between the military and the new democratic regime, even if the results were not so radical as they initially appeared to be. Instead of a transformation that resulted from the gradual accumulation of investment in the state, events in Argentina changed overnight. The Falklands/ Malvinas War simply discredited the military, forcing them to leave. The Peronists were at that time relatively weak, and the result was that the Radical Party, the traditional party of old and new professionals, came to power. The Radicals—in part because of the lack of a strong state—could not find the tools to handle the debt crisis, and they were then cast out of power. The Peronists under Menem were able to regroup, win the election, and then finally to begin to accumulate some investment in the state. The Peronists converted to economic orthodoxy by purchasing what was respectable according to foreign standards, and they pulled the leading economics think tank —Instituto de Estudios Económicos sobre la Realidad Argentina y Latinoamericana (IERRAL) in Cordoba, led by Domingo Cavallo—into the government. They also paid at least lip service to professional legal orthodoxy, offering the appearance of legality while taking advantage of the lack of autonomy of the law. Within this climate, the economists began to invest more in the state and even in the rule of law—seeking to legitimate their own positions within the state. The most obvious result is the transformation of the Argentine economy, but there have also been some transformations in the position of law.

Professional actors from outside the state, including the law firms, have been able to take advantage of the relative stability to invest more in legal institutions, including the private business law schools, alternative dispute resolution, and the beginnings of court reform. Although the court reform investment has not been very successful to date, several judges were able to combine with the government to institutionalize U.S.-style alternative dispute resolution. These various activities are part of a variety of potentially complementary investments in and around the state and law. The greatest success of the international strategies, however, remains with the thriving institutions outside the state—the think tanks and the family law firms.

In contrast to the situations in Argentina and Mexico, international legal strategies in the 1980s and the 1990s in Brazil and Chile can be understood as efforts to rebuild and reconstruct a social peace that was shattered—and to redefine the role of law and lawyers in transformed states. Corporate law firms, which especially in Chile but also in Brazil (with notable exceptions) were typically family law firms, helped preserve some role for lawyers in the economy, and they grew and prospered in the authoritarian regimes as a result of the debt crisis and the increase in international investment. They were able to make strong connections to the lawyers who served the economists controlling the economic policies of the state, especially because both the public and private spheres invested in U.S. legal technologies—and came to rely on U.S. degrees and training. Not surprisingly, the lawyers who served the central banks and the Ministries of the Economy tended to find their way into the corporate law firms. And in Brazil, the corporate law experts trained in the law and development program were able to put their expertise in the service of these major changes in the state and the economy.

There were strong similar investments in international human rights, which came to occupy strong positions in the transitions to democracy in Brazil and Chile. The Ordem dos Advogados (OAB) in Brazil and the Vicariate in Chile were among the best-known organizations promoting the cause of human rights and linking with the human rights movement abroad. Lawyers gained power for themselves and the new legal expertise through their investments in human rights. At the same time, the business law firms in Brazil and Chile began to reinvest more in the state, again drawing on internationally legitimated discourses combining liberal democracy and liberal economics. In contrast to those in Argentina and Mexico, therefore, international strategies in Brazil and Chile can be conceived as a return to law, even if a very different law legitimated by new criteria. This law is very different from the one that prevailed before this period of transformation. In key areas such as business law and human rights, in addition to others that have not been discussed, such as the environment, the orientation of these civil law countries is now very much toward the United States. International strategies in law have begun to catch up to economics, and law has begun to regain a strong position in legitimating the state.

For reasons that cannot be explored in detail here, the institutions that have been built or transformed out of these institutional strategies have prospered differentially. The corporate law firms have done very well. In Mexico, they provided an institutional base for the descendants of the elite land-owning families to build expertise and credibility to move into the state —bridging the divide that had existed since the Mexican Revolution. In Chile and in Brazil, the business law firms are providing places where technically sophisticated and well-connected lawyers can move in and out of the state. The same may be true of Argentina, but the long-standing and understandable reticence of the business lawyers to invest in the state still deters that kind of investment. There is still a wariness to invest in the state and also a heightened attention to investment abroad. The business law firms, in short, are prospering, and, although they are not the same as their counterparts in the United States or Great Britain, it is very easy to place them in a recognized category.

Public interest law, however, as found for example in human rights or the environment, has not been so successful. Although institutions that could be identified as public interest law thrived in the 1980s in at least three of the four countries (with Mexico the least successful), the return to democracy provided more opportunities in Brazil and Chile to reinvest in the state. Lawyers who were active in human rights in all these countries tended either to go into state politics or to move outside of their countries into the international domain, but in Brazil and Chile they could simply revive the political practices that had existed earlier. In addition, the international funders of the nongovernmental organizations (NGOs) who had been challenging the state tended to invest their funds elsewhere after the return to democracy. They did not initially see the need to focus on counterparts to the state. The "return to law" in Brazil and Chile was thus a return of ambitious and politically oriented lawyers to the state and its institutions.

Paradoxically, Argentina may provide the exception that will be the most successful in sustaining public interest law in the next few years. The historical lack of professional investment in the state in Argentina, described previously, makes it easier to sustain institutions—again akin to think tanks—that can operate outside the state. At the same time, however, it remains difficult to imagine that the courts in Argentina will assert the kind of autonomy that helps public interest law prosper in the United States. They have served to date mainly as weapons in political fights. But public interest law can use the media and international connections.

The situation is far from static in any of the countries. Our main purpose in this chapter was not to assess results. The important point is that international strategies have been played on very different institutional landscapes in the four countries that we studied. In Brazil and Chile, during the period that we examined, those strategies in law helped facilitate a return of the law —and the traditional families able to keep up with the new expertise—to a key place in governance. There is a belated success of law and development. In Argentina and Mexico, in contrast, international strategies did not fit the model of challenge and response. They played into complicated domestic structures of power that allowed some descendants of the traditional elite in Mexico to cross the border between public and private elites and some individuals close to PRI to upgrade the PRI governing technologies. In Argentina, international strategies have begun to transform the government, especially with respect to economic matters, but they have above all built and transformed the business law firms and the think tanks. Finally, although relatively easy to explain given Argentina's political structure, it is ironic that the country most embedded in the international market of expertise in the period we studied was the country whose field of state power was least transformed by the domestic investment of that expertise.

International strategies can be found increasingly in the law and in other professional fields and expertise. Because of the prestige and credibility of expertise made in the United States, especially economics but also law, ambitious individuals from many countries seek to build their local careers by participating in this prestige and credibility. There is therefore an increasing attention to the promotion of reform in legal education, improving the administration of the courts, and generally building the "rule of law" in Latin America. The pressure is to move to a kind of state that looks more like the government and economy of the United States. One way to explain this pressure for change would be to describe it as an emerging consensus about what a liberal democracy needs in order to thrive in today's world. Such a description makes it appear as if there is simply a demand for these particular products by elites or even by social movements. This chapter seeks to show how international strategies are used to fight palace wars and in the process produce changes and even consensual approaches out of particular investments available and attractive to certain individuals and groups. And at the same time, the comparison of the four countries we studied shows that the impact of similar international strategies in different structural settings is bound to be different. Again, rather than see a converging demand, we see that some similar patterns of foreign investment lead to very different outcomes—in particular with respect to the position of law—in different countries.

The return to—or establishment of a new position for—law can take the form of hybrids that emerge outside the traditional frameworks of courts and legal education. Examples include the development of arbitration or mediation outside the courts and the development of law schools attached to business schools. It is important to see these other places where law can play a new role, even though they do not correspond to institutions that have typically been examined in sociological studies of legal change. Finally, to recall the processes that are producing these changes, we note that this fragmentation and hybridization that we characterize in part as a return to law can perhaps better be seen as a return to "dependent law," as the transformations relate closely to hegemonic processes.

Notes

1. Of course, most lawyers in these countries still have relatively traditional practices grounded in the civil codes. Our focus is on elite practices not only because of the role they have in attracting people into the legal profession and structuring major developments in the economy and state, but also because the more elite sector is crucial in defining the position of law and its importance in defining the rules of the game for the economy and state.

2. Put another way, we do not wish to portray these people as omniscient or rational strategic actors. Perhaps some members of the elite have privileged information that allows them to be more strategic than others, but the point is to see the accumulation of strategies in relation to what is available and what is not—and what seems to be attractive for whatever reason at the time.

3. The "failure" in Brazil produced a quite strong group of corporate lawyers who were given very valuable expertise and credentials that could be used to serve foreign investors and the economic change that took place later. These lawyers helped rewrite corporate law and intellectual property law, for example, to make it more akin to the requirements of international investors—with approaches that were very U.S. oriented.

4. The position of the U.S. economists then made further gains in both places with the debt crises of the 1980s.

References

Bourdieu, Pierre. 1996. *The state nobility: Elite schools in the field of power.* Stanford, Calif.: Stanford University Press.

Bourdieu, Pierre, and Loic Wacquant. 1992. *An invitation to reflexive sociology.* Chicago: University of Chicago Press.

Dakolias, Maria. 1995. A strategy for judicial reform: The experience in Latin America. *Virginia Journal of International Law* 36:167.

Dezalay, Yves, and Bryant G. Garth. 1996. *Dealing in virtue: International commercial arbitration and the construction of a transnational legal order.* Chicago: University of Chicago Press.

———. 2002. *The internationalization of palace wars: Lawyers, economists and the international reconstruction of the state.* Chicago: University of Chicago Press.

Gardner, James. 1980. *Legal imperialism: American lawyers and foreign aid in Latin America.* Madison: University of Wisconsin Press.

Haggard, Stephan. 1985. The politics of adjustment: Lessons from the IMF's extended fund facility. *International Organization* 39 (3):505–34.

Lynch, Dennis. 1981. *Legal roles in Colombia.* Uppsala, Sweden: Scandinavian Institute of African Studies.

Merryman, John Henry. 1977. Comparative law and social change: On the origins, style, decline and revival of the law and development movement. *American Journal of Comparative Law* 25:457.

Pérez-Perdomo, Rogelio. 1988. The Venezuelan profession: Lawyers in an inegalitarian society. In *Lawyers and society, Vol. II, The civil law world*, edited by R. Abel and P. Lewis. Berkeley: University of California Press.

Smith, Peter H. 1996. *Talons of the eagle: Dynamics of U.S.–Latin American relations.* New York: Oxford University Press.

Trubek, David, and Marc Galanter. 1974. Scholars in self-estrangement: Some reflections on the crisis in law and development studies in the United States. *Wisconsin Law Review* 1974:1062–1102.

Williamson, John. 1990. What Washington means by policy reform. In *Latin American adjustment: How much has happened?* edited by J. Williamson. Washington, D.C.: Institute for International Economics.

World Bank. 1998. *Beyond the Washington Consensus: Institutions matter.* Washington, D.C.: World Bank.

Yergin, Daniel, and Joseph Stanislaw. 1998. *The commanding heights: The battle between government and the marketplace that is remaking the modern world.* New York: Simon & Schuster.

CHAPTER 14

SLADE: A Memoir

JOHN HENRY MERRYMAN

THIS IS THE second of two brief memoirs of law and development projects of the 1960s and 1970s in which the writer was centrally involved. The first described the Chile Law Program (CLP), in which the Stanford Law School supported Chilean law deans and professors in their efforts to reform Chilean legal education and research.[1] In this memoir I revisit SLADE (Studies in Law and Development), which was initiated and based at the Stanford Law School. Unlike the CLP, which was an action program, SLADE was an inquiry,[2] in which we set out to acquire systematic, comparable information about law and social change from the documented experiences of six nations in Spanish America and Mediterranean Europe in the decades following the end of World War II.

Origins of SLADE

In 1970, under a grant from the Ford Foundation to review the law and development literature and assess the field, I began to discuss with colleagues some ideas that eventually contributed to the intellectual structure of SLADE.[3] During the same period I was encouraged by Bayless Manning, then dean of the Stanford Law School, to approach the Agency for International Development of the U.S. Department of State (AID) for support of a research program in which these emerging ideas could be put into practice. The following language from the grant application states the general objective of the proposal:

I am grateful to Lawrence Friedman, Rogelio Pérez-Perdomo, and José Juan Toharia for suggestions and criticisms.

Though it is widely recognized that strong legal institutions are essential to sound national growth, little is yet known about the actual functions of law and legal institutions in the development process. There is clear need for a new body of theory and method—a "social science" of law and development—to provide the intellectual framework for effective study, research and decision-making.

The developing world is heterogeneous in its legal forms and institutions. Useful study and research in law and development require close familiarity with the legal institutions and cultures of specific countries. Latin America and Mediterranean Europe together form a coherent, relatively homogeneous culture area, and the work under this Grant will center on less developed countries within it. The knowledge gained through this effort will contribute to the understanding of law in its relation to economic and social change in the developed as well as the developing world.

AID responded with a generous grant. We enlisted a distinguished advisory committee,[4] and the work of translating the general objective into a research design began with a series of three multidisciplinary seminars held at Stanford in the fall and winter of 1971–72.[5] During the same period a two-day working conference was held at Stanford with law professors Kenneth L. Karst (UCLA), Stewart Macaulay (Wisconsin), Henry J. Steiner (Harvard), and David M. Trubek (then of Yale).

The advisory committee, the seminars, and the conference exposed us to a wide variety of expertise and experience and helped us define the core of the eventual research design. We decided that our research goal would be to collect systematic, comparable data on social, economic, and legal change within nations in the Spanish America–Mediterranean Europe culture area. We also decided that the data collection would be carried out by lawyer–social scientist "national scholars" from each of the nations who would be invited to work closely with us in elaborating the research design. The choice of nations to include in the study was governed by two principal considerations: the desire to represent some of the social, economic, and cultural variety within Spanish America and Mediterranean Europe and the availability of qualified, empirically inclined social scientists who could be persuaded to join us as national scholars.[6]

The national scholars joined us at Stanford in the spring and summer of 1972 for an intensive period of study and discussion that produced the complete research design. In the autumn of 1972 they returned to their nations for three years of field research and the compilation of data. During the fieldwork we met with them in three working conferences to discuss and resolve problems arising in the field, to make needed adjustments to the research design, and to assure comparability of research results. As the fieldwork progressed, Professor David S. Clark joined SLADE as associate director in 1973, with primary responsibility for maintaining contact with the national scholars and for the eventual compilation and publication of the data. In 1975–

76 the national scholars returned to Stanford to work up their field research results and begin preparation of national monographs. A volume describing SLADE and setting out a compendium of the data compiled in the study (hereinafter called the data volume) was published in 1979.[7]

Nature of the Inquiry

SLADE was an inquiry undertaken in order to build and test theory using quantitative information and methods. Because our field of interest was, in the first instance, law and development, it became necessary early in the design of the inquiry to adopt reasonably precise meanings for the two key concepts: "development" (which we defined as "social change in developing nations") and "law" (which became "legal systems"). It soon became clear that a third variable was needed, which we called "legal culture."

DEVELOPMENT

Most uses of "development" are programmatic; development is something to be brought about, a defined end to be achieved. We sought, however, to avoid commitment to any one among the many competing views of the nature of social progress (taking "social" in the broad sense to include the economic and cultural) or of the proper choice of strategies for achieving it. We were interested in social change, whether or not it comported with any of the conventional models of progress or development. It followed that any nation in which there was significant social change was, for our purposes, "developing." As social change occurs in all nations, the category was all-inclusive, and development became simply social change.

The notion of development as social change relates law and development to law and society. This is both convenient and potentially fruitful, because it gives law and development a disciplinary home, access to a group of interested colleagues, and a vital and extensive relevant literature. Most important of all, association with law and society provides a paradigm: law and development can be viewed through the lenses of the social sciences. This provides an alternative to doctrinal legal scholarship, one more amenable to inquiry and to quantitative measures and methods.

Our approach to social change was quantitative. The emphasis was on social measurements, and qualitative information was used primarily as an aid to understanding and interpreting them. The period we studied ran from the end of World War II, 1945, to the most recent year for which it seemed possible to acquire comprehensive data, 1970. Annual data for each year in the period, where available, provided twenty-six measurements of each indicator. Variations from one year to another in these social measures were our indicators of social change.

As excellent collections of social system variables were readily available, we collected only selected social indicators: basic data on demography, the labor force, education, gross domestic product, and similar structural features of society. The principal limitation of published social indicators was that they usually were based only on nationwide statistics. The comparison of national aggregates, although useful, fails to reflect the variety within national societies and their legal systems. We captured some of that variety through the use of regional data.

The basis of our regionalization was primarily socioeconomic, rather than geographic. We aggregated data from areas that were similar in economic structure, extent of urbanization, and productivity, indicators that significantly correlate. The research design contemplated six regions: the national capital and five others based on the percentage of the economically active population engaged in agriculture: urban (15–20 percent), semiurban (33–37 percent), semiagrarian (41–47 percent), agrarian (53–60 percent), and traditional (61–67 percent). As a result, each country (except Peru, where different regions were sampled rather than compiled) was divided into three to five socioeconomic regions that, together, constituted the whole nation.

LAW

The decision of what to study under the rubric "social change" was relatively easy. There was a substantial literature on social change and on social indicators, a strong tradition of empirical social research, and a sophisticated methodology, all of which expressed a large area of consensus. There were important differences among social scientists, but they existed, for the most part, within a single paradigm and did not call the paradigm itself into question.

Law was different. There was no strong tradition of empirical, quantitative, scientific, hypothesis-testing, theory-building inquiry. Legal scholarship was, as much of it still is, primarily concerned with doctrine; it was qualitative and practical or philosophical and normative. Law was perceived primarily as a body of rules. We were attracted to a working conception of law that was more amenable to the general stance of quantitative, longitudinal inquiry and more likely to lead to fruitful conjunction with the working notion of social change just described.

Such a working conception had to meet additional criteria: we wished to provide a basis for asking questions, rather than assuming or giving answers. We wanted to avoid as far as possible the implicit imposition of an ideology. Our working conception of law should be sufficiently open to admit the variety of legal reality of the six nations in SLADE (and ideally would be more generally applicable). It should have sufficient structure to provide a useful

TABLE 14.1

Analytical Framework

	Institutions	Actors	Processes	Resources consumed
Legislative				
Administrative				
Judicial				
Private ordering				
Law enforcement				
Legal education and legal professions				

framework for empirical research. We found no such working conception of law ready-made, and so we made our own.

We began with the observation that in every nation it was possible to identify institutions, actors, and processes that were generally regarded by people within these nations as "legal," as forming part of the "legal system." This prevailing characterization of institutions within a given society provided the basis from which we drew our working conception of the legal system in that society. Because the characterization could be expected to vary from one society to another, the actual size, shape, and internal configuration of the legal system in one nation was likely to vary from those in others. A working conception of the legal system that admitted such variations and that allowed for their accurate representation was a "hospitable" one, and we tried to capture a measure of this kind of hospitality in SLADE.

Table 14.1 illustrates the analytical framework we employed to represent the legal system.

The categories listed across the top of the grid are general categories that are relatively independent of culture, time, and space. All legal systems, indeed all social systems, have institutions, actors, and processes and consume resources. Particularly in the 1970s, when the Soviet Empire was still a major presence, it could be objected that the categories listed on the left side of the grid were valid only for the Western liberal tradition, which finds it useful to divide governmental activities into legislative, administrative, and judicial. Objection could also be made that to treat "private legal ordering" as a major legal category gave further evidence of a Western liberal bias when contrasted with nations in which the society and economy were governed by central planning and the role of private legal ordering was relatively minor.

Still, we chose these categories because they were useful and familiar, because they were built into our own legal culture, because they worked well in the six SLADE nations, and because there were no equally useful alternative categories available.

By "legal institutions" we meant the organized units staffed by legal actors that do the work assigned by society to the legal system. Such institutions include, among others, legislatures, administrative agencies, courts, and faculties of law. "Legal actors" are the people who fill assigned roles in the legal system: judges and judicial staff, legislators and legislative staff, administrators, law-enforcement personnel, advocates, notaries, and law professors. Within the "legal processes" category would fall such basic and obvious matters as legislation, litigation, law enforcement and administration of the law, private ordering, and legal education. "Resources consumed" by the legal system refers to the amount of social product that goes into its maintenance and operation. This translates most conveniently into institutional budgets authorized, appropriated, and spent, and in the fees paid to lawyers, notaries, and public institutions or officials for legal services.

THE QUANTITATIVE DESCRIPTION OF LEGAL SYSTEMS

One of our objectives was to advance the idea that legal systems could be usefully described in quantitative terms. That it may still be unusual to talk quantitatively about law is due more to the traditions of legal scholarship than to any inherent difficulty in measuring legal system components and processes. Many such measurements commonly exist in the form of judicial statistics, police statistics, budget information for legal institutions, and so forth. It is a relatively small conceptual step from data of this kind to the idea of a set of measurements of sufficient variety and coherence to represent the legal system.

Measurement as a way of describing legal systems offers several major attractions. For one, it can provide an additional way of looking at familiar things. Just as in chemistry one must do both quantitative and qualitative analysis in order to establish the composition of a substance or define a process, so in order to provide a full description of a legal system, both kinds of information are important. Legal measurements are not a substitute for the more usual (and generally more qualitative) approaches; they are a useful addition to them.

The quantitative stance directs our attention to matters that are readily measurable or countable. One kind of measurement suggests another, and soon a quite distinct group of related measurements—constituting a different but potentially useful approach to representation of the legal system— emerges. One attraction of a quantitative description lies in the ease and precision with which numbers can be treated. When the descriptive units are quantitative, quantitative methods can be used to interpret them. Where the numbers have statistical significance, statistical methods can be used.

The SLADE research design had to accept that some kinds of desired information would not be available to us. In particular, we could not expect to have access to police and internal security information. This is an important part of the legal system, but information about it in foreign nations is too sensitive to permit inquiry, particularly by a foreign research project. The result is a serious gap that can be filled only partially (and unsatisfactorily) from existing sources.

Except where legislative and executive acts are counted to provide a measure of the relative use of the legislator and the executive in lawmaking, we did not attempt to deal at all with legal rules and their content. One reason is that they do not lend themselves to significant measurement. Another is that rules of law in nations within the same legal tradition (as in SLADE) closely resemble each other in wording and in form. From our point of view the important differences are in the "legal systems" and, as will appear, in the legal cultures in the six nations. Legal rules may cast light on legal measurements, but they are not a primary object of our inquiry.

We sought to transform the scheme illustrated in Table 14.1 into specific measurements. For some categories, such as the judiciary, this was rather easily done. Courts were the main *institutions*: we wanted to know how many courts there were and of what kinds (administrative, labor, criminal, civil, and so forth). The principal judicial *actors* were judges and judicial staff; how many of them were there and of what kinds? The principal judicial *processes* were litigation and ex parte judicial action; how many of what kinds were instituted, withdrawn or lapsed, or completed? How many were appealed? How long did litigation last? How much money was appropriated for and spent by the judiciary? Other categories were less easy. How does one acquire systematic quantitative information about private ordering of legal relations through contracts, conveyances, wills, gifts, and the like? Our approach was through the records kept by notaries who, in the SLADE nations, draft and authenticate many of the legal documents used in private ordering

QUANTITATIVE COMPARATIVE LAW

Once we have acquired quantitative descriptions of legal systems, quantitative comparison becomes possible. Comparative law has traditionally been qualitative: comparisons of the substantive content of rules of law, of legal doctrine, of legal concepts. Quantitative comparative law is a novel and potentially fruitful complement to the more traditional qualitative approach. Thus, it is interesting that the lease is merely another type of contract in

Italy, whereas it is a conveyance of an interest in land in Massachusetts, but it is also interesting, though in a different way, that there were over four times as many judges per capita in Italy as there were in Peru.

Although the term "comparative law" is commonly used only for national or legal family comparison—for example, comparing U.S. and French law, or common law and civil law—the range of potentially interesting types of comparison is much greater than that. Another obvious kind of comparison is longitudinal. The same kinds of measurements of the same things taken at different times show whether change has occurred and, if it has, the direction and magnitude of the change. All of our legal measures were taken over time; in the ideal case we acquired annual data for each of the years 1945–70, providing twenty-six measurements of that variable for each nation. The fact that these twenty-six sets of legal measures apply to the "same" legal system—that is, to legal institutions, actors, processes, and resources consumed within the same society—allows a presumption of continuity that makes interpolation and extrapolation permissible.

Comparative law of a more familiar kind compares different legal systems at the same time, rather than the same one at different times, and is sometimes characterized as "horizontal" comparative law. For this purpose our units of comparison were nations and regions, and three levels of horizontal comparison were contemplated: intranational (the comparison of different regions within the same nation), cross-national (the comparison of national legal systems), and cross-regional (the comparison of regions within different nations). With twenty-four regions distributed among six nations, the possibilities for horizontal comparison were substantial. The difficulty of regionalizing legal measures, however, meant that the regional data were less complete than the national data, and this of course limited the potential for productive regional comparisons.

LEGAL SYSTEMS AND SOCIAL CHANGE

Our working assumptions can be summarized as follows: we assumed that the legal system is a part—a nonautonomous subsystem—of society. Social events (that is, events occurring outside the legal system; for example, an increase in population) and legal events (that is, events occurring within the legal system; for example, an increase in the number of trial courts) are related to each other in some systematic way. This proposition, which seems intuitively true and, indeed, obvious, is crucial to SLADE. Figure 14.1 illustrates the matter.

The $\Delta S_1 \leftrightarrow \Delta S_2$ equation in Figure 14.1 illustrates relationships of concern to the general sociologist: the (nonlegal) social consequences of (nonlegal) social change. The $\Delta L_1 \leftrightarrow \Delta L_2$ equation illustrates relationships that are relevant to SLADE—the legal system consequences of legal system

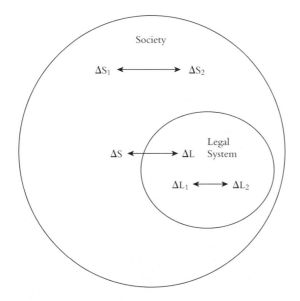

FIGURE 14.1 Social–Legal Interactions

change—but do not necessarily involve development. Our primary interest was in the relationships illustrated by the $\Delta S \leftrightarrow \Delta L$ equation—the interaction between social change and legal change.

Our assumption was that some kinds of social change and some kinds of legal system change are associated, so that if one occurs, it is reasonable to expect to find the other. This assumption suggested the important question of whether social change produced legal system change, or was the opposite the case? Our working assumption was that the influence ran both ways, but we expected the stronger effect to be that of social change on legal systems. This suggests that social change is more often and more importantly the independent variable and the legal system change the dependent variable. As a general proposition, where there is a correlation, social change causes legal system change. For example, increasing population and increasing criminal litigation may be correlated, but it is doubtful that criminal litigation produces population growth.

LEGAL CULTURE

Some kinds of social change have little or no legal system consequences. Others have significant legal system consequences. What is it that determines whether a given social change is of one kind or another? We can suppose that two kinds of influence are at work. One is the set of cultural attitudes, deeply rooted and firmly held, that determine the way "outsiders"—people in society who play no regular legal system role—perceive and define the legal system and expect it to be (or not to be) used. We call this set of attitudes the "external legal culture." The external legal culture directs the forces released by social change and controls the way these forces impinge on the legal system. The second influence is found in attitudes *within* the legal system —the attitudes of "insiders," which are also deeply rooted and firmly held. The culture of lawyers, judges, and other legal actors conditions the extent to which the legal system is receptive to the implications of social change and modulates the direction and force of such implications. We call these attitudes the "internal legal culture."

To a large degree one would expect the external and internal legal cultures in a society to overlap; many attitudes of insiders and outsiders about the proper structure and operation of the legal system are the same. Indeed, a large part of this consensus is frozen into legal rules about the structure, jurisdiction, and operation of legal institutions, the definition and regulation of legal roles, and the unfolding of legal processes. Such rules may be thought of as crystallizations of central features of the legal cultures. They are found in constitutions, laws governing the judiciary, codes of civil and criminal procedure, laws governing the public administration, laws governing admission to the bar, and so forth.

One would also expect to find that the gloss of meaning attributed to these rules would, to a certain extent, be shared by outsiders and insiders. Beyond the core of agreement, however, we should expect to find differences at the edges. Insiders and outsiders will often have somewhat different attitudes toward and perceptions of the legal system. Where these differences become excessive—where the gap between the external and internal legal cultures becomes too great—outsiders will consider the legal system unresponsive, and legal professionals will believe that people are making improper legal demands. For example, if individuals (for example, environmentalists, members of minority groups) seeking to assert important interests are prevented from presenting their cases in court by rules about standing to sue, a clash of legal cultures may be taking place.

Even the healthiest (in legal terms) of societies will show some differences between the external and internal legal cultures. This "cultural gap" is one determinant of the boundary that separates the legal system from the rest of society; the greater the gap, the more formidable the boundary. In the SLADE legal culture study we were interested in measuring this gap and in observing how these measurements changed between 1945 and 1970.

The legal culture category raised special problems and eventually generated a separate research operation. Information on legal culture is uncommon, and we found no prior attempt to develop an analysis of legal culture that would lend itself to empirical research of the sort we contemplated. We sought a method of detecting and measuring changes in legal culture between 1945 and 1970. As our research actually began in 1972, we could not use interviews and questionnaires, nor was a stratified sample of interviewees who represented prevailing attitudes for different dates in the 1945–70 period readily available to us.

Instead, we examined materials published during 1945–70 and analyzed their attitudes about law. In effect we "interviewed" these publications and scaled expressed or implied responses to our questions. The publications "interviewed" were newspapers and legal periodicals. The newspapers were selected to cover a left-center-right political spectrum. We hoped that they would reflect what we have called the "external legal culture." The legal periodicals were our principal source of internal legal culture.[8]

We can summarize our basic assumptions as follows: (1) social change takes place over time and can be measured by the use of social indicators; (2) the external legal culture modulates the forces released by social change and directs them toward or away from the legal system; (3) the internal legal culture affects the way the legal system receives the impact of social change; and (4) social change, as molded by the legal culture, brings about changes in the legal system. Accordingly, four kinds of variables are involved in this study. SLADE's ultimate aim was to examine the extent to which events in the social and legal systems could be explained by these variables.

SLADE was, in large part, an exploration of unknown terrain. Social indicators, external and internal legal culture data, and legal indicators were the categories of observation that we set out to record during the exploration. With these observations we hoped we could begin to map several great unexplored territories: the quantitative aspects of legal systems, quantitative comparative law, and the relations between social and legal change.

Results

The AID grant that funded SLADE expired in 1976, by which time we had completed the field research. We had acquired and organized a substantial body of social and legal data on the SLADE nations and had carried out an imaginative legal culture study through content analyses of newspapers and legal periodicals. We then applied to AID for a follow-up grant to support systematic study and interpretation of the large body of SLADE data. The agency, whose interest in law and development had by then moderated or taken other directions, declined to support our request. We accordingly completed preparation and publication of the data volume,[9] which sets out the social and legal indicators but not the legal culture data, and brought SLADE to a close. Most of the national scholars published interesting national studies in which they made use of the research results,[10] but there has never been a concerted and directed effort to produce comparative studies based on the large body of SLADE data.

The situation might be unkindly but accurately summed up in this way: we acquired a great deal of comparative information, but we did not do very much with it. A more positive way of putting things might be to say that the data we collected continue to present a reservoir of unexploited interpretive opportunities for comparative study. However one puts it, the fact is that our ambitions for the quantitative description of legal systems, quantitative comparative law, and quantitative study of the relations between social and legal change are still largely unaccomplished. For a few years I organized interdisciplinary seminars at Stanford in an attempt to mine the SLADE data, but they were sporadic efforts that produced work of only marginal interest, and eventually they ceased.

It is a disappointment, and something of an embarrassment, that so little published comparative work has resulted from so much effort. I often brood about it and try to think of convincing, if not consoling, explanations. At times I think of the SLADE data as a well-fortified castle, rumored to contain great treasure, that easily repels the occasional brave knight or clever sorcerer seeking access to its riches. The riches probably are in there, but it will take a planned assault by an imaginatively organized and well-armed force prepared for a long siege to overcome the castle's defenses. When we applied to AID for the supplementary grant, we suspected that interpretation would be difficult; and we were prepared to organize and conduct a sustained program of interpretation of the SLADE data. When our application was denied, that effort had to be abandoned. The relatively meager results of my subsequent sporadic approaches to the data, and that of others, have indirectly confirmed our judgment.[11] That is not the way to go at it. Still, the data have been published and could have been interpreted by others, and a few have bravely tried, but with little apparent result.

And so I must search for an explanation. Let me try this one. The SLADE enterprise came late in the curve of enthusiasm for hard social science—for the use of quantitative information about institutions, actors, and processes to form the basis for generalizations and predictions about law and society. By the time our data were published, the disciplinary style had changed, and scholars had begun to find it more interesting and productive to look elsewhere. There may also have been, for a few years, a kind of professional forbearance, a proprietary assumption that those of us who directed and conducted SLADE would take the lead in interpreting "our" data and that it would be bad form for others to show too much interest. By the time it became clear that we were not going to do the job, disciplinary styles and interests had continued to move away from the hard social science model, and both the research design and the data were now beginning to seem passé.

The other part of this explanation has been implied in earlier paragraphs: the SLADE research design was unusually ambitious, and the body of data we produced had imposing dimensions. Perhaps we tried to put our arms around too much of social and legal reality, so that our data-gathering reach exceeded our interpretive grasp. Interpretation was no small undertaking; it could be expected to take years of multidisciplinary effort, and the potential payoff was both uncertain and remote. Might we have produced, or stimulated, more productive interpretation of a more compact universe of data? Or was the crucial strategic error a different and more basic one: the simple failure to treat both data gathering and interpretation as essential components of a single scholarly enterprise and to insist from the start on funding for both?

Conclusion

What remains of the SLADE enterprise, aside from the data and the group of studies that are immortalized in the monographs and periodicals cited earlier? Is there some large truth, some cosmic social-legal insight, languishing within the data, waiting for the well-funded and abundantly staffed hero or heroine who will storm the castle and free it at last from its prison? We do not know.

Some observers have suggested that SLADE was in advance of its time. Perhaps so. After twenty-five years there is evidence of renewed scholarly interest in SLADE. At the conference held at Stanford in September 1999, an international group of younger scholars and SLADE veterans discussed papers that, in different ways, referred to and built on the ideas that underlay our work; this volume incorporates those essays. Some of the younger participants may eventually try their hands at mining the SLADE data. Their demonstration of renewed interest in the quantitative study of comparative law and social change is reassuring. SLADE lives.

Notes

1. John Henry Merryman, "Law and Development Memoirs I: The Chile Law Program," *American Journal of Comparative Law* 48 (2000): 481.

2. The distinction between law and development "action" and "inquiry" is discussed in John Henry Merryman, "Comparative Law and Social Change: On the Origins, Style, Decline and Revival of the Law and Development Movement," *American Journal of Comparative Law* 25 (1977): 457; republished in John Henry Merryman, *The Loneliness of the Comparative Lawyer and Other Essays in Foreign and Comparative Law* (Boston: Kluwer Law International, 1999; hereinafter *Loneliness*), 435.

3. The working document during this period, entitled "A First Essay in Law and Development," was widely circulated but never published, although parts of it made their way into a variety of other publications, including two articles that were stimulated by this opportunity to read and reflect on law and development: "Comparative Law and Scientific Explanation," *Law in the USA in Social and Technological Revolution* 81 (1974), republished in *Loneliness*, 478; and the article cited in note 2.

4. My Stanford colleague Lawrence Friedman became centrally involved early in SLADE and was effectively codirector of and a major intellectual contributor to the project throughout. The advisory committee was composed of Stanford professors Gabriel A. Almond (political science), John Barton (law), Alex Inkeles (sociology), and Victor Hao Li (law).

5. The following colleagues from Stanford and elsewhere joined in these seminars: Gabriel L. Almond (political science), John Barton (law), Jane Fishbourne Collier (anthropology), Thomas Ehrlich (law), Max Gluckman (anthropology, Manchester), Alex Inkeles (sociology and education), John J. Johnson (history), Kenneth L. Karst (law, UCLA), Roy Lave (industrial engineering), Joseph E. Leininger (law), John W. Lewis (political science), Philip Lewis (law, Oxford), Victor Hao Li (law), Gerald M. Meier (business), John W. Meyer (sociology), Robert A. Packenham (political science), Robert Rabin (law), Clark W. Reynolds (food research), David L. Rosenhan (psychology and law), Wilbur Schramm (communications), Eugene J. Webb (psychology and business), and John D. Wirth (history).

6. These were Professor Edmundo Fuenzalida Faivovich of Chile, Dean Carlos José Gutierrez (assisted by Professor Ricardo Harbottle) of Costa Rica, Professors Sabino Cassese and Stefano Rodotà of Italy, Dr. Miguel Wionczek and Lic. Maria Luisa Leal Duk of Mexico, Professor Lorenzo Zolezzi Ibarcena of Peru, and Professor José Juan Toharia of Spain. In 1973 Dr. Wionczek and Lic. Leal withdrew from SLADE, and Professor Fernando Rojas Hurtado of Colombia joined us.

7. John Henry Merryman, David S. Clark, and Lawrence M. Friedman, *Law and Social Change in Mediterranean Europe and Latin America: A Handbook of Legal and Social Indicators for Comparative Study* (Dobbs Ferry, N.Y.: Oceana Publications, 1979). This volume, which is now out of print, contains the legal and social indicators but not the legal culture data. A CD-ROM containing the entire body of data is on file in the Stanford Law Library.

8. The legal culture data are available on CD-ROM in the Stanford Law Library. See note 7.

9. See note 7.

10. S. Cassese, "Questione amministrativa e questione meridionale: Dimensioni e reclutamento della burocrazia dall'unità ad oggi" (Milano, 1977); E. Fuenzalida and F. Lagreze, "La investigación empírica en derecho," in *Derecho y Sociedad*, edited by G. Figueroa (Santiago, 1978); Fuenzalida et al., *Fluctuaciones de la demanda por justicia en función del Cambio Social* (Santiago, 1973–74); Fuenzalida, "Los conflictos laborales y el sistema legal en la Region VII (ODEPLAN, 1968) entre 1945 y 1970," *Revista Chilena de Derecho*, 4 (1–6) (1977):93–137; Gutiérrez, "Los jueces de Costa Rica," *Revista de Ciencias Jurídicas* 22 (1975):71; Gutiérrez, "Cantidad y cualidad de la función notarial en Costa Rica," *Revista de Ciencias Jurídicas* 27 (1975):19; Gutié-

rrez, "El desarollo de un sistema jurídico," *Revista Judicial* 5 (1977):61; Gutiérrez, *El funcionamiento del sistema juridico* (San José, Costa Rica: Ediciones Juricentro, 1979); J. Toharia, "Derecho y desarrollo: El caso de España," *Documentación Jurídica* 17 (1978): 42; L. Zolezzi, *Derecho y desarrollo: Perspectivas de análisis* (Lima: Pontificia Universidad Católica del Perú, Fondo Editorial, 1978).

11. There are references to SLADE and some use of the data in John Henry Merryman and David S. Clark, *Comparative Law: Western European and Latin American Legal Systems* (Indianapolis: Bobbs-Merrill, 1978); John Henry Merryman, David S. Clark, and John O. Haley, *The Civil Law Tradition: Europe, Latin America, and East Asia* (Charlottesville, Va.: Michie, 1994); Clark, "Civil Litigation Trends in Europe and Latin America Since 1945: The Advantage of Intracountry Comparisons," *Law & Society Review* 24 (1990):549; Clark, "The Legal Profession in Comparative Perspective: Growth and Specialization," *American Journal of Comparative Law* 30 (Supp. 1982):163; Clark, "Civil Litigation, Access to Justice, and Social Change Research Issues in Longitudinal Court Studies," *Southern Illinois University Law Journal* 12 (1988):713–29; Clark, "Adjudication to Administration: A Statistical Analysis of Federal District Courts in the Twentieth Century," *Southern California Law Review* 55 (1981):65–152; Clark and Merryman, "Measuring the Duration of Judicial and Administrative Proceedings," *Michigan Law Review* 75 (1976):89–99; Merryman, "Comparative Law and Scientific Explanation," in *Law in the USA in Social and Technological Revolution*, 81 (1974), republished in *Loneliness* (1999), 478; "Population, Civil Litigation and Legal Science," in *Studi in onore di Vittorio Denti*, vol. 1, 181 (1994), republished in *Loneliness* (1999), 505.

Index

Italic page numbers indicate material in tables and figures.

abortion: and Brazilian law, 80, 81
Abraham, Muci, 460
Academy of Political and Social Sciences
  (Venezuela), 460
acción de cumplimiento (Colombia), 177n9
Acción Democrática (Venezuela), 450, 451,
  452
Administrative Council for the Judiciary
  (Colombia), 155
administrative courts: in France, 193, *193*; in
  Italy, 228; in Spain, 393–95, 403n18
Administrative Procedure Act (Italy), 234
adoption: and Argentine family courts, 42;
  and Brazilian homosexuals, 75
adult literacy: in Brazil, 69
Agrarian Reform, Law of, 433
Alfonsin, Raul, 21–22, 23, 35–36, 45
Allende, Salvador, 113, 114, 115
American Bar Association, 373n4
amnesty: and Brazilian political prisoners,
  90; and Italian criminal cases, 253, 255,
  258
amparos: in Argentina, 38; in Mexico, 293,
  305, 309–10
Andrés Bello Catholic University, 457, 458,
  461, 463
Anti-Drug Law of 1993. *See* Stupefacient
  and Psychotropic Substances, Organic
  Law on Abuse of
antitrust authority: in Italy, 235
appeals courts: in France, 214–15; in Italy,
  266, 267–69; in Puerto Rico, 365, 367,
  368–69, 374n19; in Spain, 382–83

apremios: in Argentina, 37, 39
arbitration: in Brazil, 76, 91; in Italy, 231–32
Arbitration Law of 1996 (Brazil), 76
Argentina: adoption cases in, 43; bankruptcy cases in, 39, 54; bar association in,
  26; and citizens' access to justice, 46–50;
  constitutional reform in, 22; crime rates
  in, 23–24; debt collection cases in, 37,
  38, *39*, 46, 49; democracy in, 21–22; divorce cases in, 42–43, 46, 55; eviction
  cases in, 38, 49; family cases in, 38, 42–
  43, 49–50, 55; family courts in, 29; and
  foreign legal investment, 487–88, 491–
  93; judges in, *13*, 29, 30, 32; judicial system in, 27–33; juries in, 32; labor cases
  in, 38, 40, *41*, 46, 49–50; law firms in, 27,
  92; law professors in, 32; law students in,
  8, 26; lawyers in, *10*, 26–27; legal aid in,
  29; legal education in, 26; legislative production in, 24–25; litigation in, 33–48,
  50–56; mediation in, 32; military rule in,
  21, 44–45, 53–54; political corruption
  in, 31; social structure changes in, 22–23;
  state terrorism in, 25; succession proceedings in, 38, 40–42, 49; Supreme Court
  in, 27–28, 30, 32; urbanization in, 43–44
Arguas, Margarita, 32
Asociación Civil Primero Justicia (Venezuela), 454
Asonal Judicial (Colombia), 145
assassinations: in Colombia, 137, 145–46
Association of American Law Schools,
  373n4

Association of the Brazilian Press, 71
Atacama University, 119
Attorney General's Office of Colombia,
135–36, 146–49, 152, 169–72, 176n3
attorneys, 9–12, *10*; in Argentina, 26–27;
in Brazil, 83–84, 90–91; in Chile, 115,
130; in France, 185–89, 195, 206–7,
215n1; in Italy, 228–29, 233–34; in
Mexico, 330; in Spain, 388–91; in Venezuela, 464–66
Audiencia Nacional (Spain), 382–84
Austria: and public opinion of judicial system, *397*
avocats: in France, 185, 195, 206–7, 215n1
avvocati: in Italy, 228–29
Aylwin, Patricio, 109, 118, 119, 121, 131n5

Banco Central de la República Argentina,
25
bankruptcies: in Argentina, 39, 54
Bañados, Adolfo, 129–30
bar associations: in Argentina, 26; in Brazil,
71, 89; in Mexico, 330
barrios: in Venezuela, 434–35
Bascuñán, Antonio, 121
Belgium: and public opinion of judicial system, *397*
Bello, Andrés, 112
Berlusconi, Silvio, 222, 243, 272
bipartisanism: in Colombia, 138–39
blacks: in Brazil, 78, 98, 99
Borsalino Clan, 451, 470n9
Boyars of the State (Italy), 224
Brasil. *See* Brazil, regional disparities in
Brazil: abortion law in, 80, 81; adoption law
in, 75; adult literacy in, 69; and amnesty
for political prisoners, 90–91; arbitration
in, 76, 91; bar association in, 71, 89;
Catholic Church in, 71, 74, 99; child labor laws in, 78; citizenship laws in, 78–
79; collective rights in, 76–77; Constitutional Assembly in, 71, 72; consumer
protection in, 78; and the death penalty,
79; divorce law in, 74; drug trafficking in,
79, 80, 98; economic changes in, 69–70;
euthanasia law in, 81; family law in, 74;
and foreign legal investment, 483–86,
494–95; habeas corpus in, 76; homicide
in, 79; and homosexuals, laws pertaining

to, 74–75, 78; individual rights in, 70,
76–77; judges in, *13*, 83, 84, 89–90, 91;
kidnapping in, 79, 80; labor cases in, 82–
83; law professors in, 89; law students
in, *8*, 85–88; law schools in, 85–89,
103n66; law firms in, *11*, 91–92; lawyers
in, *10*, 83–84, 90–91; life expectancy
in, 69; litigation in, 81–83; marriage law
in, 74; mediation in, 91; organ donation
law in, 80; organized crime in, 80; penal
code in, 75; police in, 98; political corruption in, 72–73, 76; prisoners in, 75,
90; Protestantism in, 99; racial discrimination in, 78, 98, 99; regional disparities
in, 67, 73; religious discrimination in, 78;
robbery in, 79, 80, 97–98; sexual harassment laws in, 80–81; small claims courts
in, 75, 76; social movements in, 72, 90,
101n8; Supreme Court in, 82, 90; terrorism in, 79; theft in, 79, 97–98; and trade
agreements, 67, 70; traffic laws in, 77; urban violence in, 79–80, 95–96, *96*; voting rights in, 78
Brewer-Carías, A. R., 460
bribery: and Venezuelan prisoners, 451
Büchi, Hernán, 118
Buenos Aires: poverty rates in, 23; lawyers
in, 27
Bush, George H. W., 141
business bar: in France, 206–9

Caldera, Rafael, 417
Cali cartel, 141
Canada: incarceration rates in, 272; law
firms in, *92*
Cardoso, Fernando Henrique, 71, 72, 90, 92
Carlos, Juan, 400n3
Carpizo, Jorge, 490
Carta de los Notables (Venezuela), 417, 455,
468
Cassese, Sabino, 240
Catholic Church, 1; in Brazil, 71, 74, 99;
in Chile, 115; in Colombia, 140, 157; in
Venezuela, 432–33
Cavallo, Domingo, 493
Center of Legal Research, Andrés Bello
Catholic University, 463
Central University of Venezuela, 456–57,
458, 461, 462, 463

Centro de Documentación y Capacitación Electoral (Mexico), 321
Centro de Estudios Publicos (Chile), 121
CEPAL. *See* Comisión Económica para América Latina y el Caribe
Cerda, Pedro Aguirre, 115
Chávez, Hugo, 418, 468
Chicago Boys, 485–86
Chiesa, Mario, 277n14
child custody: and Puerto Rican law, 362; and Venezuelan law, 432–33, 446
child labor: and Brazilian law, 78
child support: and Venezuelan law, 446
Children and Adolescents, Law of the Rights of, 459
children's rights: and Colombian law, 158
Chile: Catholic Church in, 115; and coffee exports, 139; and computerization of courts, 121; concentration camps in, 114–15; and constitution of 1980, 116–18; customs duties in, 115; decree-laws in, 115, 117; environmental protection in, 129; family law in, 126–27; and foreign legal investment, 483–86, 494–95; habeas corpus in, 115, 117; health care in, 117; human rights in, 130; institutional senators in, 117, 118; judges in, 13, 121–24; Justice Ministry in, 121; labor cases in, 38, 40, 41, 46, 49–50; law firms in, 11; law schools in, 119; law professors in, 130; law students in, 8, 119, 120; lawyers in, 10, 115, 130; marriage law in, 127–28; marxism in, 113; military dictatorship of, 114–16; pensions in, 117; police in, 130; recourses of protection in, 117, 124, 125, 126; socialism in, 113; suffrage in, 113; Supreme Court in, 117, 118–19; tariffs in, 115; universities in, 117, 119; violence in, 114–16, 126–27; workers' rights in, 115
Chile Project, 485–86
Christian Democratic Party: in Chile, 113; in Italy, 220, 222, 243, 247, 249
Ciampi, Carlo, 249
Citizen's Constitution (Brazil), 72
citizens' rights: in Colombia, 148
citizenship: and Brazilian law, 78–79
civil cases: in Argentina, 35–43; in France, 190–91, 191; in Italy, 230, 259; in Mexico, 311; in Puerto Rico, 356; in Spain, 390–91, 392–93
civil code: in Spain, 381–82; in Venezuela, 432–36
civil courts: in Colombia, 163–69; in Italy, 226, 227–28; in Venezuela, 446
Civil Procedure, Code of (Venezuela), 427, 436–37
civil rights: in Mexico, 300
civil service: in France, 224; in Italy, 229
civil war: in Colombia, 141, 145
Clark, David S., 240, 500
clean hands investigations: in Italy, 222, 249
coffee exports: Chile and, 139
cold war, 483–85
collective rights: in Brazil, 76–77
collegiate circuit courts: in Mexico, 305, 306–7, 308–9
Collor, Fernando, 71, 72, 92
Colombia: antiterrorism statute in, 144; assassinations in, 137, 145–46; bipartisanism in, 138–39; Catholic Church in, 140, 157; children's rights in, 158; citizens' rights in, 148; civil courts in, 163–69; civil war in, 141, 145; conflict resolution in, 153–56; Constitutional Assembly in, 135, 141, 147, 150, 151, 156; Constitutional Court in, 151, 155, 156–58; constitutional justice in, 156–62; corruption in, 135, 142, 149, 152–53; courts of public order in, 149–50; and crimes against people, 171; criminal courts in, 151, 169–73; criminal investigations in, 146; criminal justice system in, 150–51; cultural preservation in, 158; debt collection in, 165–66, 167–68; declaratory trials in, 163, 167; discrimination in, 157; drug trafficking in, 140, 141, 149, 150; drug use in, 157; euthanasia law in, 157; executive powers in, 143–45, 149, 151; executory trials in, 163, 166, 167; guerrilla warfare in, 137, 140; homicide in, 137, 150, 171; human rights in, 140, 142, 152, 178n12; judges in, 13, 142–53, 155; judicial personnel in, 155; judicial reform in, 146–53; juries in, 150; justices of the peace in, 154; kidnapping in, 150; labor cases in, 159; labor strikes in, 144; law students in, 8; lawyers in, 10; military

Colombia (*continued*)
courts in, 151–52; misdemeanors in, 150;
organized crime in, 141, 142, 144; pensions in, 158; plea bargaining in, 150; and
plebiscite of 1957, 142–43; police in, 151;
prisoners in, 151; property crimes in, 171;
public order courts in, 149–50; religious
equality in, 157; secret judges and witnesses in, 150; social services in, 158;
street crimes in, 151; student protests in,
144; students' rights in, 158; Supreme
Court in, 143, 153, 156; territorial divisions procedures in, 155; terrorism in,
144, 149, 179n22; tutela actions in, 156,
157, 158–62, 178n13; violence in, 135,
137; white-collar crime in, 142
Comisión Económica para América Latina
y el Caribe (CEPAL), 483, 491
Comisión Nacional de Derechos Humanos
(Mexico), 315–16
Comissão Parlamentar de Inquérito (Brazil),
73
commercial rights: and Venezuelan law,
446–47
Committee of 24 (Chile), 115, 130
Communist Party: in Italy, 247–48; in Venezuela, 415
community property: and Puerto Rican law,
362
computerization: and Argentine judicial system, 32; and Chilean courts, 121
concentration camps: in Chile, 114–15
conciliateur: in France, 193–94
conciliation: in Mexico, 304
Conference of First Presidents of Courts of
Appeal (France), 205
conflict resolution: in Colombia, 153–56
consciousness of legality, 66
Conseil d'État (France), 201
Conseil supérieur de la magistrature
(France), 202–3, 217n18
Consejo General del Poder Judicial (Spain),
379–80
Consejo de la Magistratura (Argentina), 32
Consejo Superior de la Judicatura (Colombia), 155
Consorcio Justicia (Venezuela), 464
Constitutional Assembly: in Brazil, 71, 72;
in Colombia, 135, 141, 147, 150, 151,
156

Constitutional Chamber (Venezuela), 469
Constitutional Court: in Colombia, 151,
155, 156–58; in Italy, 221, 225, 228,
233–34, 248, 259–60, 271
constitutional justice: in Colombia, 156–58
constitutional reform: in Argentina, 22; in
Italy, 236; in Venezuela, 418
Constitutional Tribunal (Chile), 117
consumer protection: in Brazil, 78
contract law: in France, 192–93
Contreras, Manuel, 129–30
Convention on Children's Rights, 459
Convertibility Plan (Argentina), 38
Copei, 417, 450, 452
Córdoba: civil case rate in, 37; justice administration in, 28; legislative production
in, 25; litigation rates in, 36
Córdoba University, 26
corporate law: in France, 206–9
Corporación de Promoción Universitaria
(Chile), 121
Correa de la Cerda, Hernán, 121
corruption: in Argentina, 31; in Brazil, 72–
73, 76; in Colombia, 135, 142, 149, 152–
53; in France, 199; in Italy, 222, 271–72;
in Venezuela, 417–18, 422, 449–52, 466,
470n9
Corte Federal y de Casación (Venezuela),
449
Cossiga, Francesco, 249
Costa Rica: judges in, *13*; law students in, *8*;
lawyers in, *10*
Council of Development (Venezuela), 460
Council for the Economy (Italy), 221
Council of Europe, 244
Council of Europe Court, 231
Council of the Federal Judiciary (Mexico),
329, 330
Council of the Judiciary: Italy, 221, 226–27;
Mexico, 317, 318
Council of State (Italy), 231
Court of Cassation (Italy), 229–30, 245,
248–49, 259, 268–69
Court of Justice of the European Commu-
nities (Spain), 382
courts of assize: in Italy, 259, *264*, 265–66,
280n45
courts of public order: in Colombia, 149–
50
Craxi, Bettino, 249

Creel, Santiago, 491
crimes against people: in Colombia, 171
crime reporting: in Mexico, 301–2
criminal amparos: in Mexico, 310
criminal cases: in Italy, 230–31; in Mexico, 311; in Spain, 391, 395
criminal convictions: in Italy, 252–56
criminal courts: in Colombia, 151, 169–73; in Italy, 226, 227–28, 259–60
criminal investigations: in Colombia, 146; in Mexico, 302–3
criminal justice agreements: in Mexico, 334
criminal justice system: in Colombia, 150–51; in France, 196–200
criminal litigation: pyramid of, 160–71, 173
Criminal Procedure, Organic Code of, 443, 455, 456
Criminal Procedure, Code of, 431, 444, 445
criminal prosecution: in Mexico, 301–3
criminal trials: in Venezuela, 443–45
cultural preservation: in Colombia, 158
customs duties: in Chile, 115

DEA. *See* Diploma of Advanced Studies
death penalty: in Brazil, 79; in France, 204, 211; in Spain, 384–85
debt collection: in Argentina, 37, 38, *39*, 46, 49; in Colombia, 165–66, 167–68; in France, 195; in Venezuela, 447–48
decisions: and Colombian civil courts, 168–69; and French civil courts, *190*; and tutela actions, 162
declaratory trials: in Colombia, 163, 167
decree-laws: in Chile, 115, 117
defendants: and tutela actions, *161*, 161–62
democracy: in Argentina, 21–22; in Venezuela, 466–67
Democratic Action Party (Venezuela), 449–50, 451, 452
democratic deficit syndrome, 401n9
democratization, 3–6, 52–53
Denmark: and public opinion of judicial system, *397*
deregulation: in Mexico, 300
DESS. *See* Diploma of Specialized Higher Studies
Diego Portales University, 119, 121, 130
DINA (Chilean secret police), 130
Diploma of Advanced Studies (DEA), 186

Diploma of Specialized Higher Studies (DESS), 186, 187
Dirección General Impositiva (Argentina), 25
Direct Elections Now (Diretas Já, Brazil), 71
discrimination: in Brazil, 78, 98, 99; in Colombia, 157
district courts: in Mexico, 305, 306, 307, 310
divorce: and Argentine law, 42, 46, 55; and Brazilian law, 74; and French law, 191–92; and Venezuelan law, 432–33, 446
Divorce Act (Argentina), 42
Di Tella Foundation, 488
drug trafficking: in Brazil, 79, 80, 98; in Colombia, 140, 141, 149, 150; in France, 198; in Mexico, 334; in Spain, 383
drug use: in Colombia, 157; and Italian prisoners, 258; in Venezuela, 429, 430–31
drunk driving: and French law, 199
dual training: and French lawyers, 189
due process: and tutela actions, 160; in Venezuela, 431–32

EC. *See* European Community
École nationale d'administration (France), 200–201
École nationale de la magistrature (France), 188–89, 217n17
economic growth: and Argentine litigation, 43–46; in Italy, 242–43
economic rights: in Venezuela, 425
education, higher: in Argentina, 26–27; in Brazil, 85–86; in Colombia, 159; in France, 185–87; in Italy, 229; in Mexico, 294; and tutela actions, 159–60. *See also* law schools; private universities; public universities
ejecutivos (Argentina), 37, 39
Electoral Court (Mexico), 305, 311–12, 321
electoral system: in Mexico, 297–98
employment: and Brazilian citizenship, 78–79; disputes in Mexico, 304; and tutela actions, 160
England: incarceration rates in, 272; law firms in, *92*
Environment, Penal Law of the, 429
environmental protection: in Chile, 129; in Mexico, 303–4

environmental rights: in Mexico, 333–34
Escuela de la Magistratura (Argentina), 32
Estatuto da Mulher Casada (Brazil), 74
European Community (EC), 205, 222, 377.
    See also European Union
European Court of Human Rights, 260
European Court of Justice, 222, 234
European Union (EU): and the death pen-
    alty, 408n42; and Italy, 222, 232–33, 235,
    237, 243–44; and Spain, 377, 382
euthanasia: and Brazilian law, 81; and
    Colombian law, 157
evictions: and Argentine law, 38, 49
executive branch: in Colombia, 143–45,
    149, 151; in Italy, 225–26; in Mexico,
    298–99; in Venezuela, 424–25, 427–28
executory trials: in Colombia, 163, 165, 167
extortion: in Italy, 251; in Venezuela, 443

Falklands/Malvinas War, 21–22, 31, 493
family cases: in Argentina, 38, 43, 49–50,
    55; in France, 191–92; in Puerto Rico,
    366–67
family courts: in Argentina, 29
family law: in Brazil, 74; in Chile, 126–27;
    in Puerto Rica, 362; in Venezuela, 430,
    432–33
fascism, 221, 223, 245, 256
federal district courts: in Mexico, 312–14
Federal Fiscal Tribunal (Mexico), 303
feminization. *See* women
finance-sector corporations: and Colombian
    civil courts, 166–68
Finland: and public opinion of judicial sys-
    tem, 397, 399
Fiscalía General de la Nación (Colombia),
    135–36, 146–49, 152, 169–72, 176n3
Fondo Rotatorio de Justicia (Colombia), 143
Ford Foundation, 484, 485, 488
foreigners: and Italian prisons, 258
Forza Italia, 222, 243
France: administrative courts in, 193, *193*;
    administrative jurisdictions in, 215; ap-
    peals courts in, 214; business bar in, 206–
    9; and citizens' recourse to justice, 189–
    96; civil cases in, 190–91, *191*; concilia-
    teur in, 193–94; contract law in, 192–93;
    corporate law in, 206–9; corruption in,
    199; cours d'assises in, 215; court of cassa-
    tion in, 215; courts of first instance in,

214; criminal justice system in, 196–200;
    and the death penalty, 204, 211; debt col-
    lection in, 195; divorce law in, 191–92;
    drug trafficking in, 198; and education,
    higher, 185–87; family cases in, 191–92;
    houses of justice and law in, 199; immi-
    gration law in, 198; intoxicated motorists
    in, 199; and Italian political affairs, 223;
    judges in, *13*, 197, 200–206; labor cases
    in, 198–99; labor unions in, 203; law
    firms in, *11*, *92*, 205, 207–9; law profes-
    sors in, 187; law schools in, 185–89; law
    students in, *8*, 185–89; lawyers in, *10*,
    185–89, 195, 206–7, 215n1; legal aid in,
    195–96, 216n12; legal services in, 203,
    207–8; magistrates in, 185, 215n1; medi-
    ation in, 194–95, 199; police in, 197;
    property crimes in, 198; prosecutors in,
    200–206; and public opinion of judicial
    system, *397*; socialism in, 203, 204; theft
    in, 198; victim mobilization in, 199–200
Frei Ruiz-Tagle, Eduardo, 118, 121, 129
Frente Nacional (Colombia), 139, 140
Friedman, Lawrence, 1, 240
Fuenzalida, Edmundo, 240
Fuerzas Armadas Revolucionarias de Co-
    lombia, 177n7

Garzón, Baltasar, 130–31, 131n6, 407n41
General Council of the Judiciary (Spain),
    379–80
Germany: law firms in, *92*; and public opin-
    ion of judicial system, *397*
Gini coefficient, 57n7
globalization, 3–6
Greece: and public opinion of judicial sys-
    tem, *397*
guerrilla warfare: in Colombia, 137, 140
Gutiérrez, Carlos José, 240
Guzman, Juan, 407n41

habeas corpus: in Brazil, 76; in Chile, 115,
    117
Harbottle, Ricardo, 240
health care: in Chile, 117
health professionals: and Puerto Rican
    courts, 361
health services: and tutela actions, 159
High Court of the Federal District (Mex-
    ico), 312–14

Higher Council of the Magistracy (France),
202–3, 127n18
Higher Court of Salvaguarda (Venezuela),
452
Holland. *See* Netherlands
home ownership: in Venezuela, 434
homicide: in Brazil, 79; in Colombia, 137,
150, 171; in Italy, 251, 252; in Venezuela,
442
homosexuals: and Brazilian law, 74–75, 78
House of Deputies (Chile), 118–19
houses of justice and law: in France, 199
human rights: in Chile, 130; in Colombia,
140, 142, 152, 178n12; in Mexico, 333–
34; in Venezuela, 422

immigration: and French law, 198
individual rights: in Brazil, 70, 76–77; in
Italy, 259–60
Institute of Criminology (Venezuela), 462
Institute of Penal Sciences and Criminology
(Venezuela), 462
Institute of Political Studies (Venezuela),
462
Institute of Public Law (Venezuela), 460
Institute of Social Securities (Colombia),
162
Institutes of Health and Social Prevention
(ISAPRES), 117
institutional senators: in Chile, 117, 118
Instituto de Especialización Judicial (Mex-
ico), 321
Instituto de Estudios Económicos sobre la
Realidad Argentina y Latinoamericana,
493
Instituto de Estudios Superiores de Admin-
istración (Venezuela), 463
Instituto de Investigaciones Jurídicas (Mexico), 331, 490
Instituto de la Judicatura Federal (Mexico),
321
Instituto de Seguros Sociales (Colombia),
162
Instituto Tecnológico Autónomo de Mexico, 490
intellectual cold war, 483–85
international agreements: in Mexico, 332–
34
International Monetary Fund, 417
intoxicated motorists: and French law, 199

intrafamilial violence: and Chilean law,
126–27
investigations: and Venezuelan criminal
cases, 441–42
Ireland: and public opinion of judicial system, *397*
ISAPRES. *See* Institutes of Health and Social Prevention
Italy: administrative courts in, 228; antitrust
authority in, 235; appellate courts in, *266*,
267–69; arbitration in, 231–32; avvocati
in, 228–29; civil courts in, 226, 227–28;
civil cases in, 230, 259; and clean hands
investigations, 222, 249; Constitutional
Court in, 221, 225, 228, 233–34, 248,
259–60, 271; constitutional reform in,
236; corruption in, 222, 271–72; Court
of Cassation in, 229–30, 245, 248–49,
259, 268–69; courts of assize in, 259, *264*,
265–66, 280n45; criminal cases in, 230–
31, 253, 255, 258; criminal convictions
in, 252–56; criminal courts in, 226, 227–
28, 259–60; economic growth in, 242–
43; and education, higher, 229; executive
branch in, 225–26; extortion in, 251;
homicide in, 251, 252; incarceration rates
in, 272; individual rights in, 259–60;
judges in, *13*, 226–27, 235–36, 245–49,
272–73; judicial independence in, 246–
47; judiciary in, 229–32; Justice Ministry
in, 226, 271; justices of the peace in, 231;
kidnapping in, 251; law-decrees in, 225;
law firms in, *11*; law students in, *8*, 233–
34; law professors in, 229, 233–34; lawyers in, *10*, 228–29, 233–34; legal stereotypes in, 234; litigation in, 231; misdemeanors in, 256, 258; notaries in, 229;
organized crime in, 274; penal code in,
257–58, 260, 262, 271; penal decree proceeding in, 263; penal court system in,
259–60; plea bargaining in, 263; police
in, 260; political affairs, and French
influence on, 223; and positivism in law
textbooks, 234; preliminary inquiries in,
260–61; preture in, 260–63; preventive
detention in, 254, 257–58; prisoners in,
258; prisons in, 256–58; privatization in,
232, 244; procuratori in, 228–29; prosecutors in, 226–27, 237n1, 245–49, 260;
and public opinion of judicial system,

Italy (*continued*)
  397; recidivist convictions in, 253–54;
  referenda for repealing laws in, 233; regional law-making councils in, 225, 233;
  robbery in, 251; statutes in, 276; summary trials in, 262–63; and Tangentopoli
  investigations, 249, 277n14; terrorism in,
  271; theft in, 251, 253, 258; tribunali in,
  263, *264*, 265, *266*, 267; welfare state in,
  224–25

Japan: civil case rate in, 37; law firms in, *92*
jeito, 96, 104n79
Jiménez, Marcos Pérez, 414, 424, 439, 460
Jospin, Lionel, 203
Judge of Guarantee (Chile), 129
judges, 12–15, *13*; in Argentina, 27–33; in
  Brazil, 83, 84, 89–90, 91; in Chile, 121–
  24; in Colombia, 142–46, 152–53, 155;
  in France, 197, 200–206; in Italy, 226–
  27, 235–36, 245–49, 272–73; in Mexico,
  293, 305–12, 316–19, 327–30; in Puerto
  Rico, 357–61, 365–70; in Spain, 385–
  87; in Venezuela, 437–40, 449–52, 454–
  56, 465, 470n9
Judicial Academy (Chile), 121, 125
Judicial Career, Law on the, 450
judicial corruption: in Venezuela, 451–52,
  470n9
judicial creativity: in Spain, 381–82
judicial independence: in Italy, 246–47; in
  Puerto Rico, 359
judicial police: in Italy, 260
judicial privileges: and Colombian police,
  151
judicial protagonism, 176n2
judicial reform: in Colombia, 146–53; in
  Venezuela, 454–56
Judicial School (Spain), 385
Judiciary, Decree of Reorganization of the,
  455–56
Judiciary, Law of the, 359–61, 365, 367,
  369
Judiciary Law, Organic, 449, 450
Judiciary, Organic Law of the, 359
Juicio a las Juntas (Argentina), 31
juntas de conciliación y arbitraje (Mexico),
  304
Junta Federal de Cortes Supremas Provinciales (Argentina), 32

juries: in Argentina, 32; in Colombia, 150;
  in Spain, 384–85
justice: and Argentine citizens' access to,
  46–50; and French citizens' recourse to,
  189–96; and Spanish citizens' use of,
  388–95; and Venezuelan citizens' access
  to, 452–54
justices of the peace: in Argentina, 29; in
  Colombia, 154; in Italy, 231; in Puerto
  Rico, 365; in Venezuela, 454, 455
Justice Ministry: in Chile, 121; in Italy,
  226, 271; in Spain, 379; in Venezuela,
  437–38
Justice of the Peace, Law on, 455, 456
juvenile courts: in Venezuela, 446

Karst, Kenneth L., 500
kidnapping: in Brazil, 79, 80; in Colombia,
  150; in Italy, 251

labor cases: in Argentina, 38, 40, *41*, 46, 49–
  50; in Brazil, 82–83; in Chile, 117; in
  Colombia, 159; in France, 198–99; in
  Puerto Rico, 364; in Spain, 390, 393;
  in Venezuela, 448
Labor Law, Organic, 448
labor strikes: in Colombia, 144
labor unions: in France, 203
Lago, Ricardo, 109
Landless Movement (Brazil), 72
law-decrees: Italian, 225
law enforcement: in Mexico, 293, 301–4.
  See also police
law firms, *11*, 11–12, *92*; in Argentina, 27;
  in Brazil, 91–92; in France, 205, 207–9;
  in Mexico, 320–21, 323–24; in Venezuela, 465
law professors, 6–9; in Argentina, 32; in
  Brazil, 89; in Chile, 130; in France, 187;
  in Italy, 229, 233–34; in Mexico, 331;
  in Venezuela, 459–63
law scholarship: in Mexico, 322–23,
  344n59; in Venezuela, 459–63
law schools: in Brazil, 85–89; in Chile, 119;
  in France, 185–89; in Mexico, 320–21,
  323–24; in Puerto Rico, 358, 359; in
  Venezuela, 458
law students, 6–9, *8*; in Argentina, 26;
  in Brazil, 85–88; in Chile, 119, *120*; in
  France, 185–89; in Italy, 233–34; in

Mexico, 319–20; in Puerto Rico, 361; in Venezuela, 457–59
lawsuits, 12–15
lawyers, 9–12, *10*; in Argentina, 26–27; in Brazil, 83–84, 90–91; in Chile, 115, 130; in France, 185–89, 195, 206–7, 215n1; in Italy, 228–29, 233–34; in Mexico, 330; in Spain, 388–91; in Venezuela, 464–66
Lawyers' Code of Ethics (Venezuela), 454
legal aid: in Argentina, 29; in France, 195–96, 216n12
legal culture, 2, 507–9
Legal Education Committee of the Bar Association (Brazil), 88
Legal Education Specialists, Committee of, 88
legal ideology, 65–66
legal services: in France, 203, 207–8; in Puerto Rico, 360
legality: consciousness of, 66
Legislative Committee (Venezuela), 427
legislative process: in Mexico, 298–300; in Venezuela, 426–28
legislative production: in Argentina, 24–25
Letelier, Eugenio Velasco, 115
Letelier, Valentín, 112
life expectancy: in Brazil, 69
litigation: in Argentina, 33–48, 50–56; in Brazil, 81–83; in Italy, 231; in Puerto Rico, 369; in Venezuela, 446–49
"litigotiation," 168
Luxembourg: and public opinion of judicial system, *397*

Maastricht Treaty, 237, 243, 244
Macaulay, Stewart, 500
Madrazo, Jorge, 490
magistrates: in France, 185, 215n1
Magistrats' Trade Union (France), 203
Magistratura Democratica (Italy), 247, 248
Magistratura Indipendente (Italy), 247, 248
Malvinas (Falkland) War, 21–22, 31, 493
mani pulite investigations: in Italy, 222, 249
marriage: and Brazilian law, 74; and Chilean law, 127. *See also* divorce
Married Woman, Statute of the (Brazil), 74
Marxism: in Chile, 113; in Italy, 272
mediation: in Argentina, 32; in Brazil, 91; in France, 194–95, 199

Menem, Carlos, 22, 25
Mercosur (Brazil), 67, 70
Merryman, John Henry, 239–40, 241, 270
Mexican Revolution, 288–89, 293
Mexico: amparos in, 293, 305, 309–10; bar association in, 330; civil cases in, 311; civil rights in, 300; collegiate circuit courts in, 305, 306–7, 308–9; conciliation in, 304; constitution of, 295–98; crime reporting in, 301–2; criminal cases in, 311; criminal investigations in, 302–3; criminal justice agreements in, 334; criminal prosecution in, 301–3; deregulation in, 300; district courts in, 305, 306, 307, 310; drug trafficking in, 334; and education, higher, 294; electoral system in, 297–98; employment disputes in, 304; environmental protection in, 303–4; environmental rights in, 333–34; executive branch in, 298–99; federal district courts in, 312–14; federal judiciary in, 305–12; and foreign legal investment, 486–87, 489–91; human rights in, 333–34; and international agreements, 332–34; judges in, 293, 305–12, 316–19, 327–30; judiciary in, *13*, 316–19, 327–30; law enforcement in, 293, 301–4; law firms in, *11*, *92*, 330–32; law professors in, 331; law scholarship in, 322–23, 344n59; law schools in, 320–21, 323–24; law students in, *8*, 319–20; lawyers in, *10*, 330; legal education in, quality of, 323–24; legal elite in, 326–27; legislative process in, 298–300; and NAFTA, 334; and National Commission of Human Rights, 314–16; and normative constitution, efforts toward, 296–98; police in, 302; political rights in, 300; private universities in, 320, 321, 323; privatization in, 300; prosecutors in, 302–3; public officials in, 327; public universities in, 323; state judiciaries in, 322, 330; Supreme Court in, 298, 305–6, 317, 318, 327, 329–30; and trade agreements, 334; unitary circuit courts in, 305, 306, 309
military courts: in Colombia, 151–52
military justice system: in Venezuela, 440
military rule: in Argentina, 44–45, 53–54
Ministerio Público (Venezuela), 437, 456
Miracle Rain case (Venezuela), 470n9

misdemeanors: and Colombian law, 150; and Italian law, 256, 258; and Spanish law, 392

Mitterand, François, 186, 204

modernization: of Argentine judicial system, 32–33; of Chilean legal system, 121

Movimento per la Guistizia (Italy), 247

Movimento dos Sem-Terra (Brazil), 72

municipal judges: in Puerto Rico, 365

NAFTA. *See* North American Free Trade Agreement

National Commission of Human Rights (NCHR), 314–16, 490

National Commission Against the Illicit Use of Drugs (Venezuela), 430

National Congress (Venezuela), 424–25

National Constituent Assembly (Venezuela), 455–56, 468–69

National Council of Scientific Research (Venezuela), 462

National Council of Universities (Venezuela), 457, 458

National Court (Spain), 382–84

National Electoral Council (Colombia), 155

National Environmental Policy of 1981, Law of, 76

National Front (Colombia), 139, 140

National Plan for Judicial Reform (Argentina), 28

National School of Administration (France), 200–201

National School of Magistracy (France), 188–89, 201, 202, 217n17

National Security Council (Chile), 117, 118

National Security, Law of, 79

National Stadium of Santiago, 114–15

National University in Mexico City (UNAM), 487, 489. *See also* School of Law of the UNAM

natural law theory, and Brazilian legal studies, 88

Nazis, 216n15

NCHR. *See* National Commission of Human Rights

Netherlands: civil case rate in, 37; incarceration rates in, 272; and public opinion of judicial system, *397*

Netto, Antonio Delfim, 485–86

normative constitution: and Mexican efforts toward, 296–98

North American Agreement on Environmental Cooperation, 341n24

North American Environmental Commission, 341n24

North American Free Trade Agreement (NAFTA), 317, 334, 341n24, 490

notaries: in Italy, 229; in Spain, 388, 391

Ocampo, José Gabriel, 112

Office of the Administration of the Courts (Puerto Rico), 366, 367, 373n10, 373n12

oil: crisis of 1973, 184, 415; and Venezuelan economy, 419

Operación Condor (Spain), 383–84, 406n39

Ordem dos Advogados (Brazil), 494

Order of Lawyers (Chile), 115, 130

organ donation: in Brazil, 80

organized crime: in Brazil, 80; in Colombia, 141, 142, 144; in Italy, 274

Pacto de Punto Fijo (Venezuela), 414, 415, 418

Papon, Maurice, 216n15

Parliamentary Commission on Investigation (Brazil), 73

Partido Revolucionario Institucional (Mexico), 298, 487, 490

Partido dos Trabalhadores (Brazil), 90

PDVSA. *See* Petróles de Venezuela S.A.

penal code: in Brazil, 75; in Italy, 257–58, 260, 262, 271; in Venezuela, 429–32

penal courts. *See* criminal courts

penal decree proceeding: in Italy, 263

Penal Procedure Code (Italy), 257–58, 260, 262, 271

Penal Process, Organic Code of, 427

pensions: in Chile, 117; in Colombia, 158

Pérez, Carlos Andrés, 417, 425, 468, 471n20

Perón, Isabel, 21

Perón, Juan, 21, 52

personnel, judicial branch: in Colombia, 155; in Puerto Rico, 365–66; in Spain, 385–87

Peru: law firms in, *11*; law students in, *8*; lawyers in, *10*

Petróleos de Venezuela S.A. (PDVSA), 447, 465

Pinochet, Augusto, 108, 118, 130–31, 407n41
Pizani, Rafael, 450
plaintiffs: and Colombian civil courts, 166–68, *167*; and tutela actions, 160–61
plea bargaining: in Colombia, 150; in Italy, 263
plebiscite of 1957 (Colombia), 142–43
Plenário Pró-Participação Popular (Brazil), 72
police: in Brazil, 98; in Chile, 130; in Colombia, 151; in France, 197; in Italy, 260; in Mexico, 302; in Venezuela, 422, 441, 443
Political Constitution of 1925 (Chile), 115
political corruption: in Argentina, 31; in Brazil, 72–73, 76; in Colombia, 135, 142, 149; in Venezuela, 417–18
political rights: in Mexico, 300
Portugal: and public opinion of judicial system, *397*
positivism: and Brazilian legal studies, 88; and Brazilian penal code, 75; and Italian law textbooks, 234
Prebisch, Raul, 491
preliminary inquiries: in Italy, 260–61
preventive detention: in Italy, 254, 257–58
Primero Justicia. *See* Consorcio Justicia
prisoners: in Brazil, 75, 90–91; in Colombia, 151; in Italy, 258; in Spain, 395; in Venezuela, 451
prisons: in Italy, 256–58; in Venezuela, 445–46
private universities: in Chile, 117, 119; in Mexico, 320, 321, 323
privatization: in Italy, 232, 244; in Mexico, 300
Pro-Popular Participation Plenary (Brazil), 72
Procuraduría Agraria (Mexico), 315
Procuraduría de Defensa del Menor y la Familia (Mexico), 314
Procuraduría Federal del Consumidor (Mexico), 314
Procuraduría Federal de Protección al Ambiente (PROFEPA), 303–4, 314
procuratori: in Italy, 228–29
PROFEPA. *See* Procuraduría Federal de Protección al Ambiente
professors. *See* law professors

Program for Promotion of Researchers (Venezuela), 462
Programa Venezolana de Educación-Acción en Derechos Humanos (Venezuela), 464
property crimes: in Colombia, 171; in France, 198
property regimes: and married couples in Chile, 127, *128*
property rights: in Venezuela, 446–47
Propiedad Horizontal, Ley de, 433
prosecutors: in France, 200–206; in Italy, 226–27, 237n1, 245–49, 260; in Mexico, 302–3; in Spain, 387
Protestantism: in Brazil, 99
Provincial Supreme Court (Argentina), 32
Public Ministry (Chile), 129, 131
public officials: and legal training in Mexico, 327
public opinion: of EU judicial systems, 397–98; of French justice systems, 189–90; of Mexican legal culture, 335–37; of Spanish judicial system, 396–400
public order courts: in Colombia, 149–50
Public Patrimony, Law of Protection of the, 430
Public Patrimony, Organic Law of Protection of the, 429, 431
public universities: in Brazil, 103n66; in Chile, 117; in Mexico, 323
Puerto Rico: and Americanization of the law, 353–54, 356–58; appeals courts in, 365, 367, 368–69, 374n19; child custody in, 362; children's rights in, 362–63; civil cases in, 356; and community property law, 362; and constitution of 1952, 358, 359; defense theory in, 353–54; family cases in, 366–67; family law in, 362; health professionals in, 361; judges in, 357–61, 365–70; judicial independence in, 359; judicial personnel in, 365–66; justices of the peace in, 365; labor cases in, 364; law schools in, 358, 359; law students in, 361; legal services in, 360; litigation in, 369; municipal judges in, 365; social services in, 366–67; and the Spanish legal system, 357–58; Supreme Court in, 365, 367, 369–70; theft in, 364; violence in, 364

Quebec: family mediation in, 194

racial discrimination: in Brazil, 78, 98, 99
Radical Party (Argentina), 21–22
Reagan, Ronald, 141
recidivist convictions: in Italy, 253–54
recourses of protection: in Chile, 117, *124*, *125*, *126*
referenda: and repealing Italian laws, 233
Reforma, La, 400n3
regional councils: and Italian law-making, 225, 233
religious discrimination: in Brazil, 78
religious equality: in Colombia, 157
Rental Properties, Law of, 435
rents: and Venezuelan law, 433–34, 435
retirement income: and tutela actions, 159
Revolution in Liberty (Chile), 113
robbery: in Brazil, 79, 80, 97–98; in Italy, 251
Rodotà, Stefano, 240
Rojas, Fernando, 240
Roman law, 1

Salvaguarda del Patrimonio Público, Ley de, 452
Samper, Ernesto, 134, 135–36, 141, 151, 176n1
Sanabria, Edgar, 423
Santa María University, 457, 458
Sarney, José, 71–72
Sársfield, Vélez, 25
Scalfaro, Oscar, 249
School of Law of the UNAM, 321, 331
schools: and tutela actions, 159–60
secret judges and witnesses: in Colombia, 150
Serpa, Horacio, 135–36
sexual harassment: and Brazilian law, 80–81
SLADE. *See* Studies in Law and Development
small claims courts: in Brazil, 75, 76
social issues: and Italian judiciary, 248
social movements: in Brazil, 72, 90, 101n8; and Colombian antiterrorism statute, 144
social rights: in Venezuela, 425
social services: in Colombia, 158; in Puerto Rico, 366–67
socialism: in Chile, 113; in France, 203, 204
Socialist Party: Italy, 220, 222, 247, 248, 249; Venezuela, 452

sociology: and Venezuelan law schools, 462
sodium nitrate: and Chilean exports, 112
Solar, Luis Claro, 112
Solidarity, Vicariate of, 115, 130, 494
South Africa: incarceration rates in, 272
Spain: administrative courts in, 393–95, 403n18; appeals courts in, 382–83; and citizens' use of justice, 388–95; civil cases in, 390–91, 392–93; civil code in, 381–82; criminal cases in, 391, 395; and the death penalty, 384–85; drug trafficking in, 383; judges in, *13*, 385–87; judicial creativity in, 381–82; judicial independence in, 379–80; judicial personnel in, 385–87; judicial system in, 392–95; juries in, 384–85; Justice Ministry in, 379; labor cases in, 390, 393; law firms in, *11*; law students in, *8*; lawyers in, *10*, 388–91; misdemeanors in, 392; National Court in, 382–84; notaries in, 388, 391; prisoners in, 395; prosecutors in, 387; and public opinion of judicial system, 396–400; Supreme Court in, 379, 381, 382–83; terrorism in, 383; traffic cases in, 392; violence in, 395
State Council (Colombia), 153, 155, 177n5
state of emergency: and Colombian executive powers, 143–45, 149, 151
state judiciaries: in Mexico, 322, 330
state terrorism: in Argentina, 25
Steiner, Henry J., 500
stereotyping: and Venezuelan police, 443
Straw, Jack, 131n6, 407n41
street crimes: in Colombia, 151
student protests: in Colombia, 144; in Venezuela, 456
students' rights: in Colombia, 158
Studies in Law and Development (SLADE), 240, 291; and development inquiry, 501–2; and law inquiry, 502–4; and legal culture, 507–9; and legal systems inquiry, 506–7; origins of, 499–501; and quantitative comparative law, 505–6; and quantitative description of legal systems, 504–5; research results of, 509–11
Stupefacient and Psychotropic Substances, Organic Law on Abuse of, 429, 430
Suárez, Adolfo, 400n3

succession proceedings: in Argentina, 38, 40–42, 49
summary trials: in Italy, 262–63
Superior Council of the Judiciary (Italy), 235–36
Superior Magistracy Council (Italy), 245–49, 259
Supreme Court: in Argentina, 27–28, 30, 32; in Brazil, 82, 90; in Chile, 117, 118–19; in Colombia, 143, 153, 156; in Mexico, 298, 305–6, 317, 318, 327, 329–30; in the Philippines, 51; in Puerto Rico, 365, 367, 369–70; in Spain, 379, 381, 382–83; in Venezuela, 417, 424–25, 438, 449–52, 468
Supreme Court of Justice, Organic Law of the, 438
Sweden: incarceration rates in, 272; and public opinion of judicial system, *397*
symbolic capital, 480

Tangentopoli investigations (Italy), 249, 277n14. *See also* mani pulite investigations
tariffs: in Chile, 115
Task Force on the Family (Chile), 127
territorial divisions procedures: in Colombia, 155
terrorism: and Brazil, 79; and Colombia, 144, 149, 179n22; and Italy, 271; and Spain, 383. *See also* state terrorism
theft: in Brazil, 79, 97–98; in France, 198; in Italy, 251, 253, 258; in Puerto Rico, 364
Toharia, José Juan, 240
tort cases: and judicial costs, 49
trade agreements: in Brazil, 67, 70; in Mexico, 334
Trade and Development, United Nations Committee on, 491
traffic cases: in Spain, 392; in Venezuela, 447–48
traffic laws: in Brazil, 77; in France, 199
Transitional Article 24 (Chile), 116
Treaty of Assunción (Brazil), 70
Treaty of Maastricht. *See* Maastricht Treaty
Treaty of Rome, 222
Tribe of David (Venezuela), 451
Tribunal Supreme de Justicia (Venezuela), 469

tribunali: in Italy, 263, *264*, 265, *266*, 267
tribus system: in Venezuela, 451
Trubek, David M., 500
tutela actions: in Colombia, 156, 157, 158–62, 178n13

UNAM. *See* National University in Mexico City
Unified Parties for Democracy (Chile), 118
Union of Parties for Democracy (Chile), 109
Unità per la Costituzione (Italy), 247, 248
unitary circuit courts: in Mexico, 305, 306, 309
United Kingdom: and public opinion of judicial system, *397*
United States: Attorney General's Office in, 147; civil case rate in, 37; criminal mediation in, 194; and French bar association, 208; incarceration rates in, 272; and Latin American educational reform, 484; law firms in, *92*; and litigiotiation, 168; and Mexican domestic legal system, 334; and NAFTA, 317, 334, 341n24, 490; and Puerto Rican law, 353–54, 356–58
University of the Andes, 457
University of Carabobo, 457
University of Chile, 115–16, 121, 483
University of Puerto Rico, 358, 359, 372n3, 373n4
University of Recife, 483
University of Sao Paulo, 483
University of Zulia, 457, 462, 463
universities: and tutela actions, 159–60. *See also* private universities; public universities
Universities, Law of, 460
urban violence: in Brazil, 79–80, 95–96, *96*
urbanization: in Argentina, 43–44

Vargas, Getúlio, 94
Venezuela: barrios in, 434–35; Catholic Church in, 432–33; child custody in, 432–33, 446; child support in, 446; and citizens' access to justice, 452–54; civil code of, 432–36; civil courts in, 446; civil process in, 436–37; commercial rights in, 446–47; and constitution of 1961, 424–26, 449; constitutional reform in, 418; corruption in, 417–18, 422, 449–52,

Venezuela (*continued*)
470n9; criminal investigations in, 441–42; criminal trials in, 443–45; debt collection in, 447–48; democracy in, 466–67; divorce law in, 432–33, 446; drug use in, 429, 430–31; due process in, 431–32; economic rights in, 425; executive branch in, 424–25, 427–28; extortion in, 443; family law in, 430, 432–33; home ownership in, 434; homicide in, 442; human rights in, 422; judges in, *13*, 437–40, 449–52, 454–56, 465, 470n9; judicial reform in, 454–56; Justice Ministry in, 437–38; justices of the peace in, 454, 455; juvenile courts in, 446; labor cases in, 448; law firms in, *11*, 465; law professors in, 459–63; law scholarship in, 459–63; law schools in, 458; law students in, *8*, 457–59; lawyers in, *10*, 464–66; legislative process in, 426–28; litigation in, 447–49; military justice system in, 440; and oil revenues, 419; penal code in, 429–32; police in, 422, 441, 443; prisoners in, 451; prisons in, 445–46; property rights in, 446–47; rent laws in, 433–34, 435; social rights in, 425; student protests in, 456; Supreme Court in, 417, 424–25, 438, 449–52, 468; traffic cases in, 447–48; tribus system in, 451; voters in, 426; welfare state in, 421–23
victim mobilization: in France, 199–200
violence: in Brazil, 79–80, 95–96, 97; in Chile, 114–16, 126–27; in Colombia, 135, 137; and Colombian judiciary, 145–46; in Puerto Rico, 364; in Spain, 395

Violencia, La (Colombia), 137, 144
voters: and proposing Venezuelan legislation, 426
voting rights: in Brazil, 78

Wales: incarceration rates in, 272; law firms in, *92*
war on drugs, 141. *See also* drug trafficking; drug use
Washington Consensus, 479, 490
welfare state: in Italy, 224–25; in Venezuela, 421–23
West Germany: civil case rate in, 37
white-collar crime: in Colombia, 142
women: and Argentine judiciary, 32; and Argentine law faculties, 26; and Brazilian legal profession, 87–88; and Chilean suffrage, 113; and denunciations of intrafamilial violence, 127; and French law schools, *186*, 188; and French magistracy, 201–2; and Italian criminal convictions, 254; and Italian magistracy, 245; and Mexican legal profession, 331–32; and Puerto Rican law, 360–64; and Spanish judicial staff, 386; and Venezuelan civil code, 432; and Venezuelan penal code, 430
Workers Party (Brazil), 90
workers' rights: in Chile, 115
World Bank, 479
World Trade Organization, 334

Zagrebelsky, Gustavo, 248
Zolezzi, Lorenzo, 240